THE YOUNG EAGLE

THE YOUNG EAGLE

The Rise of

Abraham Lincoln

KENNETH J. WINKLE

Taylor Trade Publishing
Dallas, Texas

*My greatest debt belongs to my family, especially my parents,
who instilled in me a lifelong love of both learning and teaching,
and my son, Michael, whose inquisitive nature and
effervescent spirit over the years have never failed to refresh
my own. Together, they provide a constant reminder of our highest
purpose as historians—preserving the past to enlighten the minds and
brighten the lives of the next generation.*

Designed by David Timmons

Published by Taylor Publishing Company
1550 West Mockingbird Lane
Dallas, Texas 75235
www.taylorpub.com

Library of Congress Cataloging-in-Publication Data

Winkle, Kenneth J.
    The young eagle : the rise of Abraham Lincoln / Kenneth J. Winkle.
        p. cm.
    Includes bibliographical references and index.
    ISBN 0-87833-255-3 (cloth)
    1. Lincoln, Abraham, 1809–1865. 2. Lincoln, Abraham, 1809–1865—Childhood
and youth. 3. Presidents—United States—Biography. 4. Lincoln family. I. Title.

E457 .W77 2001
973.7'092—dc21
[B]   00-048822

10 9 8 7 6 5 4 3 2 1

Printed in the United States of America

Contents

Acknowledgments

During the years I have devoted to researching and writing this book, many people and organizations have generously offered advice and encouragement to help the project move forward. During the initial stages of the work, I received summer release time through a National Endowment for the Humanities Summer Stipend and a Cora Friedline Faculty Summer Fellowship awarded by the University of Nebraska Research Council. Institutional support from the University of Nebraska included a Layman Award from the Research Council to purchase newspapers and other documents on microfilm. Over the years, the Department of History, under the leadership of Benjamin G. Rader, Lloyd E. Ambrosius, and Dane K. Kennedy, provided a crucial degree of encouragement and support. The staff of the university's Love Library, particularly Gretchen Holten-Poppler, were always eager to aid my search for documentary materials. The History Department's Holland Fund supported the purchase of the microfilm edition of the Herndon-Weik Papers. Toward the end of the project, the department's Clay Thomas Fund enhanced this book by funding the inclusion of a generous selection of photographs.

Beyond the resources of the University of Nebraska, a great number of archivists and librarians offered their help and encouragement. In particular, I would like to single out the staffs of the Illinois State Historical Library, the Illinois Regional Archives Depository at the University of Illinois–Springfield, and the Sangamon Valley Collection of the Lincoln Library, all in Springfield, Illinois, who were unstinting of their time and energy in answering my many queries and requests for source materials. Toward the end of the project, Thomas F. Schwartz, Secretary of the Abraham Lincoln Association; Kim Bauer, Curator of the Henry Horner Lincoln Collection of the Illinois State Historical Library; Mary Michals, Department Head of the Audio-Visual Collections of the Illinois State Historical Library; Leanne Garland, Archivist/Librarian of the Abraham Lincoln Museum in Harrogate, Tennessee; and Cindy Van Horn, Registrar of the Lincoln Museum in Fort Wayne, Indiana, generously expedited the process of locating and acquiring photographs to add a welcome visual dimension to the book.

Over the years, I have presented preliminary results of my research before a variety of audiences, including the Abraham Lincoln Association, the Organization of American Historians, the Social Science History Association, the Society for Historians of the Early American Republic, the Abraham Lincoln Association of the Mid-Atlantic, the American Historical Association–Pacific Coast, the American Statistical Association, the Conference on Middle Western Regionalism at Miami University, the Missouri Valley Conference, the Mid-America Conference, and several Civil War Roundtables, including the Chicago, Milwaukee, and Lincoln, Nebraska, chapters. Last year, I delivered the Thirteenth Harmon Memorial Lincoln Lecture at Washburn University. In the process, I have been blessed with a wealth of advice from the many commentators who shared their thoughts on those occasions. They are far too numerous to mention by name, but all of them have earned my gratitude and helped me to improve the final product. At the University of Nebraska, the members of the Nineteenth Century Group read early drafts of three chapters and offered incisive comments. I would like to single out Benjamin G. Rader, Timothy R. Mahoney, and Wendy Katz for special thanks.

As they neared completion, sections of this book have appeared in print. Portions of Chapters 5, 11, 16, 19, and 23 appeared, respectively, in *The Lincoln Newsletter*, *The Journal of the Abraham Lincoln Association*, *Civil War History*, *The Journal of Social History*, and *Middle Western Regionalism*, edited by Andrew R. L. Cayton and Susan Gray. I would like to thank the editors of those journals, Barbara Hughett, Thomas F. Schwartz, John T. Hubbell, and Peter Stearns, as well as their anonymous referees, for helpful advice.

Less formally, Lincoln scholars from around the country have been extremely generous in offering help and encouragement in a variety of forms as this book took shape and neared completion. A few merit special mention. Tom Schwartz is a forceful champion and gracious patron of Lincoln scholars whose enthusiasm and advice have boosted many Lincoln projects on their way, including my own. Through both encouragement and example, Jean Baker sharpened my analysis of Lincoln's personal and political life. She graciously read the final manuscript and offered insightful suggestions. Michael Burlingame has generously shared his unsurpassed knowledge of Lincoln source materials and, although our conclusions diverge at some points, he read the final manuscript and offered crucial encouragement. Over the last quarter century, Allan G. Bogue has generously afforded both inspiration and advice and, in this instance, read the final manuscript with his usual keen eye and good humor. Finally, my colleague at the University of Nebraska, James Rawley, himself a Lincoln biographer, has provided constant encouragement and advice through the life of this project. Since he retired from teaching thirteen years ago, Jim has generously suggested many fruitful lines of inquiry, and he read the manuscript as it neared completion. Although I always welcomed my colleagues' advice, I did not always accept it, and they of course bear no responsibility for the result.

As the manuscript moved toward press, the editors at Taylor Publishing worked with skill, insight, and expedition to improve it. I would like to single out Michael Emmerich, Fred Francis, Maura Keese, and Delia Guzman for managing to make the experience a rewarding and even enjoyable one while offering their encouragement and expert advice.

Introduction

The Young Eagle

Five years before his death in 1887, Joshua Speed, the truest friend that Abraham Lincoln ever made, pondered the unfathomable achievements of the sixteenth president. "For me to have lived to see such a man rise from point to point, and from place to place, filling all the places to which he was called, with honor and distinction, until he reached the presidency, filling the presidential chair in the most trying times that any ruler ever had, seems to me," he marveled, "more like fiction than fact." Watching Lincoln rise, he likened his friend to a "young eagle," stretching his wings to catch the wind that was America and leaving the world below him to soar to the horizon beyond. "None but a genius like his could have accomplished so much, and none but a government like ours could produce such a man," he concluded. "It gave the young eagle scope for his wing."[1]

The image was apt. No one but Lincoln could have made that remarkable rise upward, escaping the world that gave him flight and bidding others to follow. But as he soared above, he caught just the right breezes, social and political currents—"a government like ours"—that drove his flight forward. Invisible yet tempestuous, the winds of change that transformed America during his lifetime helped lift this young eagle. Setting his sights on the distance, he felt the nudge and the tug of these uncertain currents but used them to reach his ultimate destination. Family and community, society and politics—each played a part in shaping his character, honing his instincts, and finally teaching him to soar.

Lincoln himself disparaged his own parentage and childhood rather than granting them much credit for preparing him for his flight upward. He actually exaggerated his humble origins to accentuate his own rise from obscurity to distinction. An astute mythmaker, Lincoln self-consciously grounded his entire political career within the context of a personal triumph over inherited adversity. During his very first campaign for public office, he declared that "I was born and have ever remained in the most humble walks of life." Three decades later, Lincoln was still sounding the theme of his modest beginnings. Running for president in 1860, he noted that both his parents had descended from "undistinguished families—second families, perhaps I should say" and depicted his youth as physically hard and culturally unrewarding. The biography Lincoln authorized for his presidential campaign pictured his parents as "poor and uneducated" and concluded that "It would be difficult to conceive of more unpromising circumstances than those under which he was ushered into life." By denigrating his own origins, Lincoln simultaneously identified himself as a "common man" and celebrated his own self-improvement. Although a polished speaker, adroit politician, and prosperous attorney, Lincoln yet remained a "self-made man" who "grew up in full sympathy with the people."[2]

This "log cabin myth" served Lincoln well in life but has forever haunted his posthumous reputation. Following his lead, biographers have reiterated the self-made myth, vastly overstating Lincoln's humble beginnings, denigrating his ancestry, impugning his parents' character, and questioning their legitimacy and even his own. This "hereditary" impeachment of Lincoln began with his longtime law partner, William H. Herndon, and flourished throughout the late nineteenth century. The controversy over hereditary handicaps, including genetic deficiencies, spawned a long-running genealogical debate that, as John Y. Simon put it, "infected the Lincoln literature with acrimony and nonsense." Eventually, during the early twentieth century, historians settled the issue of the Lincolns' legitimacy and that debate subsided. Genetics aside, however, biographers still point to the cultural bleakness of Lincoln's upbringing, accentuating his parents' poverty and illiteracy as inherited handicaps that Lincoln heroically overcame during his single-minded rise to eminence.[3]

In light of its broad cultural appeal and stubborn popular persistence, this self-made myth warrants more objective and systematic consideration than Lincoln biographers have thus far paid it. Lincoln was indeed born and reared in humble circumstances, and yet he achieved far greater prominence than all but a few of his contemporaries. Biographers frequently cite Lincoln's unlikely, meteoric rise as a sign of his extraordinary personal qualities, whether intelligence, persistence, humanity, eloquence, or ambition. But that is only half the story, and it considers Lincoln in isolation, as a heroic individual, literally a "self-made" man. In fact, his dramatic rise from frontier poverty to political, professional, and personal success occurred within a specific, indeed unique, historical context that was utterly novel and would never occur again. Lincoln's early life deserves a detailed dissection that examines his experiences within a broad social and cultural context, compares Lincoln to his contemporaries, identifies the specific disadvantages he overcame, and considers more precisely how he overcame them, charting the winds, so to speak, that caught his wings and lifted this young eagle upward.[4]

THE YOUNG EAGLE

CHAPTER I

Undistinguished Families

Abraham Lincoln was characteristically reserved about his own origins and early life. At his death, he left only two brief autobiographical accounts, both written grudgingly during his 1860 presidential campaign and encompassing a mere nine pages of his *Collected Works*. Lincoln's reticence on this subject has in fact led one recent biographer to predict pessimistically that "Historians are forever doomed to ignorance about the early life of Abraham Lincoln." Like most Americans, however, Lincoln was keenly interested in the scant information he had inherited about his own family's history. In fact, he devoted about one-seventh of his two brief autobiographies to retelling the story of his parents, ancestors, and relatives. Lincoln had only fragmentary knowledge of his own ancestry and recognized what he did know as little more than "vague tradition." He could trace his lineage back only two generations and only as far afield as Pennsylvania. "Further back than this," he wrote, "I have never heard any thing." As a result, he exaggerated his family's southern origins by mistakenly labeling his grandfather a native Virginian. In fact, the Lincoln family had deep roots in New England, and his grandfather was born in Pennsylvania. Lincoln's family had shallow southern roots. His father, Thomas, was the first Lincoln to be born in the South, and he himself was the last.[1]

The American Lincoln line began in 1637 with three Lincoln brothers who emigrated from Hingham, England, and settled in Hingham, Massachusetts. In England, the 1630s witnessed a deep depression in East Anglia and the West Country, especially among linen weavers, as well as a growing persecution of puritan religious dissenters. The result was the Great Migration, during which thousands of East Anglians fled England for Massachusetts. A veritable stream of Lincolns made the journey from the old Hingham in East Anglia to the new Hingham in America, where they flourished. By 1680, sixty Lincolns lived in the town. In fact, one-fourth of the townspeople were named Lincoln. One of the Lincoln brothers, Samuel, a weaver's apprentice, disembarked at age eighteen to establish the American

Lincoln line that led, six generations later, to Abraham. Samuel Lincoln found linen weaving an impractical livelihood in Massachusetts, so he acquired some land and probably farmed to feed his family. There his son Mordecai was born in 1657. Most of the immigrants to Hingham moved on again, but Samuel Lincoln remained rooted there for the rest of his life. His son, however, left Hingham as a young man to seek opportunity elsewhere, beginning a long family tradition of moving in search of greater opportunities. "The American Lincolns" (see Table 1.1) summarizes the genealogy of the Lincolns over two centuries, focusing on the steady movement of the family during six generations and tracing each Lincoln male in the direct descent from Mordecai to Abraham, from his place of birth to his place of death. The table also records the number of major moves accomplished by each of the Lincoln men and the total migration distance covered by each generation.[2]

The Lincoln family stayed in New England for only one generation before beginning a steady intergenerational trek southward and then westward. Like most migrants, the Lincolns did not travel directly west but instead followed natural topographical features, in this instance sweeping southward along the Allegheny Range into Virginia's Shenandoah Valley, only later spilling westward into Kentucky through the Cumberland Gap. Mid-Atlantic settlers frequently adopted this route. Daniel Boone's family, for example, undertook the same journey beginning in 1750. Boone himself was born in Pennsylvania to a family of immigrant English weavers. The Boone family trekked southward along the Alleghenies into Virginia and North Carolina and then westward into Kentucky. The Lincoln family's migration occurred during the fourth generation, under Lincoln's grandfather Abraham, who—like Boone—was born in Pennsylvania, raised a family in Virginia, and then took them westward to Kentucky.[3]

The Lincolns' subsequent migration to Illinois brought the family back to the North but only after the fifth generation, represented by Lincoln's father, had been born and reared in the South. As a result of this swing around the Alleghenies, Abraham Lincoln could claim to be a southerner by birth but hailed from New England and Mid-Atlantic ancestry as well. However, the family's southern sojourn was relatively short. Not one of Lincoln's direct ancestors spent his entire life within the South. Only Thomas and Abraham were born there, and they left the region for the North at ages thirty-eight and seven, respectively. Thomas was born in the Shenandoah Valley, the route that carried thousands of northerners through the Alleghenies, and Abraham was born along the Old Cumberland Trail, which carried thousands of southerners northward into the Midwest.

The Lincolns were an extremely migratory family, accomplishing a six-generation, two-hundred-year odyssey that took them nearly two thousand miles from Massachusetts to Illinois and back east again to Washington, D.C., by 1861. Every generation of American Lincolns moved. But they

TABLE 1.1
The American Lincolns

	Life Span	Place of Birth	Son's Place of Birth	Place of Death	No. of Moves	Lifetime Migration Distance
1. Mordecai Sr.	1657–1727	Mass.	Mass.	Mass.	2	9 mi.
2. Mordecai Jr.	1686–1736	Mass.	N.J.	Pa.	3	120 mi.
3. John	1716–1788	N.J.	Pa.	Va.	3	299 mi.
4. Abraham	1744–1786	Pa.	Va.	Ky.	2	576 mi.
5. Thomas	1778–1851	Va.	Ky.	Ill.	6	708 mi.
6. Abraham	1809–1865	Ky.	Ill.	D.C.	5	1,098 mi.

practiced a "step migration" that occurred in distinct stages, with each generation making its own crucial contribution. Not one of the Lincoln men stayed put in one place through an entire lifetime. After the first generation, each of the Lincolns lived in at least three different colonies or states. Significantly, too, each of the Lincolns became more migratory than his father before him. Without fail, their lifetime migration distance increased dramatically from one generation to the next, from a mere nine miles in the first generation to more than one thousand in the sixth generation—Abraham Lincoln's. This acceleration reflects the growing propensity of migrants throughout American history to move longer distances, responding to mounting population pressure in the East, the increasing ease of travel, and the westward progression of the frontier. The later Lincolns also moved more frequently, and the number of moves they made rose from only two during the first generation to five in the sixth. Abraham Lincoln might well have increased that number had he lived beyond 1865.[4]

The Lincoln family's American journey began with Samuel Lincoln, the future president's great-great-great-great-grandfather. Samuel stayed put in Hingham once he arrived, raising four sons to adulthood. Following a typical pattern, he kept one son at home while the others left Hingham to establish families elsewhere. Abraham Lincoln's first American-born ancestor—Mordecai—moved as a young man to the neighboring town of Hull, where he learned the trade of blacksmithing and then married. After a few years, he moved a second time to nearby Scituate, the northernmost outpost of Plymouth colony, located just outside the Hingham town line. Reflecting the limited frontier opportunities available in colonial New England, men of his era typically moved fewer than sixteen miles while their parents lived. When he died at seventy, Mordecai had moved all of nine miles from his birthplace in Hingham. But Mordecai's short move southward sparked

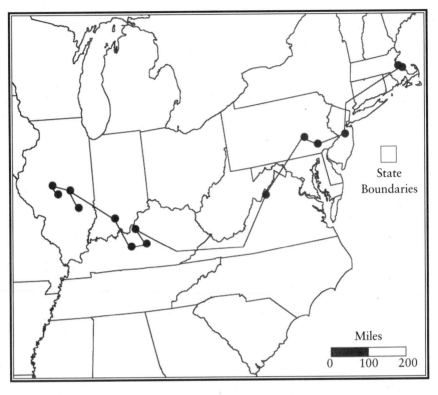

a century-long trend that eventually took the Lincoln family as far south as Virginia's Shenandoah Valley. Mordecai also established a Lincoln family pattern by losing a wife but quickly remarrying. He worked as a blacksmith but probably also farmed to feed his family. Like his father before him, Mordecai kept one son at home while the others moved on to establish families elsewhere.[5]

His son and namesake, Mordecai Lincoln Jr., moved southward to New Jersey with his brother Abraham. They settled in Freehold, the seat of Monmouth County in the region known as East Jersey. East Jersey resembled New England, with compact settlement in closely spaced towns and a strong Presbyterian heritage. Freehold was a small market town situated on New Jersey's fertile coastal plain, and there Mordecai married and raised a family of six children. In a personal history similar to his father's, he worked as a blacksmith and lost a young wife but soon remarried. Freehold lay on the Burlington Road that ran to the Delaware River and Philadelphia beyond. Attracted perhaps to the renowned iron-making district in southeastern Pennsylvania, Mordecai made a second move farther southward at

THE YOUNG EAGLE

age forty-seven to Pennsylvania, settling first in Chester County and then Berks County. A frontier area along the Schuylkill River fronting the Allegheny Mountains, the region mixed native-born farmers together with immigrants, mostly Germans and Scots-Irish. Here, Mordecai started a second family with his new wife but died after only three years at age fifty.[6]

Mordecai Jr. established a pattern that every succeeding Lincoln practiced, moving to another colony or state as a boy or young man, marrying in that intermediate location, fathering at least one son there, and then moving with his family to yet a third destination, where he died. This pattern recurred unerringly through five generations, from 1686 to 1865. Typically, each of the Lincolns moved once as a child or young adult within the shelter of a family, married in that new location and started a family of his own, and then moved on again with his wife and children. Not one of the Lincoln men, until Abraham in the sixth generation, ever moved alone. This practice was not peculiar to the Lincolns but was entirely typical in a society that emphasized family ties rather than individualism. Before the advent of modern agricultural techniques, many if not most farm families practiced this traditional policy of "escape and repeat." Families would deplete the soil on their farms, "escape" to new lands in the West, and—after a generation or so—"repeat" the process, moving ever westward. Mordecai Jr. initiated this strategy for the Lincoln family.[7]

Born in New Jersey, Mordecai's oldest son, John, married and raised a family in Pennsylvania, where he sired son Abraham, the future president's grandfather. This Pennsylvania sojourn, which lasted less than one generation, reinforced the president's erroneous impression that "The family were originally quakers, though in later times they have fallen away from the peculiar habits of that people." The "ridge country," which included the majestic Blue Ridge, naturally beckoned Mid-Atlantic settlers southwestward. In fact, families from farther north spent an average of only seven to ten years in Pennsylvania before moving on southward. After 1760, a growing land scarcity in southeastern Pennsylvania impelled thousands of Midlanders westward along the Great Philadelphia Wagon Road that ran through Lancaster, York, and Gettysburg, Pennsylvania. They then spilled southward along the Virginia Road, the major migration route among settlers bound for the interior. Within this dominant migration stream, the Lincolns mingled with the Boones, and the two families intermarried. The Boones moved southward, along the Alleghenies into Virginia's Shenandoah Valley, and the Lincoln family followed. John Lincoln moved his family to Virginia when his son Abraham was twenty-four and became known ever after as "Virginia John."[8]

This migration established what Lincoln considered his ancestral home, a knot of five Lincoln brothers living in Rockingham County, Virginia, just east of the Alleghenies. During the eighteenth century, the Shenandoah Valley was the major migration channel for northern settlers swooping southward around the mountain barrier and heading westward through the Cumberland Gap. Renowned as "the easiest and most heavily traveled approach to the Wilderness Road," the valley hosted many Mid-Atlantic settlers whose eventual destination was Kentucky or the Midwest. The Shenandoah Valley was therefore more a temporary way station for the Lincoln family than an ancestral home. After 1776, the valley was settled largely by Pennsylvanians and German immigrants and not by southerners at all. The valley's settlers usually maintained their Pennsylvania connections, and Philadelphia, reached by the Virginia and Philadelphia wagon roads, remained the valley's economic and cultural focus well into the nineteenth century.[9]

Rockingham County sat squarely in the center of the Shenandoah Valley and was the most mountainous and sparsely settled county in the region. Small, independent yeoman farmers who eschewed slavery and owned few slaves dominated this frontier area. Here, Abraham Lincoln, the president's grandfather, married, settled on a farm near his parents' home, and raised a family of five children. By the late 1770s, the area began to commercialize, and the population density reached five per square mile. The first phase of Trans-Allegheny settlement began in the midst of the American Revolution, and the main focus of westward emigration was Kentucky. Rockingham County, in particular, sent a cluster of settlers to central Kentucky's Bluegrass region. Indeed, the Daniel Boone family lived near the Lincolns on Linnville Creek, a tributary of the Shenandoah, but stayed for only a year or two before moving on again. Daniel Boone himself led an emigration to Kentucky in 1779, escorting more than one hundred pioneers through the Cumberland Gap along Boone's Trace. Abraham Lincoln joined this huge Boone party and thus became the first true westward migrant among the Lincolns. Following a family pattern, four of the five Lincoln brothers moved westward, while one of them remained in Rockingham County to inherit his father's farm.[10]

In 1780, Abraham Lincoln sold his farm in Virginia and left his family behind to visit Kentucky. There he bought two tracts of land totaling twelve hundred acres. Two years later, the entire family—Abraham and Bathsheba Lincoln and their five children—moved westward to Kentucky and conflict with Native Americans. The American Revolution had provoked a long military struggle with western Native American tribes. In 1775, the Continental Congress recognized the Ohio River as a permanent boundary between Indians and whites, granting Kentucky to white settlers and relegating the Indians to Ohio. The Shawnees, who dominated the region, resisted. Now, during peacetime, the movement of thousands of whites into Kentucky revived this conflict. The Shawnees reluctantly abandoned Kentucky, moving their villages north of the Ohio River, but they continued to attack white settlements to the south. Kentucky militiamen retaliated by launching raids deep into Ohio, burning the Shawnees' villages, killing their chiefs, and forcing the Indians farther northward. Settled in Lexington, Kentucky, the ancestors of Lincoln's future wife, Mary Todd, played a conspicuous role in this campaign against the Shawnees, with Colonel Levi Todd leading the Fayette County militia and commanding Daniel Boone.[11]

White squatters began to settle north of the Ohio, and the U.S. Army reported an "almost incredible" migration that escalated the conflict. In 1786, the Shawnees reluctantly ceded their lands in southern Ohio but received no compensation and faced famine. George Washington himself complained that squatters "roam over the Country on the Indian side of the Ohio, mark out lands, Survey, and even settle them. This gives great discontent to the Indians," Washington concluded, "and will unless measures are taken in time to prevent it, inevitably produce a war with the western Tribes." Between 1783 and 1787, this predictable war raged, and Native Americans may have killed more than three hundred white settlers in Kentucky. In September 1786, eight hundred Kentucky militiamen, including Daniel Boone, launched an unauthorized retaliatory strike north of the Ohio, destroying four Shawnee towns, burning corn, and taking hostages. The Shawnees fled still farther northward. The first half of 1786, in particular, brought renewed Native American attacks along the Ohio River, claiming even more lives than the fighting of the Revolutionary period.[12]

Unluckily, the Lincoln family arrived in Kentucky in the midst of this conflict. In May 1786, a Native American, probably a Shawnee, killed Abraham Lincoln, the future president's grandfather. Lincoln and his three sons—Mordecai, Josiah, and Thomas—were clearing a field for planting, just east of Louisville on the Ohio River, when Native Americans attacked. The father died instantly. Josiah ran to a nearby fort, and Mordecai fled into the family's cabin while the youngest son, Thomas, who was eight, simply sat by his dead father's side. From within the cabin, the oldest brother, Mordecai, pointed a gun through a chink in the logs and killed his father's attacker. Abraham Lincoln's death, as his grandson and namesake recalled seventy-five years later, plunged his family into a life of "reduced circumstances" and turned young Thomas into a "wandering laboring boy." Thomas proved the most migratory of all the Lincolns, making six major moves and a trek of over seven hundred miles during his lifetime.[13]

In later life, Lincoln astutely labeled his family "undistinguished." Although extremely migratory, they were essentially typical of their time. Historians have demonstrated repeatedly that migration has been a predictable fact of life for American families since early in the colonial era. During this period, probably only one in five men did *not* move during his lifetime. Oldest sons often inherited the family farm, while younger sons were forced by circumstances to move on. Evidence suggests that, for most Americans, the typical length of residence in any single location was a mere nine years. Colonial families traditionally employed migration as a strategy in their quest to accumulate land and pass it on to their sons. Such a "lineal family" functioned best not by staying put but by moving westward to settle on fresher, cheaper, and more abundant land. The Lincolns represented such a lineal family moving west, their intergenerational step migration stretching from Massachusetts Bay southward through the Shenandoah Valley and westward into Kentucky. The Lincolns represented substantial landowners who moved every half-generation in an attempt to achieve family security and pass on land to their sons. Never migrating as individuals but only with their families, the Lincoln men each made two primary moves—the first as an unmarried boy or youth in a family and the second as a mature adult with children of his own. This migration strategy placed primary emphasis on family security and employed group migration as part of a family survival strategy.[14]

Historians long ago demolished the myth that most westward migrants were young, single men. Far from disrupting families, westward migration actually represented an important strategy for keeping a family together and augmenting its critical resources. Westward movement to new lands could hold a family together and improve its economic situation while the resulting family stability could facilitate the process of settlement itself. Family organization eased the journey westward, and two or three families might join together and strike out for a common destination. Such pioneer families had a much better chance of succeeding and staying put in their new frontier homes.[15]

As a typical westering family, the Lincolns took all the usual wagon roads westward, following the classic migration routes renowned in early American history. The Burlington Road ran through New Jersey to the Delaware River and Philadelphia. The Great Philadelphia Wagon Road led westward through southeastern Pennsylvania to the Potomac. The Virginia Road picked up there and ran southward into the Shenandoah Valley. The Great Valley Road then ran up the valley to the Cumberland Gap, through which more than three hundred thousand pioneers poured westward into Kentucky. Finally, the Wilderness Road, blazed by Daniel Boone, led on through Kentucky all the way to Louisville on the Ohio River. Running consecutively, these major roads channeled the Lincoln family's migration history, drawing them southward around the Allegheny Mountains, westward through the Cumberland Gap, and northward again to the Ohio River and beyond. From the second generation on, in fact, each of the Lincoln men was born and died within a short distance from one of these major migration routes westward.[16]

As a result, Abraham Lincoln's cultural heritage was a composite, containing elements of three culture hearths—Yankee, Mid-Atlantic, and Upland South. In fact, Lincoln had deep roots in the North but relatively shallow roots in the South. Traveling westward, the Lincoln family skirted the coastal South and settled in a peripheral region dominated more by Pennsylvanians than by southerners. Even within the Shenandoah Valley, the Lincolns selected the one county, Rockingham, that in its emphasis on subsistence farming and its aversion to slavery least resembled the plantation South. After leaving the Shenandoah Valley and swooping westward around the Alleghenies, the Lincolns followed the Wilderness Road as far northward as it ran. The first Abraham Lincoln was breaking land in Jefferson County, near Louisville on the Ohio River, when he died. His grandson and namesake was born near the Old Cumberland Trail just fifty miles south of Louisville. Through five generations, the Lincoln family followed well-worn trails from New England through the Upper South and on westward into the Ohio Country. Abraham Lincoln inherited an ancestry that prepared him fully for the cultural ambiguity that awaited him on the prairies of Illinois.[17]

CHAPTER 2

A Wild Region

When the future president's grandfather Abraham died in 1786 at age forty-two, he was the youngest of the Lincoln men to die. His early death irrevocably altered his family's fortunes. During the colonial period, the death of a father quite often broke apart his family and scattered his children. In the words of the future president, the youngest son, Thomas, now became "a wandering laboring boy, and grew up litterally without education." Left fatherless at age eight, he lived for long stretches with uncles in Tennessee and Kentucky. Thomas's legacy to his own son was not landed property but rather continued migration northward to free territory.[1]

Moving to improve their lot was something that the Lincoln family well knew how to do. Thomas's two sisters remained in Kentucky, but he and both his brothers eventually moved northward. Many Kentucky yeomen, like Thomas Lincoln, with roots in western Virginia and eastern Pennsylvania, disapproved of slavery and eventually moved north of the Ohio River. Lincoln's father and both his uncles followed this pattern. His uncle Josiah moved just north of the Ohio River to Harrison County, Indiana, and his uncle Mordecai established a Lincoln clan in Hancock County, Illinois, on the Mississippi River across from Iowa. Lincoln's aunts married native Kentuckians who apparently preferred to remain in slave territory. They established a southern line of Lincolns that remains lost to history.[2]

At age twenty-five, Thomas Lincoln moved to Hardin County, Kentucky. He settled in the county seat, Elizabethtown, living near an uncle and apprenticing as a joiner. Working hard, he eventually acquired a sizable farm just north of the town. Three years later, in 1806, Thomas married Nancy Hanks, like him a native Virginian. The Lincolns moved back to Elizabethtown, where Thomas bought two town lots, built a log cabin, and worked as a carpenter. In 1808, the Lincolns bought another farm eighteen miles southeast of town. Here, in Hardin County, which was named after a relative of Mary Todd, Abraham Lincoln was born on February 12, 1809. When Abraham was two years old, the family moved yet again to a farm on

Knob Creek, the first home he could remember. Far from destitute, Thomas Lincoln owned three farms simultaneously during Lincoln's boyhood. Still, his holdings were modest compared to those of his father, whose early death had definitely taken the Lincolns down a notch in the world. Lacking a father's example, perhaps, Thomas managed his land holdings carelessly for the rest of his life. In short, Thomas devoted little, if any, attention to leaving his son Abraham a landed patrimony of his own.[3]

Thomas and Nancy Lincoln moved three times during their first five years of marriage, and the story of Lincoln's early life is largely a reiteration of the kind of repeat migration that carried so many settlers, by fits and starts, to the Illinois frontier. Foretelling the future of this pioneer family, the Knob Creek farm faced the Old Cumberland Trail that drew thousands of southerners from Nashville to Louisville every year on their way to Indiana and Illinois. In the fall of 1816, when Lincoln was seven, his father decided to move his family out of Kentucky entirely, northward to Indiana. Thomas was thirty-eight, the same age his father had been when he had moved his own family from Virginia to Kentucky. In later years, Lincoln credited a growing disillusionment with slavery as one of his father's motives for leaving Kentucky. But he justifiably cited a controversy over land titles as the main reason. Because of a primitive system of recordkeeping, land claims "shingled" or overlapped like shingles on a cabin roof. As a result, almost one-half of Kentucky's pioneers lost their land through faulty titles. Thomas Lincoln lost his first two farms in this way, which grieved his son after he became a lawyer and may well have encouraged Lincoln's early interest in surveying as a career. Thomas now faced the loss of his Knob Creek farm, as well. The U.S. government was selling land in Indiana for two dollars an acre and securing all titles according to the Congressional Survey System, a vast improvement over the old metes and bounds system practiced in Kentucky and much of the South. As a region of free labor, cheap land, and secure land titles, the Old Northwest promised greater economic security for this yeoman family. They joined the First Great Migration, begun the year before, that carried thousands of other Upland Southerners farther north and west.[4]

Dennis Hanks, an illegitimate cousin of Lincoln's mother, pictured the Knob Creek farm as "knotty—knobby as a piece of land could be—with deep hollows—ravines—cedar trees Covering the parts—knolls—knobs as thick as trees could grow." Indiana represented a decided improvement. In typical pioneer fashion, as his own father had done before him, Thomas Lincoln went ahead alone to scout out a new home. He built a flatboat out of yellow cedar, loaded up the family's furniture, household goods, and tools, and floated down the winding creeks to the Ohio River. Crossing the Ohio by ferry, he located a 160-acre claim—a quarter section—in Spencer County, Indiana, seventeen miles north of the river. He marked the four corners by blazing trees and building "brush heaps," and then returned to Kentucky to retrieve his waiting family. Abraham had an older sister, Sarah (a younger brother had died in infancy), and the four Lincolns mounted two horses and a wagon, bringing along two feather beds, and made a two-week, hundred-mile trek to their new home in Indiana.[5]

Crossing the Ohio River, the Lincoln family gained three major benefits. First, they left a southern slave state for a region of free labor, where yeoman families such as theirs could support themselves in dignity and aspire to reach the top of the social scale without resorting to the ownership of slaves. Second, land titles were much firmer, facilitating social mobility through the secure ownership of land and the promise of accumulating more. Finally, the Wilderness Road that passed through southern Indiana reached farther westward into Illinois, eventually leading the family even deeper into the developing Midwest. Otherwise, southern Indiana society presented few novelties.

Indiana exhibited the most southern character of any of the midwestern states. Spencer County, in particular, was an enclave of transplanted Kentuckians, with almost one-half of its settlers originating just south of the river and another one-quarter just east in Ohio. Resembling Knob Creek in many respects, this hilly southern region of Indiana was called "the Knobs." The lack of transportation sheltered self-reliant families from the commercial economy that ran along the Ohio River. In a typical year, 150 flatboats floated past on the Ohio, carrying a quarter-million bushels of corn, 100,000 barrels of pork, 10,000 hams, and 2,500 head of cattle. Away from the river where the Lincolns settled, however, families fed, clothed, and housed themselves, depending on neighbors to provide the few necessities that they could not produce without help.[6]

Lincoln pictured this Pigeon Creek home as "a wild region, with many bears and other wild animals still in the woods." Native Americans had ceded the land to the federal government just twelve years earlier, but the Lincolns never saw any of the original inhabitants. Abraham Lincoln remembered the region as "an unbroken forest; and the clearing away of surplus wood was the great task ahead." Large for his age, Lincoln "had an axe put into his hands at once; and from that till within his twenty-third year, he was almost constantly handling that most useful instrument." Thus began his famous career as an axe-handler. Observing a typical pioneer pattern, the Lincolns devoted only one day to building a log cabin, and there they wintered. The family survived the winter on wild game, hunting deer and turkey, and spent these otherwise idle months cutting down trees and underbrush to clear six acres of woodland to sow in the spring. Eventually the Lincolns tended ten acres of corn, five of wheat, two of oats, and one of meadow. Like many frontiersmen who combined occupations, Thomas Lincoln farmed in the summer and worked wood in the winter as a cabinet-maker and house joiner. He continued his Kentucky habits and, like other pioneers, merely "squatted" on the land for the first year. Then he and two neighbors traveled sixty miles to the federal land office at Vincennes to make the required one-quarter initial payment on their land claims.[7]

During Lincoln's youth, on both the Knob Creek and Pigeon Creek farmsteads, his family practiced classic subsistence agriculture. Originally, the Indiana farm was isolated and self-contained, a literal wilderness without neighbors, roads, or towns. Indeed, the Lincoln family had to cut a road through the trees to reach their claim. They arrived without "hogs—cows—chickens, or such like domestic animals," and they ate wild game, a staple of the southern frontier diet. "We always hunted," Dennis Hanks remembered; "it made no difference what came for we more or less depended on it for a living—nay for life." Families depended on meat during the winter, and—in the absence of money—animal skins served as legal tender. Even when the corn came in, the nearest mill lay seventeen miles through the forest, on the Ohio River, and it ground only enough grain for home consumption rather than sale. "It was a little bit of hand[-drawn] horse mill," as Dennis Hanks remembered, "the ground meal of which a hound could Eat as fast as it was ground. Yet this was a God Send."[8]

Without improved transportation, commercial agriculture was difficult and risky, and the Lincolns learned this truth the hard way. While in Kentucky, Thomas occasionally ventured out by flatboat, personally escorting his pork down the Ohio and Mississippi rivers all the way to New Orleans. He walked back home, in typical pioneer fashion, but earned only a "little profit" for all this trouble. In a subsistence economy, commercial agriculture was both a luxury and a gamble, and one year Thomas lost everything. "He sold one entire load on a credit," another relative, Augustus Chapman, remembered, "& never realized a cent." In Indiana, the Lincolns traded at the nearest town, Gentryville, only for goods that they could not produce themselves. Thomas "Jest Raised a Nuf for his own use he Did Not Send any produce to any other place Mor than Bought his Shugar and Coffee and Such Like." Subsistence represented the best guarantee of survival in a pioneer economy, and fortunately the Lincoln farm could supply almost all of the family's needs. "Lincolns Little Farm was well Stocked with Hogs, Horses & cattle," Chapman reminisced with apparent pride, as well as "a fine crop of Wheat corn & Vegetables." The Lincolns tanned their own leather, made their own shoes, wove their own cloth, and sewed their own clothing, all by hand. Through a chain migration, Thomas Lincoln summoned in-laws and cousins from Kentucky to form a knot of reliable neighbors in the forest to engage in cooperative farming and local exchange. They were joined by a handful of in-laws, Nancy Lincoln's cousin Dennis Hanks and her uncle and aunt, Thomas and Elizabeth Sparrow.[9]

All did their share, and husband and wife observed the traditional sexual division of labor. In this seasonal economy, Thomas supplemented farming with carpentry, building cabinets and joining his neighbors' houses "at odd times" during the winter. His wife ran the household and bartered with the neighbors. "Mr Lincoln & Mrs Lincoln Each worked a head at their own business," Dennis Hanks remembered, "Thomas at farming—Cabinet making—& hunting: She at Cooking—washing—sewing—weaving &c. &c." Of course, Hanks's "&c. &c" concealed a multitude of nameless household duties. Nancy "done all the trading for the family & had the entire management of the Children." The frontier mother clothed her family in the traditional homespun and buckskin. According to Chapman, "Their clothing was all made on looms and the material from which it was made was also made at home." As typical southern settlers, the Lincolns raised cotton and flax, which they "picked carded & spun with their own hands." Early on, the men and boys wore buckskin pants and coonskin caps against the cold. Later, the family kept some sheep, in traditional New England fashion, and Nancy's loom wove linsey-woolsey for the winter. Pioneer families purchased cloth or clothing only on extraordinary occasions, such as a wedding. Thomas Lincoln bought his wedding clothes from a store in Elizabethtown, Kentucky, and these may have been the last clothes that he ever purchased.[10]

After two years, in 1818, Nancy Lincoln grew sick and died of a frontier ailment known as "milk sickness." The family's cattle ate a weed called poison snakeroot and passed on its toxins through their milk. Nancy developed a case of the "trembles" and died within days. Lincoln found himself motherless at age nine. Such early bereavement was far from unusual, however, and historians have traditionally overstated the psychological impact of his mother's death. Until the twentieth century, mothers rarely lived to see all their children reach adulthood, usually leaving behind at least one minor child. During this period, in fact, perhaps one-fourth of all children lost a mother or father before age fifteen. Until life expectancy began to rise, which occurred between 1850 and 1880, the early death of a parent was an all-too-familiar experience for one generation after another within the typical family. As late as the twentieth century, 35 to 40 percent of all American families lost a parent, either father or mother, before all the children reached adulthood. Lincoln shared this experience of childhood bereavement with both his father and mother, his stepsisters and stepbrother, his future wife, and eventually two of his sons. Indeed, of the five generations of Lincolns who preceded Abraham, all of them experienced the early death of either a wife or a mother. Like most Americans of his time, Lincoln inherited a family tradition of parental loss, which most surely prepared him for that seemingly inevitable event.[11]

Psychohistorians have made much of Lincoln's famous brevity in referring to his own mother's death. In his two autobiographies, for example, he devoted a half sentence—a mere eight words—to the event, writing simply that "In the autumn of 1818 his mother died." From a demographic perspective, however, his experience was unexceptional, even commonplace. Only in hindsight, after life expectancy began to rise dramatically at midcentury, did parental death come to seem tragic and unnatural. Lincoln himself apparently saw little reason to elaborate on such a widely shared experience and left it to his readers to imagine and empathize with his loss. His mother's death was painful, of course, but did little, if anything, to set him apart from his contemporaries.[12]

The loss of a parent was not unusual among American presidents of this period, either. During the nineteenth century, exactly one-half of American presidents suffered parental loss before reaching adulthood—losing their mothers, fathers, or even both parents as children. More than one-fifth of the presidents lost their mothers, as Lincoln did. Another two-fifths lost their fathers. Three of the presidents—roughly one in seven—lost both parents before reaching adulthood. Presidents sharing this characteristic with Lincoln include Thomas Jefferson, James Monroe, Andrew Jackson, William Henry Harrison, Rutherford B. Hayes, James Garfield, and Grover Cleveland, and both Lincoln's immediate predecessor, James Buchanan, and his immediate successor, Andrew Johnson.[13] Throughout American history, in fact, more than one-third of American presidents have lost at least one parent in childhood. About one in seven lost their mothers, about one in three lost their fathers, and fully one in ten lost both parents before reaching adulthood. Viewed in context, Lincoln's experience with parental loss appears thoroughly unremarkable. As he observed philosophically two decades later, "The death scenes of those we love, are surely painful enough; but these we are prepared to, and expect to see. They happen to all, and all know they must happen. Painful as they are, they are not an unlooked for sorrow."[14]

Beyond its predictability, the pain of a mother's death was frequently softened by several nineteenth-century social realities. Traditionally, mothers dominated child-rearing only until boys could perform farm labor. Fathers typically gained parental control over their sons at about age seven, when mothers accordingly receded in importance. Lincoln himself wrote that he was large for his age and "had an axe put into his hands" when he was seven, two years before his mother's death. Even when children kept their mothers beyond infancy, in practice they were often raised by older sisters. Twelve-year-old Sarah Lincoln undoubtedly learned housekeeping from her mother and, after Nancy's death, she cooked, kept house, and did what was necessary to raise young Abraham. Even had her mother lived, she would have done much of this for Abraham to free their mother for more productive work on the farm, such as spinning thread, weaving cloth, and churning butter.[15]

Within a subsistence economy, widowers found it difficult to manage a household alone, especially one with children. Predictably, the Lincoln family soon fell into a kind of frontier squalor. According to Dennis Hanks, the children grew "wild, ragged, and dirty." During the early nineteenth century, the most typical and sensible response to the loss of a wife and mother was simply to find a new one. As historian Catherine Clinton observed of southern families, "A second marriage was not uncommon for widow or widower, especially one in reduced circumstances." This practice was also something of a Lincoln family tradition. Of the five generations of Lincoln men who preceded Abraham, three lost their wives, and every one of them remarried. Fourteen months after Nancy Lincoln died, Thomas did what he must have considered the only sensible thing and went off to fetch his children a new mother. In doing so, he also followed a traditional pattern by marrying a woman considerably younger than he (by ten years) and younger than his first wife (by four years).[16]

Lincoln's new stepmother was Sarah Bush Johnston, a widow from back in Elizabethtown, Kentucky. The Bush family came to Kentucky around 1780 and settled in Hardin County. Sarah's father became a substantial landowner in the region and raised a family of seven children. Sarah married Daniel Johnston in 1806, the same year in which Thomas Lincoln married Nancy Hanks, but the marriage represented a step downward for Sarah, and she and her new husband depended on five hundred acres of land that she brought into the marriage. By 1810, however, the land was gone, and legal records showed that the couple were "Without funds." Still, they reared three children, two girls and a boy. In 1814, when the Hardin County jailer died of cholera, Daniel Johnston took his place. The new post, while welcome, was a mixed blessing, because the family moved into the jail, and Sarah had to feed the prisoners. After a year and a half, in 1816, Daniel died.[17]

For the next three years, Sarah endured the unhappy fate of "an honest poor widow," as one of her neighbors described her. Still, she seems to have fared better without her husband, moving into a cabin near Elizabethtown that she was able to buy a year later. The Lincolns had known the Bushes while they lived in Hardin County. Nancy Hanks Lincoln and Sarah Bush Johnston had been friends, and Thomas Lincoln had traveled to New Orleans with one of Sarah's brothers. According to family tradition, Thomas now returned to Elizabethtown and surprised Sarah with a sudden marriage proposal. He agreed to pay off her debts, and on December 2, 1819, they married. As historian Louis Warren observed, "It was a fine testimonial to the good character and high standing of Thomas that he could return to Hardin County where had lived with his first wife for ten years and to Elizabethtown where he had brought her as a bride, and claim another in marriage." Thomas, age forty-one, and Sarah, age thirty-one, now joined their families together.[18]

For both of them, such a remarriage had stronger strategic rather than romantic implications. In recalling their marriage in old age, Sarah referred to Thomas as "Mr. Lincoln." The strategic motivation may have been more compelling for Sarah, a widow with three children, than for Thomas. As Clinton emphasized, "widowhood was a particularly unpleasant prospect

LINCOLN'S STEPMOTHER, SARAH BUSH LINCOLN. THE YOUNG LINCOLN
EMBRACED HER AS "A GOOD AND KIND MOTHER."
Courtesy of the Illinois State Historical Library.

for a southern woman. It often meant the breakup of the home and break-down within the family." Little wonder that Sarah willingly exchanged her home in Elizabethtown for a cabin in the wilderness. She undoubtedly viewed Thomas as a godsend and, as she put it, "landed in Indiana," a phrase that conveys a sense of success. In Sarah, Thomas chose wisely. She did her best to make the cabin, which she found "tolerably Comfortable," into a home. She was "neat & tidy" and "Knew exactly how to Manage children. She took an espic[i]al liking to young Abe." Lincoln soon accepted her as "a good and kind mother."[19]

The two families were a good fit. Sarah gained a new father for her three children, and Thomas gained a stepson—at age ten, one year younger than Abraham—to help work his farm. Sarah insisted on roof repairs to keep out the rain and snow, and the three boys—Abraham Lincoln, John D. Johnston, and Dennis Hanks—slept in the cabin's loft. The three girls—Sarah Lincoln, Elizabeth Johnston, and Matilda Johnston—slept below in a new bed that Thomas built for them. Sarah agreed that Indiana was "wild—and desolate," but introduced a new, urban insistence on cleanliness into the wilderness. "I dressed Abe & his sister up," she remembered, so they "looked more human." She brought a table, a bureau, a set of chairs, and sundry other household accouterments into the cabin and asked Thomas to put in a wooden floor. According to family tradition, she also reignited the young Abraham's love of learning by bringing three books from Kentucky—*Webster's Speller*, *Robinson Crusoe*, and *The Arabian Nights*. Legend holds that Dennis Hanks chided Lincoln for reading *The Arabian Nights*, which he dismissed as "a pack of lies." Lincoln's response revealed a growing reverence for the power of words to stir the imagination. "Mighty fine lies," he retorted.[20]

The Lincolns lived in Indiana for fourteen years and, as Lincoln put it, "There I grew up." Growing up on the Indiana frontier mostly meant working hard, even as a boy, because survival was uncertain. Dennis Hanks remembered everyone "working, chopping, toiling, woman, child, and man." As dependent children, sons were traditionally expected to contribute about seven years' worth of labor to the family economy before leaving home. As Lincoln summed it up, "I was raised to farm work." Soon another Hanks cousin, John, relocated from Kentucky, and all the relatives worked together to raise the frontier staple, corn. John Hanks remembered that he and Lincoln "worked bare footed—grubbed it—plowed—mowed & cradled together—plowed Corn—gathered it & shucked Corn." Indiana, Lincoln recounted gloomily, offered "absolutely nothing to excite ambition for education. Of course when I came of age I did not know much." Indeed, Lincoln educated himself, and John Hanks remembered that when the boys returned from the fields, Lincoln "would go to the Cupboard—Snatch a piece of Corn bread—take down a book—Sit down in a chair—Cock his legs up as high as his head and read."[21]

By 1820, the Lincolns counted eight families settled within a mile of their claim and another six within two miles. Most of their neighbors were fellow Kentuckians, and two of the families hailed from back in Hardin County. Pioneers preferred to live in a "settlement," a half dozen or so families of relatives and neighbors farming within a few miles of each other. The most reliable neighbors, of course, were relatives. The Sparrows had died of the same "milk sick" that claimed Nancy Lincoln, but the family quickly turned other neighbors into relatives through intermarriage. In 1821, Dennis Hanks married Sarah Lincoln's oldest daughter, Elizabeth Johnston, and the couple settled down to work an adjoining farm. They bore four children in Indiana and another four in Illinois. Hanks was now related to the Lincolns by blood, through Nancy Hanks, and by marriage, through Sarah Johnston. Five years later, Sarah's daughter Matilda Johnston married another Hanks cousin, Squire Hall, and they eventually bore eight children of their own. The result was more a clan than a family. As Augustus Chapman put it, "three families came together." The clan grew even larger when Abraham Lincoln's sister, Sarah, married into the neighboring Grigsby family at age nineteen. The Grigsbys were North Carolinians who lived for a time in Kentucky before settling in Spencer County, about three miles south of the Lincoln cabin. In accordance with tradition, the couple married in her father's cabin but settled on a farm near the groom's family, about two miles southward, and the Lincolns now had in-laws in the neighborhood.[22]

Surrounded by relatives, neighbors, and friends, the Lincoln family felt economically secure. Their farm flourished, and they engaged in the kind of neighborly reciprocity that characterized the advancing frontier. A decade after arriving in Indiana, the Lincolns were farming about forty acres of land. Along with two of his neighbors, Thomas Lincoln relinquished one-half of his 160-acre claim, turning it back to the government, preferring a secure title to less land. The most successful farmers reinvested their profits and bought more land, and Thomas purchased an adjoining twenty-acre plot already under cultivation, giving him outright title to one hundred acres of farmland. By the time the family moved to Illinois, they had a surplus of "about 100 hogs and 4 or 5 hundred bushels of corn," which they sold to one of their neighbors.[23]

To contribute to the family's survival, Thomas Lincoln, like most frontier fathers, "hired out" his son to neighbors. In the absence of cash, most of young Abraham's work was exchanged—or "changed"—and repaid later in labor rather than money. Dennis Hanks remembered Lincoln "occasionaly changing work with the Neighbors which was customary in those days." Like most rural youths, Lincoln hired out for the first time at age thirteen or fourteen. According to neighbor and in-law Nathaniel Grigsby, the boy worked mostly "at hom[e] on his fathers 'farm." But he also exchanged labor with neighbors and worked for wages on his family's behalf. Grigsby later remembered that "he ocaisially took Jobs of claring or making fense rails Sometimes he worked on the ohio river." Clearly, young Abraham's labor was essential to his family's survival. But this labor exchange also testifies to the Lincolns' economic interconnectedness with other families in the neighborhood and their growing ability to spare Abraham to work within the local farm economy.[24]

Labor drew Lincoln farther and farther afield from his family. He "swapped" labor with neighbors, especially relatives, to help them expand their farms—clearing land and splitting fence rails—and bring in the crucial harvest. In-law Nathaniel Grigsby remembered that "He worked for me frequently—a few days only at a time," pulling fodder to feed his livestock. "Abe worked for us at various times at 25 cents per day," Elizabeth Crawford recalled. "Worked hard & faithful." Working for his family drew Lincoln to some of the neighboring towns. By the time he was fifteen, Lincoln was hauling wool to the town of Princeton, forty miles distant, to have it carded in preparation for his stepmother's spinning wheel. On one occasion, he carried eighteen pounds to the carding mill, "on a flea-bitten gray mare." In the absence of cash, he had to pay a "toll" of one-sixth of the wool to the miller.[25]

As a youth, Lincoln found himself cutting cord wood all day on his father's account. Significantly, this early experience with labor exchange inadvertently turned into a poignant lesson in frontier economics. Expecting, too optimistically, to be paid in cash, Lincoln received payment in "store goods" instead. Turning the setback to his own advantage, he selected a length of white cloth as payment, and he later had it sewn up into a shirt. Setting aside his drab homespun, Lincoln now donned "the first white shirt he ever had in his life." While the primitive frontier economy required Lincoln to exchange his labor for goods rather than money, it allowed his first glimpse of the emerging market in manufactured goods that would soon replace subsistence and transform the American economy forever.[26]

At seventeen, Lincoln found a job working on a ferry on the Ohio River. Here he acquired an interest in river transportation that influenced his early political and economic views. Two years later, Lincoln traveled by flatboat all the way to New Orleans. James Gentry, the merchant who founded Gentryville, hired Lincoln and his own son Allen to float a load of produce all the way down the Ohio and Mississippi rivers to the Gulf Coast, the West's leading market. This seven-hundred-mile journey emphasizes the crude transportation and marketing facilities available to farmers and merchants in the early Midwest. In the absence of a local market, farmers often accompanied their own produce to New Orleans rather than selling it, as they would later, to local wholesalers. Indeed, the "Orleans Boat" was often the only practical connection between a frontier community and the outside world. In this way, Lincoln participated in the "triangular trade" that characterized the region. Farmers floated produce down the Mississippi to New Orleans, where merchants used their profits to ship cotton and sugar to cities on the East Coast. There, factories churned out manufactures that reached midwestern markets by floating down the Ohio River. This New Orleans trip broadened Lincoln's geographical and cultural horizons, giving him a glimpse of the world beyond the confines of his family farm, and represented his initiation into the practice of black slavery within the Deep South.[27]

At age eighteen, Lincoln earned his first real dollar, an occasion he remembered for the rest of his life. Working on the Ohio River, he hauled some trunks aboard a steamboat for a couple of travelers and was astounded when they each tossed him a half-dollar. "I could scarcely credit," he recalled as president three decades later, "that I, a poor boy, had earned a dollar in less than a day." According to reminiscence, Lincoln declared that "you may think it a very little thing, and in these days it seems like a trifle, but it was the most important thing in my life." A bit later, Lincoln and stepbrother John D. Johnston went to the Ohio River to work on a canal, and each received a silver dollar. Augustus Chapman remembered that "This is the first silver dollar Lincoln ever had or owned of his own & of it he was very proud." In this barter economy, a man's first dollar held more than symbolic significance. It represented a memorable introduction to an emerging market economy driven by money rather than exchange. Lincoln undoubtedly spoke for many such farm boys when he summed up his feelings: "The world seemed wider and fairer before me."[28]

The widening world drew the Lincoln family farther westward. John Hanks, Nancy Hanks Lincoln's first cousin, joined the Lincoln clan in Indiana six years after they arrived. Seven years older than Abraham Lincoln, he lived with the family for two years and then bought a farm next to theirs. He married in 1826 and two years later decided to move to Illinois, settling near Decatur, on the Sangamon River thirty miles east of Springfield, where he bought a farm that he lived on for the rest of his life. In typical pioneer fashion, Hanks beckoned his in-laws with descriptions of Illinois' rich prairie soil. Dennis Hanks went out to visit and decided to move his family to rejoin his cousin John. He talked Squire Hall into the idea, and so the families of both of Sarah Lincoln's daughters prepared to move westward to Illinois. Dennis Hanks remembered decades later that Sarah "could not think of parting with them," and so the entire clan decided to move west to Decatur, Illinois.[29]

This time, however, the family went westward without Lincoln's sister Sarah. At age twenty, a year after marrying, she died in childbirth. By the time he was eighteen, three out of five members of Lincoln's immediate family—mother, brother, and sister—were dead. Like many resilient pioneer families, however, this fragmented family survived—indeed it grew. Thomas, as patriarch, now headed an extended family of thirteen members, his own family and those of his two stepdaughters. As Dennis Hanks recalled, "We all went—Lincolns, Hankses, and Johnstons all hanging together." Experienced at moving, the family began to prepare for the journey several weeks in advance. They sold their farm to an in-law, Charles

Grigsby, and their farm surplus to a neighbor to amass a sizable nest egg of almost five hundred dollars. Thomas Lincoln built the wagons that transported the three united families.[30]

Although he had just turned twenty-one the previous month and was now legally an adult, Lincoln made this journey westward with his family rather than staying in Indiana. During this period, perhaps only one-third of farm youths stayed with their families beyond age twenty-one as Linclon did. He recognized the significance of his choice and noted his age in both of the autobiographical sketches that he wrote for his presidential campaign. In March 1830, this Lincoln–Hanks–Johnston clan, as they thought of themselves, left for Illinois in three covered wagons and settled near Decatur on the northern bank of the Sangamon River.

James Gentry, the local storeowner, recalled years later that, "I well remember the day when the Lincolns started for Illinois. Nearly all the neighbors were there to see them leave." During fourteen years, they had turned their farm in the wilderness into a comfortable home with dependable neighbors, and now they headed for a new frontier to start all over again.[31]

CHAPTER 3

I Came to Illinois

Illinois, like the rest of the Midwest, was originally explored and settled along its rivers. The first Euroamerican towns in the region were French settlements along the Mississippi River, south of the Missouri River. These eighteenth-century French towns—Cahokia, Kaskaskia, Fort du Chartres, and Prairie du Rocher—hugged the Mississippi and never contained more than a few hundred settlers. After the United States acquired this territory in 1783 and secured it in the War of 1812, American settlers began to enter the region, taking up the southern wooded triangle between the Mississippi, Ohio, and Wabash rivers. Illinois Territory was established in 1809, the year in which Abraham Lincoln was born. Before the appearance of roads, settlement centered on rivers, creating a chain of American towns at the mouths of major tributaries of the Ohio and Mississippi—Shawneetown at the mouth of the Wabash, Lawrenceville near the mouth of the Embarrass, and Kaskaskia at the mouth of the Kaskaskia River. The heart of this early settlement was the American Bottoms, 600 square miles lying between the mouth of the Kaskaskia and the mouth of the Illinois, so named to distinguish the area from Spanish possessions west of the Mississippi.[1]

Between 1815 and 1830, whites aggressively extinguished Native American land titles, established regional transportation routes, most notably the Erie Canal, and carved out six new western states in a mere five years. Illinois achieved statehood during this period of vigorous expansion, in 1818. Southern settlers dominated the early Illinois frontier. Southerners tended to travel to Illinois by water routes, principally the Ohio, Cumberland, and Tennessee rivers, and they established river towns once they arrived, taking up rich bottom lands and advancing only slowly upriver into the wooded interior. As a result, initial settlement in Illinois followed a frontier line that moved from south to north. During the 1820s, settlement spread rapidly northward along the Mississippi and Illinois rivers, and especially into the region between the two rivers, the Military Bounty Lands, in which War of

1812 veterans claimed nearly 3 million acres of land donated by the federal government.[2]

Before the availability of railway travel in the 1850s, migrants to the Midwest followed the most convenient roads and especially waterways to their new homes. Southerners spilled westward by land through the Cumberland Gap and along the Wilderness Trail into Kentucky and Tennessee. The Tennessee, Cumberland, and Kentucky rivers subsequently carried them by water to Illinois. Mid-Atlantic settlers crossed the Alleghenies in Pennsylvania and then traveled the Ohio River and later the National Road westward. New England settlers traveled the Erie Canal, completed in 1825. After 1830, steamboats on the Great Lakes began to carry northern settlers directly to the Illinois prairies by way of the budding city of Chicago. Once the earliest settlers established a new home, they encouraged relatives and neighbors to follow. Through this process of "chain migration," successful settlers lured family and friends to follow them westward, sometimes even "sponsoring" them in their new homes.[3]

Traditionally, southerners hesitated to leave the wooded South to settle the prairie grasslands of northern Illinois. Indeed, many southerners, the "woodsman" Daniel Boone most prominent among them, avoided the Illinois prairies altogether and moved farther westward to Missouri. There, they continued two southern traditions, woodland agriculture and black slavery. Northern Illinois's prairie terrain and the state's rejection of slavery in 1824 worked together to confine southern settlers to the lower third of the state. This "Little Egypt," centered on Cairo, later achieved notoriety as an outpost of southern racism. Northern settlers, however, took up the prairie in earnest, fanning out from Chicago and Lake Michigan westward and southward, especially along the Illinois River, mingling with southerners in the Sangamon Country. The result was a striking series of cultural layers of Deep South, Upper South, Middle Atlantic, and New England settlements running south to north in Illinois. The pioneers hailed from four "culture hearths" in the East—the Lowland South, primarily the Carolinas and Tennessee; the Upland South, including Virginia, Maryland, and Kentucky; the Midlands region of New Jersey, Pennsylvania, and Ohio; and New England, which included New York.[4]

Regional clustering, chain migration, and channeling produced a complex pattern of sectional layers in Illinois that followed latitude but also reflected cultural influences. Nineteenth-century Illinois contained five culture regions. The Lowland South region, settled by Tennesseeans and Carolinians, represented the initial core of settlement in the woodlands that lay between the Wabash and the Mississippi rivers. Upland Southerners, dominated by Kentuckians, settled farther north along the Mississippi, Illinois, and Sangamon rivers in Illinois's interior. The Upland South region hugged these major rivers and bisected the Sangamon Country. A second core area, commonly dubbed Yankeeland because it was dominated by New Yorkers,

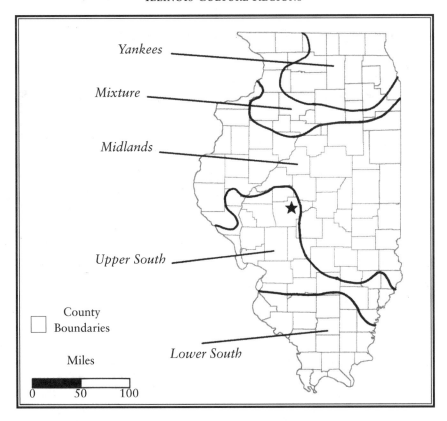

Yankees

Mixture

Midlands

Upper South

County
Boundaries

Miles

Lower South

0   50   100

spread westward and southward from its hub at Chicago. A fourth region, the Midlands, settled primarily by Ohioans and Pennsylvanians, separated the southern and northern zones. Shaped like an hourglass, this Midlands region flared out along the Indiana border to the east and the Mississippi River to the west, but was pinched in the middle by southerners moving northward and Yankees moving southward along the Illinois River. A final transitional zone mixed Midlanders and Yankees in the region between Springfield and Chicago.[5]

The Sangamon Country lay at the extreme northern edge of the Upland South region and therefore straddled the boundary between the southern and Midlands culture regions. Lincoln, a Kentuckian, hailed from Illinois's Upland South cultural hearth, which enjoyed a slight numerical dominance in central Illinois. Sangamon County, in particular, sat in the middle of a central transition zone among three dominant culture areas. By 1850, in fact, the area exhibited a rough balance among Upland Southerners, Midlanders, and Yankees. Overall, Upland Southerners and Midlanders each

---

I Came to Illinois

represented about one-third and New Englanders about one-fourth of the native-born population. The single largest group was Kentuckians, followed closely by Pennsylvanians and New Yorkers. Lowland Southerners, dominated by Tennessee natives, represented a relative handful of the population.[6]

The first white settlers to reach the region around Decatur were traders who built a trading house on the Sangamon River in 1816 to barter with Native Americans. According to tradition, up to five hundred Native Americans would camp at the spot to acquire eastern manufactured goods. Around 1825, white encroachment forced the Native Americans westward, after which only small groups of Native Americans traded at the post. The first permanent settler was a Yankee from Connecticut, Leonard Stevens, and he was soon joined by three South Carolinians, the Ward brothers— Jerry, John, and James. Stevens settled on the north side of the river, and the Ward brothers on the south side. The Sangamon River soon became a widely acknowledged dividing line between northern and southern settlers. The "Stevens settlement" attracted northerners, while the "Ward settlement" on the south side of the river attracted southerners from Tennessee and the Carolinas. "Those comprising the Stevens settlements were from New York, Virginia and Ohio," according to reminiscence, "and were called Yankees by those of the other settlement who were from the Carolinas and Tennessee. The feeling between the two settlements was not very friendly, and fights were not uncommon." Legend holds that a melee erupted over whether to locate Decatur in the northern or the southern settlement. Significantly, the Lincolns settled on the northern, "Yankee" side of the river. Lincoln went out of his way three decades later to remember that "His father and family settled a new place on the North side of the Sangamon river."[7]

Originally, most settlers lived in the two settlements facing each other across the river. Around 1828, however, "a wave of immigration poured into the county, and the settlements began rapidly to extend up and down the river." Macon County was established in 1829, with Decatur as the county seat. When the Lincolns arrived in the following year, they found a general store and tavern, ten or twelve cabins lining two streets, a post office that had just opened the week before, and a courthouse under construction. By coincidence, they found their cousin John Hanks chinking and daubing the new courthouse, a two-story log building in which Lincoln later practiced law. Hanks led the family downriver to a spot six miles past his own claim and helped them establish a new home. As they did in Indiana, the family remained squatters during their first year in Illinois, a common frontier practice. "Persons emigrating to the county usually selected their locations and commenced their improvements on government land," an early historian recalled, "and waited until they were able to amass from the scanty resources enough to purchase the forty or eighty acres—as the case might be—at the sales at the land office at Vandalia." In fact, the Lincolns never bought their Macon County farm, and the claim remained government land until a subsequent settler bought it five years later.[8]

Hanks gave the family a load of logs that he had prepared in advance, and "Here they built a log-cabin," in Lincoln's words, "into which they removed." Thomas Lincoln knew how to join a cabin without using nails, but like most pioneers, the family had brought a precious few that they salvaged from their old cabin in Indiana. The Lincolns clung to the woodlands where a "fringe of timber" lined the waterways, and they only edged out onto the prairies. "At that day there were but few people who dreamed even of the large prairies becoming settled and put into cultivation," noted one early account. "Many of the early settlers made 'clearings,' and started their little farms in the timber, as they had been accustomed to do in the States from which they came." The Lincolns selected a plot of land at the prairie margin, "at the junction of the timber-land and prairie," as Abraham Lincoln recalled. The wooded portion of their claim provided logs for house construction, rails for fencing, and firewood for the winter. The prairie portion afforded the luxury of planting without the onerous labor of clearing trees. Lincoln now exchanged his axe for a hoe and "broke prairie," laboriously peeling off the thick sod to reveal the rich, black soil beneath. In their first year, the family broke ten acres of ground and planted it in corn. Their relatives and neighbors held a "railing party" to split enough rails to fence the farm. The result was an extended Lincoln-Hanks family, with John Hanks and his brothers Charles and William farming nearby.[9]

As he had done in Indiana, Lincoln exchanged labor with his neighbors, but this time he worked on his own account. Neighbors recollected that he "worked among the farmers, picking up enough to clothe himself." He split rails and chopped wood with his famous axe but also broke prairie with a team of four oxen. Legend held that he broke fifty acres of prairie during his first year in Illinois. In a typical agreement, Lincoln split rails for John Hanks's sister, receiving a single yard of homespun jeans cloth for each batch of four hundred rails he split. He worked until he had enough cloth, "richly dyed with walnut bark," to make a pair of trousers. Labor exchange also provided him with room and board. "His home with his father thenceforth was but nominal," legal colleague Henry C. Whitney recalled years later. "He really lived with families for whom he worked as a hired laborer." Working with neighbors also introduced Lincoln to his lifelong passion, politics. According to legend, the youth was plowing a field near Decatur when he "heard cheering upon 'the square,' so turned his oxen into a corner, vaulted the fence, and went to see what was 'going on.'" He listened to a Democratic speaker and then jumped up onto a stump to deliver his first political speech, urging the improvement of the Sangamon River.[10]

His search for work eventually drew him away from his family forever. Despite the dreams of improvement and all the acres of broken prairie, the

Sangamon Country remained a wild and dangerous land. "There were deer in the woods and the prairies," Jane Martin Johns, who grew up near Decatur, wrote decades later, "and sometimes they came so near to the houses that they could be seen from the open door. Wolves lurked in the thickets and tall grass, and often showed themselves openly." Flocks of wild turkey and prairie chickens by the hundreds inhabited the timber and foraged in the fields for grasshoppers and grain hidden within the harvest stubble.[11]

The family's first winter introduced them to the worst ravages of the Illinois frontier. Between Christmas 1830, and New Year's Day 1831, a horrible blizzard devastated the land. When it cleared, three feet of snow blanketed the prairies. "Then came a rain, with weather so cold that it froze as it fell, forming a crust of ice over this three feet of snow, nearly, if not quite, strong enough to bear a man." For two weeks, temperatures never surpassed twelve below, and the Deep Snow, as pioneers called it, lingered for more than two months. In all, thirty-one snows fell during that legendary winter. Hunters who braved the weather disappeared without a trace along with their horses and dogs, only to reappear, frozen where they fell, during the spring thaw. Wild animals—deer, turkey, and small game—stuck fast in the ice-covered drifts and fell easy prey to wolves, roving dogs, and hunters. Pioneer farmers had no time to harvest their corn before the snow blanketed their fields, and they watched their livestock starve. Cut off from precious gristmills, settlers ground their own cornmeal at home with crude mortars and pestles to gather a handful of grain for daily bread.[12]

Long after falling, the snow drifted across the prairies, driven by a relentless northwest wind, a new experience for farmers who hailed from the South. Settlers broke through the snowdrifts with ox-teams pulling road scrapers, but the drifts quickly re-formed across the windswept prairies. Travelers laboriously "wallowed" through this rippling sea of snow until they packed it down into roadways, and they sleighed and sledded on narrow ribbons of ice until spring. When the snows melted at last, these ice-roads remained, silver threads glistening like a web across the newly green prairie. With the other pioneers, the Lincolns suffered mightily during the Deep Snow. Caught short of corn, the family had to borrow from their new neighbors. Abraham Lincoln and John Hanks walked across the frozen Sangamon to reach a horse-powered mill on the southern side. The mill's owner opened the fence to his cornfield, and the two cousins gathered what was left of the grain, which they hauled back home on a sled pulled by oxen.[13]

During these months of enforced idleness, Lincoln made his first Illinois connections and his first plans to strike off on his own. John Hanks was an experienced flatboatman who had made a dozen trips down the Ohio and Mississippi rivers to New Orleans. Now he found work floating a load of pork, corn, and live hogs to New Orleans for Springfield merchant Denton

Offutt. Lincoln also had experience as a raftsman, and he and his step-brother John D. Johnston agreed to join Hanks and Offutt on the journey to New Orleans, floating together down the Sangamon, Illinois, and Mississippi rivers. As the Deep Snow thawed, the three young men set out to meet Offutt—described by contemporaries as a big talker, a "gasy—windy—brain rattling man"—in a Springfield tavern.[14]

During a typical spring thaw, the melting snows ran off the level prairie, forming freshets that flooded the many creeks and small rivers that drained the countryside around Springfield. As this Deep Snow melted, however, the usual "rivulets" swelled into gushing torrents, rendering travel by land impossible and travel by water difficult and dangerous. "The county was so flooded," Lincoln recalled, "as to make traveling by land impracticable." Instead, the three young kinsmen bought a large canoe and paddled it down the Sangamon River into Springfield. Lincoln remembered this canoe trip as "the time and manner of A's first entrance into Sangamon County." Leaving his father's family behind him at last, Lincoln appeared in Springfield in March 1831. Paddling a canoe, he arrived in his future home as a self-described "strange, friendless, uneducated, penniless boy"—the son of an "undistinguished family" indeed.[15]

CHAPTER 4

Springfield, Ills

T he first white settlement in the Sangamon Country appeared in the same year Illinois achieved statehood. In 1818, Elisha Kelly, a North Carolinian, ventured into the region to hunt deer and settled the high ground between two ravines along Spring Creek, a tributary of the Sangamon River. During this territorial period, southern settlers filled the wooded lower third of the state and began edging out onto the prairies. Kelly went back to North Carolina and talked his father and four brothers into joining him in Illinois. Two of Kelly's sisters also arrived, but they moved on to Missouri within thirty days to avoid losing their six slaves. More families arrived continually and spread out over the area, but for several years the "Kelly cabins" remained the center of settlement.[1]

By this time, the Sangamon Country lay at the northern edge of white settlement in Illinois. One old pioneer remembered that "The Sangamon river was about the dividing line between the white settlers and the Indians." Within a few years, however, enough settlers had straggled into the Sangamon Country to demand their own county. Their main concern was not local self-governance but simply the inconvenience of doing official business at the county seat, Edwardsville, seventy miles south near the Mississippi. Because of the distance, settlers got little in exchange for their taxes, which they paid in the form of raccoon skins grudgingly handed over to county officials who periodically swept through the neighborhood. The legislature created Sangamon County in 1821. The settlers held their first election at the house of Elisha Kelly's brother John and elected three county commissioners—southerners William Drennan, Zachariah Peter, and Rivers Cormack. This county board met the next day and appointed Charles R. Matheny clerk of the county commissioners court. Matheny built a one-room log cabin to house his growing family, took on all the county offices except sheriff, and became something of a one-man government. Still, this was not yet much of a government. According to one old settler, "All these offices heaped upon him did not give him a bare support."[2]

The commissioners' first task was to choose a temporary county seat, as the law stipulated, "as near the centre of the population of said county as circumstances will admit." Commissioners Peter and Drennan surveyed the neighborhood, which numbered nine widely scattered families, and quickly "designated a certain point in the prairie near John Kelley's field, on the waters of Spring Creek, at a stake marked Z. & D., as the temporary seat of justice." They named the spot Springfield. "This place had been selected as the temporary county seat, to accomodate the squatters until the survey and sale of land and until a permanent site could be selected," according to an old settler. "One reason for selecting this place was that there were more settlers in this vicinity than in any other part of northern Illinois, with whom the judge and lawyers could find quarters."[3]

A Kentucky merchant named Elijah Iles arrived on horseback a while later to found the settlement's first store. Iles's father was a native Pennsylvanian who migrated to Kentucky in 1790 and married a relative of frontiersman David Crockett. The Iles family exemplified the kind of simple rusticity that characterized the self-reliant Kentucky pioneers who dominated early Springfield and counted Lincoln among their number. Living in a one-room log cabin in Bath County, Kentucky, just east of Lexington, the Ileses shifted for themselves. Iles recalled that "My mother, with her wool cards, spinning wheel, and loom, manufactured all the clothing worn by herself and the family, except the buckskin pants worn by the men and boys." But the Iles family also typified the notorious southern dependence on black slave labor to get ahead in the world. After Iles's mother died in childbirth when he was six, his father bought a slave woman to keep house and raise the children. Iles went to school for two winters, a frontier education similar to Lincoln's, but then his father gave him three hundred dollars to buy a herd of cattle to graze in Kentucky's hilly backcountry. Iles doubled his money after three years and then, like Daniel Boone before him, set out for the interior of Missouri to hunt, graze, and farm.[4]

At age twenty-two, in 1818, Iles reached the Boone's Lick Country of Missouri, where he bought and sold "government land," the newly released public domain, on speculation. During a visit back to Kentucky in 1821, Iles crossed Illinois on horseback and "heard of a district called the Sangamon valley, north of St. Louis one hundred miles, then just settling, said to be very fertile." Deciding to take a look, Iles followed the stakes of a team of surveyors who were laying out the National Road from Vincennes, Indiana, to Vandalia, the new capital of Illinois. The trail was easy to follow because "the wagon hauling the stakes made deep ruts" in the soggy prairie loam. Iles found nine families living near the Sangamon on the future site of Springfield and liked what he saw.[5]

Iles traveled back to Missouri to sell his land and collect his debts. At age twenty-five, he returned to Springfield with his saddlebags full of Spanish silver. "I hunted around and found the stake that had been stuck for the beginning of a town named Springfield," he later remembered, "and then bargained for the erection of a store house, to be set near the stake." This "store house," in pioneer fashion, was literally a store and a house in one. Iles lived in one room of the two-room cabin and conducted his business in the other. This was the first store in Sangamon County and the beginning of the town of Springfield. Iles went on to dominate the new town economically during its first decade.[6]

Iles intended to speculate in land, but the U.S. government was not yet selling land in the Sangamon Country, so he concentrated on becoming a merchant. "I had gained some little experience in selling goods," he recalled, "which determined me to use what money I had in merchandising until the land sales should take place." Typically of the man, Iles went into business on a grand scale. He traveled to St. Louis, the only place in the region that sold goods at wholesale, and purchased twenty-five tons of wrought iron, dry goods, and groceries. He hired five men to tow a chartered boat—pulling on a rope 300 feet long—150 miles up the Illinois River to the mouth of the Sangamon. Iles then spent the next month hauling the twenty-five tons of goods by wagon the remaining fifty miles to Springfield. His gamble paid off, and for the next two years he held a virtual monopoly on the trade of the region. Farmers trekked from up to eighty miles around to buy necessities at Iles's store. Spanish silver, the only available currency, was scarce, so customers paid him in frontier commodities that he could trade wholesale at St. Louis—homemade cotton and linen cloth, butter, honey, and beeswax.[7]

After selling out his first stock of goods, Iles locked his store, left the key with the one-man government, Charles Matheny, and went back to St. Louis to buy more goods. When he returned, he found that his store had been robbed and nearly cleaned out, one hazard of doing business on the frontier. He now returned to his real passion, land speculation. Before the first government land sale, all the settlers in the area were officially squatters. Iles claimed a quarter-section of land around Springfield and, to ward off rival bidders, "told all who chose to settle in the place that if I got the land I would give each a lot."[8]

The government opened a land office at Springfield in 1823 with Pascal Enos Sr. as the first receiver. Enos was a New Englander who married at age twenty-one and moved west to Cincinnati at the close of the War of 1812. Enos and his new wife moved almost immediately to St. Charles, Missouri, where Pascal Jr. was born, then to St. Louis, and yet again to St. Clair County, Illinois, in the American Bottoms. When President Monroe appointed the elder Enos the first receiver of the U.S. Land Office in Springfield, the young family made their fifth move in eight years and landed in Springfield. Enos quickly made connections with Iles, who was by now the wealthiest speculator in the district, and the two joined forces to profit from Springfield's impending growth, buying all the land around Springfield and carving it into quarters. At the first land sale, according to a witness, they

ELIJAH ILES. A SHREWD MERCHANT AND LAND SPECULATOR, ILES WAS ONE OF
SPRINGFIELD'S FOUNDERS AND AN EARLY LINCOLN SUPPORTER.
Courtesy of the Illinois State Historical Library.

faced "no opposition" and in one stroke simply "purchased Springfield." In
1825, the legislature appointed a commission to locate a permanent seat for
the county. Legend holds that when the commissioners arrived, Springfielders wined and dined and so exhausted them on a roundabout tour of
prospective townsites that they gave in and selected Springfield. The law
required the new county seat to donate thirty-five acres for public use. In a
shrewd maneuver practiced by many town founders during this period, Iles

and Enos personally donated the land, securing the county seat, and assuring the town's continued growth.[9]

The primary role of the Sangamon County commissioners, of course, was to establish a system of justice. In the summer of 1821, they appointed constables and justices to keep peace and built a jail that was so crude the sheriff refused to occupy it. Iles recalled that, without a jail, "We erected a whipping-post, as we had laws to punish theft or other lawless acts. If convicted, the culpret had to be whipped upon his bare back." The county hurriedly erected a log courthouse, "chinked outside and daubed inside" to keep out the winter cold. The biggest problem was public finance, because the county had no tax base until the settlers could buy their own land. The commissioners responded by carving the Iles and Enos donation into town lots for sale to raise revenue. During the 1830s, fashion dictated a town square, so the commissioners reserved some of the land in the center of town for county buildings. They also tried, but failed, to fund major projects through "subscription," providing half of the funds in hopes that private donations would make up the difference.[10]

A second major task was to create a rudimentary infrastructure facilitating settlement, travel, and trade. The county's crude amenities hampered initial settlement. The Sangamon River was barely navigable, and the region had no real roads. As Lincoln discovered on his first visit to the village, spring flooding made rivers more a hindrance than a help to transportation, and travelers rode randomly across the prairie rather than following recognized roads. The lack of bridges forced a troublesome dependence on unreliable private ferries. In fact, the county's first ferry was nothing more than a canoe: "Persons could be taken over safe and dry, animals could swim, and wagons were taken to pieces, and with their loads were carried over, piece by piece." Elijah Iles remembered reaching the Sangamon River and finding nothing but "a horn left on the south side, opposite the ferry, to be blown by persons desiring to cross." Iles blew on the horn for several hours with no result. He tried again the next day and still failed to raise the ferryman. Finally, on the third day, "by loud and continuous blowing," he managed to hail the ferry and cross the river. Another hindrance was the lack of regular mail service. Bad weather sometimes delayed the mail for up to three weeks and prohibited the circulation of newspapers entirely.[11]

Newcomers considered accommodations equally unreliable. Early Springfield's only hotel was a two-room cabin run by Gershom Jayne, the town's first doctor, and his wife. The Jaynes lived in one room and lodged travelers in the other. Newcomers had to board with established families or simply camp out in their wagons while building their first homes. Others lived in the courthouse temporarily. Early settlers made regular seventy-mile trips on horseback to buy food before their first crops came in. Throughout the 1820s, the county commissioners worked to facilitate transportation and trade. Between 1821 and 1826, the county licensed three ferries over the Illinois River, three over Salt Creek, and two over the Sangamon. In exchange for licenses, the ferries charged regulated fares, 6½¢ for "footmen" and horses and 50¢ for a "wagon and Team of 4 head of brutes." The county also licensed taverns, which were havens for travelers and newcomers, as well as groceries and "houses of entertainment," a total of eighteen in the first five years, one-half of them in Springfield. In exchange for a $3 license, tavern keepers posted prices of 25¢ for each meal, 12½¢ for each night's lodging, and 12½¢ for "single feed for horse." In the absence of a tax base, the county let private enterprise build the initial infrastructure. In this form of "mixed enterprise," the county both encouraged and taxed private activity by issuing licenses while protecting the public and shaping development through heavy regulation.[12]

In 1822, Springfield consisted of a store, a hotel, a blacksmith's shop, a courthouse, and a jail, all fashioned from logs. Three years later, the village had 150 inhabitants and one street, running east and west. In March 1825, the county commissioners ordered Springfield "laid off into lots by some skillful surveyor," and the first land sale took place in May. East-west streets were numbered, and north-south streets were named for U.S. presidents. The county retained a public square, bounded by Washington, Adams, Fifth, and Sixth streets, which eventually developed into a prosperous business district. A new brick courthouse, completed in 1831, was the town's centerpiece. Business blossomed, and the county began licensing retail trade. In 1832, Springfield was incorporated as a town.[13]

Springfield attracted typical pioneer families, whose experiences go far to challenge the romantic stereotype of migrants moving westward in wagon trains. Families usually traveled alone or with one or two other families, and rarely in covered wagons. Single settlers typically rode on horseback, and a surprising number of families bought or rented horses, carriages, and boats to take them westward, testifying to the rudimentary and unorganized modes of travel available before the advent of railroads. Migrants to Springfield almost never traveled in the legendary wagon or emigrant "train," and only one family remembered coming west in a classic "prairie schooner." Heading west as three families, linked through marriage, the Lincolns were thoroughly typical, crowding into three wagons and finding their own way westward.

Just two early settlers reported trekking west in a wagon train or as part of a "colony." Charles Phelps remembered coming west "with a colony who traveled from Massachusetts by way of the New York canal to Buffalo, by lake to Detroit, by land across the country one hundred and sixty miles and thence by canoes down the St. Joseph, Kankakee, and Illinois rivers." Robert Zimmerman, a painter and chair maker from Pennsylvania, started west alone, traveling by stage and then joining a wagon train purely by accident. After missing the stage at Terre Haute, Indiana, and discovering that only one coach came through each week, he started westward on foot with a few other migrants. "Arriving at the Okaw river in Illinois they found a company of emigrants from Tennessee, numbering one hundred and twenty wagons, with a corresponding number of men, women and children, all waiting until the men could construct a bridge for the teams to cross." Zimmerman joined the wagon train, "riding and walking alternately," and parted with the Tennesseeans at Springfield.[14]

Although the earliest settlers used a surprising number of transportation modes and routes on their way west, they followed several general patterns. Families typically left their homes in the East during the fall, just after the harvest, and traveled during the usually unproductive months of late fall and early winter, reaching Illinois in early spring, at the beginning of the next planting season. These farmers therefore sandwiched their migration between two growing seasons, an otherwise idle time in an agricultural society. The Sullivan Conant family is a good example, leaving Massachusetts in the fall of 1830 with their four children. The Conants spent four fall and winter months traveling by wagon, canal boat, raft, and steamboat from Massachusetts to Illinois. The winter journey was difficult, however, and one hundred miles from their destination, their youngest child died. They continued their trek overland, riding a sleigh into Springfield on the four feet of snowpack that the Deep Snow left behind. Similarly, the Eliphet Hawley family left Albany, New York, in the fall. Unlike the Conants, however, they wintered in Pittsburgh until spring to accommodate the birth of a child. The Hawleys joined another family in buying a boat, which took them down the Ohio to Shawneetown. They continued their journey overland, reaching Springfield in April 1822 with the same horses and wagons with which they had begun their journey. Their decision to winter in Pittsburgh may have allowed them to add rather than lose a child on their way west. The Lincolns were also typical in this respect. They left Indiana between growing seasons, arriving in Illinois in March, just in time for the spring planting.[15]

Old settlers preferred water routes, where available, rather than traveling by land. Rivers—particularly the Ohio and Mississippi—stood out in their memories. One couple remembered dashing across the icebound Mississippi in the dead of winter, literally leaping onto the ice while it was moving, "jumping the open space between the ice and the shore." Most early settlers, even New Englanders, preferred the southern route to Illinois—following the Ohio and Mississippi rivers—rather than traveling overland. As one settler put it, "Any route to Illinois by way of Chicago, in those days, was not to be thought of, as that place was just emerging from the condition of an Indian trading station." Only two settlers reported traveling overland from Chicago, a bumpy, eight-day journey by stagecoach that cost twenty-five dollars in gold. The convenience of the river journey is exemplified in the route Abraham Freeman traveled from Ohio. Freeman reached

Fort Wayne, Indiana, by land, but rather than traveling in a straight line westward to Springfield, he traveled by boat down the Wabash, down the Ohio, and up the Mississippi, "working his passage, as he had no money." Landing at St. Louis, Freeman walked the remaining one hundred miles to Springfield to join his uncle. Abraham Lincoln, of course, arrived in Springfield by water, paddling a canoe down the Sangamon.[16]

Undoubtedly the most important single route to Illinois focused on the forks of the Ohio at Pittsburgh, gathering settlers from New York, Pennsylvania, and Maryland and funneling them downriver. Settlers found their way to Pittsburgh by a surprising variety of routes—by road, river, and canal—and then simply floated down the Ohio all the way west. The John family left western New York in 1840 and traveled by canal, lake, and stagecoach to Pittsburgh, then by steamboat down the Ohio River. They bought a horse and wagon at New Albany, Indiana, crossed the Wabash at Vincennes, and arrived in Sangamon County during a driving spring rain. The family reminisced that "the prairie was covered with water, and they could only disern the path by observing where the grass did not rise above the water." Remarkably, this family's journey from New York to Illinois consumed a mere five weeks, dramatizing the speed made possible by the water route westward.[17]

Sangamon County was the most populous in Illinois when Lincoln arrived, hosting thirteen thousand settlers, most of them farmers. Despite Springfield's rapid growth, this remained fundamentally an agricultural society, with four-fifths of employment devoted to working Sangamon County's widely scattered farmsteads. Despite frontier dangers, the first settlers spread out as far as possible. As one pioneer wife and mother reminisced—or lamented—"They did not select their homes so near each other as one would suppose." Another settler remembered that "at this time it took at least 10 Miles square to constitute a Neighborhood and a woman would think nothing of picking up a child and walk 4 or 5 Miles to visit a Neighbor." Farmers preferred to take up land that was partly timbered, to provide logs for housing, fencing, and firewood. The first families, mostly southerners, avoided the prairies and settled along the timbered creekbeds. As a result, every creek "became the nucleus for a community." When the Barnett family reached Springfield in 1829, they found "about two hundred inhabitants, mostly living in log cabins near the timber." As a native Kentuckian remembered, "the population was sparse, the settlements being near the timber, and around the prairie, no one dreaming that those vast prairies would ever be entered." Soon, however, all of Sangamon County's timbered land had been taken up. By 1832, the *Sangamo Journal* warned prospective settlers that the county was "pretty well filled up on the borders of the prairies." Throughout his life, Thomas Lincoln exemplified this southern preference for creekbed settlement. Born on Linnville Creek, he built homes throughout his life on a series of creeks—Nolin Creek, Knob

Creek, and Pigeon Creek—and died on a homestead along Muddy Creek.[18]

After filling up the timber in central Illinois southern-born farmers now began a reluctant transition to prairie agriculture. The William Drennan family's experience was typical. As South Carolinians, the Drennans originally "had not the slightest idea of cultivating the prairie." They practiced cooperative agriculture with two other families, clearing the timber from fifteen acres of woodland and planting corn and pumpkins. While fencing in their fields, however, they inadvertently enclosed less than an acre of prairie. One of the boys in the family playfully picked up a hoe and peeled back the thick prairie sod. The men, who "laughed at the idea as ridiculous," cultivated the tiny patch of prairie anyway and were amazed at the result. Other settlers similarly discovered—and soon boasted—that they could make a farm "by merely fencing it in and ploughing—no chopping—no logging—no stumps." Experience quickly overcame tradition, and settlers began filling in the prairies between the creekbeds, being sure—like the Lincolns—to include a few acres of woodland within their claims. Latecomers agonized over this "timber question," hoping to strike just the right balance between timberland and prairie. As one early settler remembered, "At that early period the Settlers made it a point to Secure choice lots of timber land, to go with their prarie land." After 1830, more prairie land was taken up than timber, and after 1840 there was no more timberland left at all. Lincoln's personal transition from axe to hoe exemplified the more general movement from the shelter of the timber onto the open prairie.[19]

This rich, grain-growing region specialized in corn and hog production, two traditional frontier staples. The county produced almost twice as much corn as wheat and more than three times as many hogs as cattle in 1840, two signs of a southern agricultural heritage. Manufacturing, mostly performed by self-employed craftsmen in crossroads villages, occupied just one-sixth of the workforce. Merchants and professionals, who dominated Springfield's early economy, were an economic elite representing less than 5 percent of Sangamon County's workforce. In this rudimentary farm economy, commerce and manufacturing were relatively undeveloped, reflecting a subsistence rather than commercial orientation.[20]

Still, Lincoln's rural and agricultural origins did little to prepare him for the more urban world he encountered once he arrived in Springfield. When Lincoln reached the Sangamon Country in 1831, he found a familiar farm economy centered on a stable family organization. The town of Springfield, however, was a great exception, a budding urban outpost of commerce and enterprise that violated the general pattern of family organization and rural self-sufficiency. The fullest depiction of Springfield during the winter of 1830–31, just before Lincoln arrived, appears in a "census" that the Old Settlers' Society prepared in 1859. Zimri A. Enos, younger son of Pascal Enos Sr., and one of the society's organizers, compiled a list that reconstructed the population of Springfield during the winter of the Deep Snow.

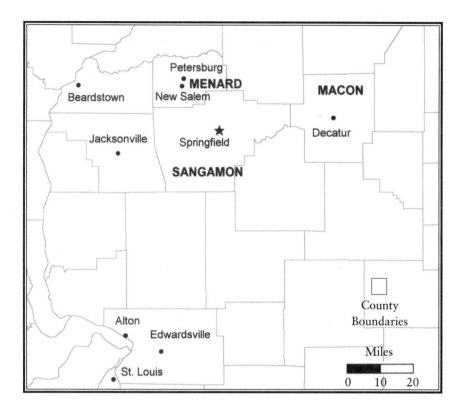

According to Enos's reconstruction, Springfield differed dramatically from the rest of Sangamon County. A village of just under 700, Springfield was dominated by adults, and adult men in particular. In 1831, two-thirds of all Springfielders were adults, 424 adults as compared to 241 children or dependents. And two-thirds of all adults were men. Springfield was clearly an exceptional frontier outpost that attracted single men, without families, who likely were just leaving their parents' farms, as was Lincoln, and looking for work in a shop, in a grocery, or in an urban profession.[21]

The village was not a community of families, for the most part. Men outnumbered women by more than two-to-one, and fewer than one-half of the men in Springfield were married. Single women were almost unheard of, and all but two of the 134 women in Springfield were married. Apparently, few single adult women settled in Springfield, and if they did, they married almost immediately once they arrived. Pioneer reminiscences suggest that most men traveled back East or visited older parts of Illinois to find wives to fetch home to Springfield.[22]

Linkage with the U.S. Census of 1840, taken nine years later, drives home the stunning population turnover typical of frontier settlements like Springfield. Among adult men, only one-fifth of the settlers of 1831 remained in the community until 1840. Population turnover was highest among single settlers, with married men twice as likely as single men to remain in Springfield throughout the 1830s. Only one in seven single settlers put down roots in the town. This large population of single men was extremely fluid, and Springfield represented a kind of way station for single settlers seeking a niche on the western frontier. Given its skewed sex ratio, Springfield was not a likely place to find a wife, nor did it provide much hope of employment for unskilled and uneducated men. Single men, like Lincoln, found settling down difficult and moving on an easy thing to do.[23]

When Lincoln arrived in Springfield, no one could have been very surprised to see yet another young man show up in the town, but they might well have been shocked to see him eventually succeed. Springfield provided few employment opportunities for a young Kentuckian who, by his own admission, was "raised to farm work." The farmers and farm communities of central Illinois were largely self-sufficient, if only because of the vast distances and crude transportation facilities that separated them from towns, markets, and one another. Farmers came to town rarely—"about once in a few months," according to a contemporary estimate—and only to secure commodities and services that they could not provide for themselves or obtain from neighbors. Springfield therefore offered a limited variety of urban services.[24]

Enos's reconstruction of Springfield in 1830–31 lists the occupations of 119 men, who practiced thirty-one different occupations. Less than half of all employment was manual in character. Various building trades—carpentry, brickmaking, plastering, and cabinetmaking—occupied one-fifth of all employed men in literally building the town. A smattering of craftsmen—blacksmiths, saddlers, hatters, tailors, watchmakers, and a gunsmith—served both the townspeople and farmers who made periodic visits from the countryside. Only seven farmers lived in Springfield. Most work was entrepreneurial or professional, with merchants representing the largest occupational group in the town. Already, Springfield hosted ten lawyers, nine doctors, and six ministers. Together, these three professions accounted for one-fifth of all employment.[25]

Beyond farming and railsplitting, Lincoln had rudimentary occupational skills and little preparation for urban life. Unlike his father Thomas, who worked part-time as a joiner, Lincoln had never lived in a town and did not possess a craft of any kind. In Indiana, he had worked as a ferryman and flatboatman and possibly as a store clerk, but only briefly. In Springfield, Lincoln had to compete with settlers educated at Yale and Princeton, while his own education amounted to a year or two in the notorious "blab schools" of the Indiana frontier, in which students essentially taught themselves by reading aloud to one another.[26]

Storekeeping, his only option, was itself extremely competitive. Springfield's storekeepers typically arrived with large amounts of capital or eastern connections, and Lincoln had neither. The best clerks were trusted friends and especially relatives. When Elijah Iles needed a clerk, for example, he hired John Williams, the son of a family friend back in Kentucky, who moved to Springfield to fill the position. Williams lived with Iles, married into his family, and eventually took over the business. Such "sponsored" migration was the best guarantee of success for a young migrant. Besides, a good deal of employment in the town was part-time or seasonal, particularly schoolteaching, surveying, and government service. Quite a few men—about one in six—cobbled together several occupations just to make ends meet.[27]

Lincoln was not prepared to compete in this emerging urban, commercial world. Migrating to a city proved even more difficult than staking a claim in a desolate forest, clearing fields, and splitting rails. Lincoln needed social and intellectual rather than merely manual skills, and by his own admission he "did not know much." Settling in a town also demanded sponsorship or social connections, which were traditionally provided by a young man's family. Confronting these realities, the "strange, friendless, uneducated, penniless boy" moved on, down the Sangamon, westward with the current, likening himself to a piece of driftwood floating aimlessly down the river.[28]

CHAPTER 5

By Himself at New Salem

Lincoln helped build a flatboat for the journey from Springfield to New Orleans. Along with stepbrother John D. Johnston, cousin John Hanks, and the merchant Denton Offutt, he set out floating down the Sangamon River. Twenty miles downstream from Springfield, the river turned abruptly northward, and upon a high bluff overlooking this bend, on the western bank of the Sangamon, sat the little village of New Salem. Two years earlier, two southern settlers, James Rutledge and his nephew John Cameron, had built a mill on the Sangamon at the foot of this bluff. To provide power for their mill, Rutledge and Cameron dammed the Sangamon to create a mill pond. Rutledge's mill dam now caught hold of Lincoln's flatboat as it floated down the river. As the village's residents gathered to watch this welcome diversion from frontier tedium, Lincoln took charge and directed a complicated maneuver to float the craft over the dam.[1]

By all accounts, Lincoln was the picture of rusticity in his blue denim jacket and jeans, homemade shoes, and broad-brimmed straw hat. One old settler, Caleb Carman, remembered the young Lincoln as "very od" and "very curious" on first meeting, but Carman later concluded that "after all this bad Apperance i Soon found to be a very intelligent young man." After a day and a night in New Salem, the sorry-looking crew floated to the mouth of the Sangamon, down the Illinois, and on to the Mississippi. Hanks remembered that they "rushed through Beardstown in a hurry—people Came out & laughed at us." Lincoln spent a month in New Orleans, took a steamboat back up to St. Louis, and then walked the ninety miles home to Decatur.[2]

During the trip to New Orleans, Denton Offutt took a liking to Lincoln and offered him a job clerking in a store he promised to open in New Salem. Meanwhile, the horrible winter of the Deep Snow convinced the rest of Lincoln's family to return to southern Indiana. Far from being unusual or an admission of defeat, this impulse was entirely predictable among newcomers. The Deep Snow, and Illinois winters in general, often induced chills and fever, or what was known as "ague" or simply the "Illinois shakes." "When you had the chill you couldn't get warm," remembered an early Spring-fielder, "and when you had the fever you couldn't get cool." The dreaded "shakes" were renowned as "a terror to newcomers," especially native southerners. Another newcomer to the region, Stephen T. Logan, recalled that "Very soon after I came I began to get the symptoms of the chills and fever, and then I wished I had never left Kentucky." The recommended home remedy, possum fat and corn, rarely proved effective. Some settlers, including the Lincolns, bought patent medicines that were equally unavail-ing. Logan remembered that "In those days I have often seen ten wagons going back to where I saw one coming this way." Another early settler, William Butler, recalled simply that "I hated the country." While Lincoln floated by raft to New Orleans, the rest of his family retraced their steps to Indiana. On the return trip, according to family legend, the group made acquaintances in Coles County, Illinois, who convinced them to stay. There, Thomas and Sarah Lincoln settled down and lived the rest of their lives, sur-rounded by the families of the three Johnston children. Thomas lived another twenty years and Sarah another thirty-eight.[3]

After the journey to New Orleans, Lincoln's stepbrothers and cousins rejoined their families and returned to farming. Johnston and Dennis Hanks moved to Coles County to establish an extended Lincoln clan on the Goosenest Prairie. Lincoln paid a brief visit to his parents' home and helped his father build a log cabin for the thirteen members of the Lincoln-Johnston-Hanks clan. Lincoln's nephew later recalled that the family moved the cabin down the road a few months later and, at Lincoln's insistence, added a second room to afford his father and mother more privacy. Then he "announced his intention 'of cutting entirely adrift from the old life'" and parted from his family for good. In July 1831, at age twenty-two, Lincoln arrived in New Salem, on his own for the first time.[4]

Lincoln joined the other single settlers in Sangamon Country who were attempting to settle down without the advantage of a family or friends. Three-fourths of all successful settlers arrived within families. One-half had been married for an average of ten years and already had children. Only one-fourth of all successful settlers arrived without a family. Settling with a family was a prescription for success. Settling without one was a prescrip-tion for failure.[5]

As a single settler in the Sangamon Country, Lincoln could count on a one-in-seven chance of making good and settling down for as long as ten years. Further, he could expect to devote the next seven years just to putting down roots and getting established before he could even think about mar-rying and starting a family. In fact, like most of the region's single men, Lin-coln's stepbrother and cousin were mere transients along the river rather than genuine settlers. Lincoln was part of the new "urban drift" that was beginning to draw sons away from farming toward nonmanual occupations in towns and cities. He was the first of the Lincolns to live alone, without at least one family member settled in the same community. He hailed from a decidedly rural, agricultural, and landed heritage. In Illinois, 85 percent of Lincoln's contemporaries worked as farmers, and scarcely one in forty lived in towns or cities. His own upbringing had prepared him for a respectable life of farming. Yet Lincoln pursued an urban career, a profession, at a time and in a place in which fewer than one in fifty men harbored such lofty aspirations.[6]

New Salem proved a good place for Lincoln to spread his wings. A settlement of perhaps thirty families gathered around the mill site, the village represented a transition between the rural, backwoods farm country in which Lincoln grew up and the dynamic, urban society of Springfield that he was not yet prepared to enter. Beyond teaching him to work hard to provide for himself and his family, farming had done little to prepare Lincoln for life. In New Salem, he could sample an assortment of urban occupations and learn new skills. As "the second town in the county in population and importance," New Salem allowed Lincoln to experiment, fail, and finally find a calling before moving on to Springfield, the principal city in the region. The villagers liked Lincoln and helped him grow and mature in various ways. "Here," Lincoln put it simply, "he rapidly made acquaintances and friends." He "stopped indefinitely" and ended up staying for the next six years.[7]

When Lincoln arrived, New Salem was a typical country village, a cluster of log cabins on a bend in the river, providing essential services, such as milling, for several knots of settlers clustered along the timbered creekbeds. According to his son Robert, James Rutledge's mill was the first in the county and "supplied a large section of country with its meal, flour, and lumber." The mill attracted more settlers, who demanded other essential services. As one observer described this familiar process, "Wherever the mill commences its operations, there is the gem of the thriving village." Farmers from far-flung inland settlements—Clary's Grove, Concord, New Market, Sand Ridge, Sugar Grove, and Indian Point—all depended on the mill to grind their grain. As one settler remembered, "All of these communities met at Salem every Saturday to trade and to hear what was going on in the different localities." While waiting for their grist, farmers had time to patronize a store, a craftsman, a tavern, even a doctor. "After the mill was built at Salem it was a big thing," according to reminiscence, "and people came from fifty miles around, and sometimes waited a week for their grist." The village eventually boasted a mill, a ferry, three general stores, a cooper, a blacksmith, a wheelwright, a hatter, a tanner, two doctors, and a handful of private homes. New Salem officially came into existence in 1829 with the opening of its post office. Most of the settlers were subsistence farmers who patronized the ten to fifteen families in the village for the few goods and services they could not provide for themselves. Largely self-sufficient, New

Salem was, as Robert Rutledge remembered, "isolated from the great world outside."[8]

Lincoln gained a hasty introduction to the harsh realities of life in the Sangamon Country. The farmers' main dilemma was marketing their produce. The Sangamon River, shallow and full of snags, was navigable only for flatboats, rather than keelboats, and then only during the spring thaw. Instead of trusting the unreliable river, farmers usually marketed their crops directly overland, hauling their produce in wagons forty to fifty miles to the Illinois River, on which steamboats carried them down to markets at St. Louis and Alton on the Mississippi. Some farmers traveled directly overland the one hundred miles to St. Louis, a ten-day or two-week journey. Whatever the route, dependence on overland transport cut deeply into potential profits. The typical farmer had to "give one half of his manufactured produce . . . to carry the other half to market."[9]

Overland trade hampered farming and inhibited urban development. Springfield's early merchants moaned that "a large share of the products of the neighborhood go directly to the Illinois or Mississippi river without taking Springfield *en route*." Because of heavy transportation costs, wheat fetched only half as much in Springfield as it could in Alton, so farmers shipped five times as much wheat directly to the Mississippi as they milled in Springfield. One old settler remembered hauling a wagon load of corn to Springfield. The load cost $1.37½ to haul, and he received only one dollar for all twenty bushels of corn. Meat packing was also slow to develop, because farmers drove most of their cattle to St. Louis and Alton on foot. This meant feeding their corn to hogs and cattle. As one farmer complained, corn "in its original shape, will not bear the cost of five miles land carriage." Denton Offutt, for example, accumulated three thousand to four thousand bushels of corn. Instead of shipping the corn, however, he had to feed it all to a thousand hogs that could then be herded to market. Wielding his famous axe, Abraham Lincoln split the rails that fenced in the hogs while they fattened.[10]

Another miller, Andrew Heredith, founded a town that he called, appropriately enough, Millville. In 1836, Heredith set out for St. Louis with fifteen hundred hogs, feeding them along the way on corn that he hauled on a caravan of wagons. Unfortunately, the hogs were caught on the open prairie during an ice storm and froze to death. Despite the hazards of these long drives, as late as 1840, Sangamon County supported only four butchers and meat packers to process hogs and cattle. Farmers and merchants therefore shared a common interest in improving transportation. As one observer summed it up, "It must be obvious to every reflecting mind that the only drawback upon the prosperity of this interior portion of Illinois is the want of the means of transportation to market."[11]

Problems with transportation, of course, ran in two directions, and farmers had as much trouble buying manufactured goods as they did in marketing their produce. Farmers who marketed produce annually in St. Louis or New Orleans bargained for a year's worth of manufactured goods to haul back home. "A few neighbors would load a boat together and take turn about going with it down to New Orleans," a pioneer recalled in her old age. "They would get sugar, coffee, and a barrel of molasses, and a 'cone of white sugar' for Madam's tea drinkings." Another old settler "went annually to St. Louis, with strained honey and deer-skins, and exchanged them for groceries and other necessaries for the family." Before the development of a local market for manufactured goods, St. Louis merchants advertised their wares in the Sangamon Country in hopes of winning customers on their annual visits to the Mississippi. The trip to market was notoriously time-consuming and tedious, requiring up to two weeks on horseback. Isolated by long, overland distances, farmers had every incentive to attempt self-sufficiency instead.[12]

Farmers made do with a sophisticated system of home manufacturing that they had developed back East. Before the advent of factories and the appearance of reliable and efficient transportation systems, Americans met most of their needs through family-based production, within a system that historians have labeled the "household economy." In a largely subsistence economy, like that on the Illinois frontier, families worked mostly to meet their own immediate needs rather than producing goods for sale on the market. "They were entirely satisfied if they could secure sufficient food and be comfortably clothed in their simple homespun attire," according to one reminiscence. Farm families produced a wide variety of products rather than specializing in one or a few staple, cash crops. Most important, of course, were foods for the table—grain, meat, vegetables, and fruits—and fabrics for clothing—wool, linen, and cotton cloth. Before the development of a market economy, the farmer's highest priority was not to achieve a profit but simply to provide for his own family.[13]

In the Sangamon Country, families produced many manufactured goods themselves, bartered with neighboring families, and patronized craftsmen in their own communities. For this reason, families depended on each other, migrating and living together as they went west. One lesson of the prairie, according to an old settler, was simply that "one family could not live alone." Home manufacture depended on neighborly relations as well as a gender division of labor within the family. Men and boys worked outside—in the fields and forests, tending crops, hunting game, and chopping wood. Women and girls usually worked inside or near the house, performing a vital economic function by manufacturing items for home consumption, such as clothing, soap, and candles. "The duties of the household were discharged by the female sex," remembered one pioneer nostalgically, "who attended the dairy, performed the culinary operations; spun, wove, and made up the garments for the whole family; carried the water from the springs, and performed much other laborious service, from which females, and especially mothers, in a more advanced state of society are exempted."[14]

Weaving, and cloth production in general, was the most important occupation of women and girls. "When the first settlers came there were no stores filled with dry goods, as there are now," a pioneer recalled, "and if the goods had been in the country there was no money to buy them. The only way families could supply themselves with clothing was to produce the materials and manufacture their own goods." Northern settlers typically raised sheep—"as extensively as the wolves would permit"—to produce woolen cloth. The first southern settlers brought their own cotton, flax, and hemp seed with them, planted a patch, and worked the fiber themselves. Women and girls "picked the seed by hand, carded it on hand cards, spun it on wheels designed for spinning wool or flax, wove it into cloth, and made it into garments for men and women's wear." The work of growing cotton or raising sheep, picking cotton seeds from the fiber, carding and spinning the fibers into thread, and weaving it into cloth was as vital to family survival as all the farm work in the fields. A loom was as indispensable as a plow "where all were dependent on the work of their own hands for the entire clothing of themselves and families." One pioneer mother, Mrs. Achsa Colburn, made a loom by hand using an axe, a hand saw, a drawing knife, an auger, a chisel, and corn cobs. On this handmade loom, she wove hundreds of yards of cloth for her family of fourteen children.[15]

This "women's work," like all farm work, was seasonal. Farmers planted cotton and flax in the spring, and in the summer the cotton had to be picked and seeded and the flax fulled, or cleaned and thickened. "We children had to lie before the fire and pick the seed from the cotton boles," a pioneer daughter remembered, "before we could go to bed." Spinning cotton and flax occupied the fall and winter months to provide cooler clothing for the summer ahead. Elizabeth McDowell Hill described her mother's spinning corner—"Mama's corner," as she remembered it—filled with a "big and little wheel, loom, warping bars, spool rack, and twenty four spools to wind the warp on." The large wheel spun wool and cotton, while the small wheel spun flax. "Near the place of light was her little wheel," she recalled, "and very few moments passed without some of this outfit being in motion." In late fall, the women would set up a loom in the middle of the cabin or—like Lincoln's mother, Nancy—in a little shed. Then they wove the thread they had just finished spinning, and "the merry whirr of the wheel and the regular 'bat bat' of the loom was heard to a late hour of the night." As a child of these years later reminisced, "You could hear the weavers go whack—whack—during the fall and winter all over the country."[16]

In the spring, just as the women had finished the cotton and linen cloth, "the men washed and sheared the sheep, then the wool was turned over to the women, and 'wool-pickings' were next in order." They spent the spring and summer spinning, weaving, and dyeing wool in time for winter. "The hum of the spinning wheel, was our daily music, during the season of manufacturing our own wool for winter wear," one pioneer woman reminisced. "At that season you [could] not enter a cabin without being greeted by the odor of the old fashioned dye pot, which had to have a warm spot in the corner of the chimney." Underclothing retained its natural color, "but for outer garments, and particularly ladies' dresses, something better was required." A few early settlers brought dyes along with them, including indigo and madder, but "for greater variety and color," most relied on native barks, including black walnut, butternut, oak, and hickory, as well as roots, hazelnut husks, and sumac berries. One old settler claimed that "it was in those days a Common thing to see the trees Stripped of Bark as high up as a woman could reach."[17]

Women were adept at spinning and weaving cotton, linen, and wool, and they sometimes dyed thread to weave stripes and other patterns into their cloth. Home production introduced a tremendous variety of fabrics, weaves, and colors into frontier apparel, and pioneer women and men were experts at judging the quality and texture of homespun and factory-woven cloth. A contemporary description of a Springfield man provides a glimpse of the curious mix of fabrics and colors that must have enlivened frontier attire: "He wore a blue mixed Ky. janes [jeans] coat, double breasted blue cloth vest, white wool hat, brogan shoes, black merino cravat, red silk pocket handkerchief with square white spots, [and a] woolen comfort." Cloth production was hard work, and few women remembered it fondly, but it afforded frontier families an important measure of economic independence. Moreover, it granted female family members, in particular, a vital economic function. Women's and girls' unrelenting labor is one reason married settlers with children fared so much better than single men in early Springfield.[18]

Through home manufacture, families made their own soap, candles, shoes, and sugar, processing a wide variety of agricultural by-products and avoiding "tedious trips to St. Louis and the river." Soap was boiled from ashes and lard, and candles dipped or molded from tallow. Shoes, a prized possession, were made at home, and settlers sometimes walked long distances barefoot, carrying their shoes to make them last. Beyond the family, farmers engaged in extensive exchange relationships with neighbors. Mary Elizabeth Quillan remembered her family boarding two young women at the height of spinning season "who would come and spin from morning until night, six days in the week, six weeks at a time." Her family also took in an itinerant shoemaker who worked the family's leather and "spent several weeks in getting the family shod" before moving on to the next household. Such labor exchange also produced the cabin raisings, corn shuckings, wood choppings, and quilting bees so celebrated in frontier folklore. As one settler put it, "all took a part at the work." Labor was "swapped" rather than hired for money, and "Custom—an unwritten law—settled the matter of work and wages."[19]

Labor exchange reflected the necessity of community cooperation in a new country. One settler remembered that "it was no uncommon thing for a man to go 8 or 10 miles to help a Neighbor harvest or raise a house—all felt their Dependence in those days." Another pioneer recalled that "No matter if we lived miles apart A community interest made neighbors of us all." A pioneer mother, Jane Martin Johns, remembered that "The sewing bees and quiltings were all day affairs which began at 9 o'clock in the morning and lasted till 12 at night." For isolated farm women, such cooperative labor naturally took the form of a social event. "Before nine o'clock the house was full," Johns reminisced. "All the beds but one had been taken down to make room for the company. One bed was reserved to 'put the babies on,' and it was occupied by from one to half a dozen all day." The women "worked, and worked and talked," she concluded. "They had all learned the art of doing these two things at the same time, else they could never have talked, for they had to work."[20]

Beyond relieving the unremitting social isolation, however, labor exchange also drove home a stinging economic reality, the painful scarcity of money on the Illinois frontier. Old settler Maxwell Campbell recalled that "for the first five years after coming to the county he never had a cent of money." Throughout American history, frontier regions generally advanced more quickly than existing financial institutions could supply them with money or credit. So pioneer farmers bartered from necessity. Thomas Beam tried to sell his corn crop in the fall of 1830. "After making it known in all the settlement," he remembered, "he was unable to get an offer for his crop at any price in money, but he traded it for a barrel of whisky, traded that for a three year old steer, and finally sold that for $10.00."[21]

Families could not supply all their "necessaries," especially the so-called "tropical goods," such as coffee, tea, sugar, and tobacco, products that did not grow in a northern climate. Some essential services, especially milling, required a trip to the nearest village. Without money, farm families bartered for services as well as goods. The first settlers trekked sixty to seventy miles to Edwardsville near the Mississippi simply to grind corn to eat, a two-week journey on horseback. The county's first mill was horse-powered, and customers had to bring their own horses to turn the wheel. The burrs, made of "loose stones picked up on the prairies," could only grind corn, not wheat, and accommodated no more than ten bushels a day. Millers customarily took a "toll" of one-fifth of the grain they milled. When John Hay opened his cotton mill in 1833, he exchanged spun cotton for raw cotton and used blind horses to turn his wheel, advertising optimistically that "Cash will be accepted." Later, the replacement of animal and water power with steam concentrated milling in towns and cities. A Springfield miller promised that

"Persons coming from a distance can at all times have their grinding done by staying over night." Farmers provided their own materials—leather, tallow, wood, and wool—to be worked by neighboring craftsmen.[22]

Rural self-sufficiency limited interactions between town and country, inhibiting urban growth and ironically leaving townspeople to feed themselves. "I suppose it is known to most of us," a Springfielder complained in 1836, "that there is not a farmer in this county who raises vegetables to supply our market, for a livelihood." Subsistence agriculture in the countryside challenged the market orientation of the growing town and enforced a degree of involuntary subsistence. "Our vegetable market, (if we can be said to have one,) is so notoriously bad," another townsman complained, "that persons who desire to have even the commonest vegetables in their proper seasons and of even a tolerable qualtity are forced to cultivate them themselves, or go without." As a result, agricultural activities continued to mingle with urban enterprises in Springfield for decades. Like farm wives in the country, Springfielders kept gardens and orchards to supply their tables. Their hogs, poultry, and other farm animals ran wild on the public streets. Even as a flourishing lawyer in Springfield, Lincoln kept a backyard garden and milked his own cow. The preferred alternative, of course, was commercial agriculture and a market. One observer stated the obvious: "There are but few of our citizens who would not prefer purchasing vegetables to raising them."[23]

For both farmers and townspeople, merchants were the region's most important economic link with the outside world. Exemplified by Elijah Iles, Springfield's merchants invested money, time, and effort in hauling goods from St. Louis to stock necessities that farmers could not produce for themselves. Amid home consumption and the lack of money, however, merchants initially did sporadic business, and as late as 1829 Springfield had only three small stores. The town's stores typically served only eight customers a day, and most customers bought only one item. Offut's store closed at 7:00 P.M., but in this leisurely economy most business took place between 9:00 and 3:00. Further, trade was seasonal, rising and falling with the rivers. Business slackened in winter and summer but increased when the waters rose during the spring and fall. Merchants therefore traveled to market to stock their shelves only twice a year, when the rivers were navigable, advertising their traditional "spring stock" and "fall stock" of goods. Farmers came to town during these seasons to market produce and to trade. "The rivers are up," noted one Springfielder during a rainy autumn, "and business of every kind is improving." When their goods were exhausted, merchants quit for the season and simply closed their stores, which typically comprised an extra room in their own homes.[24]

A representative general store stocked just sixty different products (as opposed to the sixty thousand or more a grocery might keep on hand today) and advertised them all in detail to let farm families know what was available. Goods fell into five categories, the most important of which were the tropical goods—sugar, coffee, molasses, tea, tobacco—that were imported through New Orleans from the South, the West Indies, or Asia. Manufactured goods included window glass, sperm oil for lanterns, sealing wax for closing letters, knives and iron tools of all kinds, razors, lead pencils and steel pens, paint, and gunpowder. A third category was preserved foods, which supplemented winter diets. They included raisins, currants, dried fruits of all kinds, canned fish such as herring, sardines, and anchovies, crackers in the proverbial cracker barrel, and smoked meat, such as bacon and ham. Raw materials for home manufacture represented a fourth category—bar lead for making musket balls, wick for dipping candles, pint flasks for bottling homemade whiskey, lime for whitewashing cabin walls, and china heads for making dolls. A final category, liquor, supple mented home-fermented cider and whiskey with a wide variety of imports, including wine, gin, brandy, champagne, ale, porter, and Madeira.[25]

Along with land speculators, merchants were the frontier's capitalists, frequently welcomed for introducing scarce cash into the local economy. But they were also scorned as agents of long-distance trade who drained money from the area. As early as 1832, the *Sangamo Journal* observed gloomily that "The pressure for money in our State, is already extensively and severely felt. Every dollar which our merchants receive, is of necessity carried out of the country; and their demands are such that they will be compelled to collect their debts, although it may take from the State every dollar." Bowing to the inevitable, merchants joined in the local exchange system based on barter. They accepted payment in wheat and other agricultural staples, typically advertising that groceries "will be sold low for Cash or any kind of Country Produce." One pioneer wife and mother put it simply: "For a pound of butter we paid four bushels of corn." According to another, "For a yard of common printed calico, they asked half a dollar, or a bushel of wheat." Some merchants spelled out their preferred terms of trade, which might be seasonal or geared to a particular wholesale market. A local merchant with too many hats on hand, for example, announced that he would "take in exchange for hats, Bacon, Flour, Wheat, Oats, Corn, and Pork, and Furs of all kinds."[26]

In this way, local merchants not only supplied necessities to farmers but began to market surplus produce as wholesalers. As one observer described this evolving system, "It is the business of agriculture and manufactures to furnish the surplus, and most of the means for commerce; and it is the business of merchants to purchase them and take them to the distant markets." As the local economy developed, merchants became literal "middlemen" between farmers and distant markets. Farmers could now sell their produce locally without traveling personally to St. Louis or New Orleans. Many farmers, however, viewed merchants as monopolists who cornered the market for manufactured goods and produce. "The sale of wheat has been confined, here, to a few merchants," one farmer complained, "who first made heavy profits on their sales of goods to us, and then, by monopolising the wheat trade made another profit." Farmers recognized the incompatibility of independence and profits, and it stung. The *Sangamo Journal* drove the point home: "Without merchants there can be no commerce, there may be independence but no wealth." As commerce—and wealth—increased, farm families began to prosper but were bound to lose their traditional economic independence.[27]

Still, Denton Offutt's new store seemed like a godsend to the farm families who patronized New Salem. The store—like New Salem itself—owed its existence to the harsh realities of this subsistence economy. Without efficient transportation, farmers could not carry their produce more than twenty miles to market. Rural villages grew up to serve a hinterland of ten to twenty miles in radius, about the distance a farmer's wagon could travel in a day. In fact, a state legislative committee reported that a man and horse could travel about thirty miles a day. Farmers wanted a village no more than fifteen miles away, so they could travel there and back in a day. This pattern explains New Salem's location twenty miles downriver from Springfield. The thin population and scant money supply of such a pioneer economy could support only a few merchants profitably, and the average store in Illinois served about 340 people. As a result, most merchants could not specialize and operated general stores, selling a little of everything. One early merchant remembered his general store "embracing dry goods, groceries, hardware, books, medicines, bed-clothes, matresses, in fact every thing that the country needed."[28]

Because they had a "captive market," general stores were unpretentious and dark inside, with small glass windows and narrow doorways. A typical general store was twenty feet wide and thirty feet deep, and the "counters and shelves along the store's right side were devoted to dry goods; those on the left side to groceries, tobacco, sundries, and patent medicine." At fourteen by sixteen, Offutt's store was on the small side. To save space, merchants sold bulk goods, stocking their wares in the barrels and shipping crates in which they arrived. Clerks had to hoist two-hundred-pound crates into and out of wagons, down into the cellar, or up into the eaves with a windlass. Clerking was therefore a job for young men, and clerks were valued as much for their brawn as their brains. In fact, one New Salem resident recalled Lincoln's relationship with Offutt this way: "Offut brought some goods wares & merchandise up from Beardstown and Lincoln put them up—unboxed them & put them up on shelves." Lincoln also hauled sacks of grain between the mill and the store and split enough rails to fence in a thousand of Offutt's hogs. Mixing physical labor with mental work, Lincoln called himself "a sort of Clerk" in Offutt's store.[29]

Like most other merchants, Offutt bought his goods in St. Louis. As a New Salem resident later reminisced, a typical merchant "made a trip to St.

WILLIAM GREENE. AFTER SHARING A COT WITH LINCOLN AS HIS
"ASSISTANT CLERK" IN NEW SALEM, GREENE GREW INTO A SHREWD
BUSINESSMAN AND WEALTHY LANDOWNER.
Courtesy of the Illinois State Historical Library.

Louis in the spring and fall. First going to Beardstown; he would then take a steamboat to St. Louis and would stay a week or so." Others, like Springfield's Elijah Iles, traveled all the way to Philadelphia to select their stock. As Iles recalled, "At that day the merchants went east in December and rode to Philadelphia on horseback to buy their goods. These were hauled over the mountains and sent by water to St. Louis." They were next shipped upstream by boat to Beardstown and then hauled overland by wagon to New Salem. Such high transportation costs allowed big markups—up to 100 percent. In the words of one pioneer, "As these storekeepers exercise a sort of monopoly over a certain district, their profits are great, and they often become wealthy."[30]

Still, storekeeping was a risky venture, operating largely on credit. Without money, most customers had to "buy on account." Merchants did not develop the modern "one-price" system until after the Civil War. Instead of putting prices on their goods, storekeepers marked them with secret codes. They then bargained with each customer individually, engaging in a "contest of wits" to settle on the best price. Storekeepers sized up each customer according to ability to pay and tacked on 20 to 30 percent for credit purchases. To help size up customers, Offutt hired a local boy, William Greene, to work alongside Lincoln, using his familiarity with the area's farmers to negotiate good prices on credit. As Greene later put it, his job was to "Tell Lincoln who *was* good." With the addition of this assistant, Lincoln gained the lofty title of "Chief & head Clerk."[31]

Storekeepers extended credit to perhaps two-thirds of their customers. In good times a store represented an economic boon, and storekeepers were welcome members of their communities. Extending so much credit, however, required storekeepers, in turn, to borrow their goods on credit from wholesalers. Unlike cash, credit was readily available, and country merchants routinely borrowed their goods from wholesalers for up to one year at anywhere from 6 to 10 percent interest. This system gave storekeepers an entire year to stock their goods, sell them on credit, and receive payment from their customers. Repayment, however, was haphazard, and storekeepers typically got serious about it just before their semiannual buying trips to St. Louis or Philadelphia. The following announcement was typical: "Money Wanted. Intend to start on the 10th of August, to the Eastern Cities, to purchase Goods; my friends and customers that are indebted to me, would confer a favor by letting me have a little CASH."[32]

In this system of "long credits," any economic disruption, such as the Panic of 1837, could prove disastrous to merchants and farmers alike. When a storekeeper's notes fell due, he was required to call in all of his customers' debts. "The consequence," according to one early settler, "was that the notes were not paid and were sent to a lawyer for collection, and then it would be as much trouble to get the money from the lawyer as from the customer." Under these circumstances, the country store became a bane to the farming community rather than a blessing. "The farmer," one of them moaned, "at the end of twelve months, finds himself, perhaps, as unable to pay as at first, and consequently we see 4 or 5 Magistrates and Constables fattening at the farmer's expense."[33]

Storekeepers routinely accepted agricultural produce, known as "country pay," in exchange for their merchandise. Offutt probably bartered more goods than he sold for cash. A rival merchant, for example, recalled that Offutt "Exchanged some Goods Principally Sugar & Coffee for Wheat." Merchants sometimes stocked these farm products in their stores as groceries but more often shipped them to the nearest city to pay their wholesalers. The local merchant would store the produce—typically nonperishable goods, such as bacon, lard, butter, and beeswax—wait until the river rose in the spring or fall, and then ship it to market. As one pioneer put it, "they grind the corn they obtain from the farmers, for the purpose of sending it to New Orleans, or some other place where it can be readily sold."[34]

Under this process, known as "agricultural collection," the country merchant served simultaneously as retailer and wholesaler for his rural customers. When money was particularly scarce—after the Panic of 1837, for example—barter became essential, and some merchants opened "exchange stores" that operated exclusively on barter. Such general stores fit comfortably into the system of barter that characterized the local, family economy. Still, the storekeeper took all the risks for his customers, storing their produce for future sale, assuming substantial transportation costs, and testing the vagaries of the market. As a result, merchants typically exercised aggressive economic leadership in their communities, taking an active interest in wholesale markets, banking, and especially transportation improvements.[35]

Offutt's store was the third to open in a village that could support only one or at most two. Samuel Hill opened New Salem's first store in the fall of 1829 and ran it nonstop throughout the village's history. The second store had a checkered career and was run by a half-dozen merchants, including Lincoln, during its rocky eight-year existence. Offutt's store appeared relatively late, two years after the town's founding. Compounding this disadvantage, Offutt was erratic and unreliable. His clerk Bill Greene called him a "wild—recless—careless man,—a kind of wandering horse tamer." A local farmer remembered him as "a wild, harum-scarum kind of a man, and I think not much of a business man." Predictably, as Lincoln put it succinctly, "In less than a year Offutt's business was failing." Soon after luring Lincoln to New Salem, Offutt simply disappeared. Left alone to fend for himself, Lincoln was essentially stranded in New Salem.[36]

CHAPTER 6

He Rapidly Made
Acquaintances and Friends

Despite his brief residence in the village, Lincoln's sojourn in New Salem made a lasting personal impression. Nearly thirty years after arriving, Lincoln devoted over one-fourth of the space in his autobiographies to the six years he spent there. Still, of all the distinct periods of Lincoln's life, these years in New Salem are perhaps the most obscured in legend. A tiny, pioneer village, New Salem produced few reliable records to document its short, ten-year history. Lincoln's earliest biographers, several of whom were his personal friends, had little first-hand knowledge of his life during these New Salem years. As a result, they relied heavily on pioneer reminiscence or even sheer legend to fill in the gaps. Long after his death, New Salem residents were still boasting about their lifelong friendships with Lincoln and particularly the help they offered him as a young man. Lincoln himself gave every indication of valuing these connections, maintaining many of them until his death and commemorating with apparent tenderness these "friends who had treated him with so much generosity." In New Salem, Lincoln noted, he "rapidly made acquaintances and friends," perhaps more of them than during any other period of his life. As one of his neighbors put it simply, Lincoln "Knew every man, woman & child for miles around."[1]

The New Salem legend emphasizes Lincoln's unique personal qualities—his fabled congeniality and good humor, his native intelligence, and his perseverance. Yet Lincoln's intense personal relationships and numerous personal debts in New Salem reflect penetrating social realities as well. New Salem was part of a pioneer society that emphasized barter, labor exchange, and personal reciprocity within a family setting. Although ostensibly on his own for the first time, in New Salem Lincoln remained firmly enmeshed within a family economy. New Salem's rudimentary social development fostered—essentially demanded—personal relationships founded on trust, sharing, and mutual aid. This is exactly what New Salem's pioneers remembered about Lincoln, and what he remembered about New Salem.

The New Salem legend is replete with anecdotes that emphasize exchange, sharing, and generosity. "There are many tales told of homely service rendered him," according to Lincoln biographer Ida Tarbell. "There was not one of them who did not gladly 'put on a plate' for Abe Lincoln when he appeared, or would not darn or mend for him when she knew he needed it." Lincoln's neighbors gladly lent him books, a horse, or a saddle when he needed one, and Lincoln reciprocated. "If a traveler 'stuck in the mud' in New Salem's one street, Lincoln was always the first to help pull out the wheel. The widows praised him because he 'chopped their wood;' the overworked, because he was always ready to give them a lift." Tarbell observed quite correctly that "with one and all he was at home." But she mistook Lincoln's generosity as a remarkable personal peculiarity rather than an ordinary social obligation: "He possessed in an extraordinary degree the power of entering into the interests of others, a power found only in reflective, unselfish natures endowed with a humorous sense of human foibles, coupled with great tenderness of heart."[2]

Such ready reciprocity, however, says as much about New Salem—and Lincoln's situation in the community—as it does about the young man's nature. Subsistence agriculture was based on a family organization, and given the importance of home production, anyone found it difficult, indeed nearly impossible, to live alone. Before the twentieth century, in fact, very few Americans ever lived alone. Traditionally, almost all Americans—adults as well as children—lived together in families. Throughout the entire nineteenth century, the proportion of single-member households held steady at less than 4 percent, rising only during the twentieth century and particularly in the modern era. This traditional emphasis on families rather than individuals is particularly striking in early Sangamon County. Incredibly, in 1830, out of a total population of almost thirteen thousand men, women, and children, only two residents of the county lived alone. The two exceptions were a single man in his fifties and a single woman in her sixties, both of whom may have been recently widowed.[3]

Most single people who had left home boarded with other families. During the nineteenth century, boarding represented a predictable and accepted stage in the life cycle, occurring during young adulthood, in the interlude between leaving one's family of birth and establishing a new family of one's own. Before the Civil War, about one-fifth of all American families took in boarders. Boarding performed several important functions in a subsistence economy, allowing young adults to live independently of their own families without having to take on the considerable burden and expense of establishing and maintaining a new household. The elaborate process of food and cloth production that most Americans learned as children continued to take place, as it was virtually bound to do, but within the context of a surrogate family.[4]

Boarders could move freely from place to place, leaving one family behind and joining a new one with relative ease, and so the practice facilitated mobility among young adults. Boarding was particularly important for rural-to-urban migrants with few social connections and little experience in towns and cities. Finally, boarding performed an important economic function in a subsistence economy. In the absence of money, boarding represented a kind of exchange or barter, in which young workers exchanged their labor or services for room and board in established households. For this reason, many young men and women boarded with their employers, accepting part or even all of their wages in kind.[5]

Lincoln boarded the whole six years that he lived in New Salem. From the time he left his family at age twenty-two until his marriage at age thirty-three, Lincoln never lived alone. Like many young men of this period, Lincoln started out living and sleeping where he worked, in Denton Offutt's store. By night, the clerks slept on blankets on the same counters that they tended during the day. Lincoln's fellow clerk, Bill Greene, recalled that they both slept among the crates and barrels in Offutt's back storeroom. Lincoln and Greene, in fact, "slept on the same cott & when one turned over the other had to do likewise." Meanwhile, Lincoln ate or "boarded" (the term referred to a table top) at the Rutledge Tavern or with local families. "Each morning the two clerks, and sometimes the proprietor, would wend their way down the slanting road which led to the bottom land northward," according to Lincoln's friend and fellow lawyer Henry Whitney, "and proceed up the State road for three-quarters of a mile to a primitive farmstead owned by one Bowlin[g] Greene, where they would get their breakfast, generally of bread and milk." Offutt paid Lincoln fifteen dollars a month, and Lincoln spent one dollar a week on board, so boarding Lincoln was a good way for families to come by a little cash in this subsistence economy.[6]

After Offutt's store closed, Lincoln lived and boarded with other families in New Salem, including the village's two founders, James Rutledge and John Cameron. Because he routinely visited families in the neighborhood for weeks on end, the villagers seem to have taken turns boarding Lincoln. As one settler reminisced, Lincoln "staid at our house 2 or 3 weeks at a time." When Lincoln was unemployed or "idle," friends would take him in to help with the harvest or some other chore. To earn his keep, Lincoln could chop wood or thresh wheat, and later read a newspaper or write a legal document. As farmer James Short remembered the often informal arrangement, "Frequently when Mr L was at my house he would help me gather corn." Several women in the community took the young Lincoln under their wings. Bennett Abell's wife, Elizabeth, accepted particular responsibility for Lincoln. "She evidently liked Lincoln, his genial manner and disposition to make himself agreeable," an early friend remembered. "He boarded with Mrs. Able—she washed for him and he generally lived there in a sort of home intimacy."[7]

Boarding proved advantageous for Lincoln, as for most young adults. It allowed him to settle down and settle in quickly after arriving as a stranger in New Salem. It brought him into close contact with the two founding families of the village, the Rutledge and Cameron families. Yet it allowed him to leave New Salem when he was ready to do so, with few personal entanglements to hold him back. Boarding allowed Lincoln to move to Springfield and settle down quickly, making the acquaintance of the leading families of that community, as well.

Lincoln, of course, had more practical reasons for boarding. In this subsistence economy, a young, single man had neither the skills nor the means to provide food and clothing for himself. This was partly the result of the traditional gender division of labor. As Lincoln's stepmother, Sarah Bush Johnston, recalled later with apparent pride, "I cooked his meals for nearly 15 years." Like most men of his era, Lincoln showed no interest at all in food preparation. "He Sat down & ate what was set before him, making no complaint," his stepmother remembered; "he seemed Careless about this." In New Salem, Lincoln boarded with several "surrogate families," who took up where his stepmother left off and similarly provided his food and clothing. In fact, Lincoln seems to have been welcome in quite a few homes in the village, perhaps all of them. Robert Rutledge recalled that Lincoln would "pass from one house in the town to an other, or from one crowd or squad of men to an other, apparently seeking amusement." He not only sought amusement in his neighbors' homes but also sustenance. J. Rowan Herndon, with whom Lincoln boarded for a time, recalled that the young man ate pretty much whatever his friends and neighbors provided him. He "was fond of fruit [and] Nuts," Herndon remembered, "& allway Reach for his Share of such things as they were frequently Brought to him By his friends." Hannah Armstrong, who lived on a farm four miles from the village, recalled that "Abe would Come out to our house—drink milk & mush—Corn bread—butter." Similarly, whenever Lincoln visited farmer James Short, "he invariably asked his wife for some bread & honey."[8]

Lincoln was equally undiscriminating in his dress. His stepmother reminisced that he "was tolerably neat and clean only—Cared nothing for clothes" and "was Careless about these things." Herndon agreed that "as to his Dress he was Rather Slouchy iff his Close were whole & Clean he seemed to Be satisfied as he was only able to Dress in Common Cloths." Like everyone else in the settlement, Lincoln could not afford to buy clothing, so he employed a local seamstress to make his clothes for him, out of homespun. Hannah Armstrong recalled that "I foxed his pants—made his shirts." As a result, his typical attire was a "blue cotton round about coat, stoga shoes, and pale blue casinet pantaloons which failed to make the connection with either coat or socks, coming about three inches below the former and an inch or two above the latter." (Cloth, of course, was at a premium, and Lincoln's six-foot-four-inch frame put heavy demands on the local supply.) Rather than an emblem of poverty, however, Lincoln's clothing bespoke his membership in a subsistence economy dominated by home production—indeed his full acceptance into the self-reliant families and community of New Salem. Although picturesque, Lincoln's attire was typical—as Robert Rutledge noted, "such as worn by all the inhabitants of the village."[9]

Far from representing a self-reliant pioneer during these years in New Salem, Lincoln—like most men of his era—could not even feed and clothe himself. Although legally an adult, until his marriage Lincoln remained a boarder, dependent on a series of surrogate families during his first dozen years as an adult. The intermediate status of boarding blurred the boundary between childhood and adulthood, and in New Salem men of any age remained "boys" as long as they boarded or apprenticed. One pioneer remembered the region around New Salem hosting "The Clary's Grove boys, the Island Grove boys, the Sangamon River boys and the Sand Ridge boys, each designated by the part of the country from which they came." Boarding also obscured the distinction between family and community. Lincoln himself conflated the two by habitually referring to older men in the neighborhood as "Uncle" and older women as "Aunt." James Short, for example, was "Uncle Jimmy," and Hannah Armstrong became "Aunt Hannah."[10]

During the nineteenth century, a prolonged period of young adulthood represented a distinct stage in the life cycle of most Americans. Traditionally, children passed through three stages on their way to adulthood—dependence, semidependence, and independence. Dependence ended around age ten when a child began to work productively, either at home, as an apprentice, or hired out to neighbors. Semidependence represented a long, undefined transitional stage during which an adolescent left home, acquired an occupation, and made other important life decisions. True independence began only with marriage and the formation of a family of one's own.[11]

According to this definition, as a distinct stage in life, semidependence—or simply "youth"—lasted far longer during the past than it does today. Historian Joseph Kett has aptly characterized "youth" during the nineteenth century as a "time of indecision between ages 15 and 25." Such semidependence was characterized by a long series of tentative steps toward independence that started sooner in life and lasted longer than their modern equivalents. Milestones included starting to work at home, hiring out for the first time, leaving home, choosing an occupation, initiating a courtship, marrying, and acquiring a new home. Today, such transitions often occur in just a few years, with semidependence typically bracketed between graduation from high school and receipt of a college degree. Indeed, today several major transitions, such as graduating from college, starting a career, marrying, and establishing a new home, can occur within a short period or even simultaneously. During the nineteenth century, however, the transition might well last for two decades, with "youth" or semidependence spanning ages thirteen to thirty-four.[12]

Lincoln's extended period of youth was therefore typical (see Table 6.1,

Table 6.1
Lincoln's Transition to Adulthood

	Age	Location
Starting to work at home	7	Indiana
Hiring out for the first time	13–14	Indiana
Leaving home	22	Decatur
Initiating a courtship	26–27	New Salem
Choosing an occupation	27	New Salem
Marrying	33	Springfield
Acquiring a new home	34	Springfield

"Lincoln's Transition to Adulthood"). Lincoln's long transition to adulthood began at age seven when he started working—"earning his keep"—on his family's Indiana farm. It ended when he married at age thirty-three and acquired a home of his own at age thirty-four. Intermediate steps included leaving home, choosing an occupation, and courting. The two most important milestones, leaving his parents' home and acquiring a home of his own, were separated by a dozen years. By contemporary standards, Lincoln's life cycle was neither precocious nor dilatory. Family historians have concluded that boys were expected to start working at about age seven, leave home at twenty-two or twenty-three, and form families of their own by their early thirties. In each of these respects, Lincoln was right on target.[13]

Lincoln's years of boarding in New Salem, helped him bridge the gap between his father's farm in Indiana and the urban environment of Springfield, and the Lincoln legend is replete with references to the many important, personal debts he accumulated during his sojourn in New Salem. Here Lincoln developed his first personal relationships—professional, political, and romantic—beyond his family circle. Three decades later, in a passage of elegant ambiguity, Lincoln acknowledged his own semidependence during this period when he remembered leaving his family and living "for the first time, as it were, by himself at New-Salem."[14]

In this prolonged and unsettled period of youth, Lincoln had plenty of company. Most frontiers in American history have experienced both a skewed age distribution, attracting younger settlers, and an unbalanced sex ratio, attracting more men than women. A preponderance of young people in their twenties and thirties settled the western frontier and produced a ratio of 150 men for every 100 women. As historian Jack Eblen concluded, "It seems clear that single men over forty tended to stay home, while those between twenty and forty sought out the frontier." The Sangamon Country was typical in this regard. The region's population was extremely youthful. In 1840, almost one-half of all adults living in Sangamon County were in their twenties. This classic "pyramidal" age structure reflected not only the nation's youthfulness in general—the median age was only seventeen—but also the generational winnowing worked by the western frontier. Further, men far outnumbered women, by an imposing 24 percent, typical of western settlements. This unbalanced sex ratio affected every age group—men in their twenties, men in their seventies, and every age in between. This gender imbalance was probably the result of settlement patterns rather than mortality, appearing consistently within every adult age group. Below age twenty, however, the sex ratio was almost evenly balanced. Simply put, far fewer women than men settled in the Sangamon Country as adults, but roughly equal numbers of males and females arrived with their families as children.[15]

Both the skewed age distribution and the unbalanced sex ratio made an important impact on the region's social and demographic character, as well as on Lincoln's personal and professional development. Men outnumbered women by nearly one-quarter. This meant that one in every five men in Sangamon County was not married and, more important, had little immediate prospect of finding a wife. The single largest age group, in fact, was young men in their twenties. They comprised almost one-half of all adult males, and there were simply too few eligible women in their age group. Throughout Sangamon County, more than six hundred men, 70 percent of them in their twenties and thirties, had to remain single indefinitely for the lack of an available partner. Contemporaries understandably bemoaned the scarcity of marriage-age women in the region. In 1832, for example, the Springfield *Sangano Journal* cautioned that "Our present stock of girls seem in a fair way of 'being used up,' soon."[16]

Further, the glut of young men set up an intense competition for housing, work, and wives. Men boarded with families for the lack of a wife and home. They accordingly remained "boys" throughout their twenties, wandering from job to job and place to place in search of a home, employment, and a wife. A scarcity of women virtually defined local patterns of courtship and marriage. The unbalanced sex ratio encouraged later marriages among men but earlier matches among women. Men had to wait until their late twenties or early thirties to take a wife, but women found themselves in great demand as teenagers. Up to 1840, in fact, men in Springfield married at age twenty-seven, on average. Women, by contrast, married at an average age of nineteen.[17]

This eight-year age difference in the typical marriage probably reflected frontier necessities more than general cultural expectations. The typical Springfield couple who married *before* moving to Illinois observed a different pattern. Springfield men who married back East took a wife two years sooner on average, at age twenty-five. Their marriage partners were also two years older than the typical bride in Springfield, age twenty-one on average. The typical eastern bride waited until reaching legal adulthood before marrying and leaving home. A more balanced sex ratio back East therefore encouraged a smaller age difference in marriage—four years—as compared to the eight-year difference evident in the Sangamon Country. The ten-year age difference between Lincoln and his wife, Mary, was therefore predictable, reflecting the same social realities underlying the general Springfield pattern.[18]

In fact, single women remained scarce well into the 1840s. As late as 1845, for example, the *Springfield Register* declared that "Indeed, we believe, there are but twelve (we have not counted them) *marriageable* females now in this city, which has a population of 4000 inhabitants; and, if we are not in error, eleven of these are *engaged!*" The problem was simply that "the girls all get married a few months after they get here." Implying that most eligible husbands were getting along in years, the *Register* complained that "some whiskered gentleman comes along and whisks her off before you know it; and the next thing you hear of her she is milking her own cows, churning her own butter, and perhaps, *nursing her own babies!*" Most young men simply had to bide their time until a home, a career, and a wife all came their way. Lincoln, like other men, had to wait patiently for all three until his late twenties and early thirties. This demographic reality may have contributed to Lincoln's seeming aloofness or indifference toward women as a youth. As one of his New Salem companions reminisced, "He didn't go to see the girls much. He didn't appear bashful, but it seemed as if he cared but little for them." As another New Salem acquaintance summed it up many years later, "at that time I think neither Mr. Lincon nor my self were in a Situation to Enter into what Mr Seward would Call 'Entangling Alliances.'"[19]

In New Salem, the most visible result of the age and gender imbalance was the domination of public life by single, young men, who naturally fell in together. After leaving their families and coming to town, young men entered an "associational" culture, gathering together in groups of their own making. This "male youth culture" represented a new phenomenon, reflecting novel patterns of family life, economic organization, and migration. In the absence of public institutions designed to educate or occupy youths outside the context of a family, young men voluntarily formed their own groups or "societies." Young men's associations of all kinds focused on work (trade associations and mechanics' institutes), self-improvement (lyceums and libraries), or camaraderie (military companies and clubs). Again, Lincoln was typical. "He always liked lively, jovial company, where there was plenty of fun & no drunkenness," a companion recalled, "and would just as lieve the company were all men as to have it a mixture of the sexes."[20]

When Lincoln arrived in the Sangamon Country, he found a lot of young men but little organization. New Salem, in the words of one early settler, was "a great place of resort for the young men." Robert Rutledge pictured young men lounging about the village's only street grouped into "crowds" or "squads." In this seasonal agricultural society, men devoted their considerable leisure time to traditional masculine pursuits, including horse racing, card playing, cockfighting, and athletic competitions of all kinds. Until the mid-1800s, Americans participated in unorganized, spontaneous games rather than formal sporting events. Rural villagers, especially southerners and frontiersmen, practiced simple "folk games," such as running, jumping, and wrestling, that allowed them to test and compare their athletic skills. These contests encouraged and rewarded "masculine" traits, including strength, speed, and courage, that were valued on the frontier. Other sports showcased occupational skills essential to frontier survival, such as shooting, axe-handling, and riding. Farmers even engaged in threshing contests both to hone and to demonstrate their harvesting skills. Such sports appealed in particular to the "bachelor subculture" of young, unattached men who dominated village life.[21]

Lincoln's physical prowess won him immediate respect and recognition in New Salem. Standing six-feet-four-inches tall and weighing more than two hundred pounds, Lincoln towered over most of his contemporaries. Renowned for his physical stature, he stood at least eight inches taller than the average American man of his day. A close friend reminisced that "Mr L. was very fond of out door recreations & sports, and excelled at them." Others recalled that Lincoln "would play at vari[ou]s games," such as jumping, running, hopping, pitching quoits, swimming, and shooting. Such competitions were simultaneously tests of strength and masculinity—"trials," as they were known—and exhibitions of occupational skill. "Among the settlers in a new country," according to one reminiscence, "from the nature of the case, a higher value is set upon physical than mental endowments." The famed rail-splitter Lincoln would show off both his strength and skill by grabbing two axes by the ends of their handles and raising them, elbows locked, straight over his head. Robert Rutledge remembered New Salem's games as tests of both strength and occupational prowess, and in both categories Lincoln excelled. "Trials of strength were very common among the pioneers," he recalled. "Lifting weights, as heavy timbers piled one upon another was a favorite pastime and no workman in the neighborhood could at all cope with Mr Lincoln in this direction."[22]

Physical contests often began with a challenge and frequently escalated into wrestling matches that historian Elliot Gorn identified as "southern backwoods brawling." Young southern men, especially the "lower sort," engaged in no-holds-barred, "rough-and-tumble" competitions to test their manhood and decide their social status. According to the tradition of "southern honor," status was conferred by the community as a reward for a public display of courage, physical prowess, or endurance. An insult, whether real or imagined, conferred dishonor and would often provoke a physical challenge. The resulting public brawl, according to Gorn, was a "fierce struggle for status" that could make or break a man's reputation. Writing in 1837, philosopher Ralph Waldo Emerson observed that "The Southerner asks concerning any man, 'How does he fight?' The Northerner asks, 'What can he do?'" As Robert Rutledge summed it up with considerable understatement, "an appeal was often made to physical strength to settle controversies."[23]

As an outpost of the Upland South, New Salem developed a reputation as a rough-and-tumble frontier town. Games of skill or chance easily escalated into physical challenges and brawls. According to Lincoln's friend and patron "Uncle" Jimmy Short, for example, "New Salem & the surrounding country was settled by roughs and bullies, who were in the habit of winning all the money of strangers at cards, & then whipping them in the bargain." New Salem youths followed the southern tradition of frequenting taverns, which hosted both their sports and the resulting imbroglios. William Clary opened a grocery in the village that sold mostly liquor and doubled as a tavern. Clary's brother John was the first settler in the area, establishing a knot of cabins that became known as Clary's Grove. The Clarys were from Tennessee and settled in Clary's Grove with an extended clan of intermarried families that included the Armstrongs. Jack Armstrong, a young man of twenty-eight when Lincoln arrived in New Salem, led a gang of toughs called the Clary's Grove boys. Known as a "regular bully," Armstrong and the Clary's Grove boys frequented Clary's grocery whenever they came to New Salem. "After filling up on whiskey," according to one early settler, they "were ready for a racket among themselves, though preferably with strangers."[24]

As a newcomer to the village, Lincoln had to pass muster with the Clary's Grove boys. His longtime law partner, William H. Herndon, declared ominously that "A stranger's introduction was likely to be the most unpleasant part of his acquaintance with them." Lincoln's introduction, in typical rough-and-tumble fashion, began with a boast that soon escalated into a challenge. Denton Offutt and William Clary, as rival storekeepers in a small village, naturally had reputations to polish. In 1831, Offutt, "gasy-windy" as ever, bragged that his store clerk—Lincoln—could "throw" Clary's brother-in-law, Jack Armstrong. The boast escalated into a bet of five dollars—serious money in a barter economy. Any affair of honor was meaningless without an audience, so predictably "All the men of the village and quite a number from the surrounding country were assembled."[25]

As a Kentuckian, Lincoln was versed in the art of rough-and-tumble fighting. Back in Hardin County, affairs of honor had substituted for local justice. As an acquaintance of the Kentucky Lincolns testified, "In Most of Cases they Setteled all their difficulties out of the Court House at some pub-

JACK ARMSTRONG. LINCOLN WRESTLED HIM TO GAIN ACCEPTANCE
INTO THE ROUGH-AND-TUMBLE WORLD OF NEW SALEM.
Courtesy of the Illinois State Historical Library.

lic gathering or old fashioned Ky–Knock down was the order of the day." Physical confrontation resolved disputes, satisfied everyone's honor, and—above all—confirmed social status: "Unless a Man Could boast of whipping some body he was not taken up in the best of Society." When the fight was over, the combatants would "get up drink make Friends & all went on well." As "ritualized behavior," rough-and-tumble fighting restored order rather than disrupting it and made friendships rather than producing enemies. Each confrontation went through a time-honored cycle: "Men drink together, tongues loosen, a simmering old rivalry begins to boil; insult is given, offense taken, ritual boasts commence; the fight begins, mettle is tested, blood redeems honor, and equilibrium is restored."[26]

Dennis Hanks remembered Thomas Lincoln engaging in just such a fight back in Kentucky: "Mr. Lincoln's friends thought him the best man in Kentucky and others thought that a man by the name of Hardin was a better man—so the two men through the influence of their friends met at a tavern." All the ingredients were there for a classic rough-and-tumble: rivalry and brag, the boasting of one's friends, a trip to a tavern, and the struggle for honor. Shorter than his son, but stocky and barrel-chested, Thomas—according to family tradition—triumphed. As Hanks told the story, "the two men had a long & tedious fight and Lincoln whipped Hardin without a scratch." In retelling the tale, Hanks ended with a flourish, saving the most important ingredient for last: "They did not fight from anger or malice but to try who was the strongest man—to try manhood."[27]

Soon came the time for the son to try his own manhood, to clarify his status within a new community. Accounts of the resulting Lincoln-Armstrong match vary. This scrape cannot have been too serious: Armstrong was a constable, and in fact Lincoln had recently voted for him. Contemporaries disputed the outcome, some claiming that Lincoln won the match, others remembering that he lost, and still others reporting a draw. Armstrong was a smaller man than Lincoln—ten inches shorter and forty pounds lighter—and he was five years older. Still, like any mythic foe, he was "in the prime of life, square-built, muscular, and strong as an ox." Both men used their wits. Armstrong, however, was "tricky in wrestling," while Lincoln, the thinker, was "a scientific wrestler." "They wrestled for a long time," witnesses agreed "without either being able to throw the other."[28]

The outcome, of course, was irrelevant: win, lose, or draw, simply in standing his ground Lincoln proved his manhood. In the process, he "took the matter in such good part, and laughed the matter off so pleasantly that he gained the good will of the roughs and was never disturbed by them." In the tradition of Robin Hood and Little John, there were laughs and handshakes all around, and the Clary's Grove boys accepted the newcomer. "They held no grudges after their fights," according to one reminiscence, "for this was considered unmanly." Afterward, Jack Armstrong welcomed Lincoln into his home for a week or more at a time, and his wife Hannah fed and clothed the young man. Lincoln, in return, "would chop wood, do the chores and help Jack on the farm," as Hannah remembered. Lincoln bounced the Armstrongs' children on his knees as he sat before the fire. The great wrestling match, in short, drew the extensive Armstrong family inside the growing circle of the likeable Lincoln's "fictive kin."[29]

Looking back on Lincoln's early life in New Salem, Robert Rutledge recounted the youth's obvious abilities, both intellectual and physical, and repeated his father's measured judgment that "there was more in Abe's head than wit and fun." According to James Rutledge, "all he lacked was culture." In 1857, twenty-six years after the legendary encounter, Jack Armstrong's son Duff was accused of murdering a man in a drunken brawl, in yet another rough-and-tumble. With no other resources, Jack's widow Hannah turned to Lincoln, now a prominent lawyer and politician in Springfield. Lincoln took the case, waived his fee, and waged a brilliant legal battle. In a celebrated rhetorical performance, he held the courtroom spellbound and won his old friend's son a surprise acquittal. This episode offers perhaps the most poignant indication of the vast cultural improvement, the lofty flight upward, on which the young eagle was preparing to embark.[30]

CHAPTER 7

Time and Experience

Whenever Lincoln felt called upon to offer advice about how to get ahead in life, he looked back on his own youth to frame an answer. While a congressman in Washington in 1848, he received a request from his young law partner, William Herndon, for such advice. Lincoln, quite typically, pondered the question and then frankly admitted that "I hardly know what to say." After searching for an answer, however, Lincoln soon found it within himself. The key to success was self-improvement. "The way for a young man to rise," Lincoln wrote, "is to improve himself every way he can." To Lincoln, self-improvement meant a combination of hard work and a single-minded, unwavering pursuit of knowledge. "You have been a laborious, studious young man," Lincoln reassured his young partner. "You can not fail in any laudable object, unless you allow your mind to be improperly directed."[1]

Several years later, Lincoln's stepbrother John D. Johnston turned to him for similar advice. Hearing about Johnston's proposal to move from Illinois to Missouri at age forty, Lincoln reacted with undisguised scorn. He virtually commanded Johnston to stay where he was and to concentrate on working hard. "*Go to work*," Lincoln intoned, "is the only cure for your case." But on this occasion Lincoln added crucial advice on how *not* to succeed in life. "Squirming & crawling about from place to place," Lincoln declared bluntly, "can do no good." His stepbrother's restless movement was a waste of resources and a needless diversion from self-improvement. Indeed, moving was pointless, because hard work would pay off anywhere. "If you intend to go to work, there is no better place than right where you are; if you do not intend to go to work, you can not get along any where." The seeds of success lay within.[2]

Abraham Lincoln is closely identified with Springfield, Illinois, because there he practiced a profession, raised a family, rose to prominence, and won the presidency. In fact, the importance of Springfield in Lincoln's personal, professional, and political development makes it easy to forget that he spent the first half of his life just getting there. Lincoln moved to Springfield at age twenty-eight, precisely halfway through his lifetime of fifty-six years. During the first half of his life, Lincoln made four major "horizontal" moves. He undertook the first two migrations as a youth with his family, to Indiana and Illinois, and the third and fourth alone as a young man, to New Salem and Springfield. After he reached Springfield, however, he settled down and stayed put for the next twenty-four years. The second half of his life is a story of "vertical" movement, as Lincoln remained firmly rooted in Springfield but now moved upward in the social scale.[3]

In this sense, Lincoln inhabited two different worlds. The world into which he was born was the traditional subsistence economy that empha-sized family, self-sufficiency, cooperation, and patrimonial migration. Inhabiting this world, the Lincoln family, like most families of their age, practiced a spare lifestyle that pursued mere survival rather than improve-ment as its fundamental goal. Migration—as a family—was an important and frequent means to that end. By contrast, the new world that Lincoln entered was the emerging market economy that rewarded individual initia-tive, competitiveness, commercial enterprise, and entrepreneurial impulse. One's goal was no longer mere survival as a family but economic and social improvement, measured most trenchantly by individual success. This new world rewarded not movement but persistence, celebrating dogged perse-verance and rootedness in a permanent home, even in the face of numerous tribulations and abundant temptations to move on.[4]

From this perspective, Lincoln spent the first half of his life wending his way through, and eventually out of, the first world. His journey to Spring-field sought improvement through moving, particularly the crucial move-ments from South to North and from farm to city. Running for his first pub-lic office in 1832, Lincoln wrote that "I was born and have ever remained in the most humble walks of life." This statement was eminently true but, fur-ther, the image of "walks" was apt. Lincoln's success in New Salem and his eventual acceptance into Springfield were accomplished largely through movement from place to place, as the Lincoln family—and later Lincoln himself—tested a variety of "walks" out of the traditional world of the colonial era and into the emerging one of the nineteenth century.[5]

In a comprehensive examination of the experience of growing up, histo-rian Harvey Graff identified three primary "paths" that boys and young men have followed on their way to adulthood throughout American his-tory. Extending Graff's scheme to include the Lincolns puts their experi-ences into broader perspective. The first "path," familiar to the colonial era, was the traditional one of following one's ancestors into a family enterprise, usually farming. As Graff outlined this traditional path, "Sons followed in the footsteps of their fathers, within the bonds and bounds of family, typi-cally in settled farming areas but also in migrations to the frontier and in artisanal or professional work."[6]

This traditional path describes the first four generations of Lincolns in

WILLIAM HERNDON, LINCOLN'S THIRD LAW PARTNER. AFTER LINCOLN'S DEATH,
HERNDON TRIED TO PIECE TOGETHER LINCOLN'S LIFE BY COLLECTING A TROVE OF
REMINISCENCES FROM FAMILY, FRIENDS, AND COLLEAGUES.
Courtesy of the Illinois State Historical Library.

America. These Lincolns practiced a patrimonial strategy of farming for a living while keeping a growing family together by moving generationally to frontier areas that offered more and better land. Fathers passed land down to their sons, not to launch them into new and better careers but simply to perpetuate a traditional farming lifestyle, to perpetuate a traditional, independent existence. Graff identified a second path to adulthood that appeared late in the colonial era, during Thomas Lincoln's youth. This "transitional" path coincided with the economic upheaval of early industrialization that would eventually foreclose the traditional path into farming and divert young men into a new, urban and commercial world. The transitional path, according to Graff, exhibited "Discontinuity, uncertainty, shifting expectations, and shifting locations."[7]

Thomas Lincoln amply fills out Graff's depiction of an unsure and hesitant innovator following such a "transitional" path to the future. Finding himself suspended between the two "worlds," Thomas Lincoln did indeed endure "discontinuity, uncertainty, shifting expectations, and shifting locations" as he steered his way through life without the help of a traditional patrimony. He took the new, transitional path through necessity, of course, upon the early death of his father. Graff observed of the transitional path that "there is little of the conscious choice of route and destination" that would later characterize career selection in young adulthood. According to Graff, "The traditional path for sons could be disrupted by deaths in the family, scarcity of land, or opportunities for economic development." Thomas experienced all three.[8]

As a transitional figure, therefore, Thomas could hardly help but seem unsure, even confused. After all, he inhabited the shifting zone between the two economic worlds, a pioneer of sorts on the fringe of both worlds but at home in neither. Part-time farmer and part-time craftsman, Thomas succeeded fully in neither world and has therefore been judged a failure in both. Still, he made immense contributions to the Lincoln family and to his son, in particular. Thomas was the first of the American Lincolns to attempt—and accomplish—a "betterment" migration, designed to improve his family's lot by striking out in new directions rather than following old ones. Presiding over the Lincolns' crucial movement from South to North, from farm to town, and from agriculture to trade, Thomas led his son away from the old world and pointed him in the direction of the new. Thomas was the most mobile of all the Lincolns, and his son Abraham similarly needed to move *horizontally*, to situate himself in the emerging northern, urban, commercial economy, before he could take root and begin to move *vertically*—to "rise." This he learned from his father Thomas.[9]

Graff identified a final "path" to adulthood that, not surprisingly, describes that of Abraham Lincoln. A new "emergent" path originated in the early nineteenth century just as Lincoln was coming of age. This path diverged from the traditional one by encouraging young men to pursue careers of their own making. The great economic transformation of the early nineteenth century provided new occupational choices and granted young men the novel luxury of sampling a wide variety of careers before choosing one to pursue, a process historian Robert Wiebe labeled a "revolution in choices." "Hallmarks of the emergent path," according to Graff, "include conscious choice and self-direction, a search for opportunities including social mobility, the instrumental use of further (especially higher) education, and risk-taking in the commercial marketplace."[10]

Significantly, the young Lincoln practiced all four of these "emergent" strategies. He chose just such a path at age twenty-two when he left his family behind to become a storekeeper in New Salem. The six years Lincoln spent in New Salem therefore represent a decisive, defining period in his life, during which he explored and eventually chose an "emergent path" all his own. A small, crossroads farming village, New Salem provided a bridge of sorts for Lincoln's passage from the old world to the new. Lincoln now made the transition from patrimonial to entrepreneurial settlement, from mere subsistence to a commercial economy, from agriculture to trade and eventually a profession. The skills and experience he acquired in this fledgling village prepared him to make the final move of his youth to the growing, commercially oriented town of Springfield.

Lincoln began his process of self-improvement in New Salem. He reminisced that "After he was twenty-three and had separated from his father, he studied English grammar, imperfectly of course, but so as to speak and write as well as he now does." Lincoln may have studied briefly with the village schoolmaster, Mentor Graham, but he was largely self-educated. Old settlers remembered Lincoln as a voracious reader. Retreating to the woods, walking through the village with a book tucked under one arm, or sitting by a fire, "He used to read a great deal, improving every opportunity, by day and by night." Here he acquired his lifelong habit of foregoing sleep to read, think, and write in solitude. "Used to sit up late of nights reading," James Short remembered "& would recommence in the morning when he got up." Most of his reading was utilitarian, designed to improve his mind and his prospects rather than to amuse. Short "never knew of his reading a novel." Instead, "History and poetry & the newspapers constituted the most of his reading." As his closest friend, Joshua Speed, observed, "No matter how ridiculous his ignorance upon any subject might make him appear, he was never ashamed to acknowledge it; but he immediately addressed himself to the task of being ignorant no longer." Fellow storekeeper William Greene agreed that "he never saw anyone who could learn as fast as Lincoln."[11]

In the Sangamon Country, educational opportunities were rare but not unheard of. Five New Salem youths attended Illinois College, a church-sponsored academy that opened in 1830 in the neighboring town of Jacksonville. Colleges began proliferating after 1830 as more and more farmers' sons left rural areas and began to fashion nonmanual careers in towns and cities. The traditional "accidental education" afforded to young farmboys soon gave way to a more systematic, morally grounded schooling offered by academies and common schools. Despite his own "accidental education," however, Lincoln soon gained the attention of New Salem's elders. He attended a debating society headed by tavern owner James Rutledge and astonished his audience with his eloquence and poise. "As he arose to speak," Robert Rutledge recalled many years later, "his tall form towered above the little assembly. Both hands were thrust down deep in the pockets of his pantaloons. A perceptible smile at once lit up the faces of the audience, for all anticipated the relation of some humorous story. But he opened up the discussion in splendid style to the infinite astonishment of his friends."[12]

Mostly, however, Lincoln studied alone. As a New Salem acquaintance recalled, "When his associates would return in the Evening to their various homes he would go to his reading." Lincoln's later preparation for law, in particular, was profoundly solitary. J. Rowan Herndon concluded that "his object was to study and Be By himself." William Greene agreed that "Mr. Lincoln had no Teacher." In one of his autobiographies, Lincoln himself wrote pointedly, perhaps proudly, that "He studied with nobody." In such a setting, success required extraordinary self-discipline and perseverance—no longer physical work but a new style of labor. Along with the rest of his culture, Lincoln was undertaking a crucial shift from manual to mental work. The rise from manual labor in boyhood to mental work in manhood represented a crucial achievement of the self-made man. Rising men like Lincoln celebrated—and some no doubt exaggerated—the manual labor they had performed as boys. Lincoln himself wrote that at age seven he "had an axe put into his hands at once; and from that till within his twenty-third year, he was almost constantly handling that most useful instrument." One hallmark of a truly self-made man, therefore, was an inexorable rise from manual to mental labor, usually accomplished through diligent self-education. "Abraham Lincoln, whether as boy or man, was not enamored of steady, hard work," friend and legal colleague Henry Whitney observed years later; "he preferred a variety of tasks, chiefly mental labor."[13]

Self-education, however, seemed out of place in a pioneer culture, even one on the verge of a commercial revolution. Lincoln therefore received little encouragement to forego manual labor to read and think. Back in Indiana, for example, the young man's penchant for reading and writing had earned him little more than a reputation for laziness. John Romine, who hired the boy, recalled much later that "Abe was awful lazy: he worked for me—was always reading & thinking—used to get mad at him." Dennis Hanks agreed that "Lincoln was lazy—a very lazy man—He was always reading—scribbling—writing—Ciphering—writing Poetry &c. &c." In fact, the Lincoln family had to hire him out for books to get him to work—

"bought him, I think the Columbian Orator or American Preceptor," Hanks remembered. Even in New Salem, Lincoln's solitary reading habits earned him an unflattering reputation. In Springfield, Stephen T. Logan, cousin of Mary Todd and later Lincoln's law partner, heard about the lazy young newcomer. As he later reminisced, "The impression that I had at the time was that he was a sort of loafer."[14]

Only much later did anyone recognize this diligent reading, thinking, and writing as hard work, in fact a new and important kind of labor. As Nat Grigsby put it, "Abe worked almost alone from the head." Indeed, during these years Americans redefined work itself, drawing a new distinction between physical and mental labor and enthusiastically endorsing the latter. Lincoln's stepmother made the distinction clearly: "Abe was a good boy; he didn't like physical labor—was diligent for Knowledge—wished to Know." His father as Nat Grigsby reminisced, "taught him to work but never learned him to love it." Thomas, of course, tried to teach his son manual rather than mental labor.[15]

Like the other self-made men of his age, Lincoln made the shift from manual to nonmanual work through a systematic program of self-improvement that depended for its success on rigorous self-discipline. After his death, his stepmother described the system of self-education that he developed as a boy and practiced for the rest of his life. "Abe read all the books he could lay his hands on—and when he came across a passage that Struck him, he would write it down," she reminisced. "He would rewrite it—look at it—repeat it—He had a copy book—a kind of scrap book in which he put down all things and this preserved them." The result was an amazing ability to absorb and retain facts that may have seemed innate but instead reflected hours of solitary mental labor. "He must understand Every thing—even to the smallest thing—Minutely & Exactly," as his stepmother recalled. "He would then repeat it over to himself again & again—sometimes in one form and then in another & when it was fixed in his mind to suit him he became Easy and he never lost that fact or his understanding of it." This painstaking practice of "becoming easy" with the knowledge he absorbed allowed him to reach back into his memory and provoke the "instant astonishment" of audiences for the rest of his life. As New Salem's schoolmaster, Mentor Graham, observed, "He was regular in his habits punctual in doing anything that he promised or agreed to do his method of doing *any* thing was very systematic."[16]

In short, the young Lincoln succeeded by single-mindedly pursuing mental work, pursuing it through every opportunity that came his way, following every new "walk" that appeared, taking it as far he could, wherever it led. Flatboatman, store clerk, miller, militiaman, merchant, postmaster, surveyor, legislator, and finally lawyer—one opportunity led to another, and usually a better one. Historians have depicted Lincoln as an aimless, even befuddled youth, as he tried to seek his own way in the world. As one recent biographer portrayed him, for example, "He was trying to put together the fragmented pieces of his personality into a coherent pattern."[17]

If in hindsight his path seems aimless, it simply reflects the bewildering array of new opportunities that constantly appeared as the new commercial economy unfolded before him. In his ambition to rise, Lincoln had few role models to follow, least of all his father. As they educated themselves, Lincoln and the other self-made men of his era puttered along in fits and starts, groping their way forward in new and untested directions. They followed, in E. Anthony Rotundo's estimation, "a path to manhood that was less clearly marked than today." With so few institutions of self-advancement and such scant precedent for self-improvement, "There was little system to the passage of a boy through his years of education, and there was even less system in the process that gave him credentials for a life in commerce or the professions." In Graff's formulation, the new "paths" to success were as yet "unpaved."[18]

During the early nineteenth century, Americans experienced a "revolution in choices," as a host of new opportunities and especially vocations became available for the first time. Americans accordingly began to consider youth a "choosing time," a time to make important decisions. As such, youth represented an extended period of both growth and opportunity but also self-doubt and indecision. In New Salem, during his twenties, Lincoln chose both his vocation—law—and his lifelong avocation—politics. By modern standards, Lincoln came late in life to his profession, at age twenty-seven. During his lifetime, however, men typically took their time in choosing careers. Young men simply felt little pressure to settle on an occupation. Historian Joseph Kett, for example, observed a "lack of intense social pressure on young men to decide on vocations," so that "the problem of career choice did not arise before 1860 with its later intensity." Lincoln himself reminisced that in New Salem "He studied what he should do," and apparently he was not in much of a hurry to decide.[19]

Coming of age in an agricultural community a stone's throw from Springfield gave Lincoln a panoramic view of the social and economic life of the Sangamon Country. During six years in New Salem, Lincoln practiced as many occupations, to make ends meet and to make up his own mind. As historian Burton Bledstein has pointed out, "Career patterns in the mid-nineteenth century were still uncertain as men jumped from profession to profession." Rather than representing aimless indecision, "Such a system encouraged young men, however unprepossessing but alert, to try their hands at different trades." Prolonged youth and occupational fluidity combined to produce what Joseph Kett described as "a certain amount of stumbling about before one was settled in a calling." By his own account, Lincoln rejected a manual occupation, blacksmithing, as well as a profession, law—he "rather thought he could not succeed at that without a better education." Instead, he did his own fair share of "stumbling about" by settling on a career as a merchant.[20]

In the region's villages and towns, storekeeping was an honorable occupation that naturally attracted any ambitious young man. Merchants were the region's natural leaders and boosters, luring capital from outside the community and commanding respect from within. Sporting a leisurely pace and seasonal rhythms, a store might sell only ten items on an ordinary day, affording young merchants the leisure to read books and newspapers, socialize, and politick. Storekeeping was so appealing a vocation that during its brief existence New Salem boasted twenty-one store owners. But insecurities haunted the life of any storekeeper. Merchants bought their goods in the East on long-term credit and were therefore constantly in debt. They in turn sold most of their goods to their customers on credit and therefore depended on their clientele to settle up before the notes came due. As a result, merchants needed to invest more than their own time and labor into their stores. Successful store owners began with enough capital to start a store and to see it through the lean times, and they needed reliable commercial connections back East.[21]

Storekeeping was therefore an extremely speculative venture that attracted entrepreneurial settlers—young, single men who, like Springfield's Elijah Iles, could bring money into the region and risk losing it. The most successful stores were partnerships, through which merchants pooled resources and reduced competition. Relatives, especially brothers, made the most reliable partners, but rival merchants sometimes fell in together and then fell out again. Most New Salem merchants—thirteen out of the twenty-one—worked with partners. The village boasted seven such partnerships, three of them involving brothers. One exception to the preference for partnerships was Lincoln's first employer, Denton Offutt, who arrived in Illinois alone and therefore operated at a disadvantage. Born near Lexington, Kentucky, Offutt inherited some property from his father, a horse farmer. He sold this patrimony, however, to speculate in farm produce in the Sangamon Country, floating corn and pork down to New Orleans in hopes of making a profit. Offutt operated on a grand scale, at one point offering four thousand bushels of seed corn for sale in New Salem. His New Salem store proved to be something of an afterthought, however, and Offutt never commanded enough capital or commercial connections to stay afloat for long. When his notes fell due at the end of the year, he simply left the region. Still in his twenties, Offutt was young and ambitious enough to head south, start over, and launch a new and more successful career as a horse tamer.[22]

Like Lincoln and Offutt, most of New Salem's merchants were southerners—in fact Kentuckians—and most of them failed miserably in business. For many merchants, storekeeping proved a fleeting flirtation, even a gamble, representing a brief urban experience and a lost opportunity of their youth. When they foundered, they either left the region entirely or sold out to a competitor, settled down, and tried another occupation. Significantly, the village's most successful merchants were northeasterners. A handful of "Yankee traders" ended up dominating New Salem. Southerners generally arrived with families, but Yankees tended to arrive as individuals or sometimes with unrelated business partners.

New Salem's first and most successful store owner, Samuel Hill, was a Midlander from New Jersey. He came to Illinois via Cincinnati, arriving at age twenty-nine as a single settler. Hill opened his store in 1829 in partnership with John McNamar, a native New Yorker who, like him, was a twenty-nine-year-old single settler. McNamar was the quintessential entrepreneurial migrant, leaving his family behind to strike out west in hopes of making a fortune in some city or town. Not only did he leave his family behind, he left his identity behind as well, arriving as John NcNeil to prevent his family from finding him. His son later tried to justify this deception, explaining that McNamar's father "had a large family and John being the oldest, was looked to by the others for support." Instead, McNamar "wanted to establish himself financially and believed that, if they could find him, the whole family would pile on him and prevent him from accumulating anything." A classic single, entrepreneurial settler, McNamar placed his own advancement ahead of family ties. He therefore moved west alone and incognito to seek his fortune in Illinois.[23]

Hill and McNamar bought their goods in Cincinnati, shipped them to St. Louis by river, and then headed straight for the Sangamon Country. Like Elijah Iles before him, McNamar "set out on a voyage of Discovery on the praries of Illinois." He considered New Salem a promising "business point" and promptly built "a Magnificent Store house for the Sum of fifteen Dollars." This "magnificent store" became known as the Hill-McNeil Store and thrived for the next decade, supplying coffee, tea, sugar, salt, whiskey, and sundries to the area's far-flung families. Hill, a stereotypical Yankee, had enough capital, business sense, and commercial connections to survive. Simply put, he maintained the largest inventory in the area, spending a week or two in St. Louis every spring and fall, selecting his merchandise. As one early settler put it, "Hill had the largest stock of goods in town," indeed "all the kinds of goods that the people called for."[24]

As a shrewd "Yankee trader," Hill became New Salem's wealthiest resident. McNamar, however, sold out his interest in 1832 and went back East for three years. When he returned, he opened a new store with John Allen, the village physician, as silent partner. Significantly, Allen was a fellow Yankee, a native Vermonter and graduate of Dartmouth Medical School. Still, despite this boost, McNamar could not hope to weather the worst economic storm, the Panic of 1837. He later reminisced that "the crash of 37 induced us to close out with considerable loss." Like Denton Offutt, McNamar left New Salem in 1837, but he opened another store in nearby Petersburg. Along with most of the area's would-be merchants, however, McNamar eventually gave up storekeeping and returned to farming. Hill alone managed to weather the storm, building the largest home in New Salem—the only two-story house in the village—which stood next to his store as a visible monument to his commercial success. In fact, Hill was the only merchant who managed to stay in business throughout the life of New Salem. According to one account, Hill was a "mercantile king" who "generally had things his own way." He was also a tough competitor. "He had the rowdy part of the community for his comrades," one early settler remembered. "Though not much of a man physically when he had a grudge against a man he could hire some old bluffer to whip him." But even the tenacious Hill eventually had to concede to New Salem's demise. In 1839, he moved his store to Petersburg when the all but abandoned village of New Salem died at last.[25]

During his first few years in New Salem, Lincoln viewed the world through the eyes of a storekeeper, and his commitment to self-improvement embraced the village as well. Before he left New Salem, Denton Offutt rented the mill from the Rutledges and recruited Lincoln to run it. As a merchant and miller, Lincoln's livelihood, like the village itself, depended on the river. The Sangamon powered the mill, but the river was crucial to the store as well, promising a cheap connection by water with St. Louis and other commercial centers. Improved transportation was not essential to subsistence farmers, who could trade with their neighbors and occasionally with merchants. If nothing else, they could ride the fifty miles to Beardstown or the hundred to St. Louis once or twice a year.

An improved river, however, was essential for commercial agriculture. As one observer put it, "The farmer who lives near a navigable stream, is able to transport his produce to a foreign market, with a mere fractional expense, compared to that he is driven to the necessity of incurring if he transports by land." Above all, reliable and cheap transportation was crucial to the area's merchants, who accepted all kinds of commercial risks during the normal course of business. Merchants collected the farmers' produce as payment for goods, stored it through the winter, shipped it to St. Louis in the spring, and bought more goods in return. The small commercial component of the local economy therefore proved the most vocal in supporting improved transportation—or simply "improvements," as they became known. Only one in forty men were merchants, but they were natural community leaders in the growing campaign to fund improved transportation.[26]

Along with other merchants, Lincoln looked to the river to connect the Sangamon Country to the world beyond. During his first spring in New Salem, Lincoln became personally involved in an ambitious scheme to navigate the Sangamon. In January 1832, Vincent Bogue, a Springfield merchant and miller, announced triumphantly that he would ascend the Sangamon in a chartered steamboat, the *Talisman*, during the spring thaw. He advertised a stock of spring goods that the boat would carry up the Sangamon. He also promised Springfield's merchants that he would carry off all of their accumulated produce when the boat steamed back down the river to St. Louis. Reporting this news, the *Sangamo Journal* proclaimed optimistically that "We seriously believe that the Sangamo river, with some little improvement, can be made navigable for steam-boats, for several months in the year."[27]

A group of influential Springfielders led a subscription drive to subsidize the venture. Headed by Elijah Iles, Bogue's underwriters comprised prominent merchants, lawyers, and physicians, including the Todd family patriarch, John Todd. As the *Talisman* puffed upriver, Bogue called for a dozen men, "having axes with *long* handles," to meet him at Beardstown at the mouth of the river to clear branches from the banks and snags from the bottom as the boat puffed upstream. Lincoln—as a former axe handler and budding storekeeper—now cast his lot with the Springfield merchants and joined this hardy crew. In March, the *Talisman* appeared as promised and docked at Bogue's mill five miles downstream from Springfield, spilling forth tons of hardware, lumber, sugar, coffee, chocolate, liquor, soap, candles, and dry goods.[28]

The *Sangamo Journal* crowed with delight that "Springfield can no longer be considered an inland town." A local poet who witnessed the landing wrote that "Some thought the world was at an end,/And heav'n in mercy this did send." The *Talisman* did indeed seem heaven-sent. As one settler recalled, "The people then believed that the Sangamon would always be navigable for steamboats and they were wild with excitement with the outlook for Springfield's prosperity." The delirium was short-lived, however. The spring was unusually dry, and the river fell quickly, forcing a desperate retreat downstream after only a week. Acting as assistant pilot, Lincoln helped to guide the *Talisman* on a tedious two-week journey back down to Beardstown as the water continued to fall. The desperate pilots used long oars to try to steer the boat into the middle of the river. "The steamer was continually running into the banks of the river and into the tops of trees that grew on and over the banks of the river," one witness remembered, "and the result was that the cabin and upper parts of the boat were badly broken and injured."[29]

Reaching New Salem, the boat threatened to snag on Rutledge's mill dam. As the local poet put it, "when we came up to Salem dam,/Up we went against it, *jam*!" Desperate to return to Beardstown, the boat's crew insisted on tearing down the dam. The mill's owners, Rutledge and Cameron, declared that the river was unnavigable and that their dam was therefore legal and should remain. In a compromise between the steamboat and the mill, the *Talisman* crew removed and then replaced a section of the dam to allow the boat to pass. Stephen T. Logan remembered that the boat was "nearly torn to pieces" during its discouraging two-week retreat. The long-awaited steamboat arrived at Beardstown "in a ruinous condition." Bogue lost money on this maiden voyage and fled from Illinois. Like Denton Offut before him, Bogue headed south and later turned up in New Orleans. The *Talisman*, however, scattered nothing but debts in its wake, for some of which Lincoln was held personally responsible. In fact, the *Talisman* was the only steamboat ever to venture so far upstream on the Sangamon. Four years later, another steamboat, the *Utility*, attempted to paddle upriver to Springfield but struck low water at Petersburg. Unable to move upriver or retreat downstream, the boat simply tied up indefinitely. It sat idle until the villagers dismantled it, salvaging the wood for lumber and the glass for windows. The *Utility*'s engine powered the town's first steam mill. According to one reminiscence, "there was not a house in the town that was not orna-mented with some of the Utility." Together, these two futile voyages drama-tized the pressing need for large-scale improvements to make the Sangamon River navigable if commercial agriculture were to become a reality.[30]

The frenzy to improve the Sangamon and open the region to commercial development caught up the young Lincoln, and he committed himself per-sonally to the project. In less than a year at Offut's store, Lincoln had won the villagers' confidence by building a reputation for enterprise, honesty, and good humor. With the help and encouragement of local politicians—as Lincoln put it, "encouraged by his great popularity among his immediate neighbors"—he ran for the state legislature in the spring of 1832. By all accounts, Lincoln came easily to politics. Politics also came naturally to any storekeeper. Stores and taverns frequently hosted spontaneous political gatherings, and perhaps one-fourth of frontier merchants held some kind of elective office. New Salem merchant Samuel Hill, for example, furnished the use of his store's front porch to many a politician. "Hill's store was headquarters for all political discussions," according to one reminiscence. "The farmers would congregate there and discuss the questions of the day." As William Herndon, Lincoln's future law partner, summed it up, the village storekeeper "took the only newspaper, owned the only collection of books and half the property in the village; and in general was the social, and often-times the political head of the community."[31]

Merchants had many qualities that recommended them as political lead-ers. They often possessed the most learning—and leisure—within their com-munities. With their adroit penmanship, practiced arithmetic, and easy familiarity with both townsfolk and farmers for miles around, storekeepers made astute election clerks. Clerking at elections was a position of trust awarded to the most dependable members of any community. Lincoln clerked at an election about a year after he arrived in New Salem, a sign of both his growing stature and his familiarity with the villagers. In fact, Lin-coln supplanted trusted schoolteacher Mentor Graham in this capacity.

Graham himself remembered that "He performed the duties with great felicity—much fairness and honesty & impartiality." Significantly, the election took place at the house of a merchant—John McNamar—or, as Lincoln recorded it, "at the house of John McNeil." Significantly, too, Lincoln's fellow clerk at the election was William Greene, his assistant clerk from those early days at Offutt's store.[32]

At gatherings such as this, Lincoln gained the attention of Bowling Green, the village's justice of the peace and the precinct's political leader. A North Carolina native, Greene was a member of the vast Armstrong clan that dominated the neighborhood, and in fact was Jack Armstrong's half-brother. Forty-five years old in 1832, Green qualified as one of the elders in this youthful pioneer community. A large, jolly man affectionately known as "Pot," Green presided over the elections that introduced Lincoln to politics as well as the informal courtroom that introduced him to the law. Known as a "reading man," Green lent an intellectual air to the pioneer community. Although a Jacksonian, Green was Lincoln's first political patron. He and his wife boarded Lincoln from time to time, and "Pot" and "Aunt Nancy" soon became his fictive kin.[33]

The area's merchants, like those in Springfield, tended to support the Whig Party, with its commitment to improved transportation, banks, and a paper currency. Historian Lewis Atherton estimated that three-fourths of frontier merchants were Whigs. Samuel Hill, New Salem's most successful merchant, was a New Jersey Democrat, but his partner, John McNamar, was a committed Whig. In fact, the old settlers made McNamar the butt of a joke that illustrated his political perseverance. Heading to the polling place, McNamar heard that his son, who happened to be mentally challenged, had voted Democratic. "Huh," he muttered, "*All the damn fools vote that ticket.*"[34]

Lincoln, of course, proclaimed proudly that he was "Always a whig in politics." In 1832, however, no real parties, either Whig or Democratic, had yet formed in Illinois. In the absence of parties, voters usually supported a local favorite. In fact, between the War of 1812 and the 1820s, there was only one national party, the Democratic-Republican. A two-party system began to emerge slowly during the 1820s, however, when Andrew Jackson twice battled John Quincy Adams for the presidency. Jackson's disciples gradually coalesced into the Democratic Party, while Adams's supporters eventually became Whigs. This new system appeared first in presidential contests at the national level, only slowly filtering down to the state and local levels. Parties appeared last in the new, western states, such as Illinois.[35]

Well into the 1830s, Illinois, like other new states, boasted temporary, personal cliques rather than real parties. This "struggle between personal factions" focused on Ninian Edwards, Illinois's first territorial governor and later U.S. senator. An "Edwards party" competed with an "anti-Edwards party" for political control of the state. Despite its personal focus, the Edwards party generally supported internal improvements, banks, and a high, protective tariff, later features of Whig economic policy.[36]

As historian Edward Pease concluded, "Till 1832 national issues in general did not take a strong hold on the people or influence seriously the alignment of factions." In that year, Henry Clay challenged Jackson for the presidency, urging an aggressive economic program to boost national development, focusing on banks, internal improvements, and a protective tariff. In a dramatic stroke, President Jackson vetoed the federal recharter of the Bank of the United States, winning broad public support for a more decentralized economic program. Throwing the "Clay men" into disarray, Jackson won a second term handily. In Illinois, the opposition remained disorganized through most of the campaign. Rather than endorsing a single candidate, Jackson's opponents held an Anti-Jackson convention in Vandalia, as they put it, "to concentrate the opposition." They nominated a slate of Anti-Jackson electors, which included Springfield merchant Elijah Iles. The delegates agreed on principles, however, supporting the Bank of the United States, domestic manufactures, and internal improvements, which soon became the trinity of Whig party doctrine.[37]

Still, in central Illinois national parties and issues mattered less than a candidate's personal popularity and his view on local affairs. Historian Richard McCormick concluded that as late as 1832 "elections to the state legislature continued to be fought on the basis of personalities." When it came to personality, of course, Lincoln was New Salem's favorite. John McNamar reminisced that "I do not think there was any party Politics hereabout in those days candidats for Election basing their Claims upon Local Hobeys." The most important "local hobey" in the New Salem district was improvement of the Sangamon, on which Lincoln was an expert. Despite his affinity for the emerging Whig Party—Lincoln called himself "an avowed Clay man"—Jacksonians in the neighborhood threw their support behind him. As Stephen Logan remembered, "they were mostly democratic, but were for Lincoln on personal grounds."[38]

Without any party machinery to nominate a candidate, political aspirants put themselves before the voters—or had their friends do so—by publishing campaign letters in local newspapers. Lincoln himself termed this "an established custom" and had doubtless perused many campaign letters in the newspapers he read so voraciously. Now, he carefully crafted a long "communication" to the voters to support his own candidacy for the legislature. This first written testament of Lincoln's political views drew heavily on his single year's experience in the Sangamon Country rather than on any coherent partisan ideology. Parties had barely made their appearance in the politics of the county. Lincoln therefore addressed his letter to the "independent voters" and focused self-consciously on "local affairs."[39]

His underlying theme clearly embraced improvement, both economic and cultural, and transportation improvement in particular. "Time and experience have verified to a demonstration," Lincoln declared, "the public utility of internal improvements." He enthusiastically endorsed a wide range of improvements—"the opening of good roads," "the clearing of navigable streams," and the construction of canals and railroads—to address what he saw as the county's primary problem, access to markets. Lincoln the storekeeper declared that "exporting the surplus products of its fertile soil, and importing necessary articles from abroad, are indispensably necessary."[40]

Lincoln recognized railroads as the ideal form of transportation. "No other improvement that reason will justify us in hoping for," he wrote, "can equal in utility the rail road." Lincoln clearly looked at the issue from a commercial perspective. He praised railroads as "a never failing source of communication, between places of business remotely situated from each other." His own adventures on the Sangamon River and his experience as a merchant and miller undoubtedly had convinced him of their superiority. "Upon the rail road the regular progress of commercial intercourse is not interrupted by either high or low water, or freezing weather, which are the principal difficulties that render our future hopes of water communication precarious and uncertain." Still, Lincoln rejected railroads for the Sangamon Country as too expensive. He also knew that a proposed railroad running from the Illinois River to Springfield would bypass New Salem and render river transport—and New Salem—obsolete. With the impending voyage of the *Talisman* undoubtedly in the back of his mind, Lincoln cast his lot, both politically and personally, with the river. "The improvement of Sangamo river," Lincoln concluded in an appeal to the favorite local issue, "is an object much better suited to our infant resources."[41]

Lincoln was an authority on river transportation. Fascinated with the subject, years later he patented a method for floating vessels through shallow water. He now portrayed himself, quite justifiably, as an expert on the ebb and flow of the Sangamon. "From my peculiar circumstances," he wrote, "it is probable that for the last twelve months I have given as particular attention to the stage of the water in this river, as any other person in the country." He went on to detail an ambitious plan for improving the river: "whatever may be its natural advantages, certain it is, that it never can be practically useful to any great extent, without being greatly improved by art." The "art" he had in mind would completely reshape the river, straightening out its meandering "zig zag course," literally moving the river out of its old channel and forcing it into a new one. The new course would cut the distance between New Salem and Beardstown in half and increase the velocity of the current, granting New Salem virtual control over the trade of the Sangamon Country. "I believe the improvement of the Sangamo river," he concluded, "to be vastly important and highly desirable to the people of this county."[42]

Lincoln next turned to a subject of vital concern to merchants and any-one else engaged in a commercial economy—interest rates. Storekeepers, above all, operated on borrowed money, and Lincoln considered interest rates "exorbitant." High rates of interest were a "baneful and corroding system" that injured the "general interests of the community" by draining money from the region. Lincoln now called for a usury law to cap interest rates in Illinois. As a storekeeper, Lincoln had personal experience with such extremely high rates. His employer, Denton Offutt, had borrowed money at 60 percent interest, ten times the usual rate available to merchants. Offutt desperately needed money to keep his store afloat, and Lincoln may have been partly responsible for repaying this loan. Offutt eventually defaulted, and as Lincoln ran for the legislature the store "was failing—had almost failed," as Lincoln later put it. In his campaign letter, he acknowledged that "in cases of the greatest necessity" such high rates of interest might be justified. Given his experiences in the Offutt store and his uncertain prospects, one of the "cases of the greatest necessity" he anticipated may well have been his own. Taken together, these pleas for improved transportation and lower interest rates indicate a commercial slant to Lincoln's emerging political perspective.[43]

In a paragraph inspired perhaps by an awareness of his own belated intellectual awakening, Lincoln labeled education "the most important subject which we as a people can be engaged in." Lincoln hoped that "every man may receive at least, a moderate education," which of course was his own personal goal. He recommended especially the reading of history, his favorite subject, but also the scriptures, which so heavily influenced his own development as a writer. Here was an evolving link between public improvement and personal self-betterment. Widespread education would encourage "morality, sobriety, enterprise and industry," elevating these virtues from merely personal into general social values. Eventually Lincoln, like other Whigs, would implicitly conflate personal development with national improvement and the public good, viewing Improvement as beneficial to both society and individuals.[44]

In closing, Lincoln declared his own modesty and excused his age (he was twenty-three), two rhetorical devices that would resurface time and again throughout his public life. He also openly denigrated his own origins—for the first but not the last time—by declaring that "I was born and have ever remained in the most humble walks of life." Finally, he acknowledged his lack of two social and political advantages: "I have no wealthy or popular relations to recommend me." Overall, Lincoln's letter was narrowly focused. It targeted a local constituency in the northwest corner of Sangamon County that hoped for commercial development and pinned those hopes on improvement of the Sangamon. Still, at age twenty-three, Lincoln had found his lifelong avocation, and later his passion—politics.[45]

CHAPTER 8

He Went the Campaign

Lincoln's first political campaign was unexpectedly interrupted by a military one, the Black Hawk War, the last Euroamerican assault on Illinois's native inhabitants. The Sac and Fox tribes who, though they had separate chiefs, were affiliated aand lived and travelled together, originated in Ontario but moved westward before 1700 under pressure from the Iroquois, the powerful confederation that dominated the Great Lakes region during the American colonial period. Before the Revolution, the Sacs and Foxes controlled a vast stretch of the Mississippi Valley bounded roughly by the Wisconsin and Illinois rivers to the north and east and the Missouri to the south and west. The Sacs' principal tribal village, Saukenuk, was located at the mouth of the Rock River near present-day Rock Island, Illinois. Here, Black Hawk was born into the Sac tribe in 1767.[1]

Traditionally, the Sacs and Foxes planted corn at Saukenuk in the spring and then headed westward to hunt buffalo on the Great Plains during the summer. As fall approached, they returned to Saukenuk to harvest their crops. As white settlers moved westward, however, the Sacs and Foxes began to feel pressure to relinquish their tribal lands. Game grew scarce, and they increasingly depended on American and British manufactured goods, which they acquired through the fur trade. In 1804, the Sacs and Foxes signed a treaty negotiated by William Henry Harrison, governor of Indiana Territory. Under the Treaty of 1804, Sac and Fox leaders ceded 50 million acres of their land to the United States, including all of their land east of the Mississippi River, opening the Illinois country to white settlement. One important provision of the Treaty of 1804 guaranteed the Native Americans the use of the land until the government sold it to white settlers.[2]

During the War of 1812, many Sacs and Foxes, including Black Hawk, sided with the British and fought the Americans. The Americans clearly wanted the tribes' land, while the British merely traded with them and in fact promised to restore their ceded territory should they win the war. During the war, Ninian Edwards, governor of Illinois Territory, ordered his militia to destroy three Sac and Fox villages along the Illinois River to break their resistance. Meanwhile, Edwards persuaded neutral Sacs and Foxes to move west of the Mississippi River to Iowa. At Saukenuk, a new leader, Keokuk, emerged as a village war chief to represent the growing majority of Sacs who favored cooperation. Black Hawk's band, however, continued to fight, defeating an American force under Major Zachary Taylor in two battles at the mouth of the Rock River in 1814.[3]

After the war, Sac and Fox leaders signed a treaty of peace with the Americans. Many of the Native Americans followed Chief Keokuk in a voluntary removal across the Mississippi to Iowa, where they clashed with the Sioux. A minority, however, remained peacefully at Saukenuk. Tensions later mounted when U.S. forces built a fort on Rock Island, which the Sacs considered a sacred place. Additionally, during the 1820s, the remaining Sacs grew increasingly dependent on trade with the whites, and their traditional society steadily deteriorated. They became economically dependent on the British in Canada and traveled there frequently to plead for food, manufactured goods, and arms. Americans began to suspect a military plot and labeled the remaining Sacs the "British Band." Led by Black Hawk, the Sacs argued that they had been tricked into selling their land under the Treaty of 1804. Governor Edwards now demanded that the federal government remove all of the Native Americans from Illinois or his militia would do the job The War Department agreed to remove the Native Americans by 1829.[4]

White squatters began to invade the region in advance of government land sales. Most of the Sacs and Foxes strove to maintain peace with the settlers, but Black Hawk's band asserted their right to remain in the Rock River Valley until the government sold the land. For two summers, Black Hawk's band actually lived side by side with white squatters in Saukenuk. A white settler even occupied Black Hawk's own house. Meanwhile, the federal land office in Springfield, headed by John Todd, Mary Todd's uncle, began selling this prime farmland. Still, Black Hawk, who was a traditionalist, determined to remain at Saukenuk, his birthplace, citing its religious significance for the Sacs. Despite signing a treaty requiring the tribe to remain west of the Mississippi and to break all ties with the British, Black Hawk, now sixty-five, led his band of eight hundred men, women, and children back into Illinois with the avowed purpose of planting their spring crop in their traditional homeland.[5]

Black Hawk hoped to win support from allied tribes and the British in Canada for this reassertion of Native American sovereignty in northern Illinois. He determined to avoid war and intended only to plant crops for the summer and then leave for the winter, believing that the Americans would not attack an openly peaceful band. As the Sacs traveled up the Rock River, however, they gathered up like-minded Foxes, Kickapoo, and Winnebago until their numbers swelled to almost two thousand. During April and May

1832, hysteria swept through the white settlements of northern and central Illinois. The U.S. Army commander, General Henry Atkinson, called on Illinois Governor John Reynolds to raise a mounted militia. About seventeen hundred Illinois militiamen volunteered to serve alongside Atkinson's 340 regular army troops. As Atkinson's infantry followed on foot, the mounted militiamen surged ahead under orders to locate Black Hawk and "kill Injuns." Moving slowly up the Rock River into Wisconsin, Black Hawk, outnumbered and protective of his band's women and children, decided to surrender. Instead of dealing with Black Hawk's emissaries, however, the militiamen, untrained and inexperienced, attacked the Native Americans, provoking a bloody counterattack in which a few dozen Native Americans routed the volunteers. Known as Stillman's Run, this skirmish claimed eleven militiamen and ruined any chance of a peaceful resolution.[6]

Black Hawk now decided to cross the Mississippi back into Iowa. His band continued up the Rock River into Wisconsin in hopes of circling north and west around the approaching army, all the while raiding white settlements for food. Meanwhile, President Jackson ordered Atkinson to "attack and disperse them." On May 21, a Potawatomi war party killed fifteen white settlers, prompting Governor Reynolds to call for two thousand more militiamen. Black Hawk's hoped-for Native American allies never materialized. In fact, the Americans recruited members of the Potawatomi, Winnebago, Sioux, Menominee, and Stockbridge tribes to help run down Black Hawk and his band. They also arranged for Sioux and Menominee warriors to stand by west of the Mississippi should the band get that far. In a further escalation, Jackson put General Winfield Scott, a hero of the War of 1812, in command. Troops caught up with the Native Americans after they turned westward and attacked them as they tried to cross the Wisconsin River.[7]

On August 1, 1832, Black Hawk's band reached the Mississippi, their numbers thinned to five hundred through warfare and starvation. Before they could cross the river, however, the steamboat *Warrior* appeared and drove them back with gunfire. The next day, Atkinson's infantry overtook them at last. In the resulting massacre, dubbed the Battle of Bad Axe, Black Hawk's band was almost completely annihilated. One witness reported that "The Inds. were pushed litterally into the Mississippi, the current of which was at one time perceptibly tinged with the blood of the Native Americans." Anywhere from 150 to 300 Native Americans died in the battle while perhaps 100 managed to cross the Mississippi. These few stragglers were soon cut down or taken prisoner by the Sioux. Overall, the U.S. government enlisted ten thousand militiamen to defend the frontier against Black Hawk and his followers. Perhaps one thousand Native Americans died during this "small and foolish war," as one historian has justifiably described it.[8]

Black Hawk himself survived and surrendered. Along with other Sac

BLACK HAWK. IN A TRAGIC TREK ACROSS NORTHERN ILLINOIS, THE SAC AND FOX
CHIEF LED A PORTION OF HIS TRIBE IN FUTILE RESISTANCE
AGAINST DISPOSSESSION.
Courtesy of the Illinois State Historical Library.

and Fox leaders, he was escorted in leg irons to Jefferson Barracks south of St. Louis by Lieutenant Jefferson Davis. Originally sentenced to ten years of imprisonment, Black Hawk was eventually released after taking a tour of Washington, D.C., and other eastern cities that was meant to awe him into submission. The Sacs and Foxes as a whole paid a heavy penalty for Black Hawk's resistance. Although most of them had removed voluntarily from Illinois, they were forced to sell most of the eastern half of Iowa. They were required to remove within a year and thereafter never "reside, plant, fish, or hunt, on any portion of the ceded land." In this so-called Black Hawk Purchase, the United States obtained 6 million acres for a mere ten cents an acre. As punishment for their supposed complicity in the Black Hawk War, the Winnebago were required to cede all of their lands east of the Mississippi and remove westward to a much smaller tract of land in Iowa. As a reward for his compliance, Keokuk received the title of civil chief, at last displacing Black Hawk as undisputed leader of the Sacs and Foxes. Black Hawk himself died in 1838. Within a year, his bones were dug up and put on display in a museum.[9]

Lincoln took part in the Black Hawk War as an Illinois volunteer. After Governor Reynolds activated the state militia, Sangamon County organized eleven companies containing just over five hundred volunteers. Seventy men, including some of the Clary's Grove boys, gathered near New Salem to organize a company. Units chose their own officers, and in yet another indication of Lincoln's growing reputation—and "to his own surprize"— this company named him captain. Jack Armstrong served as Lincoln's sergeant. Lincoln was perhaps the youngest captain in the county; he was younger than eight of the other ten whose ages are known. Discipline in militia units, however, was notoriously lax, so initially this election proved a mixed blessing. A contemporary observer concluded that "there are few more ridiculous scenes than a militia muster," in which the men assumed "every variety of posture or position—some sitting, some lying, some standing on one foot, some on both." Uniforms were unheard of and weaponry was crude, with "every variety of coat and shirt sleeves, and every variety of weapon—among the latter, however, the corn-stalk, umbrella and riding whip predominating." Poet William Cullen Bryant saw the volunteers and called them "unkempt and unshaven." Lincoln had his hands full just keeping his men in line. John Todd Stuart, who served under him, admitted that "Lincoln had no military qualities whatever except that he was a good clever fellow and kept the esteem and respect of his men." Lincoln's company enrolled for thirty days and was sworn briefly into federal service. They marched to Rock Island on the Mississippi, making camp near Saukenuk. They next marched up the Rock River and then moved southward to Ottawa, but saw no action.[10]

After mustering out his company at the end of thirty days, Lincoln had satisfied his own military obligation. Instead of returning home like most of his men, however, Lincoln reenlisted immediately. Legend holds that Colonel Zachary Taylor rallied the militiamen and persuaded three hundred of them, including Lincoln, to reenlist. Lieutenant Robert Anderson, later the Union commander at Fort Sumter, mustered Lincoln into a company led by Springfield merchant Elijah Iles. Iles commanded a cavalry unit whose mobility permitted the men to act as scouts and spies. Such elite companies attracted wealthier members of the community, who could provide their own horses and therefore enjoyed greater autonomy. As historian John Mahon described such volunteers, "The wealthier among them tended to join the cavalry, which was exclusive because it was expensive, while clerks and shopkeepers enrolled in grenadier, light, and other elite infantry companies." Iles's elite, mounted unit of twenty-day volunteers consisted of former officers from disbanded units. In this sense, Lincoln's unexpected election as captain had elevated him from the infantry to the cavalry, from the ranks of clerks and storekeepers to the select company of Springfield's merchants, lawyers, and physicians. Although he served as a private under Iles—and had to borrow a horse—this was a decided step upward. Earning ten times the pay of an infantryman, Lincoln now had the opportunity to meet and befriend several influential Springfielders. All three of the company's officers employed camp servants. Iles brought his store clerk, John Williams. In a temporary reversal of fortune, Lincoln found himself soldiering alongside Elijah Iles and standing a cut above store clerk John Williams, who had been reduced to the status of camp servant. This mounted company tried—but failed—"to find out where the Indians were," according to Stuart. "There were Indians all about us, constantly watching our movements," he reminisced. The company rode to Galena but saw no real action.[11]

After leaving Iles's command, Lincoln enlisted for a third and final time in another spy company, commanded by Captain Jacob Early. Early, a Springfield physician and minister, had served as a private under Lincoln, and the two men now reversed their roles. In Early's company, Lincoln got his closest look at the war, helping to bury five men who had been killed by Native Americans. "The red light of the morning sun was streaming upon them as they lay heads towards us on the ground," Lincoln reportedly recounted years later. "And every man had a round, red spot on top of his head, about as big as a dollar where the redskins had taken his scalp." Lincoln marched with the company as far north as the White River Valley in Wisconsin, where he was mustered out after thirty days. Awakening one morning to find their horses stolen, Lincoln and messmate George Harrison—later a physician—had to walk back to Peoria. There, they bought a canoe and paddled it down the Illinois River to Havana. Lincoln walked the rest of the way back home to New Salem.[12]

Historians have traditionally portrayed Lincoln as a reluctant warrior. In later years, Lincoln often made light of his eighty-day military career, recalling that "I had a good many bloody struggles with the musquitoes;

and although I never fainted from loss of blood, I can truly say I was often hungry." In fact, Lincoln was an enthusiastic soldier, proud of his military service and especially his election as captain. In 1859, he reminisced that "I was elected a Captain of Volunteers—a success which gave me more pleasure than any I have had since." A year later, after winning the Republican nomination for president, he still declared that "he has not since had any success in life which gave him so much satisfaction." Indeed, Lincoln admitted feeling "elated" during the campaign.[13]

Examination of enlistment rosters from the Black Hawk War confirms the exuberance apparent in Lincoln's own testimony. All white males age eighteen to forty-five were eligible for militia duty, and during the campaign just under one-quarter of Sangamon County's eligible militiamen volunteered (see Table 8.1 "Sangamon County Militiamen in 1832"). Of course, young men without families were more likely to serve, as were those without farms to tend during the summer. Married men with children and other obligations could hire substitutes to serve in their place, as did New Salem's cooper, Henry Onstot. Onstot's son later recalled that "As my father had a family of small children, and could not well go, he hired a substitute." The price, however, was substantial: thirty dollars and a rifle.[14]

Probably the most eager volunteers and substitutes were single men. Significantly, the 505 volunteers nearly equalled the 600 unmarried men in their twenties and thirties who so skewed Sangamon County's sex ratio. Lincoln, of course, belonged to this minority of men who were unencumbered by a family or farm. Even among the volunteers, however, Lincoln joined a still smaller minority who reenlisted after their initial terms of service had expired. Three-fourths of Sangamon County's militiamen served in only one company. One-sixth reenlisted once and therefore served in two companies. Fewer than 6 percent of the volunteers served in three or more units, as did Lincoln. Put more starkly, of the 2,284 eligible militiamen in Sangamon County, only thirty or 1.3 percent served as long as Lincoln did. Lincoln himself acknowledged this distinction in both of his autobiographical sketches when he wrote simply that he "went the campaign."[15]

Lincoln's military service undoubtedly had several motivations. As a young, single man, Lincoln may have simply gotten caught up in the general pioneer impulse to fight Native Americans, joining "the Patriock Boys to Defend the frontier setters of this State from the savages tomahock and skelping knife," as one old settler phrased it. Further, militia duty was an important component of the young men's associational culture to which Lincoln now belonged. Militia duty epitomized the kind of bachelor subculture that Lincoln had enjoyed since arriving in New Salem. Indeed, John Todd Stuart concluded that "the whole thing was a sort of frolic." Soldiering allowed these young men to put aside their work, camp outside, drink liquor, play cards, and wrestle. "Being midsummer," remembered George Harrison, Lincoln's messmate, "our Idle days were mostly spent under the

TABLE 8.1

Sangamon County Militiamen in 1832

	Number	Percentage of Eligible Men	Percentage of Volunteers
Eligible men	2,284	100.0	
Volunteers	505	22.1	100.0
Volunteers in one unit	392	17.1	77.6
Volunteers in two units	83	3.6	16.4
Volunteers in three or more units	30	1.3	5.9

forest trees in the sitting or horizontal position." Lincoln wrestled with his men, who numbered some of the Clary's Grove boys, and reputedly lost only one match. Such youthful sport crossed racial lines, and the volunteers competed with their Native American allies. "Our red boys and white, would frequently race against each other, and sometimes wrestle," Harrison recalled. "In a short race, the white boys generally beat, but a very long race generally, if not always, resulted in favor of the Indians." Such fraternization was not limited to physical pursuits. "Chess, Checkers, & Cards, were among the favorite plays or amusements, of both Indians and whites," Harrison reminisced. Militia musters and training days, with their elaborate uniforms and ostentatious drill, were a traditional holiday from the humdrum routine of rural village life. As a child of these years later recalled, "Muster days which would come in August were red letter days." Indeed, after returning from the Black Hawk War, Lincoln enlisted yet a fourth time as a captain in the Illinois militia. This conspicuous military service boosted Lincoln's popularity within the district. One old settler recalled simply that Lincoln "became very popular whilst in the army."[16]

Volunteers were also disproportionately urban—young craftsmen, clerks, and professionals who were understandably beguiled by the colorful spectacle of an ostentatious muster on the village green, as well as the prospect of an officer's commission. Above all, merchants like Lincoln tended to volunteer. Militia companies often mustered at the general store, the natural focus of any rural village. Community leaders in peacetime, merchants often took the lead as well during times of war. As historian Gerald Carson concluded, "The storekeeper was, like as not, an officer."[17]

Beyond his personal situation in New Salem, Lincoln inherited a family tradition of militia service. Back in Virginia, his grandfather and namesake, Abraham Lincoln, had served as a captain in the colonial militia. Known ever after as Captain Abraham, he served in the Revolutionary War and quite possibly fought Native Americans during the Cherokee Wars of the 1770s. Lincoln's family included three militia captains who fought in the

Revolution and a captain in the Kentucky militia who fought Native Americans. Lincoln's own father, Thomas, served in the Kentucky militia. The Lincolns apparently took pride in these military exploits and preserved them as family traditions. In particular, the family venerated Captain Abraham, who died at the hands of Native Americans—as Lincoln put it, "not in battle, but by stealth, when he was laboring to open a farm in the forest." According to William Herndon, Thomas Lincoln "retained a vivid recollection of his father's death, which, together with other reminiscences of his boyhood, he was fond of relating later in life to his children." Similarly, Lincoln's uncle Mordecai, who witnessed his father's death and killed a Native American during the confrontation, acquired "an intense hatred of the Indians—a feeling from which he never recovered." Lincoln's own reaction to the death of his grandfather remains obscure, but in 1854 he wrote that "the story of his death by the Indians, and of Uncle Mordecai, then fourteen years old, killing one of the Indians, is the legend more strongly than all others imprinted upon my mind and memory."[18]

The only motive for volunteering that Lincoln ever acknowledged was financial. As he recalled nearly thirty years later, "Offut's business was failing—had almost failed,—when the Black Hawk war of 1832—broke out." On the verge of unemployment, he volunteered. Lincoln earned about $125 for eighty days of service, equivalent to over eight months' salary clerking for Denton Offutt. Additionally, twenty years later, when Congress granted land bounties to veterans of U.S. military service, Lincoln claimed two tracts, totaling 160 acres, in Iowa. He received 120 acres of bounty land one week before he was elected president. Lincoln retained this land until he died and wrote with seeming satisfaction in one of his autobiographies that "He now owns in Iowa, the land upon which his own warrants for this service, were located." Tangibly or intangibly, this windfall may have compensated Lincoln for the patrimony he lost when his grandfather Abraham died at the hands of a Native American. Captain Abraham's early death proved a turning point for the Lincoln family, plunging his son Thomas—and eventually his grandson Abraham—into a childhood of what he euphemistically labeled "narrow circumstances."[19]

Finally, many Americans considered the removal of Native Americans essential to national development. One motive of the militiamen who fought the Native Americans was to protect what they considered their property. Rather than an ignorant rabble, many of them represented the rising generation of landowners, merchants, and speculators who were investing their own labor, fortunes, and families in the economic improvement of the region. "Most of the volunteers," concluded historian John Mahon, "were men of substance who saw in volunteer units instruments by means of which they could help defend what they owned." More generally, many militiamen undoubtedly agreed with President Andrew Jackson when he declared that "The States which had so long been retarded in their improvement by the Indian tribes residing in the midst of them are at length relieved from the evil." This link between fighting Native Americans and improvement echoes in Lincoln's pride in his military service and in his depiction of his grandfather's untimely death "when he was laboring to open a farm in the forest."[20]

The Black Hawk War coincided with the legislative elections, and the military and political campaigns blended imperceptibly together. Nine of Sangamon County's thirteen candidates for the Illinois House volunteered. They took this opportunity to solicit votes from the militiamen, getting to know them and delivering impromptu stump speeches during the campaign. Lincoln, who "went the campaign," returned to New Salem too late to stump for the legislature. Still, he took pains to have his military service noticed in the *Sangamo Journal*, which announced that "Some weeks ago we gave a list of those candidates of this County (omitting, by accident the name of Capt. LINCOLN, of New Salem,) who were on the frontiers periling their lives in the service of their country." In the county's at-large election for four state representatives, three of the four winners had served in the Black Hawk War. During Lincoln's first term in the legislature, more than two-thirds of his colleagues were Black Hawk War veterans. This time, however, Lincoln ran eighth in a field of thirteen. Still, he won 92 percent of the votes in his precinct. This was, Lincoln recalled with pride, "the only time he was ever beaten on a direct vote of the people." Three months later, Lincoln voted for Henry Clay for president. The rest of New Salem cast 70 percent of their ballots for the wildly popular "Indian-fighter" Andrew Jackson.[21]

CHAPTER 9

The Store

Lincoln received a lump payment of $125 for his military service. With this windfall in mind, perhaps, he now "studied what he should do." This pioneer region offered many opportunities. Lincoln's $125 would fetch an eighty-acre farm in the area, but apparently Lincoln never considered farming. He did consider learning a trade—blacksmithing—but then rejected the idea. An education was another possibility, even in this frontier village. Five New Salem youths—including two former merchants—attended college, a remarkable commitment to education within a rural community of this size (as late as 1870, only 1 percent of all Americans attended college). All five attended Illinois College, which opened in 1830 in Jacksonville. A college education, however, virtually required the support of a family. Parents and other family members, often sisters, would support a youth in college or, at a minimum, agree to dispense with his labor.[1]

With the support of his family, Lincoln's assistant clerk, William Greene, attended Illinois college after Offutt's store failed. As a friend reminisced, Greene "was the second son and never worked on the farm." He went off to Jacksonville "with $20.00 in his pocket and a homespun suit of clothes." A church-sponsored school, Illinois College allowed students to earn their tuition through manual labor. Greene studied for three years, paying his tuition by working for 10 cents an hour. Similarly, tavern owner James Rutledge returned to farming in 1833 and sent his son David to Illinois College. Just before her death, Rutledge's daughter Ann was making plans to attend Jacksonville Female Academy, which opened in 1833. These colleges were not yet age-segregated, and they enrolled youths of all ages who hoped to improve their prospects. Law was always a possibility. David Rutledge, for example, went on to become a lawyer. The son of another villager earned a law degree from a college in Louisville, Kentucky. But Lincoln rejected law while lamenting that he did not have "a better education." He later wrote, perhaps with some regret, that "He was never in a college or Academy as a student; and never inside of a college or accademy building till since he had a law-license."[2]

Lincoln, like many others, was swept up in the flurry of speculative activity. The arrival of the *Talisman* and proposals to improve the Sangamon River raised hopes of an economic boom in the region's towns and villages. Instead of investing in an education, a skilled trade, a profession, or a farm, Lincoln reaffirmed his commitment to a career as a merchant by investing in yet another store. Lincoln formed a partnership with William Berry, the son of a local minister and one of the corporals in his militia company. With Lincoln the senior partner at age twenty-three, the firm of Lincoln and Berry attempted what seventeen other storekeepers found impossible—challenging Samuel Hill as New Salem's leading merchant.

Lincoln and Berry quickly got involved in a complicated series of financial transactions. They bought a store building from two merchants and a stock of goods from three others. In this way, they hoped to reduce competition by consolidating all of Samuel Hill's rivals into a single store. From a different and more realistic perspective, however, they bailed out five of New Salem's foundering merchants by opening a new store of their own. Brimming with optimism, the partners ran what Lincoln later described as "*the* store." Hampered by the scarcity of money in the local economy, the partners put up personal notes, horses, land, and their military pay to stave off the inevitable. As William Herndon described the transaction, "not a cent of money was required—the buyer giving the seller his note and the latter assigning it to someone else in another trade." This store was larger than Offut's, twenty feet square, with two rooms. Like all the other southern merchants in New Salem, however, Lincoln and Berry failed miserably. As Lincoln observed through twenty-five years of hindsight, "Of course they did nothing but get deeper and deeper in debt." With too little capital to invest and no eastern connections, the partners borrowed heavily. In less than a year, like most other stores, this one "winked out."[3]

This last attempt at storekeeping ended bitterly. Deep in debt, Lincoln and Berry sold out to two other fledgling merchants who wanted to try their own turn at storekeeping. Berry enrolled in Illinois College but died in 1835. As unlimited partners, the two were liable for each other's debts, so Lincoln now began paying off the entire debt for the ill-fated store. In the space of two years, Lincoln had amassed obligations of over five hundred dollars through his various commercial ventures involving Offutt, Bogue, and finally Berry. Lincoln now retreated into the local barter economy that was so hospitable and familiar to him. "He was now without means and out of business," he put it plainly, "but was anxious to remain with his friends who had treated him with so much generosity, especially as he had nothing elsewhere to go to." In other words, his neighbors tolerated, even sympathized with, his brief speculative career. He now "procured bread, and kept body and soul together" by throwing together several part-time employments. He split rails, ran a mill, kept store for Sam Hill, harvested crops, tended a still, clerked at local elections, and served as the New Salem agent for Springfield's Whig newspaper, the *Sangamo Journal*. Without a family to help him out, Lincoln depended heavily on his fictive kin. At one point, Lincoln's belongings were put up for public auction to meet his obligations. Without being asked, "Uncle" Jimmy Short stepped forward, bought them back for $120, and returned them to the grateful Lincoln.[4]

By itself, debt meant little to people engaged in subsistence farming and a barter economy. All of them were indebted, in one way or another, to relatives, neighbors, and friends. As long as Lincoln could board with a family, earn his keep with his own labor, and barter for necessities, no one would have noticed much of a change in his circumstances. In New Salem, Lincoln had always been indebted—for the board, goods, and labor he exchanged with his neighbors—but he had always been able to repay those debts in kind, "working them off" through his own labor. Such personal debts were necessary in a traditional society and actually helped to bind the community together.

Lincoln's commercial debt, however, was new and different in several ways. Commercial debts had several novel characteristics. First, they were frequently impersonal, owed to strangers rather than to relatives, friends, and neighbors who could be counted upon and trusted within a personal relationship. Second, commercial debts could be multilateral. Rather than representing a bilateral, personal relationship between borrower and lender, they could involve third parties with little personal involvement in the transaction. Third, they were negotiable. They could be bought and sold at a discount or profit to virtually anyone with enough money to buy them. Fourth, commercial debts could be geographically distant, transcending the local community to involve strangers, banks, and corporations in far-flung financial markets. Fifth, commercial debts, unlike personal obligations, could be legally enforced. Above all, these debts required repayment in money, which was scarce within the region's subsistence economy. In short, commercial debts could be both complex and unforgiving. During this period, as historian Steven Mintz summed it up, "Relations between creditors and debtors became more impersonal, with lenders relying less on a borrower's reputation and more on contracts and the threat of imprisonment."[5]

Negotiability was a novel feature of debt that was only beginning to gain acceptance with the emergence of the new commercial economy. Negotiability of debt meant that Lincoln might borrow money from a friend and neighbor but ultimately find himself indebted to strangers in distant commercial cities. In this way, Lincoln eventually became obligated to strangers outside New Salem, including wholesalers in St. Louis and Cincinnati. His debts ultimately landed him in court when his creditors sued for repayment in the normal course of their business. Years later, "Uncle" Jimmy Short tried to sum up Lincoln's tangled legal mess this way: "Radford sold out his stock of goods to W G Greene and Greene sold out to Lincoln & Berry. Lincoln & Berry gave their note for 400$ to Greene, and Greene assigned it to Radford. Radford assigned it to Peter Van Bergen." In short, Lincoln and Berry paid for their store by giving their personal note to William Greene. Greene, with debts of his own, "assigned" the note to Reuben Radford to pay them off. Radford in turn sold the note to satisfy his own debts to Van Bergen, a Springfield merchant. Van Bergen, whom one of Lincoln's friends labeled "a prairie Shylock," later sued for payment of the note, which was now thrice-removed from Lincoln and Berry. The two partners also bought goods from James and John Rowan Herndon and similarly became indebted to their creditors as well.[6]

Such negotiability was ultimately necessary for the growth of a commercial economy in the region, because it helped to bring in needed capital from distant markets. Assignable notes also served as a form of money in a cash-starved economy. But the negotiability of personal debt also had more immediate, personal implications for Lincoln, entangling him within the new credit mechanisms of the emerging national economy, for better or for worse. Men without families were more likely to end up indebted to strangers and to suffer the worst consequences of the increasingly impersonal commercial economy.[7]

Many of New Salem's commercial debtors, like Offutt and Bogue, simply fled the region, leaving others to sort out the financial tangles they left behind. Similarly, the Trent brothers, whose store was deep in debt, disappeared from New Salem overnight, along with their families and all their belongings. The villagers awoke the next morning and wondered at the absence of smoke spiraling from the store's chimney. Most villagers were suspicious of the growing commercial economy, with its impersonal relationships and capricious ups and downs, and so they sympathized with these luckless neighbors who chose to sneak off into the night. These local speculators, after all, brought needed capital into the community while attempting to meet local economic needs. Their neighbors tolerated them, as long as their capital remained in the community. As one historian of New Salem observed, "This method of paying debts was of common occurrence in those days and did not excite the inhabitants, provided the remnant of goods on hand were left." Lincoln ended up repaying several other people's debts in this fashion. Other merchants who failed took up new occupations or simply returned to farming, slipping back into the subsistence economy from which they had so briefly emerged.[8]

Rather than fleeing the territory or returning to farming, Lincoln stayed in New Salem and made good his debts. In fact, he went to extraordinary lengths to repay all his debts and those of others at a time when many debtors simply shrugged off such commercial obligations. Historians disagree over the size of Lincoln's debt and how long he spent in repaying it. Estimates range from five hundred to eleven hundred dollars and from five to fifteen years. William Herndon claimed that Lincoln was still repaying his debts as a congressman in Washington in 1848, and fellow lawyer Henry Whitney remembered Lincoln paying off the debt "about the year 1850." Subsequent biographers have argued that Lincoln recovered financially before he left New Salem in 1837.[9]

At any rate, the debt lingered and stung, and Lincoln eventually dubbed it the "National Debt," a phrase that suggests not only its size but also its character. This was no personal, informal debt like those commonplace to a local barter economy, which could be repaid in kind—and with gratitude—at the next opportunity. Unlike Lincoln's previous debts, these were payable only in money and belonged to strangers from as far away as Cincinnati. In short, this was a formal, impersonal, commercial debt, to be repaid with interest under court order, a truly "national" debt befitting the emerging national economic system. By going to such great lengths to repay it, Lincoln implicitly signaled his understanding and acceptance of the new commercial order of things. He simultaneously reiterated his commitment to his chosen community by staying put and repaying his neighbors.

Lincoln overcame this self-inflicted adversity and learned a lesson from it. Far from letting this potentially dispiriting and compromising episode of his youth tarnish his reputation, Lincoln turned it into a personal asset. He went out of his way to fashion a reputation for painstaking and scrupulous honesty. When Lincoln the storekeeper overcharged a customer by 6½¢, he walked three miles to correct the error. When he charged another customer for four ounces of tea she did not receive, he promptly closed the store to deliver the tea personally. As New Salem's postmaster, a federal position, Lincoln earned an even wider reputation for honesty and responsibility. In answer to a request for a receipt, for example, postmaster Lincoln replied in high dudgeon: "The law requires Newspaper postage to be paid in advance and now that I have waited a full year you choose to wound my feelings by insinuating that unless you get a receipt I will probably make you pay it again."[10]

He won praise for keeping the post office's money separate from his own, apparently an unusual practice that was not compulsory. After he left the post office, he took charge of $17, which he kept in a sock. As one old settler retold the tale, "It was all 6¼, 12½, 25, and 50 cent pieces," coins that were scarce in the region. Despite the considerable temptation to borrow some of the money to keep body and soul together, he repaid the post office agent to the penny. According to legend, "Mr. Lincoln straightened himself up and, looking the agent square in the face, said: 'No, sir, I never make use of money that does not belong to me.'" Rather than sullying his character, repaying all of his debts earned Lincoln a lifelong reputation for honesty and honor. In the words of the legend, Lincoln "straightened himself up" under the burden of this personal misfortune.[11]

J. Rowan Herndon, one of the merchants who sold Lincoln his store, later reminisced that "I believed he was thoroughly honest, and that impression was so strong in me I accepted his note in payment of the whole. He had no money," Herndon concluded, "but I would have advanced him still more had he asked for it." Surely Lincoln recognized that in an impersonal, commercial economy a reputation for honesty could be worth more than money itself. George Washington, according to legend, won his reputation for honesty by admitting a youthful transgression, chopping down a cherry tree. Now "honesty" had come to mean much more than simple truthfulness. Lincoln won his reputation for honesty through his scrupulous handling of money, the highest virtue within the emerging commercial order. Indeed, as a youth in New Salem, deep in debt, Lincoln earned the lifelong nickname "Honest Abe." For the rest of his life, his word was as good as gold. As one of Lincoln's campaign biographers emphasized in 1860, "after a manly struggle with certain adverse circumstances for which he was not responsible, he relinquished the business, finding himself encumbered with debt—which he afterwards paid to the last farthing."[12]

Historians have often faulted Lincoln for poor judgment in opening a store and poor business sense in running it. But Lincoln's checkered career as a storekeeper resulted in an enhanced rather than tarnished reputation, especially when his conduct is compared to that of all the other merchants in New Salem. The village hosted a total of twenty-one merchants, a remarkable number for a community that never claimed more than two dozen families during its brief existence. By any literal standard, only one of them—Samuel Hill—truly succeeded as a merchant. Hill opened the first store in the village in 1829 and stayed in business for a decade, moving his store to Petersburg after New Salem went into decline, indeed just as the village died. In Petersburg, Hill's business prospered, and there he reputedly "accumulated a fortune." When he died in 1857, he left an estate valued at nearly one hundred thousand dollars. Apart from Hill, the remaining twenty merchants all sold out or folded after anywhere from a few weeks to a few years in business. William Greene owned a stock of goods for only a few hours before selling it for a tidy profit—to Lincoln and Berry.[13]

A more flexible definition of success, however, puts the merchants' commercial careers in truer perspective. Table 9.1 "The Fate of New Salem's Merchants" divides New Salem's twenty-one merchants into three groups: fatalities, fugitives, and survivors. The three fatalities were former merchants who died in or near New Salem during this period. The eight fugitives were merchants who sold or lost their stores and left the area, usually under disreputable circumstances. The ten survivors represent merchants who stayed in the area and therefore "survived" their commercial careers.

TABLE 9.1
The Fate of New Salem's Merchants

	Birthplace	Settlement Strategy
Fatalities		
William F. Berry	South (Ky.)	Family
James Rutledge	South (S.C.)	Family
George Warburton	North	Single
Fugitives		
Isaac P. Chrisman	South (Va.)	Family
St. Clair Chrisman	South (Va.)	Family
William Clary	South (Tenn.)	Family
James Herndon	South (Ky.)	Family
John Rowan Herndon	South (Ky.)	Family
Denton Offutt	South (Ky.)	Single
Henry Sinco	South (Ky.)	Single
Martin S. Trent	South (Va.)	Family
Survivors		
John Allen	North (Vt.)	Single
Abner Y. Ellis	South (Ky.)	Family
Nicholas A. Garland	South (Va.)	Family
William G. Greene	South (Tenn.)	Family
Samuel Hill	North (N.J.)	Single
Abraham Lincoln	South (Ky.)	Single
John McNamar	North (N.Y.)	Single
Reuben Radford	South (Va.)	Family
James McGrady Rutledge	South (Ky.)	Family
Alexander Trent	South (Va.)	Family

The survivors managed to stay in Menard and Sangamon counties, all but one of them fashioning a career in some other field. The table also presents the merchants' birthplaces (divided into North and South) and their settlement strategies (single or family settlement).[14]

Three of the merchants died shortly after giving up their stores. William Berry's death at age twenty-four is the most notorious. According to tradition, Berry succumbed to alcohol abuse, and his drinking habits precipitated the demise of the Lincoln-Berry Store. As one old settler put it bluntly, "Bill Berry turned out bad and became a drinking man and gambler, and died a total wreck." William Herndon labeled him an "idle, shiftless fellow." After ending his partnership with Lincoln, however, Berry seemed headed in a better direction, attending Illinois College in Jacksonville and winning election as village constable. In reality, he may have succumbed not to drunkenness at all but to tuberculosis, which claimed two other family members.[15]

Another fatality, James Rutledge, was one of New Salem's founders and kept the village's only tavern. He became a merchant when he acted briefly as a silent partner in Henry Sinco's store, selling out when Sinco went broke. The Rutledge family's fortunes deteriorated when New Salem went into decline beginning in 1832. Rutledge sold his tavern and left the village, moving several miles downriver to the Sand Ridge area. There, he and his family settled on a farm owned by fellow merchant John McNamar. A few months after typhoid fever killed his young daughter Ann, Rutledge died of the same disease, in December 1835.[16]

The third fatality, George Warburton, was one of the more promising merchants in the village. With his brother's backing, he represented a St. Louis merchant, Hezekiah King, and billed himself as Warburton & King when he opened his store in New Salem in 1831. According to tradition, Warburton was "a man of fine business qualities, an excellent scholar, and without an enemy, except his appetite for strong drink." The old settlers recalled the lifelong bachelor not at work but at play, racing horses and getting "pritty tight." Fellow storekeeper John McNamar remembered simply that he "soon Closed out, the country not having improved his morels." Within a year, Warburton had sold his store to the Chrisman brothers and began to speculate in land, buying several hundred acres around the eventual site of Petersburg. In fact, he was one of the cofounders of the new county seat. Peter Lukins, a shoemaker from Kentucky, lived in New Salem for a year and then moved two miles north. There, he laid out the new town on 160 acres that he owned in partnership with Warburton. Warburton and Lukins squabbled over what to call the town, each favoring his own given name. According to legend, the two men played a game of cards to choose between Georgetown and Petersburg, and Peter Lukins won. But the partners were poor promoters. They soon sold the townsite to a more enterprising investor, another New Salem resident, John Taylor, who hired Lincoln to resurvey the town. Both Warburton and Lukins reputedly turned to drink and soon succumbed to their vices. Lukins opened a tavern in Petersburg but was soon "found dead in his bed, the result of hard drink." Warburton's fondness for both liquor and horses proved his own undoing. In 1840, he fell off his horse while crossing a stream and drowned in six inches of water. With public opinion torn between accident and suicide, a jury of inquest ruled noncommitally that "he died by his own act." But local legend forever had it that he "ended his wretched existence by suicide, throwing himself in the Sangamon river."[17]

The eight fugitives left New Salem under a cloud and never returned.

Isaac and St. Clair Chrisman were Virginians who bought out George Warburton but went too deeply into debt. They soon sold out and went west. William Clary was the brother of John Clary, who founded Clary's Grove. William Clary briefly ran a "grocery," which sold some provisions but was chiefly a saloon. Clary's grocery was the scene of most of the rough-and-tumbles between the Clary's Grove and River Timber boys. Like the Chrismans, Clary soon sold out and headed west, to Texas, where he dropped out of the historical record.

James and John Rowan Herndon were cousins of Lincoln's future law partner, William Herndon. Rowan Herndon, or "Row," befriended Lincoln when he boarded the young man. The Herndons built a store in New Salem but soon sold out to Lincoln and Berry. As James Herndon put it with a tinge of sour grapes, "I didn't like the place and sold out to Berry." Row fell victim to a scandal when he killed his wife by shooting her through the neck while cleaning his shotgun in their cabin. Suspicions of murder haunted the brothers. "The sentiment was about evenly divided as to whether it was accidental or by design," according to one account. Apparently at James's urging, the brothers moved westward to Adams County on the Mississippi, but rumors followed them there and continued to dog Row. Returning Herndon's friendship, Lincoln tried to help dispel the rumors. Row Herndon remarried and returned to farming, working on the side as a butcher and constable. His brother James made ends meet as a butcher, painter, and harness maker.

The most notorious of the fugitives, of course, was Denton Offutt, who talked a big story but fled New Salem after nine months, leaving Lincoln and his debts behind him. When he left New Salem, Offut rejoined his family and returned to the agricultural economy, raising livestock in Kentucky with two brothers, who were "established farmers." He later moved to Missouri with one of his brothers and ended his career training horses with a traveling circus in Georgia. Near death from consumption, he finally showed up in Washington in 1861 to ask the president-elect for a job.

Another big talker, Henry Sinco, was born near Richmond, Virginia, in 1800. He moved to Kentucky in 1820, where he became a plasterer and chimney builder. He arrived in New Salem by 1830 and went into business with James Rutledge. According to Rutledge's son David, Sinco "bought a bunch of horses for the southern market and went broke on them." Sinco returned to his native Kentucky in 1834. He later moved to Indiana and then Iowa, where he farmed until his death in 1873.

Finally, the Trent brothers, Alexander and Martin, arrived in New Salem in 1829. They originally ran a ferry but, like many young men in the village, succumbed to the allure of storekeeping. They bought William Clary's grocery in 1832 and then bought out William Berry when his partnership with Lincoln ended. Overextended and deep in debt, they "left the country between two suns" and never paid Berry for his goods. Their disappearance left Lincoln to repay Berry's debts after the young man died. As one old settler put it, "they Rann off Leavng Lincoln the Burden to Bar as Berry Dide soon after." Several years after the brothers' flight, Alexander Trent reappeared in Petersburg and somehow managed to get back on his feet as a carpenter, although he was the least prosperous of all the former merchants who remained in Menard County. He moved to nearby Mason County in 1858. His brother Martin, however, disappeared, either dying in 1833 or 1834 or moving westward and changing his name.[18]

The ten survivors, by contrast, left New Salem as the village declined but eventually resettled nearby in either Sangamon or Menard counties. Six of them stayed in Menard County, while four of them, including Lincoln, resettled in Springfield. Only one of them—Sam Hill—remained a merchant. The other survivors fit a broad working definition of success that takes into account the occupational fluidity of this period. The survivors failed as storekeepers but not so badly as to ruin their reputations or resort to flight. Like Lincoln, they worked hard to stay in the area and recoup their credit in the face of their reverses. William Greene, for example, earned a reputation—similar to Lincoln's—for working hard to repay his debts. "You see," he wrote in later years, "I always wanted to keep my credit." Above all, the survivors adapted by choosing new, sometimes better occupations that would allow them to stay and help them succeed. In this sense, occupational flexibility was a sign of long-term success rather than short-term failure, a source of strength rather than weakness. Americans of the period admired adaptability—"an extensive array of skills," as historian James O. Robertson put it—that was best exemplified by Ben Franklin. Lincoln's climb up the occupational ladder, after all, reflected an extraordinary occupational flexibility that carried him through ten different occupations in a mere six years.[19]

Comparing the three groups points to several patterns. First, almost one half—ten of twenty-one—of New Salem's merchants remained in the area and therefore qualify as survivors. Almost all of the Survivors put down deep roots, and all of them, save Lincoln, ultimately died in the area. Given a typical persistence rate of 20 percent over a single decade, New Salem's merchants were remarkably stable. Indeed, they were more than twice as stable as the average resident of the area. Typically, New Salem's merchants either left the area immediately after losing their stores or stayed for the rest of their lives. In this fashion, storekeeping winnowed out the more transient members of the community from the diehard permanent residents. Weathering the turbulent economic seas of the 1830s apparently required or engendered a lifelong commitment to remain in the area. William Greene left Illinois for a few years but then returned, nostalgically buying the site of Clary's Grove, his boyhood home, and settling down. Greene died in 1894, seventy-three years after arriving in the Sangamon Country with his parents. James McGrady Rutledge, James Rutledge's nephew, also spent seventy-three years in the area, arriving with his family at age twelve and dying in 1899.[20]

Second, comparing the survivors with the fugitives provides some clues about the ingredients of success and failure in Lincoln's New Salem. Every one of the fugitives, for example, was southern-born. In a village legendary for its roots in the Upland South, three of the ten survivors were Yankees. One of the old settlers declared, with little exaggeration, that "The inhabitants were all from Kentucky and Virginia." Yet a handful of northern entrepreneurs, a knot of stereotypical "Yankee traders," dominated the area's commercial economy. Working together as partners or alone, Sam Hill, John McNamar, and John Allen used their valuable eastern connections to maintain New Salem's most successful stores. All three Yankee traders in New Salem were survivors.[21]

Further, the merchants' settlement strategies affected their success or failure. Family settlers, who arrived with wives, children, parents, brothers, or some combination of relatives, were much more likely to fail as merchants and to flee the area. In fact, only two of the eight fugitives—Offutt and Sinco—were single settlers. Three-fourths of the fugitives arrived with families. Among the survivors, however, four of the ten were single settlers, including the three most successful merchants in the village—Hill, Allen, and McNamar. Single men were better able to take advantage of rapidly changing opportunities, make frequent occupational moves, and shift for themselves between occupations. In short, they were more flexible in the face of a capricious commercial economy. They could take greater risks and reap larger rewards than the family men could. Agriculture favored family settlers, but single settlers were more successful in commerce. Southerners were more likely to travel within families, while northerners were more apt to travel alone. This gave the three Yankee traders an even greater advantage over their rivals in New Salem.

The New Salem merchants, therefore, confirm an essential ingredient of the self-made ethic. In the commercial world of the merchant, families no longer represented assets but could prove substantial liabilities. In an emerging urban economy that rewarded competitiveness, flexibility, and individual enterprise, single men were better off. In New Salem, the self-made ethic flowered in the careers of Samuel Hill, John Allen, and John McNamar. Arriving as a single settler from New Jersey, Hill married only when his commercial success seemed assured and went on to dominate New Salem's economy. Six years after arriving in New Salem, the thirty-five-year-old Hill married an eighteen-year-old woman and went on to raise two children. The Hills also adopted "Uncle" Jimmy Short's daughter when he went to California during the Gold Rush. Hill outlasted the death of the village and, as a true survivor, literally picked up his store and moved it to Petersburg.[22]

Like Sam Hill, John Allen arrived as a single settler. He married three years after arriving in New Salem, when his career as a physician and part-time merchant seemed secure, but his wife died two years later. Allen moved to Petersburg in 1838 and soon remarried there, raising a family of six children and remaining a part-time entrepreneur. Known as "a shrewd business man and a good collector," the physician built the largest medical practice in the region. Most of his patients, however, were farmers, who had to pay for his services in kind. Allen shrewdly turned this situation to his own advantage. He routinely asked for payment in hogs and collected two or three hundred a year. "He would barrel up the lard and make bacon of the hogs, and by spring he would have one thousand dollars worth of provisions to take to St. Louis," Onstot recalled. "By this way he would collect most of his bills." In the midst of a barter economy, the Yankee physician shrewdly used his mercantile expertise to turn a healthy profit as middle-man between the region's farmers and the meatpackers of St. Louis. By 1840, Allen owned four lots in Petersburg and eight farms in the area.[23]

Among all the merchants who inhabited New Salem, McNamar was the most unabashed "self-made man." A native New Yorker, he arrived without a family, promising to stay only until he had, as he put it, "made his pile." He opened the village's first store with Sam Hill in 1829. As the store flourished, McNamar courted the daughter of the town's founder, tavern owner, and fellow merchant, James Rutledge. McNamar and Ann Rutledge became engaged to marry in 1832, three years after McNamar arrived in New Salem. But McNamar abruptly sold out to his partner to go back home to visit his family. By the time he returned in 1835, Ann Rutledge was dead. McNamar went into partnership with John Allen and bought the luckless Trent brothers' store when they went out of business. McNamar and Allen survived for two years, qualifying as a limited success. But the store went under during the Panic of 1837. When New Salem died, the partners relocated to Petersburg and briefly operated a store there. McNamar married and had four children.[24]

By 1850, however, McNamar was clearly down on his luck. His wife was dead, and he was living in a hotel room in Petersburg, leaving his four children scattered about, boarding with farm families in the countryside. This low point in his life left him "knocking about Petersburg some Eight or Ten years," as he put it. Within a decade, however, McNamar had rebounded. In 1855 he married "Uncle" Jimmy Short's daughter. Leaving Petersburg, he settled on a farm and reassembled his children. Despite some fleeting successes, therefore, McNamar's career as a merchant was ill-starred. He spent twenty years seeking his fortune in the Sangamon Country, as a partner in at least three different stores. But for him as for others, storekeeping proved incompatible with a stable family life. Only when he returned to the traditional livelihood of farming did he find any real success, both personal and professional. As a farmer, he accumulated a substantial estate and, according to one county history, "reared a respectable family."

Upon his death at age seventy-eight, "He was respected in the community where he lived," and he lived not in a village, town, or city but on a farm.[25]

The careers of Hill, Allen, and McNamar followed a common pattern that presaged long-term success. Each was a Yankee who arrived in New Salem as a single settler and plunged into storekeeping. The three were nearly identical in age, born in 1800 or 1801 and therefore around thirty when they arrived. Each of them went into business with a partner. All three married only after establishing a store that seemed to promise success, between ages thirty-three and thirty-eight, when the average age at marriage in the county was twenty-seven. All three moved to Petersburg, opening stores in the new county seat as New Salem fell into decline. Lincoln shared some similarities with these more successful merchants. He arrived as a single settler, deferred marriage until age thirty-three, and left New Salem in 1837. But there were important contrasts. Lincoln, of course, was a southerner, he settled in Springfield after leaving New Salem, and he abandoned storekeeping forever. Above all, he was younger than the "Yankee traders" by nearly a decade. This age difference meant that Lincoln was simply not yet ready to take full advantage of the opportunities that New Salem had to offer.[26]

A final look at the longer-term success of the survivors puts the impact of Lincoln's commercial career in broader perspective (see Table 9.2 "The Surviving Merchants in 1850"). By 1850, only Samuel Hill remained a merchant. The others survived either by falling back on a former occupation or adopting a new one. Both William Greene and James McGrady Rutledge returned to farming, their family's traditional livelihood. John Allen continued his medical practice. Nicholas Garland and Reuben Radford slipped back into the manual trades. Only three of the survivors climbed the occupational ladder after losing their stores. Both John McNamar and Abner Ellis held government offices in 1850, while Lincoln practiced law. McNamar, however, soon returned to farming, while Ellis went back into business as a merchant. Lincoln alone made a permanent jump up the occupational ladder after his brief mercantile career.[27]

Yet all of the men were affected by their youthful careers as merchants in New Salem. They all remained enmeshed, for good or ill, in the commercial economy that they had helped to create in the Sangamon Country. Several of them became part-time entrepreneurs. Greene, for example, invested his profits widely and wisely, amassing a veritable fortune as a gentleman farmer. As old settler T. G. Onstot remembered him, "He always had a tact and talent for making money—what the world terms shrewdness." Greene invested in land, banks, and transportation, becoming a railroad director. He founded several towns, including Greenview, which bore his name. He owned a woolen mill and a coal mine and invested in gold and silver mines out West. Renowned as "a wealthy farmer and banker," Greene became the wealthiest of the New Salem merchants, eventually worth six hundred

TABLE 9.2
The Surviving Merchants in 1850

	Occupation	Age	Wealth*	Household Head
Sangamon County				
Abner Y. Ellis	postmaster	46	$ 950	yes
Nicholas A. Garland	waggoner	44	$ 350	yes
Abraham Lincoln	attorney	41	$ 0	yes
Reuben Radford	carpenter	47	$ 0	no
Menard County				
John Allen	physician	49	$7,000	yes
William G. Greene	farmer	43	$3,000	yes
Samuel Hill	merchant	50	$2,500	yes
John McNamar	assessor	50	$1,500	no
James McGrady Rutledge	farmer	35	$2,000	yes
Alexander Trent	carpenter	52	$1,000	yes

* Real property owned in 1850 and reported in the U.S. Census of 1850.

thousand dollars. Above all, he lent his money liberally. "He was the money king of this county," Onstot recalled, "and any man who needed money could always be accommodated, though the rate was often 5 per cent a month." A lifelong entrepreneur, Greene told Onstot "that he scarcely ever lost a debt, and that the man would always find him on hand early in the morning." During the Civil War, Lincoln appointed Greene collector of internal revenue in the district. Greene died with his reputation as "a prominent man of the county" firmly intact.[28]

Along with Lincoln and Hill, Greene and Allen were the clear winners in the struggle to get ahead in this new commercial economy. But there were losers as well. The two manual workers, Nicholas Garland and Reuben Radford, experienced the dark side of the emerging culture. Approaching middle age by 1850, both men had failed to improve. Born in Virginia, Garland came to the Sangamon Country as an adult with two children, arriving in 1832. He opened a store in New Salem that folded quickly. After this brief and disappointing career as a merchant, Garland's life continued even further downhill. He moved into the country and bought a farm, working intermittently as a farmer, cabinetmaker, and miller. At one point, he rather desperately constructed a horse-powered mill on the prairie outside Springfield to grind grain and saw lumber. Garland's wife died in 1844, however, leaving him a widower with six children ages two to twelve. He struggled during the next five years, giving up farming and moving to Springfield. There he married a widow, but this second wife died three years later.[29]

Twice widowed, Garland remarried quickly, to a woman who bore him a new family of five children. In all, Garland raised thirteen children. Storekeeping, however, had done little to improve the Garland family's lot in life. By 1850, Garland had given up cabinetmaking and resorted to manual labor. He went to work as a wagon driver in Springfield and employed his sixteen-year-old son as a teamster to make ends meet. His son attempted a brief career as a newspaper editor in Springfield but soon left the city to practice farming. Garland's interlude as a storekeeper did little to prepare him or his family for the urban, commercial order of things to come. [30]

Another obvious casualty of storekeeping was Reuben Radford. The son-in-law of a prosperous Springfield merchant, Radford showed promise as "a man of experience, a member of a family of merchants." He took over the Chrisman brothers' store as payment for a debt they owed him, selling the villagers "salt, pepper & such like things—with whiskey." Radford was never popular in New Salem, however, and he managed to keep his store open for only a few weeks. During one of his visits back to Springfield, the Clary's Grove boys came to New Salem and broke up the store in a drunken brawl. Radford sold his stock of goods immediately to William Greene at a hefty discount. Within hours, Greene sold the goods to Lincoln and Berry to earn a handsome profit of his own. William Herndon remembered the episode, and he sided with the villagers. "I knew Radford and his wife, and good Lord deliver me from such people," he reminisced. Radford, in his estimation, was like most New Salem merchants, "a vile, blustering, crazy fool." Run out of the village, Radford headed steadily downhill. A family man in fits and starts, Radford divorced his wife Catherine only to remarry her seven years later. In 1840, the irascible Radford, a committed Democrat, had a run-in with Lincoln at a local election, and the two men almost came to blows. At the time, Radford was running a railroad, but within two years he was bankrupt. By 1850, he was working as a carpenter in Springfield with no property to call his own. Separated from his wife yet again, Radford lived in the home of his son-in-law, who was also his business partner. Then things got even worse. Radford soon had a falling-out with his son-in-law, and they dissolved their partnership. Within a year, he and his wife divorced. (Lincoln and Herndon represented him in court.) In 1855, Radford married again but died five days later at age fifty-two.[31]

Without exception, biographers have portrayed Lincoln's brief commercial career as an unmitigated disaster. Viewed in broad perspective, however, Lincoln was quite arguably the greatest beneficiary of New Salem's commercializing economy. He did not, it is true, succeed as a storekeeper. Only one of New Salem's twenty-one merchants could claim that hard-won honor. Lincoln, however, was clearly a survivor, belonging to the minority of merchants who managed to stay in the area. More important, he was the only one who rose occupationally into a profession when his mercantile career ended. In 1850, Lincoln still felt the lingering effects of his famous "National Debt" and declared no property in the U.S. Census. Occupationally, however, Lincoln was a flourishing lawyer in Springfield, the state's capital. Within his avocation, politics, he was a former legislator and member of Congress and arguably the most powerful Whig in Illinois. Storekeeping did not make Lincoln rich, yet this brief experience provided an indispensable bridge between the old world and the new, between the agricultural, subsistence economy that dominated the region and the emerging commercial culture of the nation's growing cities. Lincoln's long and famous leap from flatboatman to lawyer seems unimaginable without the intermediate step of storekeeping.

Viewing Lincoln's employment experiences as a deliberate progression from manual to mental occupations renders the Lincoln-Berry Store as an essential step upward. As Harvey Graff concluded, "For some young men on traditional as well as more clearly transitional or emergent journeys, the opportunities and risks of commercial exchange transformed their paths and reoriented their destinations." In this sense, Lincoln's short-term failure as a merchant may have "reoriented" him in the direction of his eventual profession, law, as well as his avocation, politics. It therefore proved personally advantageous in the long run. Rather than a needless and ill-considered diversion from Lincoln's path to greatness, "*the* store" may have represented an indispensable interlude in the young man's deliberate progression upward.[32]

CHAPTER 10

This Procured Bread

Three government positions—one federal, one state, and one local—helped budding politician Abe Lincoln through several lean years. These government positions were important to Lincoln because he needed to earn cash to repay his debts. Government offices were the best source of real money in this pioneer economy. In 1833, Lincoln won presidential appointment as U.S. postmaster at New Salem. The post office was the primary source of federal patronage before the Civil War, and every presidential election prompted the removal of thousands of postmasters across the country and their replacement with supporters of the victorious party. Democratic President Andrew Jackson was the first to politicize the post office, during the late 1820s and early 1830s. Although Lincoln opposed Jackson's reelection in 1832, he won appointment anyway, probably because, as he put it, the position was "too insignificant, to make his politics an objection." Besides, in New Salem there was not yet any party regularity to enforce.[1]

The job of postmaster was essentially a part-time position. As in most communities in the country, New Salem's mail was carried on horseback in saddlebags. The mails left and arrived at New Salem only once each week. Until 1825, there was no home delivery of mail at all, and thereafter home delivery carried an extra charge of up to two cents per letter. Free mail delivery did not begin until 1863, when Lincoln was president. In the absence of mailboxes, letters had to be hand delivered to the addressees, and in a community with little cash in circulation, most people avoided paying postage by picking up their own mail whenever they visited town. As a result, this position was leisurely. The pay was commensurate with the responsibility. Postmasters were not salaried but earned a commission on their receipts. As postmaster, Lincoln probably earned no more than twenty dollars a year. He was paid in cash, however, and the post office was a crucial source of money in a subsistence economy such as this.[2]

Lincoln received other benefits as postmaster. He was exempt from militia and jury duty, could send mail free of charge, and could read all the newspapers that came through his office. Less tangibly, he had a chance to become acquainted with virtually every resident in the neighborhood. Finally, the post office was the only vestige of the federal government in New Salem. Besides the land office in Springfield, it was the sole federal outpost in the county. Lincoln therefore raised his status a notch by serving as a federal official and working in an "office" for the first time. Lincoln held this leisurely, plum position for the next three years.[3]

The post office job brought people into New Salem to meet Lincoln. His next appointment, as a surveyor, drew him out into the countryside. Rapid settlement of the prairie created a demand for surveyors to mark off farms, run roads, and lay out whole towns, dividing them into lots for sale. Illinois authorized counties to appoint official surveyors to see the work done correctly. Such positions were lucrative, because business was brisk—land sales around Springfield were reaching their peak—and surveyors pocketed their own fees. Sangamon County's surveyor, John Calhoun, was a distant relative of South Carolina's fire-breathing senator of the same name. A Yankee, Springfield's Calhoun was born in Boston but pioneered in the Mohawk Valley as a young man, studying law in New York before reaching Illinois just in time to experience the Deep Snow. Like his southern namesake, Calhoun was a Democrat who had a reputation as a brilliant orator and formidable political opponent. In later years, Lincoln judged him the best speaker he ever debated. After serving in the Black Hawk War, Calhoun won appointment as county surveyor and, despite their political differences, appointed Lincoln his deputy. According to tradition, Lincoln heard second hand that Calhoun wanted to appoint him deputy surveyor. Lincoln "walked to Springfield to see Mr. Calhoun and told him that he would accept the appointment if he had the assurance that it would not interfere in any way with his political obligations and that he might be permitted to express his opinions as freely as he chose." Calhoun agreed, and the two men began a lifelong personal and political relationship. They became bitter political opponents but remained personal friends for the next two decades.[4]

Lincoln borrowed money for a horse and for the next four years rode the prairie, platting farmers' claims, drawing township lines, and running roads to open up the country. He studied surveying assiduously and developed a lifelong interest in geometry that he later recognized as an important step in his self-education. Surveying took Lincoln up to one hundred miles from New Salem, so he met people and made friends over a much wider area. All but the smallest jobs took at least two days, and marking off a new townsite could occupy months, so Lincoln boarded with local families until the work was done. Surveying also strengthened Lincoln's interest in transportation. Whenever a road was planned, a surveyor had to lay it out, and Lincoln met quite a few of the region's local boosters and endorsed various petitions asking the legislature to authorize roads. Real estate transactions often required a property line to be run, so Lincoln became privy to land deals, both large and small, throughout the region. He routinely witnessed deeds, mediated disputes, and settled lawsuits between property owners. As Lincoln later reminisced, "This procured bread, and kept soul and body together."[5]

More important, Lincoln won the confidence of the area's land speculators. In 1834, Elijah Iles, Springfield merchant and Lincoln's captain during the Black Hawk War, sent Lincoln to survey New Boston, a townsite on the Mississippi River in which Iles had invested. Two years later, Lincoln surveyed the town of Huron, a speculative venture involving some of Springfield's wealthiest investors—lawyer John Todd Stuart, cousin of Mary Todd and Lincoln's legislative colleague and first law partner; lawyer Stephen T. Logan, another relative of the Todds and Lincoln's second law partner; another lawyer, Ninian Edwards, Mary Todd's brother-in-law and a wealthy merchant; Springfield's first physician, Gershom Jayne; newspaper editor Simeon Francis; and wealthy merchant James Adams.[6]

Huron was part of a plan to shorten the distance from Springfield to Beardstown by digging a canal between the Sangamon and Illinois rivers. The canal would connect with the Sangamon at the site of Huron. The platting of Huron demonstrates the close link between transportation improvement and land speculation. Speculators would back a transportation improvement—a steamboat or a canal—and then buy up land at crucial townsites that stood to benefit. According to one early settler, for example, the voyage of the *Talisman* "induced almost every man who had land on the river above high water mark to lay it out in town lots." Lincoln himself bought one share of stock in the proposed Beardstown and Sangamon Canal and forty-seven acres of land near Huron. Like many other "paper towns," however, neither the canal nor the town ever materialized, and the meticulously subdivided land reverted back to farming. In all, Lincoln divided at least five new towns into lots for various speculators. He thus became involved in the buying and selling of land, rather than simply working it with an axe or a hoe, and he began to invest in local real estate. Swept up in the "land and town lot fever" of the mid-1830s, Lincoln bought two town lots, not in New Salem at all but in his future home, Springfield. In short, surveying broadened Lincoln's interests, introduced him to influential Springfielders, and drew him further into the emerging commercial economy. As Robert Rutledge summed up Lincoln's career as a surveyor, he "engaged in a good business in the profession."[7]

Building on his growing reputation in the region, Lincoln ran for the legislature for a second time in 1834. His election to this state office provided the bridge he needed to leave New Salem and enter Springfield at last. Coming during a nonpresidential election year, this campaign turned even more on personalities than the last one had. With personal followings still outweighing political parties, Lincoln won the support of Whigs and Democrats alike. Lincoln's friends later reminisced that New Salem Democrats traded votes for Lincoln in other parts of the county in hopes of electing him over incumbent legislator John Todd Stuart. If so, the arrangement backfired and ended up electing both men instead. Still, winning bipartisan support proved a difficult balancing act, and Lincoln ran without publishing a campaign letter. Instead, Simeon Francis made a simple announcement in his *Sangamo Journal*: "We are authorized to state that A. Lincoln, of New Salem, is a candidate for Representative for this County." Lincoln did little campaigning. His roles as militia captain, postmaster, and surveyor had won him a wide reputation, and he finished second in the field of thirteen. Decades later, a political ally recalled that "Lincoln was run by a sort of common consent without party lines being drawn very tight as to him, but that voters of all parties rather encouraged his candidacy." With party lines still ambiguous, Lincoln voted for a Democrat for Congress two months later.[8]

Attempting to explain why Lincoln was such a popular candidate, William Butler, a close friend and fellow Whig, remembered a thousand reasons: "Well it is hard to say just why. It was because of the standing he had got in the county, and especially the prominence given him by the his captaincy in the Black Hawk War—because he was a good fellow—because he told good stories, and remembered good jokes—because he was genial, kind, sympathetic, open-hearted—because when he was asked a question and gave an answer it was always characteristic, brief, pointed, *a propos*, out of the common way and manner, and yet exactly suited to the time place and thing—because of a thousand things which cannot now be remembered or told." John Todd Stuart remembered that during Lincoln's first campaign he "acquired a reputation for candor and honesty, as well as for ability in speech-making. He made friends everywhere he went—he ran on the square—and thereby acquired the respect and confidence of everybody."[9]

In this first elective victory, Lincoln won 64 percent of the countywide vote. In fact, Lincoln more than doubled his vote between 1832 and 1834, demonstrating the boost to his reputation that his service as militia captain, postmaster, and surveyor had provided. Significantly, dozens of Springfield notables lined up behind Lincoln, including John Todd, patriarch of the Todd-Stuart-Edwards family and Mary Todd's uncle; John Todd Stuart; Stephen T. Logan; Elijah Iles; Charles Matheny, Sangamon County's "one-man government"; all three Francis brothers—Simeon, Josiah, and Allen—prominent in the emerging Whig organization; physician Gershom Jayne; William Wallace, another physician and Lincoln's future in-law; Archer Herndon, patriarch of the far-flung Herndon clan; his son William, Lincoln's future law partner; John Calhoun, county surveyor and Lincoln's boss; Hugh Armstrong, Jack Armstrong's brother and Springfield representative of the Armstrong clan; and John Hay, head of an influential Whig family. (Ninian Edwards voted for only one representative, his wife's cousin, John Todd Stuart. Two years later, in 1836, Edwards swung into line and voted for Lincoln.) Lincoln won all these votes without a campaign letter and with almost no campaigning. According to Stuart, "All the prominent Clay men here and in other parts of the county were for him." The outlines of an emerging Whig party were now visible in Springfield, and most of its members were early supporters of Lincoln.[10]

In November 1834, Lincoln borrowed $200 for a new suit of clothes and rode off to the state capital at Vandalia. As a legislator, Lincoln was a thoroughgoing Whig who consistently supported the three-part economic program of his idol Henry Clay—internal improvements, a system of banks, and a protective tariff. According to tradition, a typical Lincoln campaign speech during this period found him standing on a stump or a box and declaring that "My politics are short and sweet, like the old woman's dance. I am in favor of a national bank. I am in favor of the internal improvement system and a high protective tariff. These are my sentiments and political principles. If elected, I shall be thankful; if not, it will be all the same."[11]

Above all, Lincoln supported government-funded improvements in transportation. As historian Daniel Walker Howe concluded, "Of all items in the Whig program, internal improvements held the greatest appeal for the young Lincoln." A pioneer of the period remembered that "He would generally speak on the subject of internal improvement and of the great resources of the State of Illinois, of its advantages over other states, and of the wonderful opportunities that lay in store for the young men of Illinois if they would only improve them." Beyond its personal appeal for Lincoln, improvement was widely popular throughout Illinois and transcended party lines. As historian Paul Simon observed, "The one thing all candidates agreed on was the development of Illinois resources through a system of internal improvements." As the legislature crafted an ambitious scheme of government-backed canals and railroads, Lincoln lent his "all-out support."[12]

Between 1834 and 1836, parties at long last solidified in Illinois. The presidential election of 1836 provoked a scramble to crown a successor to the retiring incumbent, Andrew Jackson. Jacksonians hoped to avoid a divisive contest by holding their first national nominating convention and unanimously annointing Vice President Martin Van Buren as Jackson's heir apparent. The emerging Whigs were far less organized. In the absence of a national convention, two candidates, Daniel Webster and William Henry Harrison, divided the opposition along sectional lines, East and West. Democrats suffered a similar division when southerners championed the candidacy of Hugh Lawson White, a Democratic senator from Jackson's home state of Tennessee. White was a staunch Jacksonian in his opposition to internal improvements, a national bank, and a protective tariff. But he

JOHN TODD STUART, LINCOLN'S FIRST LAW PARTNER. AS A POLITICIAN, HE WAS
KNOWN TO FRIENDS AS "JERRY SLY" AND TO ENEMIES AS "SLEEPY JOHNNY."
Courtesy of the Illinois State Historical Library.

appealed to disaffected Jacksonians, especially southerners, who viewed
Van Buren's nomination as evidence of an undemocratic "dictation" by
northern Democrats. So in 1836, Van Buren ran as Andrew Jackson's hand-
picked successor against two Anti-Jacksonians—Harrison, popular in the
West, and Webster, popular in the Northeast—and one disaffected Democrat—the southerner Hugh Lawson White.[13]

In Illinois, many Jackson supporters, especially native southerners,
refused to support Van Buren for president and instead campaigned for
White. In New Salem, staunch Jacksonian Bowling Green led a movement

of disaffected Democrats who supported White. Opposition voters settled on William Henry Harrison as their best chance to defeat Van Buren. Together, White and Harrison supporters ran a "Union Anti–Van Buren Ticket" to concentrate the opposition against Van Buren. Nevertheless, claiming both a popular incumbent and a superior organization, Democrats won Illinois handily with 55 percent of the vote. The combined White and Harrison ticket, however, won both Springfield and Sangamon County, which soon emerged as reliable Whig territory within a solidly Democratic state.[14]

Lincoln ran for reelection in 1836. In June, he published a campaign letter in the *Sangamo Journal* that addressed only one specific issue, internal improvements, calling for federal aid to states in constructing canals and railroads. "Whether elected or not," Lincoln wrote, "I go for distributing the proceeds of the sales of the public lands to the several states, to enable our state, in common with others, to dig canals and construct railroads, without borrowing money and paying interest on it." Lincoln also indicated a broadened view of representation in which he embraced the entire county as his constituency rather than simply New Salem. "If elected, I shall consider the whole people of Sangamon my constituents," he promised, "as well those that oppose, as those that support me."[15]

Significantly, Lincoln ended his letter by declaring his support for Hugh Lawson White. "If alive on the first Monday in November," he pledged, "I shall vote for Hugh L. White for President." This declaration was both politically safe and personally beneficial. White won New Salem with 66 percent of the vote. Still, it dramatizes the growing power of presidential politics and national party organizations to draw local political lines. In 1832, Lincoln had appealed to "independent voters" on a purely local issue, improvement of the Sangamon River. In 1834, Lincoln had won support from both parties by depending on his personal popularity and remaining silent on most issues. In 1836, Lincoln felt it necessary, or at least helpful, to identify himself with a presidential candidate and to lend his support. This act clearly distinguished him as an Anti-Jacksonian and suggests his growing commitment not only to issues but to a party and party organization. The declaration demonstrates both that local candidates could now ride the coattails of a popular presidential contender and that local politicians were beginning to play key roles within nationally organized presidential campaigns. Lincoln not only won reelection to the legislature but received the largest number of votes in the county. He thus led the "Long Nine"—Sangamon County's legislative delegation of seven representatives and two senators—in both height and popularity. True to his word, in November Lincoln voted for Hugh L. White for president. In Springfield, John Todd, John Todd Stuart, and Ninian Edwards all voted for White and Lincoln, as did the town's leading merchant, Elijah Iles.[16]

For two years, Lincoln served simultaneously as U.S. postmaster, state legislator, and deputy county surveyor, rivaling Springfield's Charles Matheny as a "one-man government." Youths such as Lincoln frequently patched together several unrelated occupations before choosing a career. According to historian Joseph Kett, "Occupations simply did not have the rigid quality that they later acquired, and, in practice, many people had more than one occupation." Such experimentation was part and parcel of the social fluidity that was drawing so many farmboys into the burgeoning urban professions. Young men could tread several paths before deciding which one to pursue. As Kett put it, young men could now "switch from occupations to professions," which is exactly what Lincoln now decided to do. During his first term in the legislature, Lincoln roomed with John Todd Stuart, who encouraged him to study law. Lincoln borrowed some law books and studied them in his spare time. After two years, he earned his law license and joined the county's occupational elite, the 2 percent of adult men who practiced professions.[17]

Lincoln's personal success was propitious, because New Salem was on the verge of failure. Throughout its history the village had engaged, by necessity, in the kind of "urban rivalry" that pitted towns and cities throughout the Midwest in a continuous struggle for survival. All along, New Salem had competed for settlers, trade, investment, and improvements with other towns in central Illinois, including Springfield, Jacksonville, and Peoria. All of the village's transportation schemes—navigating the Sangamon, improving it, digging a canal, and laying a railroad—were attempts to get a leg up on these competitors.[18]

During the 1830s, New Salem waged four such struggles, in all of which Lincoln played a prominent part. First, the villagers hoped to demonstrate that the Sangamon River was navigable for steamboats. This hope soared but then plummeted in 1832 when Vincent Bogue's *Talisman*, with Lincoln at the helm, made its desperate retreat downriver to Beardstown. Second, the villagers proposed improving the Sangamon for steamboat navigation. Lincoln's first election campaign in 1832 featured this proposal. The improvement campaign coincided with a speculative flurry in land and townsites along the river, a "rage for new towns" that produced five hundred new townsites in Illinois over a mere two years. But when the prospects for improving the Sangamon dimmed, New Salem's growth peaked, around 1833, and then waned. By 1836, the village had declined so much that it lost its coveted post office, which was crucial to any community's economy and indeed its self-identity.[19]

Thereafter, New Salem competed not for urban growth so much as survival. In the mid-1830s, Springfield waged a long campaign to replace Vandalia as the state capital. Hoping to win the capital—and a corresponding economic boost—for the Sangamon Country, New Salem supported Springfield, which lay on the Sangamon. When Illinois held a referendum on the subject in 1834, New Salem's voters backed Springfield against its rivals

Jacksonville and Peoria. Three years later, Springfield won this long legislative battle, in which Lincoln figured prominently. Lincoln "was at the head of the project to remove the seat of government here," Stephen Logan remembered; "it was entirely entrusted to him to manage."[20]

Springfield's victory assured it own future. But this emerging city now threatened the growth of smaller towns and villages nearby. Indeed, New Salem had to fight one last battle for survival. For years, Sangamon County's small-town and rural residents had proposed dividing the county into several smaller ones. In 1839, the northwest corner of Sangamon County became Menard County, and New Salem campaigned to become the county seat. Its main rival was a new town, Petersburg. Petersburg lay on the Sangamon River only two miles downstream from New Salem but was much more accessible than the village on the bluff. As deputy county surveyor, Lincoln surveyed Petersburg, spending two months carving the grandiose townsite into sixty-four blocks of eight lots apiece. As state legislator, Lincoln sponsored the town's incorporation. When the choice of a new county seat approached, a legislative delegation swept through the area examining the rival townsites. One witness remembered the entourage arriving in New Salem with "twenty-five or thirty men on horseback, the only way men traveled then, with about a dozen dogs following."[21]

Despite this raucous visit, Petersburg won out, and New Salem was doomed. Actually, many New Salemites had already moved to Petersburg, and now a general exodus ensued. One by one, the villagers literally picked up their houses and stores and carted them off by wagon the two miles downstream to Petersburg. By 1840, a mere decade after its founding, New Salem simply disappeared. Only one building remained in the village, Sam Hill's two-story house, the only two-story building in the settlement. Hill built the house in the spring of 1835, just before his marriage and while New Salem's future still looked bright. Hill at last moved his store to the new county seat but had to leave the two-story house behind, where it stood as a sort of memorial to the life and eventual passing of New Salem. The village had struggled to survive throughout its history yet managed to live little more than a decade.[22]

Lincoln had left New Salem three years earlier. Practicing the kind of "sponsored" migration that was the best guarantee of success, John Todd Stuart invited Lincoln to move to Springfield to become his law partner. Lincoln had grown considerably in New Salem; indeed, he had outgrown the village. In six years, he had risen from flatboatman and storekeeper to lawyer and state legislator. Now he had a profession, a law partner, and many friends waiting for him in Springfield. If still penniless, he was no longer strange, uneducated, nor friendless. On April 15, 1837, Lincoln packed his belongings into a pair of saddlebags and rode a borrowed horse the twenty miles upriver to Springfield, to join his "old friend" Stuart in a new career in law and politics.[23]

CHAPTER 11

The Way for a Young Man
to Rise

L incoln was among a small minority of young men—ambitious, innovative, and self-directed—who pursued self-improvement with single-minded zeal. The means to the end may have changed, and changed frequently. But the end—self-improvement—remained the same. As one path closed, another opened, in a long, deliberate climb upward in the social scale. Table 11.1 "Lincoln's Climb up the Occupational Ladder in Sangamon County" provides a rough approximation of the "occupational ladder" that prevailed in Sangamon County in 1840 and matches it against Lincoln's own occupational rise. As defined by the U.S. Census, Sangamon County's occupational ladder had four "rungs" in 1840. The table arrays them from the most inclusive at the bottom—farming—to the most exclusive—learned professions—at the top.[1]

By this definition, during his six years in New Salem, Lincoln climbed steadily upward on the occupational ladder from the bottom rung to the top. He arrived in Illinois as a farmer, along with four-fifths of his peers. When he left farming to live in New Salem, he cast his lot with the one-fifth of his peers who pursued nonagricultural livelihoods. In New Salem, Lincoln persistently worked his way upward from the manual callings of flatboatman and miller to the commercial occupations of store clerk and merchant, practiced by only one in forty of Lincoln's peers. Finally, at age twenty-eight, Lincoln became a lawyer, joining the 2 percent of his peers who similarly practiced a profession. Overall, 95 percent of Sangamon County's breadwinners practiced manual occupations. Fewer than 5 percent of Lincoln's peers performed "mental" labor, as he did. In particular, Lincoln's experience as a merchant appears as a crucial intermediate step or "rung" on the occupational ladder, facilitating his climb from the third rung—the skilled trades—to the top rung—the professions.

Lincoln had abundant company in accomplishing this meteoric personal rise. The American economy boomed after 1815 and particularly during the 1830s. This "Jacksonian Boom," as it came to be known, rested on a dramatic expansion of agricultural production that coincided with a massive

TABLE 11.1
Lincoln's Climb up the Occupational Ladder in Sangamon County

Lincoln		Sangamon County, 1840	
Occupation	*Age*	*Occupation*	*Percent*
Lawyer	28–52	Professions/Engineers	1.9
Legislator	25–33		
Surveyor	24–28		
Postmaster	24–27	Commerce	2.5
Merchant	23–24		
Militia captain	23		
Store clerk	22–23	Manufactures/Trades	15.7
Miller	22–23		
Flatboatman	22		
Farmer	7–22	Agriculture	79.9

upsurge in westward settlement. This unprecedented wave of expansion crested during four years, 1832–1836, and western land sales reached a historic peak during the 1830s, topping out in 1837. The period 1830–1837 also brought a tremendous rise in farm prices, which rose 50 percent between 1834 and 1837 alone. Rising wheat and corn prices fueled an unremitting expansion, which coincided with Lincoln's arrival in Illinois and his youth in New Salem.[2]

Precisely during this momentous western economic boom, Lincoln came of age, improved himself, and explored his options. His admission to the bar and his move to Springfield occurred in early 1837, just as the boom crested and began to decline. His timing could not have been more fortunate. As historian Richard Hofstadter observed, "If historical epochs are judged by the opportunities they offer talented men to rise from the ranks to places of wealth, power, and prestige, the period during which Lincoln grew up was among the greatest in history, and among all places such opportunities were most available in the fresh territory north and west of the Ohio River."[3]

During the early decades of the nineteenth century, the relatively sudden appearance of so many new "emergent" paths transformed not only Lincoln personally but American culture as a whole. Historian Joyce Appleby has charted the appearance of an "American entrepreneurial culture" during the first three decades of the nineteenth century. During this period of formative commercial organization, a generation of young American men came of age and aggressively took advantage of the full range of new economic avenues becoming available to them for the first time. "The elaboration of a national market," according to Appleby, "depended on many, many young men leaving the place of their birth and trying their hand at new careers." Instead of following—and honoring—the traditional paths blazed by their parents and ancestors, these young innovators struck out on their own in a dramatic burst of individualism that carried significant risks but also promised substantial rewards. "The range and sweep of enterprise in this period are awesome," Appleby concluded, "suggesting the widespread willingness to be uprooted, to embark on an uncharted course of action, to take risks with one's resources—above all the resource of one's youth."[4]

In the process, a minority of pioneering entrepreneurs redefined "success" in American culture through a "shifting of loyalties from home and habit to self and progress." Success no longer meant maintaining the integrity and independence of a lineal family while passing on a patrimony to the next generation. Young men now sought immediate, tangible, personal rewards in a new, hectic competition for individual success. In transcending traditional economic and social values, these innovative entrepreneurs refocused American culture away from families and tradition and toward individual achievement and change. In transforming American cultural ideals, they set an example for future generations. As Appleby concluded, "Their lives served as models of innovation in a society losing all desire to replicate past ways of doing things." In short, they became America's "new cultural heroes."[5]

Appleby did not examine Lincoln as one of these new "heroes." But in their willingness to break with tradition, their disdain for their families, and their zest to succeed, Appleby's "new cultural heroes" emulate no one more so than the young Lincoln. In fact, Appleby's depiction of these budding entrepreneurs fairly resonates with echoes of Lincoln's life experiences and the posthumous Lincoln legend. Citing their autobiographies, for example, Appleby portrayed her subjects as struggling with their parents, and particularly their fathers, in pursuit of an adequate education. As a result they frequently complained—or boasted—about the paucity of their formal schooling. "My education had been sadly neglected," one of them reminisced. "I could hardly read or write intelligibly, and had passed rapidly and carelessly through the common rules of Arithmetic."[6] This memory echoes, almost eerily, Lincoln's recollection in his own autobiography that he "grew up, litterally without education. . . . Still somehow, I could read, write, and cipher to the Rule of Three."[7] Both Lincoln and the new cultural heroes were largely self-taught. With rare exceptions, the new cultural heroes exhibited a "self-nurtured love of learning."[8] Similarly, Lincoln wrote that "He regrets his want of education, and does what he can to supply the want."[9]

For the new cultural heroes, their fathers' resistance to education was the greatest source of friction within their families, frequently causing a breach with their parents over their lack of encouragement. The result was a formulaic "denial of the father's contribution to the son's life" that became almost mandatory in autobiographies of the age. In short, the new cultural heroes claimed most of the credit for their own successes in life and granted their fathers little or even none at all.[10] In unison with Appleby's new cultural heroes, Lincoln could confidently declare, with no apparent sense of remorse or irony, that "he could not say that he ever had an ancestor older than his father." Lincoln's father himself, of course, is notorious for contributing virtually nothing to his son's education. According to Lincoln, he "never did more in the way of writing than to bunglingly sign his own name."[11] A novel and growing social distance from one's family was utterly pervasive among the budding entrepreneurs and says far less about Lincoln personally than about his emerging culture. "Rendering their fathers as failures," according to Appleby, "was also a way of burning their bridges."[12]

Far from relying on their families for a start in life, Lincoln and the new cultural heroes were eager to leave their families behind them. Just as Lincoln left both farming and his family with little apparent regret, Appleby discovered that among her subjects "the opportunity to quit the family farm is presented as a deliverance. In retrospect, no regret or nostalgia appears. Moving on meant moving out to a larger world." Like Lincoln, many of Appleby's youths never looked back, cutting their family ties, even to the extent of never seeing their parents again. Others struggled to reconcile their individual ambitions with society's expectation that they care for their aging parents. Lincoln's testy insistence that stepbrother John D. Johnston tend his parents' farm echoes a similar "arrangement" one of Appleby's subjects forged with an older brother. "What seems remarkable about these accounts," Appleby observes, "is the display of early independence, with the son's ambition juxtaposed against the father's failure."[13] Hence, the popular denigration of Thomas Lincoln as a ne'er-do-well and the fabled depiction of Lincoln's own ambition as "a little engine that knew no rest."[14]

Rising through their own exertions and owing little to tradition and even less to their families, the new entrepreneurs acquired the label of "self-made men." In the first book-length examination of the self-made man in America, published in 1848, John Frost posed this definition: "A self-made man means one who has rendered himself accomplished, eminent, rich, or great, by his own unaided efforts." More recently, historian Richard Weiss defined the self-made ethic as "The belief that all men could achieve material success by living according to certain ethical rules of conduct." Lincoln, of course, became the quintessential self-made man, as well as the greatest American cultural hero of all. As John Cawelti concluded in his dissection of the nineteenth-century self-made ethic, "the legend of Lincoln was the highpoint." The phrase "self-made men," in fact, was coined by Lincoln's own intellectual hero, Henry Clay, in 1832. Just nine years later, Lincoln himself acquired the label "self-made man."[15]

Arising in the pivotal 1830s, the self-made ethic justified the single-minded pursuit of opportunity. The industrializing economy no longer rewarded the conservative stewardship of family resources. A dazzling array of new occupational choices beckoned young men to towns and cities, offering new opportunities far beyond the fixed horizons of a family farm. The new economy rewarded innovation, initiative, and above all individualism. The word "individualism" first appeared in 1827 in England and in an American context in 1835. By the 1830s, the transition to a new market economy demanded a generation of youths who were willing to forego the traditional security of a family, to take personal risks in the pursuit of profit, and to seize upon opportunities whenever and wherever they appeared.[16]

The myth of the self-made man smoothed that potentially acrimonious transition. Departing from the traditional celebration of the family as the foundation of any stable society, the self-made ethic now celebrated individual advancement, even when achieved at the expense of one's family. No longer representing both the source and the measure of any man's success in life, the family now seemed an impediment to economic advancement. Henry Clay coined the term in defense of manufacturers who *earned* their wealth rather than inheriting it. Speaking in the U.S. Senate, Clay declared that "almost every manufactory known to me is in the hands of enterprising self-made men, who have whatever wealth they possess by patient and diligent labor." Self-improvement, not family, was the new source of wealth in America. Inherited wealth and security now seemed less relevant to a fluid and dynamic industrializing economy.[17]

As John Cawelti summed it up, the self-made ethic held that "mobility was completely dependent on the will and actions of the individual, that a man could make of himself what he would, and that the individual who failed had only himself to blame." A solid family foundation was not only unnecessary to success in life but might even prove burdensome. Humble beginnings spurred the individual to greater exertions in pursuit of success. "When he becomes successful," Cawelti observed, "the American self-made man likes to boast of his achievement, to exaggerate the obscurity of his origin." A simple, rural childhood became not only a handicap to be overcome but also a badge of honor. Self-made men eagerly exaggerated, indeed glorified, their humble beginnings. Rising apart from—even in spite of—his family background, the self-made man cut a democratic figure, befitting an emerging democratic age. Not only was family unnecessary and even unwelcome, indeed it was invidious, smacking of inherited distinctions and aristocratic privileges amid the new celebration of the common man. Lincoln, concluded historian Irvin Wyllie, another student of the self-made ethic, "in accepting the success values of his age, associated them with the economic advance of the common man."[18]

The self-made man, of course, had both to merit and to earn his success. The seeds of success lay within the individual rather than society itself. As Ralph Waldo Emerson summed it up, "the reason why this or that man is fortunate is not to be told. It lies in the man; that is all anybody can tell you about it." Success, it seemed, must be actively cultivated within the individual rather than passively received from one's family. Viewing their families as largely irrelevant amid the shift from farm to city, ambitious youths now learned to help themselves. The new culture of achievement demanded a regimen of self-culture or "self-help." A veritable cult of self-improvement emerged to encourage young men to nurture a host of inner qualities that readily became values within the new society. Self-reliance, industry, frugality, sobriety, loyalty, and honesty all became hallowed virtues, along with the once forbidden qualities of competitiveness, individualism, and ambition.[19]

The young Lincoln's qualifications as a self-made man are exemplary. A humble, rural background was a virtual prerequisite for self-made success. As Irvin Wyllie observed, "Along with the glorification of poverty in the success cult's ideology went the glorification of rural childhood." Lincoln's humble beginnings glorified both. Lincoln himself remarked that "it is a great piece of folly to attempt to make anything out of me or my early life. It can all be condensed into a single sentence, and that sentence you will find in Gray's Elegy: 'The short and simple annals of the poor.' That's my life, and that's all you or anyone else can make of it." Lincoln's disclaimer did double duty, emphasizing both his humble beginnings and his modest demeanor. The self-made man was, after all, in John Cawelti's phrase, "the veritable apotheosis of modesty."[20]

Self-made men were also precocious. "The early signs of intelligence that aroused the attention of outsiders," according to Appleby, "formed an important element in the social transaction that effected the break with home." Put simply, self-made men were astute enough, even as youths, to see new opportunities beckoning from far beyond the horizons of their own families. Families therefore became impediments to both their educations and their success. "A boy at home seldom has a chance," a nineteenth-century self-help manual intoned. "Nobody believes in him,—least of all his relations." As Lincoln summed up his own experience at home, "There was absolutely nothing to excite ambition for education. Of course when I came of age I did not know much." The predictable breach with one's family almost invariably centered on education. "Intelligence, an aptitude for learning, an early gift for reading, a yearning for more schooling," according to Appleby, "these were the notes that, in retrospect, orchestrated the movement from home and justified the rupture, if not in the eyes of parents, clearly for the departing sons." Hence, Lincoln's own recollection that "After he was twenty-three, and had separated from his father, he studied

English grammar." Here, Lincoln clearly associated his "separation" from his father with the elaboration of his own education.[21]

Many other of Lincoln's recollections mirror those of the proverbial self-made man. Occupational choice was crucial and, in fact, was a novel experience for most Americans. Men could now choose their own careers rather than passively heeding a "calling." Similarly, Lincoln self-consciously "studied what he should do." Debt and similar temporary setbacks were virtually inevitable in a mercurial economy that emphasized risk. Self-made men faced them stoically. "I kept my business to myself," one of Appleby's subjects reminisced, "and maintained my credit until I struggled pretty well through my indebtedness, living economically and wasting nothing." Lincoln, too, waged "a manly struggle with certain adverse circumstances for which he was not responsible," according to a campaign biography. "He relinquished the business, finding himself encumbered with debt—which he afterwards paid to the last farthing."[22]

Migration to a city was also crucial. "Many self-help handbooks," according to Wyllie, "therefore encouraged farm boys to leave home," as Lincoln did. On leaving home, emotional detachment was essential. "The capacity to sever the actual emotional links to the family," according to Appleby, "seems an important factor." Lincoln's emotional distance from his parents, of course, is legendary. In his own autobiography, Lincoln remembered that he stayed in New Salem through the lean times of his youth because "he had nothing elsewhere to go to." His father Thomas and his stepmother Sarah, like the parents of America's other self-made men, now amounted to "nothing." Above all, Lincoln rose dramatically. He entered New Salem alone, as an uneducated flatboatman, and left for Springfield six years later as a lawyer and legislator.[23]

So exemplary was Lincoln's rise from obscurity to success that Horatio Alger himself enshrined it forever as part of the rags-to-riches myth. In 1883, the author published *Abraham Lincoln, the Young Backwoods Boy; or, How a Young Rail Splitter Became President*, written for young readers. Of course, by the time Alger appropriated Lincoln, the rags-to-riches myth had long since been reduced to little more than a routine formula, what Carol Nackenoff called "ritual repetition" and "formula writing." Two years earlier, Alger had published a biography of the recently assassinated James A. Garfield and now applied the same basic formula to a popular portrayal of Lincoln. A prolific writer, Alger easily stretched the basic facts of Lincoln's life to suit his own purposes. "In this story, which I have made as attractive as I am able, I make no claim to originality," he admitted. "I have made free use of such materials as came within my reach." Alger seems to have depended heavily on William Herndon's collection of reminiscences. But he went well beyond biography to turn Lincoln's life into an allegory on success and failure—in short, to incorporate Lincoln into the rags-to-riches myth. Lincoln fit the mold perfectly.[24]

The typical Horatio Alger story focuses on a boy who leaves his home and family in the country for a new life in the city. Making his own way in the world, the boy is both tempted and tested by the novel vices of an emerging urban, industrial society. The classic Horatio Alger story therefore presents, in Nackenoff's words, a "dangerous passage, in which the hero is torn from community and family and their moral influence to be thrown among strangers in the city." Nackenoff views this journey as an allegory in which the adolescent boy represents the young republic undertaking its perilous voyage from youth to maturity. "The story is a rite of passage from boyhood to manhood during which the youth must undergo many trials," according to Nackenoff. "The completion of the passage yields a young adult whose virtue is firm; the adolescent of the Republic attains manhood."[25]

To Alger, success came through "virtue," meaning the maintenance of traditional values—industry, frugality, sobriety, honesty—in the face of temptation and the jarring shock of social change. During the nineteenth century, factories and cities undermined the traditional moral system grounded in family, farm, and community and therefore threatened both Alger's heroes and the young republic. Cut off from family and community, youths had to develop their own internal moral codes. They made mistakes but also learned lessons on their passage through the new and dangerous world.[26]

The quintessential Alger hero, according to historian Daniel Rodgers, was "the poor boy who made his own way in the world by a steady growth in moral habits." The lessons of life must therefore be learned through experience, not inherited from family. To dramatize this crucial self-reliance, Alger typically orphaned his heroes early in life. Even if parents lived, they were usually unable to help their sons materially or morally as they set out on their solitary journeys. Hence, the typical Alger hero, in Nackenoff's words, is an "orphan or apparent orphan," an individual without a family or at least without a family that matters. "With uncertain parentage and lacking place, station, or fixed identity," Nackenoff concluded, "the Alger 'orphan' creates his or her own identity and selfhood." In short, he becomes a self-made man.[27]

Alger's Lincoln was indubitably self-made. He was "a rough youth, born and reared in the backwoods, without early educational advantages, homely and awkward." His stark boyhood left him unprepared to venture out into a complex and competitive world. But the seeds of redemption, indeed of greatness, lay within, for Lincoln had "a good heart." To fit the rags-to-riches mold, however, Lincoln's greatness had to flower from within himself and without the help of his family. Unfortunately for Alger, Lincoln was no orphan. Alger therefore had to orphan Abraham Lincoln in some other way, denying him parents in practice if not in fact, making him an "apparent orphan" for his young readers. More specifically, Alger removed

Thomas Lincoln morally if not physically from the young boy's life. Alger portrayed Thomas as a careless and ineffectual parent, clearly inferior in character and of no help at all to his son. Thomas was "shiftless and unambitious." He was uneducated and, worse, failed to educate his son, leaving him a "stranger to schools and colleges." He was inferior in achievement. As Alger took pains to delineate, "Thomas Lincoln was a carpenter. He did not, however, understand his trade very well, and, though he was employed in small jobs, there is no evidence that he was ever employed to build a house, or was considered competent to do so." Thomas was not competent to "build a house," meaning—allegorically—that he was unable to make a home.[28]

Determined to give Abraham Lincoln a plain rural heritage, Alger concluded that Thomas was not really a carpenter at all but a simple farmer: "In fact, he derived but a small income from his trade, and probably looked upon himself rather as a farmer than a mechanic." Thomas, in other words, inhabited the old world rather than helping to introduce his son to the new one. Thomas was so inferior in every way to his famous son that Alger took the trouble to compare their physical statures. Thomas "was much shorter than his son Abe, being an inch or two under six feet." (This still would have left Thomas at least two to three inches taller than the average man of his day.) Characteristically, Alger summed up Thomas's many deficiencies in a way that the youths of the Gilded Age were sure to appreciate—in material terms. Thomas was such a poor provider for his family—let alone a good role model for his son—that "The possessions of the Lincolns were altogether beneath the notice of even the poorest tramp."[29]

Historian Daniel Rodgers identified the main characters who inhabit the various Alger stories as "autonomous boys" and "crippled fathers." Alger, like many Lincoln biographers both before and since, portrayed Abraham as supremely autonomous—a spiritual orphan—and Thomas as a decided "cripple," both mentally and morally. While denying their fathers any recognition for their own personal success, the self-made men of the period were more willing to concede a beneficial influence to their mothers. Lincoln, for example, reputedly declared to William Herndon, "God bless my mother; all that I am or ever hope to be I owe to her."[30]

As compensation for Thomas's deficiencies, in fact, Lincoln enjoyed the tutelage of two "good and kind" mothers. Alger granted Nancy Hanks and Sarah Johnston all the credit for the little learning and ambition that the Lincoln family enjoyed. In so doing, Alger at least had to praise Thomas for marrying well. Reversing traditional gender roles, Alger had Nancy Hanks teaching Thomas Lincoln to write. Thomas "could write his name, having learned this much from his first wife, Abe's mother, but he never had the ambition or perseverance to go farther up the hill of learning." His choice of Sarah as his second wife was also propitious: "It was a piece of good fortune for himself and his children, that, shiftless and unambitious as he was, he should have won a wife so much more capable and energetic than himself." But Alger typically denigrated Thomas even while praising his choice of Sarah. This second marriage was the result of "good fortune" rather than intelligence or ambition on Thomas's part. His shrewd choice of Sarah, his long journey back to Elizabethtown, and his offer to pay all of Sarah's outstanding debts counted for nothing. In short, "luck" rather than "pluck" won him his second wife. Alger even offered his readers the choice tidbit that "She was an old flame of Mr. Lincoln, but had rejected him, being able, as she thought, to do better." Only the death of Sarah's first husband made her available to marry Thomas.[31]

To drive home Abraham Lincoln's singular achievement in life, Alger also took pains to denigrate his stepbrother, John D. Johnston. Johnston, of course, had made the critical mistake of staying at home on the farm with Thomas and Sarah rather than venturing out into the wider world. As a result, Johnston "was a rolling-stone, idle, shiftless, and always hard up." The story of Johnston's move to Arkansas and his early death became a homily on the virtues of hard work and the imprudence of restless migration. As Alger summed it up, "Shiftless people are very apt to think they can earn a living away from home better than at home." Alger reprinted Lincoln's testy letter to Johnston with the observation that "Nothing can be plainer, or more in accordance with common sense than this advice." Success, like greatness, lay within, and so did failure. No one could flee hard times or poor luck because "the trouble is in themselves, not in their surroundings." Johnston clung to the traditional, subsistence lifestyle of the Lincolns' past and therefore chose to replicate the simple life that Thomas Lincoln had led. In an ironic role reversal, Sarah received the credit for making Thomas's son a success, while Thomas bore the blame for making Sarah's son a failure.[32]

Alger's rendering of Lincoln, of course, had a moral. As Carol Nackenoff put it, "In Alger's moral universe, all real men were self-made, for one was not born virtuous. Virtue and true manhood required work." Hence the emphasis on hard work embodied in Lincoln's legendary youth. "Abe is not to be pitied for the hardships of his lot," Alger concluded. "That is the way strong men are made." Hardship, or rather a young man's *response* to hardship, bred greatness.[33]

Historians have roundly labeled the self-made ethic a myth, the "self-made myth." They have also questioned Lincoln's faith in the self-made ethic even as he espoused it. For most Americans through most of our history, the self-made ethic may well have been little more than mythical. Whatever the objective merits of the self-made ethic, however, it worked for Lincoln, and he believed in it. When Lincoln arrived in New Salem, he occupied the bottom of the occupational ladder, with the 80 percent of his peers who farmed for a living. During his six years in the village, however, Lincoln single-mindedly worked his way upward. Exploiting every available resource and seizing every opportunity to improve himself, he progressively joined the minority of 20 percent who practiced nonagricultural occupations, then the 5 percent who performed nonmanual work, and finally the 2 percent who practiced professions.

Through most of his life, Lincoln practiced the self-made ethic as well as preaching it. Even more, he came to personify it. The ideal of improvement—and particularly self-improvement—infused Lincoln's view of America and helped to make him the "great common man" that he was. In Lincoln's youth, in New Salem, hard work, individual effort, self-improvement, and persistence all paid off, if not for most of his peers, at least for Lincoln.

CHAPTER 12

More Painful Than Pleasant

As he lay dying in Coles County, Illinois, Thomas Lincoln called for his son, Abraham, to come to his bedside for a final farewell. One hundred miles away, in Springfield, Abraham Lincoln refused to come, concluding that "if we could meet now, it is doubtful whether it would not be more painful than pleasant." Five days later, Thomas Lincoln died. His son did not attend his funeral. In fact, this wrenching episode was merely the climax of two decades of emotional estrangement between this father and son. After leaving home at age twenty-two, Abraham Lincoln rarely saw or wrote to his father and stepmother. For twenty years, he never invited them to visit him in Springfield. They never met their daughter-in-law Mary Lincoln nor their own grandchildren. Lincoln named his fourth son Thomas to honor his father after his father died, but he never called him Thomas, giving the boy a nickname instead—Tad.[1]

Psychohistorians have constructed complex and sometimes fanciful psychological interpretations of this apparent father-son breach, posing long-lasting emotional implications for Lincoln's personal life and political career. Even the most judicious explications of this father-son relationship, such as that proposed by John Y. Simon, rely heavily on psychological rather than cultural explanations. Simon brilliantly dissected the Lincolns' relationship and then argued convincingly that Lincoln had little reason to feel ashamed of his father's family. Thomas Lincoln was a respectable, landowning farmer who was broadly typical of the time and place in which he lived. "In order to understand the relationship between father and son," Simon concluded with ample justification, "no denigration of Thomas is necessary." But Simon then posed two psychological conflicts between Thomas and Abraham Lincoln. First, Abraham Lincoln's ambitions "exceeded his father's expectations and could not be fulfilled under his father's roof." Second, Lincoln felt jealous of his stepbrother, John D. Johnston, who was about his own age and stood in as a surrogate son for Thomas after Abraham, in his own words, "separated from his father."[2]

A systematic examination of the Lincolns' family history, however, points to a cultural rather than psychological analysis of their relationship. At the end and the beginning of their lives, respectively, Thomas and Abraham Lincoln experienced, and grappled with, several major transitions in their society and culture that made a profound impact on American family life. In particular, two great social and cultural transitions helped to open a gulf between the father and his son. First, America began a dramatic economic transformation during the early nineteenth century that historians call the Market Revolution. In a subsistence economy, families produce most of the goods they consume—particularly food and clothing—working at home and working by hand. Under this system of "home manufacture," families work primarily to feed and clothe themselves, acquire and maintain a farm, and pass this farmstead on to future generations. Farmers practice "safety-first farming," worrying about earning a profit through commercial sale of a surplus only after feeding and clothing their own families. Profit and accumulation take second place to family survival and security.[3]

Until 1820, probably three-fourths of all production occurred at home for family consumption rather than for sale. As late as 1840, families spun more yarn and wove more cloth—to clothe themselves—than did all American textile mills combined. Beginning around 1815, however, the advent of factory production and improved transportation increasingly allowed families to replace homemade goods with factory products. The new market economy encouraged families to produce cash crops for commercial sale and to purchase necessities and even luxuries that they had once produced for themselves. As a result, home production peaked around 1810 in the East and around 1830 in the West and then declined. In fact, the "family economy" that Lincoln discovered when he arrived in the Sangamon Country in 1831 was just reaching its peak, and it soon began to decline. By the 1840s, factory production and commercial agriculture had come to dominate the northern economy.[4]

The Market Revolution, with its emphasis on mechanized production in factories, encouraged the growth of industrial and commercial cities, especially in the North and West. Families lost many of their traditional economic functions as the market economy provided new ways to produce and to consume. Rather than waiting patiently to inherit their fathers' farms, many young men began seeking new employment opportunities in the cities, as craftsmen or better yet as nonmanual workers in the growing middle class of merchants, clerks, managers, and professionals. The market therefore emphasized individual opportunity rather than family security, rewarding initiative and ambition rather than tradition and stability.[5]

As part of the Market Revolution, the venerable system of patrimonial settlement gave way to new patterns of migration. Under patrimonial settlement, families had been paramount above individual aspirations. Traditionally, the family was important, if not essential, to individual success. During two centuries, such patrimonial "family auspices" had carried five generations of Lincolns step-by-step from Massachusetts to Illinois. The Market Revolution, however, stimulated a new pattern of migration—"entrepreneurial settlement"—that drew young men as individuals away from their families to growing towns and cities. As part of this "urban drift," the family lost its centrality and, indeed, became increasingly irrelevant to the swelling ranks of young "career" migrants. In place of family background, individual achievement took precedence.[6]

During this period, fathers in particular lost their privileged, patriarchal status within their own families. "The ability of a father to transmit his 'status position' to his children declined," according to family historians Stephen Mintz and Susan Kellogg. "By the early nineteenth century, families were finding it increasingly difficult to pass on their status by bequeathing land or a family to their offspring." In this new culture of achievement, Lincoln could safely declare, with little exaggeration or even regret, that "he could not say that he ever had an ancestor older than his father." From a social and cultural perspective, Lincoln's aloofness from his family reflected not so much personal shame, guilt, jealousy, or ambition but simply his family's growing social and economic irrelevance within the emerging market economy.[7]

John Y. Simon is quite right that no impeachment of Thomas Lincoln's character is necessary to explain his relationship with his son, but probably no psychological inquiry is recommended either. The apparent breach between father and son reflected a clash of the traditional social system with an emerging new one. In the new entrepreneurial economy, Lincoln no longer needed his father's landed patrimony. In fact, he spurned it. The rise of the entrepreneurial ethos did indeed coincide with a decline in the Lincoln family's land holdings. But the most prosperous farming family—and the most understanding father—would have had trouble holding the young Abraham Lincoln to the land. Throughout America, as Mintz and Kellog observed, fathers' authority within their own families was on the wane: "The declining ability of fathers to transmit land to their sons undermined the traditional basis of paternal authority." In fact, "Fathers increasingly were expected to acquiesce in the early independence of their sons." The nature of Lincoln's ambitions—urban, entrepreneurial, eventually professional—rendered his family's rural, landed heritage little help to him and largely meaningless.[8]

From this perspective, Thomas Lincoln appears as a transitional, rather than tragic, figure. Born in the late eighteenth century, during the American Revolution, Thomas came of age within an agricultural society that measured a man's success by the extent of his land holdings. Denied his expected patrimony by his own father's early death, Thomas straddled the boundary between the old society and the new. A halfhearted farmer, he flirted with an urban lifestyle, practicing carpentry as a trade and living in a town for five years as a young man. After leaving the South for the more openly entrepreneurial North, he became a farmer but only a part-time one. Dennis Hanks's son-in-law, Augustus Chapman, remembered Thomas "part of the time working at his trade & at other times on his farm." Like many part-time farmers, he practiced several occupations simultaneously. As Chapman put it, "his business chie[f]ly was farming but he was a cabinet maker and a carpenter." Rather than experiencing an economic decline, as measured by his continually dwindling acreage, Thomas partook in the more general economic transition that was shifting emphasis from agriculture to trade, from farm to town and eventually to city. In fact, Thomas himself dabbled in long-distance trade to New Orleans. Thomas "Made Several trips down the River while he lived in Ind taking flat Boats loaded with produce Principally Pork," according to Chapman, but "from these trips he realized but little profit simply turning what he raised on his Farm into cash." As a part-time farmer, Thomas forsook the old society. As a part-time entrepreneur, he acknowledged the new one. In both endeavors, he led the way for his son Abraham.[9]

Thomas Lincoln should not be judged by the size of his land holdings, just as Abraham Lincoln should not be evaluated by that traditional standard of success. Thomas's tragedy was that he inhabited the uncertain boundary between the old and new economic worlds but achieved success in neither. In the traditional landed society, Thomas was a smallholder who repeatedly lost the lands he possessed rather than accumulating new and better ones. Dennis Hanks remembered that Thomas "at time[s] accumulated considerable property which he always managed to make way with about as fast as he made it." An "unlucky Man," Thomas "Was very unfortunate in most of his attempts to accumulate property or money." One of the Lincolns' in-laws, Nathaniel Grigsby, remembered Thomas Lincoln as "not a lazy man" but a "piddler—always doing but doing nothing great." Thomas "had but few wants and Supplied these. He wanted few things and Supplied them Easily." In fact, Thomas's land holdings continually dwindled—from 826.5 acres to 200 acres in Kentucky, to 160 acres in Indiana, to 120 acres and finally 80 acres in Illinois. Later in life, his trouble keeping land provoked a withering lecture, along with a humbling twenty-dollar handout, from his son. Yet Thomas was equally feckless as an entrepreneur. In both Kentucky and Indiana, Thomas tried commercial agriculture, floating his crops down the Ohio and Mississippi rivers all the way to New Orleans. He walked back home, in typical pioneer fashion, but earned only a "little profit" for all his trouble. One year, in fact, Thomas lost everything. While living in Kentucky, Thomas decided to float his pork down the river to New Orleans. An aspiring entrepreneur, he offered to carry his neighbors' pork as well. On the river, he met "a couple of sleek fellows" who offered to float the load to New Orleans "on a credit," in Dennis Hanks's phrase, but never paid Thomas a penny. In attempting the transition from the old economic system to the emerging new one, Thomas achieved too little in either world and in neither instance could bequeath much of value to his son.[10]

The Market Revolution not only transformed the American economy, but also the American family. As a result, a second great cultural transformation, one that focused on family life, further divided father from son. Thomas and Abraham Lincoln stood at a portentous crossroads between the traditional and the modern family. The traditional family was a cooperative economic unit, in which all members were expected to contribute to the good of the whole. More economic than emotional in its foundations, the traditional family emphasized home production, either on a farm or in a shop, and required everyone to suppress individual aspirations and to work for the survival and advancement of the family.[11]

The emerging modern family, by contrast, put greater emphasis on emotional rather than economic ties among its members. The new market economy increasingly called on men to work away from home, and the modern family therefore emphasized individual rather than collective economic advancement and gratification. Family members, especially wives and children, were expected to soothe and nurture men as breadwinners who left their homes by day to compete in the emerging workaday world of the city. The traditional family, which historians have labeled "cooperative," began to decline sometime between the American Revolution and 1830. It increasingly gave way to the modern family, labeled "companionate" because it emphasized affection rather than economic obligation. This transition in the American family reached its climax just as Abraham Lincoln was coming of age.[12]

In the eighteenth-century cooperative family, every member had an economic function, a traditional role within the family. Parents and children literally worked together, usually at home on a farm or in a shop. In his study of the changing meaning of adolescence, Joseph Kett has thoroughly documented the economic foundations of the parent-child relationship in the cooperative family. In a traditional farming society, children were above all an economic asset, and rational calculation rather than affection dominated the parent-child relationship. "Parents and children were not unfeeling toward one another," Kett observed, "but as long as children lived, affection had to be kept in check."[13]

The traditional family was first and foremost an economic system, and fathers and sons had socially prescribed obligations to one another. A father had to have enough children so that his family could function as an economic unit. More specifically, he had to produce enough adult children to support himself and his wife in their old age. In fact, most aging Americans had no other support beyond their adult children. In their study of aging, historians Howard Chudacoff and Tamara Hareven emphasized that after "the loss of a spouse, older people had to rely on assistance from their children." A father also had to employ his children productively, for the family's benefit, between ages seven and twenty-one. Sons might work at home—on a farm or in a shop—or away from home as an apprentice or hireling, not on their own account but to support their families. Finally, a father had to give his sons a start in life when they reached adulthood, in the form of land, capital, or education—a patrimony. A son, in his own turn, was expected to work as a child for the good of the family and to support his aging parents after reaching adulthood.[14]

During this age of family transition, however, neither Thomas nor Abraham met these traditional standards. For his part, Thomas produced just enough children so that only one of them reached adulthood. With the death of his wife, daughter, and younger son, Thomas depended for sustenance, all too precariously, on a single son. According to historian Richard Bushman, "Property and children were the only means of support when strength and health eventually failed." Without much property, Thomas leaned heavily on his son Abraham. In a traditional, agricultural society, producing only one adult son could prove a grave economic blunder. Thomas's slip seemed so egregious, in fact, that it provoked posthumous rumors that questioned his manhood. Decades later, for example, William H. Herndon portrayed Thomas as sterile—"cut, fixed, castrated," as he put it. Thomas was the first of the Lincolns to produce only one adult son. Still, Thomas landed on his feet and partially recovered by quickly remarrying a widow with three children, including a son about Abraham's age. This "blended" family was more functional in the present and afforded an able-bodied stepson, John D. Johnston, to provide for the future.[15]

The young Lincoln worked hard for his family's benefit, both at home and as a hireling. Indiana neighbor and in-law Nathaniel Grigsby remembered that Thomas Lincoln was "a man of limited means so that it became necessary for Abraham to work from home." He "ocaissally took Jobs of claring or making fense rails Sometimes he worked on the ohio river." But as an only son, Abraham worked mostly "at hom[e] on his fathers farm." Indeed, Kett observed that "in the quasi-contractual relationship between fathers and sons, the obligation to work lay heavily on the son." But at manhood, this obligation ended and a new one began. In exchange for a start in life in the form of land, capital, or education, sons were obligated to support their aging parents. As a result, Chudacoff and Hareven have noted, young adults "confronted the dilemmas of having to help their parents just at the point when they were struggling to achieve autonomy." Typically, aging parents prevailed on one of their sons to stay near home, which was in fact a Lincoln family tradition. "This dilemma," according to Chudacoff and Hareven, "could easily generate conflicts of interest within the family."[16]

The traditional barter economy emphasized family, but the rising market economy encouraged independence. Traditionally, sons were obligated to work for their fathers between ages seventeen and twenty-one, indeed, to turn over their wages to them if they worked away from home. The new cash economy, however, beckoned many young men, including those who were underage. A substantial minority of young men now left home before age twenty-one—with or without their fathers' consent—to work "on their own account." Lincoln, too, succumbed to this temptation. In Indiana, one of Lincoln's neighbors remembered that the young man asked for his help in finding work before his legal obligation to his father had ended. When Lincoln was still twenty, "Abe came to my house one day and stood around about timid & Shy. I Knew he wanted Something. I said to him—Abe what is your Care. Abe replied—"Uncle I want you to go the River—(the Ohio) and give me Some recommendation to some boat." I remarked—"Abe—your age is against you—you are not 21, yet." "I know that, but I want a start," said Abe. I concluded not to go for the boys good—did not go."[17]

Only after turning twenty-one did Lincoln get his "start" in the market economy. According to biographer Ida Tarbell, before moving to Illinois Lincoln cobbled his money together and bought thirty dollars' worth of notions—"needles, pins, thread, buttons, and other little domestic necessities." Trekking westward, the young Lincoln peddled sundries to other pioneers out of the family's wagon. He doubled his money and wrote back to Indiana boasting of his commercial success. In this way, the young Lincoln turned a patrimonial migration into a literal "entrepreneurial" one. As historian Norman A. Graebner concluded, "Even as a youth in Indiana, Lincoln identified emotionally with that progressive frontier element which preferred commerce and movement to farming." Without a doubt, the emerging market economy promised far greater opportunities and rewards than mere subsistence ever could. In an oft-quoted exchange, Lincoln reputedly told Indiana neighbor John Romine that "his father taught him to work but never learned him to love it." In a lesser-known passage, Romine rejoined that Lincoln "didn't love work but did dearly love his pay." Such was the allure of the new commercial economy.[18]

Throughout his own life, however, Thomas Lincoln remained enmeshed in the kind of traditional, cooperative family that had characterized his youth. He moved westward to be sure but to benefit his family rather than pursue any individual aspirations. Historians have labeled Thomas a footloose wanderer who "roved about" for much of his life, an unflattering reputation that Louis A. Warren aptly dubbed "the shiftless father myth." In fact, whenever Thomas Lincoln moved, he invariably engaged in family rather than individual migration. As a boy, he moved with his father Abraham from Virginia to Kentucky. After his father's death, he lived with his mother in Washington County, Kentucky, well into his twenties. As a young man, he moved to Elizabethtown, Kentucky, to live with his uncle Hananiah Lincoln and then, for less than a year, to Tennessee to live with another uncle, Isaac. He probably boarded while learning and plying his trade but never lived in a community alone without one or more family members—father, mother, uncle, or siblings—settled nearby. After marrying, Thomas continued to move fairly frequently but only with his family and never as an individual. Growing up, Abraham Lincoln lived in a relatively stable family and moved only twice before coming of age, living a full fourteen years on one homestead in Indiana.[19]

As he moved northward and westward, Thomas always practiced group migration, as the patriarch of a growing, extended family. Throughout his adult life, in fact, Thomas's role as patriarch grew in importance precisely as the family he headed grew in size. After moving from Kentucky to Indiana, for example, Thomas attracted a knot of in-laws—Nancy Hanks's cousins, Dennis and John, and her uncle and aunt, Thomas and Elizabeth Sparrow—augmenting his family to create what was then known as a "settlement." After his wife's death, Thomas enlarged this family yet again by remarrying and adding a third family, the Johnstons, to the growing clan. Through his two marriages, in fact, Thomas bound three families together—the Lincolns, the Hankses, and the Johnstons. Further, in their isolated Indiana settlement, the Hanks and Johnston families intermarried. Sarah Johnston's daughter Sarah married Nancy Hanks's cousin Dennis, and daughter Matilda Johnston married another Hanks cousin, Squire Hall. The resulting Lincoln-Hanks-Johnston family was therefore cemented by four marriages that made all of its members kin by blood, marriage, or sometimes both. Sarah and Matilda Johnston's children, for example, were related to Abraham Lincoln by both blood, through Nancy Hanks, and marriage, through Sarah Johnston. This Lincoln migration therefore typifies the kind of "clan-based" migration that brought Upland Southerners to the Illinois frontier as members of extended families, including three generations as well as nonlineal relatives such as aunts, uncles, and cousins.[20]

The Lincoln-Hanks-Johnston clan also typifies the resilient cohesion of families ravaged by the early death and family disruption that characterized the westward-moving frontier. Of the six members of Thomas Lincoln's generation, two were dead (Nancy Hanks and Daniel Johnston), two were widowed and remarried (Thomas and Sarah Lincoln), and two were illegitimate (Nancy and Dennis Hanks). Yet the family survived by living, working, and moving together, as well as intermarrying. This resiliency resembles the kind of "kinship imbeddedness" that helped southern families, both black and white, survive the continued buffeting engendered by the region's prevalent social trends of ceaseless westward migration, separation, early death, and illegitimacy. The same resiliency enabled these three southern white families to survive. By the time of his migration from Indiana to Illinois, therefore, Thomas was acting as patriarch of a thirteen-member extended family consisting of the reassembled remnants of three others, the Lincolns, Hankses, and Johnstons. As Dennis Hanks recalled, "We all went—Lincolns, Hankses, and Johnstons all hanging together." As the oldest member and the link that connected the three families, Thomas Lincoln was clearly the patriarch and the chief decisionmaker.[21]

In Coles County, the families created a dense, interwoven network of neighboring farms and mutual support. Naming patterns attest to the emotional as well as physical closeness of this extended family. John D. Johnston named his first son after Thomas Lincoln and his second after his stepbrother Abraham. He named two other sons after his brothers-in-law, Squire Hall and Dennis Hanks. In return, Squire Hall named his first son John Johnston Hall. As partriarch of a growing, landed family, Thomas could afford to let his own land holdings decline. He increasingly grew to depend on his two sons-in-law and, most important, on his stepson, John D. Johnston.[22]

Abraham Lincoln's relationship with his stepmother, Sarah, has undergone frequent analysis. But historians have never dwelt upon the relationship John D. Johnston developed with his stepfather, Thomas. Sarah became a "good and kind mother" to Abraham Lincoln, but did Thomas become a "good and kind father" to his stepson? John Johnston lost his father when he was only six and gained Thomas as his stepfather when he was nine. Thomas and his young stepson apparently developed a genuinely loving relationship, enjoying many common interests, such as hunting and fishing. Johnston stood at Thomas's side through three decades, between ages nine and forty, indeed until Thomas died. By all accounts, Thomas Lincoln was a generous and loving man. Fifty years later, Sarah Lincoln's granddaughter recalled that Thomas "made a good living, and I reckon he would have got something ahead if he hadn't been so generous. He had the old Virginia notion of hospitality—liked to see people sit up at the table and eat hearty, and there were always plenty of his relations and grandmother's willing to live on him." In 1836, Lincoln's assistant clerk, William Greene, visited Coles County. After staying overnight with Thomas, Greene agreed that "his Manors wer what might be termed Back[w]oodsish yet they were easy so much so that I allmost would say they were polished." Greene decided that Thomas was simply a "good old man." Indeed, a neighbor recalled that people in the vicinity knew him as "Uncle Tommy," emblematic of the fictive kinship that bound cooperative neighbors together. Dennis Hanks similarly concluded that Thomas "loved his Relitives Do any thing for them he could No Better Man then old Tom Lincoln."[23]

Just as Sarah Lincoln supposedly prepared her stepson Abraham to make his own way in the world, Thomas prepared his stepson John for a life of subsistence agriculture. Indeed, Thomas and his stepson entered into a complex series of mutually supportive land transactions that spanned twenty years. During their first few years in Coles County, Thomas Lincoln and John Johnston squatted together on forty acres of government land. In 1833, Johnston bought forty acres, which he sold to his stepfather the

THE YOUNG EAGLE

LINCOLN'S FATHER THOMAS. SCORNED BY POSTERITY AS A NE'ER-DO-WELL,
HE EARNED THE RESPECT OF CONTEMPORARIES WHO SWORE THAT THERE WAS
"NO BETTER MAN THEN OLD TOM LINCOLN."
*Abraham Lincoln Library and Museum, Lincoln Memorial
University, Harrogate, Tennessee.*

More Painful Than Pleasant

following year. Three years later, Johnston bought a second forty-acre farm in a different part of the county known as the Goosenest Prairie. Planning yet another group migration, Thomas bought an eighty-acre plot adjoining Johnston's forty, and in 1837 the two families moved together to the Goosenest Prairie. For three years, from 1837 to 1840, Thomas and Sarah Lincoln lived in a one-room cabin with Johnston, his wife, and their two infant sons, Thomas and Abraham. Together, the two adjoining farms represented a traditional survival strategy known as a "family holding," in which relatives shared their resources. "Parcels making up a family holding nearly always abutted," according to historian Susan Gray. "Contiguity made economic sense, for it enabled a family to maximize its resources."[24]

In March 1840, Thomas Lincoln bought Johnston's forty-acre homestead—at the nominal government price of $1.25 an acre—and cobbled it together with his own land to create a farm of 120 acres. He was now sixty-two and undoubtedly considered this his final homestead. As historian Charles Coleman concluded, "These land transactions were neither speculative nor highly profitable. He was attempting to secure an estate for his old age, and in this he succeeded. At the time of his death and for the eleven years preceding, he owned the land upon which he lived." In all, Thomas had spent nine years putting together his retirement farm, buying eighty acres from his stepson and moving jointly with him to the Goosenest Prairie. This deliberate Lincoln-Johnston venture represented the kind of intergenerational support and family cooperation that was essential to both stepfather and stepson, enmeshed as they were in a traditional farm economy. It was less important to the son and stepbrother Abraham, who had spent the same decade, the 1830s, carving out a career without any help at all from his family, in the village of New Salem and eventually the town of Springfield.[25]

In fact, Abraham and Thomas eventually turned patrimony on its head in an ironic parody of the traditional father-son relationship. In 1841, Lincoln bought his father's forty-acre homestead for two hundred dollars to keep it secure but gave Thomas and Sarah a lifelong tenure in the land. In this fashion, after leaving the farm for the city, the upwardly mobile son provided a "patrimony" of sorts for his own father. All the while, Lincoln maintained an emotional distance from this plot of land. He owned it for the rest of his life yet told his closest friend Joshua Speed that "I have no farm, nor ever expect to have." He also reported no real property in the U.S. Census of 1850. Quite possibly, he never mentioned the arrangement to anyone, including his wife.[26]

Clearly, Thomas Lincoln had failed his son in his final obligation: to provide him a patrimony of some kind, either land, an education, or a skill. As Lincoln summed it up, "when I came of age I did not know much." According to historians Steven Mintz and Susan Kellogg, "Parental authority was reinforced by control of property (land) or a craft skill that could be transmitted to the children." On either count, Thomas Lincoln held little sway over his son. To support them as they grew older, Lincoln's parents turned to his stepbrother, John Johnston, and to his cousins, the Hankses, to fill his place. John Johnston, for one, "thought that Abe did not Do a Nuff for the old people." According to Dennis Hanks, "they be cum Enimes for awhile on this ground." Lincoln seems to have settled on Johnston as a more dependable and perhaps compliant surrogate. He implored Johnston to stay in Coles County rather than leaving for St. Louis or California. He paid his stepbrother to stay on the Goosenest Prairie and help his parents, offering to match every dollar Johnston could earn if he stayed "close to home." Lincoln's money, offered indirectly through Johnston, served as a substitute for his own presence.[27]

Far from feeling jealous of his stepbrother or his cousins for minding his father's farm, Lincoln may have felt relieved at the lifting of this traditional responsibility. Historian Susan Gray has pointed out that the commercial economy of this period "shifted the conception of patrimony from land to capital." In this sense, Thomas Lincoln and his stepson John Johnston continued to value land as the ultimate resource long after Abraham Lincoln had learned to value capital. Instead of accepting land from his father to get a start in life, Lincoln offered his father and stepbrother capital to provide them necessary security within the new economy. Rather than a cynical rejection of farming as a livelihood, this offer quite probably represented a sensible accommodation to the new, modern realities of life. In a commercial economy, fathers could help their sons simply by releasing them from the traditional obligation to work their farms. Thomas Lincoln provided his son this advantage, at least.[28]

Still, unlike his son, Thomas Lincoln undoubtedly felt more at home in the traditional, agrarian society in which he spent his final decades. Fairness to Thomas requires a comparison of his economic standing with that of his neighbors on the Goosenest Prairie in which he made his final home. Thomas and his family arrived in Coles County in the summer of 1831, during a major wave of immigration into the county. They settled in Pleasant Grove Township, near the southern border of the county, an area settled mostly by southerners, including many Kentuckians. This was resoundingly an agricultural society, and Thomas mirrored the 97 percent of his peers who farmed for a living. In an agricultural society, of course, the most obvious measure of success or failure is land. Superficially, Thomas comes up short according to this measure, reporting a mere one hundred dollars in real property in 1850. In fact, the average farmer in the area owned more than sixteen hundred dollars in land, and Thomas's holdings left him in only the 21st percentile among his peers. Including the forty acres that Abraham Lincoln bought on his father's behalf, however, would lift Thomas to the 29th percentile, which is more respectable but still not an impressive record for a lifetime of farming.[29]

But in the traditional, agrarian world—unlike the emerging commercial economy—wealth was not everything. The ultimate goal was survival as a family on a plot of land that was their own and that was sufficient to support the independence of the household, a situation that was often called "competence." According to this more subtle standard, Thomas Lincoln was far more successful. Family was clearly important on the Goosenest Prairie, where no one lived alone. The average household size was between five and six members, and one household contained seventeen people. Agriculture depended on large families to provide labor, both outdoors and indoors, and household size was therefore an important measure of competence. In 1850, Thomas Lincoln was the head of a household of nine members, putting him near the top of the ladder in terms of household size, in the 92nd percentile. Indeed, only eight households in the entire settlement were larger than Thomas Lincoln's.[30]

At the age of seventy-two, Thomas Lincoln managed to maintain one of the largest households in his community. In fact, only two household heads were older, one seventy-three and another seventy-five. The average household head was forty-one, and Thomas stood in the 98th percentile in terms of his age. Taking his relatively advanced age into account, therefore, maintaining a household at all was a real achievement, let alone keeping one of the largest households in the area. Like many other men of his generation, Thomas may well have valued a large family and a secure competence far more than any material success. In short, Thomas Lincoln was a solid family man, if not a wealthy individual.

In May 1849, Johnston wrote Lincoln to tell him that his father was dying. "I hast to inform you That father is yet a Live & that is all & he Craves to See you all the time & he wonts you to Come if you ar able to git hure," Johnston wrote, "for you are his only Child that is of his own flush & blood & it is nothing more than natere for him to crave to See you." These anguished sentiments were a distinct statement of the patrimonial lineage that traditionally bound together a father and his son. Abraham was "his own flush & blood," and, as Johnston acknowledged, it was "nothing more than natere" for a father to live—and die—with his only son in mind. Indeed, this last request suggests genuine affection for his son. Thomas clearly took comfort in his family, going out of his way to embrace Mary Lincoln, whom he had never met. Johnston wrote that "he wonts me to tell your wife that he Loves hure & wants hur to prepare to meet him at ower Savours feet." Johnston's own grief was palpable. "I wright this with a bursting hart," he confided. "I won you to make an effort Come, if you are able to get hure."[31]

Dennis Hanks's son-in-law, Augustus Chapman, also wrote to Lincoln, telling him that Thomas "is very anxious to See you before He dies & I am told that His Cries for you for the last few days are truly Heart-Rendering. He wishes you to come & see Him instantly if you possibly can." Thomas had never seen his own grandchildren, and Chapman now urged Lincoln to bring them to his bedside. "If you are fearfull of Leaving your family on account of the Children & can bring them With you," he suggested, "we would be very Glad for you to bring them." Chapman promised to "do all we can to render your stay agreeable." Before Lincoln could respond, however, Chapman wrote back to say that the illness had been a false alarm. "I now Have the pleasure of informing you that your Father is not only out of all Danger but that he is not afflicted with a Disease of the Heart," Chapman wrote. In fact, Thomas would "doubtless be well in a Short time." Before this second letter reached him, however, Lincoln had already left for Coles County.[32]

Beyond bringing his son to his bedside, however, this false alarm proved unfortunate for Thomas. Nearly two years later, in the winter of 1850–51, he took sick again, but his son may have dismissed this illness as another false alarm. Lincoln thought of it as his father's "present sickness" rather than his final one. Lincoln, in fact, did not reply to the first two letters he received from John Johnston. At last, Dennis Hanks's daughter, Harriet Chapman, who had briefly boarded with the Lincolns in Springfield, wrote a letter that evoked an answer. Lincoln now crafted a dispirited and detached letter, not to his father at all but to his stepbrother. "I received both your [letters, and] although I have not answered them, it is n[ot because] I have forgotten them, or been uninterested about them," he confided, "but because it appeared to me I could write nothing which could do any good." Lincoln declined to visit Coles County, one hundred miles from Springfield, citing sickness in his own family. Mary was suffering a bout of "baby-sickness" which seemed "not dangerous." Lincoln, who was now a lawyer, added that "My business is such that I could hardly leave home now."[33]

Apart from these practical considerations, Lincoln asked Johnston to tell their father that "if we could meet now, it is doubtful whether it would not be more painful than pleasant." Lincoln went on to offer some sentiments that were sure to comfort his deeply religious father, urging him to depend on God: "He notes the fall of a sparrow, and numbers the hairs of our heads; and He will not forget the dying man, who puts his trust in Him." He closed by putting aside whatever earthly estrangement separated father from son by calling on Thomas to await a blessed reunion in heaven, where "he will soon have a joyous [meeting] with many loved ones gone before; and where [the rest] of us, through the help of God, hope ere-long [to join] them." According to Johnston, Thomas Lincoln believed that God "has a Crown of glory, prepared for *him*." Five days later, Thomas died at age seventy-three. His son did not attend his funeral.[34]

Thomas represented the last—perhaps the only—link between the two stepbrothers, who had come to inhabit such starkly different worlds. Thomas's death provoked a rupture between Abraham Lincoln and John

Johnston, confirming the pivotal role he had played for so long as patriarch of the Lincoln-Hanks-Johnston clan. Lincoln inherited his father's eighty-acre farm but sold it back immediately to Johnston for one dollar, retaining a dower right for Sarah Lincoln as long as she lived. Lincoln clearly expected Johnston to farm the land to help support his mother. Instead, Johnston made plans to move westward. The year before Thomas Lincoln's death, Johnston's wife had died, after fifteen years of marriage. Soon after Thomas's death, Johnston remarried a much younger woman whose father lived in Arkansas. With Thomas gone, Johnston now decided to move west to join this new extended family. This migration undoubtedly made sense to Johnston. After all, he was simply doing exactly what the Lincoln family had always done, moving generationally to new land farther west. Johnston had moved from Kentucky to Indiana as a boy to join the Lincoln family, and he had moved with them to Illinois as a young man. He was now moving yet again westward as a mature man of forty with a wife and children, as the Lincoln men had traditionally done. Johnston had spent twenty years in Coles County beside his stepfather and now proposed moving away only after the old man had died. His mother, Sarah, had other relatives—daughters, sons-in-law, and grandchildren—to provide for her future.[35]

To finance the move, however, Johnston proposed selling the eighty acres that Lincoln had sold to him, on Sarah's behalf. This news provoked a withering letter from his stepbrother. Lincoln simply did not understand the logic that would prompt Johnston to move yet again westward. He wrote that he "can not but think such a notion is utterly foolish." Lincoln accused Johnston of laziness for not staying in Illinois and working harder. "Can you there, any more than here, raise corn, & wheat & oats, without work?" he asked. "If you intend to go to work, there is no better place than right where you are," he advised, and "if you do not intend to go to work, you can not get along any where." Casting Johnston's plans in the most unflattering terms, Lincoln told him that "Squirming & crawling about from place to place can do you no good." Above all, Johnston's proposal clashed with Lincoln's plans for supporting his stepmother. "I feel that it is my duty to have no hand in such a piece of foolery," he wrote. "I feel that it is so even on your own account; and particularly on *Mother's* account." Writing again five days later, however, Lincoln agreed to allow Johnston to sell the land for three hundred dollars to support Sarah. Johnston eventually sold the farm to Squire Hall's son, one of Sarah Lincoln's grandchildren, to keep the land in the family. Lincoln himself retained ownership of the forty-acre homestead on Sarah's behalf.[36]

Nothing better reveals the two men's differing conceptions of family than an episode that happened precisely at this same moment. During his correspondence with Lincoln about his move westward, Johnston asked his stepbrother to take in his son Abraham, who was about thirteen years old, so he could get an education. Traditionally, many farm families "bound out" their sons at around age eleven to thirteen to work or learn new trades. Relatives—especially uncles—were the preferred sponsors. "As to Abram," Lincoln wrote, "I do not want him *on my own account*; but I understand he wants to live with me so that he can go to school, and get a fair start in the world, which I very much wish him to have." Lincoln told Johnston that "if I can make it convenient to take him, I will take him, provided there is no mistake between us as to the object and terms of my taking him." In fact, Lincoln never took him in, and he never came to Springfield. Despite the tone of the letter, Lincoln did not act out of unkindness. From his perspective and in his experience, family was simply unimportant, indeed unnecessary, in the struggle to succeed in the new, urban world. Rather than a reciprocal family obligation, helping a nephew, even a namesake, was now simply a matter of personal "convenience."[37]

In February 1852, Johnston and his family moved to Marion County, Arkansas, in the Ozarks, where Johnston bought a new farm for $160. Lincoln's advice, however, proved all too true. Johnston apparently could not "get along any where." Within a year, he had moved back to Coles County. Lincoln had predicted that "my life upon it, you will never after, own a spot big enough to bury you in." On April 1, 1854, John D. Johnston died at the age of forty-three, leaving an estate valued at less than $56. Johnston's fate, however, was far from unique. Like his stepfather before him, he was a pioneer who continually sought a better piece of land for his family farther westward. Historian James O. Robertson depicted this kind of ceaseless westward movement as thoroughly typical of the age, a recurrent feature within American cultural history. Pioneers took the land from the Native Americans, broke it, and prepared the way for the "civilizers," who built towns and brought refinements. Yet the pioneers lost their independent way of life precisely as the land they cleared grew civilized. According to Robertson, "they ceased to live a frontier life when the frontier moved beyond them."[38]

One solution was simply to keep moving: "Very often, like Tom Lincoln and his family, they sold out and moved on." Pioneers "often found themselves rejected or ostracized by the communities that grew up around them, their language and behavior too uncouth, too dirty, too uneducated, too primitive for the people who brought 'the civil parts of the world' to their doorsteps." Such was the fate of Thomas Lincoln and his stepson, John Johnston. Instead of moving, there was another solution—to stay put and become civilized. "Others, like Abraham Lincoln, would follow another pattern, from self-education to school to storekeeping to the law to the political life of settled, complex communities," Robertson observed. "They chose civilization, and so rejected the possibility of remaining frontiersmen." This was the gulf that separated Lincoln from his family. He "chose civilization," while they "remained frontiersmen."[39]

Historian Charles Coleman observed of Abraham and Thomas Lincoln that "the father and son relationship, while not particularly congenial, was a normal one." Within the context of the wrenching changes wracking American society during the early nineteenth century, and especially the dramatic transformation of father-son roles within the family, the relationship, although "more painful than pleasant," was indeed normal. Historians have traditionally faulted Lincoln for his inattention to his family, both economic and emotional. Like his contemporaries, however, Lincoln stood at the puzzling threshold between the old society and the new. Befuddled himself, his father Thomas provided little guidance or material help as Lincoln prepared to enter this new, urban world. Reciprocal economic obligations meant little in a traditional family that lacked a usable patrimony. In this new society, Abraham Lincoln owed his father little.[40]

Lincoln sought self-advancement and security in an emerging urban society, achieving independence by pursuing his own aspirations, both economic and personal, not by trying to live out those of his father, or those of any of his forebears. He looked to the future rather than the past as guide to living his own life. Historian E. Anthony Rotundo has identified this era's new individual freedom as "self-made manhood," a shift from communal obligations to individual success. "Men rejected the idea that they had a fixed place in any hierarchy," according to Rotundo. "And they ceased to see themselves as segments in an unbroken family line."[41]

This certainly held true for Lincoln. Thomas's generation had begun to break the traditional economic ties that held the cooperative family together. By the 1830s, the long Lincoln family line that stretched from Hingham to Springfield had lost most of its importance for its upwardly mobile son. With the decline of tangible economic ties, emotional ones soon emerged to bind the members of the modern family together. In Lincoln's youth, however, emotional ties were as yet only a glimmer within the family of the future. Looking backward on the old family could, understandably, prove quite painful. Looking forward to a new one could seem very pleasant indeed.

CHAPTER 13

Never Again to Think of Marrying

By the time Lincoln was twenty-eight, he was well on his way to achieving independence. In this traditional society, however, true manhood did not arrive until a man married, established a home of his own, and started a family. For a variety of reasons, Lincoln had trouble finding a wife. Temperamentally, Lincoln felt uncomfortable around eligible women, preferring the company of men or married women. His rough manners and appearance appealed to the sensibilities of southern men who valued rustic simplicity and honor above Yankee refinement and dignity. But they also endeared him to older women who strove to instil a modicum of gentility into this young diamond in the rough. Surrogate "aunts," such as Jack Armstrong's wife Hannah, James Rutledge's wife Polly, and—in Springfield—William Butler's wife Elizabeth all drew him into their family circles as a welcome visitor. In fact, Lincoln's relationship with his friends' wives generated neighborhood humor and friendly innuendo. Jack Armstrong, for example, openly joked that Lincoln had sired one of his sons, an insinuation that "plagued Abe terribly," which was of course the entire point of the jest. The episode also reveals that even Lincoln's friends considered him perfectly harmless, even a joke, as a romantic rival.[1]

This frontier society limited opportunities for courtship and marriage. The region's unbalanced sex ratio set up a tremendous competition for wives, pushing the age at marriage downward for women but adding two extra years to the bachelorhood of the typical man in the region. Friends often competed for the favor of the same woman, and women quite often courted several men simultaneously, giving rise, for example, to the oft-repeated legend that Abraham Lincoln and Stephen Douglas were romantic as well as political rivals. Other cultural realities compounded the scarcity of eligible partners. In this pioneer society, single men who moved westward married considerably later than youths born in Illinois, typically sacrificing five years of married life to complete the settlement process. Ethnic preferences also limited the marriage pool. Natives and immigrants exhibited little intermarriage, with more than nine-tenths of native-born men marrying native-born women. Among natives, northerners and southerners rarely intermarried. Among immigrants, 70 percent of southern-born men married southern-born women. One-half of Kentucky men marryied Kentucky women. Each of these cultural considerations limited Lincoln's choice of partners and his marriage prospects. Lincoln's economic situation was a final and perhaps definitive influence. Until he could support a family through a trade, business, or profession, he had little hope of winning a wife.[2]

Above all, during Lincoln's youth, standards of courtship and marriage were undergoing a dramatic transition. Just as family life was shifting from an economic to an emotional foundation, women began demanding a greater emotional investment from suitors during courtship. The traditional, "strategic" marriage had joined a couple together for the mutual economic advantage of their families. Women sought husbands whose economic positions would enhance the fortunes of their families as well as their own. Parents therefore exercised a strong if not determining influence over the choice of marriage partners, and prospective mates sought the blessing if not the permission of parents. Traditionally, a man visited his prospective father-in-law to ask his permission to marry his daughter, often before discussing the subject with his intended bride. In a more than symbolic gesture, fathers literally "gave away" their daughters during the wedding ceremony. As paternal authority declined, however, marriage began evolving into a union of two individuals rather than two families. Couples formed emotional bonds that superceded and sometimes even flouted economic considerations. The new "companionate" marriages that were emerging put a premium on emotional compatibility, transforming courtship into an often turbulent period of personal testing and emotional turmoil.[3]

Although "young poor and awkward," and thus a poor candidate for marriage, Lincoln formed two romantic attachments in New Salem. Lincoln boarded with James and Polly Rutledge, whose third child, Ann, was four years younger than he. Remembered poetically as "a gentle Amiable Maiden without any of the airs of your city Belles but winsome and Comly withal a blond in complection with golden hair," she was quite probably the most eligible woman in New Salem. The daughter of one of the settlement's founders, she was a good candidate for a strategic as well as companionate match. Three of the village's merchants all pursued her—Lincoln, Sam Hill, and John McNamar, who was still using the name McNeil. As Ann's brother Robert remembered, "A friendship grew up between McNeil and Ann which ripened apace and resulted in an engagement to marry."[4]

Nine years older than Lincoln, McNamar seemed a much better prospect to marry and head a family, owning one-half of a successful store and soon a piece of farmland in the area. Ann seemed an equally good match, but soon the Rutledges fell on hard times. A year after Lincoln arrived, James Rutledge sold his tavern as well as his eighty acres of land. As a rising merchant in the village, John McNamar snatched up forty acres of it as well as a plot of land belonging to one of the town's other founders, John Cameron. McNamar intended to settle his father's family there once they followed him to Illinois. An ill-timed sickness in his family, however, upset his plans and called him back to New York. McNamar sold his half of the store to his partner, Sam Hill, and rode back East on a horse named Charley, whom he still revered thirty years later as "a hero of the Black Hawk war." He stayed in New York for the next three years. "One of those Long interminable fevers that Sometimes occur in the East came into My Fathers family and prostrated Every member thereof except myself," he explained thirty years later, "and continued for Months making victims of three of them one of whom was my Father."[5]

The engagement was probably more strategic than emotional on both sides. Although still engaged to marry, McNamar stopped writing to Ann during his three years' absence. In an attempt to rebound economically, the Rutledge family moved onto McNamar's land to farm it as tenants, and Ann undoubtedly hesitated to break the engagement for fear of dislodging her family. According to the Rutledges, Lincoln began a secret courtship with Ann during McNamar's absence. Their relationship "resulted in an engagement to marry, conditional to an honorable release from the contract with McNamar." Before she could break her engagement with McNamar and make a new one with Lincoln, however, Ann Rutledge died of typhoid fever in August 1835. McNamar returned a few weeks after her death with nothing to show for his long engagement except a lock of hair, a "small Braid or Tress of Ann Rutleges Hair much worn and aparently moth eaten," as he described it decades later.[6]

Historians have fiercely debated Lincoln's engagement to Ann Rutledge, focusing on its impact on his later life and even questioning its existence. For many years, Lincoln's biographers denied that the engagement took place. Lincoln and Rutledge never corresponded, even when he spent three months in Vandalia serving in the legislature. Ann Rutledge's name appears in none of his surviving letters. The relationship gained public notice only after Lincoln's death, when he could not answer the rumors. Thirty years after Ann Rutledge's death, William Herndon delivered a series of lectures in Springfield claiming that the grief Lincoln felt over losing Ann plunged him into a lifelong depression that he never overcame. Herndon also suggested that Lincoln never truly loved another woman, including his wife Mary. Pointing to the overwhelming testimony contained in reminiscences as well as Lincoln's genuine grief, recent biographers have accepted the engagement as fact. Lincoln mourned so long and deeply that he suffered the first of two so-called "crazy spells" that he endured during his life. Friends tried to console him and harbored him in the their homes, hiding objects, such as razors, that might tempt him to consider suicide.[7]

In addition to reminiscences, circumstantial evidence points to the existence of an engagement. Lincoln and Rutledge were just the right age to contract a marriage. At her death, Rutledge was twenty-two and Lincoln was twenty-six. In 1835, the typical bride and groom in Sangamon County were twenty-one and twenty-five. Both of them were Kentuckians, which would have facilitated and even recommended the match. (Lincoln, of course, later married a Kentuckian.) Relatives remembered that they planned to marry only after completing their educations, Lincoln by earning his law degree, which he accomplished during the following year, and Rutledge by attending Illinois College, which she was preparing to do when she died.[8]

Rutledge most likely viewed her engagement to McNamar in strategic rather than emotional terms, especially after he apparently jilted her in the same manner that he had earlier abandoned his family, leaving her available for an emotional attachment to Lincoln. For his part, Lincoln could undoubtedly see strategic advantages to marrying a descendant of the prestigious Rutledge family of South Carolina, one of whose members signed the Declaration of Independence. Boarding with the Rutledges put Lincoln on intimate terms with Ann, providing an advantage that McNamar, who boarded with the Camerons, would have lacked. Finally, the grief that he expressed at her death was so deep and uncharacteristic that it must have reflected the loss of a love deeply felt.

Complicating any analysis of Lincoln's romance with Rutledge is his second, puzzling courtship, which he commenced just a year later. Lincoln frequently visited Dr. Bennett Abell and his wife Elizabeth, who lived one mile north of New Salem in what was described as a "little log Cabbin on the hill South of Petersburg." Lincoln was in fact staying with the Abells when Ann Rutledge died. "It was a great shock to him and I never seen a man mourn for a companion more than he did for her," Elizabeth Abell remembered. "He made a remark one day when it was raining that he could not bare the idea of its raining on her Grave[;] that was the time the community said he was crazy[;] he was not crazy but he was very disponding a long time." During the next year, Abell devised a plan to return to Kentucky, fetch her sister Mary Owens, and arrange a marriage with Lincoln. She may have had several motives: making a good match for her sister, bringing her to New Salem through a chain migration, and distracting Lincoln from the shock of Rutledge's death.[9]

Lincoln had met Mary Owens three years earlier and, by his own account, considered her "inteligent and agreeable" and was therefore "well pleased with the project." Owens was a year older than Lincoln, which was unusual but not an insurmountable obstacle to the match. One-sixth of marriages contracted in Sangamon County before the Civil War featured a wife who was older than her husband.[10] When Owens reached New Salem, Lincoln obligingly commenced a courtship. Hailing from a wealthy and aristocratic Kentucky family, Owens expected Lincoln to observe all of the niceties of a genteel courtship, something she soon found Lincoln entirely unable or at least unwilling to do. A series of incidents revealed Lincoln as an inattentive and even inconsiderate suitor. When riding across a dangerous creek, Owens noticed Lincoln "never looking back to see how I got along; when I rode up beside him, I remarked, you are a nice fellow; I suppose you did not care whether my neck was broken or not. He laughingly replied, (I suppose by way of compliment) that he knew I was plenty smart to take care of myself." As she recollected three decades later, "I thought him lacking in smaller attentions." Owens's cousin described another episode in which she attempted to test Lincoln's feelings for her, and he came up short. She deliberately missed an appointment with Lincoln and expected him to follow her to the house of Mentor Graham, who was her cousin. Instead, Lincoln refused and turned back sullenly to New Salem. These episodes led Owens to the conclusion—which she confided in Lincoln—that "You would not make a good husband Abe." Much later, she reflected "not that I believed it proceeded from a lack of goodness of heart, but his training had been different from mine, hence there was not that congeniality which would have otherwise existed."[11]

Misreading Owens's emotions, Lincoln continued the courtship. "I mustered my resolution," he recounted a year later, "and made the proposal to her direct; but, shocking to relate, she answered, No." Accepting the refusal as another "test" and thus a challenge, Lincoln persisted. "I tried it again and again, but with the same success, or rather with the same want of success." Too socially sensitive, he was devastated at the rejection, "mortified, it seemed to me, in a hundred different ways." In a pathetic misapprehension of his own situation, Lincoln believed that Owens considered him too humble to make a worthy mate. "Lincoln thought that as he was Extremely poor and Miss Owens very rich that it was a fling on him on that account," according to Owens's cousin. "This was at that time Abes tender spot." Confirming Lincoln's economic perspective on the courtship, he wrote Owens after he moved to Springfield to caution her that any marriage to him would throw her into unaccustomed poverty. "I am afraid you would not be satisfied," he warned. "There is a great deal of flourishing about in carriages here, which it would be your doom to see without shareing in it. You would have to be poor without the means of hiding your poverty." Instead, Owens simply wanted a more considerate and attentive husband. "Abe was mistaken in his guesses," according to Owens's cousin, "for wealth Cut no figure in Miss Owens Eyes." As Owens put it so eloquently, "Mr. Lincoln was deficient in those little links which make up the great chain of womans happiness." Dissatisfied with the uncultured Lincoln, Mary Owens left Illinois, returned to Kentucky, and married two years later. "The last message I ever received from him was about a year after we parted in Illinois," she remembered. "Mrs. Able visited Ky. and he said to

MARY OWENS. SHE REBUFFED LINCOLN'S PROPOSALS AFTER CONCLUDING
THAT HE LACKED "THOSE LITTLE LINKS WHICH MAKE UP THE GREAT
CHAIN OF WOMANS HAPPINESS."
Courtesy of the Illinois State Historical Library.

her in Springfield, Tell your Sister, that I think she was a great fool, because
she did not stay here and marry me. Characteristic of the man."[12]

The affair was indeed characteristic of Lincoln. Summoning the barest
of emotional responses to the woman he hoped to marry, the best that he
could do was to assure her that "I have not been pleased since I left you,"
and "I can not see you, or think of you, with entire indifference." Herndon
agreed that "Lincoln had none of the tender ways that please a woman."
Rather than reacting to Owens's rejection with grief, he felt nothing but bit-

terness and reacted by penning one of the cruelest letters that he ever concocted. Writing a year later to the wife of a legislative colleague, Orville Browning, Lincoln lampooned the entire episode and cast the most unflattering—and undeserved—aspersions against Mary Owens. Lincoln clearly viewed the proposed marriage to Owens in entirely strategic rather than emotional terms. Betraying the faintest emotional involvement in the whole affair, he told Eliza Browning that he "saw no good objection to plodding life through hand in hand with her" and that he "began to suspect that I was really a little in love with her." The experience of such a public courtship and such a humiliating rejection left him thoroughly embittered. "I have now come to the conclusion never again to think of marrying," he wrote Browning, "and for this reason; I can never be satisfied with any one who would be block-head enough to have me."[13]

The contrast with his emotional relationship with Ann Rutledge could not have been greater. The Owens engagement was as passionless as possible for a man who was proposing marriage. A traditional, strategic courtship, it originated through the efforts of a well-meaning matchmaker, had the blessing of the bride's family, took place within the aegis of a watchful community, and evoked little emotion from either party. Lincoln urged a coldly rational decision on Owens's part, posing only his poverty and not his want of passion as an objection to the match. On her side, Owens expected Lincoln to observe the formalities of a traditional courtship. Had it been consummated, the match would have been a mere marriage of convenience. Lincoln's relationship with Ann Rutledge, by contrast, was a true romance, calling forth an overwhelming passion on the part of the man who could not publicly proclaim his love and then tragically lost his lover. In this sense a more modern relationship, it flouted the conventions of polite society by endangering Ann's family, violating her betrothal to another man, and taking place in strict privacy, indeed secrecy.

In New Salem, Lincoln contracted two marriages out of entirely different motivations. His courtship of Mary Owens was loveless yet convenient. His romance with Ann Rutledge was passionate yet decidedly inconvenient for everyone involved. Both experiences left him embittered. Despite his resolve "never again to think of marrying," he needed to forge a relationship that occupied a middle ground somewhere between these two agonizing extremes.[14]

CHAPTER 14

Well, Speed, I Am Moved!

In April 1837, Abraham Lincoln and his new law partner announced to the world that "J. T. Stuart and A. Lincoln, Attorneys and Counsellors at Law, will practice, conjointly, in the Courts of this Judicial Circuit.—Office No. 4 Hoffman's Row, up stairs. Springfield, april 12, 1837." Three days later, Lincoln left the dying village of New Salem behind him and rode the twenty miles to Springfield on a borrowed horse, to join "his old friend, Stuart," in the practice of law. Springfield had changed dramatically since Lincoln's first appearance six years earlier. While New Salem was waging a life-and-death struggle just to survive, Springfield was thriving. Passing through Springfield as the Deep Snow melted in the spring of 1831, Lincoln had found a small frontier village of only 692 settlers. Three years later, the population had nearly doubled to around 1,200. Just a few months before Lincoln moved to Springfield, a local resident, George Rice, compiled a census, counting 1,879 men, women, and children, an increase of more than 50 percent over three years. The town had defeated its urban rivals, captured the state capital, and now attracted 450 new residents annually.[1]

Population growth stimulated a building boom, with seventy-five new houses going up during the preceding year. Two-thirds of them were humble but respectable single-story frames. The rest were grander—two-story frame houses or the kind of "brick palaces" that signified prosperity and indeed permanence. Business was booming, and upon Lincoln's arrival there were already 174 retail establishments in the town. A third of them, carpenters and painters, were devoted to building the town's homes and businesses. The region's crude transportation did not allow the importation of brick, and the townspeople supported five brickyards. By 1840, Springfield was the second-largest city in Illinois, with just over twenty-five hundred people, well over half the size of its fledgling northern rival, Chicago.[2]

As he attempted to settle down and rise in the world amid the social whirl of Springfield, Lincoln faced several distinct advantages and disadvantages. Lincoln's six years in New Salem facilitated—indeed enabled—his entry into Springfield society. Lincoln had formed several strong personal connections among the townspeople—merchants and lawyers, in particular—and important political alliances throughout the region. After six years of diligent work and self-discipline, he had a hard-won law license in hand. Not quite penniless, Lincoln owned land in Springfield when he arrived, a lot he sold five days later for seventy-five dollars, probably to cover his moving expenses. He still bore the burden of his National Debt, however, and spent the next decade repaying the creditors who had financed his youthful experiment in storekeeping at New Salem. Although he arrived alone, he was still courting Mary Owens, daughter of a prominent Kentucky family with relatives in the area. Still, success remained uncertain, and Lincoln referred to his prospective legal career as an "experiment."[3]

Largely because of his six-year sojourn in New Salem, Lincoln was something of a latecomer to Springfield. A close look at Lincoln's peers who lived in the town between 1830 and 1860 demonstrates that the typical Springfielder arrived in 1833, four years ahead of Lincoln. The typical Springfielder was also four years older than Lincoln, which put him at a considerable social and economic disadvantage. By the time Lincoln arrived, there were already eleven lawyers in the town and an established legal profession. "Leaving the field of his youthful sports, pleasures, and pains, where he was the leading man, he came to a bar then considered the best in the State, and perhaps as good as any in the West," in Joshua Speed's estimation. As Speed summed it up, "Then began with him the real battle of life."[4]

Lincoln had been the only lawyer in New Salem, but now he faced daunting professional competition. During this period, the typical lawyer in Springfield was between thirty-five and thirty-nine years old, so Lincoln's youth and relative inexperience were real disadvantages. Mason Brayman, another lawyer who arrived about the same time and became Lincoln's friend, wrote home to his parents optimistically that "I am doing tolerably well in my business here." But then he added ominously, "There are a large number of lawyers." Two years later he had to inform his sister that "I have made but a bare living thus far." In short, Lincoln was starting out all over again with an uncertain future and at the bottom of a new profession. Little wonder that "He entered with diffidence upon his new career," as Speed remembered.[5]

Arriving alone in the town, as Lincoln did, represented another handicap. A contemporary observer noticed two kinds of settlers arriving in Springfield, "young men who are just commencing to act for themselves, and fathers of families, who wish to see their children settled around them." Most of Springfield's early settlers arrived within stable families, and only a minority arrived alone. In a subsistence economy, single settlers had a difficult time surviving and were twice as likely as married settlers to pull up stakes after a few years and leave the region. Only one in seven single men managed to stay in Springfield for as long as a decade. The most successful settlers established a family before reaching Springfield, back East or en route to Illinois. Throughout the American West, in fact, about three-quarters of all settlers arrived with families—either wives and children, parents or siblings, or some combination of relatives—and Springfield reflected this general pattern.[6]

Families usually traveled west together as a group, but "chain migration"—as practiced by Lincoln's family—represented an important variation on the pattern. After their mother's death, for example, John Todd Stuart and his brothers considered reuniting in Springfield. "If you, from your knowledge of the state of things in Illinois, think a change might be made to advantage," Stuart's brother Robert wrote in 1834, "communicate with us on the subject." D. T. Stuart also mused that "We are now a divided family. You are in the distant west. I am in the east. Ma is in heaven." Later, he wrote wistfully that "I have always thought that Ill. was to be my home ever since you settled there." Mason Brayman also dreamed of luring his parents from New York to Springfield. "I have been thinking of your coming to *Illinois*," he wrote in 1841. "Land is cheap here, and more fertile than with you." Settlers often prevailed upon friends and former neighbors to visit and then relocate. "I called on some *old friends* below Springfield, and finding more than I knew of staid 10 days in the county, and am highly pleased with the place and the people," Joseph Street recorded in 1827. "i was very much solicited to settle amongst them, and at last purchased a farm."[7]

Beyond such dreams of reuniting a family in the West, the best strategy for assembling a family in Springfield was to arrive with one. Overall, married men with families accounted for more than one-half of all early settlers. These family men typically married at age twenty-five, usually in their home states, and spent the next decade—their late twenties and early thirties—back East, establishing a family. On average, they bore two living children in the East and came to Illinois with a mature, nuclear family in hand ten years after marriage. The typical married settler therefore arrived in Springfield at age thirty-five with a wife and two children, and then went on to raise four more children, for a total of six. Such established families, of course, had a much improved chance of success in settlement. Married men were thirteen years older on arrival than were single settlers. Often, they already had a profession, business, or established farm to sell back East. On arrival, they enjoyed free labor in the form of a wife and two children. Already established back East yet still growing, these families represented the ideal pioneers. They brought resources from the East, contributed to the western economy immediately on their arrival, and were better positioned to benefit from frontier opportunities.[8]

As they were throughout the American West, single men—"young men who are just commencing to act for themselves"—were the exception in

Table 14.1

Regional Origins of Settlers in Springfield Before and After 1830

	Before 1830	1830 and After
New England	12.9%	42.2%
Midlands	6.5%	30.0%
South	80.9%	27.8%

Springfield, representing only one-fourth of all settlers. Single settlers came to Springfield at age twenty-two on average, just a year after reaching their majority but before starting a family of their own. During the nineteenth century, men usually left home around age twenty-two, so these single settlers were probably heading west immediately after parting from their families. They arrived without relatives and usually without resources, such as an education, a business, or a farm. Often possessing little more than youthful optimism, single settlers spent their twenties getting established in new homes, starting a farm, clerking in a business, or apprenticing in a trade or profession. As a result, they postponed marriage until age thirty, five years later than the married settlers and about eight years after arriving. Because they delayed marriage, single settlers ended up forming smaller families than did the married settlers, bearing an average of only four children during their lifetimes. Compared with married settlers, they lost five years of family life, on average, in their struggle to succeed, marrying only once they had made a place in the world.[9]

Although Lincoln's solitary situation put him at a decided disadvantage in Springfield, his Kentucky heritage represented a real asset. The general Illinois pattern of southern settlers followed by northerners held true in this specific community. Southern settlers were first to arrive in Springfield, settling on average in 1831—the year of the Deep Snow. They were followed by the typical New England settler, who arrived in 1835, and finally by the typical Midlander, who settled in 1836. Before 1830, therefore, Springfield was an outpost of the Upland South, and four-fifths of all settlers in the town were southerners. After 1830, however, northerners began arriving in full force, with New England settlers predominating at 42 percent and Midlanders representing a close second at 30 percent. Southern settlers were suddenly a minority. After 1830, only one-quarter of Springfield's settlers hailed from the South (see Table 14.1).[10]

Fortunately for Lincoln, southerners—and particularly Kentuckians—represented the most important culture hearth in Springfield. A Yankee visitor saw this clearly and concluded that "their early possession of the soil gave the Southern pioneers an influence which their present relation to the population does not suggest." Kentuckians were the single largest settle-

---

ment group in Springfield, representing one in ten Springfielders as late as 1850. As a Kentuckian, Lincoln fit right in and would have represented a welcome addition to the community's dwindling Kentucky contingent. Kentuckians were adept at practicing chain migration, which exaggerated their influence by creating networks of extended families, friends, and political allies throughout central Illinois. The Bluegrass region of central Kentucky, in particular, contributed a small, close-knit, family-centered oligarchy that dominated Springfield socially, economically, and politically throughout the nineteenth century. Lincoln's new partnership with John Todd Stuart granted him a crucial entree into Springfield society that boded extremely well for his success.[11]

The roots of the influential Todd-Edwards-Stuart family lay in Ireland, from which David and Hannah Todd emigrated in 1737. Settling in Pennsylvania, the Todds raised three sons, Levi, Robert, and John, who went west together to Kentucky in 1775. Among the first white settlers to cross the Appalachians, the three Todd brothers were founders of Lexington, Kentucky, in the heart of the Bluegrass, and they named the town after the celebrated battle in Massachusetts that had recently sparked the War for Independence. The family prospered, and eventually an extended family of forty Todds dominated the social and political life of the Bluegrass region. The eldest Todd brother, Levi, was a lawyer and surveyor who fathered thirteen children, naming his seventh child after his brother Robert. The younger Robert Todd attended Kentucky's Transylvania University, which his family had helped to establish near their home in the center of Lexington. He studied law and was admitted to the bar, but as a southern gentleman he never practiced his profession. Robert Todd fathered sixteen children with two wives and, in the process, became the patriarch of one of the most distinguished families in Kentucky. Beginning a tradition of dynastic marriages that his descendants would carry on in Springfield, Robert Todd married a cousin, Eliza Parker, daughter of another of Lexington's old founding families. Between 1812 and 1825, Eliza Parker Todd bore seven children. The third child, born in 1818, was Mary Ann Todd, named after an aunt, her mother's sister.[12]

Mary Ann Todd might well have matured and married in Lexington, where her father thrived as a wealthy slave owner, bank president, state legislator, and vocal Whig. In 1825, however, her mother Eliza died after childbirth at age thirty-one. Her death left Mary motherless at six and eventually provoked a bitter schism among the Todds. Instead of mourning at least a year in proper aristocratic fashion, Robert Todd began a courtship while attending the legislature in Frankfort. Within six months, he proposed to Elizabeth Humphreys and within a year and a half he remarried. The new Elizabeth Todd went on to bear nine children in the next fifteen years. The Parker family never forgave Todd for his unseemly haste, and Eliza Todd's children resented their stepmother. Beyond personal conflicts, family tradi-

THE YOUNG EAGLE

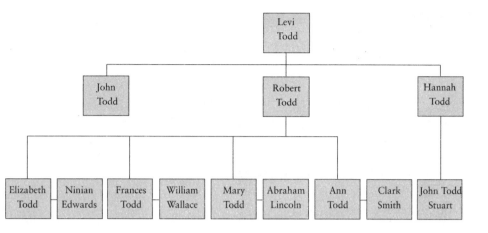

tion held that Eliza Todd's children grew critical of slavery, while their step-family increasingly rose to the institution's defense. Like so many southern families, the Todds moved off westward during the next generation, and eventually only one of Robert Todd's many sons remained in Lexington. In 1827, the Todds began a long process of chain migration that established an extended family cluster in Springfield.[13]

John Todd Stuart, Lincoln's law partner and Mary Todd's cousin, was the son of Robert Stuart, a Presbyterian minister who was born in Virginia and moved west to serve as professor of languages at Transylvania University in Lexington. Robert Stuart met and married Hannah Todd, sister of Robert S. Todd, patriarch of Lexington's wealthiest and most influential family. Named after Hannah Todd's brother John, John Todd Stuart was born near Lexington. As a youth, he attended Centre College in Danville, Kentucky, and studied law. The Todd and Stuart families practiced a classic chain migration to Springfield that eventually included Mary Todd. The first family member to reach Springfield was John Todd, Robert Todd's brother and Mary Todd's uncle. Like his brother Robert, John Todd attended Transylvania University. Rather than study law, however, John Todd chose medicine as his profession and attended the Medical University of Philadelphia, in his father's native Pennsylvania. John Todd returned to Lexington, where he married in 1813 at age twenty-six, practicing his profession and serving as surgeon general of Kentucky troops during the War of 1812. After practicing medicine in both Lexington and Bardstown, Kentucky, in 1817 he relocated to Edwardsville, Illinois. Ten years later, he was called to Springfield as register of the U.S. Land Office. Todd made Springfield his lifelong home, became one of the town's eminent physicians, and

---

raised a family of six children. He played a leading role in the town's economic development, political organization, and religious life. Above all, his arrival initiated a steady migration stream of Kentucky Todds that eventually made him the patriarch of a budding dynasty in Springfield.[14]

In 1828 at age twenty-one, John Todd Stuart traveled ten days on horseback to join his namesake and uncle in Springfield. Arriving as a single settler, Stuart lived with his uncle John during his first few years in town, in a form of "sponsored migration." He delayed marriage for the next nine years while becoming established as one of Springfield's foremost attorneys. He served in the Black Hawk War of 1832 and then returned to be elected to his first term in the legislature. After rooming with Lincoln during his second term, Stuart ran for Congress in 1836 but lost. He married in 1837, the same year that his partnership with Lincoln began, to a woman who was the daughter of a general and the niece of a judge. He and his wife went on to produce six children. Stuart was barely a year older than Lincoln, and yet he was the "senior" partner who sponsored the younger man's entree into Springfield society. As a Todd, he possessed the entire range of advantages that Lincoln lacked—a Lexington heritage, family connections, a college education, and an early arrival in Springfield. Stuart inherited all of the refined social graces prized by the Kentucky Todds. Renowned as "one of the handsomest men in Illinois," Stuart was six feet tall "with a noble forehead and large dark eyes. He was courtly and dignified in his carriage, and had an easy, affable address." He was the perfect role model for the young Lincoln. Above all, he shrewdly recognized the seeds of success in his uncouth, younger colleague.[15]

With two of its men ensconced securely in Springfield, the Todd family now began a five-year process of sending its daughters, one by one, to join them. Robert's eldest daughter Elizabeth made a crucial dynastic contribution to the family by marrying Ninian W. Edwards in 1832. Edwards was a member of another distinguished Kentucky, and later Illinois, family. His father, also named Ninian, was a prominent attorney and chief justice of the Court of Appeals in Kentucky. Just after his son's birth in 1809, the elder Ninian Edwards became the first governor of the new Illinois Territory, and the family moved to the territorial capital at Kaskaskia. The younger Ninian Edwards maintained his family's Kentucky roots, however, studying law at Transylvania University in Lexington. There he met and married Elizabeth Todd. When the elder Governor Edwards died of cholera, the new governor appointed his son attorney general of Illinois. The newly married couple, age twenty-three and nineteen, now moved to Vandalia, Illinois's new state capital.[16]

Encouraged by Todd and Stuart or perhaps by their example, Edwards soon resigned his office and moved to Springfield to practice law. There he joined Stuart as one of the town's eminent attorneys. As typical married settlers, Ninian and Elizabeth Todd Edwards went on to rear four children.

Edwards had been groomed for a distinguished career in law and politics, and he fulfilled his promise. Edwards was an early Whig, "tall and slender, and in manner mild and courteous." Together, John Todd, John Todd Stuart, and Ninian Edwards headed what was generally known in Springfield as the "Todd-Stuart-Edwards family" or, more derisively, "*the aristocracy.*"[17]

The Edwards home became the center of the Todd family circle and gained renown as the focus of Springfield's budding social and cultural life. More important, it became the frontier outpost of the Kentucky Todds in Illinois. Robert Todd now sent his daughters, one by one, to board with the Edwardses, to enjoy Illinois society, and to make good marriages. The next Todd to arrive was Frances, who obeyed the Todd tradition of sponsored migration by paying $150 to board with the Edwardses, thereby escaping the disharmony of her stepmother's household. Maintaining a busy social schedule, sister Elizabeth introduced Frances to Springfield society, especially the eligible young professionals who were now gathering in the town. Frances soon met and married a young physician, William Wallace of Pennsylvania. The couple moved into a Springfield boarding house, the Globe Tavern, opening a place in the Edwards home for yet another Todd daughter. In 1839, after an extended visit to size up the situation, twenty-one-year-old Mary Todd moved in with the Edwardses to grace Springfield's social scene and to look for a husband of her own.[18]

The final link in the family chain stretching from Kentucky to Springfield was cousin Stephen T. Logan. Logan studied law and in his youth conducted a practice in Kentucky. He married at twenty-three, and he and his wife had eight children. In 1832, Logan joined his relatives the Todds in Springfield, arriving relatively late, at age thirty-two. Bringing with him an established reputation as an outstanding lawyer, Logan went into partnership with Edward Baker, one of Lincoln's closest friends. He was twice elected circuit court judge but resigned both times to resume private practice, which he considered more lucrative. After Lincoln left his partnership with John Todd Stuart, he served as Logan's junior partner for three years, 1841–1844. Nine years older than Lincoln, Logan was an ardent Whig who served four terms in the Illinois legislature. Judge Logan, as he was known, ran for Congress in 1848 to succeed Lincoln but lost what had been considered a safe seat. Never much of a popular campaigner, Logan lost another election in 1855 and was, in fact, "worse beaten than any other man ever was since elections were invented," in Lincoln's judgment.[19]

The Todds of Kentucky orchestrated an impeccable family settlement strategy. Conducting an elaborate chain migration, they established a secure family outpost in Springfield and then painstakingly settled sons and daughters there one by one in a process that spanned well over a decade. Through sponsored migration and strategic marriages, Springfield's Todd-Stuart-Edwards family virtually guaranteed success to each of its new members. By 1850, the family's five patriarchs numbered two physicians and three attorneys who together owned land exceeding forty thousand dollars in value. Family, education, connections, wealth, and status knit the Todd-Stuart-Edwards family into the kind of "core community" that could dominate Springfield's social, economic, and political life for generations to come. Above all, the family conducted a model patrimonial migration from Kentucky to Springfield. The contrast with Lincoln's arrival could hardly have been more striking.[20]

As a lawyer, a prominent member of the Todd-Stuart-Edwards family, and an old settler, John Todd Stuart was virtually destined for public service. If nothing else, one-fourth of all lawyers in Springfield held a political office, five times the rate of the average resident.[21] Like Lincoln an early supporter of Henry Clay, Stuart was instrumental in organizing the emerging Whig Party in central Illinois. During his first campaign for the legislature in 1832, Stuart simultaneously worked in the futile attempt to elect Clay to the presidency. He later joined Lincoln as one of the Long Nine that represented Sangamon County in the legislature. Outside the political arena, Stuart was an early town booster, working to capture the state capital for Springfield, attending internal improvement meetings and conventions, advocating the establishment of common schools, helping to organize local voluntary associations, and speculating in land. He was also an early leader of the "colonization" movement in Springfield, which advocated the removal of free African Americans to Africa. After two terms in the Illinois House, Stuart ran as a Whig for Congress in 1836 but lost. He ran again in 1838 and won an extremely close election, defeating Democrat Stephen Douglas by a mere thirty-six votes out of thirty-six thousand cast. The narrow victory prompted an abortive contest from Douglas but helped to turn the political tide toward the Whigs, who held onto the congressional seat for a solid decade, just long enough to send Lincoln to Congress. Although an effective legislator, Stuart had a reputation for indolence and was apparently far from a rousing campaigner. Legislative colleagues knew him as "Jerry Sly," but as a stump speaker Democrats taunted him as "Sleepy Johnny" and delighted in comparing him to Rip Van Winkle awakening from his long slumber. "The last we saw of him, he was rubbing his eyes open at a corner of the street, with his arms raised above his head, giving a most portentous yawn," the Springfield *Illinois State Register* charged during one of his re-election campaigns. "After all his boasting that he was sure of six thousand majority, without stirring from home, we marvel much, that he should have had energy enough to arouse himself from his lethargy, and sufficient condescension to visit the people at all."[22]

After forging a promising partnership with Stuart, Lincoln's next preoccupation was to find a place to live. Springfield's population boom posed a real problem. "Our town is already filled with strangers," the editor of the *Sangamo Journal* observed in 1839, "and some difficulty is experienced in finding accommodations for all of them." As the town pressed outward, houses impinged on the nearby farmland. But the building boom raised land prices toward the center of town beyond the reach of many, "and real estate holds a high price, especially near the most business part of the City." In the midst of its boom, Springfield experienced a serious housing shortage. This was a long-term problem that persisted as the town continued to grow. "Our town is full of people," was the complaint a decade later. "Not an empty house can be found. Next year more buildings must go up.—We must have them." Newcomers had real difficulty finding a place to settle. "The number of houses in a new country, is barely sufficient to accommodate the inhabitants," warned *Illinois Monthly Magazine*, "and, in the infancy of society, but few dwellings contain superfluous apartments.—The new comers must, therefore, either be crowded into the houses of the settlers, which are already filled with inmates, or they must erect buildings, which, in the first instance, are merely temporary." Helping to ease the problem, Springfield hosted four public houses, in which prospective residents could board while looking for a place to live. Just a year after Lincoln arrived, Elijah Iles built the American House, a "gigantic building" that opened with a gala attended by 200 townspeople.[23]

Like most boom towns, Springfield attracted more than its share of young, single men. George Rice's census revealed a steeply skewed sex ratio in the town. Overall, there were 1.7 adult men for every adult woman. Further, most of the men in the town were young, like Lincoln. Fully 60 percent of them were in their twenties. Lincoln's age group, twenty-five to thirty, was the most prevalent, comprising an astounding one-third of all adult men in Springfield. Lincoln's peer group exhibited a discouraging sex ratio of 2.6 men for every woman. Put simply, between two and three prospective grooms competed for every woman who was about Lincoln's age. This unbalanced sex ratio held tremendous consequences for Springfield's youths, putting a premium on both economic opportunities and marriage partners, throwing young men into a novel "youth subculture," and— most immediately for Lincoln—creating a shortage of housing for anyone who lacked a family.[24]

Just as in New Salem, most single men in Springfield were boarders. Clerks and craftsmen typically slept where they worked, in the stores they tended or the workshops where they toiled during the day. Lodging houses, as they were called, were a good investment amid a transient population of young men, and they proliferated. Two years after Lincoln arrived, for example, a Springfielder posted a simple announcement: "Thirty Rooms to Rent. The subscriber keeps in good order and repair thirty rooms suitable for family residences;—good water and healthy situated." Lodging houses came in two varieties. "Rooming houses" offered a place to live but offered no meals. "Boarding houses," which were more expensive, provided meals at scheduled times in a formal dining room and thus provided more of a family atmosphere. Roomers therefore had a place to sleep but had to fend for themselves at mealtime. As a result, young men often roomed in one place but boarded in another.[25]

Because there was only one restaurant in Springfield when Lincoln arrived, boarding was in demand and helped quite a few townspeople supplement their incomes. A good example is William W. Watson, who was a confectioner and therefore well situated to feed the town's roomers. In 1840, he announced simply: "Boarders. The subscriber will take six or eight Boarders, without lodging." A typical fee for boarding was $2.50 a week, so Watson could earn an extra $20 a week by feeding boarders. Amid the housing shortage, hotels also sprang up—five of them by 1839—to help fill the void. Hotels offered a wider range of services, including rooms, meals, and livery service, to new residents as well as travelers. A typical hotel owner promised that "His table will be furnished with the best provision the market affords. He will pay particular attention to his stables—where horses shall be furnished with corn or grain, and otherwise be well taken care of." In short, "It will be his object at all times to make his house, *the home* of the traveller."[26]

Lincoln's immediate task on moving to Springfield was to find just such a home. His first stop was a cabinetmaker's shop, where he contracted to have a bedstead constructed. Then he headed to Abner Ellis's general store to buy bedding—"mattress, blankets, sheets, coverlid, and pillow." Ellis was a former New Salem merchant, one of the "survivors" who had sold out and moved to Springfield, like Lincoln. In fact, Lincoln had briefly clerked for him in New Salem. Two years older than Lincoln, Ellis was a native Kentuckian and a staunch Whig, like Lincoln, as well as a fellow old settler who had settled in the region very early, in 1825. These associations likely beckoned Lincoln to Ellis's store. In 1837, Joshua Speed was a partner in the store and was clerking there on the day that Lincoln walked in. Speed shared many similarities with Lincoln, and the two quickly became lifelong friends. Sixty years later, Lincoln's son Robert called Joshua Speed "the most intimate friend my father ever had." In fact, Lincoln's wartime secretaries and eventual biographers John Nicolay and John Hay singled Speed out as "the only—as he was certainly the last—intimate friend that Lincoln ever had."[27]

Speed was five years younger than Lincoln, only twenty-two years old when they met. A fellow Kentuckian, he was born into a wealthy family on a plantation five miles outside Louisville. His father, John Speed, was a judge, a planter, a substantial landowner, and the master of more than seventy slaves. Named after his mother's father, Joshua Fry Speed was the fifth among ten children. His family educated him in private schools to prepare him for a professional career. While in college, however, Speed fell ill and after recuperating at home decided to strike out on his own. He worked as a clerk for two or three years in the largest mercantile house in Louisville and, after this apprenticeship, moved to Springfield in 1835. Speed spent

JOSHUA SPEED. LINCOLN ROOMED WITH SPEED DURING HIS FIRST FOUR YEARS IN
SPRINGFIELD CALLING HIM "THE MOST INTIMATE FRIEND" HE EVER HAD.
Courtesy of the Illinois State Historical Library.

the next seven years working as a merchant in the Illinois capital. Despite poignant differences in their family backgrounds (Speed hailed from the slave-owning planter class, Lincoln from the independent yeomanry), the two hit it off immediately. Lincoln may have seen something of himself in the young store clerk who looked into the future with optimism. In addition, both were Kentuckians who had come to Springfield alone after rejecting the career paths of their fathers. Both were ambitious young men who aspired to succeed while working with senior partners who were already established in Springfield. Both were confirmed Whigs. Both were at sea amid the bubbling social turmoil of the burgeoning boom town. Lincoln was, as Speed put it, "almost without friends." The two men became instant companions.[28]

Speed was already familiar with Lincoln, whose reputation as a speaker preceded him to Springfield. "I had not seen him for the first six months of my residence there," Speed recalled, "but had heard him spoken of as a man of wonderful ability on the stump." The young clerk had his first look at Lincoln when he spoke in Springfield while running for reelection to the legislature in 1836. Like most of Lincoln's acquaintances throughout his life, Speed was initially put off by the young man's appearance, finding him "a long, gawky, ugly, shapeless, man." But the young Abraham's eloquence soon won him over. "I remember that his speech was a very able one," Speed concluded, and the youth "produced a profound impression." Simply put, "The Crowd was with him." And soon so was Speed.[29]

Decades later, Speed remembered vividly that fateful Saturday in April when "Lincoln came into the store with his saddle-bags on his arm." Learning that the bedding would cost seventeen dollars, Lincoln confessed that "I have not the money to pay." This rude introduction to Springfield's budding cash economy left him visibly discouraged. "As I looked up at him I thought then, and think now," Speed recalled, "that I never saw a sadder face." The young clerk suggested that Lincoln share his room above the store. "He took his saddle-bags on his arm, went up stairs, set them down on the floor, and came down with the most changed countenance. Beaming with pleasure he exclaimed, 'Well, Speed, I am moved!'"[30]

The persistent housing shortages that characterized any frontier enforced a virtually instantaneous intimacy, and the two became fast friends. As Lincoln reminisced as president, "I slept with Joshua for four years." With the young lawyer and store clerk ensconced in the room above, the store became a focus of the town's young male subculture. "After he made his home with me, on every winter's night at my store, by a big wood fire, no matter how inclement the weather, eight or ten choice spirits assembled, without distinction of party," Speed reminisced. Newcomers to the area, especially adults, often had trouble making new friends. As another young settler wrote back home, "people of your age and mine cannot change their Location with equal facility as younger people it is more difficult to leave old friends and acquaintance and form New one." In Joshua Speed, Lincoln made a friend who could introduce him to many others.[31]

Lincoln roomed with Speed but boarded with William Butler. Butler was a fellow Kentuckian and committed Whig who was twelve years older than Lincoln. During the War of 1812, when he was only fifteen, Butler served as a messenger for General William Henry Harrison. After the war, he worked as a deputy circuit court clerk in Kentucky, where he befriended Stephen T. Logan, cousin of Mary Todd. In 1828, already thirty-one years old, he followed Logan to the Sangamon Country, where he bought a farm that he worked with his father. A restless youth, Butler had no intention of remaining permanently. He traveled extensively, spending months away from home in St. Louis and Nashville. His father died, however, and according to Butler "I was therefore forced to remain here." Saddled with the unwelcome responsibility for running a family farm, Butler declared simply that "I hated the country." But he "was thus occupied in taking care of my farm and generally looking after my father's family which was thrown upon my care." At age thirty-five, he married Elizabeth Rickard, the daughter of a local family, and raised three children, naming his first son Speed. In 1836, Logan, who was now a judge, appointed him clerk of the circuit court. Butler was one of the first Springfielders to encounter Lincoln, when he and his cousins were building their flatboat for Denton Offut. Like Speed, Butler was initially unimpressed. Lincoln was "not prepossessing—he was awkward and shabbily dressed." Lincoln broke prairie on Butler's farm, and the two served together in the Black Hawk War.[32]

While Lincoln was in the legislature, Butler had some business in Vandalia, and the two traveled back home to Springfield on horseback. Decades later, Butler reminisced that Lincoln seemed restless and explained that "All the rest of you have something to look forward to, and all are glad to get home, and will have something to do when you get there. But it isn't so with me. I am going home, Butler, without a thing in the world." Still deep in debt, Lincoln admitted that "I dont know what to do." When they reached Springfield, Butler secretly paid some of Lincoln's debts and carried his saddlebags to his house. He invited Lincoln to board with his family "and make my house your home."[33]

Lincoln boarded with Butler for the next five years. "You know he was always careless about his clothes," Butler recalled. "In all the time he stayed at my house, he never bought a hat or a pair of socks, or a coat. Whenever he needed them, my wife went out and bought them for him, and put them in the drawer where he could find them." Elizabeth Butler lent a welcome feminine touch to the solitary man's meager existence. Despite their youthful intimacy, Butler eventually had a falling out with Lincoln, and their friendship ended bitterly. When Lincoln served in Congress a decade later, Butler asked him for an appointment to the federal land office, but apparently Lincoln refused. According to Gershom Jayne's son William, who was a mutual friend, Butler "swore he would be revenged on Lincoln." True to his word, Butler worked surreptitiously to block Lincoln's election to the Senate in 1855. Lincoln's brother-in-law, Ninian Edwards, who had become a Democrat, sympathized with Butler. "Had I been Lincoln and had been taken in as Butler did Lincoln," he reasoned, "I certainly would have given him an office."[34]

Lincoln's four-year tenure as Stuart's junior partner provided him with a solid professional and political apprenticeship. Junior partners ordinarily conducted a good deal of the ordinary business of any law firm, and Stuart, who was absorbed in politics, gave Lincoln a lot of responsibility. Lincoln routinely wrote legal documents for the firm and signed Stuart's name. The Sangamon County circuit court met only four weeks each year, so Lincoln began his famous routine of "riding the circuit," pleading cases in the courts of other counties throughout central Illinois. As a result, he traveled for weeks at a time, a tiresome schedule that was facilitated by the system of boarding. While away from Springfield, Lincoln simply boarded in other towns. Representing clients who typically paid a five-dollar fee, Lincoln had to work incessantly to cobble together a living. Although lawyers were steeped in the region's budding cash economy, Stuart and Lincoln occasionally received payment in kind. One of Stuart's clients made him a coat worth fifteen dollars, and one of Lincoln's offered him six dollars' worth of board. Still, during his first year of practice, Lincoln earned enough to buy two lots in Springfield from Elijah Iles.[35]

While Lincoln minded the law firm, Stuart engaged in politics, running for Congress a second time in 1838. Lincoln engaged in both a political and a legal apprenticeship by campaigning for Stuart, as well as for his own re-election to the legislature. Lincoln wrote letters on Stuart's behalf to the *Sangamo Journal* and to Whig leaders in the district critical of the Democratic candidate, Stephen Douglas. "We have adopted it as part of our policy here, to never speak of Douglass at all," he joked. "Is'nt that the best mode of treating so small a matter?" Enlivening the contest between Stuart and Douglas was their nearly daily contact within legal circles. Stuart and Lincoln squared off against Douglas in a sensational murder trial that dragged on throughout the summer. The partners defended the accused murderer of Jacob Early, a doctor and Methodist preacher who had been Lincoln's captain during the Black Hawk War. Three days before the election, the campaign turned violent. During a debate, Stuart grabbed Douglas and picked him up. Douglas responded by biting Stuart's thumb. Stuart defeated Douglas both in the courtroom and on the stump, winning both the murder trial and the election to Congress.[36]

When Stuart left for Washington, he entrusted Lincoln with all of the firm's business. Stuart's first term in Congress gave Lincoln a taste of national politics. He corresponded with Stuart regularly, about the business of the firm and local political affairs, and asked him for help in organizing Illinois Whigs. Lincoln's work was truly "half legal, half political," as one of his friends put it. Lincoln now came into his own as a lawyer and a politician. He argued cases in Springfield, rode the circuit throughout central Illinois, sat in the legislature, wrote editorials for the *Sangamo Journal*, and campaigned for William Henry Harrison. On the day Stuart left for Washington, the self-confident Lincoln opened the firm's fee book and wrote the entry, "Commencement of Lincoln's Administration."[37]

CHAPTER 15

A Community of People

Politics took root very slowly in the Sangamon Country. Until the mid-1830s, government was fundamentally local and addressed the mundane concerns of daily living. Most people looked to government to solve immediate problems of local concern and watched warily as national issues and parties slowly intruded into the affairs of everyday life. At its creation in 1821, Sangamon County inherited a skeleton government that focused on facilitating settlement and economic growth. County government was fragmentary, consisting of three commissioners, elected annually, who convened irregularly, as needed, to help the county develop. After providing the barest essentials, such as building a courthouse and a jail, imposing a county tax, drawing township lines, and establishing school districts, the commissioners sat back to hear the demands of their constituents.[1]

Such a "negative" government intervened only when called upon to dispense services that the community could not provide for themselves. The Commissioners Court spent most of their time considering petitions for the opening of a road, the building of a bridge, the relief of a pauper, or the licensing of a mill. In 1829, for example, their minute book recorded that "J. T. Stuart presented a petition to the Court that Second Street in the Town of Springfield be opened." When permission was granted, the villagers went ahead and laid out the street themselves. In theory, the commissioners granted only those requests that contributed to the public good. In this "government by petition," simple requests might require just a single signature, but petitions demanding more elaborate or controversial actions might attract hundreds.[2]

During the county's infancy, transportation remained the most pressing concern. In its first five years, the commissioners licensed eight ferries to span rivers and creeks and then authorized dozens of roads to connect the ferries. A typical road petition argued that "We consider the road of great importance not only to the Country through which it passes, but to the travelling community." Samuel Musick, for example, received a license to open a ferry across Salt Creek, and then the commissioners approved a road running from the ferry through New Salem and on toward Jacksonville. They appointed Abraham Lincoln "to view said road and said Lincoln to act as surveyor." Fittingly, during Lincoln's first year in the state legislature, he introduced a bill allowing Musick to build a toll bridge at the same spot, which was his first proposal that ever became a law.[3]

The commissioners also appointed dozens of road viewers to keep the new roads in good repair and divided the county into road districts, each with a supervisor to maintain them. To make the job easier, they bought one road scraper for each district in the county, which helped clear the roads during the winter of the Deep Snow. Additionally, the county's "estray pen" held runaway horses until their owners could claim them. To accommodate travelers and settlers, the commissioners began licensing taverns, public houses, and groceries. Licenses were cheap but provided revenue to the county and allowed the commissioners to regulate prices. Taverns, for example, paid a $3 fee and were limited to charging 12½¢ for a night's lodging, 25¢ per meal, and an equal amount for a half-pint of French Brandy. During the county's first five years, eighteen taverns appeared, nine of them in Springfield. The county also licensed nine mills to grind grain and saw lumber. The seventy-mile trips to the old county seat, Edwardsville, now came to end. Echoing Lincoln's call for transportation improvements, the commissioners also tried, in vain, to facilitate navigation on the Sangamon River.[4]

Justice consisted of a county sheriff, appointed by the commissioners, and a varying number of constables to keep peace in the rural villages that dotted the prairie. Three justices of the peace heard minor cases, imposing fines for routine offenses, such as three dollars for assault and battery. Jury trials took place in the circuit court, which sat at John Kelly's house until the first log courthouse was finished. Justice was a routine, everyday affair until 1826, when a blacksmith killed his wife in a drunken rage. Two days later, a jury, headed by Bowling Green as foreman, found him guilty. The execution was public, and "almost the entire community" turned out to watch the condemned man hang. As late as 1832, the jail was "quite a harmless affair here, having been entirely tenantless for the last three months," a local newspaper editor boasted. Criminal justice in the county was a mostly humdrum exercise in keeping the peace. "Indeed, the equilibrium of our social affairs is scarcely ever broken in upon except in some case matrimonial—and even then, our friend, the parson, or some worthy justice, so expeditiously unites the sundered elements of society." Despite these simple beginnings, the Sangamon County circuit court became the primary arena in which Abraham Lincoln later practiced law. Here Lincoln argued more than twenty-five hundred cases over the next quarter century, nearly half his caseload during his entire legal career.[5]

The commissioners also oversaw the county's poor. Initially, there was no almshouse, and the county auctioned adult paupers to the highest bidder. Once "farmed out," they earned their keep by working for local families. Overseers of the poor, appointed by the commissioners, typically provided one dollar per week for "dieting and clothing" paupers. Orphans, or any children who became public charges, were apprenticed to local families. Boys were apprenticed until age twenty-one, girls until they turned eighteen. Thirteen-year-old Mary Elizabeth Orr, for example, was apprenticed to John Delany, an Irish shingle maker, ostensibly "to learn the art and mystery [of] Domestic Housewifery," but in reality to serve as his housekeeper for the next five years. Orr's indenture of apprenticeship prohibited her from marrying as well as frequenting "Taverns, Alehouses, Tipling Shops or houses of Ill fame," while requiring Delany to provide her with "good wholesome and sufficient meat, drink, washing, [and] lodging," until she turned eighteen.[6]

Orphaned boys were bound out to learn husbandry by working alongside local farmers. In 1834, eight-year-old Howard Vandegrift was apprenticed to learn carding and cotton spinning in John Hay's recently opened carding mill. This followed Hay's announcement that "He wishes to employ a few hands. Boys 10 or 12 years of age would be preferred. He also wishes to purchase a few blind horses." In 1844, Martha Reed bound out her three-year-old son Charles as an apprentice "to learn the Art & Mystery of Farming." At the end of the apprenticeship, the boy would receive "a new Bible and Two new Suits of clothes. Suitable and proper for his condition."[7]

The ostensible goal of such apprenticeships was to situate paupers and orphans within a wholesome, family setting while minimizing the expense of feeding, clothing, and housing them. As the number of paupers swelled, however, the commissioners responded by confining them to the county jail. The local jailer became the "supervisor of all the poor of both City and County," a local reformer complained. "By this jail arrangement, the difference between the criminal and the unfortunate poor, is almost lost sight of." In 1839, the legislature authorized counties to open almshouses to provide "indoor relief." The Sangamon County commissioners established the county's first almshouse in 1851 when they bought a farm two miles north of Springfield. They ended the practice of farming out paupers to local families and now required them all to live and work on the new "poor farm."[8]

Clearly, this was government on a small scale. Three years after its establishment, the county collected a meager six hundred dollars in taxes and twenty-three dollars in fines. "In the whole of this wealthy and extensive county, there is not a single bridge constructed in whole or in part by the County," a local resident complained bitterly in 1834. "To a considerable extent, the demands on our county treasury, will cease, after the completion of the jail." This fragmentary government focused on opening the region to settlement through improved transportation and accommodations, while addressing the most egregious cases of want and criminality in a rural society. When new towns were incorporated, they became self-governing and relieved the county government of its most complex problems.[9]

The Commissioners Court inaugurated the county's first town by ordering Springfield "laid off into lots by some skillful surveyor," and the legislature created Springfield in 1832. Until becoming a city in 1840, Springfield was governed by a town board consisting of a president and four trustees. During Springfield's eight years as a town, the trustees met once a month, and their president presided over the town in place of a mayor. The five board members were elected, but politics played little role in town government. At a typical election, voters gathered at the polling place between 8:00 and noon on a Monday morning and chose trustees through a voice vote. The town board appointed all other town officers, including a treasurer, a corporation attorney, a constable, a graveyard sexton, and street commissioners.[10]

During the 1830s, the trustees' major preoccupation was town building. Rapid growth produced a kind of urban squalor unbefitting a new state capital, and the town and its citizens worked hard to improve it. In 1832, Springfield's trustees fixed the town's limits at one square mile and stipulated, for the sake of orderly and esthetic growth, that the court house would remain the centerpiece of the town and that "the lines of the said town shall conform to the same parallels as are now fixed for the streets." The trustees mandated the opening of alleys to facilitate waste disposal and deliveries, imposing fines against anyone who fenced them in. They appointed street commissioners and charged them with keeping the roads in good repair for a mile in every direction from the courthouse. Springfield remained a rural outpost, and animals still had the run of the streets. The trustees prohibited the indiscriminate dumping of "dead carcases" and required the street commissioners to remove them. They began to prohibit a host of familiar agricultural practices that were increasingly considered nuisances in a town. Hogs, for example, could no longer roam freely. To prevent rabies, other ordinances targeted dogs running loose within the town. A Board of Health, consisting of seven doctors, among them Stuart's uncle John Todd, was charged with suppressing "filth of any description," including the stagnant pools that bred mosquitoes and disease. These efforts were new to an emerging urban government sitting in the middle of a prairie. The agricultural landscape was now expected to stop at Springfield's town limits.[11]

Population growth put a premium on public health and safety. When a single case of cholera appeared in 1832, the Board of Health promptly set up a hospital well outside "the business parts of the town" to contain the disease. In 1834, the *Sangamon Journal* tried to counter Illinois's reputation as an unhealthy environment by crowing that not a single soul had died during the previous seven months, labeling Springfield "one of the healthiest towns in the United States." The next month, however, cholera broke out again and claimed seventeen townspeople in less than a month. During this period, a traveler remembered, "People sometimes refused to let us stay all night when they found we were from Sp[ringfield] where cholera was." Life and health remained uncertain, and Springfielders depended on private physicians to treat a wide assortment of ordinary diseases. When Lincoln arrived, there were eighteen doctors and four druggists. Indeed, physicians were the third-largest occupational group in the town. Lincoln's future brother-in-law, the well-to-do Dr. William Wallace, was a partner in Springfield's largest drugstore. Wallace advertised over one hundred varieties of drugs, dyes, paints, oils, and perfumes, including forty-one different patent medicines "just received from the Eastern Cities," to prevent and treat common diseases. Lincoln himself enjoyed robust good health but constantly consulted physicians, including his brother-in-law, for the latest medical advice on warding off disease.[12]

Soon after Lincoln arrived, Springfield's official size quadrupled when the trustees extended the town limits to one mile east, west, north, and south from the center of the public square. The town now encompassed four square miles. The edge of town, in particular, represented a transitional zone in which rural customs only gradually succumbed to the emerging urban lifestyle. "The small enclosures, near the City, that have been in cultivation for several years, are giving way," according to one observer, "and buildings are stretching out into the prairies in every direction." The sprawling town sat uneasily in the midst of a once-wild prairie. As late as 1845, wolves still roamed the outskirts. "The weather and the depth of the snow for a few days past have been strong temptations to many of our citizens to enjoy the sport of running down prairie wolves," according to one chilling account. "The sportsman mounts his horse, and with a good 'hickory club,' pursues the animal into the prairies, where he generally overtakes, and despatches him." The town was impinging on nature, and "the destruction of wolves, in consequence, has been very great." Despite fencing and farming, the prairies left an indelible impression, and prairie fires routinely lit the nighttime sky. "Monday evening the prairie south of the City was lit up with fire," the editor of the *Illinois State Register* rhapsodized in 1840. "The scene was beautiful. The night was dark, and as we viewed the fire from the State House, we were filled with delightful emotions." Springfielders felt secure in their attempts to banish the uncertainty of nature to the distant and still-wild horizons.[13]

One-sixth of the entire county's population now lived in Springfield, crowded within a mere four square miles. Springfield's boomtown atmosphere bred a host of growing pains and a steady demand for civic improvements. During this transition from farm to city, animals continued to intrude on everyday life. The town board could ban hogs, but horses remained a daily necessity. For the sake of decorum, the trustees discreetly prohibited the "indecent exhibition of horses," and anyone who "put or let a stallion to a mare" was subject to a five-dollar fine. Soon, even the running of horses in town became a crime, and they were required to walk rather than "gallop, canter or run." Early on, the town mandated the construction of sidewalks. A generous twelve feet in width, the sidewalks signified Springfield's status as a "walking city," in which most people walked to and from work. Brick sidewalks graced the public square, and a town ordinance prohibited the running of horses on any brick or stone walkway.[14]

Like the booming population, the growing number of horses who did the daily work of transportation in any town remained a persistent problem. Homeowners kept their horses in sheds that abutted alleyways, as Lincoln eventually did, but boarders and travelers needed to rent accommodations for their animals or rent the animals themselves. Livery stables began to dot the town as the countryside receded. Gershom Jayne, the town's first doctor and tavern keeper, and perhaps not coincidentally a member of the Board of Health, opened the first livery stable in 1832. "The stable will be well furnished with the best feed the country affords and horses will be kept by the week, day, or feed," he promised. The Springfield Livery Stable also offered "a good two and a four horse coach, in which they can carry persons to any point in the country." To ensure safety and reliability, Jayne promised that "they will employ none but careful drivers, and faithful Ostlers." Although Springfield was small enough to qualify as a "walking city," horses remained essential for long-distance travel and transport. At midcentury, one in twenty Springfielders worked with horses for a living, as teamsters and draymen, saddlers and wagon makers, or horse dealers and liverymen.[15]

In the absence of adequate fencing, which was an expensive investment, horses often strayed, and "estray" notices filled the newspapers. Quite a few were stolen. In 1840, for example, the *Sangamo Journal* warned its readers to "Look out for Horse thieves—Several horses have been stolen from this city and vicinity within a few days past." The state's attorney general warned that the horse thieves had formed an "organized ring" that was operating beyond the reach of the government. "Such persons generally live in the vicinity of a forest of timber or a heavy thicket of underbrush," he cautioned, "so that they can conveniently hide away men, horses, &c. for weeks and months, if necessary, to avoid all suspicion and pursuit." He stopped short of recommending the lynching that seemed to work closer to the frontier but advised that "By proper vigilance on the part of honest men these head quarters of scoundrels can be broken up, and when the leaders are dispersed the death blow will be given to the whole gang, and not till then."[16]

In 1841, Springfielders responded by creating the Society for the Suppression of Horse Thieves. A recently formed company of mounted lancers agreed to help in the effort and pledged to "parade opposite the market house by signal, mounted, armed and in fatigue dress, for the purpose of pursuing the thief or thieves." Lincoln himself was not immune. In 1836, he ran an all-too-familiar notice: "Strayed or Stolen, From a stable in Springfield, 18th inst, a large bay horse, star in his forehead, plainly marked with harness, supposed to be eight years old." Lincoln promised that anyone who captured the horse "shall be liberally paid for their trouble."[17]

Beyond the threat of horse thieves, the gathering of so many rootless young men combined with the town's wide-open atmosphere and keen political competition to breed a daily threat of violence. Early on, the town's trustees imposed a spate of ordinances "against drunkenness, and using of profane language, and riots," along with "unlawful gaming or riotous conduct" and the like. Springfielders could no longer shoot off firearms in town, light bonfires, or carry torches. The trustees passed the town's first noise ordinance when they prohibited "disturbing the peace of the town of Springfield, by meeting together and blowing upon horns and other instruments, drumming upon kettles and other articles, and making other unusual and undefinable noises."[18]

Gambling was a bigger problem that the trustees were unable to address. Like the residents of other boomtowns, Springfielders decided to take matters into their own hands. In 1834, the *Sangamo Journal* announced that "A meeting of the Citizens of Springfield will be held at the Court House on this afternoon, (Saturday,) at 4 o'clock, for the purpose of devising means to suppress Gaming in this place. All persons friendly to the object are invited to attend." Five years later, the trustees acknowledged that the problem had resumed. "Springfield is at this time infested with a horde of gamblers, who have recently arrived among us," they warned, "and who are a nuisance to our citizens, and an injury to the character of our community." Unfortunately, "the laws furnish a very inadequate remedy for these evils." The trustees now called a public meeting of citizens to address the problem outside the constraints of the law.[19]

Two years after arriving in Springfield, Lincoln himself served briefly as a town trustee. When a member of the board resigned to become a judge, the trustees appointed Lincoln to take his place. He took the oath of office from William Butler, who was now clerk of the circuit court. The town board met in the afternoon of the last Monday of each month, and the trustees received a dollar per meeting. When Lincoln joined the board, the president was Charles Matheny, Sangamon County's erstwhile "one-man government." Most of Lincoln's work during his eight months of service was decidedly routine. The trustees levied a tax of twenty-five cents on every one hundred dollars of real estate and ordered Joel Johnson's unnamed "nuisance" to be removed. They appointed Lincoln to a committee to determine "the proper width of side walks on 4th Street" and awarded liquor licenses. The trustees were guided mostly by citizen petitions requesting improvements. Petitioners bore most of the cost of opening streets and erecting bridges, but the trustees defrayed some of the cost of building the town. During Lincoln's term, for example, four petitioners, including his law partner John Todd Stuart, asked for a stone culvert to help with drainage. The petitioners paid the first three hundred dollars and one-half of the remaining cost.[20]

Serving simultaneously as a state legislator, Lincoln missed most of the meetings of the town board. Still, his service to Springfield signified his growing stature in the town, and he was reelected a trustee when his partial term ran out. During Lincoln's tenure, the board's most important business was transforming Springfield from a town into a city. As a legislator, Lincoln was invaluable in boosting Springfield and helping to expand the town's powers as well as its limits. Under Lincoln's guidance, the legislature permitted the town to borrow up to one hundred thousand dollars and to order streets paved rather than simply waiting for citizen action. In 1840, Lincoln presided over a legislative committee that recommended the incorporation of Springfield as a city. Springfield could now establish a school system, set up a hospital, form fire companies, and light its streets. The charter election resulted in landslide support, and Springfield became the fourth city in Illinois, joining Chicago, Cairo, and Alton. The town board then presided over its own demise, dividing the town into four wards and overseeing the election of a mayor and four aldermen. On April 20, 1840, the new city council took office, dominated by Whigs eager to improve Springfield. Instrumental in the birth of the new city government, Lincoln left office to continue his work as a state legislator. By age thirty, Lincoln had gained experience serving the federal government as a postmaster, the state government as a legislator, the county government as a surveyor, and the town of Springfield as a trustee.[21]

As in most new communities, however, most of the work of town building lay beyond the scope of government. In the emerging tradition of self-help, the town's uprooted and ambitious youths joined together in a collective exercise in self-improvement. Young men poured in from rural areas, typically from their fathers' farms, and lost their connections to their families and communities. As compensation, they created a host of voluntary associations to occupy their time, educate themselves, and provide a boost on their way up the social ladder. Small towns and cities like Springfield, rather than the emerging metropolises, were the most likely to depend on voluntary associations to instill a fledgling sense of community in their newcomers. Government was limited, and nineteenth-century Americans were quintessentially "joiners" who organized to fill the void. An "associational culture" emerged in which private individuals banded together to address problems of general concern. By 1850, Springfield hosted forty-two different voluntary associations. Although their functions overlapped, the societies served five different purposes. Temperance societies, the first to form, appeared as early as 1831 and represented one-fourth of all the voluntary associations. Political clubs, founded by the parties during election campaigns, accounted for another one-fifth of the associations. Civic and benevolent organizations made up about one-sixth of them. Religious societies, the so-called church auxiliaries, included one-tenth of the total. Most important, however, were fraternal societies, which aimed at organizing young men, ostensibly for their own benefit. In the Springfield of Lincoln's youth, they represented one-third of all voluntary associations.[22]

Fraternal societies targeted young men who lacked families and other community ties and even permanent homes of their own. They promoted association with other youths and promised self-improvement and social advancement. Typically meeting during the evenings, they occupied workingmen in the otherwise idle hours between quitting time and turning in. The earliest fraternal organization on record was, naturally enough, the Bachelors' Club, reflecting the hefty proportion of unmarried men. First appearing in 1834, the Bachelors' Club met after work on weekday evenings in a public hall, which they probably rented. Paralleling the Bachelors' Club was the Cleopatra Club which apparently performed similar functions for young women. In 1835, the two clubs announced plans to merge into a single society. The pseudonymous secretary of the Cleopatra Club, Penelope Tenderheart, called the members into session in their sitting room "to take into consideration the proposition of the 'Bachelor's Club' for merging the two societies into one—generally and particularly." Unfortunately, the outcome of their deliberations, as well as the subsequent activities of the two clubs and their members, are lost in obscurity.[23]

Around the same time, a chess club appeared, which met at the law offices of John Todd Stuart and his first partner, Henry Dummer. Lincoln was an avid chess player who delighted in playing political friends and adversaries, and he may well have participated in the club. In 1841, a paramilitary group, the Lancers, was organized to fill in for the militia musters that periodically paraded down the main streets of smaller towns. The Lancers appealed to young men who were wealthy enough to own horses, allowing them to wear uniforms and hold offices, and permitting them, within a formal setting, simply to blow off steam. "A splendid company of Lancers is being formed in this city," a local editor noted. "A good rifle company ought to be added to the Lancers. Our spirited young mechanics are the men to form such a company." In fact, John Todd Stuart and Joshua Speed helped to organize the Springfield Artillery and Sharp Shooters. Two national organizations, the Masons and the Odd Fellows, also maintained lodges in Springfield. All these societies organized the town's "spirited young mechanics" and focused them on constructive rather than potentially disruptive activities.[24]

Self-help societies, almost by definition, focused on education. Springfield lacked public schools until 1856. Until then, private schools met irregularly and ran on "subscription," with students supporting their own teachers through tuition. The community's first school met in a log cabin in

1821, and as late as 1827 the village boasted but one schoolteacher. Five years later, Jonathan Wadley opened a badly needed school simply by announcing "School. The subscriber intends taking up school again on Monday next in his new school house, situated on the green, west of the methodist church—where he will pay every attention to the good conduct and advancement of his pupils." This was a "classical school" that taught Latin, Greek, and mathematics rather than more practical skills. Such impromptu schools abandoned any attempt at age grading and were usually segregated by gender. Mary J. Cowardin opened an "English female school" around the same time, offering Springfield's girls instruction in reading, writing, spelling, arithmetic, and the quintessential female accomplishment, needlework.[25]

By 1850, Springfield's schools included four subscription schools—the Springfield Academy for boys and the Springfield Female Seminary for girls, the Parochial School of the First Presbyterian Church, headed by two women, and the Classical School, taught by a minister. Many educated parents distrusted such irregular schooling and preferred to teach their own children. "Our *Dot*, we don't send her to school, never have, and don't intend to," lawyer Mason Brayman wrote to his sister in 1845. "We teach her at home." Like Abraham Lincoln, Dot Brayman learned to read by scouring the Bible. "She can spell with facility," her father boasted, "reads a chapter in the Bible every day." In the tradition of adult education, quite a few private schools taught business skills, such as handwriting, to upwardly mobile men and women. In 1846, for example, S. R. Wiley advertised a writing school for adults. "Ladies and gentlemen desirous of joining, in the hope of improving their knowledge in this necessary branch of education, are requested to make early application." Another school taught double-entry bookkeeping to merchants and their clerks. Public speaking was becoming a more essential skill than ever, and Thomas Lewis, a local merchant, opened an institute to cure stammering. Lewis promised "Terms moderate. (*No Cure, no Pay*)."[26]

Many adults, such as Lincoln, attempted to supplement their "accidental education" by attending lyceums. The lyceum movement began in Massachusetts in 1826 as an attempt to stimulate interest in the establishment of public schools. After Massachusetts adopted its common school system in 1836, lyceums began serving the broader purpose of diffusing knowledge among the general public. Across America, three thousand villages and towns formed lyceums that met weekly to present lectures and host debates on a wide variety of topics, practical and theoretical. Reflecting the determination of upwardly mobile youths to improve their own education, the Springfield Young Men's Lyceum formed in 1833 with founding officers who were mostly merchants and professionals, age thirty on average. They included quite a few of Lincoln's associates and friends—John Todd Stuart and Dan Stone, both lawyers and members of the legislative Long Nine;

Elijah Iles's clerk and future son-in-law and partner, John Williams; and Simeon Francis, editor of the *Sangamon Journal*. The Lyceum originally met monthly in a school room. The subject of the first debate was "Ought Capital Punishments to be abolished?" The lyceum met irregularly and in changing venues but remained the most important forum for intellectual debate in the town. A decade after its founding, the lyceum transformed from a self-help into a civic organization, the Springfield City Lyceum. During the 1850s, the group added a subscription library and reading room that charged a three-dollar annual membership fee.[27]

Far and away the most substantial fraternal organization was the Springfield Mechanics Union. "Mechanic" was a catch-all label that signified anyone who worked with his hands, and in 1840 fully 70 percent of all Springfield men were mechanics. Stretching all the way back to Benjamin Franklin's Mechanics Institute in Philadelphia, American workers enjoyed a long tradition of organizing for the sake of self-improvement. In April 1837, the same month in which Lincoln moved to Springfield, a group of mechanics met at the courthouse to address their concerns and created the Mechanics Institute. On July 4, they paraded through Springfield, escorted by "the military of the town," which included mostly mechanics, to lay the cornerstone of the new statehouse, which many of them were busy building.[28]

In 1840, the Springfield Mechanics Union received a charter from the state legislature, which Abraham Lincoln wrote as a representative of Sangamon County. As one of its first actions, in fact, the Union voted to "present Mr A Lincoln a vote of thanks for the passage of the act of incorporation." The charter organized the Union "for the purpose of improvement in literature, science, and the Arts, and for the mutual assistance of members and their families, in cases of sickness, accidental disability of body, or death." Like similar societies in other towns and cities, the Union served two functions, offering educational opportunities in the absence of free public schools and providing insurance benefits in the event of death or inability to work. Members paid a one-dollar initiation fee and monthly dues of twenty-five cents in exchange for a twenty-dollar death benefit, which essentially amounted to burial insurance. The widow and children of any member who died would receive between twenty and fifty dollars in compensation.[29]

Beyond its function as a simple "burial club," the Mechanics Union promoted self-improvement and steady habits. New members, who were required to exhibit "good moral character," had to be nominated by two other members and elected by secret ballot. No member disabled through "drunkenness, horse racing, voluntary fighting or any other vicious, improper or immoral act" would receive benefits. Finally, any member who "shall become an habitual drunkard" could be expelled. During its first few years, the Union built a new meeting hall and established a common school, hiring a schoolteacher at a salary of $250 and charging students two dollars per quarter. The goal was to establish "such low rates as would put it in the

power of every family in town to give their children the Benefits of education." By 1844, two hundred children were enrolled. A series of public lectures and addresses, delivered on the third Thursday of every month, aimed
at edifying not only mechanics but the community at large. The mechanics
invited Abraham Lincoln to deliver the inaugural lecture.[30]

During its seven-year lifespan, one-third of the town's manual laborers
joined the institute. They ranged in age from seventeen to fifty but were
twenty-nine years old on average. A few improved their lot, becoming
clerks, merchants, or shop owners, but four-fifths of the mechanics were
still practicing the same occupation a decade later. After a few years of
activity, the Mechanics Union fell on hard times. Financial problems and
resignations forced the Union to retrench. In the wake of the Panic of 1837,
the institute expelled sixteen members for failing to pay their dues. In 1846,
the school disbanded, and the Union began renting out its classrooms.
Mechanics' Hall became just another private subscription school, the lower
floor devoted to educating boys and the upper floor, girls. In the following
year, the Union sold its meeting hall, paid off its debts, forgave all its dues
and fines, and disbanded.[31]

Springfielders were indeed "joiners," creating four times the number of
voluntary associations as the typical community of its size. Among the
town's core residents, almost one-third served as officers of voluntary associations, some serving in several associations simultaneously. These inveter-
ate organizers represented the community's elite, the typical "town boosters" of the American frontier. Joiners had a long-term interest in building a
new and stable community. They were more than twice as wealthy as non-
joiners and were heavily professional in outlook. Two-thirds of Springfield's
professionals—lawyers, doctors, teachers, and ministers—were officers in a
society, club, or lodge, as opposed to only one-fourth of nonprofessionals.
Organizers were also heavily native. Only one-tenth of immigrants took
leadership roles in voluntary associations, in contrast to one in three native-
born Springfield men.[32]

Confirming their renowned commitment to community improvement,
Yankees predominated in Springfield's clubs. Southerners, in particular,
were underrepresented, reaffirming their reputation for independence and a
stronger commitment to individualism in solving problems and getting
ahead in life. As a pioneer wife and mother put it half a century later, "A
few persons must organize and sustain the net work of the civilizing
process." In the absence of a strong and intrusive local government, Springfielders made do with a host of impromptu organizations that attempted to
do just that. They sprang up as the situation demanded, flourished until
their work was done, and then receded again as the problem waned or government expanded to do the job. Within five years of Lincoln's arrival, the
first generation of rowdy Springfield youths had settled down in their societies and clubs to do the mundane work of making a living and building the

town. "Rarely a case of drunkenness is exhibited in our streets," Simeon Francis rhapsodized in 1842. "The riots that used to pain our citizens—fighting, blasphemy, reeling with drunkenness, formerly witnessed—do not now occur. There is a great, a pleasing change."[33]

Lincoln thrived within this effervescent young men's culture, developing what historian Robert Wiebe has labeled a "fraternal" sense of democracy. Gathering in small groups about the town, meeting late into the night to plan their campaigns, and dominating the public square, Springfield's lawyers and politicians created a subculture all their own. Four years after Lincoln arrived in Springfield, a newspaper editor described a typical street scene that found the most prominent young politicians and lawyers ambling up and down the sidewalks, standing in groups at street corners, and ducking into doorways to imbibe good fellowship. "Do you see that group of men at the Post Office, or at Irwin's corner, or at yonder Coffee House?" he asked. "Do you hear their conversation? Yes. It is that of friendship and entire confidence in the integrity of each other." The most important associations in Springfield, at least for the up-and-coming youths of the town, were clearly political. "Do you see them walking off after taking a friendly glass of exhilerating wine, arm in arm," he continued; "there goes Lincoln and Thomas—how friendly they meet Baker and Douglass—how social Speed and Calhoun; what openess Francis and Walters." As the editor concluded, with a shrewdness bred of his profession, these young Whigs and Democrats were now "old croneys" all.[34]

Beyond the state bar and the emerging Whig Party, Lincoln hardly needed to join a formal association. His infectious good spirits, his renowned independence, and of course his prodigious absorption in politics all set him apart from—and eventually above—the crowds of aimless young men that inundated Springfield. "He showed his superiority among them right away even while he was making rails," Stephen Logan remembered years later. "He was always independent and had generally a very good nature." As Joshua Speed put it pointedly, his friend Lincoln always assumed "a perfect naturalness. He could act no part but his own. He copied no one either in manner or style." The young men who gathered on winter nights in the storeroom below the double bed that they shared represented "a sort of social club without organization. They came there because they were sure to find Lincoln."[35]

The newly paved streets and sidewalks surrounding the town square were the natural milieu for the budding young lawyer and politician who had once entertained constituents by cracking jokes and telling stories as he split rails and harvested hay. A fellow lawyer in Springfield described the allure of the streets that was part and parcel of professional life for any rising young lawyer confronting the task of drumming up legal cases to the tune of five dollars apiece. "Lawyers were never found plodding in their offices," Milton Hay reminisced thirty-five years later. "Such an one would have waited long for the recognition of his talents—or a demand for his services." Like New Salem years before, Springfield was the perfect place for Lincoln to get out, meet people, and engage in spontaneous political debate. "There was scarcely a day or hour when a knot of men might not have been seen near the door of some leading store, or about the steps of the court house eagerly discuss[ing] a current political topic."[36]

This was the government Lincoln knew and even cherished. In 1855, Lincoln wrote two private memos to himself outlining the purpose of government. "The legitimate object of government," he pondered, "is to do for a community of people, whatever they need to have done, but can not do, *at all*, or can not, *so well do*, for themselves." Of course, the reverse was also true: whatever the people *could* do for themselves, they *should* do, without the interference of government. The "mixed" government that resulted combined the efforts of private citizens and public officials to accomplish worthwhile ends. Posing a succinct definition, Lincoln reasoned that "Government is a combination of the people of a country to effect certain objects by joint effort."[37]

Here, Lincoln, like other Whigs, clearly departed from the traditional Democratic conception of limited government—"That government is best which governs least." Transcending the people "in their separate, and individual capacities," government *required* a joint effort to succeed. Whigs celebrated associations of all kinds—corporations, societies, clubs, and movements—that could accomplish much more than the sum of all their parts ever could. The ultimate "joiners," one-fourth of Whigs in Springfield led voluntary associations, as compared to only one-tenth of Democrats. Rejecting the Jacksonian view of government as a necessary evil, Whigs praised it as a positive good. As one of Lincoln's colleagues summed it up, "Government *is* something—has positive virtues of its own." Whigs now had to decide what they—and their government—should do.[38]

CHAPTER 16

Always a Whig

Abraham Lincoln was one of the leading architects of the Whig Party in Springfield and throughout central Illinois. In his 1859 autobiography, Lincoln proclaimed proudly that he was "Always a whig in politics, and generally on the whig electoral tickets, making active canvasses." This statement signifies three different aspects of Lincoln's involvement in politics: his lifelong, personal commitment to Whig values and principles, his leadership role in organizing the party in Illinois, and his untiring contributions to the nuts-and-bolts activity of electioneering.[1]

Historians have often pondered why Lincoln became a Whig. The most obvious attraction, of course, was the party's program of economic development embodied in the American System of his idol Henry Clay. Westerners bent on developing their region's resources and improving its economic and social prospects naturally supported internal improvements, banks, and a protective tariff. Merchants, professionals, manufacturers, and commercial farmers all welcomed the arrival of the new market economy, with its cheap and reliable transportation routes, financial institutions, and commercial orientation.[2]

Whigs, in short, championed the rapid but rational economic development of the West. Democrats, by contrast, defended the traditional home economy of subsistence agriculture, family farms, and small shops. They represented farmers and craftsmen who lived beyond the reach of improved transportation and commercial institutions, such as banks, or those who felt left out and even threatened by the development of a new, national economic system. As historian Harry L. Watson summed up these differences, "Democrats were more popular in regions where the inroads of the Market Revolution were more limited, and more dreaded, than in more commercialized areas."[3]

But for many Whigs these literal "improvements"—roads, banks, and factories—were but a means to an end. Less tangibly, Whigs championed "improvement" in general—economic and social, moral and personal—

which they lumped together as "progress." They welcomed the rational, systematic marshaling of resources characteristic of both the American System and the emerging market economy. They therefore supported an active government, centralized control, and a collective direction of the American economy and American society. "For them," Daniel Walker Howe concluded, "real progress was not likely to occur automatically; it required careful, purposeful planning."[4]

That was the function of government—planning carefully for a future that promised social and moral, as well as economic, uplift. Government should intervene actively to foster development, to shape progress, rather than simply reacting piecemeal to provide the bare necessities of life to its constituents. At their first state political convention, for example, Illinois Whigs summed up their principles by endorsing Henry Clay's American System, advocating a national bank, government-funded internal improvements, and a high tariff to protect domestic industry from foreign competition. President Andrew Jackson's veto of the recharter of the Bank of the United States, in particular, was "calculated to bring distress and ruin upon thousands of our citizens, and especially those residing in the Western Country." With their own transportation needs in mind, Illinois Whigs demanded federal help in building roads and canals and, significantly, "in removing obstructions to navigation in our rivers." Finally, the new party supported federal "aid and protection of domestic manufactures," to boost the development of shops and factories that could compete with imports in producing goods for an emerging commercial market. Jackson's supporters in Illinois, by contrast, opposed the creation of a national economic system, as symbolized by the national bank, and welcomed the bank's destruction as a blow for liberty.[5]

The Democratic idea of progress was not the centralized development of transportation routes, cities, and factories but rather the extension of rural agriculture—family farming—farther westward. Democrats supported government actions to dispossess Native Americans, to reduce the price of public land, and to enable squatters to claim the land they farmed. They celebrated the traditional Jeffersonian ideal of independent farmers tilling the soil without interference from government, asking just enough help to acquire a secure homestead at a reasonable cost.[6]

The Whig vision of improvement through federally aided development was particularly appealing to Springfielders, who turned their city into a Whig stronghold within Illinois. Springfield was consistently regarded as an anomalous Whig island amid a sea of Illinois Democrats, who reviled Springfield as a "foul 'spot' upon the state." Whigs countered by celebrating the city as "a green spot in the great desert" of Democratic Illinois. Springfield Whigs typically counted on majorities of 60 percent in presidential elections, while even the neighboring precincts in rural Sangamon County routinely voted Democratic. Throughout the life of the Whig Party,

TABLE 16.1
The Presidential Vote in Springfield, 1832–1848

	Whig	Democratic	Free Soil
1832	45.0 %	55.0 %	
1836	65.7	34.3	
1840	63.2	36.8	
1844	57.6	42.4	
1848	59.8	38.0	2.1 %
Average	58.3	41.3	0.4

Illinois never gave a majority to a Whig presidential nominee, averaging nearly 60 percent in favor of Democratic candidates (see Table 16.1 "The Presidential Vote in Springfield, 1832–1848"). Springfield, however, reversed the pattern, casting almost 60 percent of its votes for Whigs. Central Illinois also sent Whigs, including Abraham Lincoln, to Congress for five straight terms between 1838 and 1848. Whigs dominated city government from the very beginning, electing the mayor and all four aldermen in the city's first election in 1840.[7]

Yet, like the rest of Illinois, Springfield began as a Democratic stronghold, voting for the immensely popular Andrew Jackson in 1828 and 1832. In 1832, the "Friends of Jackson," as they styled themselves, won a landslide in Springfield with 55 percent of the presidential vote. Soon, however, rapid urban growth and persistent, if oversized, dreams of commercial development boosted the Whig Party and its program of active improvement. Like much of the emerging West, Illinois lagged behind the older states in party formation and witnessed an era of personal faction between statehood in 1818 and the rise of Andrew Jackson. The state's first decade was a period of shifting personal alignments without party organization or formal nominations. As John Todd Stuart, a leading Whig and Lincoln's first law partner, later reminisced, "Ev[e]ry man became a candidate who wanted to—run on his own hook—spoke for himself." When future Democrat Peter Cartwright ran for the legislature in 1831, for example, five future Whigs, including John Todd Stuart, Pascal Enos, and Elijah Iles, ran a simple notice in the newspaper endorsing "our old friend" for the general assembly. Candidates mounted personal campaigns with little reference to national issues and organizations, leading voters to complain vociferously about "the common plan of electioneering adopted by candidates, of visiting almost every elector throughout the county or district, for the purpose of influencing their votes."[8]

Rather than promoting democracy, such a system seemed "degrading to the candidate and insulting to the elector; and prevents in a great degree our ablest citizens from suffering their names to be entered on the list of competitors for office." A Sangamon County farmer decried the candidates' preferred personal style of politics. "They will ride through the country, call on every man merely to see how his wife and children fare, and to ascertain his wants and wishes in relation to public measures," he complained. "The contests were mostly personal, and for men," Governor Thomas Ford reminisced in later years. "There are those who are apt to believe that this mode of conducting elections is likely to result in the choice of the best materials for administering government. But experience did not prove the fact to be so." As late as 1834, personal rather than partisan politics reigned in Springfield. "Political lines were not drawn at the late election in this State," the *Sangamo Journal* concluded, "and the results of that election cannot be considered as furnishing an unerring indication of public opinion in regard to the great political questions which now divide the country."[9]

The young Lincoln excelled at this face-to-face approach to politics. His legislative campaigning was simply part of the fabric of his homespun connections with ordinary people. "In those early days in Illinois, it was customary for candidates for public favor to travel through their districts and address their fellow citizens in public, and also to call at the homes and dwellings of their constituents," a fellow store clerk in New Salem remembered. "For this latter mode of canvass Lincoln was peculiarly gifted." His years of boarding, clerking, surveying, and working in intimacy with his neighbors now served him well. "It was in the family circle, around the fireside, no matter how humble and lowly, that Lincoln felt at home. He entered into conversation with the father and mother relative to their hopes and prospects in life, the schools, farm, crops, stock." Everyday concerns rather than momentous public issues endeared him to the voters. "Lincoln's experience in his early life had taught him that in the family circle, around the hearth stone, were realized and enjoyed the hopes, the aspirations and pleasures of our better natures."[10]

Throughout his four terms in the state legislature, Lincoln was a leading advocate of the Whig program of improvement. During his first term, he supported the creation of the State Bank of Illinois, headquartered in Springfield with branches in eight other towns. Lincoln sponsored local transportation improvements in Sangamon County, including state roads running to Springfield, such as the one that ran across Musick's bridge. Still dreaming of a water route linking Springfield and the Illinois River, he pushed for a canal running along the Sangamon River, which was approved but never constructed. More grandly, Lincoln supported construction of the Illinois and Michigan Canal and the Illinois Central Railroad. In 1836, he was reelected to the legislature as part of the "Long Nine" who represented Sangamon County. The Long Nine included seven southerners and two northerners. Five were lawyers, three were farmers, and one was an innkeeper. Lincoln was the tallest but youngest of the nine legislators, two months younger than his future brother-in-law, Ninian Edwards. Eight of the nine were Whigs, and they all supported the ambitious scheme of internal improvements on which the state now embarked. Sangamon County held a local internal improvements convention that called for a "broad, extended and judicious system of Internal Improvements" and sent fifteen delegates, including John Todd Stuart, to a statewide improvements meeting in Vandalia. The Vandalia meeting recommended an ambitious network of publicly financed canals and railroads, which the legislature promptly approved. The governor vetoed the plan, but the legislature overrode his veto. The improvements program proved disastrous, and Illinois spent the next forty-five years ruing the decision and repaying the enormous debt.[11]

National parties first began to intrude into Illinois politics around 1835, during the transition from Jackson to Martin Van Buren. Jackson supporters had always been divided into two factions, the "whole hog" Jackson men, who supported his policies in every detail, and the "milk and cider" faction, who admired Jackson personally but objected to parts of his program. Jackson's successor, Van Buren, was never popular in Illinois, even as vice president, because of his perceived eastern orientation. His vice presidential aspirations put new demands on Jacksonians for party regularity and provoked the first Anti-Jackson tickets in the state. As a nascent opposition party, Clay's supporters in Springfield sent a delegation to the state's first convention in 1832, which appointed an Anti-Jackson electoral ticket.[12]

Springfield's Whigs found a popular issue when the Democrats adopted their own convention system. In 1835, Democrats nominated Van Buren for president in their first national convention in Baltimore. Illinois Democrats planned a state convention to ratify his nomination, and Springfield Democrats held a caucus to choose delegates. Whigs quickly labeled the Democrats a "caucus party," warned of dictation by an "aristocracy of Office Holders," and derided Democrats as "Vannies," personal adherents to the unpopular vice president. "Heretofore, the voters of this County have been accustomed to vote as they please," the Sangamo Journal objected. "There are but few individuals here who have not, time and again, supported candidates of both parties; but this will be no longer permitted to Van Buren men." Often credited to Stephen A. Douglas, the convention system emphasized party regularity, put an end to intraparty competition, and—according to Whigs—stifled independent judgment. "The Convention System was adopted in all America about 1836," Stuart reminisced, and "it was a Van Buren Democratic measure." Many of Jackson's moderate or "milk and cider" followers in Springfield objected to Van Buren and bolted to the Whigs. The election of 1836 was a turning-point in Springfield, galvanizing Springfield Whigs in opposition to Van Buren and converting the city into a Whig stronghold.[13]

Within their state convention, Democrats divided, a substantial minority supporting Hugh Lawson White of Tennessee as the true heir to Jackson's throne. Balking at dictation by the "Van Buren Junto," Jackson men now left the party in droves. An "anti–Van Buren party" organized, holding a White meeting at the courthouse and adopting the Whig label for the first time, giving "Vannies" the opportunity to deride their opponents as "Whiggies." Even Ninian Edwards, Lincoln's future in-law and son of the state's first governor, defected to the opposition. "I believe neither in caucuses nor conventions—that all power emanates from the people," Edwards announced. "Originally in favor of General Jackson, I shall, at the next election, support the claims of Hugh L. White to the Presidency." Lincoln, too, seized this opportunity to side with the Tennessean and announced emphatically that "If alive on the first Monday in November, I shall vote for Hugh L. White for President." The opposition now organized the Union Anti–Van Buren Electoral Ticket, or simply Union Ticket. "The Van Buren party have given us no choice," these nascent Whigs insisted, "but to stand by our ticket—for we must have one—or suffer a defeat." In Springfield, White won a landslide victory with 66 percent of the vote. Democrats moaned that "the whigs of this county formed a ticket composed almost exclusively of Jackson men, and in that way revolutionized the county."[14]

In the wake of their first presidential victory in Springfield, Whigs crowed that "the Jackson men did not turn out and vote the Van Buren ticket. Though urged and importuned by all the means in the power of the party, these Jackson men could not be made to vote for Van Buren." Table 16.2 "Retention of Voters Between Presidential Elections in Springfield" displays the two parties' retention of voters between pairs of presidential elections. Between 1832 and 1836, the opposition achieved a nearly perfect continuity between Clay and White—94 percent. Significantly, however, little more than two-thirds of Democrats made the transition from Jackson to Van Buren, over 30 percent of them switching to White. This apparent failure of the Democratic convention system granted Whigs a commanding majority in Springfield that they never surrendered. The defection of Archer Herndon, father of Lincoln's future law partner and an original Jackson supporter, dramatized the bitterness provoked by the city's first experience with the convention system. "Can I not support Judge White, the faithful friend of the democratic party, without being the object of abuse?" he asked. Another Whig posed a more penetrating question: "If such caucuses become of common use, will they not have a tendency to rear up an aristocracy in this land of freedom dangerous to liberty?" Clearly, by provoking revulsion against conventions and aggravating an East-West division among Jacksonians, the election of 1836 solidified the Whig Party in Springfield. As Stuart concluded three decades later, "Sangamon Co was Democratic till 1834 and in 1836 & 7 it became Whig—Herndon & others went for *White* of Tennessee and this Settled Old Sangamon for nearly 20 y[ear]s." Support

---

TABLE 16.2

Retention of Voters Between Presidential Elections in Springfield

	Whigs	Democrats
1832–1836	94.3 %	69.6 %
1836–1840	94.0	82.0
1840–1844	93.7	94.3
1844–1848	95.6	92.5
Average	94.4	84.6

for the Whig Party peaked in 1836 in Springfield and in 1840 throughout the rest of Illinois, and so Springfield helped lead the way.[15]

Whigs continued to rail against the convention system and the parties they served but quietly perfected an organization of their own. They worked hard to counter their constituents' "anti-party" proclivities by educating them in the new logic of politics, in which parties, not candidates, won elections. "Does not every man know," they asked, "that if the Loco Focos elect their candidates, they will claim it as a victory of their party[?]" Individual aspirations had to give way to party loyalty: "Some of the whigs must be withdrawn from the convass and those only left to run the race who shall be most likely to succeed." In 1838, this strategy paid off when Whigs elected their first congressman. Lincoln's law partner, John Todd Stuart, narrowly defeated Stephen A. Douglas in a bitter contest, and Whigs held the seat for the next decade. As party lines began to filter down to the local level, however, some Whigs objected to "dictation" within their own party. Democrats fomented resistance to "the dictative course pursued by the Springfield Junto of lawyers and office holders" and supported an "Anti-Junto Whig" slate of legislative candidates, which attracted about one-tenth of Whig voters. The next year, Whigs forewent nominations for county officials, agreeing that they "would have been charged, and with some show of reason, of attempting to dictate to the voters who they should, and should not, cast their suffrages for."[16]

Whig dreams of economic growth disintegrated, and their corresponding fears of economic ruin materialized in the wake of Van Buren's election as president. A devastating depression broke out in the following year. Dubbed the Panic of 1837, the economic collapse was national in scope but hit hardest in the developing West. In May 1837, the State Bank of Illinois suspended specie payments, refusing to redeem its paper notes for gold and silver. Many Democrats, who had opposed the bank along with its paper money, rejoiced and welcomed a return to gold and silver coins. Whigs, however, defended the bank's depreciating paper currency as essential to the developing Illinois economy. The bank actually increased the number of notes in circulation, which propped up the state's economy for the next five years. At the same time, the impact of the panic on the newly adopted internal improvements system was devastating. After limping along for years, in 1841 Illinois defaulted on its interest payments. Whigs and Democrats now blamed each other for originating the internal improvements plan.[17]

In Springfield, the lingering depression boosted the Whig Party by solidifying demands for the provision of a sound currency and the opening of markets through improved transportation. Local merchants held a public meeting to defend the state bank's suspension of specie payments and to pledge confidence in the solvency of the bank. The merchants promised to continue accepting its bank notes as payment for their customers' debts. Soon, however, state bank notes had depreciated to 44 cents on the dollar, and merchants were accepting the notes only at a steep discount. Storekeepers who honored the notes at face value raised their prices to account for the difference. Already deep in debt, farmers, in particular, felt the pinch and demanded better transportation to open a market for their produce and a more stable currency to afford them higher prices when their grain did reach its market. One farmer bemoaned "the worthless and depreciated paper of the State Bank of Illlinois," and then demanded a stable currency and a new railroad. "It is a notorious fact, that when the smash in money affairs took place, almost every body was in debt." A few merchants tried to accommodate farmers by abandoning the cash system entirely. Democrat Thomas Lewis opened an Exchange Grocery that accepted "cash or country produce" as payment. Merchants began accepting wheat as payment for debts at the rate of fifty cents per bushel. After a decade of growth and economic development, Springfield had reverted to its original barter system. "Hundreds borrowed money—bought and improved farms *on credit*," lawyer Mason Brayman reported to his parents in 1841. "At this time money is scarce—the banks are winding up." Perhaps fishing for a loan or gift, he concluded that "A little money will go a great ways now."[18]

Whigs seized upon the economic collapse to preach against the evils of a hard money system and to advocate the reestablishment of a national bank. "[W]e are pretty nearly destitute of all currency—save Auditor's Warrants or State shin plasters," Simeon Francis reported six years into the crisis. "Now, our Farmers and Mechanics, and our Laborers—all men who do business, and have not money laid up,—can understand and feel the advantages of this hard money currency." Appealing for votes, he reported that corn was selling in the streets of Springfield for eight cents a bushel. "So much for a specie currency. Farmers, what do you think of it?" Some farmers began collecting wolf scalps in a mistaken belief that they would be accepted as payment for taxes. They were disappointed, however, when the legislature lowered taxes but made them payable only in gold and silver. "The People had collected State Bank paper for their taxes," Whigs moaned, "and out comes a Proclamation that the money shall not be received." In response, Democrats blamed the Whigs, and especially the famous Long Nine, for foisting the ruinous internal improvements system on the state. Democrats jokingly referred to the "Infernal Improvements." Whigs retorted, with some justice, that Democrats had supported the system with equal enthusiasm. "The Internal Improvement system of this State, in its origin, was not the work of party." Even Lincoln admitted on the floor of the legislature that the program was a "general wreck" that saddled the state with an "immense debt."[19]

In 1839, Springfield became the state capital, just as the second party system matured, and so the city began to play a special role in state-level politics, hosting the legislature, the statehouse, and both Whig and Democratic state central committees. In fact, although Whig organization was never effective outside central Illinois, Springfield Whigs now adopted the once-denounced convention system with abandon. After making their first regular nominations in 1837, their party newspaper printed the Whig ticket apologetically. "The candidates above named, are our political friends," the editor explained. "We think we wrong no one when we suggest to our political friends the propriety of supporting them." But just two years later, the same editor crowed that Illinois Whigs had hosted "the largest political Convention ever held in this State." Democrats sneered in reply that "The Federal party in this State have for many years past denounced the Democratic party for holding Conventions, calling them 'caucuses,' 'humbugs,' 'dictating assemblies,' &c. The sincerity of the Federal party may now be estimated by the People. That party has itself held one of these so much abused Conventions."[20]

Originally an opponent of the convention system, Lincoln eventually embraced it when it threatened to produce Democratic victories. He attended the Whig state convention as a delegate in 1839, won appointment as a presidential elector for Harrison in 1840, and served on the state's Whig central committee during that contest. This committee, all of whom lived in or near Springfield, wrote the most thorough "plan of organization" yet adopted in Illinois, announcing in a "secret circular" their intention to "organize the whole State, so that every Whig can be brought to the polls in the coming presidential contest." The Whig plan divided every county into "small districts," each organized by a subcommittee "to keep a CONSTANT WATCH on the DOUBTFUL VOTERS, and from time to time have them TALKED TO by those IN WHOM THEY HAVE THE MOST CONFIDENCE." Democrats promptly castigated the Whigs, including Lincoln, for "SENDING SECRET CIRCULARS all over the State, addressed to the little Whig factions in every town and precinct" and adopting the very convention system that they had once opposed. They dubbed the Whig central committee the "Springfield Junto."[21]

Lincoln continued to combine law and politics, depending on his law partner John Todd Stuart to help with the campaign, suggesting that Stuart send campaign literature to Springfield Democrats who were supporting Harrison. "Be sure to send me as many copies of the life of Harrison, as you can spare," he wrote Stuart in January. "And, in general, send me every thing you think will be a good '*war-club*.'" As a Harrison elector, Lincoln was responsible for campaigning not only in central Illinois but throughout the state, speaking at Whig rallies, barbecues, log raisings, pole raisings, and parades whenever and wherever his legal practice allowed. Probably because of his Kentucky roots, he was selected to make a grueling swing through southern Illinois to meet with Whig leaders at county seats and to debate Democratic speakers. "In 1840 Lincoln was one of the Harrison electors, and took a long trip, making stump speeches down south and over the Wabash," Stephen Logan recalled later. "It seemed to be supposed that his character and style of speaking suited the people down there more than up north." Lincoln and his opponents often traveled together from town to town, covering the same territory in debate after debate before different audiences. Democrats singled out Lincoln as one of the most aggressive practitioners of the novel party organization, a veritable "travelling missionary" for Harrison. They pictured him "ranging over the county for weeks before the election, begging, coaxing and commanding the voters to come out to the polls," along with "deputy and sub-deputy sheriffs, deputy and sub-deputy clerks of the circuit court, and the entire drove of officers and sub-officers, with other blue lights of the coon skin and Muskrat party." Overall, Lincoln devoted nearly three months to the campaign. He considered economic issues, especially banking, central to the campaign and published a pamphlet that circulated widely before the election. Along with other Whigs, he published a campaign newspaper, *The Old Soldier*, that countered Democratic attacks on the Whig nominee and provided fodder for lesser Whig speakers throughout Illinois. Election day found Lincoln still on the road and consequently unable to vote for Harrison.[22]

Democrats defended their own organization as "a convention of the People themselves to select their own candidates," while labeling the Whig organization "two or three sneaking fellows skulking into some dark corner at night." Whigs countered Democratic charges of a "midnight caucus" with the claim that "*They* set us the example of organization; and we, in self defence, are driven into it." Party organization was not yet complete, however. Whigs still emphasized issues—national issues—and presidential personalities rather than party lines, styling themselves at various times the Anti-Sub-Treasury party or the Harrison party. Emphasizing William Henry Harrison's stature as a general and pioneer, Springfield Whigs raised a log cabin, thirty-six by twenty-four feet in size, to dramatize their campaign for "Old Tippecanoe." Democrats lampooned such popular spectacles and campaign songs as Whig attempts to divert voters from real issues by dazzling them with entertainment. "What peculiar and transcendent merit is there in drinking hard cider, living in a Log cabin, riding in a canoe placed upon wagon wheels in a Prairie, or carrying a Turkey Buzzard upon a pole, which should make a man President of the United States?" they wondered. "Those who suppose the people of this country are so ignorant and degenerated as to be influenced by such contemptible and disgusting humbugs, underrate and insult their intelligence, virtue and patriotism." During this so-called Log Cabin Campaign, Democrats charged, "it was impossible for a quiet peaceable citizen to travel through the country without being constantly annoyed by the vulgar songs, which the most distinguished whig orators and the veriest blackguard grocery politicians were alike accustomed to chant." But the Whig campaign worked, winning a landslide victory of 63 percent for William Henry Harrison in 1840. In that year, Harrison attracted 94 percent of the White voters of 1836, while Democrats continued to lose support to the opposition. Only 82 percent of the original Van Buren voters in Springfield supported his reelection in 1840. Nearly one-fifth of Democrats defected to Harrison.[23]

With apparent justice, Democrats charged Whigs with hypocrisy for embracing party in fact but denouncing it in principle. "While the election is pending," they pointed out, "the Whigs cry 'No party! no party!' but when the election is over, they cry 'Party! party! We have got a majority.'" They also worried over a more ominous trend, the success of Springfield Whigs in transferring party loyalties from the presidency down to the local level. "The late election," they moaned, "turned exclusively on national politics in every part of the State." On the eve of the Harrison victory, Springfield Whigs held ward conventions in the city and nominated a mayor. "What object the leading whigs expect to gain by this policy we are wholly at a loss to perceive," a Democrat mused. "Is there any thing for the Mayor and Aldermen to do which partakes in the slightest degree of principles involving national politics?" Put even more bluntly, "we know of nothing they have to do in the way of making Presidents." The election of 1840 solidified the Whig majority in Springfield and brought party organization to the local level as well. As party loyalties trickled down from the presidency to the state, county, and city levels, Whigs discovered that mayors could indeed help elect presidents and presidents could in fact help elect mayors. Thanks to incessant Whig organization, party loyalties no longer faded between presidential elections but intensified at every level of government.[24]

National party divisions filtered down into town government as early as 1836, when Whigs and Democrats nominated Van Buren and White candidates for constable. By the time Springfield held its first city council election in 1840, the two-party system was firmly established, and a Whig won a landslide election as mayor. In the next year, the choice of Springfield's second mayor was hard-fought and produced the closest result in the city's history. The Democratic candidate, Thomas Lewis, defeated the Whig, William L. May, by a single vote, 223–222. May contested the election and

LINCOLN'S BROTHER-IN-LAW, NINIAN EDWARDS. AN EARLY POLITICAL
SUPPORTER, THE ARISTOCRATIC EDWARDS BROKE WITH LINCOLN OVER
THE SLAVERY ISSUE AND EVENTUALLY BECAME A DEMOCRAT.
Courtesy of the Illinois State Historical Library.

suggested that he and Lewis run the race all over again. When Lewis refused, the outgoing city council, which was entirely Whig, had to recount the votes and investigate the conduct of the election. The council deliberated for three days in William Watson's saloon, poring over the election records name by name and debating the validity of every vote. The council seized upon a technicality that required voters to live within their wards for at least ten days before the election. When they discovered that one voter "had changed his boarding house within ten days preceding the election," they threw out his vote. Overall, they invalidated twenty-eight of Lewis's votes as illegal and declared May, the Whig candidate, the new mayor. Whigs attempted to mute partisan repercussions by pointing out that "The election was not contested strictly on party grounds—large numbers of citizens did not vote for either of the candidates." The next year, they accused Democrats of playing politics by attempting "to make the Bank a question in the election of Mayor." Democrats had to acknowledge the impact of national divisions on city politics when they responded faintly that "Local causes governed some of the votes." But eventually they had to give in and admitted glumly that Springfield was "a whig city."[25]

Springfield's Whigs now campaigned vigorously to organize the entire state along the lines they had pioneered in Springfield, and after their humbling defeat in 1840, local Democrats followed suit. Whigs preached that "conventions are useful and necessary, and cannot be too strongly recommended. By them we allay every clashing interest, and every discordant feeling. By them we ensure unity of action and concert in every movement, and are enabled to present a single individual front at every contest." After building an elaborate and effective organization in 1840, Whigs were in an excellent position to contest the election of 1844. They began organizing Clay Clubs in 1842, two years before the presidential contest, to keep their followers mobilized between elections and to bring them out to vote in congressional and legislative elections. They watched approvingly as "country Whigs" began holding caucuses throughout the county. In Springfield, fifty Whig leaders, including Lincoln, held a meeting to nominate Henry Clay for president, a full two years before the election. The meeting pledged the "restoration of the Government to its original purity, and the people to their former state of prosperity and happiness" while denouncing President John Tyler's "treachery and imbecility" in failing to reestablish a national bank.[26]

Lincoln, who was retiring from the legislature after four terms, continued to campaign for Whig candidates and addressed the meeting. Clay's nomination by the Clay Club was timed to boost support for Whigs in the legislative elections that took place two weeks later. "The formation of this club *at that particular time*, had but one object, and that was to influence the August election," Democrats sniffed. "The candidates of the Junto for the Legislature and for Sheriff were about being *used up* here, and the *herculian* strength of Mr. Clay was sought to help them along." As bankruptcy notices continued to fill the newspapers, Whigs hammered at national issues, promising that only a national bank and a protective tariff could restore prosperity. "Now, as ever," they reiterated, "the whigs of this County, and of this State, hold as most sacred principles, the duty of the Government to provide a *uniform and sound currency for the People*, and to secure, by an *adequate tariff, protection to the industry of the country*." Whigs were learning to ride presidential coattails into office.[27]

As one of the chief architects of the Whig organization, Lincoln had to submit to its dictates. After serving four consecutive terms in the state legislature, in 1843 Lincoln made a bid to replace John Todd Stuart in Congress. Sangamon County Whigs held a meeting to choose between Lincoln and one of his closest friends and political allies, Edward Baker. "Our ears are stunned here, just now," Democrats gloated, "by the din of the Whigs, concer[n]ing Lincoln and Baker, as to which shall go to Congress from this district." They predicted that Springfield Whigs would "choke down the throats of the whigs of Tazewell, Morgan, Scott, &c. whatever candidate they please, however bitter he may be to swallow." Explaining the new system of nominations for the sake of party unity, Democrats reasoned that "Whichever candidate is defeated, is to withdraw altogether," to assure victory for a candidate from Springfield. Faced with the choice of Lincoln or Baker, Democrats concluded simply that "it would be difficult to decide which is the bigger rascal." When Baker won the nod over Lincoln, Democrats characterized the Whig caucus as a "slaughter pen" and expressed mock sympathy for its victim.[28]

After nominating Baker for Congress, the Sangamon County Whigs included Lincoln among the delegates sent to the district convention. "We had a meeting of the whigs in the county here on last Monday to appoint delegates to a district convention, and Baker beat me & got the delegation instructed to go for him," Lincoln reported gloomily to Joshua Speed. "The meeting, in spite of my attempt to decline it, appointed me one of the delegates; so that in getting Baker the nomination, I shall be 'fixed' a good deal like a fellow who is made groomsman to the man what has cut him out, and is marrying his own dear 'gal.'" The infighting proved pointless, because John J. Hardin won the nomination instead of Lincoln or Baker and eventually went to Congress. Hardin was one of Lincoln's distant in-laws. The grandson of the Kentucky militia general who lent his name to Hardin County, Lincoln's birthplace, John J. Hardin was Mary Todd's third cousin. Still, in one of his few exhibitions of lukewarm support for a Whig, Lincoln failed to vote for Hardin in the congressional election. Lincoln had to accept, however reluctantly, the decision of the very caucus that he had helped to establish.[29]

On the eve of the 1844 presidential contest, one Whig gloated that "The whigs are holding meetings very often now a days." Early in 1844, the

Sangamon County Whig central committee debated the question and officially endorsed conventions as "the most democratic mode of selecting candidates." Their rivals had to agree, responding to the Whigs' Clay Clubs by forming local organizations of their own in every county—calling them Democratic Associations because, unlike the Whigs, they did not yet have a presidential candidate to endorse. "Let us bury all local questions," one advised, "and come up once more with our democratic colors nailed to the mast head." They simultaneously vilified the well-oiled Whig machine that they now hoped to unseat. "The Junto (a score or two of deeply interested politicians of Springfield) have most extraordinary facilities to carry out their plots and plans," they warned. "They have sheriffs, collectors, surveyors and assessors with their deputies and sub-deputies, and a score of constables riding through the county constantly." So extensive was their organization that "they know how every man in the county has voted for years—they know who have split their tickets at a former election—they thus know who to 'talk to,' who to watch and who to squeeze or relieve by their foul apparatus of *justice*, kept in motion by a dozen corrupt lawyers." Democrats focused on winning the city and county as well as the White House, lamenting that "The Whigs have carried every thing in this county as usual," including "every officer from Congressman down to constable." The Whigs had perfected local organization and won, and the Democrats now concentrated on playing catch-up.[30]

Popular appeals climaxed in a deafening crescendo during the 1844 election. In January, Springfield's Whigs organized the coming campaign, announcing a slate of seven presidential electors, including Lincoln. They established a state central committee of five members, four of whom lived in Springfield. Each congressional district had its own central committee, as did each county. The Sangamon County Whig committee included Lincoln's brother-in-law William S. Wallace and his future law partner William H. Herndon. The committee enunciated six "Whig Doctrines," which included a national currency, protection for domestic industry, economy in government, noninterference of officeholders in elections, and a commitment to one presidential term. "The Whigs have a great central committee in this city, whose power appears to be unlimited," Democrats warned. "They are to determine in what districts the whigs are to run candidates for congress, and in what districts there are to be no candidates." Democrats lampooned Whig leaders as a corrupt clique standing in the way of democracy. "Lincoln, another member of the Junto," they crowed, "is a greater man than Baker. He is our jester and mountebank, and tells us stories, to make people laugh. We have had him appointed a candidate for Clay elector. This we hope will buy him off from becoming a candidate for Congress."[31]

As he had in 1840, Lincoln launched another speaking tour of central Illinois, sandwiching debates in between legal cases on the circuit. In February, William Butler reported that "Baker, Lincoln, Logan and Stuart are making speeches every night at some one of the precincts in our County to crowded houses; we confidently expect to give 1000 majority in Sangamon County for Clay." Sensing Lincoln's destiny for higher office, Democrats singled him out for vilification. A Sugar Creek voter, who obviously resented the intrusion of Springfield Whigs into local affairs, lampooned a Lincoln speech in his district. When local farmers asked him to explain the impact of a high tariff on prices, "Lincoln came near having a chicken fit, and a choking to death; but fortunately some water was procured and he got over it."[32]

In 1844, Democrats infused two new issues into the campaign in an attempt to distract voters from the region's economic ills. One of these issues was immigration. Throughout America, the arrival of Irish and German Catholic immigrants produced a backlash among Protestants. A rising group of "nativists" strove to restrict immigration, lengthen the process for obtaining citizenship, and prevent immigrants from voting. At midcentury, almost 30 percent of Springfielders were immigrants. The largest single ethnic group were the Irish, who represented about one-tenth of Springfielders. Germans were second at just over 8 percent of the population. In 1841, when John Todd Stuart ran for reelection to Congress, Democrats warned that a faction of Whig nativists were supporting Stuart and that he was working on their behalf in Congress by presenting a petition to revise immigration laws. Stuart, indeed, became a conspicuous nativist during the 1850s.[33]

Whigs and Democrats agreed that foreign-born voters were the mainstay of the Democratic Party in Springfield. Democrats framed this predilection in a positive light, portraying themselves as "the protectors of the rights of aliens." By charging that "The strong, robust, able-bodied Irishman and German who enters this State, ploughs our prairies, fells our forests, opens our roads and digs our canals, is, according to this faction, unfit to enjoy the rights of a freeman," Democrats could appeal simultaneously to immigrants and workers. Whigs fended off such claims as "demogogical" and "the last resorts of a depraved and desperate faction," charging Democrats with "herding" recent immigrants to the polls on election day. But, confirming Democratic rhetoric, Whigs consistently decried the admission of immigrants to the polling place. In 1844, Democrats launched a general accusation of nativism against the Whigs, labeling them "Native Whigs." Significantly, even Democrats acknowledged Lincoln's tolerance for immigrant voters. A series of nativistic riots in Philadelphia prompted a public meeting in Springfield at which Lincoln attempted to mute nativism within his own party by expressing "the kindest, and most benevolent feelings towards foreigners." Democrats acknowledged such tolerance as "the sincere and honest sentiments of *his heart*; but they were not those of *his party.*" Attempting to blunt the impact of Lincoln's speech, Democrats reported that "Mr. Lincoln also alleged that the whigs were as much the friends of foreigners as democrats; but he failed to substantiate it in a manner satisfactory to the foreigners who heard him."[34]

A second Democratic issue was the annexation of Texas, which had won independence from Mexico in 1836. Southern Democrats hoped to make Texas a slave state in an effort to extend the institution of slavery farther westward. In Springfield, as in other communities throughout the West, "Texas meetings" organized to call for annexation. When a Texas meeting in Springfield advocated the immediate annexation of Texas, both Lincoln and Baker spoke against it. Democrats crowed with delight when James K. Polk of Tennessee, a leading advocate of annexation, won their nomination. "A real enthusiasm has been kindled by the news of an Annexation Democratic candidate for President," they reported. They smeared Baker, the Whig candidate for Congress, as the "Santa Anna of Whiggery" for his opposition to annexation. Baker "has no mercy for Texas—and he sneers at the idea of annexation." Whigs countered by supporting the annexation of Oregon instead, urging the settlement of the Northwest and its eventual annexation as an antidote to the "Texas Humbug." During the campaign, however, their nominee, Henry Clay, dealt a major blow to this strategy when he endorsed the eventual annexation of Texas. Springfield Democrats gleefully identified the three key issues in the campaign as Texas, Oregon, and the National Bank, putting the traditional Whig economic program last.[35]

As the election neared, national issues fell by the wayside to make way for symbolic shows of Whig and Democratic strength. Democrats set out to raise a hickory pole to honor their political icon, Andrew Jackson—"Old Hickory." In July, they promised to raise a hickory pole 150 feet in height. "Let every Democrat attend;" they urged, "let the young men bring their swee[t]hearts, and the old men their wives and daughters." Whigs responded by labeling Polk supporters "Polkats" and pledging to raise an even taller pole, made of ash in honor of Henry Clay, the "Hero of Ashland." Aided by members of the Mechanics Union, Springfield Whigs assembled a pole 214 feet and 6 inches long, reputed to be the tallest in the nation. The Whig pole was eight-sided, prompting Democrats to lambaste the "eight faces" of their opponents: "Federalism—Whigism—Abolitionism—Antimasonicism—Nativeism—Tylerism—Bankism—Humbugism."

According to Whig accounts, the ash pole raising attracted a crowd of more than five thousand. Tragedy struck, however, when the pole collapsed and crushed two mechanics, killing one and leaving the other critically injured. Whigs held a ceremony to bury the victim, presided over by Charles Dresser, the Springfield minister who had married Lincoln and Mary Todd two years earlier. The local Clay Club joined the Mechanics Union in paying for the funeral. To avert another disaster, Dresser traveled personally to

St. Louis to buy a stronger rope to help raise a second pole, which Whigs now dubbed the Liberty Pole.[36]

Whigs attempted to turn the tragedy to their own benefit by insinuating that Democrats had plotted to cut the ropes. Democrats countered that Whigs had callously continued their ceremonies in disregard to the injured and dying mechanics. In the days that followed, the mechanics who had raised the pole began to fall ill, and Whigs charged that Democrats had poisoned the well on the public square. Democrats scorned the editor of the *Sangamo Journal*, Simeon Francis. "What an infamous slanderer is this Francis of the Journal," the editor of the Democratic newspaper raved. "If he was a man of any character, people out of the State would suppose us all to be fit inmates for the penetentiary. As it is, he is so base, mean, and contemptable, as to render every thing that emanates from his pen, a perfect abortion." Tempers calmed when the truth proved far less sinister. By accident, a boy had dropped a package of fly salve for horses into the well a week or so before the pole raising. Charges of malice abated, and the second pole went up without incident. But the events of that long, hot August dramatized the fever pitch of partisan politics in the midst of a hard-fought presidential campaign.[37]

The Democrats' efforts to match the Whigs' organization, along with their new drumbeat of nativism and Texas annexation, paid off. They improved their showing in the 1844 election, taking 42 percent of the vote in Springfield and carrying the state for James K. Polk. Significantly, their partisan continuity in Springfield at last topped that of the Whigs. Slightly more Democrats than Whigs stayed with their party between 1840 and 1844. The frenetic election demonstrated that both parties could embrace, perfect, and defend convention systems of equal effectiveness, form local organizations down to the precinct level, and retain more than 90 percent of their voters between presidential elections. Lincoln himself worked hard to hone and defend the convention system even when it disappointed his own political aspirations. Democrats could boast that they fielded "candidate against candidate" from the top of the ticket down, while Whigs trooped to the polls "as a band of brethren, and not like guerilla parties." The election of 1840, in which Henry Clay captured 48 percent of the vote, represented the high water mark for Whigs in Illinois. Whigs never won a statewide contest and never elected a governor.[38]

Party organization filtered down slowly from the presidential level, with personal allegiances giving way to nascent party ties in 1836. Presidential elections, and particularly the election of 1836, were more important in altering and solidifying partisan cleavages than local elections and even congressional contests. Democrats were indeed first to organize in central Illinois, but a revulsion against parties, as symbolized by the new convention system, and against Van Buren provoked rapid development of an organized opposition. As a result, Democrats toned down their convention system, giving Whigs a chance to organize Springfield. The Whigs seized it, and the election of 1836 was key to their success, strategic Democratic defections granting them an experienced core leadership. By the time former Jackson men such as Ninian Edwards and Archer Herndon returned to the Democratic fold, as they eventually did, Whig organization was complete. Democrats copied the Whig plan of organization and rebounded by 1844 but still found themselves heavily outnumbered by Whigs in Springfield.

CHAPTER 17

So Little Headway
in the World

Lincoln's rapid rise upward leveled off during his first half-decade in Springfield, languishing in something of a plateau. While the western economy was slowing and then collapsing, Lincoln was experiencing a period of missteps and indecision reminiscent of his initial years in New Salem. Leaving behind a village that was rapidly disappearing, Lincoln relinquished old friendships and began all over again at the bottom of a new and loftier social scale in Springfield. His pessimistic letters to Mary Owens exuded a genuine disillusionment with the urban social whirl that he had long coveted but from which he now felt excluded. "This thing of living in Springfield is rather a dull business after all, at least it is so to me," he confided. "I am quite as lonesome here as ever was anywhere in my life." Feeling the sting of his own want of refinement, the young lawyer focused on his practice and shunned social situations. "I've never been to church yet, nor probably shall not be soon. I stay away because I am conscious I should not know how to behave myself." Always impatient to advance, he complained to Joshua Speed that "I am so poor, and make so little headway in the world, that I drop back in a month of idleness, as much as I gain in a year's rowing."[1]

Feeling at sea in Springfield society, Lincoln launched a series of dramatic if sometimes misguided gestures to gain notice in the community. His most noble effort was a speech before the Springfield Lyceum on "The Perpetuation of Our Political Institutions." Lincoln chose this opportunity to demonstrate his ability to rise above partisan politics and, as a rising statesman, call for an end to the social disorder that threatened to engulf his nation and his community. Recounting instances of mob violence that repeatedly violated public order, Lincoln decried "the increasing disregard for law which pervades the country" and "the growing disposition to substitute the wild and furious passions, in lieu of the sober judgement of Courts." Mobs targeted African Americans, immigrants, abolitionists, and even gamblers. Lincoln spoke in the shadow of the most notorious anti-abolitionist riot in American history, which occurred in nearby Alton, Illinois, in 1837. Abolitionist Elijah Lovejoy published an antislavery newspaper in St. Louis but was forced to flee across the Mississippi to Alton in fear of his life. There he continued to publish his newspaper, taking aim at St. Louis across the river. In November 1837, an antiabolitionist mob attacked the printing press and killed Lovejoy as he tried to defend it. Lincoln did not mention Lovejoy by name but condemned the mobs that "throw printing presses into rivers [and] shoot editors."[2]

The remedy, Lincoln declared, was a simple reverence for the law. "Let every American, every lover of liberty, every well wisher to his posterity," Lincoln enjoined, "swear by the blood of the Revolution, never to violate in the least particular, the laws of the country; and never to tolerate their violation by others." Respect for the law should become "the *political religion* of the nation." Lincoln's call for law and order won him praise from influential Springfielders but held several unintended implications. Portending his attitude toward the antislavery movement in later years, Lincoln declared that "bad laws, if they exist, should be repealed as soon as possible, still while they continue in force, for the sake of example, they should be religiously observed." In the long run, Lincoln's "reverence for the laws," taken to the extreme, encouraged a lifelong moderation on the subject of slavery. In the short run, Lincoln was on the verge of providing several personal examples of "wild and furious passions" giving way to "sober judgement."[3]

Mary Todd arrived in Springfield in the spring of 1837 to visit her eldest sister Elizabeth Edwards and her husband Ninian. There she joined her older sister Frances, who was living in the Edwards home as a boarder while socializing and looking for a husband. Ensconced in their house on Aristocrat's Hill, the Edwardses introduced Mary to Springfield society, and throughout the summer she engaged in the dances, parlor games, and political debates that enlivened the new state capital. A bachelor of the period noted "the many parties, Balls sociables, accidentals, and candy pullings and last and least the sewing societies" that animated the town. Caught up in this social scene, Mary Todd returned to Lexington quite reluctantly in the fall.[4]

During her absence, her sister Frances made a good match, marrying one of the town's leading physicians, William Wallace in 1839. Wallace was born in Lancaster County, Pennsylvania, and earned a medical degree in Philadelphia. At age thirty-four, he relocated to Springfield and practiced medicine for the next twenty-five years. A steady Whig, Wallace never sought public office, but he tirelessly organized local Whigs, and he became one of Lincoln's closest personal confidants. When Lincoln was a congressman, he helped Wallace secure a federal appointment. The Lincolns named their third son William Wallace Lincoln—the beloved Willie, Mary's favorite. Like several of Lincoln's in-laws, Wallace became a Democrat during the 1850s, but at Mary's behest President Lincoln offered him a minor federal appointment during the Civil War, as paymaster of volunteers in Springfield.[5]

Both Frances Todd and William Wallace were boarders, and the couple moved into the Globe Tavern, a local hotel and boarding house, to begin their married life together. Frances Todd's departure from the Edwards home opened a spot for Mary, who promptly moved to Springfield. Historians have fiercely debated the circumstances of Lincoln's and Mary Todd's courtship, as well as the couple's engagement and marriage. Social customs among the middle and upper classes of the day dictated that courtship take place within the aegis of the woman's family and with their permission. In this patriarchal society, suitors "came calling" only after receiving an invitation from one of the men in the household. The Lincoln-Todd courtship had the blessing, at least initially, of Elizabeth and Ninian Edwards and took place in the parlor of their imposing two-story brick home. "Many courting couples throughout the nineteenth century continued to seek consent from the young woman's parents," notes historian Karen Lystra. "Scant attention, however, was paid to the young man's family. Nineteenth-century men enthusiastically supported the value of familial independence." Thomas and Sarah Lincoln never met Mary Todd, either before or after her marriage to their son. The Edwardses, however, felt a responsibility to make a good match for Mary Todd, just as they had helped Frances Todd marry well and would eventually help Mary's younger sister Ann find an equally suitable husband. They probably would have considered any romantic union acceptable as long as it contributed to the Todd family's strategic quest to forge broader social and economic connections. Ninian Edwards later admitted that he had "policy reasons" for encouraging the courtship, hoping to bind the promising young Lincoln more firmly within the family's social and political orbit.[6]

Like most of the eligible women in the town, Mary Todd entertained multiple suitors, including Lincoln's political rival Stephen Douglas. Sometime during 1840, however, Abraham Lincoln and Mary Todd discreetly made plans to marry. Courtship was growing in complexity during this era of family transition. With the decline in both parental authority and economic motivations for marrying, couples expected to cultivate an emotional intimacy during an extended period of betrothal, a process of "disclosing and explaining the self," in Lystra's words. The male ideal of dignified self-composure prompted women to seek long, drawn-out engagements to allow more time to explore their prospective husband's character and personality. Glib and emotional, Mary Todd divulged an outpouring of confidences to her suitor, but Lincoln was hesitant and possibly unable to reciprocate. "Mary was quick, lively, gay—frivalous it may be," her sister Elizabeth Edwards explained. Lincoln, however, "Could not hold a lengthy Conversation with a lady—was not sufficiently Educated and intelligent in the female line to so," she concluded. Yet Lincoln was fascinated with the lovely young woman who poured out her heart to him. "I have happened in the room where they were sitting often & often Mary led the Conversation," her sister reminisced. "Lincoln would listen & gaze on her as if drawn by some Superior power, irresistably So: he listened—never Scarcely Said a word."[7]

Despite Lincoln's fascination, however, the couple had a falling out in early 1841. After Lincoln's death, William Herndon concocted a compelling but dubious story in which his law partner left his fiancee standing at the altar on January 1. In later years, the Edwardses claimed that they changed their minds about Lincoln and discouraged the match. More likely, both members of the couple felt unready to marry, and the parting was a mutual if not amicable decision. Courtships of the period were typically fraught with anxiety. "Men hesitated to commit themselves to marry—even at some date in the indefinite future," historian Ellen Rothman has observed, "until they felt emotionally ready and could be sure of acquiring the necessary financial resources." Lincoln—and Mary Todd—undoubtedly felt unsure on both counts. "When the courtship drew to a close," according to Rothman, "even the most confident women were gripped by intense anxiety." Courting couples typically underwent a crisis precipitated by the prospective bride's demand for a clear sign of an emotional commitment on the part of her suitor. "Women threw large and small obstacles in the path of the courting male," Lystra concludes, "to measure the depth and intensity of his romantic love." Biographers have suggested that Lincoln's genuine interest in another woman and Mary Todd's feigned attentions to another man strained the relationship and led to the breach.[8]

For a year and a half, from early 1841 until late 1842, Lincoln and Mary Todd maintained a cordial distance. Mary wrote to a friend that Lincoln "deems me unworthy of notice, as I have not met *him* in the gay world for months." Longingly, she confided that "I would that the case were different, that he would once more resume his Station in Society." At the same time that the couple broke off their engagement, Joshua Speed moved back to Kentucky, and Lincoln's isolation provoked his second and final "crazy spell." Grieving over his broken engagement in a way that was far more reminiscent of his feelings for Ann Rutledge than for Mary Owens, Lincoln confided in John Todd Stuart that "I am now the most miserable man living. If what I feel were equally distributed to the whole human family, there would not be one cheerful face on the earth. Whether I shall ever be better I can not tell; I awfully forebode I shall not." Hinting at suicide, Lincoln concluded that "To remain as I am is impossible; I must die or be better, it appears to me." He neglected his duties in the legislature, was described as ill, and finally missed an entire week. Feeling the sting of his sister-in-law's unhappiness, perhaps, Ninian Edwards described Lincoln as "crazy as a *Loon*." Around this time, Speed embarked on a tentative courtship of his own, and Lincoln paid him an extended visit between August and November 1841,

ELIZABETH EDWARDS, MARY TODD'S SISTER. SHE PLAYED THE ROLE OF
MATCHMAKER FOR BOTH OF HER SISTERS BUT SOON REGRETTED THE
MATCH THAT SHE MADE FOR MARY.
Courtesy of the Illinois State Historical Library.

giving the best friends a chance to commiserate. When Lincoln returned to Springfield, he occupied himself in advising Speed about his romance. The exercise was cathartic, allowing Lincoln to share his inner thoughts and urge a reconciliation under the pretense of offering advice to a friend. He need hardly have reminded Speed that "you know the Hell I have suffered on that point." By February 1842, Lincoln could confidently announce that "I am now fully convinced, that you love her as ardently as you are capable of loving," while perhaps believing the same thing of himself.[9]

Lincoln's reconciliation with Mary Todd occurred unexpectedly yet characteristically within a political setting. Encouraged by the wife of Simeon Francis, editor of the *Sangamo Journal*, the couple began meeting at the Francis home, away from the by now disapproving eyes of the Edwards family. During the summer of 1842, the two heedlessly hatched a plot to carry their mutual political interests into the pages of the *Journal*. After the collapse of the State Bank of Illinois in February, the state auditor, James Shields, issued a circular refusing its bank notes as payment for taxes. Whigs pilloried Shields, a rising young Democrat, and now Lincoln and Mary Todd joined in. Together with Mary's best friend, Julia Jayne, the couple published a series of letters in the *Journal* that lampooned Shields. Known as the "Rebecca Letters" after their pseudonymous author, they caricatured Shields with a wit that only Abraham Lincoln could summon. When Shields demanded the true identity of the author, Lincoln gallantly took sole credit for the insults to preserve the women's honor. Shields promptly demanded that Lincoln defend his own honor and challenged him to a duel.[10]

In his defense, Lincoln had not condemned dueling during his Lyceum speech, but his behavior during the Shields affair did little to preserve the reverence for the law that he had tried to instill in his audience. Dueling was endemic within the early American political system. Before parties emerged to mobilize voters on behalf of candidates, political leaders had to depend on their personal reputations to win office. Any challenge to their honor posed a grave threat to their ability to lead. Dueling was a traditional method of defending one's honor while also displaying courage. During election season, political duels, as they were known, were a common campaign strategy. Amid the Second Great Awakening, religious reformers attacked dueling as a relic of barbarism and an unwholesome feature of democratic politics. After Alexander Hamilton's famous death at the hands of Aaron Burr, dueling began to disappear in the North. The practice lingered in the South, however, and America's most famous duelist was Andrew Jackson, whose enemies charged him with killing a dozen men in duels. With the decline of deferential politics and the rise of more popular campaigning, dueling faded as a strategy for rallying support and winning office. Ironically, mobbing—a more popular form of political violence— arose to take its place.[11]

In central Illinois, the predominantly southern political heritage lingered and promoted political violence. Illinois outlawed dueling in its constitution, so premeditated political violence was rare in Springfield. Spontaneous brawls, however, were ubiquitous, and Lincoln's Kentucky in-laws and political associates were some of the biggest offenders. In 1836, Whigs and Democrats held a debate at the courthouse that degenerated into a brawl that saw Ninian Edwards pull a pistol on a Democratic rival. During their campaign for Congress two years later, John Todd Stuart and Stephen Douglas scuffled during a debate and fought in a local tavern. "They both fought till Exhausted," a witness remembered, "grocery floor Slippery with Slop." Whigs reported that Douglas was "brawling over the District" in search of votes. Two years later, during the Harrison campaign, Douglas caned Simeon Francis. "We cannot pass a corner of the street but sounds of altercation assail our ears," a prophetic Springfielder wrote to the *Sangamo Journal*. "We cannot look into the columns of our village papers but we meet with abusive and violent communications. These signs forbode war,—duels must be the result."[12]

The most notorious act of political violence in the city's history occurred in 1838. Jacob Early, a physician and Methodist minister who was Lincoln's captain during the Black Hawk War, met a political rival, Henry Truett, in the parlor of the Globe Tavern in Springfield. Truett demanded to know whether Early had written a set of resolutions calling for his removal from office. When Early refused to answer, Truett drew a pistol, and Early picked up a chair to defend himself. Truett shot Early dead and was charged with murder. In defending the killer, Lincoln argued that the chair was a lethal weapon and that Truett therefore shot Early in self-defense. Lincoln won the acquittal, but the episode should have driven home the perils of penning anonymous communications. Just a year before Lincoln's confrontation with Shields, a duelist received two balls from a double-barreled pistol and nearly died.[13]

The impending duel with Shields therefore presented a real threat to both men's lives. Lincoln's initial reaction was to decline the challenge, noting that he was "wholly opposed to duelling, and would do anything to avoid it that might not degrade him in the estimation of himself and friends." Ironically, Dr. Merryman, who had attended the earlier duel victim and saved his life, urged Lincoln onward. Lincoln selected broadswords and seems to have had every intention of defending himself. "I did not intend to hurt Shields unless I did so clearly in self-defense," he later confided in Herndon. "If it had been necessary I could have split him from the crown of his head to the end of his backbone." To maintain his "reverence for the law," however, the lawyerly Lincoln agreed to cross the Mississippi River to Missouri, where dueling was legal, to face off against Shields at the appropriately named Bloody Island. At the last moment, John J. Hardin, a fellow Whig leader and Mary Todd's relative, convinced Shields to withdraw the challenge in a compromise that allowed both men to save face. But the "duelling business," as Lincoln termed it, was infectious. Shields soon challenged William Butler, one of Lincoln's seconds, to what Lincoln labeled "duel No. 2." A third duel loomed when one of Shields's seconds challenged Dr. Merryman. Like duel No. 1, however, the succeeding affairs ended peaceably.[14]

As biographers Jean Baker and Douglas Wilson made clear, the Shields Affair was instrumental in bringing the quarreling couple together again. Writing the Rebecca Letters resembled the kind of close collaboration that would draw Lincoln and Mary Todd together and preoccupy them during their married life—advancing Lincoln's political career. Their publication empowered Mary Todd by granting her a political voice that she never enjoyed before and never would again. Finally, the duel allowed Lincoln to demonstrate his emotional commitment to Mary Todd by defending her honor in a way that left his own intact and in fact enhanced it.[15]

With the crisis of commitment overcome to Mary's satisfaction, the couple married in November 1842. Weddings of this period tended toward simplicity. Large church weddings became fashionable only with continued urbanization, and honeymoons were unknown until transportation improved. "Most couples were married by a minister, at the bride's home, in the presence of a small group of friends and relatives," according to Ellen Rothman. Episcopal minister Charles Dresser presided over the hastily arranged ceremony in the parlor of the Edwards home, where the couple had spent so many afternoons in courtship. James Matheny stood up for Lincoln, and Julia Jayne was bridesmaid for Mary Todd. "Mr and Mrs Edwards, knew nothing of the wedding until the morning of the day," Julia Jayne's brother William recalled. "Only meager preparations could be made on so—short notice & only a few friends were present." Reacting, perhaps, to the sight of Abraham Lincoln accepting the challenge of married life, Matheny found the wedding "one of the funiest things to have witnessed imaginable—No description on paper can possibly do it justice." The event filled Lincoln with a far different emotion. A week later, he was back at work, concluding a letter to a client by observing, "Nothing new here, except my marrying, which to me, is matter of profound wonder."[16]

CHAPTER 18

A Matter of Profound Wonder

On the night Abraham Lincoln was elected president, he walked to the telegraph office in Springfield, Illinois, to follow the election returns. Mary Lincoln stayed at home and in fact locked him out of the house. According to reminiscence, Mary told Abraham "that if he wasn't at home by 10 o'clock she would lock him out. And she did so. But, Mr. Lincoln said that when she heard the music coming to serenade them she turned the key in a hurry."[1] A witness later recounted the scene as Lincoln walked home: "Across the street 10,000 crazy people were shouting, throwing up their hats, slapping and kicking one another." Through it all, "down the street walked Lincoln, without a sign of anything unusual."[2]

This story, like so many others depicting the Lincolns' sometimes stormy marriage, casts both members of the couple in all-too-familiar roles. Mary is the headstrong, even shrewish wife who resents her husband's absence from home even at this transforming moment in both their lives, and indeed the life of the nation. As on so many similar occasions during their marriage, Abraham turns to humor both to mollify his wife and to bear her reproach. Despite her demeanor, he remains "in fine spirits" and retails the anecdote the next day before a group of well-wishers. He makes the episode public, portraying himself as the victor in this domestic struggle, announcing that "he had a good joke on his wife." Lincoln left for the telegraph office as a private citizen but returned as president-elect, followed by a crowd of well-wishers whom Mary had to let into her home. Mary, by contrast, is humorless, attempting to keep her transgression private, pointedly warning her husband, "Don't ever tell that again."[3] Like most anecdotes that feature both Lincolns, this one portrays Mary negatively and Abraham favorably, and, like some others, it may be apocryphal. Still, the story rings true, and the image of the locked door provides an apt metaphor for the kind of middle-class marriage the Lincolns, like many other nineteenth-century couples, led together.

Abraham Lincoln courted and married Mary Todd during an extraordinary and unique period in American history. The early nineteenth century witnessed a dramatic transition within the institution of marriage, and within the American family itself. During the 1830s, a dynamic, new social class began to emerge in America's urbanizing Northeast. Practicing the growing range of nonmanual occupations increasingly available in commerce and the professions, a new middle class aspired to self-improvement and social reform, emphasized self-control, and defined and defended stark new gender roles, especially within marriage. Above all, this emerging Victorian culture drew sharp lines between public and private spheres. The public world outside the home, the world of work and politics, was men's domain. Inside the home, however, amid the family, women ruled. The Lincolns, who were fairly typical middle-class Victorians, observed these gender roles throughout their marriage. Outside the Lincoln home at Eighth and Jackson, Abraham Lincoln reigned supreme and roamed freely. Once he stepped inside his own house, however, culture demanded that he defer to Mary Lincoln. This is precisely why Abraham Lincoln went out alone to the telegraph office on election night and why Mary Lincoln stayed at home and felt empowered to lock the door behind him.[4]

In the America of Lincoln's youth, families had been "cooperative," resting on a strong economic foundation in which all members of the family—men, women, and children—played a productive role. Most American men were farmers, 42 percent of them as late as 1900. A smaller minority of Americans practiced manual, nonfarm trades but usually within rural settings, villages and small towns. In this preindustrial era, most husbands and fathers worked at home, typically on farms. Most food and goods were produced at home in an elaborate system of home manufacturing. Women played a crucial role in this subsistence economy, supervising dairy and poultry operations, making soap and candles, and above all producing cloth.[5]

In Lincoln's Illinois, most families continued to work together in this way until the Civil War. In 1840, two years before the Lincolns married, fully 80 percent of all men living in Sangamon County were farmers. Another 15 percent practiced manufacturing and trades, and most of those were self-employed. In 1840, only one-sixth of the county's manufacturers and craftsmen worked in shops. The rest, presumably, worked in or near their homes. Overall, more than 95 percent of the county's adult males performed manual labor. Fewer than 5 percent engaged in commerce or a profession, as Lincoln the lawyer did, and therefore qualified as members of the emerging middle class. In Springfield, the state capital, three-fourths of all workers performed manual labor, mostly in building, transportation, and skilled trades. The young Lincoln fit right into this familiar, family-based economy.[6]

The economic boom of the 1830s, however, promoted rapid industrialization and urbanization and fostered an emerging middle class. The budding factory system began calling men from farms to cities and drew them away from their homes as industrial workers, managers, merchants, clerks, and professionals. Traditional family patterns changed, and western cities now hosted a growing middle class of nonmanual workers. Farm families stopped producing most of the goods they consumed, growing cash crops for sale on a commercial market and, in turn, buying the necessities they had once made at home. Significantly, industrialization came first in the textile industry, freeing farm women from their endless rounds of spinning, weaving, dyeing, and eventually even sewing the fabric that clothed their families.[7]

In Illinois, factory goods gradually freed farm wives and daughters from the never-ending cycle of home production. The first manufactured goods appeared in general stores in Chicago and St. Louis during the 1830s, and farmers began trading for them on their twice-yearly trips to market. In old age, for example, one Illinois farmer's daughter remembered her father returning from Chicago with the first factory-made cloth she had ever seen. He announced triumphantly, "Wife and daughters, store away your loom, wheels, warping bars, spool rack, winding blades, all your utensils for weaving cloth up in the loft. The boys and I can make enough by increasing our herds and driving them to Chicago for sale." Men could now supply cloth to their wives and daughters. Freed from the constant drudgery of spinning and weaving, "The girls clapped their hands with delight."[8]

Textile production increasingly left the home for the factory. Emblematic of the shift from production to consumption was the growth of a local textile industry. In 1832, a mill opened eleven miles west of Springfield to card, spin, and weave wool. Families could now shear their sheep, take their wool to Richland Creek to be carded, spun, and woven into cloth, and then sew it into clothing at home for their own use. Soon, John Hay Sr., father of Lincoln's future White House secretary, opened a cotton factory in Springfield. He exchanged spun cotton for raw cotton for a fee payable in cash. Hay employed working-class boys ages ten to twelve, along with blind horses, to run his mill. In this fashion, the work of textile production passed from middle-class girls to working-class boys, from homes to factories.[9]

By the time Lincoln arrived in Springfield, much of the work that families traditionally performed, such as making clothes, had left the home. One-fifth of the businesses in town worked just to clothe Springfielders. Four carding machines freed Springfield's women and girls from the endless drudgery of carding wool before spinning it into yarn. But there were also nineteen dry-goods stores, where wives and mothers could buy spools of yarn and thread to do their own weaving or purchase bolts of "store-bought" cloth to sew into garments for their families. They could also patronize seven tailors to have garments custom-made for special occasions. Two clothing stores stocked the first "ready-made" wear in the region, freeing women from the last step in cloth production, sewing their families' clothing. A handful of hatters and shoemakers worked to round out the wardrobe. By 1845, ready-made clothing was manufactured in Springfield. Clothier E. R. Wiley advertised that "I have the most experienced Cutters and workmen constantly employed," and promised that "Those who favor me with a call, will be convinced that it is in their interest to buy their garments of me, rather than go to the trouble of having them made up, after the old fashion." By 1850, Wiley employed one hundred workers, ninety of them women, who manufactured 150 garments a day with the help of a steam engine. Instead of helping their mothers sew at home, working-class girls now worked in shops for wages.[10]

Food production underwent a similar transition. During Springfield's formative years, families raised their own food in their backyards. Even as a flourishing lawyer, for example, Abraham Lincoln kept a backyard garden and milked his own cow. The town, however, soon established a farmer's market to provide fresh produce from the countryside. A market master rented stalls to local farmers, who sold their produce three days a week. Later, private markets appeared around town to supply middle-class housewives. The city's butchers, for example, reasoned that "their shops were more convenient for customers than the market house, located as they were in different parts of the city." When Lincoln moved to Springfield, there were already six groceries. Before long, only the working class continued to grow their own produce, laboring after hours in what became known as the "poor man's garden." Middle-class women now fed their families through a daily round of "marketing."[11] Springfield housewives had stopped producing goods for their families and were now largely consumers.[12]

In 1850, Springfield shops produced shoes, hats, gloves, soap, candles, furniture, flour, baked goods, candy, and twenty-five other necessities for local consumption. During the next year, ice deliveries began to supply middle-class families with refrigeration. In 1854, the city started to lay down gas lines for lighting and eventually cooking. In the same year, a Springfielder confirmed that "it is comforting to see the long strings of market-wagons, these fresh spring mornings, pouring in with their stores of produce for the city. Still more comforting it is, to notice the pots of nice butter, the baskets of fresh eggs, the barrels of fat hams, the bushels of dried fruit, and the bundles of choice fixens, as they are driven up and invitingly paraded before our stores and market rooms." Housewives now bemoaned a whole new set of middle-class inconveniences and modern problems. In 1855, for example, John Todd Stuart's wife complained that "We were expecting the gas men, to put the pipes in the house today, but they did not come." As a western state, Illinois was late in industrializing, but distinct middle and working classes began to emerge during the 1830s and 1840s, just as Abraham Lincoln and Mary Todd arrived, courted, and married. Most noticeably, agriculture declined as the mainstay of the state's economy. In 1840, farmers represented 85 percent of the Illinois workforce. By

1850 they had declined to 65 percent, and by 1860 they represented a minority, just 39 percent. Meanwhile, the middle class—practitioners of nonmanual occupations, primarily merchants, professionals, and public officials—grew steadily in numbers. They represented a mere 4 percent in 1840 but increased to 5 percent in 1850 and nearly doubled to 9 percent of the state's employed men by 1860. At Lincoln's election to the presidency, about one-tenth of Illinois families were middle class.[13]

Middle-class men left home to go to work every morning—a revolutionary process labeled the "separation of home and work"—and therefore gained status as "breadwinners" in their families. Married women stayed home, and their primary role was to maintain the household for the benefit of their husbands and children. Housekeeping became a science, and middle-class women turned nervously to a spate of new publications—domestic manuals, as well as novels and magazines—to learn its arcane mysteries. Cooking, in particular, became the new standard by which husbands and the public now judged the quality of any woman's domestic skills. New standards of cleanliness occupied housewives during the long days while their husbands labored in factories, shops, and offices. Above all, housewives were expected to spend their husbands' salaries wisely.[14]

Because women were not paid for their work, the work they did became a duty, the "domestic duty." The new ideology of separate spheres (work and politics vs. home and family) portrayed men and women as fundamentally different. Men were by nature aggressive, competitive, and shrewd, preparing them to compete in the new ruthless world of work. Women, by contrast, were assumed to be gentle, loving, and sensitive creatures, enabling them to nurture their husbands and children. These gender differences complemented each other and bound husband and wife together in a new "companionate" marriage founded on emotional attachment. Industrialization therefore reshaped not only the family but also gender roles within the family. The home became a refuge for middle-class men who expected their wives to keep house and nurture them when they came home from work. Middle-class men and women were now perceived to be exact opposites so that each could perform their complementary roles within the family.[15]

Abraham Lincoln was a classic middle-class professional. Unlike the men of Springfield's small upper class, middle-class men were self-educated and self-made. In 1850, the average age of middle-class men was forty-one, but thirty-eight for their working-class neighbors. After all, middle-calss men had to invest considerable time and effort to climb the occupational ladder, as Lincoln did so successfully. Lincoln was forty-one years old in 1850. Middle-class men were four-and-a-half times wealthier than manual workers, owning about $3,500 in real property as compared to $758. Such wealth reflected the new rewards that attended nonmanual labor and funded a novel lifestyle characterized by conspicuous consumption. The Lincolns reported no real property in the Census of 1850, reflecting the deep indebtedness that Abraham Lincoln incurred during his fledgling efforts to enter the middle class as a merchant in New Salem. By 1860, however, the Lincolns had rebounded, reporting enough real wealth to place them in the 90th percentile in Springfield.[16]

The real hallmark of the middle class, however, was not real property—land—but personal wealth, the physical trappings of genteel refinement. Lincoln never showed much interest in land and owned very little by contemporary standards. By the 1850s, however, Lincoln's five-dollar fees had grown considerably, including the five-thousand dollar fee that he won from the Illinois Central Railroad, and the Lincolns were wealthy. In 1860, they reported enough personal wealth to put them in the 99th percentile among their peers. Abraham Lincoln ranked sixteenth out of 2,225 white adult males in terms of personal wealth. Middle-class households also included more nonfamily members, 1.2 on average. They were more likely than working-class families to depend on a live-in servant to help with housekeeping and child rearing. The Lincolns routinely kept servants to help maintain their household and raise their sons. Lacking a daughter to help her meant that Mary Lincoln was more dependent on servants than most women. "By the way, you do not intend to do without a girl, because the one you had has left you?" Lincoln asked Mary while in Congress. "Get another as soon as you can to take charge of the dear codgers." In 1850, the Lincolns employed one servant, which was average—an immigrant girl from Ireland. By 1860, after their family and income had grown, they kept two servants, a boy and a girl, both from Illinois, to help Lincoln and his wife, respectively, keep up their middle-class home.[17]

Although industrialization was a largely northern phenomenon, southern birth by itself did not preclude upward mobility. Middle-class men hailed equally from the North and South. They were, however, heavily native-born. Thirty percent of native-born couples were middle-class, as compared to only 20 percent of immigrants. This distinction affected all immigrant groups—Germans, Irish, and English—about equally. The Lincolns, of course, were both native and southern-born. Not surprisingly, middle-class men played a prominent political role in Springfield. More likely to hold public office, they essentially ran the city. One in seven middle-class men held office, as compared to a mere one in twenty-five working-class men. Put differently, a majority of officeholders (57 percent) were middle-class. The Whig Party, and later the Republicans, championed the values that gave rise to industry, cities, commerce, and the middle class itself. As a result, Whigs were heavily Victorian. One-third of Whigs were middle-class, as compared to only one-fourth of Democrats. In fact, two-thirds of the middle class were Whigs. Both the Lincolns were ardent Whigs, and Abraham Lincoln was a leading Whig officeholder. Finally, most of the people Abraham Lincoln knew were also middle class. Springfielders who can be linked with Lincoln in some way through surviving records were 51 percent middle class, twice the proportion of the population at large. Those who cannot be linked with him were only 20 percent middle class.[18]

Raised to run a household and to consume rather than to produce, Mary Lincoln was poised to fulfill her role as a housewife to perfection. The Todds were one of the most eminent families in Kentucky, founders of Lexington, at the heart of the lush Bluegrass country. Mary Todd's father was a lawyer, state assemblyman and senator, investor, land speculator, and slave owner. In their fourteen-room house on Lexington's Main Street, production was the work of domestic slaves rather than family members. Freed from the performance of innumerable household duties, Mary Todd spent a decade at private girls' academies to learn how to supervise an aristocratic home and family. In this upper-class enclave, girls' most important function was to serve their families by marrying well, not to produce but rather to reproduce and raise children. The Todds educated Mary in the finest girls' boarding school in Lexington, one that they had helped to found. Her intellectual attainments fitted her to marry a rising professional man and help him strive to get ahead in a middle-class world of sometimes ruthless competitiveness.[19]

Like many newlyweds, the Lincolns spent their first year of married life together as boarders. They rented the same room in the Globe Tavern that Frances Todd Wallace had occupied with her husband after their wedding. Eight dollars a week paid for their room, all of their meals, and their washing as well. Accustomed to the splendor and social status embodied in the Edwardses' two-story brick home on Aristocrat's Hill, Mary Lincoln suffered a precipitous decline when she moved into the eight-by-fourteen-foot room in the Globe. After five years of sleeping with Speed, boarding with the Butlers, and sometimes stretching out on a bed in his law office, however, Abraham Lincoln undoubtedly viewed the room he shared with Mary as a welcome improvement. For the first time in his life, at age thirty-three, Lincoln was the head of a family.[20]

As a very public place, the Globe violated Victorian standards, forcing the couple into a close intimacy with the neighbors, with whom they shared meals in the common dining room below. Run by George Washington Spottswood, reputed grandnephew of the first president, the tavern was connected to a livery stable and accommodated up to thirty guests at a time. The Globe was a decidedly masculine environment with strong political overtones. Located a "few rods west of the State House," it was a Whig hangout during the legislative season and a polling place for elections. Lincoln was familiar with the Globe Tavern through the "jollifications" that he and his cronies held there after their political conventions. In 1837, local Whigs held a banquet there to congratulate the Long Nine for bringing the state capital to Springfield. After one noteworthy bash, according to Democrats, "It took Spotswood half of the next day after the revel to *clean the house*." The Globe also housed quite a few visitors to town, mostly men, a few families, and travelers visiting the state capital from Vandalia, Jacksonville, and even St. Louis. Abraham Lincoln undoubtedly enjoyed the male camaraderie of the tavern, but during his frequent absences Mary likely cringed at the mere thought of entering the dining room by herself.[21]

Couples who married in Springfield typically waited for two years before starting a family. Mary and Abraham Lincoln, however, were older than the average bride and groom, Mary by four years and Abraham by six, which may have encouraged them to hasten childbearing. At any rate, they wasted no time. Three days shy of nine months after her wedding, Mary Lincoln bore the first of four sons. Lincoln's ancestors traditionally named their eldest sons after their paternal grandfathers. Thomas Lincoln, for example, honored his own father by naming his first son Abraham.[22] As in so many other respects, Lincoln violated this family tradition when the newly married couple decided not to honor Abraham's father but rather Mary's.

Most Americans by this time had abandoned the practice of naming sons after grandfathers. The naming of Robert Todd Lincoln was therefore

THE GLOBE TAVERN. THIS BOARDING HOUSE WAS THE FIRST HOME OF ABRAHAM AND MARY LINCOLN AND THE BIRTHPLACE OF ROBERT TODD LINCOLN.
Courtesy of the Illinois State Historical Library.

THE LINCOLN HOUSE AT EIGHTH AND JACKSON. THE LINCOLNS TURNED IT
INTO A SHOWCASE OF MIDDLE-CLASS RESPECTABILITY AND A
COMFORTABLE HOME FOR THEIR FOUR SONS.
Courtesy of the Illinois State Historical Library.

a quaint tribute to the family patriarch and was likely an attempt on Mary's part to ingratiate herself with her father, which she had attempted to do repeatedly after the death of her mother. Abraham Lincoln, of course, felt no similar impulse and quietly acquiesced in this decision that overlooked his own father. Symbolically, the name signified the boy's inclusion in the prestigious Todd family, which Lincoln undoubtedly considered a superior legacy for his son. If the decision was strategic, it was certainly judicious. Before the end of the year, Robert Todd trekked to Springfield and gave his blessing, along with generous financial support, to the fledgling family. Filled with pride, according to family tradition, he intoned, "May God bless and protect my little namesake."[23]

A few months after Robert's birth, the couple moved into a more comfortable home, renting a cottage with four rooms on Fourth Street. A year and a half after their marriage, the Lincolns at last purchased a house. Located at the corner of Eighth and Jackson, the family called it home for the next sixteen years. The one-eighth acre, like much of the rest of Springfield, belonged originally to Elijah Iles, who sold it to Gershom Jayne, Springfield's first physician. Jayne was a speculator who held onto the land until 1839, when the Reverend Charles Dresser decided to build a new house to accommodate his wife and two children. After building the five-room, one-and-a-half-story cottage, however, Dresser fell into debt and decided to sell the house to repay it. In May 1844, the Lincolns cobbled together some of the gifts from Robert Todd and a piece of land they owned with Stephen Logan and purchased the Dresser house for fifteen hundred dollars. Lincoln's Todd family connections, not his own, made possible this final transition to middle-class respectability. Only six blocks from the center of Springfield, their new home nevertheless stood on the edge of town. Behind the house sat a woodshed, where Lincoln put his years of experience as a rail-splitter to good use by chopping wood for the fireplaces that heated the home and the kitchen stove that cooked their meals. On past the privy lay an open field in which Lincoln pastured his horse and the family's milk cow. The house was a convenient walk from Abraham Lincoln's law offices and the grocers, druggists, and dry-goods stores that Mary Lincoln frequented on her daily rounds.[24]

With a wife, son, and home of his own by age thirty-four, Lincoln had completed his long climb to independent adulthood. Less tangibly, however, the Lincolns' transition to the middle class was less than perfect. The couple often violated the very expectations that lay at the foundation of their Victorian marriage. Put simply, the new middle-class values set an impossible standard that all too often both Lincolns failed to meet. In 1842, just four months before the Lincolns married, a Springfield newspaper published an article entitled "The Happy Match," instructing middle-class husbands and wives in the new ways of married life. Clearly borrowed from an eastern newspaper, the article depicted a middle-class husband, Harry Hemphill, introducing his new wife to the secrets of a happy marriage. "Now," Harry told his wife, "it's my business to bring money into the house, and your's to see that none goes foolishly out it." In this respect, the Hemphills proved a perfect match. "He chose her, first because he loved her, and in the second place because he knew she was sensible, economical, and industrious—just the reason which influences a sensible man in his choice now." Significantly, "he thought it best that each should have a distinct sphere of action." In tune with the doctrine of separate spheres, "His business called for his whole attention; he wished, therefore, to pursue it undistracted by other cares," while "Her duties being all domestic, she was able to compass them better by turning her whole attention to them." Above all, their home was a reliable refuge from the turmoil of public life. "There he sought repose after the toil and weariness of the day, and there he found it. When perplexed and low spirited, he retired thither, and amid the soothing influence of its quiet and peaceful shades, he forgot the heartlessness of the world." In short, "While Harry was prospering in his business all went like clock work at home."[25]

Abundant evidence suggests that all did not "go like clockwork" in the Lincoln home, and historians have long debated the extent to which the couple enjoyed a "happy match."[26] For a variety of reasons, middle-class mores interfered with a happy match—and happiness itself—within the Lincolns' marriage. As an emerging ethic of family life in America, Victorianism remained untested and ambiguous. Newly married couples, especially women, were unfamiliar with its demanding dictates, its arcane domestic duties, and its unnatural gender roles. For this reason, a flood of advice literature appeared, including etiquette books for women and success manuals for men, to prepare wives and husbands for the challenging gender roles they must now fulfill. On New Year's Eve, 1846, for example, Abraham Lincoln stopped at a general store in Springfield and bought Mary two domestic manuals, "Miss Leslie's Cookery" and "Miss Leslie's Housekeeper." The timing suggests an attempt to improve Mary's housekeeping skills as part of a New Year's resolution. (Whether Abraham presented the books as a gift or bought them at Mary's direction is an intriguing but moot question.) Further, middle-class marriages were a minority. By 1860, the middle class included only one-tenth of Illinois families and only one-fourth of families in Springfield. Far too often, middle-class status was precarious. Between 1850 and 1860, three out of ten middle-class families in Springfield fell in status and slipped backward into the ranks of the working class. Maintaining a middle-class marriage, even in Springfield, was problematic.[27]

Above all, Abraham and Mary Lincoln approached their middle-class marriage from two opposing perspectives. When he married, Abraham Lincoln was just leaving the traditional folk economy in which he had been raised. He found himself *rising* into the new middle class in Springfield, taking a definite step upward. By contrast, when Mary Lincoln married, she *fell* from her perch within the comfortable upper class. As one of Mary's relatives explained, "Mrs. Lincoln came from the best of stock, and was raised like a lady. Her husband was her opposite, in origins, in education, in breeding, in everything."[28]

The middle class therefore proved a social and cultural gulf that separated the Lincolns from other families and from one another. Both Lincolns tried hard to lead a respectable middle-class marriage. This was, after all, the ideal for Americans of their age. But both often failed. Abraham Lincoln continually reverted to the traditional patterns of family life in which he had been reared. Mary Lincoln consistently attempted to reproduce the upper-class lifestyle that she found so familiar. The middle class might have become a middle ground uniting the couple who hailed from such starkly different backgrounds. Instead, it too often became a battleground, because neither partner ever successfully fulfilled the exacting strictures of the new middle class. Above all, Abraham Lincoln's vocation—law—and his avocation—politics—continually blurred the boundaries between public and private that were central to the new middle-class existence.

As a wife and mother, Mary Lincoln's foremost duty—as the fictional Harry Hemphill reiterated—was to keep a home for her husband. A lawyer who knew Lincoln made this point sympathetically: "At home he had at all times the watchful and efficient attention of Mrs. Lincoln to every detail of his daily life as regards those things she had learned were most essential to keep him at his constitutional best." As a result, "Mrs. Lincoln, by her attention, had much to do with preserving her husband's health. She was careful to see that he ate his meals regularly, and that he was well groomed. He was not naturally inclined to give much thought to his clothes, and if Mrs. Lincoln happened to be away from Springfield for a few days on a trip out of the city, we were pretty sure to be apprised of her absence by some slight disorder in Lincoln's apparel and his irregularity at meal-time." This positive contribution, however, could acquire a negative cast, as when an acquaintance heard Mary snap, "Why don't you dress up and try to look like somebody?" In short, middle-class status *empowered* Mary Lincoln but also *burdened* her with nearly complete supervision of the Lincoln family. Further, her authority ended at the front door at Eighth and Jackson. Like many middle-class couples, the Lincolns led "divided lives" together. Abraham enjoyed tremendous prestige within the public sphere that diminished the moment he stepped inside his own home. Mary, by contrast, enjoyed a domestic authority that dissolved the moment she stepped outside her own front door.[29]

For his part, Abraham Lincoln understood, without fully accepting, this middle-class separation of spheres. Like other ambitious middle-class men, Lincoln felt more at ease in his office than in his home. A colleague reminisced that "Lincoln, when in this little office, was more easy in manner and unrestrained in all respects than at any other place I ever saw him." Away from home, Lincoln—unlike Mary—had the run of the city: "He would leave to call at Diller's drug-store, or at one of the dry-goods stores, to meet a friendly group in the counting-room, or more often to meet friends at the State House, that was directly across the street from his law office, to visit the offices there, or spent an hour or two in the State Library."[30]

Like many men of his era, Lincoln clearly valued this public sphere over the private one. At one point, he conceded that "I myself manage all important matters. In little things I have got along through life by letting my wife run her end of the machine pretty much in her own way." This is a clear, indeed shrewd, assessment of the newly emerging gender roles. Still, Lincoln's "little things" were the family's domestic affairs. His "important matters" took place outside the home, in the masculine world of work and politics.[31]

All too often, Abraham Lincoln violated Victorian standards. As William Herndon pointed out, "Such want of social polish on the part of her husband of course gave Mrs. Lincoln great offence." Mary's role was precisely to enforce the very standards that her husband so frequently enjoyed flouting. "It is therefore quite natural that she should complain if he answered the door-bell himself instead of sending the servant to do so,"

MARY TODD LINCOLN. TAKEN IN 1846, THIS IS THE FIRST PHOTOGRAPH
MARY TODD LINCOLN EVER SAT FOR. IT IS THE COMPANION TO
THE PHOTOGRAPH OF HER HUSBAND ON THE COVER.
The Lincoln Museum, Fort Wayne, Indiana

one of her relatives explained, "neither is she to be condemned if, as you say, she raised 'merry war' because he persisted in using his own knife in the butter, instead of the silver-handled one intended for that purpose." To his credit, Lincoln was acutely aware of his own lack of polish and avoided awkward social situations. As Herndon put it, "For fashionable society he had a marked dislike, although he appreciated its value in promoting the welfare of a man ambitious to succeed in politics." In short, Lincoln valued middle-class mores but never mastered them. Indeed, "the consciousness of his shortcomings as a society man rendered him unusually diffident." He therefore masked his own awkwardness with a whimsical humor that seemed like indifference. One evening, Lincoln answered the front door in his shirtsleeves and admitted two women, "notifying them in his open familiar way, that he would 'trot the women folks out.'" Of course, Mary's anger was "instantaneous." Still, Lincoln seemed to enjoy flouting the genteel values that Mary cherished but that he could never master. In the White House, for example, Mary caught Abraham feeding a cat with a gold fork at a dinner party. In response, Lincoln reasoned that "If the gold fork was good enough for Buchanan I think it is good enough for Tabby."[32]

When his humor failed him, Lincoln's best recourse was to retreat, which the new separation of spheres facilitated. During social occasions at home, Lincoln drew on gender roles as a shield against unwonted gentility. According to Herndon, "at the very first opportunity he would have the men separated from their ladies and crowded close around him in one corner of the parlor," much to Mary's disgust. "He would get a crowd around him in the gentlemen's room and start a conversation," another acquaintance reminisced, "with the result that the ladies would be left alone downstairs, and would have to send some one to break up Mr. Lincoln's party, in order to get the gentlemen downstairs." More often, Lincoln would simply leave home, and contemporaries attributed his long absences to Mary. During a domestic set-to, a neighbor noted, Abraham would "suddenly think of an engagement he had downtown, grasp his hat, and start for his office." During their worst episodes, Lincoln went to work early and came home late or never came home at all. His profession, of course, abetted these absences, and he spent weeks on end riding the circuit. Lincoln attended two court terms a year in each county, spending three months on the road in the spring and again in the fall. He was gone nearly half the year. Judge David Davis summed up the popular sentiment when he concluded that "I think Mr Lincoln was happy—as happy as *he* could be, when on this Circuit—and happy no other place. This was his place of Enjoyment. As a general rule when all the lawyers of a Saturday Evening would go home and see their families & friends at home Lincoln would refuse to go home."[33]

In this fashion, Lincoln turned the Victorian separation of spheres to his own advantage. Christopher Lasch has argued that Victorians viewed the home as a "haven in a heartless world." Lincoln inverted this formula, seeking refuge away from home in the masculine public world. Work thus became a "haven from a heartless home." As Herndon stated more bluntly, "his home was *Hell*" and "absence from home was his *Heaven*." Still others put a positive face on these long absences. "The fact that Mary Todd, by her turbulent nature and unfortunate manner, prevented her husband from becoming a domestic man, operated largely in his favor," a sympathetic friend reminisced; "for he was thereby kept out in the world of business and politics."[34]

Often, however, Mary Lincoln drove her husband from home. A Lincoln neighbor, for example, reminisced that "she was seen frequently to drive him from the house with a broomstick." This unfortunate image conjures up the stereotype of a witch riding a broomstick but is in fact typically middle class. The broom was the symbol of the Victorian housewife's commitment to domestic cleanliness, a quintessentially middle-class tool of housekeeping. Still, the contrast with Springfield's working class is striking. In 1855, the *Springfield Journal* reported that "This forenoon, a German woman with a butcher knife in her hand, bare headed, in great excitement, was seen running up Sixth street, north from the square, in pursuit of a man." A proper middle-class housewife, of course, would wield not a knife but a broom.[35]

Yet Mary Lincoln, too, violated middle-class standards. As historian Michael Burlingame has emphasized, she frequently attempted to reproduce the upper-class surroundings of her youth. Herndon found her "cold and & repulsive to visitors that did not suit her cold aristocratic blood." A neighbor agreed that she "put on plenty style." Like many Victorian housewives, Mary Lincoln had trouble finding, managing, and keeping servants. A persistent labor shortage raised wages and produced a scarcity of native-born girls to work in middle-class families. There were simply too many middle-class homes in Springfield. "You can scarcely imagine a place, improving more rapidly than ours," Mary Lincoln wrote to her half-sister in 1857, "almost *palaces* of homes, have been reared since you were here, hundreds of houses have been going up this season and some of them, very elegant." As the demand for servants increased, so did the competition. Wage labor in shops, such as Wiley's clothing factory, attracted the "country girls" who had formerly moved to town to serve as maids. Wiley, for example, routinely advertised for "Two or three Girls to learn the Tailoring business."[36]

This "servant problem," as it was known, bedeviled Mary Lincoln, along with other housewives in Springfield. Raised in a plantation society, Mary Lincoln demanded abject submission from her "girls." In 1859, for example, she wrote approvingly to a confidante that "Mary, the same girl, I had last winter, is still with me, a very faithful servant, has become as submissive as possible." Facing a shortage of suitable servants, Springfielders consistently called on women and girls to come west to work as maids. "Help Wanted!" read an urgent request in a local newspaper. "We have been requested by several of our citizens to state that many families in this city are without help, and that a number of respectable females, having a knowledge of housework, could find permanent employment here, at $1.50 to $2.50 per week." During the 1840s, immigrants began to fill in for the "country girls" who had once tended house in Springfield. In 1849, Sarah McConnell wrote to her nieces in Liverpool, England, to advise that "Good girls to do housework in respectable families can readily get from one and a half to two Doll[ars] per week and good Board." One local merchant went so far as to "import" servants, paying the railroad passage of German immigrant girls from New York City to Springfield.[37]

As a housekeeper, Mary Lincoln persisted in trying to duplicate the staff of slaves who had waited on her as a child. After visiting relatives in St. Louis, she commended their gracious urban lifestyle by observing that "They live in a very handsome house, four stories, plenty of room & some Kentucky *darkies*, to wait on them." Other Springfielders took on female apprentices, including African Americans, to keep house, but the Lincolns made do with "country" boys and immigrant girls. A quarter-century later, their former Irish maid, Meg Ryan, remembered that a "cranky" and "half crazy" Mary Lincoln sometimes struck her servants and made their lives, as well as Lincoln's, intolerable. More egalitarian in nature than his wife, Abraham Lincoln often interceded, paying Ryan an extra 75 cents a week to stay on and placing his hand on her head with the plea to "Keep courage."[38]

During their early years of marriage the Lincolns could not afford a full-time servant. They addressed this "servant problem," as some other middle-class couples did, by hosting a younger relative to help with housework. After the birth of their first son, Robert, they welcomed Harriet Hanks Chapman into their home. Chapman was Abraham Lincoln's niece, the daughter of his stepsister Sarah Johnston and her husband Dennis Hanks. The sixteen-year-old girl visited Springfield from Coles County for a year and a half between 1842 and 1844. Chapman found Mary Lincoln "high strung," and the two women did not get along. Forty years later, she remembered her uncle Abraham fondly but wrote bitterly that she "would rather *Say nothing* about his Wife, as I Could Say but little in her *favor* I Conclude it best to Say nothing." Perhaps recalling this experience, when his stepbrother John Johnston suggested a decade later that his own son visit the Springfield home, Abraham Lincoln declined. In short, Mary Lincoln's aristocratic upbringing encouraged her to treat her servants like slaves and her relatives like servants. In fact, according to one neighbor, she "was quite disposed to make a servant girl of her husband." Abraham Lincoln would "get the breakfast and then dress the children" and finally "wash the dishes before going to his office," which represented a pointed violation of Victorian gender roles. While performing routine housework, Mary Lincoln once asked rhetorically, "What would my poor father say if he found me doing this kind of work." While attempting to live beyond her means, she still provoked charges of stinginess. Harriet Chapman remembered her as "vary *economical* So much So that *by Some She* might have been pronounced Stingy." She faced the perpetual dilemma of the middle-class housewife—making her home comfortable for her husband while advancing his career, all on a middle-class budget.[39]

Mary Lincoln's greatest social fault, however, was violating the quintessential middle-class virtue of her era, self-control. "An ethic of self-restraint was central to the middle-class vision of antebellum America," according to historian William Barney. "The middle class first fashioned this ethic in the family world of their domestic lives and then tried to universalize it throughout society in their reform activities." Abraham Lincoln learned self-control during the tribulations that marked his long rise upward in life, practicing frugality, self-discipline, and emotional restraint. Mary Lincoln's aristocratic childhood, however, never provided the kind of adversity that required the same kind of hard work to overcome. Harriet Chapman remembered Lincoln practicing the same kind of subdued self-restraint at home that he exhibited in the public world of law and politics. She found him "vary pleasent to all around him never did I hear him utter an un kind word to enny one." Even in the face of one of Mary's tantrums, Abraham remained the picture of stoicism, "without even Changing his Countenance, or making enny reply to his wife." A neighbor recalled that "Lincoln & his wife got along tolerably well, unless Mrs L got the devil in her: Lincoln paid no attention—would pick up one of his Children & walked off—would laugh at her—pay no Earthly attention to her when in that wild furious Condition." Even his in-laws considered Lincoln a saint who endured the tongue-lashings of the uncontrollable Mary with incredible patience and aplomb. Mary's sister Elizabeth Edwards considered her "quick, lively, gay" but added "frivalous it may be, Social loved glitter Show & pomp & power." Lincoln's law partner, William Herndon, contrasted her turbulent passion against the era's ethic of self-restraint when he called her "the wildcat of the age."[40]

In his personal as in his public life, Lincoln's own self-control was nearly perfect, yet ironically his composure earned him as much ridicule as respect. "Lincoln had no spontaneity—nor Emotional Nature—no Strong Emotional feelings for any person—Mankind or thing," David Davis complained two decades later. "Lincoln I say again and again was a peculiar man." Sister-in-law Elizabeth Edwards agreed that "I knew Mr L well—he was a cold Man—had no affection—was not Social—was abstracted—thoughtful." Like Davis, she concluded that "He was a peculiar man." John Todd Stuart similarly noted the "want of passion—Emotion" that produced a "peculiar constitution—this dormancy—this vegetable constitution." Herndon agreed that "Lincoln was undemonstrative" and "somewhat cold and yet exacting." The couple exemplified Victorian gender roles in the extreme. Mary the wife was emotional, high-strung, and sensitive, while Abraham the husband remained reticent, aloof, and calm, the perfect "man's man" of his era. They were indeed "the opposite in everything." Instead of producing domestic bliss, as every advice manual of the age predicted, the contrast in their very natures bred discord. Rather than jointly earning praise as complementary helpmeets, as a couple they won only mocking derision.[41]

As Michael Burlingame has made clear, discord within the Lincoln family arose from personal and psychological as well as social and cultural influences.[42] Yet the rules of Victorian marriage surely contributed their share of problems. Above all, the semipublic life of a politician challenged the basic premises on which Victorian marriages rested. Indeed, evidence suggests that marriages like the Lincolns' endured unusual stress during this period of cultural change. The overall divorce rate in Springfield was very low, just 1.3 percent between 1850 and 1860. But divorce rates varied dramatically across the city's occupational groups. Somewhat astoundingly, three groups—farmers, merchants, and professionals—enjoyed extremely stable marriages during the decade. Not a single household head who engaged in agriculture, commerce, or a profession divorced between 1850 and 1860. Overall, both middle-class and working-class couples experienced a thoroughly average divorce rate during the decade—1.3 percent. At the other extreme, however, one group—public officials—stood out. Officeholders suffered by far the highest divorce rate in Springfield. During the 1850s, nearly 9 percent of officeholders divorced, a stunning seven times the average. In fact, couples that Abraham Lincoln knew had a divorce rate three times higher than those he didn't know. Clearly, involvement in politics and public service put unusual stress upon otherwise typical marriages. By blurring the line between public and private life, politics, apparently, bred stormy marriages.[43] It certainly bred a stormy marriage for the Lincolns.

In this man's world, Lincoln's career choices, both law and politics, virtually defined his marriage and certainly took a heavy personal toll on his family life. Still, in their matrimonial partnership this was clearly a price that he and Mary were willing to pay. The front door at Eighth and Jackson represented—figuratively and literally—the socially defined boundary between the Lincolns' separate spheres. It also represented the boundary between the public and private worlds that the couple struggled to reconcile, sometimes unsuccessfully, together. Mary Lincoln felt that she could lock the door on election night through her socially prescribed authority within her private, domestic sphere, the home. But Abraham Lincoln's public life always took precedence over this private one. When he returned with the news of his momentous victory, Mary quite willingly unlocked the door. Abraham Lincoln's resounding success in the public sphere opened the lock, so to speak, that guarded the Lincoln home and exposed their most private moments to the world.

CHAPTER 19

Bring Forth Good Fruit

braham Lincoln's election to Congress in 1846 is best known
for the candidate's somewhat unseemly struggle to win his
party's nomination, his campaign against a Methodist preacher
who charged him with religious "infidelity," and the rather
lackluster, single term in Congress that resulted from his election. But that
election is crucial to understanding the transformation of a hard-boiled,
sometimes cynical politician who championed economic issues into a statesman who eventually confronted—and solved—the most important moral
question of his age.

Most Americans revere Abraham Lincoln as a champion of democracy
who guided the nation through its deepest crisis by adhering firmly to its
founding principles of representative government, political freedom, and
the rule of law. Lincoln's reputation as a plain-spoken democrat began to
take shape immediately after his death, guided by the judgments of personal
friends and political allies who closed ranks to portray him as the humble
yet dignified savior of the Union. As a longtime personal friend, professional associate, and political ally in Illinois summed him up, "The amazing
popularity he obtained was attributable to two things[.] He had been successful under the most trying circumstances and then he was most emphatically one of the People." Lincoln succeeded as a statesman in saving the
Union, yet through it all he remained a common man. In short, throughout
his life and especially during his presidency, Lincoln was "the representative
man of the unsophisticated People."[1]

Although his historical reputation as a democrat has seen its ups and
downs through the decades, today's standard portrait of Lincoln stresses his
deep commitment to republican principles and his liberal tolerance for dis-
senting views. In life, of course, political opponents—both northern and
southern—frequently condemned his actions as self-serving, undemocratic,
and even dictatorial. Several noted historians have also, over the years,
struck a note of realism, if not cynicism, by portraying Lincoln as a hard-
boiled, partisan politician who was not above manipulating voters and leg-

islators for his own political ends. Lincoln therefore presents a dual face to the world as both a staunch, uncompromising, and principled democrat *and* an unrelenting, shrewd, and practical politician.[2]

Lincoln, of course, was both—a champion of democracy *and* a masterful politician. He recognized that democracy is difficult to establish yet even more difficult to maintain. The ideals that he cherished, including democracy, the Union, and the end of slavery, required not just eloquent oratory to win and to defend but also strenuous exertions and constant vigilance within the political arena. Democracy rests upon and fosters popular political participation and therefore demands a mastery of the partisan, political process to work at all. Indeed, that hard-fought, workaday political process *is* democracy, as Americans know it.

Many characteristics of politics in the community that bred Lincoln confirm our worst fears about antebellum democracy—and about Lincoln as a politician. Voters faced most of the limitations on participation that we associate with the era's restrictive suffrage. Illinois's first constitution, adopted in 1818, required voters to be male, white, and legal adults but did not require citizenship nor impose a property qualification. A residence qualification required voters to live in the state for six months. Instead of relaxing suffrage restrictions, Illinois's second constitution, adopted in 1848 actually tightened them, adding U.S. citizenship and a full year's residence in Illinois as prerequisites. A venerable political rule of thumb held that one-fifth of any population was eligible to vote. In 1850, exactly 20 percent of all Springfielders were eligible voters.[3]

In addition to these legal restrictions on suffrage, differences in wealth, occupation, ethnicity, age, migration, and even geographical distance from polling places produced variations in participation, among voters and public officeholders. In Springfield as elsewhere, the paramount social influence on participation was migration. Historians have identified rates of persistence ranging from a mere one-fourth to roughly one-half of ordinary voters in any community through most of the nineteenth century. Over any particular decade, perhaps three-fourths of all eligible voters moved away, leaving a majority of newcomers to dominate the local political scene. Seven out of ten voters who were present in the city in a typical year moved away or died during the succeeding decade. In Springfield, persistence among eligible voters was a mere 29 percent. In fact, turnover was so incessant that most voters in Springfield participated in only one election in the community before moving on again.[4]

As a result, officeholders were not particularly representative of the voters who elected them. Immigrants, for example, represented 29 percent of Springfielders in 1850 and one-half in 1860. Yet only one immigrant was elected to public office during the entire decade. Officeholders were four times wealthier than the typical voter and much more highly skilled. One-fifth of all eligible voters were laborers, yet only one laborer held office during the 1850s. In this society of routine mobility, young men, in particular, could make little impact on local political life. Youths who came of age in Springfield experienced the highest rates of out-migration. A mere one-sixth of them stayed in the community long enough to vote even once. Young men coming of age in Springfield represented only twelve voters at the typical election, less than 1 percent of the active electorate. Most moved away before becoming politically active. Rates of migration were generally unrelated to party affiliation, and so Whigs, Republicans, and Democrats alike contended with similar social patterns among their respective followers.[5]

Limitations on participation, both legal and practical, made a dramatic impact on the way voters behaved, political leaders campaigned, and parties organized their followers. First, suffrage laws restricted the franchise to about one-fifth of the populace, which imposed severe limitations on the mix of political actors within the electorate. Entire segments of the population—women, African Americans, noncitizens, recent newcomers, and youths—were disfranchised and, more broadly, barred from the arena of political discourse. Legal limitations therefore narrowed the scope of public debate to the concerns of a mere slice of voters—white, adult, male citizens—who constituted a relatively homogeneous minority. Focused on this small segment of the potential political spectrum, political parties debated issues that seemed less than relevant to most of their constituents.

Second, within that minority of legal voters, migration lent a tremendous fluidity to the local electorate, selecting only the most stable members of any community for sustained participation as voters and practically barring most of them from leadership roles. The result was, third, an intense need for organization within the electorate. Finally, a small minority of settled persisters could provide that organization, as well as benefit from it, by building and maintaining political parties. In this sense, socially unrepresentative party leaders imposed an artificial political order to compensate for social disorganization among ordinary voters.

In 1846, the Seventh Congressional District virtually belonged to the Whigs. Considered a "safe seat," it was the only Whig district in the state of Illinois. Whigs first captured the seat in 1838 and won it handily throughout the next decade, holding it through five consecutive terms of Congress. For this reason, Lincoln expected to win in 1846. With 56 percent of the vote, he achieved the largest landslide in the history of the district. Comparing the congressional election of 1844, which Lincoln's friend Edward Baker won handily, with the results of the 1846 election documents the stunning turnover in the electorate. Among all the voters who participated in the 1844 election, only about one-fourth turned out for the congressional contest two years later. Seventy percent of the voters who elected Lincoln to Congress were voting in Springfield for the first time. Fortunately for Lincoln and the Whigs, their followers experienced a higher rate of persistence than did Democrats. Between 1844 and 1846, 31 percent of Whig voters persisted, while only 19 percent of Democrats returned. Lincoln and every other candidate could therefore count on only one-fifth to one-third of all voters to persist from one election to the next.[6]

At the same time, both parties benefitted from a remarkable partisan loyalty among their adherents. Historians contend that political loyalties were resilient before the Civil War, sometimes persisting for decades or even a lifetime. This was true in Springfield. Among voters who participated in both the 1844 and 1846 elections, fully 97 percent remained committed to their parties, and only 3 percent switched. Whigs enjoyed a higher consistency (98 percent) than did Democrats (92 percent). Between 1844 and 1846, only three voters switched from Whig to Democratic, and one of those was Lincoln! (Under the system of voice voting, candidates traditionally voted for their opponents.) At the same time, eleven Democrats switched and voted for Lincoln.

Whigs and Democrats could count on only a minority of their followers to turn out even two years hence, with anywhere from one-fifth to one-third of their supporters voting in consecutive elections. But within this small slice of the electorate—thanks in large part to the convention system—they could count on nearly unanimous partisan consistency. Still, most of the voters who elected Lincoln to Congress were political newcomers in Springfield without deep partisan roots or even a voting record. They were quite probably recent arrivals into the community, as well. Most of them, too, would never vote in Springfield again. Lincoln could count on nearly all Whigs to retain their partisan allegiance but only a third of them to carry over from the last election. The vast majority of voters were political unknowns. So how did Lincoln win the election of 1846?

Several political imperatives, imposed in large measure by the everyday realities of antebellum social life, shaped the kind of campaign that Lincoln, along with other candidates, had to run in order to win. First, only a small core of persistent voters carried over from one election to the next. A successful candidate had to identify them, organize them, and bring them out to vote. Second, few voters switched parties between elections. Candidates rarely wasted time and effort appealing to members of the opposing party. Third, most voters, as recent arrivals to the community, were new to the electorate. Shrewd candidates didn't begin campaigning too early, because many voters would move away. A last-minute push bore more fruit than a long-drawn-out campaign. Fourth, most voters had shallow political roots within the community. Candidates therefore preferred traditional issues with broad, national appeal, rather than controversial or merely local ones. Finally, appealing directly to new voters was not particularly cost-effective. Instead, successful candidates concentrated on controlling established political institutions and rallying core voters and, above all, core leaders. Lincoln won election to Congress by observing all of these rules.

Lincoln started campaigning for the Whig nomination nine months before the election, not among voters but only among party leaders, particularly newspaper editors. As a result of the convention system, which was now ten years old, candidates for state and federal offices no longer had to campaign directly for votes. As his legal colleague and friend Henry Clay Whitney explained, "Mr. Lincoln did not meddle with, or obtrude himself upon, his neighbors or their local matters, nor did he after 1840 personally ask them to support him for office." Instead, he concentrated on winning the support of Whig conventions, in which whole counties could swing their support toward him at a single blow.[7]

Newspapers traditionally nominated candidates to allow them to test the political waters well in advance of elections. Late in 1845, newspapers in the Seventh District began speculating on candidates for governor and Congress. Lincoln feared that former U.S. Representative John J. Hardin might be mentioned for Congress and knock him out of the running even before the race began. In November 1845, Lincoln began writing to Whig political leaders in the district. "It would give Hardin a great start, and perhaps use me up, if the whig papers of the District should nominate him for *Congress*," Lincoln cautioned Benjamin F. James, editor of the *Tazewell Whig*, the leading Whig newspaper in Tazewell County. Tazewell County lay in the northern part of the district, where Lincoln was not well known. "I wish you would let nothing appear in your paper which may operate against me," Lincoln pleaded. "You understand." Lincoln did not ask for an endorsement but simply tried to stop any movement toward Hardin.[8]

The next day, Lincoln asked the editor of the Beardstown *Gazette* to join James in delaying any recommendation for Congress. In this same letter, Lincoln staked out his own claim to the nomination, not by championing any political issues but instead appealing to the political process. "Turn about is fair play," Lincoln declared. The Whig incumbent in Congress, Edward Baker, supported him on the principle that the seat should rotate among Whig leaders in the Seventh District. "Before Baker left," according to Lincoln, "he said to me, in accordance with what had long been an understanding between him and me, that the track for the next congressional race was clear to me, as far as he was concerned." Lincoln claimed the nomination largely because it was his "turn" to succeed Whig leaders John Todd Stuart, John J. Hardin, and Edward Baker in Congress.[9]

Two days later, the Whig newspaper in Springfield, the *Sangamo Journal*, gave Lincoln a boost by proposing that Hardin run for governor. Lincoln did not write this item but approved it in advance. Soon, Lincoln was counting delegates to decide whether he had enough votes to challenge Hardin for Congress. He wrote back to James that "Upon the whole, it is my intention to give him the trial, unless clouds should rise, which are not yet discernible." Lincoln felt vulnerable in the extreme northern reaches of the district, and indeed those three counties—Putnam, Marshall, and Woodford—were the only ones he lost in the election. Early in 1846, Lincoln wrote to state senator Robert Boal to ask for his support in securing the delegation from his legislative district, which included Tazewell, Marshall, and Woodford counties, the "northern counties," as Lincoln called them. He appealed to the principle of "turn about" and asked for a "fair shake" at the nomination. "I wish you would write me, telling the aspect of things in your county, or rather your district," Lincoln requested, "and also send the names of some of your whig neighbours, to whom I might, with propriety, write." Focusing on winning the delegates from Marshall County, Lincoln then wrote to "three or four of the most active whigs in each precinct of the county."[10]

In maneuvering for the nomination well in advance of the district convention, Lincoln appealed not to voters or even potential delegates but instead to their established leaders. As part of the fabled "pyramidal" structure of antebellum politics, Lincoln worked from the top down to cobble together electoral units—precincts, counties, and entire senatorial districts—by enlisting political friends. "To succeed, I must have 17 votes in convention," Lincoln informed James in a typical passage. "To secure them, I think I may safely claim Sangamon 8, Menard 2, Logan 1, making 11, so that if you and other friends can secure Dr. Boal's entire senatorial district, that is, Tazewell 4, Woodford 1, and Marshall 1, it just covers the case." By practicing this kind of "trickle-down democracy," Lincoln could sit at the "top" of the political pyramid—in Springfield—and orchestrate his own nomination without leaving his law office.[11]

After a decade of organizing, campaigning, and forging political alliances, it no longer made sense for Lincoln to establish personal contacts with ordinary voters, to work hard between elections to keep his supporters mobilized, or even to mount a campaign very far in advance of the election. Instead, Lincoln forged connections with local Whig leaders who controlled the political process and could turn out voters on short notice on his behalf. In Springfield, Lincoln knew about one-fifth of all eligible voters and could campaign face to face. But the Seventh Congressional District contained over six thousand Whig voters in 1846, many of them newcomers, and Lincoln could never hope to reach all of them personally. Instead, he had to work indirectly through local leaders in a form of "proxy democracy."[12]

Lincoln seemed to have a political "friend" in every community. "In Woodford," he reported, "I have Davenport, Simms, Willard, Bracken, Perry[,] Travis, Dr. Hazzard, and the Clarks, & some others all specially committed." As he wrote Senator Boal, "My reliance for a fair shake (and I want nothing more) in your county is chiefly on you, because of your position and standing, and because I am acquainted with so few others." Soon after testing the waters and lining up support, Lincoln felt confident enough to propose a site for the nominating convention, suggesting Petersburg, the seat of neighboring Menard County, whose delegates he already counted as his own. Petersburg was safe territory for Lincoln because he had lived for six years in New Salem, just two miles from the city. Lincoln also chose Petersburg in an attempt to shore up the convention system itself. "They are a little disinclined, to adopt the convention system," he reasoned. "[S]ome of their prejudices would be done away by their having the convention amongst them."[13]

By 1846, the convention system was effective yet not universally accepted. Whigs occasionally mounted challenges against the convention by running independently. Now, however, in a desperate attempt to deny Lincoln the nomination, his opponent Hardin proposed abandoning the convention system entirely. In a letter to Lincoln that he later published, Hardin proposed a new system in which Whig voters would choose their nominee directly, as Hardin put it, "to leave the selection of the candidate to the Whig voters of the District." Hardin envisioned a sort of primary election in which Whig voters would assemble in their precincts and vote directly for the nominee. Hardin's intricate plan even included a provision for a run-off election in case no candidate won a majority. He also proposed that candidates refrain from campaigning outside their own counties, in an apparent attempt to mute the influence of Springfield Whigs within the district. The goal was both to unite the party and allow voters a greater voice in choosing the nominee or, as Hardin put it, "to prevent excitement between the candidates and their friends, and to leave the voters of the counties to their unbiased choice." If adopted, Lincoln's careful courting of delegates would have gained him nothing.[14]

Lincoln rejected the plan out of hand, declaring that "I am entirely satisfied with the old system under which you and Baker were successively nominated and elected to congress." He endorsed the idea of a primary election but suggested that each county decide for itself whether to elect delegates through a primary or a county convention. He also argued that restricting candidates to their own counties would favor incumbents. "[T]he fact of your having been in congress," Lincoln reasoned, "has, in various ways, so spread your name in the district, as to give you a decided advantage in such a stipulation." He also pledged party unity, quipping that "I promise to 'keep cool' under all circumstances." Hardin's proposal was designed, in the short run, to deny Lincoln the nomination but also, over the long run, to decentralize political control away from Springfield. While making the nomination process more democratic, it threatened the intricate organization forged by Springfield Whigs during the previous decade. To that extent, it also threatened Whig domination in the district.[15]

In February, Hardin heard from a Whig supporter in Tazewell that Lincoln was sure to win all the county's delegates. "The *regular succession* principle has been accepted," he wrote. "It is Abrahams turn now." Later that month, Hardin withdrew from the congressional contest to make way for Lincoln. Whigs now began selecting delegates to the district convention. In Sangamon County, the voters of each precinct were to elect five delegates to the county convention. In reality, precincts held "meetings," not elections, and "appointed" delegates. The city of Springfield constituted a precinct and selected five young Whigs, none of whom had ever held office, as delegates to the county convention. Membership in the delegation, however, was fluid. Three of the five Springfield delegates were replaced, without explanation. Not only voters but even delegates experienced substantial turnover!

The county convention nominated candidates for county offices, chose eight delegates to attend the district convention, and instructed them to vote for Lincoln. In May, the district convention met in Petersburg and nominated Lincoln, as expected. Lincoln's new law partner, William Herndon, was secretary of the convention, and his former partner, Stephen Logan, chaired the committee on resolutions. Democrats sneered that only one-half of the district's eleven counties were represented. In fact, two of Sangamon County's delegates were missing, and among the remaining six, only one had been elected by the county convention. Anticlimactically, the Springfield *Sangamo Journal* noted that "This nomination was of course anticipated—there being no other candidate in the field." The battle for the nomination had been fought and won well in advance, with only passing notice in the public press.[16]

Lincoln's years of party service, political organizing, and personal campaigning had paid off. His election to Congress was a foregone conclusion or, in the language of the time, "anticipated." The district's Whigs had an organization in place to identify, reach, and bring out their voters. Democrats pressed Lincoln to address their own perennial issue—national expansion—but he refused to bite. "Is Lincoln for 54 4[o], or is he for 'compromising' away our Oregon territory to England," the Springfield *Register* asked. "This, the People ought to know, before they vote next August. No shuffling, Mr. Lincoln! Come out, square!" But Lincoln did not "come out." He continued to campaign on tried-and-true Whig economic issues—banks, the tariff, and internal improvements. Privately, he admitted to a supporter that "individually I never was much interested in the Texas question." Maintaining public silence on the issue, he spent only two days campaigning before his nomination, in Petersburg, the site of the convention. During the general election, he delivered only seven speeches. On May 30, he spoke in Springfield in support of the Mexican War, which broke out during the contest. During a one-week campaign swing in July, he delivered six speeches in Tazewell and Marshall counties, focusing on the tariff, a perennial Whig issue. The text of none of the seven speeches he delivered during the campaign survives.[17]

Once Lincoln reached Congress, Democrats repudiated his views as unrepresentative, because he had not made them known during his campaign. "When Lincoln was elected he made no declaration of principles in regard to the war before the people, as he himself tells us in his first speech in Congress," the Springfield *Register* complained. In firm control of the political machinery in the Seventh District, Lincoln didn't need to give speeches—and certainly not make promises—to win.[18]

A last-minute challenge, however, threatened Lincoln's election. His Democratic opponent was Peter Cartwright, a Methodist preacher with an evangelistic approach to politics. Lincoln learned that Cartwright, known as "the circuit rider," had swung through the northern part of the district, the same counties that Lincoln had targeted, "whispering the charge of infidelity against me." As Lincoln's ally Senator Boal sized it up, "Cartwright *sneaked* through this part of the district after Lincoln." This was the kind of superficial, last-minute charge that might sway uncommitted voters who were unfamiliar with the candidates. Lincoln recognized this moment "as a time when he knew I could not contradict him, either in person or by letter before the election." He turned immediately to the "friends" he had already courted in Tazewell and Marshall counties. "I at once wrote a contradiction of it," he explained, "and sent it to my friends there, with the request that they should publish it or not, as in their discretion they might think proper." No one published it, but as the election neared Lincoln decided that "it was not entirely safe to leave it unnoticed." Too late to reach voters through the normal channels of partisan politics, whether Whig newspapers, rallies, speeches, or letters, Lincoln now published the letter himself, as the "Handbill Replying to Charges of Infidelity." Lincoln denied Cartwright's charges and explained his own religious views, agreeing diplomatically that "I do not think I could myself, be brought to support a man for office, whom I knew to be an open enemy of, and scoffer at, religion." He later concluded that Cartwright's "whisper campaign" had indeed cost him some votes where he was not "well known."[19]

In Springfield, where the excitement of the war overshadowed local political affairs, Whigs made little public effort to rally voters. The Springfield paper, for example, concluded that "The Mexican War, the session of Congress, the Oregon and Tariff questions, our own State campaign are subjects of absorbing interest." The understated campaign did not feature a single rally, parade, or speech, yet Lincoln won the city with 67 percent of the vote. Both parties turned out a majority of newcomers to the local political scene and maintained nearly perfect consistency among repeat voters. Tellingly, however, turnout fell from 1844, a presidential election year. Both Whigs and Democrats bemoaned the light turnout and jointly blamed it on "apathy." According to Democrats, "That old enemy—'General Apathy' seems to have pervaded not only our ranks, but those of our opponents." With the outcome "anticipated," many Whigs and Democrats stayed home, "the former from a security in their strength, and the latter from the certainty of defeat." Lincoln echoed that pervasive lack of spirit. "Being elected to Congress, though I am very grateful to our friends, for having done it," he wrote two months later, "has not pleased me as much as I expected."[20]

Lincoln had dissolved his law partnership with Stephen Logan in 1844. "I then told him that I wished to take in my son David with me who had meanwhile grown up, and Lincoln was perhaps by that time quite willing to begin on his own account," Logan later explained. "So we talked the matter over and dissolved the partnership amicably and in friendship." As his partner, Lincoln took on William Herndon, nine years his junior and another ardent Whig. Lincoln was now the senior partner in his firm, and he turned over to Herndon a great deal of the legal research and other details that no longer absorbed him. The arrangement freed Lincoln to continue traveling the circuit, engage actively in politics, and in 1847 go to Congress. Just as Lincoln had once anchored the law firm while his partner John Todd Stuart served in Congress, now Herndon acted as Lincoln's eyes and ears in Springfield.[21]

In October 1847, Lincoln left Springfield for Washington. "Mr. Lincoln, the member of Congress elect from this district, has just set out on his way to the city of Washington," the local newspaper reported by way of a farewell. "His family is with him; they intend to visit their friends and relatives in Kentucky before they take up the line of march for the seat of government. Success to our talented member of Congress! He will find many men in Congress who possess twice the good looks, and not half the good sense, of our own representative." The Lincolns now had a second son. Edward Baker Lincoln, named for his father's predecessor in Congress, was born in 1846. The four Lincolns visited the Todd family for three weeks in Lexington, Kentucky, on their way to Washington. After two years of housekeeping in their own Springfield home, the Lincolns returned to boarding in Washington. They moved into Mrs. Sprigg's boarding house, a short walk from the Capitol. Known as a Whig establishment, Mrs. Sprigg's had hosted Lincoln's predecessors in Congress, John Todd Stuart and Edward Baker. Mary Lincoln was the only congressional wife in tow. As she had in the Globe Tavern, she landed in another male enclave.[22]

The Washington winter found the four Lincolns confined to a single room. When spring arrived, Mary Lincoln gathered the two children and returned to her family in Lexington. At age thirty-nine, for the first and only time in his entire life, Lincoln had to live alone. Accustomed to sharing camaraderie and even a bed with his male roommates, not to mention his wife Mary, Lincoln abhorred this self-imposed solitude. In a poignant tribute to the couple's affections, he wrote back to Mary that "In this troublesome world, we are never quite satisfied. When you were here, I thought you hindered me some in attending to business; but now, having nothing but business—no variety—it has grown exceedingly tasteless to me."

Expressing tenderness for his sons, Lincoln told Mary, "Dont let the blessed fellows forget father."[23]

Lincoln's single term in Congress was dominated by the Mexican War. As the only Whig congressman from Illinois, Lincoln felt obligated to represent the views of the party that he had helped to build. Illinois Whigs insisted that they did not oppose the war itself but only the suspicious circumstances in which it began. "Mr. Polk's War," as they labeled it, seemed an attempt to enhance southern political power by adding new slave territory to the Union. Illinois Whigs supported the war once it was underway but wanted a speedy conclusion. The Springfield *Illinois State Journal*, the leading Whig newspaper in Lincoln's district, reiterated that "the whigs have not opposed the war measures of the administration. They have given all the men and money called for. They are for a vigorous prosecution of this war. They wish it ended."

Lincoln set out to make a major statement in opposition to Polk's handling of the war. Writing home to his law partner Herndon, Lincoln promised that "As you are all so anxious for me to distinguish myself, I have concluded to do so, before long." About a week later, he introduced his famous "Spot Resolutions." The resolutions focused on the origins of the war and particularly Polk's insistence that Mexico "invaded our territory, and shed the blood of our fellow citizens on our own soil." Lincoln asked Polk whether the "spot" on which the war began was truly American soil or the just possession of Mexico. The implication was that Polk had provoked an unnecessary war with territorial acquisition as its goal, not national honor. During the next month, Lincoln voted for an amendment labeling the Mexican War "unnecessarily and unconstitutionally begun by the President" and delivered a speech blaming Polk for starting the war.[24]

Lincoln's aggressive attack on Polk caught both his friends and enemies by surprise. Back in Springfield, the Democratic newspaper published the resolutions even before Whigs did. They portrayed Lincoln as a virtual traitor to the American cause. "He denies the justness of our cause, and asserts that the title of Mexico extends this side of the Rio Grande," they trumpeted with considerable exaggeration, "that the march of General Taylor up that river was an invasion of Mexico, and that the law of nations and the principles of justice were on the side of the Mexicans." All of this, of course, was incompatible with the views of Lincoln's constituents. "The masses in this state have committed themselves, body and soul, in favor of the war; they believe it to be just—to have been brought on by the act of Mexico, and that it could not on our part have been avoided without compromising the national honor and subjecting us to the scoff and scorn of the whole civilized world." Trying to contain the damage, Springfield's Whig newspaper published the resolutions without endorsing them. In fact, Lincoln's stand on the war reflected the conventional views of leading Whigs.

Ironically, in an attempt to use the resolutions to sully the entire Whig Party, Illinois Democrats pointed out that Lincoln's predecessor in Congress had taken exactly the same stand. Still, the Whigs of Lincoln's congressional district never supported nor repudiated his views, leaving him to stand alone.[25]

William Herndon wrote to his law partner to warn him about "extensive defections" among Whigs in his district and to dissuade him from committing "political suicide." In reply, Lincoln defended his opposition to Polk and assured Herndon that "I will stake my life, that if you had been in my place, you would have voted just as I did." He pointed out that he opposed the commencement of the war but fully supported its prosecution once it had begun, insisting that "the whigs have, from the beginning, made and kept the distinction between the two." Still, he told Herndon that "if *you* misunderstand, I fear other good friends will also." He was right. Lincoln's position proved a tremendous liability during the next congressional election. Lincoln himself had withdrawn from the contest as part of his party's traditional rotation of office, "from a wish to deal fairly with others," as he put it, "to keep peace among our friends, and to keep the district from going to the enemy." Whigs now struggled to find someone to succeed him. After his two terms in Congress, John Todd Stuart had virtually withdrawn from politics. Democrats labeled him "a retired politician, taking no part now whatever in politics." Edward Baker, favored to succeed Lincoln, announced his intention to leave Springfield for Galena. He won nomination to Congress from his new district and eventually went to Congress as the only Whig representing the state. John J. Hardin had died a hero during the Mexican War. Whigs now turned nervously to yet another member of the Todd-Stuart-Edwards clan, Lincoln's former law partner, Stephen Logan.[26]

As a result of Lincoln's audacious stand and his own political shortcomings, Logan's candidacy was doomed from the beginning. Democrats sensed an opportunity to regain the district. "The whigs have long clung to this district as their strongest position," they exulted, "but their strength is giving way at every successive poll; their majorities diminish, and they see that, at no distant day, they, must sink into the minority." They lumped Logan together with his former law partner, noting that he "unblushingly endorses the vote cast by Abraham Lincoln in Congress, denouncing the war." Logan had served three consecutive terms in the legislature, where he opposed a resolution of support for the war effort. To lead the fight against Logan, Democrats shrewdly nominated a war hero, Thomas L. Harris, who had served as a major at the Battle of Cerro Gordo. "In this district, although heretofore largely in the minority, every inch of ground will be disputed," they promised. "We are determined to efface the foul 'spot' upon the state, if within the power of human means." Meanwhile, Whigs were leaderless and divided, in a "more disorganized State than I have Ever Known Them," as David Davis moaned.[27]

LINCOLN'S SECOND LAW PARTNER, STEPHEN LOGAN. A RESPECTED LAWYER BUT
HAPLESS POLITICIAN, LOGAN WAS, IN LINCOLN'S ESTIMATION, "WORSE BEATEN
THAN ANY OTHER MAN EVER WAS SINCE ELECTIONS WERE INVENTED."
Courtesy of the Illinois State Historical Library.

Nativism and abolition joined the Mexican War as decisive issues in the
congressional campaign. Continuing their appeals to foreign-born voters,
Democrats circulated a German-language handbill claiming that Logan,
like his distant cousin Stuart, was a nativist. The growing antislavery campaign also disrupted the Whigs. During the war, David Wilmot, a Pennsylvania Democrat, proposed a proviso excluding slavery from any territory
the United States might seize from Mexico. The Wilmot Proviso was never
enacted but provoked a powerful "free soil" movement that focused on pre-

venting the extension of slavery farther into the West. Nonextensionists, or free soilers as they became known, hoped to contain the spread of slavery and eventually effect its demise. A Free Soil Party organized in central Illinois and nominated Erastus Wright to oppose Logan and Harris. Disaffected Whigs considered running a second candidate themselves. Bearing the weight of the Spot Resolutions and Whig divisions and facing off against a war hero and a Free Soiler, Whigs predicted gloomily and correctly that "Judge Logan may be beaten."[28]

In fact, Whigs lost the district for the first time in a decade. Logan lost an extremely close election by a mere 106 votes. Ominously, however, Logan ran 7 percent behind Lincoln's total in 1846 and lost ground in all eleven counties in the district. Ironically, the greatest losses occurred in Logan County, named in the candidate's honor, where Whig support fell by nearly 20 percent. Ever after, Whigs blamed Logan personally for the loss. Herndon, for example, concluded that Logan lacked "the elements of a successful politician." David Davis believed that "Logan was beat for Congress by his own folly in connection with Lincoln's momentary unpopularity." Milton Hay dismissed Logan as "a sort of half politician." Beyond Logan's personal shortcomings, Whigs cited the "military spirit" that the war engendered and argued, optimistically, that their presidential nominee would benefit from it in November. They also acknowledged the impact of the Free Soil candidate in drawing votes from Logan. "It will be seen," they lamented, "that the professed friends of 'Free Soil,' in throwing their votes on E. Wright, sent a man to Congress, to vote in favor of the extension of slavery." For his own part, Logan simply blamed "Lincoln's unpopularity among other things" for his defeat.[29]

Democrats, of course, tried to burden the entire Whig Party—and Lincoln—with the loss. "The whigs about Springfield are attributing their defeat to Judge Logan, solely," they warned, "alleging that the Judge's unpopularity brought about the result." Instead, "It was the crushing load Logan had to carry in the shape of whig principles, and the course of the whig party for the past two years. Besides his own dead weight, Logan had to carry the votes of the whig party, including Lincoln, that the war was unconstitutional and unnecessary." To celebrate their victory, Springfield Democrats organized a "glorification," firing cannons and lighting bonfires in the streets. A parade led by a brass band marched through the city. The result, they reiterated, was "The 'spot' wiped out."[30]

Lincoln himself, who was still in Washington, tried to remain above it all. "I would rather not be put upon explaining how Logan was defeated in my district," he wrote to an Illinois Whig. He speculated that turnout was low, while in fact it ran 25 percent higher than in his own race in 1846. He also admitted that Harris's military record gave him a boost. Ever the political optimist, Lincoln focused on Logan's personal unpopularity. "The most I can now say," he concluded, "is that a good many Whigs, without good cause, as I think, were unwilling to go for Logan." He therefore hoped for the best in the coming presidential election. "I dislike to predict," he wrote, "but it seems to me the district must and will be found right side up again in November."[31]

Election records reveal the stunning extent of Logan's defeat. In their own citadel of Springfield, Whig support fell by nearly one-tenth. Among Springfielders who voted in both 1846 and 1848, 12 percent of all Lincoln voters abandoned Logan to support the Democrat Harris. Astoundingly, 29 percent of the Harris voters in Springfield were former Whigs. Ominously, the Whig defections carried over to the presidential election in November. Zachary Taylor gained by 3 percent over Logan's vote but still ran 6 percent behind Lincoln's vote from 1846. The Whig decline was even worse in the rest of the district, in which perhaps 15 percent of Lincoln voters defected. Still, the Democratic victory was incomplete. Harris received only 49.8 percent of the vote. In reality, neither Democrats nor Whigs controlled the district. The Free Soiler Wright won a mere 1 percent of the vote but held the balance of power.[32]

The election of 1848 solidified the transition from traditional economic questions to moral issues that had begun earlier in the decade. In particular, the annexation of Texas and the Mexican War shifted the political focus toward antislavery. The Wilmot Proviso and the resulting free soil movement increasingly divided the Whigs, who nominated a war hero, General Zachary Taylor, to try to gloss over the issue and unite their party. As their candidate, Democrats selected Lewis Cass, governor of Michigan and a proponent of sovereignty, the idea that the people of the new territories acquired from Mexico, not Congress, should decide for themselves whether to adopt slavery in the West. As Springfield Democrats put it, "We have uniformly maintained that the question should be left to the states which may be carved out of the territory that we may acquire from Mexico. Let them have slavery if they want it." Finally, the new Free Soil Party championed the Wilmot Proviso, or the nonextension of slavery, as it was also known. Their nominee was former president Martin Van Buren of New York.[33]

In Springfield, a Free Soil Club met two weeks before the presidential election to support Van Buren. Democrats, of course, seized on nonextension as the most divisive issue among the Whigs. They recognized clearly that the free soil movement could help Cass by drawing Whig votes away from Taylor. "The 'free dirt' movement," as they put it, "will in this state absorb three whigs to one democrat." Whigs strove to keep their nonextension members from breaking ranks and labeled the Free Soil campaign a lost cause, claiming that "the votes of the free soil men, are absolutely thrown away if cast for Mr. Van Buren." Taylor's supporters argued that Van Buren had no chance to win the presidency, while a vote for Taylor would help Whigs win the election and thwart the Democratic campaign to extend slavery westward in the guise of popular sovereignty. Free Soilers' true interests recommended a vote for Taylor. In desperation, Whigs portrayed Taylor, who was a slave owner, as a free soiler, or as Democrats labeled him in derision "an out-and-out free negro, free soil, free territory, anti-annexation, anti-increase-of-the-area, candidate."[34]

Always a practitioner of the politically possible, Lincoln himself supported Taylor, largely because he believed that Henry Clay had no chance to win the presidency. "In my judgment," he wrote, "we can elect nobody but Gen; Taylor." Lincoln attended the national Whig convention in Philadelphia to witness Taylor's nomination. Although he returned to Washington, the Whig state committee named him an "assistant elector" to ensure his active support for Taylor. Lincoln gave a long address in Congress defending Taylor and mailed seventy-five hundred copies of his own speeches back to voters in Illinois. Then he embarked on a speaking tour of the Northeast on Taylor's behalf. Privately, Lincoln was already a supporter of nonextension. During his campaign for Congress, he explained to an abolitionist that he was opposed to slavery but felt bound to tolerate it in the South, where it already existed. He was committed, however, to preventing its spread westward. "I hold it to be a paramount duty of us in the free states, due to the Union of the states, and perhaps to liberty itself (paradox though it may seem) to let the slavery of the other states alone," he reasoned, "while, on the other hand, I hold it to be equally clear, that we should never knowingly lend ourselves directly or indirectly, to prevent that slavery from dying a natural death—to find new places for it to live in, when it can no longer exist in the old." Lincoln, in short, was a free soiler but not an abolitionist. He was committed to preventing the spread of slavery but was not willing to attack it where it already existed. He opposed any antislavery party simply because it had no chance of winning an election and would in fact elect a Democrat by dividing the Whigs. "By the *fruit* the tree is to be known," he concluded. Only the Whig Party could "bring forth *good* fruit" by preventing the spread of slavery westward.[35]

During his campaign for Taylor, Lincoln first made his views on slavery public, not in Illinois but in Massachusetts. In Worcester, he made the dramatic declaration that slavery was evil but went on to insist that northerners "cannot affect it in States of this Union where we do not live." Northerners could, however, prevent the spread of slavery into new territories, and that was indeed their duty, "part of our responsibility and care, and is under our control." Both Whigs and Free Soilers opposed the extension of slavery, but only the Whigs had any chance of winning the election. Although not an enemy of slavery and in fact a slave owner, Taylor "would not encourage it, and would not prohibit its restriction." The election of a Democrat, however, would hasten the spread of slavery. Returning to Illinois, Lincoln made the same point in eight speeches before local audiences, touring the northernmost counties in the Seventh District to try to keep nonextensionists in the Whig fold. The best way to stop the spread of slavery, if not overturn it, he argued, was to vote for Taylor. In November, Taylor won the Seventh District with 52 percent of the vote but lost the state of Illinois.[36]

Both the traditional economic issues and the emerging nativist crusade helped Zachary Taylor win Springfield. Taylor supporters were wealthier than Democrats and more highly skilled but also more heavily native-born.[37] Springfield's politicians found fertile ground in traditional appeals to class and occupation. Democrats claimed that the Whig Party comprised "a large portion of the Lawyers and Doctors, Merchants, and Bank Directors, stock jobbers and speculators, [who] think they can deceive the farmers and mechanics." Whigs, by contrast, made more subtle attempts to woo farmers, mechanics, and laborers to their camp by muting class antagonisms. Whigs routinely patronized the farmer as "Thou chosen man of God" and mechanics and laborers as the "hard-fisted, honest, yeomanry."[38]

In 1848, Springfield's Whigs were concentrated in the professions, public service, nonproductive occupations, and commerce. They were overrepresented by almost three to one among professionals, confirming the contemporary Democratic identification of Whigs with lawyers and doctors. Overall, four-fifths of professionals voted Whig. Whig appeals to workers also seem to have borne fruit, with "manufacturers," many of whom were skilled craftsmen and even factory owners, dividing their votes evenly between Taylor and Cass. Democratic occupations, by contrast, included manual workers, especially the building trades, transportation ("the canallers and rail road workmen," according to one Whig), and unskilled laborers. More than one-sixth of all Democrats were laborers, and almost two-thirds of unskilled workers voted Democratic in 1848. Almost two-thirds of businessmen and professionals, by contrast, voted Whig. Whigs were, in addition, wealthier than Democrats, owning about one-third more real wealth in 1850 than did Democrats. Working-class voters were an important mainstay of the Democratic Party.[39]

So were foreign-born voters. Democrats framed this predilection in a positive light, portraying themselves as "the protectors of the rights of aliens." By charging that "The strong, robust, able-bodied Irishman and German who enters this State, ploughs our prairies, fells our forests, opens our roads and digs our canals, is, according to this faction, unfit to enjoy the rights of a freeman," Democrats could appeal simultaneously to immigrants and workers. Whigs fended off such claims as "demogogical" and "the last resorts of a depraved and desperate faction," charging Democrats with "herding" recent immigrants to the polls on election day. But, confirming Democratic rhetoric, Whigs consistently decried the admission of immigrants to the polling place.[40]

In 1848, Springfield's Whigs attempted to attract immigrant voters, declaring that "the Whigs are the true friends of the foreigner." Democrats countered by warning immigrants, particularly Irish and German voters, that "whigs basely fawn and flatter while they would betray." In fact, Whig voters were heavily underrepresented among immigrants. As they did elsewhere during the period, immigrants voted heavily Democratic in Springfield, representing almost one-fourth of all Cass voters in 1848. Overall, about 70 percent of the foreign-born voted Democratic. By contrast, only about one-tenth of Whig voters were immigrants. The leading immigrant groups were the Irish and Germans, and each of these nationalities went Democratic by a majority of three to one, reflecting both their foreign birth and their liturgical religious doctrines as Catholics and Lutherans. Interestingly, breaking down native-born voters into region of birth reveals little divergence between North and South. Whigs came from the two sections about equally, so there was no obvious Yankee-Cavalier antagonism in Springfield. Breaking down the Northeast into New England and the Middle States does clarify the pattern. Whigs were heavily overrepresented among Yankees, voters born in New England. About one-eighth of all Whigs were Yankees, but only about one in twenty-five Democrats hailed from New England. Put differently, about three-fourths of all Springfield's Yankees voted Whig.[41]

In November, Taylor won Springfield with almost 60 percent of the vote. Springfield's Whigs celebrated with a "jollification" that included bonfires, a torchlight parade, cannon fire, and fireworks. A few days later, they learned that Taylor had carried the nation in spite of losing Illinois. The Democratic nominee, Lewis Cass of Michigan, had won a plurality in the state, with the Free Soil candidate, Martin Van Buren, receiving considerable support in the northern counties. In Springfield, Van Buren received only thirty-nine votes or 2.1 percent. "The Wilmot Proviso was the most absorbing question in the late Presidential election in Illinois," Springfield's Whigs concluded. "All men must admit that the whigs fought the political battle in Illinois under the banner of the Wilmot Proviso." Meanwhile, 80 percent of all defectors to Free Soil were Whigs. In Springfield, Free Soil attracted four times as many Whigs as Democrats.[42]

The lesson for Whigs was obvious. The 1840s had brought a shift from the traditional economic issues—bank, tariff, and internal improvements—that had provoked the party in the first place and toward new moral questions, primarily opposition to slavery but also nativism. Lincoln clearly recognized the strange Whig brew that included free soil Democrats or "Barnburners," nativists, and disaffected Democrats, writing that "all the odds and ends are with us—Barnburners, Native Americans, Tyler men, disappointed office seeking locofocos, and the Lord knows what." Guiding the party through this new political thicket of moral issues would be a difficult task. With Stuart retired, Baker absent, Hardin dead, and Logan defeated, Lincoln was poised to lead the way.

CHAPTER 20

God Made Us Separate

Slavery and race had always divided the people of Illinois. French settlers around Vincennes brought the first African American slaves to the Illinois Country during the eighteenth century. After the United States acquired the region, Congress enacted the Northwest Ordinance of 1787 to govern the territory. The ordinance contained a provision, Article VI, that prohibited slavery and involuntary servitude, except as punishment for a crime. Over the next half-century, the residents of the Northwest Territory and later the state of Illinois systematically set out to weaken Article VI and allow the continuation of slavery. The Northwest Ordinance exempted French slave owners from its provisions, and American settlers who already owned slaves demanded similar treatment. They petitioned for a ten-year suspension of Article VI, as well as some form of gradual emancipation that would keep African Americans in slavery until they reached a specified age, such as thirty or thirty-five. In an attempt to continue attracting southern settlers to the region north of the Ohio River, the first governor of the Northwest Territory, Arthur St. Clair, ruled that Article VI was not retroactive. Any slaves who were in the region before the ordinance took effect would remain enslaved for the rest of their lives. As a result of this subversion of the Ordinance in the Northwest and gradual emancipation plans in the Northeast, about one-sixth of northern African Americans were slaves in 1820.[1]

Succeeding decisions quickly made a shambles of the Northwest Ordinance. In 1830, William Henry Harrison, governor of Indiana Territory, which included Illinois, imposed a system of involuntary service on African Americans. Harrison legalized indentured servitude, allowing terms to run up to ninety-nine years. In 1809, Illinois Territory adopted a similar system of "registered servants." Illinois residents could "import" slaves who were under fifteen years of age and register them at the county seat. The agreement between master and slave was to be consensual, but of course slaves under the age of fifteen had little option but to agree. Typical provisions required slaves to exchange a year's worth of labor for as little as a coat or a blanket. Registered servants could be sold and resold at will, and an underground market in slaves developed in Illinois. Children born to registered servants belonged to their masters until they turned thirty-five, in the case of male slaves, or thirty among females. Masters had three options. They could renew the contract with the consent of their slaves, set them free, or sell them back into slavery in the South. In 1814, a new statute allowed Americans to hire slaves for one-year terms that were renewable for any number of years.[2]

The state's first constitution, adopted in 1818, embodied this system of one-year, renewable contracts and required the enforcement of all existing agreements. Illinois also imposed a set of severe restrictions on the rights of free African Americans within its limits. Under these restrictions, known as the Black Laws, free people of color had to file a certificate of freedom at the county seat. Overseers of the poor retained the right to expel any African American, and free blacks who wanted to enter the state needed to have a white resident post a one-thousand-dollar bond to ensure that they would not become public charges. The Black Laws denied legal and political rights, including the right to testify in court against whites and to vote or hold office. African Americans were also denied a host of social privileges, such as the right to marry whites. The admission of neighboring Missouri as a slave state in 1820 actually prompted renewed demands to reestablish slavery in Illinois. Many southern-born whites relocated to Missouri to practice the institution of slavery in its familiar, unmodified form, but many Illinois residents attempted to reinstate slavery. In 1824, they launched a campaign for a constitutional convention to do just that. The measure was popular in the southern one-third of the state, known as Little Egypt, but failed by a wide margin. The decision not to reestablish slavery slowed the pace of southern settlement in Illinois. In Sangamon County, 83 percent of the voters opposed the convention and the demand to reintroduce slavery. Most whites in early Illinois were willing to tolerate a modified form of slavery for African Americans but not complete, hereditary enslavement.[3]

Lincoln's earliest experiences with slavery occurred before he came to Illinois. He had little contact with slaves and slave owners as a boy in Hardin County, Kentucky, which was a society of mostly free, white family farmers rather than large slave plantations. About one-eighth of the population were slaves. By comparison, slaves comprised fully one-third of the population of Mary Todd's childhood home of Fayette County, Kentucky. Still, the Cumberland Road, which ran past the Lincoln cabin, presented the constant spectacle of slaves herded like cattle between Nashville and Louisville. As a boy, Lincoln similarly had little experience with free African Americans. Only 3 percent of Hardin County's black residents, twenty-eight of them, were free. Moving to Indiana isolated Lincoln even further from African Americans, both slave and free. When he left Spencer County, where in his own words he "grew up," there were no slaves and only fourteen African Americans in the entire county. His first memorable glimpses of slavery occurred on his voyages down the Mississippi River to New Orleans, and his earliest recorded racial memory originated when he was nineteen during his trip down the river with Allen Gentry. Lincoln remembered thirty years later that "one night they were attacked by seven negroes with intent to kill and rob them." During his first trip southward as an adult, guiding Denton Offutt's flatboat in 1831, Lincoln caught a glimpse of a slave market in New Orleans. His cousin John Hanks believed that this experience made an indelible mark and moved Lincoln to sympathize with African American slaves. "There it was we Saw Negroes Chained—maltreated—whipt & scourged," Hanks recalled in 1865. "I can say Knowingly that it was on this trip that he formed his opinions of Slavery: it ran its iron in him then & there." These early experiences as a youth helped to shape the racial views of the man. "I am naturally anti-slavery," Lincoln reflected as president. "If slavery is not wrong, nothing is wrong. I can not remember when I did not so think and feel."[4]

When Lincoln settled in New Salem, thirty-eight African Americans were living in Sangamon County out of a total population of more than twelve thousand. Most of them, just over two-thirds, were free. In the entire county, only one African American, Lucy Roundtree, headed an independent household. The remaining free blacks were servants living in white families. Six residents of the county, including John Todd, the patriarch of the Todd family in Springfield, owned slaves. Todd, in fact, owned four slaves, two boys and two girls, which made him the largest slave owner in the county. Local government accommodated slave owners by registering servants and apprenticing African American children. In 1835, for example, John Todd took on an eight-year-old African American girl "to learn the art and mystery of domestic housewifery" until she turned eighteen. The county commissioners followed southern tradition in recognizing slaves not as people but as property. In 1827, they imposed a tax of one-half of 1 percent "on the following personal property (viz) on slaves and indentured or registered negro or mulatto servants on pleasure carriages on Distilling on stock in trade on all horse mares mules asses and neat Cattle." They were also responsible for issuing certificates of freedom. In 1834, the commissioners duly recorded that "Macklin Shelby a colored man presented the following certificate of Freedom." Macklin offered evidence that he had sued his masters for false imprisonment and won the suit. After considering the claim, the commissioners ruled that "Macklin by virtue of said Judgment is entitled to all the privileges of a free man of colour." Macklin, of course, remained subject to the state's Black Laws, which severely circumscribed those privileges.[5]

Under this system of legalized slavery and restricted rights, African Americans continued to settle in the county during the 1830s, mostly as servants and slaves. By the time Lincoln moved to Springfield, eighty-six

African Americans lived in the town, comprising almost 5 percent of the population. The sex ratio was unbalanced, but in the opposite direction of that of whites. Almost two-thirds of African Americans living in Springfield were female, reflecting the growing demand for domestic servants and perhaps also the greater proclivity of men to run away. Despite the racism of southern-born Springfielders, the legality of involuntary servitude, and the inequality inherent in the Black Laws, an African American community was beginning to take root. On a hopeful note, the number of slaves in Springfield fell between 1830 and 1840, from eleven to five. Meanwhile, free African Americans established eleven independent households, all but one of them headed by men. Overall, two-thirds of the city's free blacks lived within African-American families. The rest were servants working for white families. Lincoln's future in-laws Ninian and Benjamin Edwards, his former employer and political adversary John Calhoun, and his friend and political ally Edward Baker all employed free blacks as servants. Even William Butler kept a free African American servant, a boy under ten, while Lincoln boarded with him. The five slave owners in Springfield included Lincoln's future sister-in-law, Elizabeth Edwards, Mary Todd's sister. In 1835, Ninian Edwards took on an eleven-year-old African American orphan girl to practice "domestic housewifery" in his household until 1842. Abraham Lincoln courted Mary Todd in a home that included an African American slave.[6]

The presence of African Americans, both slave and free, provoked a wide range of responses among white Springfielders. At one extreme, the demand for labor drew some of them into the underground market for slaves. In 1830, Pascal Enos received a letter asking him "Will you please have the goodness to ascertain if Mr. Wm Kirkpatrick has a coloured boy for sale & what he would take for him, what is his character, if sober, honest and a good hand with horses." To his credit, Enos never answered the letter, which prompted a renewed request a month later for information about the "colour boy" who was rumored to be for sale. Illinois masters often advertised for their runaway servants, just as southern slave owners were accustomed to do. A slave owner in St. Clair County, near the old French settlements, posted a notice in Springfield for a runaway African American who spoke English and French. At the other extreme, whites sometimes worked to set Springfield's slaves free. In 1831, the Commissioners Court freed a slave after a white man posted a bond on his behalf. "Henry Yates came into court and gave bond as this law requires," they reported, "in setting free a negro man named Nelson aged fifty five years."[7]

Somewhere between these two extremes, most Springfielders neither owned nor freed slaves. The most prevalent response was endorsement of the Black Laws that reduced African Americans to the status of second-class citizens, along with acquiescence in southern slavery. Racism knew no political bounds, and most Whigs and Democrats spurned all attempts to extend legal, political, or social equality to African Americans. "We are opposed to extending the right of suffrage to the blacks upon any terms," the leading Whig newspaper in Springfield, the *Sangamo Journal* argued. Rejecting the idea of a property qualification to allow only the wealthiest African Americans to vote, the *Journal* actually boasted that "we would prefer to admit the poor ones and exclude the rich ones. Of all things keep us clear of the negro who is puffed up with the idea of being master of a little property." At the mere hint of a property qualification that would allow the wealthiest blacks to vote, the *Journal* printed a crude cartoon, rendered in offensive caricature, depicting an African American casting a ballot and pushing white voters aside with the command to "Git out ob de way, poor white folks, and let gemman of 'sponsibility and qualiakashuns vote.—yah! yah! yah!" The Whig editor rejected even a modicum of legal rights as the entering wedge of both political participation and social equality. "Once admit negro testimony, and the right of suffrage, and a participation in the government, would soon follow," he warned. "There would then be but one step more—too horrid to be contemplated—and that amalgamation." The widespread fear of amalgamation remained the trump card for the opponents of any extension of rights to African Americans. "Whatever may be said to the contrary, in the Free States, as in the Slave States, it is our opinion that the black man will never be the equal of the white man," the Whig editor reiterated in 1850. "Right or wrong, we regard this as true. The races are distinct. The slightest taint of African blood, degrades the Saxon race."[8]

As a young legislator, Lincoln reflected majority opinion in opposing African American suffrage. During his first term, he voted for a resolution "that the elective franchise should be kept pure from contamination by the admission of colored votes." Running for a second term, he announced that "I go for admitting all whites to the right of suffrage, who pay taxes and bear arms." Despite his sympathy for the plight of southern slaves, Lincoln never publicly advocated the extension of political rights to African Americans until a few days before his death. He also rejected any thought of racial intermarriage. Lincoln's famous debates with Stephen Douglas made this point clearly. "I protest, now and forever, against that counterfeit logic which presumes that because I do not want a negro woman for a slave, I do necessarily want her for a wife," Lincoln insisted at Chicago. "My understanding is that I need not have her for either, but as God made us separate, we can leave one another alone and do one another much good thereby. There are white men enough to marry all the white women, and enough black men to marry all the black women, and in God's name let them be so married." Lincoln invoked God to portray racial separation as entirely natural and therefore insurmountable. Born into a slave society, Lincoln grew up within racist communities that instilled a sense of white superiority that would be difficult or even impossible to overcome. This prejudice stayed with him until his death.[9]

Whatever their opinions about free blacks, most Springfielders felt no compunction about returning runaway slaves to their masters. Runaway notices peppered local newspapers, promising rewards ranging from $100 to $250, about half a year's wages for a skilled craftsman. One notice offered $250 for an entire family—husband, wife, and four-year-old daughter—who "left my farm in my absence, and without cause." Sometimes local residents were seized as runaway slaves and forced back into slavery. In 1842, an Arkansas man claimed James Foster, who had lived in Springfield for two years, as a runaway slave. Judge Samuel Treat, who kept an African American servant in his own home, demanded proof of ownership and then surrendered Foster to his master and his fate in Arkansas. Beyond the scope of the courts, mobs sometimes ran down suspected fugitives. Several residents of a nearby town spotted two African Americans traveling to Chicago in 1845, and, on the strength of a runaway notice in the Springfield *Register*, decided to give chase. They drove the two into the woods and caught one of them in a hazel thicket. Despite his protests of freedom, he was relegated to the upper floor of the county courthouse until his captors' letter to Missouri received a reply. The rationale for the confinement was that "we have got no jail and a good many abolitionists about." In the face of hostility and suspicion, African Americans had ample incentive to leave central Illinois, so the black community lost members to slavery in the South and freedom farther North.[10]

Beyond such intermittent episodes of escape and reenslavement, the most organized response to racial tensions in Springfield was the formation of a local colonization society. Colonization was a national movement that sought to eliminate blacks from American society by sending them in "colonies" to either Africa or Latin America. The American Colonization Society formed in Washington, D.C., in 1816, mounting a campaign to create an overseas colony for African Americans. The founding members were mostly southerners, and Henry Clay presided over the meeting that organized the society. Their motives varied. Some of them were simply racists who strove to eliminate all African Americans, both slave and free, from American soil. Others hoped to undermine the institution of slavery by creating a viable alternative for slave owners who might free their slaves if they knew that they would leave the country rather than remain as free blacks. Still others genuinely believed that African Americans would be better off if they left a predominantly white country and created a black society of their own in a tropical climate. The movement produced local colonization societies in every state except South Carolina and culminated in the creation of the new African nation of Liberia in 1822.[11]

The first colonization society in Illinois formed in Vandalia, the state capital, in 1830. Springfielders were quick to endorse its mission. "We have in this State many colored people, living in degradation and poverty, who, under a government like that of Liberia, would become useful and valuable members of society," the editor of the Springfield *Journal* reasoned, "and would thus be able to give to their descendants blessings and privileges which they can never hope for in this country." In 1833, a group of Springfielders met in the Methodist Church to organize a local chapter. Charles Matheny was elected president, and John Todd Stuart was the society's secretary.[12]

This first colonization society soon lapsed and remained inactive until the end of the decade. In 1839, an auxiliary of the American Colonization Society formed at the Presbyterian Church in Springfield under the leadership of Rev. John G. Bergen. The local chapter included about one hundred members and heard an address from the secretary of the national society. The Sangamon Colonization Society grew quickly to 150 members and began meeting semiannually. The new president was Charles Dresser, the Episcopal minister who had married the Lincolns. Like the Todd and Edwards families, the Dressers employed an African American servant girl as an apprentice. Both John Todd and John Todd Stuart were vice presidents of the colonization society. Within a month, a group of Methodists joined the Presbyterians in supporting colonization. The Ladies of the Methodist Congregation in Springfield donated fifty-two dollars to send two African Americans to Liberia, returning "two of the wandering children of bereaved Africa in the bosom of their mother land," as they put it, "in the enjoyment of all the blessings of civil and religious liberty."[13]

By 1845, the colonization movement was strong enough to support a statewide organization, the Illinois State Colonization Society, organized in Springfield. Its purpose was to establish a colony of free African Americans on the west coast of Africa, as envisioned by the national society. The group intended to meet annually, with members paying annual dues of one dollar to support the venture. Colonization was a bipartisan effort but generally attracted more Whigs than Democrats. In 1848, four-fifths of the leaders of Springfield's colonization societies were Whigs. Some colonizationists may have viewed the movement as a stepping-stone to abolition. Most of them, however, probably viewed colonization as entirely consistent with southern slavery. In fact, the editor of the *Illinois Journal* labeled the local chapter "an institution antagonistical to abolitionism."[14]

African Americans overwhelmingly rejected colonization as both racist and impractical, holding anticolonization meetings in Chicago and Springfield. Still, a minority devised a plan to emigrate voluntarily to Liberia. In 1847, the Colored Baptist Association of Madison County asked Samuel S. Ball, a black Springfielder and Baptist elder, to travel to Liberia to investigate the "condition of the Republic of Liberia favorable to us in America." A native Virginian, Ball worked as a barber, like one-fourth of his black peers in Springfield. In 1848, the thirty-eight-year-old Ball left his wife and five children behind to visit Liberia, armed with a letter of introduction from the governor of Illinois. Although local Democrats reported that

"This movement is, we understand, entirely independent of the colonization and abolition societies," in fact the local colonization society financed the journey. Ball left Springfield for New Orleans in February, only to be stopped by ice on the Mississippi River. He made a second "successful" attempt to reach Liberia via Baltimore in May. When he returned, he issued a report to the Colored Baptist Association that later appeared as a thirteen-page pamphlet. Ball presented a realistic and even bleak assessment of the prospects of poor emigrants traveling to Liberia. "As to people going to that country without means," he reported, "I consider it one of the worst countries he can go to." Ball recommended a group effort, concluding that "the only way in which I would be willing to remove to Liberia, would be to go in a body; and that each family should have, before starting, sufficient means within themselves to procure them the necessaries of life." Apparently, no other Springfielders were willing or able to accompany Ball to Liberia, and by 1850 he was again practicing his trade as a barber in Springfield. Ball later wrote an ill-fated legislative bill to extend financial aid to emigrants, but in 1852, before gathering support for it, at age forty-two, he died of typhoid fever, leaving a widow and six children.[15]

Most African Americans, rejecting colonization, hoped to stay in Springfield while improving their situation. When the Illinois State Colonization Society requested legislative funding to support their mission, African Americans in Springfield held a public meeting to protest. They organized Baptist and Methodist churches in the city and, resolving that schools were "the only sure way to redeem ourselves from the bondage we are now in," mounted a campaign to open a school of their own. Recognizing their precarious condition in Springfield, African Americans called on sympathetic whites for help. Clearly "too weak in point of numbers to sustain a School permanently amongst them," the trustees organized a public supper to raise funds. "We have appointed a committee of females to solicit donations among our white friends towards making the Supper," they announced, "and we hope that their claims will not be disregarded." Striking a rare optimistic note, the local newspaper reported that "A large number of our white citizens, ladies and gentlemen attended." Despite his earlier commitment to colonization, Samuel Ball served as one of the trustees of the new "colored school." Springfield's blacks also embraced temperance as a self-reform that would improve their lot. "Nearly all the colored population of this city are members of this Society," white reformers boasted. "It has already been productive of great good to them." If nothing else, the temperance crusade provided another focal point for the African American community, which held a parade complete with banners, badges, and music, under the aegis of the Colored Baptist Association. Factional problems, however, besieged even this beleaguered community. Most African Americans were Methodists who quarreled with the Baptists of both Springfield and Jacksonville, refusing to cooperate with the Baptist Association's plans for education and colonization. A Baptist critic charged that "They must be ignorant, and do not know their own misery."[16]

A handful of white Springfielders were sympathetic toward the African American community and opposed both slavery and colonization in favor of equal rights. A few bold voices even called for the extension of political rights to landowning blacks. "Should a man who is settled in our country, and who has property, be denied the right of suffrage, because he is black?" asked a letter writer in 1836. "Freedom is but a mockery! if Negroes are not allowed the right of suffrage!" The growth of abolition societies across the North produced a counterreaction, antiabolitionism, aimed at suppressing antislavery activity as injurious to public order as well as the true interests of the nation. The most notorious antiabolitionist riot in American history occurred in nearby Alton, Illinois, in 1837, and prompted a principled response from Lincoln in his Lyceum Speech. In Springfield, antiabolitionists responded to the Lovejoy murder by holding a public meeting to head off any calls for the emancipation of slaves and the mob violence that might result. They resolved that "the efforts of abolitionists in this community, are neither necessary nor useful," arguing that abolition leaders were "designing, ambitious men, and dangerous members of society, and should be shunned by all good citizens." Instead of promoting equality, they concluded, abolitionism would only "breed contention, broils and mobs." For the moment, they were right. A few years later, when an abolitionist attempted to deliver a lecture in Springfield, a group of 150 boys disrupted the talk by making noise with sticks, boards, and horns. They drowned out the speech and threw eggs at the speaker's head. Refusing to intervene, the city police watched the spectacle and just laughed. Democrats seized on this opportunity to condemn the growing influence of "mobocracy" and to warn that abolitionism would only lead to disunion and civil war.[17]

In response to the growing antislavery movement in the North, the Illinois legislature adopted resolutions supporting slavery in the South while condemning the formation of abolition societies in the North. During his second term in the legislature, Lincoln made his initial public stand against slavery. Only six legislators opposed the resolution, including Lincoln and his colleague from Sangamon County, Dan Stone. Signaling their strong objections to the resolutions, Lincoln and Stone filed a protest. "They believe that the institution of slavery is founded on both injustice and bad policy," they wrote, "but that the promulgation of abolition doctrines tends rather to increase than to abate its evils." The protest put Lincoln and Stone on the middle ground in the debate over slavery. They could not stomach the legislature's endorsement of slavery as a "sacred" right, yet they also could not countenance the activities of abolitionists to undermine the institution. Lincoln's position harmonized with the views of most Springfielders, who avoided any connection with either southern slavery on the one hand or northern abolitionism on the other. When Lincoln ran for reelection for a third term, he received the highest vote of any candidate in Sangamon County. Reflecting pride in his early stand against slavery, Lincoln highlighted the protest in one of his autobiographies and cited its precise location in the Illinois House Journals. As the Republican nominee for president, he noted that the protest "defined his position on the slavery question; and so far as it goes, it was then the same that it is now." Thirty-five years later, Lincoln was still trying to steer a path between the rock of slavery on one side and the shoal of abolitionism on the other. He abhorred slavery as an evil but objected to abolition as a remedy.[18]

During his final term in the legislature, Lincoln once again encountered southern slavery. In 1841, he visited his old friend Joshua Speed near Louisville, Kentucky. Speed had recently inherited an opulent plantation, Farmington, on which his father had gathered more than seventy slaves. After two months, Lincoln and Speed returned together to Illinois, taking a riverboat down the Ohio to St. Louis, where they boarded a stagecoach for Springfield. On the riverboat, Lincoln witnessed the eerie spectacle of a dozen slaves chained together, as he put it, "like so many fish upon a trotline." He felt genuinely moved. "In this condition they were being separated forever from the scenes of their childhood, their friends, their fathers and mothers, and brothers and sisters, and many of them, from their wives and children," he mused with an eloquence on the subject that would soon become second nature, "and going into perpetual slavery where the lash of the master is proverbially more ruthless and unrelenting than any other where." The scene stayed with Lincoln, and fourteen years later he called its very memory "a continual torment to me." Significantly, however, Lincoln condemned the slave trade that destroyed families and sent slaves westward but not the slavery on a plantation like Farmington. Just as tellingly, he sympathized with the slaves but believed that he could do nothing to ameliorate their plight.[19]

That same attitude informed his stance on slavery while in Congress, where he first had the opportunity to confront slavery as a national problem. Already a nonextensionist in private, Lincoln's opposition to the Mexican War strengthened his views and made them public. As a moderate, however, he continued the stance that he had taken while in the Illinois legislature—that slavery was wrong, indeed evil, but that Congress had no power to interfere with it in southern states. Instead, he concentrated on attacking slavery only where Congress did have undisputed authority to end it, in the western territories and the District of Columbia. Lincoln therefore supported the Wilmot Proviso, which sought to exclude slavery from any new territory acquired from Mexico, and voted for it at least forty times. He also introduced an amendment abolishing slavery in the nation's capital. Neither measure won passage, yet Lincoln's support marked him as a moderate who would not confront slavery directly but would do everything possible to prevent its spread. During his single congressional term,

Lincoln witnessed the creation of a new and powerful antislavery crusade, the free soil movement, dedicated to attacking slavery indirectly by prohibiting it not in the South but wherever Congress had a clear power—and what Free Soilers called a duty—to end it.[20]

Beyond his lifelong commitment to political moderation, Lincoln's legal training and law practice encouraged ambivalence toward slavery. During the 1840s, he argued two "slave cases" that put him on opposite sides of the issue. The first involved a young African American woman named Nance, who was sold as an indentured servant to David Bailey in Tazewell County. Nance, who still had seven years left on her contract, told Bailey that she would not work without pay and left his service. Bailey sued Nance's previous master to recover the $432 he spent to buy the servant. Lincoln defended Bailey and argued that Nance had always been free by virtue of the Northwest Ordinance and the Illinois Constitution of 1818, which both prohibited slavery. Nance's original owner therefore had no legal right to sell her to Bailey. The Tazewell County Circuit Court agreed on the grounds that "the presumption of the law in Illinois is that every person is free without regard to color." Therefore, "the sale of a free person is illegal."[21]

The second case, which Lincoln argued six years later, put him on the other side of the issue. Robert Matson was a Kentucky slave owner who brought his slaves into Illinois every year to work his farm from planting until harvest. In 1847, his slaves ran away and sued for their freedom, arguing—as Lincoln had done six years earlier—that the Northwest Ordinance prohibited slavery in Illinois. Matson hired Lincoln to get his slaves back. Now Lincoln worked to circumscribe the effect of the Ordinance, arguing that it applied only to slaves and slave owners who were permanent residents of the state. As a resident of Kentucky, Matson had a "right of transit," allowing him to transport his slaves into or through free territory for any temporary purpose. Lincoln lost the case when the court granted freedom to Matson's slaves.[22]

Taken together, the two slave cases say little about Lincoln's attitude toward slavery and race but everything about his reverence for the law. Throughout Lincoln's rhetoric and later his policy on slavery and antislavery ran a profound commitment to do everything possible to enforce the law. As a lawyer he felt a sacred obligation to defend the interests of his clients, whatever they might be. Further, he believed that only the rule of law could preserve the republic that guaranteed freedom, ultimately, to everyone. In his Lyceum Speech, written ten years earlier, Lincoln had celebrated a reverence for law as the foundation of self-government. He therefore refused to challenge the rule of law even to advance a compelling moral reform like the end of slavery. Throughout his life, he insisted on upholding the law, which meant tolerating enslavement wherever it was legal while defending freedom wherever it was legal. He just as consistently rejected any notion of a "higher law," a form of justice of divine rather than human creation, that many abolitionists espoused in the campaign they waged against slavery.

Slavery, colonization, abolition—Springfielders embraced all three but, like Lincoln, most hewed to the middle of the spectrum. Unsuccessful at colonizing African Americans out of Illinois, white racists turned instead to restricting the immigration of any more free blacks into the state. White Springfielders had always insisted with near unanimity that "Our State is threatened to be overrun with free negroes." The common reaction to any hint of abolition was simply that "We do not want the negroes who will be thus thrown upon us." In 1848, a new constitution took the state a step forward by explicitly banning slavery. With the threat of abolition looming over the horizon, however, the new constitution also impeded the settlement of any additional African Americans. During the constitutional debates, a delegate from one of the southern counties proposed a provision prohibiting the immigration of free blacks, calling them "a great annoyance, if not a nuisance, to the people of Illinois." He claimed that free African Americans created "little settlements" whose purpose was to help fugitive slaves escape their masters. Linking his proposal to colonization, he concluded that if African Americans could not enjoy equality in Illinois, they should not be admitted at all. Delegates from northern counties responded with a proposal that would prohibit "black laws" in Illinois.[23]

Sangamon County's four convention delegates were all Whigs and included three Springfielders. The delegates from Springfield all had close ties to Lincoln. Stephen Logan and Ninian Edwards were his in-laws, and James Matheny, one of his closest friends, was best man at his wedding. The single delegate from outside the city, John Dawson, was a farmer who employed a twenty-year-old African American youth as an "indentured apprentice" to practice farming. During the debate over immigration restriction, Logan and Edwards claimed the middle ground, attempting to avoid conflict by removing any reference to immigration restriction from the constitution. Logan posed a distinction between "judgment and prejudice"— prejudice against African Americans on the one hand and a rational judgment about right and wrong on the other. He proposed that the convention leave the whole issue to the state legislature, which could make a more rational decision based on judgment rather than prejudice. The debate pitted representatives of the northern counties against the unreasoning racism of Little Egypt. Edwards also tried to play peacemaker, proposing an adjournment to allow tempers to cool overnight.[24]

As the dispute dragged on into a second day, Logan restated his compromise position, "a midway policy of leaving the matter to the Legislature." In an attempt to placate the northern counties, he insisted that he "respected the abolitionists and believed them to be honest and sincere, and was willing to listen to what they had to say." In support of the southern counties, he asked the delegates to "remember that the north was only a part of the State; that the State had two ends." Springfield, of course, lay in the middle. Balancing the demands of both sections was the key to compromise, and Logan wanted the legislature to do it. At the end of the debate, Edwards moved to omit the restrictive clause from the constitution and won the motion 71–63. The vote crossed party lines and split the state geographically, with only a handful of delegates north of Springfield opposing the motion.[25]

Rather than following Logan's advice and letting the legislature handle the issue, however, southern delegates decided to put the disputed clause to a popular vote. In April 1848, voters who ratified the new constitution were asked to consider a clause restricting African American immigration as a separate measure. The resulting vote was literally a referendum on racism, focusing on the single issue of affording African Americans an equal right to move to Illinois. Across the state, the restrictive clause won approval by an overwhelming 70 percent. Illinois joined Indiana and Oregon as the only states in the Union that restricted African American immigration in their constitutions.[26]

Voters in Springfield supported the restriction by an even greater margin, 84 percent. The restrictive clause won bipartisan support from Whigs and Democrats. In keeping with their sympathetic stance toward southern slavery and their aggressive racism, however, Democrats provided the mainstay of support, voting for restriction at the rate of 92 percent. Eighty percent of Whigs supported the measure, while two-thirds of the small Free Soil contingent in the city opposed it. Somewhat surprisingly, one-third of Free Soilers actually supported restriction of African American settlement in Illinois, suggesting that even a minority of Free Soilers were motivated by racism more than humanitarian concern for blacks.[27]

Not surprisingly, Yankees were less enthusiastic about restriction than their southern-born neighbors. Two-thirds of northeastern natives but almost nine-tenths of native southerners supported the clause. "We are men who have come here from southern and slaveholding states," a former Kentuckian insisted, "we are men who have seen the evils of a negro population, we came here to escape them, and we wish to prevent the increase within this state of that class of population more vicious and more degraded than even slaves—free negroes." An economic dimension suggested that fears of heightened competition and lower wages encouraged workers to support restrictions on African American settlement. White workers in the manual trades and transportation competed directly with African Americans, which depressed their wages and encouraged racial discrimination. As a result, unskilled laborers in Springfield supported restriction unanimously. Four-fifths of skilled craftsmen and builders also voted for the restrictive clause. Merchants and professionals were the least supportive of restriction, casting about 60 percent of their votes for the constitutional clause.

Opponents of the clause owned almost three times as much real property as supporters, confirming that economic insecurity was a primary source of racism among voters in Springfield. Colonization leaders played a conspicuous role in opposing the clause, casting 60 percent of their votes against it, which suggests that by and large colonization represented an attempt to help rather than hurt African Americans. The restrictive clause instructed the legislature to prohibit the immigration of free African Americans into Illinois, but the general assembly did not comply for another five years.[28]

Springfield's African American community had reached its zenith by 1850. In conformity with the newly adopted constitution, there were no more slaves in Springfield. Twenty-seven independent black families lived in the city, all but one of them headed by men. Four-fifths of the household heads had been born in slave states. The sex ratio had evened out, offering hope for a stable family life. In fact, nine-tenths of Springfield's African Americans lived in independent households, leaving only one-tenth to live with white families as servants. Still, there were conspicuous signs of discrimination and poverty. The African American community grew by one-third between 1840 and 1850, while the white population nearly doubled. Black families were also considerably smaller than white families, reflecting the tenuous status of free blacks within a racist community. Supporting an average of only 1.6 children, African American families were not yet self-sustaining. Economically, African American men were relegated exclusively to the ranks of manual workers. Almost one-half of them were unskilled laborers, and only three African Americans practiced skilled crafts in 1850. Men, like women, specialized in domestic service, and almost one-fourth of them were barbers. In fact, there was not a single white barber in Springfield in 1850. A local newspaper celebrated the kind of menial labor African Americans performed in its description of "Black Bill," who was renowned for "handling the white-wash brush with great dexterity, and is capital at 'sweeping-out,' 'building fires,' 'blacking boots,' 'renovating old clothes,' and such like works of art and utility." As a result of this kind of occupational segregation, African American families owned only about one-seventh as much property as the typical white family in Springfield.[29]

Critics labeled free blacks "old, decrepid, and good-for-nothing." In fact, their labor was vital to the city but was poorly rewarded. They represented one-tenth of all manual workers but owned only one-third as much property as whites practicing the same trades. The typical black man in Springfield was forty-one, only five years older than his white counterpart, and the oldest was fifty-six. Overall, the African-American community had dwindled to just 3 percent of Springfield's population and commanded a mere one-half of 1 percent of the city's real wealth. African American men were five times as likely as whites to be unemployed. Confirming the impact of racism on African Americans' economic status, full-blooded blacks fared even worse than those of mixed ancestry. In 1850, mixed-race African Americans, known as "mulattoes," owned twice as much property as their full-blooded peers, who were labeled "black." Apparently, lighter complexions contributed to a slightly higher social status. One-half of Springfield's African Americans were of mixed race, compared to about 30 percent in the rest of the North.[30]

Because of their minority status in Springfield and their poverty, African Americans were not economically viable as a subcommunity within the city. They had to develop a white clientele in order to survive. In a "walking city" such as Springfield, African Americans had no choice but to live and work in predominantly white neighborhoods. As a result, there were six distinct clusters of black families spread across the city, usually in groups of two or three houses, rather than a single "ghetto" in the modern sense. The Lincolns, for example, were surrounded by blacks. About one-tenth of all African Americans, over twenty of them, lived within a mere three blocks of Eighth and Jackson. Only about one-half of African American families had any black neighbors. Significantly, African American families who were surrounded by whites were economically better off. The residents of the black clusters owned just over one-half as much real property. Residential proximity brought more whites into contact with African Americans but usually the most prosperous, which may have disguised the true extent of black poverty in Springfield. One result of the residential clustering was the epidemics that usually claimed more blacks than whites.[31]

The 1850s was a decade of severe setbacks for free blacks living in the North. When California petitioned for admission to the Union as a free state in 1850, southerners threatened to secede. In an attempt to prevent or at least to postpone civil war, Congress enacted the Compromise of 1850. Engineered by the Whig Henry Clay of Kentucky and the Democrat Stephen Douglas of Illinois, the compromise included the Fugitive Slave Law that required federal officials to facilitate the return of runaway slaves back to their owners in the South. Free African Americans now faced a heightened threat of capture and reenslavement. The Underground Railroad developed to help fugitive slaves escape from the South and reach freedom farther North. Rumors circulated that an Underground Railroad was operating in Springfield. The presumed "conductor" was Jameson Jenkins, a mixed-race Springfielder from North Carolina. Jenkins, a drayman, was a forty-year-old family man with a wife and daughter. His wife was a native Virginian, and his daughter was born in Indiana, indicating that the trajectory Jenkins followed to Illinois probably took him through those two states. Jenkins was a fairly successful drayman, owning 50 percent more property than the average African American, suggesting that he operated his own cart or "dray." He also managed to harbor two free African American girls in his household of five. On the day that Abraham Lincoln left Springfield for Washington, Jenkins drove him to the railroad station.[32]

The Fugitive Slave Law drew a horde of southern "slave catchers" pouring northward in search of runaways. In 1850, three slave catchers ran down a band of fourteen fugitives from Missouri and Kentucky who were hiding in Springfield. Rumor held that Jenkins had been leading the slaves northward to freedom. "A general fight ensued," according to news reports, "in which there were some bloody heads and noses exhibited." The spectacle became known ever after as the "slave stampede." The slave catchers consigned a "lame negro" to the Springfield city jail and took the rest back St. Louis. Ten of the runaways, however, managed to escape during a "severe fight" that left one fugitive and one slave catcher badly wounded. When they returned to Missouri, all that the slave catchers had to show for their trouble was one African American woman and her two children.[33]

Even when they were permitted to remain in Springfield, African Americans suffered harassment at the hands of local whites. In 1851, a gang of white boys mounted a campaign of intimidation against a black woman in the city. "The house occupied by 'Violet,' a colored woman,—who minds her own business and interferes with no one,—has been assailed night after night, by a parcel of half-grown boys, for the mere purpose of distressing her, until she is now nearly a maniac," a witness reported. "On Friday night last some of these persons actually entered her house, while she, frantic, made the neighborhood ring with the cry of 'murder! murder!'" The police stood by and did nothing. Rather than condemning the episode as an instance of racist violence, however, the local newspaper simply cautioned that Violet's impending insanity would add another pauper to the city's welfare rolls. "If the corporation do not want the support of another individual," ran the warning, "they had better see to this thing in time,—if it is not now too late." Instead of prompting sympathy for free blacks, the Fugitive Slave Law and its resulting campaign of reenslavement ironically renewed calls for colonization. The increased threat of violence against blacks led the Whig newspaper to conclude that "they never can enjoy equal rights with white citizens, either in a social or political view. All efforts tending to produce such results, are an injury to the race, and destructive to the harmony and peace of the community."[34]

After returning from Congress, Lincoln retired from political office for the next twelve years. As the leading Whig in Springfield—and indeed the state—he remained an active campaigner on the most important issues of the day. Henry Clay's death in 1852 gave Lincoln the chance to summarize his views on slavery in the wake of the Compromise of 1850. In an eloquent eulogy delivered in the Hall of Representatives, Lincoln hailed Clay as a defender of liberty and a champion of moderation. To Lincoln, as for Clay, the two were not contradictory; indeed, they were complementary. Lincoln excused Clay's ownership of slaves as an inherited condition and his rejection of abolition as the reasoned judgment of a statesman who loved his country. "Cast into life where slavery was already widely spread and deeply seated," Lincoln argued, "he did not perceive, as I think no wise man has perceived, how it could be at *once* eradicated, without producing a greater evil, even to the cause of human liberty itself." Slavery was wrong, but abolition was a greater evil, threatening to destroy the very nation that was the best guarantee of liberty for all. "His feeling and his judgment, therefore, ever led him to oppose both extremes of opinion on the subject," Lincoln reasoned. "Those who would shiver into fragments the Union of these States; tear to tatters its now venerated constitution; and even burn the last copy of the Bible, rather than slavery should continue a single hour, together with all their more halting sympathisers, have received, and are receiving their just execration."[35]

Like Clay before him, Lincoln opposed the abolition of slavery "at *once*," while hoping for its eventual extinction. He strove to avoid the emerging "opposite extremes" of slavery extension among southerners, and abolition among northerners. Lincoln concluded his eulogy by embracing colonization, which he viewed as the best way to undermine slavery indirectly by making eventual abolition more acceptable to whites in both the South and the North. Colonization might lead to the ultimate extinction of slavery, improve the lot of African Americans, and even redeem Africa itself, without threatening the bonds of Union that guaranteed freedom to white Americans. Lincoln labeled such a result "a glorious consummation" for all.[36]

Lincoln's nationalism, like Clay's, counseled a moderate stand on slavery. His public endorsement of colonization came in the wake of the Fugitive Slave Act, a renewed national colonization campaign, and a growing free soil movement. Colonization represented a middle ground between the extension of slavery on one hand and abolition on the other. Colonization might head off the other two movements. In attempting to transcend such sectional interests, Clay, according to Lincoln, was a "truly national man," and at this point in his journey, so too was Lincoln. Significantly, Lincoln made this initial endorsement of colonization as part of Clay's eulogy, suggesting that he considered it a potential solution to a *political* problem, not a social one. The next year, Lincoln spoke before the local colonization society at the Presbyterian Church and addressed the annual meeting of the Illinois State Colonization Society in Springfield in 1855. Two years later, the society elected him one of its eleven managers. He continued to dream of an overseas colony of African Americans until late in his presidency, when the severity of the Civil War convinced him at last that emancipation represented the only just and practical solution to the moral dilemma of slavery. In 1852, however, the most that he could countenance was nonextension and colonization to achieve "the possible ultimate redemption of the African race."[37]

The threat and the reality of recapture, coupled with continuing and even heightened legal discrimination and physical harassment, devastated Springfield's African American community during the 1850s. The white population more than doubled during the decade, but African Americans increased by only one-third. By 1860, African Americans represented a mere 2 percent of Springfielders. Reenslavement and flight claimed more men than women, and the once-balanced sex ratio was now severely skewed. As a result, marriages deteriorated. In 1860, only 39 percent of African Americans were male. One-fourth of black families now had female heads. In 1850, only one household head was unmarried, but in 1860 more than one-fourth of household heads were single.[38]

Black households managed to grow in size during the decade, but only by taking in nonfamily members, the remnants of other families that had been shattered in the wake of the racist campaign. The situation of manual workers deteriorated. Fewer blacks were skilled craftsmen, and more were barbers or unemployed. To make matters worse, three white barbers had appeared in Springfield. All three of them were German immigrants, highlighting the new problem of European immigrants competing with African Americans for positions on the lowest tier of the city's occupational ladder. As a result of this social and economic deterioration, African American workers now owned only one-fifth as much property as their white competitors. Overall, their share of Springfield's total wealth had fallen to a mere one-fifth of 1 percent. African Americans also faced increasing racial segregation. Two-thirds of African American families now had black neighbors, up from about one-half in 1850. A cluster of seven families, headed by laborers and single women, portended the emergence of the black ghetto, commonly dubbed Badtown, that experienced racial rioting in Springfield during the twentieth century. Overall, the proportion of Illinois residents of African ancestry fell by one-third during the 1850s.[39]

The Lincolns' personal relations with free blacks were always respectful, yet they interacted with them only as the employers of servants. At least four African Americans provided domestic help for the Lincolns. Ruth Stanton, known as "Aunt Ruth," Jane Jenkins, who lived a block away, and Mariah Vance, who served as cook and nursemaid for the boys during the 1850s, helped Mary Lincoln. William H. Johnson accompanied the family to Washington as Abraham Lincoln's personal servant, tending to the president-elect during the two-week railway journey. Lincoln planned to employ Johnson as a servant and messenger, but the African American staff in the White House objected to him as too dark-skinned. Lincoln put Johnson to work keeping the fire in the furnace room until finding him a position as a laborer in the Treasury Department.[40]

Among the African Americans in Springfield, Abraham Lincoln developed the closest relationship with his barber, William Florville. A native Haitian of French ancestry, Florville also went by the names William De Fleurville and Billy the Barber, presumably according to the taste of his

WILLIAM FLORVILLE, LINCOLN'S BARBER. HIS ASSOCIATION WITH
LINCOLN AND OTHER LEADING SPRINGFIELDERS MADE HIM A WEALTHY MAN
BUT HE CHOSE TO MARCH AT THE REAR OF THE PRESIDENT'S FUNERAL
PROCESSION WITH OTHER AFRICAN AMERICANS.
Courtesy of the Illinois State Historical Library.

clientele. Florville fled Haiti as a youth of about fifteen during the revolution of 1821–22. Landing in Baltimore, he was orphaned and became a live-in servant for the family of Dr. Elias Merryman. Merryman attended William and Mary College in Virginia and then Baltimore Medical University. He and his wife Susan moved to St. Louis and then to Springfield in 1830, arriving just before the Deep Snow. Merryman fought in the Black Hawk War and then set up a medical practice in Springfield that lasted twenty years. Florville left Baltimore for New Orleans but feared re-enslavement and sought out Elias Merryman in Springfield. Traveling up the Sangamon River, Florville stopped at New Salem. Improbably, the first person he met was Abraham Lincoln. The young Lincoln invited Florville to spend the night and then sent him on his way to Springfield, where Merryman helped set him up in a barber shop. When Lincoln moved to Springfield five years later, he sought out Florville, who was in fact the only barber in town.[41]

Florville was the only foreign-born African American in Springfield. Such creoles, as they were known, tended to act as community leaders, and Florville was no exception. His barber shop thrived, and he opened other businesses, including the first laundry in the city. Tradition holds that Florville's clients were the wealthiest in Springfield. Florville began buying property on Lincoln's advice and grew rich, becoming the community's most prosperous African American. In 1850, he owned five times as much property as the average black household head, in fact almost 50 percent more than the average white man. During the 1850s, he doubled his wealth. He was known as an active leader in the African American community, contributing to charities and the city's black churches and heading the movement to found an African American school. Florville married one of Lucy Roundtree's daughters, a member of the oldest African American family in the county. Together, William and Phoebe Florville raised five children, one of whom died during the Civil War at age twenty-three after serving in the Union Army. The rest lived out their lives in Springfield.[42]

Despite his contributions to the African American community, Florville has been renowned ever since simply as Lincoln's barber, faithfully cutting the future president's hair for twenty-four years. When Lincoln died, a funeral procession accompanied his cortege through Springfield. The last of the twenty-one groups permitted to march in the column was the city's "colored persons." Invited to march near the front with white dignitaries, Florville chose instead to walk with the other African Americans at the rear of the procession that followed the martyred president to his grave.[43]

CHAPTER 21

All Passions Subdued

O f late Springfield has been noted for sobriety, order and good morals," a local resident noted in 1855. "I trust our good name is not to be lost to gratify the debased passions of a few." Ever since they founded the town, Springfielders had worked hard to create a prosperous and safe place to live. As the town grew into a city, however, its character changed dramatically. Like the town board of the 1830s, the city council that governed Springfield after 1840 pursued two sometimes contradictory goals: facilitating economic and population growth while fostering a clean and safe community. Springfield's population grew by three-quarters during the 1840s and then more than doubled during the 1850s. The housing boom that was the perennial pride of city boosters just as consistently failed to meet the ever-growing demand. Building spurts that produced four hundred new dwellings a year failed to relieve the housing shortage that Lincoln had faced when he first came to Springfield. Well into the 1850s, strangers continued to board in private homes while looking for a place to live, and many simply moved on again before finding an available house to rent. As in other market towns, the population surged every Saturday when "country traders" parked more than a hundred wagons and carts around the public square.[1]

Health and safety were prime concerns, especially with cholera periodically ravaging American cities. When a cholera epidemic threatened the nation in 1849, Springfield took steps to prevent an outbreak. Clear, cold water was considered an important preventative, and the city council focused on the public water supply. Two decades of growth had polluted Springfield's wells, prompting repeated complaints that "Our city is in an extremely filthy condition. Back yards, necessaries, ponds with putrid waters, can be seen all about." The city council now turned to rainwater, installing "water works" at the corners of the public square to catch the runoff. City boosters promised that "The drainings of the ditches are supposed to give the water an agreeable sweetness." Ten years later, the city began pumping water out of the Sangamon River and, in 1861, incorporated the Springfield Water Works Company. Meanwhile, a growing concern with cleanliness among the rising middle class, symbolized by the installation of the first bathtub in the White House in 1851, prompted the establishment of public baths in cities such as Springfield. "What is more refreshing, invigorating,—and contributes more to health and cleanliness,—these warm days, than BATHING?" a newspaper editor asked in 1846. "Mr. Johnson at the City Hotel, has a bath constantly in order. Shall not one such establishment be sustained in this city?" These cold baths, said to reinvigorate the system, soon gave way to the hot baths with soap that contributed to public health later in the century. David King, who "tried once before and failed for want of support," opened a second bathhouse behind Samuel Ball's barber shop, where "warm and cold baths can be had from six o'clock in the morning until 9 o'clock in the evening." By midcentury, middle-class families were installing their own "home shower baths," manufactured locally in Springfield.[2]

At the other extreme from water, fire posed a daily threat. The initial response was spontaneous action to douse the flames. Local newspapers were peppered with familiar announcements, such as the one in which "The undersigned begs leave to return his thanks to the citizens generally, for their energetic and successful efforts in subduing the late fire upon his premises." Springfielders gained a reputation for "superhuman skill in putting out fires." Volunteers organized a fire company, but a wave of arson during the 1850s made their task impossible. In 1851, an arsonist tried to destroy the Globe Tavern, in which the Lincolns had once kept house. "Last night, about two o'clock," the report ran, "an attempt was made to blow up or destroy the Globe Tavern.—Powder was placed in one of the middle rooms in front, and the explosion greatly injured the building." Two years later, the Old Tavern, near the railroad depot, went up in flames in another act of arson, and two years after that someone torched half a block on the west side of the public square. This "burnt district" sat for months as a reminder of public disorder. A few days later, a fire set in A. G. Herndon's stable killed five of his horses and left the irascible Democrat "severely, but not dangerously, burnt" in trying to save them. A month later, the city responded by purchasing a fire engine.[3]

The most visible affront to middle-class refinement remained the animals that continued to inhabit Springfield. As the center of a sprawling agricultural hinterland, the city welcomed the trade of neighboring farmers but suffered the consequences. Well into the 1850s, cattle trudged through town on their way to market. Early fall brought up to a hundred cattle sweeping through in a single herd. More quaintly, a drove of thirty buffaloes ran through the city in 1850. "It was something of a sight to see these animals of the plains so domesticated as to be driven like cattle," according to one witness. Dogs, who were working animals in the country, became nuisances in the city. Springfield licensed dogs from its inception, charging one dollar

THE WEST SIDE OF SPRINGFIELD'S PUBLIC SQUARE. IN ANY "WALKING CITY," THE PUBLIC SQUARE WAS THE BUSIEST—AND MOST CONGESTED—PART OF TOWN. *Courtesy of the Illinois State Historical Library.*

for male dogs and five dollars for female "sluts." The street commissioner was required to kill any dog "running at large" without a collar. Enforcement was lax, and packs of dogs subsisted by eating the offal that accumulated near the markethouse. Dogs helped to clean the city but contributed to the filth when they died. "On coming into the city from the north, the traveler has to pass near dead and putrid hogs, dogs, horses and cattle, which lie within a short distance of the road," which contributed to disease. The diseases that living dogs carried posed a greater threat, and mad dog "scares" periodically swept Springfield.[4]

In 1851, the marshal mounted an indiscriminate campaign to rid the city of strays. "Some three weeks since we saw flaming handbills posted over the city, that on a certain day our City Marshal was determined to SLAY all the canine race that were not registered with the city treasurer and had the name of the owner engraved on their collar," the *Journal* complained. "On the day specified, we find the Marshal and aids traversing our streets, firing pistols and guns about our premises, endangering the lives of women and children, frightening horses, calling puppies from our very yards and mutilating them." The marshal "murdered" thirty dogs and registered fifteen others. The campaign failed, and five years later there were

All Passions Subdued

"500 to 1,000 worthless curs in Springfield which could well be spared." The Lincoln family dog met his own violent end on the streets of the city. When they moved to Washington in 1861, Willie and Tad Lincoln left their beloved yellow dog, Fido, in Springfield, entrusting him to two playmates, John and Frank Roll. But the life of a dog was uncertain in Springfield. As John Roll reminisced years later, "one day the dog, in a playful manner put his dirty paws upon a drunken man sitting on the street curbing [who] in his drunken rage, thrust a knife into the body of poor old Fido." Unlike most of the dogs who met a similar fate, Fido was "buried by loving hands."[5]

Far less numerous than dogs but much more troublesome, the most controversial animals in Springfield were hogs. Springfield's hog ordinance dated back to 1832, but as the city grew it became a politically sensitive issue that drew lines around class, ethnicity, and race. Many poor families, especially southerners, immigrants, and African Americans, ran their hogs in the streets to make ends meet. Known as "run-away pigs," the hogs performed two functions, according to one observer: "they remove nuisances and enable the poor to raise their own pork." But as a critic complained, "These creatures, not being half-fed by their owners, prowl about at all hazards, to pick up garbage often of the most *loathsome* kind, in order to satisfy their hunger." Known affectionately as "his swineship," the so-called "city hog" ruled the streets, creating "hog-wallers" and burrowing under the plank sidewalks of the square, rooting for grubs. By 1853, a growing "hog interest" was clamoring for repeal of the prohibitory ordinance to allow hog owners to run their animals freely throughout the city. The city council obliged temporarily but then reimposed the ban just a week later. They eventually compromised by allowing hogs to roam the city for four months out of the year but scheduling a referendum to decide the matter. In April 1854, Springfield's voters trooped to the polls arrayed into the "Hog party" and the "Anti-Hogites." Hogs lost by a two-thirds vote in favor of prohibition, with every ward in the city endorsing their removal from the streets. At its next meeting, the city council duly reinstated the hog ordinance. In a scene poignant with pathos, city authorities impounded every hog in the city. "Last night, late in the night, several hog pens of our poor citizens were opened, the hogs turned out, and they have found them in the pound to-day," one sympathetic witness recounted. "These facts, unexplained, are causing much excitement among a class of citizens, who can ill afford to pay pound fees, thus unjustly imposed on them." Another critic of the ordinance noted that, with the hogs eliminated, putrid flesh was accumulating around the market house, "more than sufficient for dogs." Until the city council authorized the first sewer system in 1857, filth of all descriptions continued to disgrace the streets. "Complaints on this subject are in the mouth of every body," a local newspaper editor protested.[6]

The 1850s was a decade of general social disorder. The city's population not only doubled but changed considerably in character, as well. The decade witnessed the greatest rate of foreign immigration in the nation's history, bringing the first great wave of non-English and non-Protestant immigrants to America. In Springfield, immigrants represented about 30 percent of the population in 1850 but one-half by 1860. Irish and German immigrants, in particular, doubled in their representation in the city. At Lincoln's election to the presidency, one-fifth of Springfielders were Irish immigrants, and another one-sixth were Germans. Meanwhile, familiar sources of settlement dried up almost completely. Astoundingly, while the proportion of Irish and German immigrants more than doubled, the number of Springfielders from Kentucky rose by only nine during the decade, less than one per year. The city's booming economy also exaggerated extremes between rich and poor. By 1860, one-tenth of Springfield's men were unemployed, and the wealthiest one-fourth owned 97 percent of all the property in the city. Immigrants crowded into a squalid block of buildings on the north side of the public square known as "Chicken Row," because many of them survived by raising and selling chickens to the city's middle-class housewives.[7]

Poverty and overcrowding bred a litany of social ills. The city council continued to tend to the poor, but the typical pauper received only $2.50 a week. After rejecting the idea of a city poor house, "The Mayor was instructed to send to the County Poor House all Paupers which he may deem advantageous for the City." The council began boarding paupers in the county poor house for $10 a month. Burying the dead was even more onerous. At various times, the Committee on Paupers appropriated anywhere from $2.50 to $26 for coffins, graves, and shrouds, and on one occasion "87½ cts to Condell Jones & co for gloves for corpse." Lacking an insane asylum, the city supported "lunatics" at home. A mother petitioned the council "to provide work and sustenance for her son Henry who is represented to be crazy" but instead received $2 a week to keep him at home. Many simply slipped through the cracks. The council denied quite a few claims on the ground that the victim was not a pauper. "A maniac has been lurking about the public square for several days unprovided with the necessaries of life," the Springfield *Register* complained. "The city council would do a meritorious act by paying some attention to him." Six years later, the Springfield *Journal* reported the council's solution to the problem: "Last evening there was a poor deranged female parading our streets, and the authorities very properly put her under the charge of the jail keeper."[8]

Poverty naturally bred crime, and a "dangerous class" emerged to bedevil the city. Replacing the ubiquitous horse thieves and gamblers of an earlier generation, a new variety of criminals—burglars, "house thieves," pickpockets, vandals, streetfighters, and confidence men—all filled their niches within the Dickensian urban environment. "Mud holes in our streets, doggeries in full blast every day in the week, more especially on Sundays, when we have also firing of guns, general rows and street fights—

these are the comforts of the day," ran the complaint; "broken pavements, broken windows, broken fences, screeching and howling of drunkards—these are the comforts of the night." Burglars broke into businesses to steal goods, petty thieves stole clothes off clotheslines, and "an organized band of night-thieves" ruled the streets after dark. Knives and guns encouraged a spate of violent crimes that elevated the traditional "affairs of honor" into "deadly affrays." So many "fight notices" filled the newspapers that Springfielders had to relax their standards of tranquility. "Market street was quiet last night," one newspaper reported. "A fight came off at Phillip's Grocery about sun-down." Another editor considered the report that "There were no fights yesterday," newsworthy enough to pass along to his readers. "Is it not time that the drunken and vagabond scenes constantly witnessed about our city should be stopped?" one editor queried. "Strangers may be assured, whatever the corporation officers may think, that the respectable portion of our citizens are tired of and disgusted with them." The saloon district in Springfield became known as "Battle Row."[9]

Springfielders blamed two groups for the crime wave—immigrant men and native-born boys. Newspapers inaugurated "Police News" columns that never failed to note the nationalities of the criminals involved. A German immigrant was cut with a knife at a beer house, Irish railroad workers brawled in the Old Town, and a Frenchman killed an Irishman over a $5 debt. The Frenchman, according to the dramatic report, "drew a knife and cut the Irishman across the bowels, letting out his intestines." The "fall fighting season" was sure to erupt near election time. "During the last week," went one report, "there were eight fights and one case of horse-whipping, in which were engaged a printer, a hatter, a boarding house keeper, a book-keeper, a freight agent, and nine Irishmen." On Battle Row, a fight broke out "between about fifteen or twenty Irishmen and an equal quantity of Teutons."[10]

Even more alarming to native-born Springfielders was the behavior of their own sons, who committed most of the mischief and violence that disturbed the community. In a traditional, agricultural society, boys worked for their families until age twenty-one or later, when they gained their independence and usually moved off westward or to a city. With urbanization, however, children—especially middle-class sons and daughters—lost their productive functions within their families. For the first time in history, youths had "idle time" on their hands. "Our city is infested with hordes of idle vagabond boys, who are fast preparing themselves for the prison and the gallows," ran a typical complaint. Such "idlers" often sought early independence from their families, which their fathers could grant by posting a legal notice. "Notice is hereby given, that Isham Ware, a son of mine under age, is authorised by me, to trade for himself," John Ware declared in 1841, "but that I will, on no account, be responsible for his acts."[11]

Increasingly, however, rebellious youths who saw no future with their families ran away without their fathers' permission. Runaway notices now warned the public not just about fugitive slaves but also fugitive sons. "Runaway—My son, Micajah Shutt," Jacob Shutt, a Springfield clerk, announced in 1853. "I hereby notify all persons against harboring or trusting him on my account as I will not be responsible for any debts of his contracting." Even after coming of age, young men increasingly found nothing productive to do. With a housing shortage in Springfield and unemployment approaching 10 percent, many young men postponed marriage—to an average age of twenty-five—and simply stayed at home. In 1860, one-fourth of all adult men were still living at home with their parents. Unmarried youths who did leave home—and even newly married couples, like the Lincolns—increasingly inhabited boarding houses.[12]

Springfield, like other cities of the time, was beginning to experience a serious "boy problem." Critics bemoaned the increasing lack of parental supervision. "How many boys are now growing up without trades—because their parents are unable to make them learn trades, or masters are unwilling to have their shops occupied by boys who get their rudiments of morality from the worst trash that floats in the streets or in worse than pest houses—when they should be asleep in their beds," was a frequent complaint. "We have specimens here of what boys will do when suffered to have their own heads, and when they are permitted to hold parental authority in entire contempt." Too many youths were "left to idle about during the day, and prowl about nights without check or restraint from any body."[13]

The problem was ubiquitous, affecting all social classes. "They belong to all classes of our citizens," the Springfield *Journal* warned in a diatribe that would become a ritual during succeeding decades. "Many indulgent parents may not be aware that it is THEIR boys that steal out at back doors and are off from nine to twelve o'clock at night. Yet we recognized boys in that last night's gang, belonging to those who are looked upon as pattern men in [the] community." As many as thirty boys might gather unsupervised on a darkened corner, and street crime was the predictable result. Boys pilfered, shoplifted, stole fruit from orchards, and generally made the city "a perfect Bedlam." "The fact is, the boys in this country have no just conception of discipline," a Springfielder complained privately, "and any one who tries to keep them in order, is viewed as a 'tyrant.'"[14]

Reformers advocated private and public remedies. Heeding calls for the creation of a library to enlighten and occupy the city's youths, the Springfield Lyceum opened a subscription library and reading room in 1852. Two years later, Simeon Francis, editor of the *Journal*, founded the Young Men's Institute and served as its first president, with William Herndon joining him as vice president. Simultaneously, the first YMCA opened in Springfield. "The school life of the child is from 10 to 15," Francis reasoned in 1854. "We must educate these hundred young prowlers of night, about Springfield, or in a few years, we must enlarge our jails to hold them." In the following year, under Herndon's guidance as mayor, the city established its first public school system, in part to occupy the time of urban youths. The Episcopal Church ran a Sunday School, but calls for the establishment of public parks in the city went unheeded. More vocal critics, however, demanded police reform. In 1849, the city adopted a curfew that banned boys from assembling and "making a noise or creating any disturbance" after 8 P.M. The ordinance also prohibited boys from exploding firecrackers, pilfering fruit, beating other boys, and generally engaging in "malicious mischief" within the city limits. Any violation would result in a twenty-four-hour stay in the city jail. "We are told that it is a common occurrence for boys, from ten to fourteen years old, to be perambulating our streets after 12 o'clock at night," Simeon Francis moaned three years later in demanding enforcement. "Have we an ordinance touching this point?"[15]

Enforcement was the real problem. Springfield's original charter called for a single marshal, appointed by the city council. A few years later, the council made the office elective and added a deputy marshal. More responsive now to public opinion, the marshal won blame or praise as the crime rate rose or fell. "Our City Marshall is moving in the way of his duty," Francis noted in 1852. "This was expected. Every good citizen will thank him for it." As crime continued to grow along with the city, however, reformers demanded the appointment of assistant marshals. "Such is the amount of violations of police regulations, that we think there should be an assistant marshal in each ward, to attend to police duty when called on," Francis urged. "The Chief Marshal cannot be every where at the same moment." When authorities failed to act, citizens organized their own City Watch to prevent burglaries. Soon enough, the council responded by appointing four deputy marshals, one for each ward in the city, as well as erecting lampposts on the four corners of the public square. As predicted, however, Springfielders soon agreed that "we must enlarge our jails." The city's market house was the focus of youthful mischief. "Our market house is in a beautiful condition—a place of resort for every filthy thing having the power of locomotion," critics moaned, "and on Sundays made a perfect Bedlam by the boys and loafers who congregate there." The city opened a special "Calaboose" at one end of the market house just to round up and hold the "b'hoys," "night-disturbers," and "larkies" who bedeviled the place. By 1860, the city council had established a squad of special police constables and doubled the number of deputy marshals from four to eight—two now for each ward. The decade ended with the council looking to the experience of larger cities for help in enforcing its laws. In 1860, the council wrote to the mayor of Cincinnati "with a view to ascertain whether there is a Mace in use there, by the Police, and whether the same [can] be purchased and at what price."[16]

Stepped-up police enforcement did not reduce the crime rate but did

THE FRONT PARLOR OF THE LINCOLNS' HOME. THIS WAS THE FAMILY'S REFUGE
FROM THE UNSAFE AND UNSANITARY STREETS OF EARLY SPRINGFIELD.
The Lincoln Museum, Fort Wayne, Indiana.

keep it from rising. The overall crime rate remained steady from 1850 to
1860. Violent crimes, however, rose dramatically, tripling while the city's
population doubled. They also increased relative to other types of crime. In
1850, violent crimes represented 40 percent of all crimes prosecuted in
Sangamon County. By 1860, they accounted for 60 percent. In 1850, there
were only two murder charges in the county. In 1860, there were nine, as
well as twenty assaults, fifteen threats, four rapes, and three charges of riot.
The number of robberies tripled. In 1850, only one Springfielder inhabited
the city jail. Two years later, there were seven prisoners, one held for swin-
dling, four for larceny, and two for murder. By 1860, 1 percent of all adult
men in Springfield were in jail.[17]

Leaving the idlers and larkies, housebreakers and arsonists, mad dogs
and swine behind them to rule the streets, the members of the middle class
retreated into their families, turning their homes into a refuge from the novel
social turmoil of the city. Middle-class families strove to attain what was
called "respectability" or "gentility," an aspiration not just to achieve
wealth but to use their wealth to best advantage, displaying the cultural
accouterments and exhibiting the proper behaviors of polite society. Gentility was a social code that signified membership in an exclusive circle that
transcended the workaday hubbub of the city and all the tribulations that
bedeviled the "lower sort." Genteel Springfielders circulated in a world of

soirees, calling cards, parlor games, and picnics that emulated the aristocratic culture of eastern cities and turned their homes into islands of tranquility amid the stormy sea of city life. "A great object to be attained by all, and the only prudent course, is to acquire the habit, and so form the taste and disposition, as to make our homes the circle of content and private happiness," wrote one advocate of "domestic happiness." "This habit acquired, and a person thus favored, he can bid defiance to the turmoils that embitter public life—can enjoy that private happiness at his own fireside."[18]

The house at Eighth and Jackson was tailor-made to serve just such a purpose. "Mary Todd came into Lincoln's life at one of its most important and critical periods," one of Lincoln's legal colleagues observed. "He needed far more than most men a refined and well-appointed home." Starting life as the modest home of an Episcopal minister, the house gradually evolved into a showcase of middle-class refinement. The clapboard house—less imposing than the brick residences of Aristocrat's Hill—shows up as white in the monochrome daguerreotypes of the day. In fact, it was a subtle shade of brown, befitting the fashionable "brown decades" that preceded the later vogue for white that characterized the late nineteenth and early twentieth centuries. From a distance, the picket fence, designed to keep both dogs and hogs at bay, set the home apart from the world around it. "The fenced foreyard emerged as the most common feature of the nineteenth-century house exterior," according to cultural historian Richard Bushman. "A simple white picket fence with gate was sufficient to create the 'court yard,' to demark the zone of domestic refinement from the dirt of the street." Lawns awaited the invention of garden hoses and lawn mowers, so yards of this period exhibited shrubs and trees instead, taming nature in the name of decorative display. The first nursery in Springfield appeared in 1843 to supply city people with a taste of the rural greenery that they had left behind. By 1860, Springfield had eighteen gardeners and nurserymen.[19]

The Lincolns appreciated the refinement that shrubs and trees exuded but spurned the labor they required, hiring nurserymen to do their planting. Harriet Chapman, who lived in the home during the 1840s, remembered of Abraham Lincoln that "I never knew him to make a garden, yet no one loved flowers better than he did." Next-door neighbor James Gourley agreed that "Lincoln never planted any trees—: he did plant Some rose bushes once in front of his house." Lincoln eventually hired a Portuguese immigrant, Antonio Mendonsa, to tend his garden. Middle-class men spurned the tools that they had once wielded to till the land and typically left planting to their wives as part of their domestic management. Springfield's Horticultural Society, organized in 1849, sponsored flower shows that allowed women to display their prowess at growing and arranging flowers. As a local editor emphasized, "Most of our Ladies cultivate flowers."[20]

After climbing the front steps that elevated the house above the surrounding neighborhood, a visitor would enter the front hallway that protected the home from the world outside. Ideally, a servant would answer the door and announce the visitor by carrying a calling card upstairs to the mistress of the house. The hallway typically contained a hat rack to receive coats and hats, an umbrella stand, and a table to greet the visitor with flowers and to receive calling cards. Often a mirror provided one last opportunity to groom, while a chair or bench allowed the visitor to wait in comfort while the hosts composed themselves upstairs. Like most Victorian homes, the Lincoln house had two parlors, one in front to receive visitors and a back parlor to accommodate the family during their daily routine. Sliding doors or curtains separated the two parlors, drawing the line between public and private, which was one of the primary functions of the middle-class home. Comfort and conspicuous display demanded the finest furniture, and the Lincoln parlor featured walnut, mahogany, cherry, hickory, pine, and oak, along with a luxurious couch of horsehair, the most durable fabric of the age. Here, the Lincolns entertained their neighbors during their endless rounds of "visiting," as well as before and after the dinner parties that represented the middle-class housewife's proudest moments.[21]

Springfield's middle class enjoyed a seemingly endless round of dinner parties. "There seems no bounds to the spirit of gayety and disipation just now," John Todd Stuart's wife observed in 1855, "there has been one party and sometimes two or more, every evening for two weeks and a disposition still to keep it up." Mary Lincoln was one of the most renowned hostesses in the city. "In her modest and simple home, everything orderly and refined, there was always, on the part of both host and hostess, a cordial and hearty Western welcome," one frequent guest noted. "Mrs. Lincoln's table was famed for the excellence of many rare Kentucky dishes, and in season, it was loaded with venison, wild turkeys, prairie chickens, quail and other game." Springfield's dinner parties were stunning not only in their number but also their dimensions. Mrs. Stuart, for example, reported with understatement that "we were invited, to a little family gathering at Dr Wallaces. When arrived we found the *family* extended, including some fifty or sixty. Quite a pleasant party it was." The most memorable parties hosted fashionable visitors from the East. In 1852, Mason Brayman had a chance to "take tea" with President Millard Fillmore's sister. In tune with their improving social situation, the Lincolns, too, competed to entertain the city's loftiest social circles. In 1857, Mary Lincoln described the disappointing turnout at one of her parties. "About 500 were invited," she wrote her half-sister, "yet owing to an *unlucky* rain, 300 only favored us by their presence, and the same evening in Jacksonville Col Warren, gave a bridal party to his son." The swirling social scene was exhausting, however, especially for the hostess, and Mary Lincoln reported with undoubted understatement a "slight fatigue." Mary Stuart also moaned that "My list of acquaintances is becoming laboriously large. O, that I had strength to perform all my duties but it *is* pleasant after all to have a large circle of acquaintances." Still, these hostesses lived to entertain, and any lull in the social season would produce an abject boredom. "The Legislature has adjourned," Mary Stuart wrote in 1855. "Strangers all gone, and Springfield returned to its uniform dullness." The absence of an audience relegated her to the humdrum drudgery of housekeeping, and she reported to her daughter that "We have been soap making today, turned off nearly a barrel full this morning." A year later, she was still complaining that "there is so little incident in my limited circle, I scarcely know what to write about."[22]

In between parties, middle-class women spent most of their lives keeping house and raising families. The new Victorian morality, named for the queen who took the throne of England in 1837, consigned women to their homes to look after their children while their husbands braved the dangers of the city as providers for their families. Victorian culture elevated motherhood into an art and a science, indeed a sacred duty to raise morally upright sons and daughters.[23] As children lost their productive functions in their families, husbands and wives began controlling their fertility, bearing fewer children but devoting more time and attention to raising them. Fertility fell dramatically during the nineteenth century. In 1800, white women typically bore seven children during their lifetimes. By 1850, they were bearing an average of five, and only between three and four as the century ended. Overall, fertility fell by one-half between 1800 and 1900. Limiting fertility allowed middle-class parents to devote more time, attention, and affection to each child as an individual, nurturing and educating their children to promote future success, rather than exacting immediate economic benefits. Within the household, middle-class women took on servants, usually adolescent girls and boys, to help them keep house while their own children went to school, studied at home, and played.[24]

In the absence of artificial birth control, middle-class couples suppressed their fertility in a variety of ways. They began marrying later and delaying childbirth as a result. By the 1840s, the decade during which the Lincolns married, women in Springfield had increased their marriage age by two years, which would suppress their fertility by one child, in most cases. They also stopped bearing children earlier, thereby compressing their childbearing into a shorter period. Couples who married in Springfield bore all of their children during a period of nine years, on average, as compared to fourteen years among couples who married in the East. After completing their families, wives often retreated to a separate bedroom from their husbands to facilitate abstinence. If abstinence failed as a strategy for limiting childbearing, a variety of fertility suppressants was available to women in Springfield. Newspapers advertised "female pills" or "regulators" that came through the mail and cost as little as one dollar. Acting as abortifacients, they contained mild poisons that terminated pregnancies during the first three months. Heart-rending discoveries occasionally reminded Springfielders that the age-old practice of infanticide continued, even in this

THE YOUNG EAGLE

enlightened age that valued children as little angels. In 1852, "the remains of a new born infant, slightly covered with earth, were found in the burying ground." A year later, an infant's body was discovered in a privy. The coroner ruled that the cause of death was "violence, by an unknown hand." Two years later, a newspaper reported that "The body of an infant was found in an outhouse belonging to Mr. Houghton, in this city yesterday. It died manifestly of exposure." A widow took her baby to a nearby town, smothered it, and then returned to Springfield. In 1858, Springfield police arrested a man "on a charge of murder, by administering medicines to produce an abortion," but dismissed the charge when no witness would testify against him. Another mother literally left her baby in a basket on a neighbor's doorstep. With no other solution available, the family decided to raise the infant themselves.[25]

Whatever the method—delayed marriage, abstinence, birth control, abortifacients, or infanticide—the size of families in Springfield fell dramatically. Couples who married in Springfield bore an average of only four children, compared to the six or seven of the typical couple who married back East, a decline of over one-third. Significantly, middle-class Springfielders practiced the most rigorous regimen of family limitation. One measure of fertility control is the average period between childbirths, known as the "birth interval." Working-class women likely depended on nursing to inhibit their fertility. In Springfield, they exhibited an interval between births of 2.7 years. Middle-class couples maintained a longer birth interval of 3.2 years, probably practicing some form of artificial birth control to allow them to devote more resources to fewer children.

The Lincolns shared this Victorian commitment to family limitation. Mary Lincoln was acutely aware of the dangers of uncontrolled fertility. Her own mother bore children at a natural birth interval, every two years, but died from complications after her seventh childbirth, leaving Mary motherless at six. Her stepmother went on to bear ten children in less than twenty years. Mary Lincoln deferred her own marriage until age twenty-three, four years beyond the average age for brides in Springfield. She and Abraham Lincoln conceived their first son, Robert, a few days after their wedding but then began practicing some form of limitation, achieving an overall birth interval of 3.2 years, which was perfectly average among Springfield's middle class. Lincoln's frequent absences riding the circuit certainly facilitated abstinence, and after bearing their second son, Eddie, the couple went nearly five years without conceiving again. Eddie's death at age three, however, prompted a third conception, which occurred almost immediately. One common strategy among parents who lost an infant was to bear another as quickly as possible to compensate, in part, for the loss. Willie, the third son, was born about eleven months after his brother's death. The fourth and final son, Tad, came just over two years later.[26]

The Lincolns bore all of their children over a period of nine and one-half

---

years, which was about average for married couples in Springfield. Mary Lincoln completed her family at age thirty-four and devoted the rest of her married life to raising rather than bearing children. The couple added a second bedroom two years after Tad's birth, which was a fashion among prosperous Victorians. The second bedroom afforded privacy to wives who doted on grooming for their husbands while simultaneously facilitating abstinence. The arrangement likely indicated cooperation to attain middle-class respectability and limit fertility rather than signifying domestic discord. Mary Lincolns' family limitation may have had several motives. Both Abraham and Mary lost their mothers early in childhood and suffered emotional abuse at the hands of their distant fathers. Both vied with stepsiblings for the attention of their fathers. Family limitation allowed them to dote on their children in an attempt to compensate, or even overcompensate, for their own turbulent childhoods. Career advancement was a primary motive among middle-class parents, and the Lincolns apparently agreed that they should devote as much time and energy to that goal as possible.[27]

Abraham Lincoln was a notoriously permissive parent. Next-door neighbor James Gourley remembered approvingly that "He was Kind—tender and affectionate to his children—very—very." Harriet Chapman agreed that "I Can Say and that truly he was all that a Husband Father and Neighbor Should be. Kind and affectionate to his wife and Child." Mary Lincoln was more the disciplinarian, which was the newly prescribed role for Victorian mothers. During the early years of their marriage, the oldest child, Robert, took the brunt of her anger, and a servant remembered that "Ms L would whip Bob a great deal." Abraham Lincoln played peacemaker and generally defended his sons. After little Eddie's death, both the Lincolns seem to have become more permissive, and Willie and Tad virtually wallowed in their indulgence. Abraham Lincoln abetted and sometimes even joined them in the pranks they played on neighbors and visitors to the home. Victorian fathers generally engaged in play as a way of nurturing both their children and themselves. One acquaintance remembered Tad disrupting a meeting between his father and Lyman Trumbull, recalling that "the door opened and a boy dashed in, running as hard as he could. He was Tad." Rather than disciplining his son, Lincoln "stood up and opened wide his arms," and the visitors watched "both of them laughing and carrying on as if there was nobody looking at them." Lincoln freely admitted that "We never controlled our children much." When accused of whipping the boys, Mary Lincoln retorted that "if *I* have erred, it has been, in being too indulgent." Both of them tolerated innocent misbehavior, leading many acquaintances to detest the "brats," as Lincoln's law partner Herndon called them.[28]

In fairness to the Lincolns, they were trying to raise their sons during a period in which Victorians were redefining standards of childhood and child-rearing. As patriarchy declined and fathers began leaving home for work, mothers bore an increasing share of childrearing duties, which burdened women such as Mary Lincoln with additional responsibilities. "Moral mothers" now shouldered the burden of shaping the character of their children as well as safeguarding their physical health and safety. This "intensive" motherhood demanded constant attention and instilled anxiety and fear for children's physical and spiritual well-being. Like many middle-class mothers, Mary Lincoln was clearly an overprotective parent. Her children rarely left her sight, and when they did she overreacted. When Robert was three, Abraham Lincoln wrote in a letter to Joshua Speed that "Since I began this letter a messenger came to tell me, Bob was lost; but by the time I reached the house, his mother had found him, and had him whip[p]ed—and, by now, very likely he is run away again." Victorian mothers practiced excessive moral and physical vigilance over their children, while fathers grew more distant from the management of children. Absent most of the time, like Lincoln, they indulged their children when they had the opportunity.[29]

Eddie's death was clearly a turning point in both their lives, driving home the vulnerability of their family while heightening their emotional connection with their sons. Child mortality was an unfortunate fact of life until about 1880. In 1850, the year that Eddie Lincoln died, death claimed a stunning one in ten infants under the age of one in Springfield. Mortality among children under five, which was Eddie's age group, was considerably lower—3.5 percent—but still five times the rate of adult Springfielders. One-fourth of all Springfielders who died during the year were infants under one, and one-half were children under five. The rate of death leveled off beginning at age five. Traditionally, child mortality bred an emotional distance between children and their parents, who hesitated to make a psychological commitment until they were sure that their children would live. Parents considered procreation, as well as infant death, an act of God over which they had no control. Victorian parents, however, and especially mothers, were increasingly expected and even encouraged to grieve when they lost children. Just as conception was now viewed as voluntary, infant death came to seem preventable, heightening the sense of loss when a child did succumb. A family founded on affection rather than economic survival felt an emotional emptiness upon losing any one of its members.[30]

Eddie's death from consumption reiterated the fragility of the family even within their gated Victorian home and doubtlessly encouraged both parents to dote all the more on their two youngest children, Willie and Tad. The family's health and safety became their primary concern. Mary Lincoln developed a near-phobia about the world outdoors, in particular fretting over the intruders, dogs, and fires that continually plagued the city. During one of her husband's extended absences, James Gourley recalled, "She was crying & wailing one night—Called me and said— 'Mr Gourly—Come—do Come & Stay with me all night—you Can Sleep in the bed with Bob and I.'" On various occasions she called out "Murder!" when confronted with a stranger or "Fire, Fire!" when fat caught flame on her stove. Neighbor John Weber recalled that "one day I heard the scream—'Murder'—'Murder'. 'Murder'—turned round—Saw Mrs Lincoln up on the fence—hands up—Screaming—went to her—she said a big ferocious man had Entered her house—Saw an umbrella man come out—I suppose he had Entered to ask for old umbrellas to mend." When she summoned him to fend off a dog, he found "a little thing" that was "too small and good natured to do anything" yet managed to send Mary Lincoln into a panic. The husband, too, could overreact. When a dog bit Robert, Lincoln took him all they way to Terre Haute, Indiana, where a "mad stone" reputedly had the power to prevent rabies. In the parents' defense, Springfield was indeed a dangerous city. Intruders, fires, and dogs took their toll every day, as did the specter of infant death that stalked the streets in the form of infectious disease. The Lincolns doted on their children literally to keep them alive and appreciated them all the more in the wake of their inability to prevent little Eddie's death.[31]

The retreat of the middle class into family and home was only partially successful. The next step was to reclaim the streets and clean up the city in which they lived. Devoted to controlling their own lives at home, Victorians set out to control the community around them. Viewing stable families as the foundation of any morally upright society, the middle class became natural social reformers. Until the Civil War thrust antislavery upon the nation, the most popular reform was temperance. The temperance movement evolved through several distinct stages. The original argument against drinking alcohol focused on its physical effects on drinkers' health. The earliest advocates of temperance were therefore physicians, such as Philadelphia's Benjamin Rush. Rush and other early temperance reformers countenanced moderate drinking while crusading against intoxication. The religious revival that swept the nation in the form of the Second Great Awakening hardened the stance of temperance reformers. Protestant ministers, such as Lyman Beecher, began crusading against the consumption of any alcohol as a basic social evil and religious sin. They preached total abstinence from drinking as a key component of their campaign to purify America. In 1826, the American Temperance Society formed to promote abstinence from hard liquor. Organizing through Protestant churches, five thousand state and local temperance societies had appeared around the nation by 1834. The Illinois State Temperance Society, headquartered at Alton, eventually claimed three hundred local societies and twenty-five thousand members.[32]

Springfield's first temperance society formed in 1831, joining Presbyterians and Methodists together in a campaign to achieve what they called "total abstinence" in the community. Within two years, the Temperance Society of Springfield claimed more than one hundred members. An auxiliary, the Juvenile Temperance Society, meeting at the Presbyterian Church, targeted children eight to fifteen years old and included about sixty members. By 1835, the temperance society counted 157 adult members and eighty juveniles. Lincoln did not participate in this first phase of the temperance movement and in fact opposed it. The crusade reached its crescendo in 1838 and 1839 while Lincoln was serving in the legislature and on the Springfield town board. Sangamon County temperance advocates submitted a petition with 631 signatures that called for "the repeal of all laws authorizing the retailing of intoxicating liquors." Lincoln dutifully submitted the petitions but voted against a bill allowing counties to levy an onerous, in fact, prohibitive tax of five hundred dollars against tavern owners. Lincoln also voted against a "local option" that would have allowed the majority of the voters of any town or county to outlaw liquor. During his last term in the legislature, temperance advocates pushed for a bill to prohibit drinking entirely. Lincoln made a motion to kill it, and the House defeated prohibition by a wide margin. While Lincoln personally did not drink and maintained a lifelong reputation for absolute sobriety, he never countenanced any measure that would force his own standards or those of others on everyone. "He was a good temperance man—he Scarcely Ever drank," neighbor James Gourley remembered. "If Lincoln Ever drank it was as a medicine I think."[33]

One of the functions of the Springfield town board was to issue liquor licenses to taverns. The board charged fifty dollars for an annual license, the highest fee allowed by state law. In May 1839, however, 231 Springfield residents submitted a petition asking the trustees to stop granting liquor licenses. The board tabled the petition without discussing it. In December, two more petitions, one supporting and the other opposing prohibition, reached the board. Lincoln and two other trustees were appointed a committee to examine the petitions. Two days later, the committee reported that 269 Springfield residents supported prohibition but 281 opposed it. The board voted 4–1 to continue issuing liquor licenses while reducing them from a one-year to a two-month period. Lincoln supported the measure and continued voting to grant licenses during his remaining tenure on the board. The decision must have been popular, because all of the board members were reelected the following April.[34]

By 1839, the temperance movement had lost momentum throughout America. Total abstinence or "teetotalism," factional disputes, and financial problems during the Panic of 1837 spelled the end of the American Temperance Society and its local chapter in Springfield. In 1840, however, a powerful new temperance movement began in Baltimore with the creation of the Washington Temperance Society. Washingtonians, as they were known, lent several new features to temperance. The earlier movement had been dominated by ministers and the upper classes. The Springfield Temperance Society, for example, had been focused within the Presbyterian and Methodist churches and included five ministers among its leaders. The society included the city's wealthiest residents, who owned four times as much property as the typical Springfielder. Washingtonians, by contrast, tended to be workers who developed a secular critique of drinking as injurious to the social and economic standing of their members. Explicitly secular in focus, Washingtonian leaders did not include a single minister. Unlike the earlier movement, the Washington society also rejected political action and legislation as one of its tactics. Finally, the new movement appealed directly to drunkards, encouraging them to give up drinking voluntarily and to join the new society. Named for George Washington, a model of dignified comportment, the Washingtonians preached not coercion but self-control. Reaching drinkers directly rather than through churches or liquor ordinances required the Washingtonians to create a truly popular movement replete with fire-breathing speakers, parades, picnics, and even temperance plays, including *Ten Nights in a Bar-Room*.[35]

In 1841, a delegation from the Washington Temperance Society in Alton visited Springfield. A local society formed, which quickly gathered 350 members and sent delegations to spread the movement throughout Sangamon County, as well as founding a Juvenile Washington Temperance Society. Its goal was "to advance the cause of temperance, and especially direct its efforts to the redemption of our fellow men, who have been degraded by the use of intoxicating liquor." In the following year, Washingtonians mounted a revival and harvested hundreds of new members. "The first night they got 107 names, and they continued four nights in succession, some nights till 11 o'clock," recounted one witness. "They obtained in all 376 names—none of whom were previously members of any temperance society, and many of whom had been hard drinkers, or sots,—several rum-sellers signed, and others expressed a determination to quit the business." Numbering more than six hundred members, Washingtonians predicted that "Rum-selling and rum-drinking in Springfield has received a shock, from which we trust it will never recover." Within five years, Springfield was hosting the state Washington Temperance Convention, which proposed founding a chapter in every Illinois county and holding a Grand Temperance Rally in Alton. Soon, the Sangamon County Temperance Union emerged to combine all the societies in the county and advocate the organization of "every village, town, and city" in the temperance cause." This was truly a more popular movement than the previous one. Washingtonian leaders in Springfield were only one-half as wealthy as their predecessors in the Temperance Society, they refused to call for government prohibition of drinking, and they made inroads into both working-class and rural cultures. About one-third of their leaders hailed from the working class. They steadfastly rebuffed any hint of a religious foundation for temperance. When a Washingtonian lecturer visited in 1842, a local member advised that "we hope he will not take it unkind of us, if we suggest to him that it is not the practice in the West to discuss religious subjects in connection with Washington Temperance. We are satisfied that the cause of Temperance will succeed best while disconnected entirely from other matters." Their newspaper put it even more simply: "With party politics or religion we have nothing to do."[36]

Lincoln embraced the Washingtonian movement. John Weber, a neighbor and fellow Washingtonian, remembered traveling with Lincoln throughout the countryside organizing the movement. "During the Washingtonian Temperance Reformation, Societies were organized in most of the School houses in Sangamon County, and were attended monthly by volunteer speakers," he recalled. "Mr Lincoln and I rendered a part of this volunteers service, I frequently succeeded in getting Mr Lincoln to fill my appointment, and on all such occasions we rode together in Mr Lincolns buggy." Weber was disabled and, he explained, "he had a horse & buggy & I had none." Neighbor James Gourley agreed that "Lincoln was a great temperance man during the time of the Washingtonians—he would go a foot 5 or ten miles to talk."[37]

In 1842, Lincoln revealed his attitude not just toward temperance but toward all moral reforms when he gave a speech before the Springfield Washington Temperance Society. He faulted earlier temperance movements for trying to outlaw liquor, "legislating morality" in modern parlance. People are more likely to respond to "accents of entreaty and persuasion, diffidently addressed by erring man to an erring brother," Lincoln reasoned, than to "the thundering tones of anathema and denunciation." As a result, prohibitory legislation was simply impolitic. "When the conduct of men is designed to be influenced, *persuasion*, kind, unassuming persuasion, should ever be adopted," he counseled. "On the contrary, assume to dictate to his judgment, or to command his action, or to mark him as one to be shunned and despised, and he will retreat within himself, close all the avenues to his head and his heart."[38]

Persuasion stood at the heart of Lincoln's leadership, and from temperance he derived the general principle that "Such is man, and so *must* he be understood by those who would lead him, even to his own best interest." Reason and logic rather than coercion and prejudice were sure to conquer all evil and win over all minds and hearts. "Happy day, when, all appetites controled, all passions subdued, all matters subjected, *mind*, all conquering *mind*, shall live and move the monarch of the world." Before closing, Lincoln made one final leap, from intemperance to slavery, concluding that "the victory shall be compete—when there shall be neither a slave nor a drunkard on the earth." The same spirit of persuasion and appeal to self-control that could reform a drunkard could also free a slave.[39]

Overall, Lincoln advocated a rational and secular, rather than emotional and religious, approach to reform. William Herndon concluded that his law partner's flirtation with the Washingtonians "was damaging to Lincoln, and gave rise to the opposition on the part of the churches which confronted him several years afterwards when he became a candidate against the noted Peter Cartwright for Congress." Still, "He spoke often again in Springfield, and also in other places over the country, displaying the same courage and adherence to principle that characterized his every undertaking."[40]

The Washingtonian crusade, however, proved short-lived. As with other reforms that depended on persuasion, including abolition and colonization, results were disappointing. Temperance reformers returned yet again to prohibition. Beginning in 1843, a third movement, the Sons of Temperance, advocated prohibition, created a centralized organization, functioned as a secret society, and won attention and loyalty through dramatic pledges to abstain from drinking liquor. In Springfield, the Sons of Temperance began holding weekly meetings in 1847, organized eleven local societies throughout the county, and joined the Sangamon County Temperance Union the following year. A county-wide temperance celebration attracted fifteen hundred members from forty-three local societies. A host of affiliated societies began to dot the city. The Cadets of Temperance organized juvenile members, Templars established a Grand Temple of Honor in Springfield, and the Catholic Temperance Society of Young Men focused on appealing to non-Protestants. The movement took on a permanent footing with the opening of a Temperance Hall and the inauguration of a temperance newspaper in the city. Even more than the Washingtonians, the Sons of Temperance appealed to the working class in Springfield. About two-thirds working class in origin, their leaders owned only one-half as much property as the average Springfielder and less than one-fourth as much as the typical Washingtonian leader. Doubtlessly repelled by their emphasis on coercion, Lincoln did not participate in the Sons. "I got Lincoln to join the Sons of temperance about 1854," Gourley reminisced. "He joined & never appeared in it again."[41]

By 1852, Springfield hosted five different temperance societies—the Sons of Temperance, the Cadets of Temperance, the Temple of Honor, the Springfield City Union Temperance Society, and the Catholic Temperance Society. All of them advocated not only abstinence but outright prohibition as the best way to reform society itself. Despite its broad popular appeal, temperance was a potentially divisive issue. Originally appealing to northerners and southerners about equally, by the 1850s temperance was a heavily Yankee crusade, with northerners representing three-fifths of all temperance leaders. As one observer wrote of a temperance meeting in 1854, "The delegates come mainly from the north." Temperance was also heavily native in focus. At a time when one-third of Springfield men were foreign-born, only 2 percent of temperance leaders were immigrants. The movement was also strongly Whiggish in orientation. Three-quarters of all temperance leaders were Whigs. As the movement for prohibition gained momentum, the potential for cultural conflict grew. By the early 1850s, middle-class Springfielders were poised to embark on a political crusade combining anti-slavery, nativism, and temperance.[42]

CHAPTER 22

I Hate Slavery

In 1854, Lincoln made the dramatic and definitive declaration that "I hate slavery." Before he could do anything to halt the spread of the institution that he considered evil, however, he had to navigate his way through a thicket of party divisions, ethnic rivalries, and cultural prejudices that threatened to lead him and the nation astray. During the 1850s, three tumultuous moral issues—slavery, temperance, and nativism—reached a crescendo, overwhelming the economic questions that traditionally divided Whigs from Democrats and eventually overturning the parties themselves. In Springfield, the first sign of the coming revolution was the raucous election of 1850. Temperance advocates sponsored a referendum to end the licensing of public houses in the city. Springfield voters supported the anti-liquor ordinance in an overwhelming three-to-one landslide. The same election resulted in a tie for mayor. In a special run-off election, Democrat John Calhoun defeated his Whig opponent by a mere thirty votes, a stinging rebuke for the party that had governed the city for nearly twenty years. The temperance movement was escalating, and in the following year the legislature of Maine outlawed the manufacture and sale of liquor throughout the state. The Maine Law, as it was dubbed, stimulated a national movement for similar laws that won impressive victories in New England and soon spread to Illinois. In 1852, the Springfield Lyceum debated the Maine Law, and a Maine Law Alliance advocated a statewide ban on liquor similar to the one enacted in Springfield.[1]

The Illinois legislature stopped short of enacting a Maine Law, instead prohibiting the sale of alcohol in quantities of less than one quart, thereby outlawing taverns, saloons, and groceries that dispensed liquor by the drink. Even this partial victory was short-lived. Under popular pressure, the legislature soon reinstated the system of licensing the sale of liquor by the drink. Springfield temperance leaders were livid. "Parades and speeches would do no longer," Lincoln's friend James Matheny raged. "They had gone to the legislature; they had rolled in petitions,—numberless, uncounted. But the legislature had been bought with champaigne from St. Louis—they proved craven and treacherous." Striking a major chord that would reverberate throughout the 1850s, Matheny labeled the two parties corrupt and ineffectual and called on the people to act directly, "taking the question away from political parties, and voting for men that would represent the sentiments of the people." To circumvent the party system, which they considered corrupt, the Maine Law Alliance appointed a committee of five in each ward of the city, including Lincoln's law partner, William Herndon.[2]

Meanwhile, the two major parties were losing their hold on their traditional constituencies. The Compromise of 1850 had temporarily halted debate over the spread of slavery, and economic issues faded as Americans were swept up in a spate of moral crusades. Amid these new departures, the presidential election of 1852 produced dramatic results. Voters in Springfield supported the Whig nominee, Winfield Scott, but the state went for the Democrat, Franklin Pierce. Scott won only four states in the entire nation, and the Whig Party began a slow disintegration that eventually led to its demise. Ninian Edwards's defection to the Democrats was the first sign of the impending Whig collapse in Springfield. Edwards resigned as a Whig representative in the legislature and ran for reelection with the opposition party that his own father had abandoned twenty years before. Whigs complained bitterly that they "never supposed, that he would so soon adopt new principles, new views, coalesce with a new party, and in one short moment turn his back upon all his old political friends,—those who made him all that he is,—and seek to break down the organization of the whig party." Democrats suffered their own divisions, however, with a reform faction known as the "law and order democracy" breaking ranks. Whigs narrowly defeated Edwards in his bid to return to the legislature as a Democrat in 1852.[3]

Continuing to cut across party lines, the temperance crusaders won yet another victory in Springfield. In April 1854, William Herndon was elected mayor on a reform agenda that attracted Whigs and Democrats. Herndon undertook several needed initiatives, such as installing gas lines for lighting, expanding the police force by turning the mayor and aldermen into police officers, renting a new city hall, and laying the groundwork for a public school system. Herndon was a leader of the Temple of Honor, and a month after his election a second prohibitory referendum outlawing the sale of liquor in any quantity won approval by a small margin. Launching a personal crusade against liquor, Herndon visited the city's public houses waving the city ordinance in his hands, ordering them to close their doors. Herndon considered prohibition his administration's most important legacy to the city, noting that "the great cause of sobriety and temperance has advanced and progressed, and the good people of our city feel secure in their persons and property." As groceries cropped up right outside the city limits to sell liquor, temperance advocates renewed their efforts to enact a statewide ban.[4]

The same popular impulse for good order and public morality that drove the temperance crusade also fueled a nativist movement among native-born Protestants. The massive Irish and German immigration of the late 1840s produced a cultural backlash that sought to curtail immigration itself and the political rights of the foreign born. In 1850, a secret society called the Order of the Star Spangled Banner arose in New York City. Both nativist and anti-Catholic in motivation, the order recruited native-born men and met in secrecy to protest the growing influence of immigrants in American society and politics. When asked about the society, members were instructed to say simply that they "know nothing." The name stuck, and the Know Nothings became a potent political force during the turbulent 1850s. Launching a campaign to "reform" naturalization laws and restrict the political rights and activities of immigrants, the Know Nothings spread rapidly, establishing ten thousand local lodges and claiming 1 million members by 1854.[5]

Drawing upon disaffection within the two major parties, Know Nothings quickly entered the political arena. Although shrouded in secrecy and thus difficult to document, Know Nothings began organizing in Springfield by 1854. Whigs and Democrats accused each other of affiliation with the secret society. Whigs formally denied any association but then stated arrogantly that "We know nothing of such a society." Exuding inconsistency, they declared that "we seriously doubt its very existence," while admitting that "the organization is extending its powers rapidly in the West." An independent newspaper in Springfield hedged that "We are unable to say whether there is really a Know Nothing society here or not," but reported that the Whig editors of the Springfield *Journal* were its leaders. In response, the *Journal* retorted contemptuously that "We know nothing of the Know Nothings." The secret society won its first political victory in Springfield in 1854, electing an alderman by a single vote. The most anyone would say was simply that Know Nothings were "mysteriously scattered abroad" throughout the city.[6]

In the midst of the temperance and nativist crusades, antislavery came to the fore yet again. In May 1854, Congress passed the Nebraska Bill, which repealed the Missouri Compromise and allowed popular sovereignty to decide the question of slavery in the Kansas and Nebraska territories. Northerners of all political persuasions were appalled at the possibility of southerners reintroducing slavery into a region that had been guaranteed to freedom since 1820. Illinois senator Stephen Douglas sponsored the bill, which heightened the turmoil that followed on the heels of its dramatic passage. Springfield's Whigs were livid. "We had hoped to gain a short respite from that old din of 'Slavery Agitation,' and 'Slavery Extension' that has been warring in our country so often for the last twenty years, but it seems that it is about to be let in upon us again, more repulsive and disgusting than ever from having been so many times kicked out of doors," they ranted. "We can't conceive of a greater piece of mischief than is here set on foot by our Senator." Questioning Douglas's motives, they judged that "to deliberately raise the flood-gates of those old dammed up waters, because Mr. Douglas wants to be President, is too much of an infliction for the most forbearing patience." Lincoln himself hoped that "this Nebraska measure shall be rebuked and condemned every where." Literally overnight, the volatile Nebraska issue produced a political revolution—"a hell of a storm"—that swept across the North. As Lincoln sized it up, "The country was at once in a blaze." The Democratic Party split into two wings, with Nebraska or Douglas Democrats supporting the bill and Anti-Nebraska or Anti-Douglas Democrats opposing it. Whigs and Free Soilers castigated the bill as fresh evidence that a conspiracy of southern slave owners—the "slaveholding power," as Lincoln labeled it—was subverting the republic to extend their evil institution westward.[7]

An Anti-Nebraska coalition began to take shape, gathering up Whigs, Free Soilers, and Anti-Nebraska Democrats into it ranks. In the fall congressional elections, two-thirds of incumbent northern Democrats lost their seats. Among the forty-four northern Democrats who supported the Nebraska Bill, only seven were reelected. In 1852, Whigs had won only two northern states. In 1854, the Anti-Nebraska coalition lost only two. Republican parties began springing up at the state level, the first appearing in Michigan and Wisconsin. Republicans in other states, including Illinois, organized more slowly. The temperance and nativist movements posed a major problem. On the one hand, state and local Whig factions, especially in the East, championed the temperance movement and launched aggressive Maine Law campaigns. On the other hand, Know Nothings took an Anti-Nebraska stance that appealed to many antislavery Whigs. Temporary alliances called "fusion" parties gathered up Whigs, Free Soilers, Anti-Nebraska Democrats, and Know Nothings. Advocating abolition, temperance, and nativism in roughly equal proportions, the fusion parties took on a wide variety of names: Anti-Nebraska Party, People's Party, or simply Reform Party. Douglas dismissed them contemptuously and with a good deal of truth as "a crucible into which they poured Abolitionism, Maine liquor law-ism, and what there was left of northern Whigism, and then the Protestant feeling against the Catholic, and the native feeling against the foreigner. All these elements," he concluded, "were melted down in that crucible and the result was what was called the Fusion party." Committed antislavery leaders discovered that they had no chance of defeating Democrats without cooperating, however reluctantly, with the Know Nothings.[8]

In Illinois, a Republican Party formed in the northern third of the state but made only a faint impact in central Illinois and none at all in southern counties. The Whig stronghold around Springfield was particularly slow to organize. Whigs were reluctant to give up the organization they had spent twenty years perfecting. Bitter rivalries prevented cooperation with Anti-

Nebraska Democrats, and temperance and nativism alienated immigrant voters. The man who called himself "always a whig in politics" was particularly hesitant to join the new alliance. During the early 1850s, Lincoln spurned the temperance and nativist campaigns and by his own admission "was losing interest in politics, when the repeal of the Missouri Compromise aroused me again." He had absolutely no interest in joining any party that advocated either prohibition or nativism. The first Republican state convention, held in Springfield, was a disappointment, attracting only twenty-six delegates. Lincoln refused to participate, hoping to win a Senate seat from Illinois to help wage the antislavery campaign in Congress as a Whig. The convention established a state central committee that included three Whigs, three Free Soilers, two Democrats, and one Know Nothing. They appointed Lincoln, but he refused to serve.[9]

Victory required the simple but courageous conviction that antislavery was the only moral crusade that mattered. Lincoln had developed just such a conviction ten years earlier, and now he stood by it. He offered informal, moral leadership for the new party, dismissing prohibition and Know Nothingism as destructive distractions. Addressing a meeting of Republicans in Peoria, Lincoln emphasized the moral evil of slavery. He labeled the institution a "monstrous injustice" and reiterated that "I hate it." Yet he recognized that northerners could do nothing about slavery where it already existed, in the South. "If all earthly power were given me," he conceded, "I should not know what to do, as to the existing institution." He rejected abolition as a solution simply because most whites were racists. "Free them, and make them politically and socially, our equals?" he asked rhetorically. "My own feelings will not admit of this; and if mine would we well know that those of the great mass of white people will not." He had already demonstrated that he could not countenance "the establishment of political and social equality between the whites and blacks." The most that he could offer both African Americans and abolitionists was his refusal "to deny the humanity of the negro." Lincoln now made a commitment that he maintained publicly until he issued the Emancipation Proclamation eight years later—not to interfere with southern slavery. Instead, he reiterated his commitment to preventing the spread of the institution. Free soil or nonextension, as Lincoln preferred to call it, was a compromise between abolition and equality on the one hand and the spread of slavery on the other. Lincoln was "arguing against the EXTENSION of a bad thing, which where it already exists, we must of necessity, manage as we best can."[10]

In the fall of 1854, Anti-Nebraska candidates, two of whom were Know Nothings, won five of the state's congressional districts. "Never before have the democracy of Illinois been so completely vanquished," one Democrat moaned. The Know Nothing movement cut into Anti-Nebraska support by scaring off immigrants, who feared that "every anti-Nebraska man must necessarily be a Maine Law liquor man and a Know Nothing." Lincoln wrote to Richard Yates, who was campaigning to fill his old congressional seat, to warn him of rumors that Yates was a Know Nothing. He urged the candidate to make a prompt and definitive denial, but Democrats captured the seat anyway. Within a year, however, the temperance movement crested and began to subside. The state held a referendum on a prohibitory law that narrowly went down to defeat. Significantly, voters in Springfield rejected the Maine Law by a majority of 53 percent. Several months later, Springfielders repealed their own city liquor ordinance by an even wider margin, 58 percent. Temperance was losing its grip on popular politics. Drinking was legal again in Springfield, and opponents of prohibition gathered on the public square to celebrate. "Bon-fires were kindled, tar-barrels burned, and guns and pistols fired," according to one witness, "while yelling and screaming made night hideous generally." Prohibition was a dead letter for the foreseeable future. Now Republicans could—and did—ignore the temperance issue without fear of alienating reformers on the one hand and immigrants on the other.[11]

In 1855, the Anti-Nebraska coalition focused their efforts on electing a senator who would support nonextension. Lincoln was the early favorite for the seat, to be filled through a legislative appointment. When he recognized that he had no chance of election, however, Lincoln reluctantly but graciously swung his support to Lyman Trumbull, an Anti-Nebraska Democrat, to ensure that no Nebraska man could be elected. At this point in his life, Lincoln's fervent commitment to antislavery as a national ideal overrode even his renowned commitment to his own party. The episode convinced him more than ever that unity on the issue was vital to its success. Instinctively tolerant of cultural differences, however, Lincoln simply could not bring himself to cooperate with Know Nothings. "I am not a Know-Nothing. That is certain," Lincoln reiterated to his closest friend, Joshua Speed. "How could I be? How can any one who abhors the oppression of negroes, be in favor of degrading classes of white people?" Nativism was nearly as odious as slavery, and Lincoln would not endorse the one to assail the other. Lincoln put it more plainly to a young legal colleague, explaining that he opposed nativism simply because "he wanted to lift men up & give 'Em a chance."[12]

In a letter to Owen Lovejoy, brother of the martyred abolitionist Elijah Lovejoy, Lincoln defined the depths of his political principles. "I have no objection to 'fuse' with any body provided I can fuse on ground which I think is right," he explained. But the Know Nothings' campaign of intolerance was wrong, and Lincoln reiterated that "Of their principles I think little better than I do of those of the slavery extensionists." Lincoln resolved to stay out of any new party until nativism subsided, just as temperance had done a few months earlier. "Know-nothingism has not yet entirely tumbled to pieces," he lamented. "Until we can get the elements of this organization, there is not sufficient materials to successfully combat the Nebraska democracy with." Despite his aversion to nativism and his confidence in its eventual demise, however, Lincoln believed that a direct attack on the Know Nothings would prove counterproductive. "About us here, they are mostly my old political and personal friends," Lincoln reasoned, "and I have hoped their organization would die out without the painful necessity of my taking an open stand against them." In short, Lincoln refused to cooperate with nativists to attack slavery. But he also believed that attacking the Know Nothings at this moment would only needlessly alienate them and hurt the Republican cause in the long run.[13]

Know Nothings now founded a political party, the American Party, that rivaled the Republicans for popular support. The Illinois American Party held a convention in Springfield in 1855, adopting a platform that embraced abolition, nativism, and anti-Catholicism in fairly equal measure. More than one hundred delegates advocated toughened naturalization laws, denial of political rights to noncitizens, Bible reading in public schools, and "resistance to the corrupting influences and aggressive policy of the Romish Church." Most important for Republicans, however, the American Party platform pledged to "take open, fearless, and unreserved ground upon the great question of slavery," and thus threatened to cut into their constituency. Soon, however, the American Party split in two along sectional lines. The southern wing, called the American Party, emphasized nativism while muting its commitment to the antislavery cause. The North American Party, dominated by northern Know Nothings, advocated free soil and welcomed Protestant immigrants into its ranks. More compatible with the Republican Party, the North American Party actually nominated John C. Fremont, the Republican candidate for president. Like the temperance movement in the preceding year, Know Nothingism reached its peak in 1856 and then faded away. Republicans created a competing organization, the Know Somethings, that flourished in northern Illinois. The Know Somethings welcomed Protestant immigrants in an attempt to bring them into the Republican fold, while still advocating anti-Catholicism in an attempt to placate nativists. In 1856, the American Party met in Springfield for another state convention. This time, they avoided nativism and focused on antislavery and anti-Catholicism instead.[14]

By the early months of 1856, the Know Nothings were splitting north and south, the Illinois American Party was softening its stand on nativism, and the North American Party was on the verge of nominating Fremont for president. Lincoln was ready to enter the Republican fold at last. In January, he attended a meeting of Anti-Nebraska newspaper editors in Decatur that laid the groundwork for a statewide Republican Party. The editors kept their focus on antislavery. Avoiding nativism, they made a point of opposing changes in naturalization procedures while advocating religious toleration. They appointed a state central committee and called for a state convention at Bloomington in May. When 129 Sangamon County voters issued a call for a meeting to choose delegates to the convention, Lincoln's name headed the list. Reflecting the influence of nativism on early Republican organization, 95 percent of the signers were native-born. Among the signers who had voted in the 1848 election in Springfield, 95 percent were former Whigs. The Bloomington convention nominated for governor William H. Bissell, a former Democrat who had opposed the Nebraska Bill in Congress. They chose a slate of electors to campaign for Fremont, including Lincoln as one of two electors-at-large. Before the convention, Lincoln made his famous "Lost Speech," setting forth in his by now eloquent way the principles for which Illinois Republicans intended to fight—not temperance or nativism but antislavery. Lincoln was now officially a Republican.[15]

The new party lost the election of 1856 but firmly established itself as a competitive, national party that was unequivocally antislavery in foundation. The election was a three-way race. Republicans and North Americans nominated John C. Fremont, a former army scout and the renowned "Pathfinder of the West" who mapped the Oregon Trail. A war hero, Fremont helped to secure California during the Mexican War, and he later served as a Senator from that state. The former Democrat sympathized with nativists but endorsed the all-important Republican commitment to free soil, lending a ring of truth to the inevitable campaign slogan "Free Soil, Free Men, Fremont." The southern-focused American Party nominated Millard Fillmore, a former Whig president who advocated both nativism and compromise on the slavery issue. Democrats selected Pennsylvanian James Buchanan as their nominee. The election was really two races, with Buchanan and Fremont contesting the North and Buchanan and Fillmore competing in the South. In November, Buchanan won the presidency with 45 percent of the vote, capturing every southern state except Maryland, which went to Fillmore, along with five states in the lower North. Fremont was second, winning the upper North and establishing the Republicans as genuine contenders for the presidency in 1860. Illinois voted for Buchanan, but Republicans won the governorship, something that a generation of Whigs had never been able to do.[16]

In Springfield, Fillmore won considerable support, especially among southern-born former Whigs, and the city therefore witnessed a three-way campaign of its own. The American Party founded a campaign newspaper, the Springfield *Conservative*, which advocated compromise on the slavery issue and appealed to former Whigs and Know Nothings. A huge "Fillmore demonstration" filled the streets. Fillmore supporters in Springfield included Lincoln's in-laws and former law partners John Todd Stuart and Stephen T. Logan, Kentucky merchant Elijah Iles, Lincoln's former employer Abner Ellis, and his best man, James Matheny. The American Party wooed Lincoln but to no avail. "If to-day, Mr. Lincoln, with his influence and known position, would declare for Mr. Fillmore, it would send a thrill of joy through this land that would redound to his immortality," the

Conservative promised. "It would carry Illinois like a flash." When Lincoln supported Fremont instead, the Americans castigated him as "the *dictator* at Springfield." Lincoln not only rejected the American Party campaign but dismissed it entirely, insisting that "there are only two parties and only two questions now before the voters"—the platforms of Fremont and Buchanan. Slavery and its extension or nonextension was the only true issue in the campaign.[17]

Yet Fillmore's appeal to former southerners in Springfield remained compelling. The Lincoln home, in fact, included a Fillmore sympathizer. Mary Lincoln was even more reluctant than her husband to abandon the last, lingering remnants of the Whigs. "Altho' Mr L- is, or was a *Fremont* man, you must not include him with so many of those, who belong to *that party*, an *Abolitionist*," Mary Lincoln assured her Kentucky stepsister after the election. "In principle he is far from it—All he desires is, that slavery, shall not be extended, let it remain, where it is." Like her husband, Mary Lincoln drew a philosophical link between the treatment of immigrants and attitudes toward southern slaves, yet she arrived at a different conclusion. "If some of you Kentuckians, had to deal with the 'wild Irish,' as we house-keepers are sometimes called upon to do," she reasoned, "the south would certainly elect Mr Fillmore next time." Mary Lincoln had plenty of company. Buchanan took Springfield with a plurality of 49 percent. Fremont came in second with just under 30 percent of the vote. Over one-fifth of Springfield voters supported Fillmore, betraying an undercurrent of nativism and a telltale legacy of southern racism. Still, this first Illinois Republican campaign muted support for temperance and nativism, established the Republicans as the only viable alternative to the Democrats, and put the focus where it belonged, on antislavery. In drawing Lincoln into the Republican fold, the party won perhaps its greatest victory of all.[18]

CHAPTER 23

The Thing Is Done

After electing a Senator in 1855 and a governor in 1856, Lincoln and other Illinois Republicans set out to unseat the state's leading Democrat, Senator Stephen Douglas. That effort received a boost when a U.S. Supreme Court decision threw the Democratic Party into disarray. In March 1857, the Supreme Court issued the *Dred Scott* decision, which was designed to settle the question of slavery in the western territories. In their infamous ruling, the court denied the right of African Americans, both slave and free, to sue in federal courts, overturned the Missouri Compromise as unconstitutional, and denied the power of Congress to ban slavery in western territories. *Dred Scott* undercut the viability of free soil as a method of achieving the nonextension of slavery, which was by now the fundamental goal of the Republican Party. But it also angered many northern Democrats, who hoped that the West would remain free through the action not of Congress but through actual settlers exercising their rights under the program of popular sovereignty. Douglas faced the dilemma of standing by President Buchanan and endorsing the decision or breaking with the Democratic administration to pursue popular sovereignty as a compromise position for settling the West.[1]

In June 1857, Lincoln delivered a speech in Springfield that set out his response to the *Dred Scott* decision. He decried the Supreme Court ruling as subversive of the very foundation of the American republic. Dismissing the constitutional validity of the court's argument, Lincoln insisted that the spirit of American freedom lay not in the Constitution at all but in the Declaration of Independence. The statement that "all men are created equal" was a fundamental national goal that everyone had the responsibility to pursue and bring to fruition. "This they said, and this meant," Lincoln argued with elegant simplicity. "They did not mean to assert the obvious untruth, that all were then actually enjoying that equality, nor yet, that they were about to confer it immediately upon them." Lincoln's experience among slaves and free African Americans had taught him clearly that racial equality remained an unrealized dream. "They meant simply to declare the

ABRAHAM LINCOLN IN 1857. IN ONE OF HIS EARLIEST "LINCOLNIAN" POSES,
HIS TOUSLED HAIR BESPOKE AN ABIDING INFORMAL SIMPLICITY EVEN AS
HE STOOD ON THE BRINK OF NATIONAL GREATNESS.
Courtesy of the Illinois State Historical Library.

right, so that the *enforcement* of it might follow as fast as circumstances should permit." Lincoln's reading of the Declaration convinced him that all Americans, both black and white, had the right to enjoy freedom. The struggle in which the nation now engaged was an effort to *enforce* that right, which the founders had set out as a national ideal.[2]

But freedom was far more than a right conferred by a government in a document, even one as fundamental as the Declaration. Lincoln defended freedom as an "inalienable right" in its fullest sense, a *natural* right belonging to everyone by virtue of their humanity. He acknowledged practical barriers to equality that arose from the dissimilarity of races. "I protest against that counterfeit logic which concludes that, because I do not want a black woman for a *slave* I must necessarily want her for a *wife*," he argued. "I need not have her for either, I can just leave her alone." Equality and freedom were two different things. "In some respects she certainly is not my equal," he continued, "but in her natural right to eat the bread she earns with her own hands without asking leave of any one else, she is my equal, and the equal of all others." In this single sentence, Lincoln reaffirmed his opposition to racial equality in America while reiterating his commitment to human freedom. But his reasoning also held out promise for the *eventual* equality of the races. The ideology of "free labor" held that people had the right to dispose of their labor and enjoy its fruits as they pleased. Through diligence, education, frugality, and self-discipline, and a host of other personal virtues, African Americans could improve themselves, as Lincoln had done, and someday achieve an equality of their own making. The equality that the founders envisioned was not absolute but rather a potential for improvement that might find its fulfillment only if unencumbered by artificial restraints, such as slavery. Lincoln had benefitted immensely from the unfettered right to improve himself, and now he hoped to share those benefits with everyone else, regardless of race or ethnic heritage.[3]

Imbibing much the same hope, Illinois Republicans wanted to remove Douglas from his senate seat, and they selected Lincoln to unseat and succeed him. The election of 1858 would determine the composition of the state legislature, which would then choose a senator to send to Washington. In a bold move, Illinois Republicans nominated Lincoln as their candidate for the seat, acknowledging his personal and moral leadership of the party and designating him as the chief advocate for the Republican cause. Lincoln and Douglas agreed to a series of seven debates, one in each congressional district, between August and October 1858. In one sense, Lincoln and Douglas pursued a similar strategy to try to win the senate seat. Both of them sought to avoid the extremes within their parties and move toward the middle of the political spectrum. For Douglas, this meant finding a way to dissociate himself from the Buchanan administration. In late 1857, Douglas engineered a dramatic break with Buchanan, opposing the admission of Kansas with a constitution that recognized and protected slavery. Douglas argued that the state constitution, adopted at Lecompton, Kansas, was the result of fraud and made a mockery of the idea of popular sovereignty. Across the North, and especially in Illinois, the Democratic Party split in two. Douglas Democrats continued to defend popular sovereignty while rejecting the tactics of radical proslavery forces that had foisted the "Lecompton Swindle" on the people of Kansas and the nation. Administration or National Democrats defended the admission of Kansas, and by implication all other western territories, as slave territory by any means, fair or foul. In the wake of Douglas's rebellion, many Republicans hoped to win him over to their cause. Lincoln countered Douglas's move toward the middle and rejected any notion of a Republican Party that included Douglas and popular sovereignty. Lincoln attempted to move toward the middle of the spectrum by advocating the nonextension of slavery but disavowing any interest in either abolition or the extension of immediate equality for African Americans.[4]

During the debates, each man struggled to push his opponent out of the center and into the extremes of antislavery opinion. Lincoln launched an opening salvo by delivering his famous House Divided speech in Springfield even before the debates began. He attempted to keep Douglas out of the Republican fold by lumping him together with other administration Democrats. Narrating the history of the spread of slavery from the founding of the nation, Lincoln argued that Douglas was part of a conspiracy to overturn American freedoms. President Buchanan, Chief Justice Roger Taney, former President Franklin Pierce, and Douglas were a "dynasty" that devised a "*dark* and *mysterious*" plan to extend slavery not only westward but also northward. Lincoln predicted yet another Supreme Court decision, the next scene in the play, that would make slavery legal in northern states as well as western territories. Soon enough, northerners would discover that "the *Supreme* Court has made *Illinois* a *slave* State." Lincoln predicted that a crisis would soon envelop the nation. Like a house divided against itself, "I believe this government cannot endure, permanently half *slave* and half *free*. I do not expect the Union to be *dissolved*—I do not expect the house to *fall*—but I *do* expect it will cease to be divided. It will become *all* one thing, or *all* the other." Lincoln predicted that the southern dynasty of slave owners and their functionaries would do all in their power to make the nation all slave.[5]

Many of Lincoln's own supporters considered the House Divided speech far too radical, because it denied any middle ground for compromise between slavery and freedom. Lincoln's Edwards and Stuart in-laws "got mad at Mr L because he made the house-divided-against-itself Speech," one of them reminisced. Legal friend and political supporter Leonard Swett believed that "nothing could have been more unfortunate, or unappropriate." Chicagoan Norman Judd told Lincoln bluntly that "had I seen that Speech I would have made you Strike out that house divided part." Privately, Lincoln assured his friends that "you may think that Speech was a mistake, but I never have believed it was, and you will see the day when you will consider it was the wisest thing I ever said." The biblical allusion signaled Lincoln's refusal to compromise on the subject of slavery, and he vowed that he was "willing to perish with it, if necessary."[6]

During his second debate with Lincoln at Freeport, Douglas broke with the administration once again in an attempt to find a broad and comfortable center and thus win reelection. In his famous Freeport Doctrine, Douglas argued that the *Dred Scott* decision would make little impact on the status of slavery in the West. No matter what the Supreme Court said, the people of a territory could find legal methods of banning slavery. "Slavery cannot exist a day or an hour anywhere, unless it is supported by local police regulations," Douglas insisted. If a majority of the people of a territory oppose slavery, they will "by unfriendly legislation effectually prevent the introduction of it into their midst." Douglas had managed to revive popular sovereignty as a viable method of effecting the nonextension of slavery.[7]

Douglas recaptured the middle of the Democratic Party by dismissing the *Dred Scott* decision as essentially irrelevant. Now he attempted to dislodge Lincoln toward the extreme end of the Republican Party by accusing him of supporting abolition, racial equality, and even amalgamation. Douglas's ploy required Lincoln to expound upon his own racial views, which he considered disagreeable and consented to do only in the southern congressional districts, where Douglas's campaign of race-baiting promised to bear fruit. As he had earlier, Lincoln drew a sharp distinction between opposing slavery and supporting amalgamation. In keeping with the sentiments of most Illinois voters, he disavowed any intent to promote social, legal, and political equality between whites and blacks. Finally, he denied the charge of abolitionism but repeatedly avowed his commitment to restrict slavery to the South.

Through it all, however, Lincoln reiterated that slavery was wrong, a "moral, social, and political evil" and a "monstrous injustice." Lincoln's greatest weapon against Douglas was simply to acknowledge the humanity of African Americans. According to Lincoln, Douglas "has no very vivid impression that the negro is human; and consequently has no idea that there can be any moral question in legislating about him." Endowed with equal human rights by the Declaration of Independence and the nation's founding principles, African Americans had above all the right to be free. "It does not follow by any means," Lincoln reasoned, "that because a negro is not your equal or mine that hence he must necessarily be a slave." Northerners could not end slavery immediately, but they could restrict its spread. They could not grant equality to African Americans immediately, but they could remove the barrier of slavery that prevented them from achieving equality eventually. Government could and should not grant equality. Only self-improvement achieved through free labor could do that.[8]

With both candidates struggling to hold the political center, the election was close. Lincoln won the popular vote for state legislators, but an apportionment system that favored the Democrats gave Douglas a 54–46 margin in the legislature and ensured his re-election. Significantly, Lincoln's home county of Sangamon went Democratic, indicating that his attitude toward slavery was running ahead of that of his constituents in central Illinois. Still, the popular vote was a tremendous moral victory for Illinois Republicans and portended success in 1860. Above all, National Democrats were devastated. "The Repubicans, for months past, have been assiduously at work all over the state, getting up their clubs and meetings," they warned. "Republican speeches have already been made at nearly all the school houses, court houses and cross roads. They have taken the start of Democrats." By 1860, there were reportedly only five thousand National Democrats left in the state. Douglas's reelection to the Senate was merely a Pyrrhic victory. He defeated National Democrats in Illinois, but his views on slavery, which circulated throughout the nation in newspapers, pamphlets, and magazines, cost him dearly in the South. Most Deep South Democrats considered him unacceptable as a presidential nominee in 1860.[9]

The debates, however, won Lincoln praise as an eloquent but moderate opponent of slavery and gained him a wider following throughout the North. Little known outside Illinois until his famous debates with Douglas, Lincoln now began touring the North and West. During six months, between September 1859 and February 1860, Lincoln mounted a tour of the North to broaden support for the Republican Party and to introduce himself, as he put it, to leaders and voters in other regions, positioning himself for the presidency. Not much of a traveler, Lincoln rarely ventured outside the Old Northwest before mounting his campaign for the presidency. He nevertheless maintained a shrewd awareness of the different regions that shaped America, vied for political power, and now battled for the nation's future. Lincoln made two famous trips as a young man when he lived in Indiana and Illinois, floating pork down the Ohio and Mississippi rivers to New Orleans. Much later, his single term in Congress took him to Washington for two years, a stint that he followed up with a campaign tour of New England on behalf of Zachary Taylor. He paid several visits to Lexington and Louisville, Kentucky, visiting Mary Lincoln's family and his best friend, Joshua Speed. As a reluctant traveler, and at times an "accidental tourist," Lincoln gained most of his knowledge secondhand, as a voracious reader.

A renowned devotee of Shakespeare and Burns, Lincoln nevertheless preferred nonfiction, and his favorite reading matter was newspapers. Ensconced in their law office in Springfield, Lincoln and his partner, William Herndon, assiduously collected and scanned newspapers and periodicals from all over the country to keep an eye on events and opinions taking shape in America's different regions. Herndon remembered Lincoln as a constant newspaper reader, preferring western and southern periodicals. "He was a careful and patient reader of newspapers," Herndon recalled, "the *Sangamon Journal*—published at Springfield—*Louisville Journal, St. Louis Republican*, and *Cincinnati Gazette* being usually within his reach." Another lawyer, Henry Rankin, remembered "the student-like way in which they both steadfastly kept the political affairs of the whole Nation under attention; using all sources and, in their private conferences and discussions with each other, reviewing and sifting all conflicting opinions on national questions that came to their office table from North and South, East and West." Indeed, a close familiarity with these four regions—"North and South, East and West"—proved absolutely essential to Lincoln's success as a national leader. "Had they foreseen the political and executive battles before Lincoln," Rankin concluded, "his preparation could not have been more thorough, exact, and comprehensive to fit him for his duties as President."[10]

Running for president, Lincoln needed to address—and to balance—all four of these regions, without appearing to favor any one above the others. For the first time in his life he addressed them all. In the process, Lincoln traveled far more widely during these six months than he did during the rest of his life put together. Lincoln's campaign trip stretched from Providence, Rhode Island, on the east to Leavenworth, Kansas, on the west, a span of twelve hundred miles, and from Cincinnati on the south to Milwaukee on the north, another three hundred. During this period, Lincoln delivered seventeen major speeches in nine different states. Like most nineteenth-century presidential candidates, Lincoln did not campaign extensively for the presidency in either 1860 or 1864, and so these appearances collectively represent the only real national campaign that Lincoln ever mounted.[11]

Lincoln's speech in Cincinnati provided a keynote of sorts in his attempt to generate broad northern support for the Republican Party and his own candidacy. Before the Civil War, Cincinnati was the largest city west of the Appalachians, the "Queen City of the West," and in fact the largest city in which Lincoln had ever spoken. Lincoln himself declared that "This is the first time in my life that I have appeared before an audience in so great a city as this." Significantly, Lincoln took this opportunity not so much to address Ohioans—he had already done that in Columbus and Dayton—but rather to confront the South. Beyond his single term as a representative in Washington, Lincoln had never delivered a speech in a southern city. His visit to this border city provided an opportunity to reach a southern audience for the first time. Lincoln announced that "I propose to address a portion of what I have to say to the Kentuckians." A native of Kentucky, Lincoln knew that his reputation preceded him and now undertook the ironic task of "introducing himself to Kentuckians."[12]

Lincoln identified a line, both literal and figurative, that divided the North from the South. Literally, the line was the Ohio River, a physical boundary and an obstacle to communication, and Lincoln poignantly identified himself as an "old Ohio river boatman," familiar with the twists and turns of this natural barrier as it flowed westward. Culturally, of course, the line marked the division between freedom and slavery. Reminiscent of a later president who stood in West Berlin and insisted, "Tear down this wall," Lincoln viewed his own speech as an "opportunity to shoot across the line," not with bullets, of course, but with a greater weapon, words.

Lincoln provoked laughter by musing that "I should not wonder if some of the Kentuckians would hear me on the other side of the river."[13]

Lincoln defined a distinctive region, the Old Northwest, blessed with freedom by the Northwest Ordinance. "You here in Ohio," he pointed out, "our neighbors in Indiana, we in Illinois, our neighbors in Michigan and Wisconsin are happy, prosperous, teeming millions of free men." To Lincoln, the greatest blessing of freedom was opportunity, the kind of "right to rise" that he had himself enjoyed and indeed now embodied. In the Old Northwest, "There is no permanent class of hired laborers amongst us." Instead, "Advancement—improvement in condition—is the order of things in a society of equals." Lincoln proposed himself as an example of self-improvement. "Twenty-five years ago, I was a hired laborer," he declared. "The hired laborer of yesterday, labors on his own account today." Social mobility was the most palpable result of freedom. Significantly, however, Lincoln attributed such regional differences not to inherent social, cultural, or economic differences but to government. Democrats, he argued, exaggerated regional distinctions grounded in tradition, soil, and climate. Douglas, not Lincoln, "told the people, that there was a 'line drawn by the Almighty across this continent, on the one side of which the soil must always be cultivated by slaves.'" By denying essential regional differences, Lincoln cleverly shifted focus from climate and culture to where he felt it belonged, government. The climate and people of a region did not, and could not, make and keep it free. Only a government policy of freedom could do so. In the Old Northwest, soil and climate did not eliminate slavery—"the Ordinance of '87 kept it out." Lincoln could readily endow southerners with "good hearts in your bosoms." They simply lacked a congressional ordinance that made their region free. Every region therefore had an equal potential for freedom, and Congress had an obligation to fulfill it. In particular, the West deserved an equal chance with the Old Northwest to be free.[14]

Two weeks after visiting Cincinnati, Lincoln addressed the State Agricultural Society in Milwaukee. Before an audience of farmers, he outlined the essential ingredients that made midwestern society free. Lincoln contrasted two competing economic systems, one in which laborers were hired to work for others and one in which laborers were compelled to work. Free labor granted northerners independence through subsistence agriculture and, through commercial agriculture, social mobility. "The prudent, penniless beginner in the world," Lincoln argued with obvious reference to himself, "labors for wages awhile, saves a surplus with which to buy tools or land, for himself; then labors on his own account another while, and at length hires another new beginner to help him." The result was self-improvement through education, which was the "natural companion" of free labor. "*Free* labor," Lincoln concluded, "the just and generous, and prosperous system, which opens the way for all—gives hope to all, and energy, and progress, and improvement of condition to all."[15]

Lincoln's most important speech came last. His Cooper Institute address was perhaps the most important that he delivered before winning the presidency. Invited to New York City by a group of young Republicans, Lincoln's task was to introduce himself to eastern Republicans, the wing of his party long faithful to the more radical Charles Sumner, William Seward, and Salmon Chase. His goal was to forge a coalition between eastern and western Republicans by presenting a conservative position and counseling moderation. Lincoln acknowledged the importance of his eastern performance by preparing for it with unaccustomed thoroughness. "No former effort in the line of speech-making," according to his partner, Herndon, "had cost Lincoln so much time and thought as his Cooper Union." Lincoln had three months to work on the speech. He studied assiduously in the Illinois State Library, read old newspaper files, and consulted notebooks that he and Herndon had stuffed with newspaper clippings over the years. Fellow lawyer Henry Rankin reminisced that Lincoln pored over the speech in his office every day, making extensive revisions. Lincoln continued to revise the speech up to the moment that he delivered it. As a westerner, Lincoln also worried about his personal presentation and bought a new suit for the occasion.[16]

In New York, Lincoln refined and refocused his earlier themes. He began with an extensive constitutional argument supporting the federal government's right to restrict slavery within the western territories. The founders considered slavery *"an evil not to be extended, but to be tolerated and protected only because of and so far as its actual presence among us makes that toleration and protection a necessity."* In essence, they intended to let southerners keep their slaves but not to take them into any new region. Republicans were therefore the true conservatives, because they upheld this original principle of the founders. Southerners were the extremists who now sought to "undo what Washington did." Sounding a now familiar theme, Lincoln denied his party's sectionalism. "You say we are sectional," he stated bluntly. "We deny it." Slavery, not sectionalism, divided the nation. "All they ask, we could readily grant, if we thought slavery right," Lincoln argued; "all we ask, they could as readily grant, if they thought it wrong. Their thinking it right and our thinking it wrong, is the precise fact upon which depends the whole controversy." Southerners' defense of slavery had created the sectional rift and indeed the new sectional party. "The fact that we get no votes in your section," Lincoln reasoned, "is a fact of your making, and not of ours." Lincoln concluded by counseling fellow Republicans to leave the South alone while working to confine slavery. "We must not only let them alone," he reasoned, "but we must, somehow, convince them that we do let them alone."[17]

The election of 1860 produced four nominees for president, each proposing a different solution to the slavery issue that threatened to divide the nation. In April, the Democratic Party convened in Charleston, South

Carolina, the hotbed of southern sectionalism, and split into two wings. Delegates from the Deep South refused to support Douglas because of his commitment to popular sovereignty. Through fifty-seven grueling ballots, Douglas failed to achieve the necessary two-thirds vote to win the nomination. Delegates from eight states in the Deep South walked out of the convention, which had no choice but to adjourn. Northern Democrats reassembled six weeks later in Baltimore, a border city, to try to salvage the remnants of a national party that might present a united front on the subject of slavery. They nominated Douglas for president and adopted a platform that advocated popular sovereignty in western territories. Southern Democrats nominated a candidate of their own, John C. Breckinridge of Kentucky, who was Buchanan's vice president and a defender of slavery expansion. The Southern Democrats adopted a proslavery platform that demanded federal protection of slavery in the West. The remnants of the American Party reassembled as the Constitutional Union Party. They supported the Union, advocated compromise on the slavery issue—envisioning the redrawing of the Missouri Compromise line and its extension to the Pacific Ocean—and resurrected a variety of nativist proposals. Popular in the Upper South, the Constitutional Unionists nominated John Bell of Tennessee as their standard bearer.[18]

Republicans met in Chicago to write a platform and select a nominee. The new party could elect a president in 1860 without a single southern vote, but only if they won the North solidly. They already commanded impressive majorities in the Upper North but needed to capture the Lower North, a band of states running from New Jersey in the east to Illinois in the west, to succeed. Three states—Pennsylvania, Indiana, and Illinois—were crucial to any hope of victory. They had voted for Buchanan in 1856 but had gone Republican in 1858, so the party focused on capturing these "doubtful" states along with several others. Such a strategy counseled moderation on the slavery issue. The platform pledged Republicans not to interfere with slavery where it already existed while proposing free soil as the only way to prevent its expansion. The delegates approved a spate of economic proposals, including a moderately protective tariff, federal funding for river and harbor improvements, a transcontinental railroad, and a homestead act to distribute free land in the West. They hoped to benefit from the Panic of 1857, a deep depression that many voters blamed on the Buchanan administration, as well as attracting workers who felt the sting of the depression. Finally, the Republicans appealed to immigrant voters by pledging to maintain existing immigration laws, thus repudiating at last any lingering flirtation with nativism.[19]

The moderate platform needed a moderate nominee to head the campaign. Eastern Republican leaders, such as Chase, Seward, and Sumner, had radical reputations and represented states—Ohio, New York, and Massachusetts—that were "safe," already solidly lodged within the Republican fold. Lincoln had many advantages as a nominee. He had worked hard to establish a reputation for moderation, supporting free soil while renouncing any interest in abolition or social, legal, and political equality for African Americans. A native southerner, he hailed from an important "doubtful" state that he could virtually guarantee to the Republicans. Like most nineteenth-century presidential aspirants, Lincoln did not attend his party's convention. Instead, he sent a delegation of advisors to argue his case, including David Davis, Stephen Logan, Richard Yates, and William Butler. They argued that Lincoln was the only Republican leader who had a chance of winning the entire North and won pledges from Seward, Sumner, and Chase delegates to make him their second choice. During the balloting, Lincoln sat nervously in the telegraph office in Springfield awaiting the result. As support for the other contenders faded, Lincoln's friends sent him telegrams that grew increasingly confident in tone—"We are quiet but moving heaven & Earth"—"Prospects fair friends at work night & day"—"Dont be frightend keep cool things is working"—"Am hopeful dont be Excited." Finally, after the third ballot, the word arrived—"To Abe Lincoln We did it glory to God."[20]

Lincoln's nomination provoked three distinct reactions in the South. In the Deep South, immediate secessionists, led by South Carolina, pledged to secede from the Union immediately upon Lincoln's election, even before he became president. Conditional Unionists took a less extreme position and were willing to wait until Lincoln took office to see how he would deal with slavery. They set several conditions for their continuing loyalty, such as enforcement of the Fugitive Slave Law and noninterference with the interstate slave trade. A third group of unconditional Unionists, strong in the Upper South, pledged to remain in the Union no matter what Lincoln decided to do about slavery. The election of 1860 was really two elections, one northern and one southern. In the North, Lincoln battled Douglas, and free soil competed with popular sovereignty as the best way to stop the spread of slavery. In the South, Bell battled Breckinridge, and a commitment to the Union and compromise on slavery squared off against the threat of secession.[21]

Refusing to provide ammunition of any kind to southern secessionists, Lincoln resolved to remain silent throughout the campaign. Above all, Lincoln had no intention of altering his views to woo anyone, and a dialogue on slavery would only raise false expectations of compromise. Simply put, he believed that "his positions were well known when he was nominated, and that he must not now embarrass the canvass by undertaking to shift or modify them." Lincoln made only one speech during the campaign, from his front porch when a group of Springfielders called on him. He was so reluctant to say anything untoward that he ended one letter with the request that his correspondent "Burn this, not that there is any thing wrong in it; but because it is best not be known that I write at all." As the campaign progressed, Lincoln's caution faded and his optimism grew. In May, he judged that "The thing starts well everywhere—too well, I almost fear, to last." Then, "The nominations start well here, and everywhere else, so far as I have heard. We may have a back-set yet." Finally, in August, he wrote to a friend and political ally that "I hesitate to say it, but it really appears now, as if the success of the Republican ticket is inevitable. We have no reason to doubt any of the states which voted for Fremont. Add to these, Minnesota, Pennsylvania, and New-Jersey, and the thing is done."[22]

In November, the thing was done. Lincoln swept the entire North, except for New Jersey, which split its vote between Lincoln and Douglas. Bell's commitment to the Union dominated the Upper South, winning Virginia, Kentucky, and Tennessee for the Constitutional Union Party. Douglas took only one state, Missouri. Breckinridge captured every other slave state, where Lincoln was not even on the ballot. The election of 1860 was won in the Lower North, the "doubtful" states that had gone Democratic in 1856. The Republicans' moderate stance—and moderate nominee—made the difference. Lincoln won Indiana and Illinois with 51 percent of the vote. The Republican sweep of the North was so complete that Lincoln would have won the election even if the three other parties had all cast their votes for a single candidate. As Lincoln put it, "I think the chances were more than equal that we could have beaten the Democracy *united*."[23]

Although Lincoln avoided public appearances, Douglas stumped tirelessly across the country. In Springfield, Democrats held two parades, which together included more than six hundred wagons and four thousand people, and twenty thousand spectators. Douglas spoke in Springfield two weeks before the election. Afterward, a torchlight procession of one thousand torches and transparencies lit up the night. Springfield Republicans concluded early that "The success of the Republican Presidential ticket is now clear and unmistakable" and likened the Douglas parade to "the boy going through a graveyard at night, 'whistling to keep up his courage.'" Both parties raised their traditional flagpoles, the Republican standard rising 120 feet. Republican Wide Awake Clubs marched through the streets with torches, music, and banners, and Republicans met nightly at their new Wigwam as the election neared. Named after Chicago's meeting hall, Springfield's circular Wigwam opened during the summer of 1860 and held three thousand people. Republicans held a parade of their own, with special trains carrying 180 carloads of out-of-town visitors into Springfield, and twenty Wide Awake Clubs marched through the streets. Wagons carried a log cabin reminiscent of the Kentucky frontier, a flatboat from the New Salem days, a power loom weaving jeans from Lincoln's youth, an old settler splitting rails, and craftsmen practicing the free labor that was the promise of a Republican victory. When Lincoln arrived at the fairgrounds, the crowd demanded a speech, but Lincoln mounted a horse and rode off after delivering no more than a simple greeting. Instead, he spent most of his time receiving dignitaries from around the country, answering mail in a temporary office in the statehouse, and sitting for oil portraits, busts, and daguerreotypes.[24]

Ever the politician, however, Lincoln was passionate about winning his hometown and especially defeating his old rival Douglas. During the momentous campaign, he sought out a Republican candidate in Springfield and asked him "what measures, if any, had been adopted to get out the full republican vote." Learning that "the Republicans would probably wait until a few days before the election before any systematic effort would be made in the city," Lincoln would have none of it. "He then detailed to the candidate his plan for procuring a full vote and securing to the Republican ticket such electors as were careless or doubtful." As a result of his exertions, Lincoln narrowly defeated Douglas, by a mere sixty-nine votes. Breckinridge won 3 percent support in Springfield, and Bell captured a mere sixteen votes. Lincoln won Springfield but with only 49 percent of the vote. As in the nation itself, Lincoln was a minority president. Springfield, too, remained a divided community, like so many others, as the country descended into civil war.[25]

An Affectionate Farewell

Ayear before Abraham Lincoln was elected president, he took time out from politics to help organize an Old Settlers' Society in Springfield. Along with five dozen other longtime residents of the area, Lincoln was a founding member of the Sangamon County Historical Society. Throughout the West, "old settlers" or "pioneers," as they styled themselves, were founding societies to commemorate their past, preserve their communities' history, and keep dying memories alive. The Sangamon County Historical Society inaugurated an annual celebration of the county's pioneer past and designated October 20 as Old Settlers' Day. Like the other societies that did the work of community building, this one adopted a constitution, elected officers, and chose a committee to plan its festivities. Throughout the West, pioneer societies adopted a variety of rules for membership, but Springfield's defined an eligible "old settler" as anyone who survived the winter of the Deep Snow of 1830–31. Emblematic of Springfielders' growing sense of their city's maturity and destiny, the commemoration of Old Settlers' Day preserved old memories of historic frontier origins in the midst of stunning social development, cultural transformation, and sectional tensions.[1]

In earmarking one day a year to think about the past, the Old Settlers were celebrating a robust and simple rural society, when Springfield was a mere village, before rough-hewn simplicities gave way to the overrefined niceties of modern life. Old Settlers' Day was organized, nostalgically, in Springfield, and four-fifths of its organizers, including Lincoln, were Springfield residents. They chose a rural spot, still a wilderness, twelve miles south of the city, where pioneer Robert Pulliam, a transplanted Virginian, had built the county's first log cabin forty-two years before. On October 20, during an Indian Summer, the Old Settlers made a ceremonious three-hour pilgrimage southward across the prairie to revisit the country and to reminisce about their pioneer past.[2]

In an era before accurate record keeping and a modern sensibility of time, the unforgettable Deep Snow seemed the logical event through which to winnow true pioneers who carved a home out of the prairies from mere newcomers who settled into established farms and towns. As a local historian summed it up, "All important events are reckoned from the deep snow." On the eve of the Civil War, Springfield's Old Settlers proudly reminisced about their whereabouts when the Deep Snow fell, their struggles to survive that memorable winter, and their indebtedness to neighbors who sheltered them or lent them corn. "This is one of the land-marks of the early settlers," a nineteenth-century Springfielder recalled. "It is his mile-stone, from which he counts in dating preceding or succeeding events. He reckons the date of his coming, his marriage, and the births of his children, from it." Surviving the Deep Snow was a distinct badge of honor among Springfielders, and one that was hard earned. But the choice of the Deep Snow as the paramount "pioneer event" harbored more than merely meteorological significance. The year 1830 represented a cultural turning point in the history of Illinois. Before 1830, most settlers were southerners, who floated down or crossed the Ohio River through the southern woodlands and edged out onto the prairie openings of central Illinois. After 1830, southern settlers began giving way to New Englanders, who traveled the Erie Canal and the Great Lakes—and later railroads—to settle the northern half of the state.[3]

Commemoration of the Deep Snow represents the kind of "invention of tradition" that societies often practice in the face of sudden cultural and political change. Communities that are losing a sense of their own solidarity or feeling beleaguered by outside social and political pressures frequently "invent" traditions to bolster their own self-identity, to provide connections to a reassuring past, and resist change itself. They use invented traditions to create formal boundaries around "real or artificial communities" so that they can maintain their traditional status, authority, and social institutions. The basis of the invented tradition is repetition, creating a comforting ritual that regularly reinforces the group's self-identity. In Springfield, southerners found themselves a suddenly outnumbered cultural group that was not only losing its former social and political status but was actually coming under attack in both the region and the nation. Creating the Old Settlers' Society, limiting its membership to survivors of the Deep Snow, and establishing an annual Old Settlers' Day represented one last attempt at recapturing southerners' former status as community elders. Feeling increasingly outnumbered and besieged, southerners set out to defend and romanticize their pioneer past. Surviving the Deep Snow became, for these southerners, a literal badge of honor. "At the old settlers' annual meetings," according to one participant, "they have badges that are worn by all who were here before 1830."[4]

The first Old Settlers' Day provided a vivid reminder of smoldering sectional tensions. By accident, the festivities coincided with John Brown's raid on the federal arsenal at Harper's Ferry, Virginia. Exaggerated reports in the morning newspapers announced that fifteen to twenty northern abolitionists had joined five southern slaves in sparking a massive slave rebellion

THE REPUBLICAN NOMINEE, AUGUST 1860. SOON TO SPROUT A BEARD,
THIS COUNTENANCE WOULD RALLY THE UNION THROUGH THE
SECESSION CRISIS AND FOUR YEARS OF CIVIL WAR.
Courtesy of the Illinois State Historical Library.

that, at last telling, had swelled to two or three hundred insurrectionaries. Sectional strife now haunted the celebration, and the band conspicuously played the patriotic "Hurray for the Red, White, and Blue." The settlers circled their wagons back into the timber from which they had first emerged four decades before, and speaker after speaker decried the partisan and sectional spirit that threatened to divide their community and their nation. Old Settlers' Day was designed to be an annual commemoration, but on the next October 20, Lincoln's momentous campaign for the presidency forced a postponement of the event. The Civil War and Reconstruction delayed the next Old Settlers' Day for nearly a decade.[5]

"Old Settler" status in Illinois was rare and quite prestigious, simply because moving west was a difficult thing to do and staying put in an expansive, frontier society was even harder. Before the Civil War, thousands of newcomers scrutinized Springfield and the Sangamon Country every year, but only a relative handful succeeded in settling down as permanent residents. Most newcomers did not put down deep roots but only stayed a few seasons before moving on again. Just ten years after the Deep Snow fell, four-fifths of its survivors had already left the region. Southerners grew discouraged during this awful winter and turned back home in droves or moved on southwestward to the more familiar terrain of Missouri. Effectively stopping the northward advance of southern-style agriculture, the severe climate destroyed their tobacco and cotton crops. A disgusted Yankee rejoiced that the climate had done "much towards improving the country" by driving "the lazy, dissipated N. & S. Carolinians, Georgians, Tennesseans" back home. Lincoln's own family weathered the winter in Decatur, Illinois, just upriver from Springfield, but decided to turn around and head back south in the spring. "In the autumn all hands were greatly afflicted with ague and fever, to which they had not been used, and by which they were greatly discouraged—so much so that they determined on leaving the county," Lincoln recalled thirty years later. "They remained however, through the succeeding winter, which was the winter of the very celebrated 'deep snow.'" Among the 290 white adult males living in Springfield before the Deep Snow, 85 percent moved away or died before 1850, and 93 percent were gone by 1860. Lincoln himself joined only twenty-one other Old Settlers—a mere 7 percent of all Deep Snow survivors—who stayed in the community until the Civil War. The Old Settlers' Society honored the few real pioneers who, through hard work, family connections, or simple luck, found their way to Springfield, survived the hard years of initial settlement, and managed to remain as permanent residents for the rest of their lives. They eventually dwindled to the point that the Old Settlers' Society finally relented and allowed latecomers to join, moving the cutoff date to January 1, 1837.[6]

Lincoln was the perfect representative of these Old Settlers. Arriving in the crucial settlement year of 1830, he braved the frontier adversities symbolized by the Deep Snow and refused to give up even when his own family surrendered to discouragement and trekked back southward toward home. A southerner by birth, he came of age within a region that enjoyed a mixture of disparate cultures but managed to blend them, even as they simmered, into a unique amalgam of North and South, a sort of microcosm of the sectional tensions that would soon demand his leadership. Remembered as "one of the least pretentious" of the Old Settlers, Lincoln persevered and turned one adversity after another into a personal advantage. His remarkable struggle to overcome humble beginnings and achieve the pinnacle of success remains one of the most cherished themes within the Lincoln legend and, indeed, within all of American history.[7]

As he lived his life, Lincoln learned to recognize instinctively the differences that divided his country as well as the commonalities that could bind it together. On the verge of becoming president, he labeled himself "the representative man of the nation." Although elected by a minority of Americans—a mere 40 percent—Lincoln yet possessed an extraordinary ability to sympathize with or at least to understand the hopes and dreams, the fears and doubts, and above all the way of life of the typical American of his day. Even as president, Lincoln's connection to the American people lay rooted deep within his own ancestry—his family's history—and the wisdom that he had gathered from his own experiences—both bitter and tender moments—as he grew up, matured, and felt his life unfold within the heart of the nation. His stature as both a great and an ordinary American grew out of the journey that he made in his own life, moving as a boy from the slaveholding South to the free air of the Midwest, persevering, and rising as a youth from the humblest walks of life to the pinnacle of earthly success. Yet through it all he remained a representative in true connection with the people, primarily because the individual, personal journey that he made across the geographical and social landscape of America mirrored the nation's collective journey as well.[8]

On February 11, 1861, Lincoln stood at the back of the train that would carry him to Washington and delivered his Farewell Address to the community that had taken him in, made him a man, and raised him to the pinnacle of power. "To this place, and the kindness of these people," he admitted to a crowd of 150 neighbors, "I owe everything. Here I have lived a quarter of a century, and have passed from a young to an old man. Here my children have been born, and one is buried. I now leave, not knowing when, or whether ever, I may return." In closing, he asked that "in your prayers you will commend me," and then said simply, "I bid you an affectionate farewell."[9] In life, of course, he never did return. But he took with him to Washington the best parts of this society, etched in his memory and embodied instinctively now in his way of looking at the world. Spreading his wings in the Sangamon Country, the young eagle had tested the winds, set his sights on the horizon, caught just the right currents with impeccable timing, and soared.

Notes

INTRODUCTION

1. Douglas L. Wilson and Rodney O. Davis, eds., *Herndon's Informants: Letters, Interviews, and Statements About Abraham Lincoln* (Urbana: University of Illinois Press, 1998), 590.

2. Roy P. Basler, ed., *The Collected Works of Abraham Lincoln* (New Brunswick, NJ: Rutgers University Press, 1953), III, 511–12, IV, 60–67; John Locke Scripps, *The Life of Abraham Lincoln* (Chicago, 1860), reprint, ed. Roy P. Basler and Lloyd A. Dunlap (New York: Greenwood Press, 1968), 27, 33, 40; Lincoln, of course, was borrowing rather than creating a rhetorical device. With the rise of democratic politics during the 1820s, presidential candidates—Andrew Jackson and William Henry Harrison most successfully—consciously fostered an image of humble origins to emphasize their sympathy with voters and their own natural talents and perseverance. Edward Pessen, *The Log Cabin Myth: The Social Backgrounds of the Presidents* (New Haven, CT: Yale University Press, 1984), dissects and largely dismisses the "log cabin" origins of U.S. presidents and of Lincoln in particular (24–25, 91–92). Richard Hofstadter, "Abraham Lincoln and the Self-Made Myth," in Richard Hofstadter, *The American Political Tradition and the Men Who Made It* (New York: Knopf, 1948), 93–136, explores the myth's various ideological and personal dimensions.

3. Merrill D. Peterson, *Lincoln in American Memory* (New York: Oxford University Press, 1994), 232–43, reviews the controversy over Lincoln's ancestry. David M. Potter, *The Lincoln Theme and American National Historiography* (Oxford, Eng.: Oxford University Press, 1948); D. E. Fehrenbacher, *The Changing Image of Lincoln in American Historiography* (Oxford, Eng.: Oxford University Press, 1968); and John Y. Simon, *House Divided: Lincoln and His Father* (Fort Wayne, IN: Louis A. Warren Lincoln Library and Museum, 1987), ably put the controversy into broader historiographical context. Quote from Simon, *House Divided*, 3. During the 1920s, William E. Barton published a series of books that meticulously demonstrated Lincoln's legitimacy but questioned that of his mother; see, especially, William E. Barton, *The Lineage of Lincoln* (Indianapolis: Bobbs-Merrill, 1929). Meanwhile, Louis A. Warren, *Lincoln's Parentage and Childhood* (New York: Century, 1929), more persuasively championed both Thomas Lincoln's character and Nancy Hanks Lincoln's legitimacy.

4. As the most recent example, Mark E. Neely Jr, *The Last Best Hope of Earth: Abraham Lincoln and the Promise of America* (Cambridge, MA: Harvard University Press, 1993), entitled the first chapter of his biography, surveying Lincoln's early life, "Peculiar Ambition."

CHAPTER 1

1. Roy P. Basler, ed., *The Collected Works of Abraham Lincoln* (New Brunswick, NJ: Rutgers University Press, 1953), I, 456, IV, 60; Waldo Lincoln, *History of the Lincoln Family: An Account of the Descendants of Samuel Lincoln of Hingham, Massachusetts, 1637–1920* (Worcester, MA: Commonwealth Press, 1923), 5; William E. Barton, *The Lineage of Lincoln* (Indianapolis: Bobbs-Merrill, 1929), 33, 36, 41–42; Louis A. Warren, "Abraham Lincoln's Knowledge of His Ancestry," *Lincoln Lore*, 1308 (May 3, 1954), 1; Mark E. Neely Jr., *The Last Best Hope of Earth: Abraham Lincoln and the Promise of America* (Cambridge, MA: Harvard University Press, 1993), 1.

2. John Coolidge, "Hingham Builds a Meetinghouse," *New England Quarterly*, 34 (December

1961), 435–61, esp. 442; John J. Waters, "Hingham, Massachusetts, 1631–1661: An East Anglian Oligarchy in the New World," *Journal of Social History*, 1 (Summer 1968), 351–70; David Cressy, *Coming Over: Migration and Communication Between England and New England in the Seventeenth Century* (New York: Cambridge University Press, 1987); Ida M. Tarbell, *In the Footsteps of the Lincolns* (New York: Harper and Brothers, 1924), 7–8. Life spans, places of birth and death, and migrations were compiled from Barton, *Lineage of Lincoln*; Lincoln, *History of the Lincoln Family*; and Tarbell, *Footsteps of the Lincolns*. The table considers permanent rather than temporary moves—moves of at least one year's duration—beyond one county or, in New England, one town. These moves include:

(a) Mordecai Sr.: Hingham, Mass., to Hull, Mass., to Scituate, Mass.; (b) Mordecai Jr.: Scituate, Mass., to Freehold, N.J., to Chester County, Pa., to Berks County, Pa.; (c) John: Freehold, N.J., to Chester County, Pa., to Berks County, Pa., to Rockingham County, Va.; (d) Abraham: Berks County, Pa., to Rockingham County, Va., to Jefferson County, Ky.; (e) Thomas: Rockingham County, Va., to Jefferson County, Ky., to Washington County, Ky., to Hardin County, Ky., to Spencer County, Ind., to Decatur, Ill., to Charleston, Ill.; (f) Abraham: Hardin County, Ky., to Spencer County, Ind., to Decatur, Ill., to New Salem, Ill., to Springfield, Ill., to Washington, D.C.

Tracing the male line of descent from Mordecai in the first generation to Abraham in the sixth compares Lincoln's behavior to that of his direct male ancestors. John W. Adams and Alice Bee Kasakoff, "Migration and the Family in Colonial New England: The View from Genealogies," *Journal of Family History*, 9 (Spring 1984), 24–43, esp. 25, similarly chart the movements of only the "male patrilineal descendants" who married, "in order to have unbroken chains of descendants."

3. Barton, *Lineage of Lincoln*, 41, charts this geographical sweep along the Appalachian Front and then concludes in his idiosyncratic way that "The Appalachian Mountains caused the downward curve. Humanity is averse to hill-climbing." Ralph H. Brown, *Historical Geography of the United States* (New York: Harcourt, Brace and World, 1948), 183–86, provides an excellent overview of topographical barriers to westward settlement. See also John Mack Faragher, *Daniel Boone: The Life and Legend of an American Pioneer* (New York: Henry Holt, 1992), 28; and John F. Rooney Jr., Wilbur Zelinsky, and Dean R. Louder, eds., *This Remarkable Continent: An Atlas of United States and Canadian Society and Cultures* (College Station: Texas A&M University Press, 1982), 33.

4. Adams and Kasakoff, "Migration and the Family," 29, notes a similar trend.

5. Lincoln, *History of the Lincoln Family*, 16, 17, 20, 21; Tarbell, *Footsteps of the Lincolns*, 17, 18, 19, 27.

6. Lincoln, *History of the Lincoln Family*, 44–46, 49; Tarbell, *Footsteps of the Lincolns*, 27, 32, 34, 35, 37, 38, 40; John T. Cunningham, *New Jersey: America's Main Road* (Garden City, NY: Doubleday, 1976), 13, 51, 61; Richard P. McCormick, *New Jersey from Colony to State, 1609–1789* (Princeton, NJ: Van Nostrand, 1964), 84; Brown, *Historical Geography*, 186–87; D. W. Meinig, *The Shaping of America: A Geographical Perspective on 500 Years of History*, Vol. I, *Atlantic America, 1492–1800* (New Haven, CT: Yale Univerity Press, 1986), 138–39; James T. Lemon, *The Best Poor Man's Country: A Geographical Study of Early Southeastern Pennsylvania* (Baltimore: Johns Hopkins University Press, 1972), 42–50.

7. Clarence H. Danhof, *Change in Agriculture: The Northern United States 1820–1870* (Cambridge, MA: Harvard University Press, 1969), 257; Steven Mintz and Susan Kellogg, *Domestic Revolutions: A Social History of American Family Life* (New York: Free Press, 1988), 16; Adams and Kasakoff, "Migration and the Family," 28.

8. Lincoln, *History of the Lincoln Family*, 93–94, 99; Rooney, Zelinsky, and Louder, *This Remarkable Continent*, 33; Robert D. Mitchell, "The Formation of Early American Cultural Regions: An Interpretation," in James R. Gibson, ed., *European Settlement and Development in North America: Essays in Honour and Memory of Andrew Hill Clark* (Toronto: University of Toronto Press, 1978), 66–90, esp. 81; Robert D. Mitchell, "The Shenandoah Valley Frontier," *Annals of the American Association of Geographers*, 62 (September 1972), 461–86, 469, 477; Robert D. Mitchell, *Commercialism and Frontier: Perspectives on the Early Shenandoah Valley* (Charlottesville: University Press of Virginia, 1977), 35, 54; David Hackett Fischer and James C. Kelly, *Away, I'm Bound Away: Virginia and the Westward Movement* (Richmond: Virginia Historical Society, 1993), 61, 92; Faragher, *Daniel Boone*, 28; John W. Wayland, *A History of Rockingham County, Virginia* (Dayton, VA: Ruebush-Elkins, 1912), 428; Archer B. Hulbert, *The Paths of Inland Commerce: A Chronicle of Trail, Road, and Waterway* (New Haven, CT: Yale University Press, 1920), 49.

9. *Collected Works*, IV, 60–61; Mitchell, "Formation of Early American Cultural Regions," 81;

Brown, *Historical Geography*, 185–87; Tarbell, *Footsteps of the Lincolns*, 40-41, 54; Gregory S. Rose, "Hoosier Origins: The Nativity of Indiana United States–Born Population in 1850," *Indiana Magazine of History*, 81 (September 1985), 201–32, esp. 226. Mitchell, "Shenandoah Valley Frontier," 464, concludes that "the Shenandoah Valley provided a vital link in the major route complex for interior population migration prior to 1800. This complex originated in southeastern Pennsylvania and followed the Great Valley south and west through Maryland and Virginia into the Southern back country." Rockingham County was created in 1777; Wayland, *History of Rockingham County*, 65.

10. Mitchell, "Shenandoah Valley Frontier," 470, 473, 474, 484, 485; Mitchell, *Commercialism and Frontier*, 51, 56; Mitchell, "Formation of Early American Cultural Regions," 83; Faragher, *Daniel Boone*, 28, 203-204; Tarbell, *Footsteps of the Lincolns*, 54; John W. Wayland, *The Lincolns in Virginia* (Staunton, VA: McClure Printing Company, 1946), 25; Wayland, *History of Rockingham County*, 107.

11. Francis Paul Prucha, *The Great Father: The United States Government and the American Indians* (Lincoln: University of Nebraska Press, 1984), I, 44–45; Faragher, *Daniel Boone*, 177–225, 249–255; R. Douglas Hurt, *The Ohio Frontier: Crucible of the Old Northwest, 1720–1830* (Bloomington: Indiana University Press, 1996), 97–100.

12. Faragher, *Daniel Boone*, 216–17, 250-1; Richard White, *The Middle Ground: Indians, Empires, and Republics in the Great Lakes Region, 1650–1815* (New York: Cambridge University Press, 1991), 411, 417–418; Gregory Evans Dowd, *A Spirited Resistance: The North American Indian Struggle for Unity, 1745–1815* (Baltimore: Johns Hopkins University Press, 1992), 67, 75–76, 95; Hurt, *Ohio Frontier*, 97–100.

13. *Collected Works*, III, 511, IV, 61; William H. Herndon and Jesse W. Weik, *Herndon's Life of Lincoln*, ed. Paul M. Angle (Cleveland: World, 1942), 10; Lincoln, *History of the Lincoln Family*, 196. Lincoln wrote that his grandfather was killed "about" 1784. Barton, *Lineage of Lincoln*, 47, 53, 55, demonstrates that Lincoln's grandfather Abraham moved to Kentucky in 1782 and died there in 1786.

14. Adams and Kasakoff, "Migration and the Family," 27, 34; James A. Henretta, "Families and Farms: *Mentalite* in Pre-Industrial America," *William and Mary Quarterly*, 35 (January 1978), 3–32; John Y. Simon, *House Divided: Lincoln and His Father* (Fort Wayne, Ind.: Louis A. Warren Lincoln Library and Museum, 1987), 4; Kathleen Neils Conzen, "A Saga of Families," in Clyde A. Milner II, Carol A. O'Connor, and Martha A. Sandweiss, eds., *The Oxford History of the American West* (New York: Oxford University Press, 1994), 315–57, esp. 334; A. Gordon Darroch, "Migrants in the Nineteenth Century: Fugitives or Families in Motion?" *Journal of Family History*, 6 (Fall 1981), 257-77, esp. 265.

15. Charles Tilly and C. Harold Brown, "On Uprooting, Kinship and the Auspices of Migration," *International Journal of Comparative Sociology*, 8 (September 1967), 139–64; Darroch, "Fugitives or Families"; Robert E. Bieder, "Kinship as a Factor in Migration," *Journal of Marriage and the Family*, 35 (August 1973), 429–39; Jack E. Eblen, "An Analysis of Nineteenth-Century Frontier Populations," *Demography*, 2 (1965), 399–413; Conzen, "Saga of Families." Henretta, "Families and Farms," offers an insightful analysis of intergenerational migration strategies within families. Susan E. Gray, *The Yankee West: Community Life on the Michigan Frontier* (Chapel Hill: University of North Carolina Press, 1996), 10–11, contrasts family-based and clan-based migration.

16. Fischer and Kelly, *Away, I'm Bound Away*, 61, 72, 92; Mitchell, "Shenandoah Valley Frontier," 463, 477; Robert L. Kincaid, "Cumberland Gap, Gateway of Empire," *Filson Club Quarterly*, 15 (January 1941), 25–40; Faragher, *Daniel Boone*, 77; Rose, "Hoosier Origins," 226. Mordecai Lincoln Jr. died in Berks County, Pennsylvania, along the Great Philadelphia Wagon Road; John died in Rockingham County, Virginia, in the Shenandoah Valley; Abraham was born in Berks County, Pennsylvania, along the Great Philadelphia Wagon Road, and died in Jefferson County, Kentucky, along the Wilderness Road; Thomas was born in Rockingham County, Virginia, in the Shenandoah Valley; and Abraham was born in Hardin County, Kentucky, along the Wilderness Road.

17. Mitchell, "Formation of Early American Cultural Regions," 77. In his comprehensive survey of cultural diffusion in American history, historian David Hackett Fischer identifies the Shenandoah Valley as part of a separate cultural region—the Backcountry—that was linked with Pennsylvania rather than with Virginia and the coastal South. So deep was Lincoln's northern heritage that Fischer classifies the future president not as a southerner at all but as a New England Puritan by heritage. Fischer identifies four American "cultural regions" centered in Massachusetts, Delaware, Virginia, and the Backcountry. He views the Republican Party of the 1850s and 1860s as a coalition of all the cultural regions except Virginia and the South. Lincoln's identification with all three of the Republican

regions peculiarly fitted him to lead the party: "On his father's side, Lincoln was descended from New England Puritans who had intermarried with Pennsylvania Quakers and migrated to Appalachia and the Ohio Valley. He represented every regional component of the Republican coalition"; David Hackett Fischer, *Albion's Seed: Four British Folkways in America* (New York: Oxford University Press, 1989), 637, 836–37, 856–57.

CHAPTER 2

1. Roy P. Basler, ed., *The Collected Works of Abraham Lincoln* (New Brunswick, NJ: Rutgers University Press, 1953), III, 511, IV, 61; Louis A. Warren, *Lincoln's Parentage and Childhood* (New York: Century, 1929), 77–78.

2. Waldo Lincoln, *History of the Lincoln Family: An Account of the Descendants of Samuel Lincoln of Hingham, Massachusetts, 1637–1920* (Worcester, MA: Commonwealth Press, 1923), 202–3; Louis A. Warren, *Lincoln's Parentage and Childhood* (New York: Century, 1929), 77–78; John D. Mitchell, "The Formation of Early American Cultural Regions: An Interpretation," in James R. Gibson, ed., *European Settlement and Development in North America: Essays in Honour and Memory of Andrew Hill Clark* (Toronto: University of Toronto Press, 1978), 66–90, esp. 83; John W. Adams and Alice Bee Kasakoff, "Migration and the Family in Colonial New England: The View from Genealogies," *Journal of Family History*, 9 (Spring 1984), 24–43, esp. 31.

3. Lincoln's birthplace is now in Larue County. *Collected Works*, IV, 61; Harry E. Pratt, *The Personal Finances of Abraham Lincoln* (Springfield, IL: Abraham Lincoln Association, 1943), 3. Hardin County was named after John Hardin, a general in the Kentucky militia; Joseph Nathan Kane, *The American Counties* (New York: Scarecrow Press, 1962), 129. General Hardin was the grandfather of John J. Hardin; Dumas Malone, ed., *The Dictionary of American Biography* (New York: Charles Scribner's Sons, 1943), VIII, 245. John J. Hardin was Mary Todd's third cousin; Jean H. Baker, *Mary Todd Lincoln: A Biography* (New York: Norton, 1987), 136. Lincoln himself wrote that "My earliest recollection . . . is of the Knob Creek place"; *Collected Works*, IV, 70. Historians have reconstructed this early period from family reminiscences and legal records. According to John Y. Simon, *House Divided: Lincoln and His Father* (Fort Wayne, Ind.: Louis A. Warren Lincoln Library and Museum, 1987), 4–5, Abraham Lincoln owned 5,000 acres of land at his death, but his son Thomas owned only 348.5 acres when his own son was born.

4. *Collected Works*, II, 15, 96, IV, 61–62; Ida M. Tarbell, *In the Footsteps of the Lincolns* (New York: Harper and Brothers, 1924), 102; R. Gerald McMurtry, "The Lincoln Migration from Kentucky to Indiana," *Indiana Magazine of History*, 33 (December 1937), 385–421, esp. 399; John Mack Faragher, *Sugar Creek: Life on the Illinois Prairie* (New Haven, CT.: Yale University Press, 1986), 263; Michael J. O'Brien, *Grassland, Forest, and Historical Settlement: An Analysis of Dynamics in Northeast Missouri* (Lincoln: University of Nebraska Press, 1984), 68. Lincoln believed incorrectly that he was eight when he moved to Indiana. Lincoln's relative and childhood friend Dennis Hanks later denied that Thomas Lincoln left Kentucky because of slavery; Douglas L. Wilson and Rodney O. Davis, eds., *Herndon's Informants: Letters, Interviews, and Statements About Abraham Lincoln* (Urbana: University of Illinois Press, 1998), 36. Hildegard Binder Johnson, *Order Upon the Land: The U.S. Rectangular Land Survey and the Upper Mississippi Country* (New York: Oxford University Press, 1976), offers a detailed look at the intricacies and implications of the Congressional Survey System.

5. *Collected Works*, IV, 61; Wilson and Davis, *Herndon's Informants*, 38; Warren, *Lincoln's Parentage and Childhood*, 16. Given Lincoln's sketchy recollections, Dennis Hanks provides the fullest reminiscence of the family's early movements. Two months after Lincoln's assassination, Hanks began sending detailed accounts of the president's boyhood to William H. Herndon, Lincoln's longtime law partner. Hanks's account of the family's genealogy is hopelessly jumbled, and his description of Lincoln's Indiana years errs grievously when recounting dates and ages that can be verified through independent sources. Still, there is little reason to question the broad outlines of his narrative of the Lincolns' migration from Kentucky through Indiana to Illinois, in which he participated and which has never been a controversial component of Lincoln biography. Ida Tarbell, *Footsteps of the Lincolns*, 87, concludes that "However grateful we may be to Dennis for the color and liveliness which he has contributed to an important segment of the Lincoln story, a segment of which he knew much, he cannot be taken seriously as a genealogist." Don Fehrenbacher rightly observes that the entire Herndon-Weik Collection is "too valuable to ignore but extremely difficult to verify"; D. E. Fehrenbacher, *The Changing Image of Lincoln in American Historiography* (Oxford, Eng.: Oxford University Press, 1968), 6. Thomas Lincoln's father, Abraham, similarly traveled alone to Kentucky

to select a farm and came back to Virginia to retrieve his wife and children; William E. Barton, *The Lineage of Lincoln* (Indianapolis: Bobbs-Merrill, 1929), 53.

6. Gregory S. Rose, "Upland Southerners: The County Origins of Southern Migrants to Indiana by 1850," *Indiana Magazine of History*, 82 (September 1986), 242–63; Gregory S. Rose, "Hoosier Origins: The Nativity of Indiana United States–Born Population in 1850," *Indiana Magazine of History*, 81 (September 1985), 201–32, esp. 211; Andrew R. L. Cayton, *Frontier Indiana* (Bloomington: Indiana University Press, 1996), 267, 272, 277; Barbara J. Steinson, "Rural Life in Indiana, 1800–1950," *Indiana Magazine of History*, 90 (September 1994), 203–250, esp. 204.

7. *Collected Works*, III, 511, IV, 62; Wilson and Davis, *Herndon's Informants*, 35–43, 251; Pratt, *Personal Finances*, 4–5; Warren, *Lincoln's Parentage and Childhood*, 41–42; Rose, "Hoosier Origins," 221; Donald A. Hutslar, *Log Construction in the Ohio Country, 1750–1850* (Athens: Ohio University Press, 1992), 152, 154, notes that cabins in the Ohio Country were traditionally raised in a single day. A. Gordon Darroch, "Migrants in the Nineteenth Century: Fugitives or Families in Motion?" *Journal of Family History*, 6 (Fall 1981), 257–77, discusses augmented households.

8. *Collected Works*, IV, 62; Wilson and Davis, *Herndon's Informants*, 39, 40.

9. Wilson and Davis, *Herndon's Informants*, 99, 100, 176.

10. Wilson and Davis, *Herndon's Informants*, 40–41, 99–100, 126.

11. On parental death, see Peter Uhlenberg, "Death and the Family," *Journal of Family History*, 5 (Fall 1980), 313–20, esp. 316; Peter Uhlenberg, "Changing Configurations of the Life Course," in Tamara K. Hareven, ed., *Transitions: The Family and the Life Course in Historical Perspective* (New York: Academic Press, 1978), 65–97, esp. 78; Peter R. Uhlenberg, "A Study of Cohort Life Cycles: Cohorts of Native Born Massachusetts Women, 1830–1920," *Population Studies*, 23 (November 1969), 407–20, esp. 414; Joseph F. Kett, *Rites of Passage: Adolescence in America, 1790 to the Present* (New York: Basic Books, 1977), 15; Steven Mintz and Susan Kellogg, *Domestic Revolutions: A Social History of American Family Life* (New York: Free Press, 1988), 104. In his pioneering study of the family cycle, Paul Glick notes that in the typical family of 1890, at least one parent died before the youngest child married; Paul C. Glick, "The Family Cycle," *American Sociological Review*, 12 (April 1947), 164–74, esp. 168. According to Andrew Cherlin, "Changing Family and Household: Contemporary Lessons from Historical Research," *Annual Review of Sociology*, 9 (1983), 51–66, esp. 56, "As recently as the beginning of this century, it was still common for children to lose a parent through death." See also Carl N. Degler, *At Odds: Women and the Family in America from the Revolution to the Present* (New York: Oxford University Press, 1980), 174.

12. *Collected Works*, IV, 62; Tarbell, *Footsteps of the Lincolns*, 89. The classic critique of the psychological implications of his mother's death, and more generally the psychohistorical approach to Lincoln, is Don E. Fehrenbacher, *Lincoln in Text and Context: Collected Essays* (Stanford, CA: Stanford University Press, 1987), 214–27. Sound introductions to the rise in life expectancy include Robert V. Wells, *Uncle Sam's Family: Issues and Perspectives on American Demographic History* (Albany: State University of New York Press, 1985), 57–93; and Robert V. Wells, "The Mortality Transition in Schenectady, New York, 1880–1930," *Social Science History*, 19 (Fall 1995), 399–423. Philip D. Jordan, "The Death of Nancy Hanks Lincoln," *Indiana Magazine of History*, 40 (June 1944), 103–110, provides a clinical diagnosis.

13. Biographical information about the president's parental loss in childhood was gleaned from *Burke's Presidential Families of the United States of America*, 1st ed. (London: Burke's Peerage Limited, 1975); and William A. Degregorio, *The Complete Book of U.S. Presidents*, 4th ed. (New York: Barricade Books, 1993). Among the 22 presidents elected between 1800 and 1900, 5 (22.7 percent) lost mothers, 9 (40.9 percent) lost fathers, and 3 (13.6 percent) lost both parents. Among all 41 presidents, 6 (14.6 percent) lost mothers, 12 (29.3 percent) lost fathers, and 4 (9.8 percent) lost both parents.

14. *Collected Works*, I, 267.

15. *Collected Works*, IV, 62; Kett, *Rites of Passage*, 14, 16. According to Howard P. Chudacoff, *How Old Are You? Age Consciousness in American Culture* (Princeton, NJ: Princeton University Press, 1989), 14, "a twelve-year-old girl whose mother had died might have had to assume parental functions for younger siblings and housewife functions for her widowed father." See Mary Beth Norton, *Liberty's Daughters: The Revolutionary Experience of American Women, 1750–1800* (Glenview, IL: Scott, Foresman, 1980), 12–13, for the traditional role of daughters within farm families.

16. Catherine Clinton, *The Plantation Mistress: Woman's World in the Old South* (New York: Pantheon, 1982), 76, 78. Nancy Hanks Lincoln was born in 1784, Sarah Bush Johnston Lincoln in 1788, and Thomas Lincoln in 1778.

17. Warren, *Lincoln's Youth*, 60–62.

18. Warren, *Lincoln's Youth*, 59, 61, 63–64.

19. Wilson and Davis, *Herndon's Informants*, 99, 106.

20. Wilson and Davis, *Herndon's Informants*, 106; Warren, *Lincoln's Youth*, 65–69, 75.

21. *Collected Works*, III, 511; Wilson and Davis, *Herndon's Informants*, 455; John Modell, Frank F. Furstenberg Jr., and Theodore Hershberg, "Social Change and Transitions to Adulthood in Historical Perspective," *Journal of Family History*, 1 (Autumn 1976), 7–32, esp. 29.

22. Wilson and Davis, *Herndon's Informants*, 103; Albert J. Beveridge, *Abraham Lincoln, 1809–1858* (Boston: Houghton Mifflin, 1928), I, 40; Warren, *Lincoln's Youth*, 53, 98–99, 150–52; Steinson, "Rural Life in Indiana," 208.

23. Warren, *Lincoln's Youth*, 159, 205; Steinson, "Rural Life in Indiana," 205.

24. Wilson and Davis, *Herndon's Informants*, 94, 101.

25. Wilson and Davis, *Herndon's Informants*, 118, 126; Warren, *Lincoln's Youth*, 137.

26. Wilson and Davis, *Herndon's Informants*, 100–101.

27. *Collected Works*, IV, 62; Richard C. Wade, *The Urban Frontier: The Rise of Western Cities, 1790–1830* (Cambridge, MA: Harvard University Press, 1959).

28. According to Francis B. Carpenter, *The Inner Life of Abraham Lincoln: Six Months at the White House* (Boston: Houghton, Osgood, 1878), 96–98, Lincoln related this story to Secretary of State William H. Seward. T. G. Onstot, *Pioneers of Menard and Mason Counties* (Peoria, IL: J. W. Franks and Sons, 1902), 52; Wilson and Davis, *Herndon's Informants*, 100–101.

29. *Collected Works*, IV, 63; *History of Macon County, Illinois* (Philadelphia: Brink, McDonough, 1880), 204; Warren, *Lincoln's Youth*, 204.

30. C. M. Thompson, *The Lincoln Way* (Springfield: Illinois State Journal Company, 1913), 18; Warren, *Lincoln's Youth*, 204–7; Charles H. Coleman, *Abraham Lincoln and Coles County, Illinois* (New Brunswick, NJ: Scarecrow Press, 1955), 1–7. Norton, *Liberty's Daughters*, 75–78, vividly recounts the physical and emotional toll pregnancy and childbirth traditionally exacted on women and their families.

31. *Collected Works*, III, 512, IV, 63; Warren, *Lincoln's Youth*, 208. Susan E. Gray, *The Yankee West: Community Life on the Michigan Frontier* (Chapel Hill: University of North Carolina Press, 1996), 111, discusses homeleaving in the antebellum Midwest.

CHAPTER 3

1. D. W. Meinig, *The Shaping of America: A Geographical Perspective on 500 Years of History*, Vol. 2, *Continental America, 1800–1867* (New Haven, CT: Yale University Press, 1986), 223, 228. Malcolm J. Rohrbaugh, *The Trans-Appalachian Frontier: People, Societies, and Institutions, 1775–1850* (New York: Oxford University Press, 1978), 157–217; Francis Paul Prucha, *The Great Father: The United States Government and the American Indians* (Lincoln: University of Nebraska Press, 1984), I, 243–69; Ronald E. Nelson, ed., *Illinois: Land and Life in the Prairie State* (Dubuque: Kendall-Hunt, 1978), 6–7; Douglas R. McManis, *Initial Evaluation and Utilization of the Illinois Prairies, 1815–1840* (Chicago: University of Chicago Press, 1964), 17; William V. Pooley, *The Settlement of Illinois from 1830 to 1850*, Bulletin of the University of Wisconsin, History Series, Vol. 1, pp. 287–595, (Madison: University of Wisconsin, 1908), 315, 317; Ralph H. Brown, *Historical Geography of the United States* (New York: Harcourt, Brace, 1948), 208.

2. Rohrbaugh, *Trans-Appalachian Frontier*, 121–22; Douglas K. Meyer, "Illinois Culture Regions at Mid-Nineteenth Century," *Bulletin of the Illinois Geographical Society*, 18 (December 1976), 3–13; McManis, *Illinois Prairies*, 18; Nelson *Land and Life*, 7, 13.

3. McManis, *Illinois Prairies*, 17, 18, 89; Nelson, *Land and Life*, 8; Pooley, *Settlement of Illinois*, 322, 358; John C. Hudson, "Cultural Geography of the Upper Great Lakes Region," *Journal of Cultural Geography*, 5 (Fall/Winter 1984), 19–32, esp. 25; Robert P. Swierenga, "The Settlement of the Old Northwest: Ethnic Pluralism in a Featureless Plain," *Journal of the Early Republic*, 9 (Spring 1989), 73–105, esp. 77. Champions of westward movement within latitudinal zones emphasize geographical rather than cultural influences on settlement and include Pooley, *Settlement of Illinois*, 352; and Richard H. Steckel, "The Economic Foundations of East-West Migration during the 19th Century," *Explorations in Economic History*, 20 (January 1983), 14–36. Robert D. Mitchell, "The Formation of Early American Cultural Regions: An Interpretation," in James R. Gibson, ed., *European Settlement and Development in North America: Essays in Honour and Memory of Andrew Hill Clark* (Toronto: University of Toronto Press, 1978), 66–90, originated the concept of culture hearths. See John S. Macdonald and Leatrice D. Macdonald, "Chain Migration, Ethnic Neighborhood Formation, and Social Networks," *Milbank Memorial Fund Quarterly*, 42 (January 1964), 82–97; and

Robert E. Bieder, "Kinship as a Factor in Migration," *Journal of Marriage and the Family*, 35 (August 1973), 429–39, for the concept of "chain migration." John Fraser Hart, "Facets of the Geography of Population in the Midwest," *Journal of Geography*, 85 (September/October 1986), 201–211, esp. 207; and Meinig, *Continental America*, 264–96, discuss the arrival of immigrants by railroads. Darroch, "Fugitives or Families," 257–77, esp. 257, 259, 266–67, discusses "chain" migration and "family sponsorship."

4. According to Meinig, *Continental America*, 229, Upland Southerners "hung along the margins where there was wood for building, fuel, and fencing." Applications of the concept of cultural regions to Illinois history include John C. Hudson, "North American Origins of Middlewestern Frontier Populations," *Annals of the American Association of Geographers*, 78 (September 1988), 395–413; Meyer, "Illinois Culture Regions"; Douglas K. Meyer, "Southern Illinois Migration Fields: The Shawnee Hills in 1850," *The Professional Geographer*, 28 (May 1976), 151–60; Douglas K. Meyer, "Native-Born Immigrant Clusters on the Illinois Frontier," *Proceedings of the Association of American Geographers*, 8 (1976), 41–44; and Swierenga, "Settlement of the Old Northwest," 77, 79.

5. Hudson, "North American Origins," especially the map on 411; Wilbur Zelinsky, *The Cultural Geography of the United States*, rev. ed. (Englewood Cliffs, NJ: Prentice Hall, 1992); Meyer, "Illinois Culture Regions."

6. The Manuscript U.S. Census, Springfield, Illinois, 1850, lists 647 white adult native males; 36.6 percent were born in the Midlands, 32.4 percent in the Upper South, 25.0 percent in New England, and 5.9 percent in the Lower South.

7. *Collected Works*, IV, 63; John W. Smith, *History of Macon County, Illinois, from Its Organization to 1876* (Springfield: Rokker's Printing House, 1876), 26; *History of Macon County, Illinois* (Philadelphia: Brink, McDonough, 1880), 31; Edwin D. Davis, "Lincoln and Macon County, Illinois, 1830–1831," *Journal of the Illinois State Historical Society*, 25 (April/July 1932), 63–107, esp. 73.

8. *History of Macon County*, 31, 36, 204; Otto R. Dyle, *Abraham Lincoln in Decatur* (Washington: Vantage Press, 1957), 14, 20, 27, 28, 81; Henry C. Whitney, *Life of Lincoln* (New York: Baker and Taylor, 1908), I, 62, 64; Smith, *History of Macon County*, 33–34; Rexford Newcomb, *In the Lincoln Country: Journeys to the Lincoln Shrines of Kentucky, Indiana, Illinois and Other States* (Philadelphia: J. B. Lippincott, 1928), 81.

9. *Collected Works*, IV, 63; Douglas L. Wilson and Rodney O. Davis, eds., *Herndon's Informants: Letters, Interviews, and Statements about Abraham Lincoln* (Urbana: University of Illinois Press, 1998), 100, 456; Whitney, *Life of Lincoln*, I, 64; *History of Macon County*, 34, 36, 204; Smith, *History of Macon County*, 21; Dyle, *Abraham Lincoln in Decatur*, 23. McManis, *Illinois Prairies*, 90–91, observes that prairie land was initially taken up as an adjunct to timberland, and so the earliest settlers ringed the prairie openings with their farms. Meinig, *Continental America*, 229, notes that later settlers from the Upper South chose land at the prairie margins that was "well-proportioned with prairie and timber." The Lincolns were entirely typical in this respect. John Mack Faragher, *Sugar Creek: Life on the Illinois Prairie* (New Haven, CT: Yale University Press, 1986), 61–73, describes the impact of these preferences on patterns of settlement.

10. Dyle, *Abraham Lincoln in Decatur*, 21, 32; *History of Macon County*, 34; Whitney, *Life of Lincoln*, I, 65.

11. Jane Martin Johns, *Personal Recollections of Early Decatur, Abraham Lincoln, Richard J. Oglesby, and the Civil War* (Decatur: Decatur Chapter Daughters of the American Revolution, 1912), 259–60; Smith, *History of Macon County*, 144.

12. Power, *Early Settlers*, 62–65, 430; T. G. Onstot, *Pioneers of Menard and Mason Counties* (Peoria, IL: J. W. Franks and Sons, 1902), 135.

13. Power, *Early Settlers*, 62–63; Smith, *History of Macon County*, 144.

14. *Collected Works*, I, 320, IV, 63; Wilson and Davis, *Herndon's Informants*, 13, 44–45, 456; *History of Macon County*, 204; Benjamin P. Thomas, *Lincoln's New Salem* (New York: Knopf, 1954), 10; Springfield *Sangamon Journal*, February 2, 1831.

15. *Collected Works*, I, 320, IV, 63. The Springfield *Sangamo Journal*, February 9, 1832, recommended traveling to Springfield by water in the spring and by land in the fall.

CHAPTER 4

1. John Carroll Power, *History of the Early Settlers of Sangamon County, Illinois* (Springfield, IL: Edwin A. Wilson, 1876), 32–33, 424; Richard E. Hart, "Springfield's African Americans as a Part of the Lincoln Community," *Journal of the Abraham Lincoln Association*, 20 (Winter 1999), 35–54, esp. 39.

2. Power, *Early Settlers*, 30, 31, 32, 440; Elijah Iles, *Sketches of Early Life and Times in Kentucky, Missouri and Illinois* (Springfield, IL: Springfield Printing, 1883), 27, 28; Harvey Lee Ross, *The Early Pioneers and Pioneer Events of the State of Illinois* (Chicago: Eastman Brothers, 1899), 5. Sangamon County was part of Madison County until 1821.

3. Power, *Early Settlers*, 32; Sangamon County Commissioners Record, Illinois State Archives, Springfield, Illinois, April 3, 1821; Iles, *Sketches of Early Life*, 26, 31; *Illinois Laws*, (1821), sec. 2, January 30, 1821. The spot is now at the northwest corner of Second and Jefferson streets. Power, *Early Settlers*, 32, notes that "There is no explanation of letters used in marking the stake, but it is probable that the only two commissioners present agreed to use one initial from each of their names."

4. Elijah Iles, *Sketches of Early Life*, 5, 6, 7, 8, 9, 11, 12; Power, *Early Settlers*, 397–400.

5. Iles, *Sketches of Early Life*, 17, 23, 24; Power, *Early Settlers*, 397–400.

6. Iles, *Sketches of Early Life*, 28; Power, *Early Settlers*, 397–400.

7. Iles, *Sketches of Early Life* 26, 30, 31; Power, *Early Settlers*, 398.

8. Iles, *Sketches of Early Life*, 32, 35, 36.

9. Power, *Early Settlers*, 35–36, 284, 288–89, 398; Joseph Wallace, *Past and Present of the City of Springfield and Sangamon County, Illinois* (Chicago: S. J. Clarke, 1904), 7, 1003; James Latham to Ninian Edwards, November 12, 1823, in E. B. Washburne, ed., *The Edwards Papers; Being a Portion of the Collection of the Letters, Papers, and Manuscripts of Ninian Edwards*, Chicago Historical Society's Collection (Chicago: Fergus Printing, 1884), 211. Edward T. Price, "The Central Courthouse Square in the American County Seat," *Geographical Review*, 58 (January 1968), 29–60, esp. 37, notes that "Land for the public square, or even for the whole town, was often donated by a single landowner (sometimes a member of the site commission), who thus improved the location of his remaining property." Lewis E. Atherton, *The Frontier Merchant in Mid-America* (Columbia: University of Missouri Press, 1971), 50, notes that country stores attracted thieves.

10. Power, *Early Settlers*, 33, 35–36; Sangamon County Commissioners Record, June 4, September 4, 1821, June 6, 1825; Iles, *Sketches of Early Life*, 33. According to Power, *Early Settlers*, 34, the county commissioners substituted "Sangamon" for "Sangamo" "without any apparent reason." William D. Walters Jr., "Time and Town Squares," *Bulletin of the Illinois Geographical Society*, 22 (1980), 18–24, esp. 22, notes that "Most towns laid out in the 1830s had some type of town square."

11. Springfield *Illinois Journal*, December 5, 1852; Power, *Early Settlers*, 379, 398; Iles, *Sketches of Early Life*, 60; Springfield *Sangamo Journal*, February 16, 1832.

12. Power, *Early Settlers*, 262, 671; Iles, *Sketches of Early Life*, 60, 61; Douglas L. Wilson and Rodney O. Davis, eds., *Herndon's Informants: Letters, Interviews, and Statements About Abraham Lincoln* (Urbana: University of Illinois Press, 1998), 415; Sangamon County Commissioners Record, 1821–1826, passim. The first bridges in the county appeared in 1833. Merle Curti, *The Making of an American Community: A Case Study of Democracy in a Frontier County* (Stanford, CA: Stanford University Press, 1959), 35–54; and Paul Bourke and Donald DeBats, *Washington County: Politics and Community in Antebellum America* (Baltimore: Johns Hopkins University Press, 1995), 95–115, describe the role of government in creating an infrastructure in typical frontier counties.

13. Power, *Early Settlers*, 36–37, 44, 671; Iles, *Sketches of Early Life*, 32; Sangamon County Commissioners Record, March 18, 1825, 1831 passim.

14. Wallace, *Past and Present*, 445, 807–8; Power, *Early Settlers*, 797.

15. Louis A. Warren, *Lincoln's Youth: Indiana Years, Seven to Twenty-one, 1816–1830* (Indianapolis: Indiana Historical Society, 1959), 209; Power, *Early Settlers*, 144–45, 216, 364–65; 405–406. Ralph H. Brown, *Historical Geography of the United States* (New York: Harcourt, Brace, 1948), 184–86, surveys Trans-Appalachian migration routes.

16. Power, *Early Settlers*, 679; Wallace, *Past and Present*, 153–54.

17. Power, *Early Settlers*, 144–45. Susan E. Gray, *The Yankee West: Community Life on the Michigan Frontier* (Chapel Hill: University of North Carolina Press, 1996), 11, contrasts the speed of the water route with the more imposing southern route overland.

18. *Compendium of the Enumeration of the Inhabitants and Statistics of the United States . . . from the Returns of the Sixth Census* [U.S. Census of 1840] (Washington, DC: Thomas Allen, 1841), 87, 299, 301; Elizabeth McDowell Hill, "Illinois Women: Stories of the Pioneer Mothers of Illinois," Women's Exposition Board, 1893, Illinois State Historical Library, Springfield, Illinois, 4–5; Wilson and Davis, *Herndon's Informants*, 415; R. D. Miller, *Past and Present of Menard County, Illinois* (Chicago: S. J. Clarke, 1905), 16; John Tipton Barnett, "Biography of the Barnett Family Written by John Tipton Barnett," Illinois State Historical Library, Springfield, Illinois, 2; Douglas R. McManis, *Initial Evaluation and Utilization of the Illinois Prairies, 1815–1840* (Chicago: University of Chicago

Press, 1964), 65; Joshua F. Speed, *Reminiscences of Abraham Lincoln and Notes of a Visit to California* (Louisville: John P. Morton, 1884), 15; Springfield *Sangamo Journal*, January 12, 1830; Ralph H. Brown, *Historical Geography of the United States* (New York: Harcourt, Brace, 1948), 208.

19. Power, *Early Settlers*, 263; Mason Brayman to Father and Mother, Springfield, Illinois, December 25, 1843, Bailhache-Brayman Family Papers, Illinois State Historical Library, Springfield, Illinois; Wilson and Davis, *Herndon's Informants*, 201; T. G. Onstot, *Pioneers of Menard and Mason Counties* (Peoria, IL: J. W. Franks and Sons, 1902), 162; McManis, *Illinois Prairies*, 65; Brown, *Historical Geography of the United States*, 208–9. Power, *Early Settlers*, is replete with references to early settlers' anxiety about claiming enough timber, which was known as the "timber question"; see esp. 571.

20. Allan G. Bogue, *From Prairie to Corn Belt: Farming on the Illinois and Iowa Prairies in the Nineteenth Century* (Chicago: University of Chicago Press, 1963), 103–113, carefully dissects the relationship between corn and hogs on the Illinois priaries. The *U.S. Census of 1840*, 87, 299, 301, revealed the following occupational structure within Sangamon County: agriculture, 79.8 percent; manufactures and trades, 15.7 percent; commerce, 2.5 percent; learned professions and engineers, 1.9 percent; mining, 0.1 percent.

21. This population profile for Springfield is based on Zimri A. Enos, "Springfield Residents before the Deep Snow," Illinois State Historical Library, Springfield, Illinois. Enos compiled his list during organization of the Sangamon County Historical Society in 1859. It is superior to the U.S. Census of 1830 in several respects. The census did not contain a separate entry for Springfield, which was not yet an incorporated town, listed only the names of household heads and not their families, and did not record occupations. Enos listed 290 adult men, 134 adult women (132 of whom were married), and 241 children or dependent relatives.

22. Enos, "Springfield Residents before the Deep Snow."

23. Enos, "Springfield Residents before the Deep Snow," linked with Manuscript U.S. Census, Springfield, Illinois, 1840. The 1840 census only listed the names of household heads, and an unknown number of adult men may have remained as dependent members of another household. Twenty-eight percent of married men persisted to 1840, while 14.6 percent of single men remained in Springfield. Compare Gray, *Yankee West*, 13.

24. Roy P. Basler, ed., *The Collected Works of Abraham Lincoln* (New Brunswick, NJ: Rutgers University Press, 1953), III, 511; Springfield *Sangamo Journal*, December 15, 1838.

25. Enos, "Springfield Residents before the Deep Snow." Of 119 gainfully employed men, 62 or 52.1 percent practiced nonmanual occupations.

26. In 1860, Lincoln wrote that "he now thinks that the agregate of all his schooling did not amount to one year"; *Collected Works*, IV, 62. According to Paul Theobald, *Call School*, 45, Lincoln's education was "typical." Warren, *Lincoln's Youth*, 187, writes, without evidence, that Lincoln "may have" clerked briefly in George Gentry's store.

27. Power, *Early Settlers*, 144–45, 215, 348; Iles, *Sketches of Early Life*, 33, 39. According to Enos, "Springfield Residents before the Deep Snow," twenty men practiced multiple occupations.

28. *Collected Works*, I, 320, IV, 63–64; Benjamin P. Thomas, *Lincoln's New Salem* (New York: Knopf, 1954), 59.

CHAPTER 5

1. Roy P. Basler, ed., *The Collected Works of Abraham Lincoln* (New Brunswick, NJ: Rutgers University Press, 1953), I, 320, IV, 63–64; Benjamin Thomas, *Lincoln's New Salem* (Carbondale, IL: Southern Illinois University Press, 1954), 59; Thomas P. Reep, *Lincoln at New Salem* (Petersburg, IL: Old Salem Lincoln League, 1927), 7, 9, 26. Both Rutledge and Cameron were born in the Lower South, in Georgia and South Carolina, respectively.

2. Douglas L. Wilson and Rodney O. Davis, eds., *Herndon's Informants: Letters, Interviews, and Statements About Abraham Lincoln* (Urbana: University of Illinois Press, 1998), 429, 457.

3. *Collected Works*, IV, 64; John W. Smith, *History of Macon County, Illinois, from Its Organization to 1876* (Springfield: Rokker's Printing House, 1876), 33; Edwin D. Davis, "Lincoln and Macon County, Illinois, 1830–1831," *Journal of the Illinois State Historical Society*, 25 (April/July 1932), 63–107, esp. 101; "Stephen T. Logan Talks About Lincoln," *Bulletin of the Lincoln Centennial Association*, 12 (September 1, 1928), 1–5, esp. 1; Michael Burlingame, ed., *An Oral History of Abraham Lincoln: John G. Nicolay's Interviews and Essays* (Carbondale: Southern Illinois University Press, 1996), 18; Mason Brayman to Parents, March 16, 1851, Bailhache-Brayman Family Papers, Illinois State Historical Library, Springfield, Illinois; Charles H. Coleman, *Abraham Lincoln*

and Coles County, Illinois (New Brunswick, NJ: Scarecrow Press, 1955), x–xii, 19.

4. Eleanor Gridley, *The Story of Abraham Lincoln or the Journey from the Log Cabin to the White House* (Chicago: M. A. Donohue, 1900), 84. John Y. Simon, *House Divided: Lincoln and His Father* (Fort Wayne, IN.: Louis A. Warren Lincoln Library and Museum, 1987), 10–17, discusses the relationship among the Hankses, Johnstons, and Lincolns in Coles County.

5. *Collected Works*, I, 320. Enos, "Springfield Residents before the Deep Snow," linked with Manuscript U.S. Census, Springfield, Illinois, 1840.

6. *Compendium of the Enumeration of the Inhabitants and Statistics of the United States . . . from the Returns of the Sixth Census* [U.S. Census of 1840] (Washington, DC: Thomas Allen, 1841), 86, 87. The U.S. Census of 1840 listed four "principal towns" in Illinois—Alton, Chicago, Springfield, and Quincy. Of these four "towns," only Chicago and Springfield contained more than 2,500 people and therefore met the census definition of a city. Lincoln is an exemplar of the rising "entrepreneurial aspirations" depicted in Kathleen Neils Conzen, "A Saga of Families," in Clyde A. Milner II, Carol A. O'Connor, and Martha A. Sandweiss, eds. *The Oxford History of the American West* (New York: Oxford University Press, 1994), 315–57, esp. 337.

7. *Collected Works*, IV, 64; Charles Maltby, *The Life and Public Services of Abraham Lincoln* (Stockton, CA: Daily Independent Steam Power Plant, 1884), 26; Thomas, *Lincoln's New Salem*, 10, 11–12, 24, 61; Benjamin P. Thomas, "Old New Salem," *Bulletin of the Abraham Lincoln Association*, 29 (December 1932), 3–9. In one of his autobiographies, Lincoln highlighted his graduation from farmwork as a turning point in his life; *Collected Works*, III, 511–12. According to Howard P. Chudacoff and Tamara K. Hareven, "From the Empty Nest to Family Dissolution: Life Course Transitions into Old Age," *Journal of Family History*, 4 (Spring 1979), 69–83, esp. 81, "most female and male children left their families of orientation by about age 22 or 23."

8. Thomas, *Lincoln's New Salem*, 6, 9, 63, 101, 121; Wilson and Davis, *Herndon's Informants*, 382; Springfield *Sangamo Journal*, September 18, 1845; T. G. Onstot, *Pioneers of Menard and Mason Counties* (Peoria, IL: J. W. Franks and Sons, 1902), 217; "The Offutt Store," undated typescript, Sangamon Valley Collection, Lincoln Library, Springfield, Illinois, ii; "The Second Berry-Lincoln Store," undated typescript, Sangamon Valley Collection, Lincoln Library, Springfield, Illinois, 1.

9. Springfield *Sangamo Journal*, March 29, 1832; Springfield *Western Farmer* , March 1, 1840. The Springfield *Sangamo Journal*, April 16, 1846, complained that the Sangamon River did not become navigable for trade until June.

10. Springfield *Sangamo Journal*, March 29, 1832, October 9, 1845, May 13, July 1, August 3, 1847; Springfield *Illinois Journal*, August 15, October 24, 1849; Springfield *Register*, July 9, December 24, 1847; Springfield *Western Farmer* , October 8, 1840; Wilson and Davis, *Herndon's Informants*, 9; Power, *Early Settlers*, 145; Onstot, *Pioneers of Menard and Mason Counties*, 39–40.

11. Springfield *Western Farmer* , March 1, 1840; Springfield *Register*, August 7; U.S. *Census of 1840*, 301; Miller, *Past and Present of Menard County*, 26.

12. Springfield *Western Farmer*, July 15, 1840; Springfield *Sangamon Journal*, December 15, 1831; Springfield *Illinois Journal*, August 15, 1849; Power, *Early Settlers*, 187, 488; Elizabeth McDowell Hill, "Illinois Women: Stories of the Pioneer Mothers of Illinois," Women's Exposition Board, 1893, Illinois State Historical Library, Springfield, Illinois, 13; Mrs. Andrew McCormick, "Illinois Women," 2.

13. Miller, *Past and Present of Menard County*, 22. Excellent introductions to the household economy include Christopher Clark, *The Roots of Rural Capitalism: Western Massachusetts, 1780–1860* (Ithaca, NY: Cornell University Press, 1990); Christopher Clark, "Household Economy, Market Exchange and the Rise of Capitalism in the Connecticut Valley, 1800–1860," *Journal of Social History*, 13 (Winter 1979), 169–89; Bruce Laurie, *Artisans into Workers: Labor in Nineteenth-Century America* (New York: Noonday Press, 1989), 15–46; Mary Beth Norton, *Liberty's Daughters: The Revolutionary Experience of American Women, 1750–1800* (Glenview, IL: Scott, Foresman, 1980), 3–39; Jeanne Boydston, *Home and Work: Housework, Wages, and the Ideology of Labor in the Early Republic* (New York: Oxford University Press, 1990); Glenna Matthews, *"Just a Housewife": The Rise and Fall of Domesticity in America* (New York: Oxford University Press, 1987), 3–35; John Mack Faragher, *Women and Men on the Overland Trail* (New Haven, CT.: Yale University Press, 1979), 40–65; and John Mack Faragher, *Sugar Creek: Life on the Illinois Prairie* (New Haven, CT: Yale University Press, 1986), 96–105.

14. Springfield *Illinois Journal*, June 1, 1848; Power, *Early Settlers*, 571. Clark, *Roots of Rural Capitalism*; Norton, *Liberty's Daughters*, 3–39; Faragher, *Women and Men*, 50–65; and Faragher, *Sugar Creek*, 96–109, provide apt depictions of the gendered division of labor.

15. Power, *Early Settlers*, 73, 187, 213–14; Mrs. E. W. Logan, "Illinois Women," 23.

16. Power, *Early Settlers*, 213-14; Mary Elizabeth Quillan, "Illinois Women," 19-20; Hill, "Illinois Women," 9, 10, 20; Mary Jane Hazlett, "Illinois Women," 3; Wilson and Davis, *Herndon's Informants*, 37; Onstot, *Pioneers of Menard and Mason Counties*, 221; Miller, *Past and Present of Menard County*, 32; John W. Wayland, *The Lincolns in Virginia* (Staunton, VA: McClure Printing, 1946), 38.

17. McCormick, "Illinois Women," 2, 7; Quillan, "Illinois Women,"15; Hill, "Illinois Women," 11; Henrietta C. Jones, "Illinois Women," 4–5; Power, *Early Settlers*, 73; Wilson and Davis, *Herndon's Informants*, 415.

18. Springfield *Sangamo Journal*, March 28, May 2, 1844; Hill, "Illinois Women,"10.

19. Springfield *Sangamon Journal*, January 19, 1831; Springfield *Illinois Journal*, November 22, 1848, November 18, 1849; McCormick, "Illinois Women," 36; Jones, "Illinois Women," 5; Quillan, "Illinois Women," 17, 17–18, 18, 24; Wilson and Davis, *Herndon's Informants*, 415–17; Power, *Early Settlers*, 150; Faragher, *Sugar Creek*, 133–36. Robert E. Mutch, "Yeoman and Merchant in Pre-Industrial America: Eighteenth-Century Massachusetts as a Case Study," *Societas: A Review of Social History*, 7 (Autumn 1977), 279–302, esp. 283, puts such "cooperative work" in a broader context.

20. Wilson and Davis, *Herndon's Informants*, 417; Jane Martin Johns, *Personal Recollections of Early Decatur, Abraham Lincoln, Richard J. Oglesby, and the Civil War* (Decatur: Decatur Chapter Daughters of the American Revolution, 1912), 28–29; William Riley McLaren, "Reminiscences of Pioneer Life in Illinois, ca. 1830–1860," Illinois State Historical Library, Springfield, Illinois, 63.

21. Power, *Early Settlers*, 105, 173.

22. Springfield *Sangamo Journal*, September 1, 8, 1832, July 6, 1833, July 24, 1845; Power, *Early Settlers*, 70–71, 172, 187.

23. Springfield *Sangamo Journal*, June 11, 1836; Springfield *Illinois Journal*, November 11, 1847, June 6, August 22, September 15, 1849; Hill, "Illinois Women,"11; Wilson and Davis, *Herndon's Informants*, 453. Richard L. Bushman, "Family Security in the Transition from Farm to City, 1750–1850," *Journal of Family History*, 6 (Fall 1981), 238–56, esp. 247, puts such urban agriculture in a broader context.

24. John Tipton Barnett, "Biography of the Barnett Family Written by John Tipton Barnett," Illinois State Historical Library, Springfield, Illinois, 2; Mason Brayman to Father and Mother, Springfield, Illinois, November 30, 1847, Bailhache-Brayman Family Papers, Illinois State Historical Library, Springfield, Illinois; Springfield *Sangamo Journal*, April 8, 1842; Springfield *Illinois Journal*, April 30, 1849; Maltby, *Life and Public Services of Abraham Lincoln*, 26–27; "The Second Berry-Lincoln Store," undated typescript, Sangamon Valley Collection, Lincoln Library, Springfield, Illinois, 22.

25. Vandalia *Illinois State Register and People's Advocate*, January 19, 1838.

26. Springfield *Sangamo Journal*, November 17, 1831; Springfield *Sangamo Journal*, September 22, 1832, November 9, 1833; Springfield *Illinois Republican*, July 20, 1836; Jones, "Illinois Women," 5; Rebecca Burlend and Edward Burlend, *A True Picture of Emigration*, ed. Milo Milton Quaife (New York: Citadel Press, 1968), 108; Elizabeth A. Perkins, "The Consumer Frontier: Household Consumption in Early Kentucky," *Journal of American History*, 78 (September 1991), 486–510, esp. 506.

27. Springfield *Sangamo Journal*, July 29, August 26, 1842.

28. Joshua F. Speed, *Reminiscences of Abraham Lincoln and Notes of a Visit to California* (Louisville: John P. Morton, 1884), 21; James E. Vance Jr., *The Merchant's World: The Geography of Wholesaling* (Englewood Cliffs, NJ: Prentice-Hall, 1970), 83, 85–86; Gerald Carson, *The Old Country Store* (New York: Oxford University Press, 1954), 21, 37, 93–94; James M. Mayo, *The American Grocery Store: The Evolution of an Architectural Space* (Westport, CT: Greenwood Press, 1993), 44; Lewis E. Atherton, *The Frontier Merchant in Mid-America* (Columbia: University of Missouri Press, 1971), 142–43. By comparison, the average store in America in 1840 served 300 customers; Clarence H. Danhof, *Change in Agriculture: The Northern United States, 1820–1870* (Cambridge, MA: Harvard University Press, 1969), 29; James E. Davis, *Frontier Illinois* (Bloomington: Indiana University Press, 1998), 230.

29. Roy P. Basler, ed., *The Collected Works of Abraham Lincoln* (New Brunswick, NJ: Rutgers University Press, 1953), III, 512; Wilson and Davis, *Herndon's Informants*, 14; Onstot, *Pioneers of Menard and Mason Counties*, 72, 152; Carson, *Old Country Store*, 17, 66; Mayo, *American Grocery Store*, 52, 54; Atherton, *Frontier Merchant*, 51; Thomas J. Schlereth, *Victorian America: Transformations in Everyday Life* (New York: Harper, 1991), 143; "Offutt Store," 6-7; Mutch, "Yeoman and Merchant."

30. Elijah Iles, *Sketches of Early Life and Times in Kentucky, Missouri and Illinois* (Springfield, IL: Springfield Printing, 1883), 22; Burlend and Burlend, *True Picture of Emigration*, 67.

31. Reep, *Lincoln at New Salem*, 22–24; Atherton, *Frontier Merchant*, 18–19, 54, 142–43; Carson, *Old Country Store*, 25, 93–94; Schlereth, *Victorian America*, 143. Such "book credit" did not carry an interest charge, so merchants simply charged a higher price for credit purchases.

32. Springfield *Sangamo Journal*, July 26, 1832; Onstot, *Pioneers of Menard and Mason Counties*, 58; Atherton, *Frontier Merchant*, 18, 145; Carson, *Old Country Store*, 16, 98.

33. Springfield *Western Prairie Farmer, Journal of Agriculture and Rural Economy*, July 29, 1840; Harvey Lee Ross, *The Early Pioneers and Pioneer Events of the State of Illinois* (Chicago: Eastman Brothers, 1899), 116–17.

34. Springfield *Sangamo Journal*, April 12, 1839; Wilson and Davis, *Herndon's Informants*, 259; Burlend and Burlend, *True Picture of Emigration*, 67; Onstot, *Pioneers of Menard and Mason Counties*, 175.

35. Carson, *Old Country Store*, 20, 67; Vance, *Merchant's World*, 74, 75; Atherton, *Frontier Merchant*, 18–19; Mutch, "Yeoman and Merchant," 291; Mayo, *American Grocery Store*, 51; Perkins, "Consumer Frontier," 506.

36. *Collected Works*, III, 512, IV, 64; Wilson and Davis, *Herndon's Informants*, 18, 73; Reep, *Lincoln at New Salem*, 11–12, 14; "Second Berry-Lincoln Store," 1. New Salem fits Vance's definition of a "fundamental trading center"—"small and simple, possessing one or two commodity-combining general stores"; Vance, *Merchant's World*, 83.

CHAPTER 6

1. Roy P. Basler, ed., *The Collected Works of Abraham Lincoln* (New Brunswick, NJ: Rutgers University Press, 1953), IV, 64; Douglas L. Wilson and Rodney O. Davis, eds., *Herndon's Informants: Letters, Interviews, and Statements About Abraham Lincoln* (Urbana: University of Illinois Press, 1998), 91.

2. Ida M. Tarbell, *The Life of Abraham Lincoln* (New York: Macmillan, 1917), I, 106–107.

3. The Manuscript U.S. Census, Springfield, Illinois, 1830, included 12,960 residents, only two of whom lived alone. More recently, 29.4 percent of households in Sangamon County are single-member households; U.S. Bureau of the Census, *County and City Data Book: 1994*, 12th ed. (Washington, DC: U.S. Government Printing Office, 1994), 146. Nationally, the proportion of single-member households fell from 3.7 to 3.6 percent from 1790 to 1890; *Historical Statistics of the United States: Colonial Times to 1970*, Part I (Washington, DC: U.S. Government Printing Office, 1975), 42. Frances E. Kobrin, "The Fall in Household Size and the Rise of the Primary Individual in the United States," *Demography*, 13 (February 1976), 127–38, esp. 129; John Modell and Tamara K. Hareven, "Urbanization and the Malleable Household: An Examination of Boarding and Lodging in American Families," *Journal of Marriage and the Family*, 35 (August 1973), 467–79, esp. 467; Howard P. Chudacoff, *How Old Are You? Age Consciousness in American Culture* (Princeton, NJ: Princeton University Press, 1989), 14; Mark Peel, "On the Margins: Lodgers and Boarders in Boston, 1860–1900," *Journal of American History*, 72 (March 1986), 813–34; John Mack Faragher, *Sugar Creek: Life on the Illinois Prairie* (New Haven, CT.: Yale University Press, 1986), 86.

4. Chudacoff and Hareven, "Empty Nest," 468; Modell and Hareven, "Urbanization and the Malleable Household," 471, 472; Barbara Laslett, "The Family as a Public and Private Institution: An Historical Perspective," *Journal of Marriage and the Family*, 35 (August 1973), 480–92, esp. 485. Chudacoff and Hareven, "Empty Nest," 77, concludes that "Most people resided either in family or surrogate family settings."

5. Richard L. Bushman, "Family Security in the Transition from Farm to City, 1750–1850," *Journal of Family History*, 6 (Fall 1981), 238–56, esp. 240, 249–50; Paul E. Johnson, *A Shopkeeper's Millenium: Society and Revivals in Rochester, New York, 1815–1837* (New York: Hill and Wang, 1978).

6. Wilson and Davis, *Herndon's Informants*, 17–18, 73–74, 236–37; Charles Maltby, *The Life and Public Services of Abraham Lincoln* (Stockton, CA: Daily Independent Steam Power Plant, 1884), 27; Henry C. Whitney, *Life of Lincoln* (New York: Baker and Taylor, 1908), I, 85; Thomas P. Reep, *Lincoln at New Salem* (Petersburg, IL: Old Salem Lincoln League, 1927), 20, 23, 119. An acquaintance reminisced fifty years later that Lincoln earned $25 a month; Maltby, *Life and Public Services of Abraham Lincoln*, 26. "The Offutt Store," undated typescript, Sangamon Valley Collection, Lincoln Library, Springfield, Illinois, 5, a more reliable source, reports the figure as $15, which amounts to 50 cents per day.

7. Wilson and Davis, *Herndon's Informants*, 73–74, 382, 526; Michael Burlingame, ed., *An Oral History of Abraham Lincoln: John G. Nicolay's Interviews and Essays* (Carbondale: Southern Illinois University Press, 1996), 19.

8. Wilson and Davis, *Herndon's Informants*, 91, 92, 108, 498, 525.

9. Wilson and Davis, *Herndon's Informants*, 72, 92, 108, 387, 525. A "roundabout" was a short, close-fitting jacket worn by boys and men. "Stoga," also called stogie or stogey, was short for Conestoga, a heavy, roughly made shoe or boot. "Casinette" was a cloth combining cotton and fine wool. Foxed pants were lined with leather.

10. Reep, *Lincoln at New Salem*, 119, 124; Benjamin Thomas, *Lincoln's New Salem* (Carbondale: Southern Illinois University Press, 1954), 64–67; Reep, *Lincoln at New Salem*, 124; Tarbell, *Life of Abraham Lincoln*, I, 107; Modell and Hareven, "Urbanization and the Malleable Household," 471; Harvey Lee Ross, *The Early Pioneers and Pioneer Events of the State of Illinois* (Chicago: Eastman Brothers, 1899), 121–22. Julian Pitt-Rivers, "Pseudo-Kinship," *International Encyclopedia of the Social Sciences* (New York: Macmillan, 1968), VIII, 408–413, esp. 408, defined pseudo-kinship as "those relationships in which persons are described or addressed by kin terms (or terms derived from the idiom of kin) but do not stand in such a relationship by virtue of the principles, however they happen to be conceptualized, of descent or marriage." One example is the "avuncular role" performed by a fictive "aunt" or "uncle." For other historical manifestations of fictive kinship, see Herbert G. Gutman, *The Black Family in Slavery and Freedom, 1750–1925* (New York: Vintage, 1976), 219–24; and Jacqueline Jones, *Labor of Love, Labor of Sorrow: Black Women, Work and the Family, from Slavery to the Present* (New York: Vintage, 1985).

11. Joseph F. Kett, *Rites of Passage: Adolescence in America, 1790 to the Present* (New York: Basic Books, 1977), 29–31; Kobrin, "Fall in Household Size," 131. John Modell, Frank F. Furstenberg Jr., and Theodore Hershberg, "Social Change and Transitions to Adulthood in Historical Perspective," *Journal of Family History*, 1 (Autumn 1976), 7–32, defines this stage more broadly as a period of "youth." Michael Katz, *The People of Hamilton, Canada West: Family and Class in a Mid-Nineteenth-Century City* (Cambridge, MA: Harvard University Press, 1975), labels it a "semi-autonomous state."

12. Modell, Furstenberg, and Hershberg, "Social Change and Transitions to Adulthood," 17, 19; Kett, *Rites of Passage*, 31, 36, 45, 98; Ross W. Beales Jr., "In Search of the Historical Child: Miniature Adulthood and Youth in Colonial New England," *American Quarterly*, 27 (October 1975), 379–98. According to Chudacoff, *How Old Are You?*, 9, 12, the term youth "could apply to practically anyone between ages seven and thirty" and "by age seven children were considered capable of gradually assuming adult responsibilities."

13. For these major milestones in Lincoln's life, see *Collected Works*, IV, 62 (starting to work at home); Wilson and Davis, *Herndon's Informants*, 100; *Collected Works*, IV, 63 (leaving home); Thomas, *Lincoln's New Salem*, 133 (choosing an occupation); 21, 126 (initiating a courtship); Springfield *Sangamo Journal*, November 11, 1842 (marrying); *Collected Works*, I, 331 (acquiring a new home). Most controversial is the dating of Lincoln's first courtship. His fabled relationship with Ann Rutledge purportedly began when he was twenty-six, but his first documented romance—with Mary Owens—occurred at age twenty-seven. Taken together, Kett, *Rites of Passage*, 16; Chudacoff and Hareven, "Empty Nest," 81; and Modell, Furstenberg, and Hershberg, "Social Change and Transitions to Adulthood," esp. 18–19, profile a "typical" nineteenth-century life course.

14. *Collected Works*, IV, 64.

15. Jack E. Eblen, "An Analysis of Nineteenth-Century Frontier Populations," *Demography*, 2 (1965), 399–413, esp. 412; *Historical Statistics of the United States*, I, 19; James E. Davis, *Frontier America, 1800–1840: A Comparative Demographic Analysis of the Frontier Process* (Glendale, CA: Arthur H. Clark, 1977), 101–18; and Kett, *Rites of Passage*, 38.

16. Springfield *Sangamo Journal*, June 21, 1832.

17. Manuscript U.S. Census, Springfield, Illinois, 1850, linked with *Marriage Records, Sangamon County, Illinois, 1821–1840* (Springfield: Sangamon County Genealogical Society, 1987). Throughout this study, all inferences drawn from samples through record linkage are statistically significant at the 0.05 level.

18. Manuscript U.S. Census, Sangamon County, Illinois, 1850, linked with *Marriage Records, Sangamon County, Illinois, 1821–1840* (Springfield: Sangamon County Genealogical Society, 1987); *Marriage Records, Sangamon County, Illinois, 1841–1850* (Springfield: Sangamon County Genealogical Society, 1988); John Carroll Power, *History of the Early Settlers of Sangamon County, Illinois* (Springfield: Edwin A. Wilson, 1876), 9; Joseph Wallace, *Past and Present of the City of Springfield and Sangamon County, Illinois* (Chicago: S. J. Clarke, 1904); Newton Bateman and Paul

Selby, eds., *Historical Encyclopedia of Illinois . . . and History of Sangamon County* (Chicago: Munsell Publishing, 1912).

19. Springfield *Illinois State Register*, September 5, 1845; Wilson and Davis, *Herndon's Informants*, 91, 258.

20. Manuscript U.S. Census, Springfield, Illinois, 1830; Wilson and Davis, *Herndon's Informants*, 91; E. Anthony Rotundo, *American Manhood: Transformations in Masculinity from the Revolution to the Modern Era* (New York: Basic Books, 1993), 62; Timothy R. Mahoney, *Provincial Lives: Middle-Class Experience in the Antebellum Middle West* (New York: Cambridge University Press, 1999), 62–112; Glenn Wallach, *Obedient Sons: The Discourse of Youth and Generations in American Culture, 1630–1860* (Amherst: University of Massachusetts Press, 1997), 57–65.

21. Wilson and Davis, *Herndon's Informants*, 498; Ross, *Early Pioneers*, 121; T. G. Onstot, *Pioneers of Menard and Mason Counties* (Peoria, IL: J. W. Franks and Sons, 1902), 52; Benjamin G. Rader, *American Sports: From the Age of Folk Games to the Age of Televised Sports*, 2nd ed. (Englewood Cliffs, NJ: Prentice Hall, 1990), 25, 28.

22. Wilson and Davis, *Herndon's Informants*, 13, 17, 73, 387; *History of Macon County, Illinois* (Philadelphia: Brink, McDonough, 1880), 39. In one of his autobiographies, written at age fifty, Lincoln recorded his height as six feet four inches and his weight as 180 pounds; *Collected Works*, III, 512. His companions in New Salem, however, remembered him as weighing more in his youth. William Greene, for example, put the young Lincoln's weight at a precise 214 pounds. According to Robert W. Fogel, *Without Consent or Contract: The Rise and Fall of American Slavery* (New York: Norton, 1989), 141, in 1863–1865 the average northern-born white male was 5 feet 7.5 inches tall at age twenty and 5 feet 8.2 inches tall at age twenty-five to forty-five.

23. Wilson and Davis, *Herndon's Informants*, 385; Edward Waldo Emerson and Waldo Emerson Forbes, eds., *Journals of Ralph Waldo Emerson* (Boston: Houghton Mifflin, 1910), IV, 275; Elliot J. Gorn, "'Gouge and Bite, Pull Hair and Scratch': The Social Significance of Fighting in the Southern Backcountry," *American Historical Review*, 90 (February 1985), 18–43, esp. 18, 20, 21, 22; Bertram Wyatt-Brown, *Southern Honor: Ethics and Behavior in the Old South* (New York: Oxford University Press, 1982), 350–61.

24. Wilson and Davis, *Herndon's Informants*, 73; *The History of Menard and Mason Counties, Illinois* (Chicago: O. L. Baskin, 1879), 196; Onstot, *Pioneers of Menard and Mason Counties*, 132; Reep, *Lincoln at New Salem*, 9, 12, 24–25, 119–20; Thomas, *Lincoln's New Salem*, 12–13, 64–65; Rader, *American Sports*, 10.

25. William H. Herndon and Jesse W. Weik, *Herndon's Life of Lincoln*, ed. Paul M. Angle (Cleveland: World, 1942), 69; Wilson and Davis, *Herndon's Informants*, 13, 73–74, 386. William Clary was the brother of John Clary, who married Jack Armstrong's sister, Rhoda; Reep, *Lincoln at New Salem*, 111.

26. Wilson and Davis, *Herndon's Informants*, 256–57; Gorn, "Gouge and Bite," 42.

27. Wilson and Davis, *Herndon's Informants*, 37.

28. Wilson and Davis, *Herndon's Informants*, 73–74, 386; Thomas, *Lincoln's New Salem*, 61, 64–65; David Herbert Donald, *Lincoln* (New York: Simon and Schuster, 1995), 40–41. Historians have traditionally attributed the original challenge to the Clary's Grove boys or to Jack Armstrong himself, rather than the two competing merchants. Douglas L. Wilson, *Honor's Voice: The Transformation of Abraham Lincoln* (New York: Knopf, 1998), 19–51, presents the fullest and most comprehensive analysis of the fight and its implications for Lincoln's development.

29. Wilson and Davis, *Herndon's Informants*, 73–74; Reep, *Lincoln at New Salem*, 119; Onstot, *Pioneers of Menard and Mason Counties*, 151; *History of Macon County*, 39.

30. Wilson and Davis, *Herndon's Informants*, 386.

CHAPTER 7

1. Roy P. Basler, ed., *The Collected Works of Abraham Lincoln* (New Brunswick, NJ: Rutgers University Press, 1953), I, 497. Herndon was reacting to a snub from party elders who refused to let him address a meeting in support of Zachary Taylor's presidential nomination; Springfield *Illinois State Register*, June 30, 1848.

2. *Collected Works*, II, 111.

3. Burton J. Bledstein, *The Culture of Professionalism: The Middle Class and the Development of Higher Education in America* (New York: Norton, 1976), 105–20, drew this distinction between vertical and horizontal "visions" of American society. Jean H. Baker, *"Not Much of Me": Abraham Lincoln as a Typical American* (Fort Wayne, IN: Louis A. Warren Lincoln Library and Museum,

1988), 13, applied a similar distinction to Lincoln, contrasting Thomas Lincoln's "lateral" movement with the "vertical" movement of his son. The contrast is reminiscent of Major Wilson's dichotomy between "improvement through space" and "improvement through time" within antebellum culture; Major L. Wilson, *Space, Time, and Freedom: The Quest for Nationality and the Irrespressible Conflict, 1815–1861* (Westport, CT: Greenwood Press, 1974).

4. Baker, *Not Much of Me*, 19, similarly divided Lincoln's life between two cultures, while Richard Hofstadter, "Abraham Lincoln and the Self-Made Myth," in *The American Political Tradition and the Men Who Made It* (New York: Vintage, 1948), 93–136, esp. 106, depicted "a man living half in one economy and half in another."

5. *Collected Works*, I, 8–9.

6. Harvey J. Graff, *Conflicting Paths: Growing Up in America* (Cambridge, MA: Harvard University Press, 1995), 29. Graff identified a fourth, "female" path.

7. Graff, *Conflicting Paths*, 30.

8. Graff, *Conflicting Paths*, 30.

9. Bernard Bailyn, *The Peopling of British North America: An Introduction* (New York: Vintage, 1986), 23.

10. Robert H. Wiebe, *The Opening of American Society: From the Adoption of the Constitution to the Eve of Disunion* (New York: Knopf, 1984), 143–67; Graff, *Conflicting Paths*, 32.

11. *Collected Works*, IV, 62, 65; Douglas L. Wilson and Rodney O. Davis, eds., *Herndon's Informants: Letters, Interviews, and Statements About Abraham Lincoln* (Urbana: University of Illinois Press, 1998), 13, 90, 426. Jonathan A. Glickstein, *Concepts of Free Labor in Antebellum America* (New Haven, CT: Yale University Press, 1991), 41. Stuart M. Blumin, *The Emergence of the Middle Class: Social Experience in the American City, 1760–1900* (New York: Cambridge University Press, 1989), 66–107, dissects the shift from manual to nonmanual work in Jacksonian America. Douglas L. Wilson, *Honor's Voice: The Transformation of Abraham Lincoln* (New York: Knopf, 1998), 53–85, offers the fullest account of Lincoln's self-education.

12. Wilson and Davis, *Herndon's Informants*, 384; Thomas P. Reep, *Lincoln at New Salem* (Petersburg, IL: Old Salem Lincoln League, 1927), 114; Benjamin Thomas, *Lincoln's New Salem* (Carbondale: Southern Illinois University Press, 1954), 45; Bledstein, *Culture of Professionalism*, 241; Joseph F. Kett, *Rites of Passage: Adolescence in America, 1790 to the Present* (New York: Basic Books, 1977), 111; Don Harrison Doyle, *The Social Order of a Frontier Community* (Urbana: University of Illinois Press, 1978), 31, 32, 34.

13. *Collected Works*, IV, 62, 65; Wilson and Davis, *Herndon's Informants*, 13, 26, 92; Henry C. Whitney, *Life of Lincoln*, (New York: Baker and Taylor, 1908), I, 40; Jonathan A. Glickstein, *Concepts of Free Labor*, 41; Blumin, *Emergence of the Middle Class*, 66–107.

14. Wilson and Davis, *Herndon's Informants*, 104, 105; "Stephen T. Logan Talks About Lincoln," *Bulletin of the Lincoln Centennial Association*, 12 (September 1, 1928), 1–5, esp. 2.

15. Wilson and Davis, *Herndon's Informants*, 106–7, 113, 118.

16. Wilson and Davis, *Herndon's Informants*, 76, 106–7.

17. David Herbert Donald, *Lincoln* (New York: Simon & Schuster, 1995), 66.

18. E. Anthony Rotundo, *American Manhood: Transformations in Masculinity from the Revolution to the Modern Era* (New York: Basic Books, 1993), 7; Graff, *Conflicting Paths*; Joyce Appleby, "New Cultural Heroes in the Early National Period," in Thomas L. Haskell and Richard F. Teichgraeber III, eds., *The Culture of the Market: Historical Essays* (Cambridge, Eng.: Cambridge University Press, 1993), 163–88, esp. 180; Bledstein, *Culture of Professionalism*, 218.

19. *Collected Works*, IV, 65; Wiebe, *Opening of American Society*, 143–67; Ross W. Beales Jr., "In Search of the Historical Child: Miniature Adulthood and Youth in Colonial New England," *American Quarterly*, 27 (October 1975), 379–98, esp. 394; Joseph F. Kett, "Adolescence and Youth in Nineteenth-Century America," in Theodore K. Rabb and Robert I. Rotberg, eds., *The Family in History: Interdisciplinary Essays* (New York: Harper, 1971), 95–110, esp. 97, 109; John Modell, Frank F. Furstenberg Jr., and Theodore Hershberg, "Social Change and Transitions to Adulthood in Historical Perspective," *Journal of Family History*, 1 (Autumn 1976), 7–32, esp. 18.

20. *Collected Works*, IV, 65; Thomas, *Lincoln's New Salem*, 6, 9, 63, 101, 121; Bledstein, *Culture of Professionalism*, 163–65; Kett, "Adolescence and Youth," 109.

21. This study defines New Salem's merchants as all those who owned a stock of goods, rather than merely a store building, while living in the village. "The Second Berry-Lincoln Store," undated typescript, Sangamon Valley Collection, Lincoln Library, Springfield, Illinois, 1, 22, counts eighteen merchants in New Salem but omits William Greene, Abner Y. Ellis, and James McGrady Rutledge. Greene briefly owned the contents of a store. According to William Herndon, Ellis, a Springfield mer-

chant, lived for a time in New Salem. Benjamin Thomas also identified Ellis as "a New Salem merchant." Some historians confuse James Rutledge and his nephew, James McGrady Rutledge. Both men were briefly merchants in New Salem. See William H. Herndon and Jesse W. Weik, *Herndon's Life of Lincoln*, ed. Paul M. Angle (Cleveland: World, 1942), 91; Reep, *Lincoln at New Salem*, 32, 98, 99, 121–22; Thomas, *Lincoln's New Salem*, 85.

22. New Salem's partnerships included Hill-McNamar, McNamar-Allen, Berry-Lincoln, Sinco-Rutledge, the Chrisman brothers, the Trent brothers, and the Herndon brothers. Offutt was born between 1803 and 1807. He later published a manual on training horses that went through several editions; Denton Offutt, *A New and Complete System of Teaching the Horse on Phrenological Principles* (Cincinnati: Appleton's Queen City Press, 1848); Reep, *Lincoln at New Salem*, 98; "Dr. Denton Offutt: Horse Tamer," *Abraham Lincoln Quarterly*, 2 (September 1943), 330–33; "The Offutt Store," undated typescript, Sangamon Valley Collection, Lincoln Library, Springfield, Illinois, 1, 10–11; "Second Berry-Lincoln Store," 1–3, 24; Springfield *Sangamo Journal*, March 8, 1832.

23. Wilson and Davis, *Herndon's Informants*, 258–59; Reep, *Lincoln at New Salem*, 104–5; "Second Berry-Lincoln Store," 1. "Second Berry-Lincoln Store," 3, concludes that "the Hill-McNamar and Allen-McNamar partnerships were probably the only really successful stores in New Salem's history."

24. Wilson and Davis, *Herndon's Informants*, 258–59; T. G. Onstot, *Pioneers of Menard and Mason Counties* (Peoria, IL: J. W. Franks and Sons, 1902), 69.

25. *The History of Menard and Mason Counties, Illinois* (Chicago: O. L. Baskin, 1879), 288; Onstot, *Pioneers of Menard and Mason Counties*, 46, 76, 152, 170, 180; Reep, *Lincoln at New Salem*, 11, 104, 109; Harvey Lee Ross, *The Early Pioneers and Pioneer Events of the State of Illinois* (Chicago: Eastman Brothers, 1899), 96; "Second Berry-Lincoln Store," 1, 2, 5; Thomas, *Lincoln's New Salem*, 39, 44; *New Salem: A Memorial to Abraham Lincoln*, 3rd ed. (Springfield: State of Illinois, 1937), 63; "Hill Residence," undated typescript, Sangamon Valley Collection, Lincoln Library, Springfield, Illinois, 1–3; "The Offutt Store," undated typescript, Sangamon Valley Collection, Lincoln Library, Springfield, Illinois, 1.

26. Springfield *Sangamo Journal*, July 12, 1832; Harry E. Pratt, "Lincoln Pilots the Talisman," *Abraham Lincoln Quarterly*, 2 (September 1943), 319–29, esp. 325. According to the *Compendium of the Enumeration of the Inhabitants and Statistics of the United States . . . from the Returns of the Sixth Census* [U.S. Census of 1840] (Washington, DC: Thomas Allen, 1841), 87, 2.5 percent of employed men in Sangamon County were engaged in commerce in 1840.

27. Springfield *Sangamo Journal*, January 26, 1831; Springfield *Sangamo Journal*, February 16, 1832; Reep, *Lincoln at New Salem*, 34–35; Thomas, *Lincoln's New Salem*, 74–77.

28. Springfield *Sangamo Journal*, February 16, 1832; Reep, *Lincoln at New Salem*, 34–35; Thomas, *Lincoln's New Salem*, 74–77.

29. *Collected Works*, I, 13; Springfield *Sangamo Journal*, March 29, April 5, August 18, 1832; Thomas, *Lincoln's New Salem*, 74–77, 104–5; Pratt, "Lincoln Pilots the Talisman," 325–26; Onstot, *Pioneers of Menard and Mason Counties*, 48.

30. Onstot, *Pioneers of Menard and Mason Counties*, 158; *History of Menard and Mason Counties*, 250; Reep, *Lincoln at New Salem*, 35; Pratt, "Lincoln Pilots the Talisman," 325–26; Harry E. Pratt, *The Personal Finances of Abraham Lincoln* (Springfield: Abraham Lincoln Association, 1943), 9; "Stephen T. Logan Talks About Lincoln," 1. In 1875, Logan recalled that "I dont think I have seen so dry a season here since."

31. *Collected Works*, I, 5–9, IV, 64; Statement of John Hanks to Herndon, Hertz, *Hidden Lincoln*, 347; Thomas, *Lincoln's New Salem*, 85; Reep, *Lincoln at New Salem*, 104; Onstot, *Pioneers of Menard and Mason Counties*, 152; Lewis E. Atherton, *The Frontier Merchant in Mid-America* (Columbia: University of Missouri Press, 1971), 25, 32; Herndon and Weik, *Life of Lincoln*, 88.

32. *Collected Works*, I, 13; Wilson and Davis, *Herndon's Informants*, 9, 72–75; Kenneth J. Winkle, "Ohio's Informal Polling Place: Nineteenth-Century Suffrage in Theory and Practice," in Andrew R. L. Cayton and Jeffrey Brown, eds., *The Pursuit of Public Power: Political Culture in Ohio, 1787–1861* (Kent, OH: Kent State University Press, 1994), 169–84.

33. Thomas, *Lincoln's New Salem*, 62, 112–13, 115–16; Reep, *Lincoln at New Salem*, 99.

34. *Collected Works*, III, 512; Reep, *Lincoln at New Salem*, 107; Atherton, *Frontier Merchant*, 33.

35. *Collected Works*, III, 512. Robert V. Remini, "Election of 1832," in Arthur M. Schlesinger Jr. and Fred L. Israel, eds., *History of American Presidential Elections, 1789–1968* (New York: Chelsea House, 1971), I, 495–515, provides a brief review of the election of 1832. Good introductions to the Whig and Democratic parties appear in Harry L. Watson, *Liberty and Power: The Politics of Jack-*

sonian America (New York: Noonday Press, 1990); Daniel Walker Howe, *The Political Culture of the American Whigs* (Chicago: University of Chicago Press, 1979); Lawrence Frederick Kohl, *The Politics of Individualism: Parties and the American Character in the Jacksonian Era* (New York: Oxford University Press, 1989); Richard P. McCormick, *The Second American Party System: Party Formation in the Jacksonian Era* (Chapel Hill: University of North Carolina Press, 1966); Michael F. Holt, "The Democratic Party, 1828–1860," in Arthur M. Schlesinger Jr., ed., *History of U.S. Political Parties* (New York: Chelsea House, 1973), I: 497–571; Glyndon G. Van Deusen, "The Whig Party," in Schlesinger, *History of U.S. Political Parties*, I, 333–493.

36. McCormick, *Second Party System*, 278, 281, 287; Van Deusen, "Whig Party," 336; Theodore Calvin Pease, *The Frontier State, 1818–1848*, Vol. II of Clarence Walworth Alvord, ed., *The Centennial History of Illinois* (Chicago: A. C. McClurg, 1922), 76, 92, 105, 108, 137, 273; Paul Simon, *Lincoln's Preparation for Greatness: The Illinois Legislative Years* (Urbana: University of Illinois Press, 1965), 9.

37. Springfield *Sangamo Journal*, August 18, September 22, 29, 1832; Pease, *Frontier State*, 141, 142.

38. *Collected Works*, IV, 64; Wilson and Davis, *Herndon's Informants*, 259; "Logan Talks About Lincoln," 2; McCormick, *Second Party System*, 281.

39. *Collected Works*, I, 5–9.

40. *Collected Works*, I, 5–9.

41. *Collected Works*, I, 5–9.

42. *Collected Works*, I, 5–9, II, 32–36.

43. *Collected Works*, I, 5–9, IV, 64; "Offutt Store," 8. The Springfield *Sangamo Journal*, August 2, 1832, reprinted an article on usury laws from the *North American Review* on its front page two days before the election.

44. *Collected Works*, I, 8; Daniel Walker Howe, "Why Abraham Lincoln Was a Whig," *Journal of the Abraham Lincoln Association*, 16 (Summer 1995), 27–38, esp. 30.

45. *Collected Works*, I, 8–9.

CHAPTER 8

1. Roger L. Nichols, *Black Hawk and the Warrior's Path* (Arlington Heights, IL: Harlan Davidson, 1992), provides the definitive account of Black Hawk and the Black Hawk War. Anthony F. C. Wallace, "Prelude to Disaster: The Course of Indian-White Relations Which Led to the Black Hawk War of 1832," in Ellen M. Whitney, ed., *The Black Hawk War, 1831–1832* (Springfield: Illinois State Historical Library, 1970), I, 1–51, provides the best analysis of the conflict. Francis Paul Prucha, *The Great Father: The United States Government and the American Indians* (Lincoln: University of Nebraska Press, 1984), I, 253–57, offers a basic introduction. Cecil Eby, *"That Disgraceful Affair," the Black Hawk War* (New York: Norton, 1973), is a popular, narrative account. Despite its manifest ethnocentrism, William T. Hagan, *The Sac and Fox Indians* (Norman: University of Oklahoma Press, 1958), provides some basic facts.

2. Nichols, *Black Hawk*, 8, 12, 19, 26–27, 28; Harry E. Pratt, "Lincoln in the Black Hawk War," *Bulletin of the Abraham Lincoln Association*, 54 (December 1938), 3–13; Hagan, *Sac and Fox Indians*, 16–25.

3. Nichols, *Black Hawk*, 42, 44, 48, 50, 52, 56–57; Hagan, *Sac and Fox Indians*, 48–59. Alvin M. Josephy Jr., *The Patriot Chiefs: A Chronicle of American Indian Leadership* (New York: Viking, 1961), 211–53, provides the best account of the rivalry between Black Hawk and Keokuk.

4. Nichols, *Black Hawk*, 61, 64, 67, 76, 79, 81.

5. Nichols, *Black Hawk*, 84, 85, 88, 96, 99, 101, 105–6. Land sales began in October 1829. John Todd was Register of the federal land office in Springfield from 1827 to 1829; John Carroll Power, *History of the Early Settlers of Sangamon County, Illinois* (Springfield, IL: Edwin A. Wilson, 1876), 716.

6. Nichols, *Black Hawk*, 114, 115, 116, 117, 120, 122, 125; Wallace, "Prelude to Disaster," 51; Prucha, *Great White Father*, 255, 256, 257; Pratt, "Lincoln in the Black Hawk War," 7; Hagan, *Sac and Fox Indians*, 148–54, 156–59.

7. Nichols, *Black Hawk*, 123, 124, 125–26, 128, 129, 130–31.

8. Nichols, *Black Hawk*, 132–33, 135; Wallace, "Prelude to Disaster," 27, 29–30, 39, 41, 43–44, 47; Prucha, *Great White Father*, 254, 255; John K. Mahon, *History of the Militia and the National Guard* (New York: Macmillan, 1983), 87; Josephy, *Patriot Chiefs*, 252.

9. Prucha, *Great White Father*, 254, 255; Nichols, *Black Hawk*, 140, 142, 143; Hagan, *Sac and Fox Indians*, 195–97, 200–1, 220.

10. Roy P. Basler, ed., *The Collected Works of Abraham Lincoln* (New Brunswick, NJ: Rutgers University Press, 1953), III, 512; Springfield *Sangamo Journal*, April 17, 1840; Michael Burlingame, ed., *An Oral History of Abraham Lincoln: John G. Nicolay's Interviews and Essays* (Carbondale: Southern Illinois University Press, 1996), 8–9; Thomas, *Lincoln's New Salem*, 79–80; Whitney, *Black Hawk War*, 176–78; Wayne C. Temple, "Lincoln's Arms and Dress in the Black Hawk War," *Lincoln Herald*, 71 (Winter 1969), 145–49; Mahon, *Militia and National Guard*, 87. The muster rolls in Whitney, *Black Hawk War*, list 505 militiamen from Sangamon County.

11. Burlingame, *Oral History of Abraham Lincoln*, 9; Whitney, *Black Hawk War*, 227–28, 230n., 544–46; Thomas, *Lincoln's New Salem*, 81–83, 105; Power, *Early Settlers*, 275–76; Pratt, "Lincoln in the Black Hawk War," 8, 9; Harry E. Pratt, *The Personal Finances of Abraham Lincoln* (Springfield, IL: Abraham Lincoln Association, 1943), 11; Hagan, *Sac and Fox Indians*, 162. According to Mahon, *Militia and National Guard*, 4, members of elite militia units "came from higher-income levels than the standing militiamen."

12. Whitney, *Black Hawk War*, 227–28, 230n., 544–46; Reep, *Lincoln at New Salem*, 42; Thomas, *Lincoln's New Salem*, 81–83; Pratt, "Lincoln in the Black Hawk War," 13.

13. *Collected Works*, I, 509–10, III, 512, IV, 64.

14. T. G. Onstot, *Pioneers of Menard and Mason Counties* (Peoria, IL: J. W. Franks and Sons, 1902), 17. I estimated the number of eligible volunteers, white males age 18–45, in Sangamon County by counting the total number of white males age 20–29 and 30–39, two-fifths of the white males age 15–19, and six-tenths of the white males age 40–49 in 1830, for a total of 2,284; Manuscript U.S. Census, Springfield, Illinois, 1830. Given the population growth of these years, this is probably a conservative estimate of the number of eligible militiamen two years later in 1832.

15. *Collected Works*, III, 512, IV, 64.

16. Douglas L. Wilson and Rodney O. Davis, eds., *Herndon's Informants: Letters, Interviews, and Statements About Abraham Lincoln* (Urbana: University of Illinois Press, 1998), 6, 520, 553–54; Burlingame, *Oral History of Abraham Lincoln*, 8; Benjamin P. Thomas, *Lincoln's New Salem* (New York: Knopf, 1954), 79–80; Whitney, *Black Hawk War*, 176–78; Pratt, "Lincoln in the Black Hawk War," 4, 6; Onstot, *Pioneers of Menard and Mason Counties*, 132, 225.

17. Wilson and Davis, *Herndon's Informants*, 6; Mahon, *Militia and National Guard*, 84; Wayne C. Temple, "Lincoln's Military Service After the Black Hawk War," *Lincoln Herald*, 72 (Fall 1970), 87–89; Robert Reinders, "Militia and Public Order in Nineteenth-Century America," *Journal of American Studies*, 11 (April 1977), 81–101; Gerald Carson, *The Old Country Store* (New York: Oxford University Press, 1954), 126–28, 130–31.

18. *Collected Works*, II, 217, III, 511; Waldo Lincoln, *History of the Lincoln Family: An Account of the Descendents of Samuel Lincoln of Hingham Massachusetts 1637–1920* (Worcester, MA: Commonwealth Press, 1923), 193; William E. Barton, *The Lineage of Lincoln* (Indianapolis: Bobbs-Merrill, 1929), 51, 77; William H. Herndon and Jesse W. Weik, *Herndon's Life of Lincoln*, ed. Paul M. Angle (Cleveland: World, 1942), 11; Thomas L. Purvis, "The Making of a Myth: Abraham Lincoln's Family Background in the Perspective of Jacksonian Politics," *Journal of the Illinois State Historical Society*, 75 (Summer 1982), 148–60, esp. 151, 155, 156.

19. *Collected Works*, IV, 61, 64; Pratt, *Personal Finances*, 60; "Lincoln's Land Holdings and Investments," *Abraham Lincoln Association Bulletin*, 16 (September 1, 1929), 1–8, esp. 5. James W. Oberly, *Sixty Million Acres: American Veterans and the Public Lands Before the Civil War* (Kent, OH: Kent State University Press, 1990), provides a definitive account of the military bounties granted during the 1850s.

20. *Collected Works*, III, 511; Mahon, *Militia and National Guard*, 83; Phillip Weeks, *Farewell, My Nation: The American Indian and the United States, 1820–1890* (Arlington Heights, IL: Harlan Davidson, 1990), 33.

21. *Collected Works*, IV, 64–65; Springfield *Sangamo Journal*, July 19, 1837; Temple, "Lincoln's Military Service," 87; Pratt, "Lincoln in the Black Hawk War," 5; Benjamin P. Thomas, "Lincoln: Voter and Candidate, 1831–1849," *Bulletin of the Abraham Lincoln Association*, No. 36 (September 1934), 5; Rodney O. Davis, "'I Shall Consider the Whole People of Sangamon my Constituents': Lincoln and the Illinois General Assembly," in George L. Painter and Linda Norbut Suits, eds., *Abraham Lincoln and the Political Process* (Springfield: Lincoln Home National Historic Site, 1992), 13–23, esp. 14. The only winning candidate who did not volunteer was Peter Cartwright, a Methodist minister. Voting returns for this election vary. Earl Schenck Miers, ed., *Lincoln Day by Day: A Chronol-*

ogy, *1809–1865* (Washington, DC: Lincoln Sesquicentennial Commission, 1960), I, 29, provides the most reliable figures.

CHAPTER 9

1. Roy P. Basler, ed., *The Collected Works of Abraham Lincoln* (New Brunswick, NJ: Rutgers University Press, 1953), IV, 62, 65; Harry E. Pratt, *The Personal Finances of Abraham Lincoln* (Springfield, IL: Abraham Lincoln Association, 1943), 10; Benjamin Thomas, *Lincoln's New Salem* (Carbondale: Southern Illinois University Press, 1954), 45, 93; Burton J. Bledstein, *The Culture of Professionalism: The Middle Class and the Development of Higher Education in America* (New York: Norton, 1976), 243–44.

2. *The History of Menard and Mason Counties, Illinois* (Chicago: O. L. Baskin, 1879), 711; Thomas P. Reep, *Lincoln at New Salem* (Petersburg, IL: Old Salem Lincoln League, 1927), 98, 99, 114; Benjamin Thomas, *Lincoln's New Salem* (Carbondale: Southern Illinois University Press, 1954), 45, 93; T. G. Onstot, *Pioneers of Menard and Mason Counties* (Peoria, IL: J. W. Franks and Sons, 1902), 141; John Evangelist Walsh, *The Shadows Rise: Abraham Lincoln and the Ann Rutledge Legend* (Urbana: University of Illinois Press, 1993), 78; Don Harrison Doyle, *The Social Order of a Frontier Community* (Urbana: University of Illinois Press, 1978), 31, 32, 34; Christopher Clark, *The Roots of Rural Capitalism: Western Massachusetts, 1780–1860* (Ithaca, NY: Cornell University Press, 1990), 116; Rosalind Rosenberg, *Divided Lives: American Women in the Twentieth Century* (New York: Hill and Wang, 1992), 26.

3. *Collected Works*, IV, 65; Ellen M. Whitney, ed., *The Black Hawk War, 1831–1832* (Springfield: Illinois State Historical Library, 1970), I, 176–78; Reep, *Lincoln at New Salem*, 47; "The Second Berry-Lincoln Store," undated typescript, Sangamon Valley Collection, Lincoln Library, Springfield, Illinois, 2; William H. Herndon and Jesse W. Weik, *Herndon's Life of Lincoln*, ed. Paul M. Angle (Cleveland: World, 1942), 89, 125–28. The most detailed accounts of these financial entanglements appear in Thomas, *Lincoln's New Salem*, 87–93, 104–110; and Pratt, *Personal Finances*, 12–15.

4. *Collected Works*, IV, 65; Douglas L. Wilson and Rodney O. Davis, eds., *Herndon's Informants: Letters, Interviews, and Statements About Abraham Lincoln* (Urbana: University of Illinois Press, 1998), 74; Thomas, *Lincoln's New Salem*, 45, 101, 104–110; Reep, *Lincoln at New Salem*, 65; "Second Berry-Lincoln Store"; Pratt, *Personal Finances*, 19.

5. Steven Mintz, *Moralists and Modernizers: America's Pre-Civil War Reformers* (Baltimore: Johns Hopkins University Press, 1995), 94. Sociologists distinguish among different kinds of debts and exchanges and different kinds of money, including commercial or "market" money. See, for example, Viviana A. Zelizer, "The Social Meaning of Money: 'Special Monies,'" *American Journal of Sociology*, 95 (September 1989), 342–77; Viviana A. Zelizer, *The Social Meaning of Money* (New York: Basic Books, 1994); and Edwina Uehara, "Dual Exchange Theory, Social Networks, and Informal Social Support," *American Journal of Sociology*, 96 (November 1990), 521–57. Christopher Clark, *The Roots of Rural Capitalism: Western Massachusetts, 1780–1860* (Ithaca, NY: Cornell University Press, 1990); and Winifred B. Rothenberg, "The Emergence of a Capital Market in Rural Massachusetts, 1730–1838," *Journal of Economic History*, 45 (December 1985), 781–808, provide excellent introductions, from two different perspectives, to the nature of debt in a commercializing economy.

6. Wilson and Davis, *Herndon's Informants*, 74; Henry C. Whitney, *Life of Lincoln*, (New York: Baker and Taylor, 1908), 99. In 1875, John G. Nicolay interviewed Van Bergen about his legal suit against Lincoln but recorded that Van Bergen "Does not—or does not want to—remember anything about the levy and sale of Mr. Lincolns compass & horse"; Michael Burlingame, ed., *An Oral History of Abraham Lincoln: John G. Nicolay's Interviews and Essays* (Carbondale: Southern Illinois University Press, 1996), 33.

7. Morton J. Horwitz, *The Transformation of American Law, 1780–1860* (Cambridge, MA: Harvard University Press, 1977), 212–26, provides an indispensable analysis of negotiability of debt as a novel accommodation to a commercializing economy during the antebellum period. By contrast, Kermit Hall, *The Magic Mirror: Law in American History* (New York: Oxford University Press, 1989), 46–47, dismisses negotiability far too simply as a routine innovation of the colonial period. Susan E. Gray, *The Yankee West: Community Life on the Michigan Frontier* (Chapel Hill: University of North Carolina Press, 1996), 79–90, provides an excellent analysis of the practical implications of negotiability for a frontier community, concluding that 40 percent of legal suits involved debts that had been assigned to a third party.

8. Susan E. Gray, "Local Speculator as Confidence Man: Mumford Eldred, Jr., and the Michigan

Land Rush," *Journal of the Early Republic*, 10, (Fall 1990), 383–406, esp. 403, 406, notes the toleration of local speculators who boosted their communities' economies. The Trent Brothers similarly absconded from the neighborhood; Wilson and Davis, *Herndon's Informants*, 378; Reep, *Lincoln at New Salem*, 11, 65.

9. Herndon and Weik, *Life of Lincoln*, 90; Whitney, *Life of Lincoln*, I, 99; Pratt, *Personal Finances*, 14, 15; Onstot, *Pioneers*, 83; Thomas, *Lincoln's New Salem*, 106, 107, 108, 110; Reep, *Lincoln at New Salem*, 103. Zarel C. Spears and Robert S. Barton, *Berry and Lincoln, Frontier Merchants: The Store that "Winked Out"* (New York: Stratford House, 1947), go to unrealistic extremes to exonerate Berry and argue that Lincoln accrued no debt at all from the partnership.

10. *Collected Works*, I, 121; Eleanor Gridley, *The Story of Abraham Lincoln or the Journey from the Log Cabin to the White House* (Chicago: M. A. Donohue, 1900), 92–93.

11. Reep, *Lincoln at New Salem*, 33; Benjamin P. Thomas, "Lincoln the Postmaster," *Bulletin of the Abraham Lincoln Association*, 31 (June 1933), 3–9, esp. 7–8; Onstot, *Pioneers of Menard and Mason Counties*, 89, 90.

12. John Locke Scripps, *Life of Abraham Lincoln* (Chicago, 1860; reprinted, Bloomington: Indiana University Press, 1961), 64; Thomas, *Lincoln's New Salem*, 88. According to Lincoln's closest friend, Joshua Speed, who first met him in 1836, Lincoln acquired the nickname "Honest Abe" while living in New Salem; Joshua F. Speed, *Reminiscences of Abraham Lincoln and Notes of a Visit to California* (Louisville: John P. Morton, 1884), 16, 20.

13. Wilson and Davis, *Herndon's Informants*, 377; Onstot, *Pioneers of Menard and Mason Counties*, 180; Reep, *Lincoln at New Salem*, 11, 46; Benjamin Thomas, *Lincoln's New Salem* (Carbondale: Southern Illinois University Press, 1954), 105; "Hill Residence," undated typescript, Sangamon Valley Collection, Lincoln Library, Springfield, Illinois, 1. This study defines New Salem's merchants as all those who owned a stock of goods, rather than merely a store building, while living in the village. "Second Berry-Lincoln Store," 1, lists eighteen merchants, overlooking William G. Greene, James Rutledge, and James McGrady Rutledge.

14. Specific sources of information about the merchants' birthplaces, settlement, and fates includes:

ALLEN: Reep, *Lincoln at New Salem*, 108; Manuscript U.S. Census, Menard County, Illinois, 1850; "The Offutt Store," undated typescript, Sangamon Valley Collection, Lincoln Library, Springfield, Illinois.

BERRY: Reep, *Lincoln at New Salem*, 65, 103; Onstot, *Pioneers*, 233; Spears and Barton, *Berry and Lincoln*, 14–15.

CHRISMAN: *The History of Menard and Mason Counties, Illinois* (Chicago: O. L. Baskin, 1879), 203, 311; Thomas, *Lincoln's New Salem*, 38.

CLARY: Reep, *Lincoln at New Salem*, 12; Molly McKenzie, "A Demographic Study of Select New Salem Precinct Residents," undated typescript, Sangamon Valley Collection, Lincoln Library, Springfield, Illinois, 181, 183.

ELLIS: Wilson and Davis, *Herndon's Informants*, 178; John Carroll Power, *History of the Early Settlers of Sangamon County, Illinois* (Springfield, IL: Edwin A. Wilson, 1876), 285; Thomas, *Lincoln's New Salem*, 85; Manuscript U.S. Census, Sangamon County, Illinois, 1850.

GARLAND: Power, *Early Settlers*, 324–25; Manuscript U.S. Census, Sangamon County, Illinois, 1850.

GREENE: Reep, *Lincoln at New Salem*, 23, 115; *History of Menard and Mason Counties*, 709–14; Manuscript U.S. Census, Menard County, Illinois, 1850.

HERNDON: *Collected Works*, I, 150; Reep, *Lincoln at New Salem*, 117; Spears and Barton, *Berry and Lincoln*, 12; Thomas, *Lincoln's New Salem*, 114; Manuscript U.S. Census, Adams County, Illinois, 1860.

HILL: Wilson and Davis, *Herndon's Informants*, 258; Manuscript U.S. Census, Menard County, Illinois, 1850.

LINCOLN: *Collected Works*, IV, 60–67; Manuscript U.S. Census, Sangamon County, Illinois, 1850.

MCNAMAR: Wilson and Davis, *Herndon's Informants*, 258-60; Manuscript U.S. Census, Menard County, Illinois, 1850.

OFFUTT: Reep, *Lincoln at New Salem*, 98; "Dr. Denton Offutt: Horse Tamer," *Abraham Lincoln Quarterly*, 2 (September 1943), 330–33; "The Offutt Store," undated typescript, Sangamon Valley Collection, Lincoln Library, Springfield, Illinois, 1; McKenzie, "Demographic Study," 84–85.

RADFORD: Spears and Barton, *Berry and Lincoln*, 31–33; Manuscript U.S. Census, Sangamon County, Illinois, 1850.

RUTLEDGE, J.: Wilson and Davis, *Herndon's Informants*, 380–87; Reep, *Lincoln at New Salem*, 98, 99.

RUTLEDGE, J. M.: Reep, *Lincoln at New Salem*, 32, 121–22; Josephine Craven Chandler, *New Salem: Early Chapter in Lincoln's Life* (Springfield, IL: Journal Printing Company, 1930), 34; F. N. Pond, "The Memoirs of James McGrady Rutledge," *Journal of the Illinois State Historical Society*, 29 (April 1936), 76–88; Manuscript U.S. Census, Menard County, Illinois, 1850.

SINCO: Spears and Barton, *Berry and Lincoln*, 24; Springfield *Sangamo Journal*, March 8, 1834; McKenzie, "Demographic Study," 99, 103.

TRENT: Reep, *Lincoln at New Salem*, 11, 65; Chandler, *New Salem*, 36; *New Salem: A Memorial to Abraham Lincoln*, 3rd ed. (Springfield: State of Illinois, 1937), 130; Fern Nance Pond, "New Salem's Miller and Kelso," *Lincoln Herald*, 52 (December 1950), 26–41, esp. 30, 40; Manuscript U.S. Census, Menard County, Illinois, 1850; McKenzie, "Demographic Study," 106, 108–109, 111.

WARBURTON: Wilson and Davis, *Herndon's Informants*, 259; *History of Menard and Mason Counties*, 289; Onstot, *Pioneers*, 65; Reep, *Lincoln at New Salem*, 115. Warburton's place of birth remains a mystery, but R. D. Miller, *Past and Present of Menard County, Illinois* (Chicago: S. J. Clarke, 1905), 91, noted that he was from "the east," a term that generally connoted the Northeast as opposed to the South.

15. Onstot, *Pioneers*, 233; Herndon, *Herndon's Lincoln*, 88, 90. Zarel Spears, a descendent, launched a spirited defense of Berry's character in Spears and Barton, *Berry and Lincoln*, labeling Lincoln's "National Debt" a fiction and Berry himself a scapegoat for Lincoln's ill luck as a merchant.

16. Most historians confuse James Rutledge with his nephew, James McGrady Rutledge. Like the Rutledge family themselves, Thomas Reep carefully distinguished between the elder James and his nephew, who was known as McGrady. Wilson and Davis, *Herndon's Informants*, 383, 545–46; Reep, *Lincoln at New Salem*, 7, 14, 45, 99.

17. Wilson and Davis, *Herndon's Informants*, 14, 174, 258–59; Springfield *Sangamo Journal*, July 17, 1840; Reep, *Lincoln at New Salem*, 11, 55, 115; *History of Menard and Mason Counties*, 289, 311; Onstot, *Pioneers*, 165; Thomas, *Lincoln's New Salem*, 48, 55; McKenzie, "Demographic Study," 113; R. D. Miller, *Past and Present of Menard County, Illinois* (Chicago: S. J. Clarke, 1905), 19, 91, 93, 94.

18. *Collected Works*, I, 150; Springfield *Sangamo Journal*, January 25, 1833, March 8, 1834, July 19, 1853, July 20, 1853; Wilson and Davis, *Herndon's Informants*, 378, 380–87; *History of Menard and Mason Counties*, 203, 311; Reep, *Lincoln at New Salem*, 11, 12, 13, 14, 23, 45, 46, 65, 98; Manuscript U.S. Census, Adams County, Illinois, 1860; Spears and Barton, *Berry and Lincoln*, 12, 133; Thomas, *Lincoln's New Salem*, 20; *New Salem: A Memorial to Abraham Lincoln*, 53; Wilson and Davis, *Herndon's Informants*, 460, 755.

19. Onstot, *Pioneers*, 82; James Oliver Robertson, *American Myth, American Reality* (New York: Hill and Wang, 1980), 143.

20. A comparable persistence rate, for Springfield from 1831 to 1840, was 20.7 percent; Zimri A. Enos, "Springfield Residents Before the Deep Snow," Illinois State Historical Library, Springfield, Illinois, linked with the Manuscript U.S. Census, Springfield, Illinois, 1840. *History of Menard and Mason Counties*, 711–12; Reep, *Lincoln at New Salem*, 32, 111, 115 121–22; Chandler, *New Salem*, 34; Pond, "James McGrady Rutledge."

21. Onstot, *Pioneers*, 159; Marc Egnal, *Divergent Paths: How Culture and Institutions Have Shaped North American Growth* (New York: Oxford University Press, 1996), 87–101; Gray, "Local Speculator as Confidence Man."

22. "Hill Residence," 25.

23. Onstot, *Pioneers*, 186; Reep, *Lincoln at New Salem*, 109; "Allen Residence," undated typescript, Sangamon Valley Collection, Lincoln Library, Springfield, Illinois, 1, 18, 26, 27.

24. Wilson and Davis, *Herndon's Informants*, 252–53, 258–60, 492–93, 545–46.

25. Manuscript U.S. Census, 1850 and 1860, Menard County, Illinois; Wilson and Davis, *Herndon's Informants*, 493; *History of Menard and Mason Counties*, 209; Reep, *Lincoln at New Salem*, 11, 49, 108, 109; Thomas, *Lincoln's New Salem*, 56.

26. The parallel careers of Hill, Allen, and McNamar include:

	Year of Birth	Year of Arrival	Year of Marriage	Year of Departure
Samuel Hill	1800	1829	1835	1837
John Allen	1801	1831	1834	1838
John McNamar	1800	1829	1838	1837

27. Manuscript U.S. Census, Sangamon and Menard Counties, 1850 and 1860.

28. Onstot, *Pioneers*, 141; *History of Menard and Mason Counties*, 287, 353, 712, 713, 714; Reep, *Lincoln at New Salem*, 114; Wilson and Davis, *Herndon's Informants*, 751; Miller, *Past and Present of Menard County*, 106.

29. Power, *Early Settlers*, 324–25; Spears and Barton, *Berry and Lincoln*, 25.

30. Manuscript U.S. Census, Sangamon County, Illinois, 1850; Power, *Early Settlers*, 324–25; Spears and Barton, *Berry and Lincoln*, 25.

31. Manuscript U.S. Census, Sangamon County, Illinois, 1850; Springfield *Sangamo Journal*, November 11, 1842, January 25, 1851; Springfield *Illinois State Journal*, September 9, 1855; Wilson and Davis, *Herndon's Informants*, 377, 475, 530; Emanuel Hertz, *The Hidden Lincoln: From the Letters and Papers of William H. Herndon* (New York: Viking Press, 1938), 213; *History of Menard and Mason Counties*, 710–11; Power, *Early Settlers*, 720; Reep, *Lincoln at New Salem*, 11, 45, 46; Spears and Barton, *Berry and Lincoln*, 31; Earl Schenck Miers, ed., *Lincoln Day by Day: A Chronology, 1809–1865* (Washington, DC: Lincoln Sesquicentennial Commission, 1960), 65; McKenzie, "Demographic Study," 20, 97–98; Divorce Index, Sangamon County, Illinois, October 1825–October 1899, Illinois Regional Archives Depository, University of Illinois, Springfield, Illinois.

32. *Collected Works*, IV, 65; Harvey J. Graff, *Conflicting Paths: Growing Up in America* (Cambridge, MA: Harvard University Press, 1995), 32; Reep, *Lincoln at New Salem*, 49; Ida M. Tarbell, *In the Footsteps of the Lincolns* (New York: Harper and Brothers, 1924), 190; Benjamin Thomas, *Abraham Lincoln: A Biography* (New York: Knopf, 1952), 36; Stephen B. Oates, *With Malice Toward None: The Life of Abraham Lincoln* (New York: Harper, 1977), 26; David Herbert Donald, *Lincoln* (New York: Simon and Schuster, 1995), 49.

CHAPTER 10

1. Roy P. Basler, ed., *The Collected Works of Abraham Lincoln* (New Brunswick, NJ: Rutgers University Press, 1953), IV, 65; Burton J. Bledstein, *The Culture of Professionalism: The Middle Class and the Development of Higher Education in America* (New York: Norton, 1976), 172. Benjamin P. Thomas, "Lincoln the Postmaster," *Bulletin of the Abraham Lincoln Association*, 31 (June 1933), 3–9, is the best synopsis of Lincoln's service as postmaster.

2. *Collected Works*, IV, 65; Thomas, "Lincoln the Postmaster," 3–9; Benjamin P. Thomas, *Lincoln's New Salem* (New York: Knopf, 1954), 94–95; Don E. Fehrenbacher, "Political Uses of the Post Office," in Don E. Fehrenbacher, *Lincoln in Text and Context: Collected Essays* (Stanford, CA: Stanford University Press, 1987), 24–32; Wayne Fuller, *RFD: The Changing Face of Rural America* (Bloomington: Indiana University Press, 1964), 8, 11; Thomas J. Schlereth, *Victorian America: Transformations in Everyday Life* (New York: Harper, 1991), 179.

3. Thomas, "Lincoln the Postmaster," 3–9; Benjamin P. Thomas, *Lincoln's New Salem* (New York: Knopf, 1954), 94–95.

4. Springfield *Sangamo Journal*, March 9, 1833, September 12, 1835; John Carroll Power, *History of the Early Settlers of Sangamon County, Illinois* (Springfield: Edwin A. Wilson 1876),167; Joseph Wallace, *Past and Present of the City of Springfield and Sangamon County, Illinois* (Chicago: S. J. Clarke, 1904), I, 45; T. G. Onstot, *Pioneers of Menard and Mason Counties* (Peoria, IL: J. W. Franks and Sons, 1902), 249. As deputy surveyor, Lincoln crossed party lines to vote for the Democratic Calhoun in the 1835 legislative election; Earl Schenck Miers, ed., *Lincoln Day by Day: A Chronology, 1809–1865* (Washington, DC: Lincoln Sesquicentennial Commission, 1960), I, 50. At the same election, Lincoln also voted for Thomas M. Neale to succeed Calhoun as surveyor, and Neale reappointed Lincoln deputy. Adin Baber, *A. Lincoln with Compass and Chain* (Kansas, IL: privately printed, 1968), provides the best summary of Lincoln's career as a surveyor. According to Douglas R. McManis, *Initial Evaluation and Utilization of the Illinois Prairies, 1815–1840* (Chicago: University of Chicago Press, 1964), 65, land sales at the Springfield land office peaked between 1831 and 1835 and then declined. John Mack Faragher, *Sugar Creek: Life on the Illinois*

Prairie (New Haven, CT: Yale University Press, 1986), 39–43, provides a good introduction to the work and methods of surveyors in the Sangamon Country. Elections were conducted *viva voce* in Sangamon County until 1849.

5. Lincoln wrote that "He studied and nearly mastered the Six-books of Euclid, since he was a member of Congress"; *Collected Works*, IV, 62. According to Simon Singh, *Fermat's Enigma: The Epic Quest to Solve the World's Greatest Mathematical Problem* (New York: Doubleday, 1997), 46, until the twentieth century Euclid's *Elements* was "the second-best-selling book in the world after the Bible." Interestingly, both books were extremely influential in Lincoln's intellectual development.

6. Harry E. Pratt, *The Personal Finances of Abraham Lincoln* (Springfield, IL: Abraham Lincoln Association, 1943), 18; Miers, *Lincoln Day By Day*, 40, 55, 56.

7. Douglas L. Wilson and Rodney O. Davis, eds., *Herndon's Informants: Letters, Interviews, and Statements About Abraham Lincoln* (Urbana: University of Illinois Press, 1998), 384; Sangamon County Commissioners Record, Illinois State Archives, Springfield, Illinois, March 3, 1834; Harry E. Pratt, *The Personal Finances of Abraham Lincoln* (Springfield, IL: Abraham Lincoln Association, 1943), 18; Onstot, *Pioneers of Menard and Mason Counties*, 20, 40. Thomas, *Lincoln's New Salem*, 111–12; Miers, *Lincoln Day By Day*, 40, 55, 56; *The History of Menard and Mason Counties, Illinois* (Chicago: O. L. Baskin, 1879), 101. Lincoln undoubtedly bought the town lots as an investment; he sold them after a year at a profit.

8. Springfield *Sangamo Journal*, April 26, August 6, 9, 1836; Michael Burlingame, ed. *An Oral History of Abraham Lincoln: John G. Nicolay's Interviews and Essays* (Carbondale: Southern Illinois University Press, 1996), 20–21; Thomas, *Lincoln's New Salem* 16–17, 21, 55, 57; Paul Simon, *Lincoln's Preparation for Greatness: The Illinois Legislative Years* (Urbana: University of Illinois Press, 1965), 15–16, 18; Benjamin P. Thomas, "Lincoln: Voter and Candidate, 1831–1849," *Bulletin of the Abraham Lincoln Association*, No. 36 (September 1934), 5–6. Lincoln mistakenly remembered receiving the largest vote in the 1834 election, in which he came in second; *Collected Works*, IV, 65. In fact, the *Sangamo Journal* mistakenly reported Lincoln as the top vote-getter and the next week corrected their error, which probably contributed to Lincoln's confusion; Springfield *Sangamo Journal*, August 9, August 16, 1834.

9. Burlingame, *Oral History of Abraham Lincoln*, 10, 20.

10. Manuscript Poll Books, Sangamon County, Illinois, Illinois State Historical Library, Springfield, Illinois, 1834, 1836; Burlingame, *Oral History of Abraham Lincoln*, 11; Theodore Calvin Pease, *Illinois Election Returns, 1818–1848*, Vol. 18 of *Collections of the Illinois State Historical Library* (Springfield: Illinois State Historical Library, 1923), 262, 275; Reep, *Lincoln at New Salem*, 111.

11. Thomas, *Lincoln's New Salem*, 85.

12. Daniel Walker Howe, *The Political Culture of the American Whigs* (Chicago: University of Chicago Press, 1979), 264–65; Simon, *Lincoln's Preparation for Greatness*, 45, 50; Harvey Lee Ross, *The Early Pioneers and Pioneer Events of the State of Illinois* (Chicago: Eastman Brothers, 1899), 122; Reep, *Lincoln at New Salem*, 73; Norman A. Graebner, "The Apostle of Progress," in Cullom Davis, Charles B. Strozier, Rebecca Monroe Veach, and Geoffrey C. Ward, eds., *The Public and the Private Lincoln: Contemporary Perspectives* (Carbondale: Southern Illinois University Press, 1979), 71–98. According to Joel Silbey, "'Always a Whig in Politics': The Partisan Life of Abraham Lincoln," *Papers of the Abraham Lincoln Association*, 8 (1986), 21–42, esp. 25, "His voting record in the state legislature was that of a conventional Whig."

13. Glyndon G. Van Deusen, "The Whig Party," in Arthur M. Schlesinger Jr., ed., *History of U.S. Political Parties*, (New York: Chelsea House, 1973), I, 333–493, esp. 336; Theodore Calvin Pease, *The Frontier State, 1818–1848*, Vol. II of Clarence Walworth Alvord, ed., *The Centennial History of Illinois* (Chicago: A. C. McClurg, 1922), 273; Joel H. Silbey, "Election of 1836," in Schlesinger and Israel, *American Presidential Elections*, I, 577–600; and Richard P. McCormick, "Was There a 'Whig Strategy' in 1836?" *Journal of the Early Republic*, 4 (Spring 1984), 47–70, provide solid introductions to the election of 1836. Richard P. McCormick, *The Second American Party System: Party Formation in the Jacksonian Era* (Chapel Hill: University of North Carolina Press, 1966), 278, 281, 287, concludes that "Ultimately, around 1835, parties formed behind opposing presidential candidates."

14. Springfield *Sangamo Journal*, April 18, 25, May 23, 1835.

15. Springfield *Sangamo Journal*, June 13, 1836.

16. Springfield *Sangamo Journal*, June 13, 1836; Manuscript Books, Sangamon County, Illinois, Illinois State Historical Library, Springfield, Illinois, 1836. Mark Neely, "The Political Life of New Salem, Illinois," *Lincoln Lore*, No. 1715 (January 1981), 1–3, argues that New Salem was a Whig

rather than Democratic district. In fact, voting figures for New Salem have survived for only three years—1832, 1836, and 1838. In both 1832 and 1838, New Salem was heavily Democratic. The precinct's support for White in 1836 can therefore more properly be interpreted as a temporary defection of southern Democrats opposed to Van Buren rather than a reflection of underlying, long-term Whig sympathies.

17. *Collected Works*, IV, 65; *Census of 1840*, 87; Joseph F. Kett, "Adolescence and Youth in Nineteenth-Century America," in Theodore K. Rabb and Robert I. Rotberg, eds., *The Family in History: Interdisciplinary Essays* (New York: Harper, 1971), 109.

18. Harry N. Scheiber, "Urban Rivalry and Internal Improvements in the Old Northwest, 1820–1860," *Ohio History*, 71 (October 1962), 227–39.

19. James E. Davis, *Frontier Illinois* (Bloomington: Indiana University Press, 1998), 210–12. Good introductions to urban rivalries in the Midwest include Scheiber, "Urban Rivalry"; and Timothy R. Mahoney, *River Towns in the Great West: The Structure of Provincial Urbanization in the American Midwest, 1820–1870* (New York: Cambridge University Press, 1990), 198.

20. "Logan Talks About Lincoln," 3.

21. *History of Menard and Mason Counties*, 209, 293; Onstot, *Pioneers of Menard and Mason Counties*, 20–21; Baber, "Lincoln with Compass and Chain," 123–26.

22. Wilson and Davis, *Herndon's Informants*, 13; Reep, *Lincoln at New Salem*, 11, 104, 125; "Hill Residence," 1; *History of Menard and Mason Counties*, 209.

23. *Collected Works*, I, 320, IV, 65.

CHAPTER 11

1. *Compendium of the Enumeration of the Inhabitants and Statistics of the United States . . . from the Returns of the Sixth Census* [U.S. Census of 1840] (Washington, DC: Thomas Allen, 1841), 87; Kenneth J. Winkle, "Abraham Lincoln, Self-Made Man," *Journal of the Abraham Lincoln Association*, 21 (Summer 2000), 1–16. The U.S. Census of 1840 included two additional categories for occupations that were not practiced in Sangamon County—navigation of the ocean and navigation of canals, lakes, and rivers. A seventh category—mining—claimed only three practitioners and has therefore been excluded from the county's occupational ladder.

2. Peter Temin, *The Jacksonian Economy* (New York: Norton, 1969), 17–22, 68–69; Douglass, C. North, *The Economic Growth of the United States, 1790–1860* (New York: Norton, 1966), 136–37; Malcolm J. Rohrbough, *The Land Office Business: The Settlement and Administration of American Public Lands, 1789–1837* (New York: Oxford University Press, 1968), 271–94.

3. Richard Hofstadter, "Abraham Lincoln and the Self-Made Myth," in *The American Political Tradition and the Men Who Made It* (New York: Vintage, 1948), 99.

4. Joyce Appleby, "New Cultural Heroes in the Early National Period," in Thomas L. Haskell and Richard F. Teichgraeber III, eds., *The Culture of the Market: Historical Essays* (Cambridge, Eng.: Cambridge University Press, 1993), 163–88, esp. 166.

5. Appleby, "New Cultural Heroes," 171, 187.

6. Appleby, "New Cultural Heroes," 173–78.

7. Roy P. Basler, ed., *The Collected Works of Abraham Lincoln* (New Brunswick, NJ: Rutgers University Press, 1953), III, 511.

8. Appleby, "New Cultural Heroes," 176.

9. *Collected Works*, IV, 62.

10. Appleby, "New Cultural Heroes," 177, 178.

11. *Collected Works*, III, 61; John Y. Simon, *House Divided: Lincoln and His Father* (Fort Wayne, IN: Louis A. Warren Lincoln Library and Museum, 1987), 5.

12. Appleby, "New Cultural Heroes," 178.

13. Appleby, "New Cultural Heroes," 173, 176, 177.

14. William H. Herndon and Jesse W. Weik, *Herndon's Life of Lincoln*, ed. Paul M. Angle (Cleveland: World, 1942), 304.

15. *Quincy Whig*, January 1, 1841, quoted in Paul Simon, *Lincoln's Preparation for Greatness: The Illinois Legislative Years* (Urbana: University of Illinois Press, 1965), 231; John Frost, *Self-Made Men of America* (New York: W. H. Graham, 1848), iii; Richard Weiss, *The American Myth of Success: From Horatio Alger to Norman Vincent Peale* (New York: Basic Books, 1969), 6; Appleby, "New Cultural Heroes," 188; John G. Cawelti, *Apostles of the Self-Made Man* (Chicago: University of Chicago Press, 1965), 44, 95; Irvin G. Wyllie, *The Self-Made Man in America: The Myth of Rags to Riches* (New York: Free Press, 1954), 9–10.

16. Wyllie, *Self-Made Man*; Cawelti, *Apostles*; E. Anthony Rotundo, *American Manhood: Transformations in Masculinity from the Revolution to the Modern Era* (New York: Basic Books, 1993), 18–20. According to *The Oxford English Dictionary*, 2nd ed. (Oxford, Eng.: Clarendon Press, 1989), VII, 880, the Frenchman Alexis de Tocqueville was the first to apply the word "individualism" to America in his *Democracy in America*, first published in 1835.

17. Wyllie, *Self-Made Man*, 10.

18. Wyllie, *Self-Made Man*, 10, 24, 154; Cawelti, *Apostles*, 2, 44. Don Harrison Doyle, *The Social Order of a Frontier Community: Jacksonville, Illinois, 1825–70* (Urbana: University of Illinois Press, 1978), 108–118, analyzes the role of the self-made ethic within a neighboring community.

19. Wyllie, *Self-Made Man*, 29, 32, 38–50, 96, 141, 170; Ralph Waldo Emerson, *Emerson's Complete Works* (Cambridge, MA: Riverside Press, 1883), III, 92.

20. Douglas L. Wilson and Rodney O. Davis, eds., *Herndon's Informants: Letters, Interviews, and Statements About Abraham Lincoln* (Urbana: University of Illinois Press, 1998), 57; Wyllie, *Self-Made Man*, 24.

21. *Collected Works*, III, 511, IV, 62; Appleby, "New Cultural Heroes," 172, 182; Matthew H. Smith, *Successful Folks: How They Win* (Hartford, CT: American Publishing Company, 1878), 204, quoted in Wyllie, *Self-Made Man*, 28.

22. *Collected Works*, IV, 64-65; John Locke Scripps, *Life of Abraham Lincoln* (Chicago, 1860; reprinted, Bloomington: Indiana University Press, 1961), 64; Appleby, "New Cultural Heroes," 184.

23. *Collected Works*, IV, 64–65; Appleby, "New Cultural Heroes," 182; Wyllie, *Self-Made Man*, 28; Burton J. Bledstein, *The Culture of Professionalism: The Middle Class and the Development of Higher Education in America* (New York: Norton, 1976), 175.

24. Horatio Alger Jr., *Abraham Lincoln, the Young Backwoods Boy; or, How a Young Rail Splitter Became President* (New York: American Publishers, 1883), 78, 302; Horatio Alger Jr., *From Canal Boy to President or the Boyhood and Manhood of James A. Garfield* (New York: H. M. Caldwell, 1881), 5; Carol Nackenoff, *The Fictional Republic: Horatio Alger and American Political Discourse* (New York: Oxford University Press, 1994), 55. Alger wrote his biography of Lincoln three years before William Herndon's appeared but seems to have been heavily influenced by Ward Hill Lamon's *Life of Abraham Lincoln, 1847–1865* (Boston: James R. Osgood, 1872), which itself depended heavily on the reminiscences Herndon gathered after Lincoln's death.

25. Nackenoff, *Fictional Republic*, 11, 34.

26. Nackenoff, *Fictional Republic*, 45, 56; Weiss, *American Myth of Success*, 5, 50.

27. Nackenoff, *Fictional Republic*, 45, 56; Daniel T. Rodgers, *The Work Ethic in Industrial America, 1850–1920* (Chicago: University of Chicago Press, 1978), 140.

28. Alger, *Abraham Lincoln*, 30–31, 276, 302; Nackenoff, *Fictional Republic*, 45.

29. Alger, *Abraham Lincoln*, 12, 30–31. According to Robert W. Fogel, *Without Consent or Contract: The Rise and Fall of American Slavery* (New York: Norton, 1989), 141, in 1863–1865 the average northern-born white male was 5 feet 7.5 inches tall at age 20 and 5 feet 8.2 inches tall at age 25–45.

30. Alger, *Abraham Lincoln*, 13, 30, 31; Herndon and Weik, *Herndon's Life of Lincoln*, 3; Rodgers, *Work Ethic*, 140.

31. Ruth Bloch, "American Feminine Ideals in Transition: The Rise of the Moral Mother, 1785-1815," *Feminist Studies*, 4 (June 1978), 100–26; Jan Lewis, "Motherhood in the Construction of the Male Citizen in the United States, 1750-1850," in George Levine, ed., *Constructions of the Self* (New Brunswick, NJ: Rutgers University Press, 1992), 143–63. Besides Herndon, Caroline Dall was one of the first to denigrate Lincoln's family background, and particularly Thomas, writing in 1867 that Lincoln's "step-mother—a woman far superior to any whom Thomas Lincoln could have hoped to win in any state of society but one which made a man a necessary protector to every woman—seems to have been his first and best friend"; Caroline H. Dall, "Pioneering," *Atlantic Monthly*, 19 (April 1867), 403–416, esp. 409.

32. Alger, *Abraham Lincoln*, 139, 142, 144.

33. Alger, *Abraham Lincoln*, 33; Nackenoff, *Fictional Republic*, 46.

CHAPTER 12

1. *Collected Works*, II, 96–97.

2. *Collected Works*, IV, 62; John Y. Simon, *House Divided: Lincoln and His Father* (Fort Wayne, IN: Louis A. Warren Lincoln Library and Museum, 1987), 10, 13, 15, 18. Dwight Anderson, *Abraham Lincoln: The Quest for Immortality* (New York: Knopf, 1982), esp. 13–61; and George B.

Forgie, *Patricide in the House Divided: A Psychological Interpretation of Lincoln and His Age* (New York: Norton, 1979), both present complex psychological interpretations of Lincoln's relationship with his father. Each author, however, mentions Lincoln's real father Thomas a mere three times.

3. The most accessible introductions to the vast literature detailing the Market Revolution include Bruce Laurie, *Artisans into Workers: Labor in Nineteenth-Century America* (New York: Noonday Press, 1989), 15–46; Sean Wilentz, "Society, Politics, and the Market Revolution, 1815–1848," in Eric Foner, ed., *The New American History* (Philadelphia: Temple University Press, 1990), 51–71; Christopher Clark, "Household Economy, Market Exchange and the Rise of Capitalism in the Connecticut Valley, 1800–1860," *Journal of Social History*, 13 (Winter 1979), 169–89; Christopher Clark, *The Roots of Rural Capitalism: Western Massachusetts, 1780–1860* (Ithaca, NY: Cornell University Press, 1990); Charles Sellers, *The Market Revolution: Jacksonian America, 1815–1846* (New York: Oxford University Press, 1991); Clarence H. Danhof, *Change in Agriculture: The Northern United States, 1820–1870* (Cambridge, MA: Harvard University Press, 1969); Jeanne Boydston, *Home and Work: Housework, Wages, and the Ideology of Labor in the Early Republic* (New York: Oxford University Press, 1990); and Glenna Matthews, *"Just a Housewife": The Rise and Fall of Domesticity in America* (New York: Oxford University Press, 1987), 3–35.

4. Laurie, *Artisans into Workers*, 17, 24.

5. On the rise of the new urban middle class during the early nineteenth century, consult Stuart M. Blumin, *The Emergence of the Middle Class: Social Experience in the American City, 1760–1900* (New York: Cambridge University Press, 1989); Mary P. Ryan, *Cradle of the Middle Class: The Family in Oneida County, New York, 1790–1865* (New York: Cambridge University Press, 1981); Paul E. Johnson, *A Shopkeeper's Millenium: Society and Revivals in Rochester, New York, 1815–1837* (New York: Hill and Wang, 1978); and Richard L. Bushman, "Family Security in the Transition from Farm to City, 1750–1850." *Journal of Family History*, 6 (Fall 1981), 238–56.

6. Kathleen Neils Conzen, "A Saga of Families," in Clyde A. Milner II, Carol A. O'Connor, and Martha A. Sandweiss, eds., *The Oxford History of the American West* (New York: Oxford University Press, 1994), 337.

7. Simon, *House Divided*, 5; Steven Mintz and Susan Kellogg, *Domestic Revolutions: A Social History of American Family Life* (New York: Free Press, 1988), xv, 54. See A. Gordon Darroch, "Migrants in the Nineteenth Century: Fugitives or Families in Motion?" *Journal of Family History*, 6 (Fall 1981), 257–77, esp. 270, for the concept of "urban career migration."

8. Mintz and Kellogg, *Domestic Revolutions*, 18, 54. G. S. Boritt, *Lincoln and the Economics of the American Dream* (Memphis: Memphis State University Press, 1978), dissects Lincoln's lifelong commitment to an economic system founded on the free market.

9. Douglas L. Wilson and Rodney O. Davis, eds., *Herndon's Informants: Letters, Interviews, and Statements About Abraham Lincoln* (Urbana: University of Illinois Press, 1998), 94, 100; Louis A. Warren, "Thomas Lincoln Goes to New Orleans," *Lincoln Lore*, 1101 (May 15, 1950), 1. Most historians, such as Simon, *House Divided*, 6, depict the Lincolns as falling into economic decline during their fourteen years in Indiana.

10. Wilson and Davis, *Herndon's Informants*, 97, 100, 113; Eleanor Gridley, *The Story of Abraham Lincoln or the Journey from the Log Cabin to the White House* (Chicago: M. A. Donohue, 1900), 47; Harry E. Pratt, *The Personal Finances of Abraham Lincoln* (Springfield, IL: Abraham Lincoln Association, 1943), 61; Warren, "Thomas Lincoln Goes to New Orleans"; Michael Allen, *Western Rivermen, 1763–1861: Ohio and Mississippi Boatmen and the Myth of the Alligator Horse* (Baton Rouge: Louisiana University Press, 1990), 79.

11. For an excellent introduction to the emergence of the modern family between the American Revolution and 1830 and the family's increasing emotional content, see Carl N. Degler, *At Odds: Women and the Family in America from the Revolution to the Present* (New York: Oxford University Press, 1980), 3–25; and Mintz and Kellogg, *Domestic Revolutions*, 43–65.

12. Degler, *At Odds*, 3–25; Mintz and Kellogg, *Domestic Revolutions*, 43–65.

13. Joseph F. Kett, *Rites of Passage: Adolescence in America, 1790 to the Present* (New York: Basic Books, 1977), 23.

14. Howard P. Chudacoff and Tamara K. Hareven, "From the Empty Nest to Family Dissolution: Life Course Transitions into Old Age," *Journal of Family History*, 4 (Spring 1979), 69–83, esp. 77.

15. Emanuel Hertz, *The Hidden Lincoln: From the Letters and Papers of William H. Herndon* (New York: Viking Press, 1938), 206; Bushman, "Family Security," 243.

16. Wilson and Davis, *Herndon's Informants*, 94; Kett, *Rites of Passage*, 29; Chudacoff and Hareven, "Empty Nest," 77, 81. Echoing Grigsby, G. S. Boritt, "The Right to Rise," in Cullom Davis, Charles B. Strozier, Rebecca Monroe Veach, and Geoffrey C. Ward, eds., *The Public and the*

Private Lincoln: Contemporary Perspectives (Carbondale: Southern Illinois University Press, 1979), 57–70, esp. 63, noted that Lincoln "knew, better than Emerson did, that the 'Man With the Hoe' was 'covetous of his dollar.'"

17. Wilson and Davis, Herndon's Informants, 124. Susan E. Gray, The Yankee West: Community Life on the Michigan Frontier (Chapel Hill: University of North Carolina Press, 1996), 110–18, provides in indispensable analysis of this transition, concluding that more than two-fifths of men born in Kalamazoo County, Michigan, between 1810 and 1830 left home before age 21.

18. Ida M. Tarbell, The Life of Abraham Lincoln (New York: Macmillan, 1917), I, 48; Wilson and Davis, Herndon's Informants,118; Norman A. Graebner, "The Apostle of Progress," in Davis, Strozier, Veach, and Ward, Public and the Private Lincoln, 71–98, esp. 72.

19. Louis A. Warren, "The Shiftless Father Myth," Lincoln Kinsman, 32 (February 1941), 1–8; Benjamin Thomas, Abraham Lincoln: A Biography (New York: Knopf, 1952), 5–6. Thomas Lincoln's two sisters lived near Elizabethtown; Ida Tarbell, Footsteps of the Lincolns, 117.

20. Charles H. Coleman, Abraham Lincoln and Coles County, Illinois (New Brunswick, NJ: Scarecrow Press, 1955), x–xii, 3; Gray, Yankee West, 10–11.

21. Charles H. Coleman, Abraham Lincoln and Coles County, Illinois (New Brunswick, NJ: Scarecrow Press, 1955), 1–7; Donald R. Wright, African-Americans in the Early Republic, 1789–1831 (Arlington Heights, IL: Harlan Davidson, 1993), 75; Herbert G. Gutman, The Black Family in Slavery and Freedom, 1750–1925 (New York: Random House, 1976).

22. Coleman, Abraham Lincoln and Coles County, x–xii, 19.

23. Wilson and Davis, Herndon's Informants, 145, 176; Coleman, Abraham Lincoln and Coles County, 52, 55, 131.

24. Coleman, Abraham Lincoln and Coles County, 20, 28, 35, 39; Gray, Yankee West, 97.

25. Coleman, Abraham Lincoln and Coles County, 41, 55.

26. Collected Works, I, 262–63. Lincoln paid $200 for the forty acres John Johnston had sold to Thomas Lincoln for $50 the previous year and stipulated that Johnston could buy it back from him for $200 after the death of Thomas and Sarah. This plot of land became known in the family as the "Abraham Forty." Simon, House Divided, 13, suggests that "Lincoln's continued ownership of the homestead guaranteed that his parents would not show up destitute in Springfield and that political opponents could not capitalize on their poverty."

27. Collected Works, II, 15–16, III, 511; Wilson and Davis, Herndon's Informants, 176; Mintz and Kellogg, Domestic Revolutions, xviii; Pratt, Personal Finances, 60–62. Simon, House Divided, 13, 14, observes that "the total of Lincoln's support remains small. Despite Lincoln's concern for his stepmother's welfare after his father's death, she received no documented gifts of cash prior to 1864" and "Lincoln probably ceased his support about 1848, just when his finances improved."

28. Gray, Yankee West, 102, 110, 117.

29. The History of Coles County, Illinois (Chicago: William LeBaron, 1879), 407, 409, 417; Charles Edward Wilson, History of Coles County (Chicago: Munsell, 1906), 623, 639–40. This analysis compares Thomas Lincoln to the other household heads who practiced agriculture in the same U.S. Census district, Muddy Precinct, in 1850, as recorded in the Manuscript U.S. Census, Coles County, Illinois, 1850. Among all household heads, 96.8 percent were farmers. Among all employed men, 94.2 percent were farmers. Putting the value of Abraham Lincoln's land at $50—the price John D. Johnston paid for it originally—raises Thomas Lincoln's holdings from $100 to $150 and his percentile rank from 20.9 to 28.6.

30. Manuscript U.S. Census, Coles County, Illinois, 1850.

31. David C. Mearns, The Lincoln Papers (Garden City, NY: Doubleday, 1948), I, 179; Coleman, Abraham Lincoln and Coles County, 128.

32. Mearns, Lincoln Papers, 178–79, 180; Coleman, Abraham Lincoln and Coles County, 128–29.

33. Collected Works, II, 96–97; Coleman, Abraham Lincoln and Coles County, 129–31; Simon, House Divided, 11. During his earlier illness in 1849, Thomas had entreated his son, through John Johnston, "to prepare to meet him in the unknown world, or in heven, for he thinks that ower Savour has a Crown of glory, prepared for him"; Mearns, Lincoln Papers, 179.

34. Collected Works, II, 96–97.

35. Coleman, Abraham Lincoln and Coles County, xi–xii, 141.

36. Collected Works, II, 111–13; Coleman, Abraham Lincoln and Coles County, 144. Johnston sold the eighty acres to John Hall for $250.

37. Collected Works, II, 113. In 1844 and 1845, Dennis Hanks's daughter Harriet had lived with

the Lincolns in Springfield to attend school but, according to William Herndon, Mary Lincoln treated her as a servant; Simon, *House Divided*, 11.

38. Robertson, *American Myth, American Reality*, 142.

39. *Collected Works*, II, 97, 111; Coleman, *Abraham Lincoln and Coles County*, 128, 144–45; James Oliver Robertson, *American Myth, American Reality* (New York: Hill and Wang, 1980), 142.

40. Coleman, *Abraham Lincoln and Coles County*, 128.

41. E. Anthony Rotundo, *American Manhood: Transformations in Masculinity from the Revolution to the Modern Era* (New York: Basic Books, 1993), 18–19.

CHAPTER 13

1. Douglas L. Wilson and Rodney O. Davis, eds., *Herndon's Informants: Letters, Interviews, and Statements About Abraham Lincoln* (Urbana: University of Illinois Press, 1998), 386, 482, 527; Ward H. Lamon, *The Life of Abraham Lincoln: From His Birth to His Inauguration as President* (Boston: James R. Osgood, 1872), 163; Douglas L. Wilson, *Honor's Voice: The Transformation of Abraham Lincoln* (New York: Knopf, 1998), 109–112.

2. Manuscript U.S. Census, Sangamon County, Illinois, 1850, linked with *Marriage Records, Sangamon County, Illinois, 1821–1840* (Springfield: Sangamon County Genealogical Society, 1987), *Marriage Records, Sangamon County, Illinois, 1841–50* (Springfield: Sangamon County Genealogical Society, 1988), and *Marriage Records, Sangamon County, Illinois, 1851–1860* (Springfield: Sangamon County Genealogical Society, undated); Wilson and Davis, *Herndon's Informants*, 623.

3. Ellen K. Rothman, *Hands and Hearts: A History of Courtship in America* (New York: Basic Books, 1984), 87–176; Karen Lystra, *Searching the Heart: Women, Men, and Romantic Love in Nineteenth-Century America* (New York: Oxford University Press, 1989); John D'Emilio and Estelle B. Freedman, *Intimate Matters: A History of Sexuality in America* (New York: Harper and Row, 1988), 55–84; Daniel Scott Smith, "Parental Power and Marriage Patterns: An Analysis of Historical Trends in Hingham, Massachusetts," *Journal of Marriage and the Family*, 35 (August 1973), 419–28.

4. Wilson and Davis, *Herndon's Informants*, 252, 353, 383, 545; Thomas P. Reep, *Lincoln at New Salem* (Petersburg, IL: Old Salem Lincoln League, 1927), 32–33, 40.

5. Wilson and Davis, *Herndon's Informants*, 252, 258, 353, 383, 545–46; Reep, *Lincoln at New Salem*, 40.

6. Wilson and Davis, *Herndon's Informants*, 258, 383, 545; Reep, *Lincoln at New Salem*, 40. Dr. John Allen, McNamar's future business partner, managed the farm on McNamar's behalf while he was in New York.

7. Wilson and Davis, *Herndon's Informants*, 493. John Evangelist Walsh, *The Shadows Rise; Abraham Lincoln and the Ann Rutledge Legend* (Urbana: University of Illinois Press, 1993), provides the fullest historiographical review of the Rutledge engagement. The leading opponent of the validity of the engagement was J. G. Randall, *Lincoln the President: Springfield to Gettysburg* (New York: Dodd, Mead, 1945), II, 321–42. John Y. Simon, "Abraham Lincoln and Ann Rutledge," *Journal of the Abraham Lincoln Association*, 11 (Summer 1990), 13–33; and Douglas L. Wilson, "Abraham Lincoln, Ann Rutledge, and the Evidence of Herndon's Informants," *Civil War History*, 36 (December 1990), 301–23, provide persuasive arguments that have revived interest and confidence in the engagement as a formative episode in Lincoln's early development. David Herbert Donald, *Lincoln* (New York: Simon and Schuster, 1995), 55–58; and Wilson, *Honor's Voice*, 114–18, accept the engagement as fact. Wilson, *Honor's Voice*, 118–29, provides the most judicious analysis of this first "crazy spell."

8. Manuscript U.S. Census, Sangamon County, Illinois, 1850, linked with *Marriage Records, Sangamon County, Illinois, 1821–1840*. Wilson, "Abraham Lincoln, Ann Rutledge, and the Evidence of Herndon's Informants," offers a masterful review of the relevant reminiscences.

9. Roy P. Basler, ed., *The Collected Works of Abraham Lincoln* (New Brunswick, NJ: Rutgers University Press, 1953), I, 117; Wilson and Davis, *Herndon's Informants*, 533, 556–57.

10. The average age difference in this minority of marriages was 2.7 years; Manuscript U.S. Census, Sangamon County, Illinois, 1850, linked with *Marriage Records, Sangamon County, Illinois, 1821–1840*, *Marriage Records, Sangamon County, Illinois, 1841–50*, and *Marriage Records, Sangamon County, Illinois, 1851–1860*; *Collected Works*, I, 117; Wilson and Davis, *Herndon's Informants*, 265.

11. *Collected Works*, I, 117; Wilson and Davis, *Herndon's Informants*, 248, 262, 530–31;

556–57. Olive Carruthers, *Lincoln's Other Mary* (Chicago: Ziff-Davis, 1946), represents a pioneering look at Lincoln's second engagement, but Walsh, *Shadows Rise*, 111–22, provides the most accessible and authoritative account.

12. *Collected Works*, I, 78, 119; Wilson and Davis, *Herndon's Informants*, 256, 263, 531.

13. *Collected Works*, I, 55, 94, 117, 119; William H. Herndon and Jesse W. Weik, *Herndon's Life of Lincoln*, ed. Paul M. Angle (Cleveland: World, 1942), 342. Michael Burlingame, *The Inner World of Abraham Lincoln* (Urbana: University of Illinois Press, 1994), 123–39, analyzes Lincoln's general attitude toward women.

14. *Collected Works*, I, 119.

CHAPTER 14

1. Lincoln received his law license in the fall of 1836. At the same time, Stuart dissolved his partnership with Henry E. Dummer, who moved to Beardstown. Springfield *Sangamo Journal*, April 1, 1837; Roy P. Basler, ed., *The Collected Works of Abraham Lincoln* (New Brunswick, NJ: Rutgers University Press, 1953), IV, 65; Joshua F. Speed, *Reminiscences of Abraham Lincoln and Notes of a Visit to California* (Louisville: John P. Morton, 1884), 21; Zimri A. Enos, "Springfield Residents Before the Deep Snow," Illinois State Historical Library, Springfield, Illinois; Springfield *Sangamo Journal*, August 9, 1834, December 17, 1836; *Compendium of the Enumeration of the Inhabitants and Statistics of the United States . . . from the Returns of the Sixth Census* [U.S. Census of 1840] (Washington, DC: Thomas Allen, 1841), 84–87. Rice is listed in the Manuscript U.S. Census, Sangamon County, Illinois, 1840.

2. Springfield *Sangamo Journal*, April 1, 1837.

3. *Collected Works*, I, 320, IV, 63; Speed, *Reminiscences of Abraham Lincoln*, 21; Douglas L. Wilson and Rodney O. Davis, eds., *Herndon's Informants: Letters, Interviews, and Statements About Abraham Lincoln* (Urbana: University of Illinois Press, 1998), 590; "Lincoln's Land Holdings and Investments," *Abraham Lincoln Association Bulletin*, 16 (September 1, 1929), 1–8, esp. 2.

4. Speed, *Reminiscences of Abraham Lincoln*, 20. This peer group includes all white adult men who persisted in Springfield in two or more decennial U.S. censuses between 1830 and 1860 and for whom information on place of birth, date of arrival, date of marriage, and number of children appears in the following county histories: John Carroll Power, *History of the Early Settlers of Sangamon County, Illinois* (Springfield: Edwin A. Wilson, 1876), 9; Joseph Wallace, *Past and Present of the City of Springfield and Sangamon County, Illinois* (Chicago: S. J. Clarke, 1904); Newton Bateman and Paul Selby, eds., *Historical Encyclopedia of Illinois . . . and History of Sangamon County* (Chicago: Munsell Publishing, 1912). The sample includes 130 of Lincoln's peers. Gregory S. Rose, "Information Sources for Nineteenth Century Midwestern Migration," *Professional Geographer*, 37 (February 1985), 66–72, assesses the value of county histories for studying migration patterns. John C. Hudson, "North American Origins of Middlewestern Frontier Populations," *Annals of the American Association of Geographers*, 78 (September 1988), 395–413, uses county histories to map settlement patterns in the Midwest. Hudson concludes that analysis of 200 early settlers is sufficient to establish the general pattern for an entire county. This study employs a sample of 130 early settlers for the city of Springfield.

5. Springfield *Sangamo Journal*, December 17, 1836; Mason Brayman to Father and Mother, Springfield, Illinois, December 25, 1843, and Mason Brayman to Sister, Springfield, Illinois, January 13, 1845, Bailhache-Brayman Family Papers, Illinois State Historical Library, Springfield, Illinois; Speed, *Reminiscences of Abraham Lincoln*, 20. Springfield lawyers were 35 years old on average in 1850 and 39 years old on average in 1860; Manuscript U.S. Census, Springfield, Illinois, 1850 and 1860.

6. Springfield *Sangamo Journal*, February 2, 1834; Jack E. Eblen, "An Analysis of Nineteenth-Century Frontier Populations," *Demography*, 2 (1965), 399–413; John Mack Faragher, *Sugar Creek: Life on the Illinois Prairie* (New Haven, CT: Yale University Press, 1986), 53–60. The comparison of single and married settlers' persistence was calculated from Zimri A. Enos, "Springfield Residents before the Deep Snow," Illinois State Historical Library, Springfield, Illinois, linked with the Manuscript U.S. Census, Springfield, Illinois, 1840. Among the 130 early settlers sampled, 53.8 percent were married on arrival, 26.9 percent were single, and 19.2 percent were children who arrived in Springfield with family members. James E. Davis, *Frontier America, 1800–1840: A Comparative Demographic Analysis of the Frontier Process* (Glendale, CA: Clark, 1977), 57–61, emphasizes and analyzes the scarcity of single men on the frontier. James W. Adams and Alice Bee Kasakoff, "Migration and the Family in Colonial New England: The View from Genealogies," *Journal of Family His-*

tory, 9 (Spring 1984), 24–43, esp. 32, similarly finds nuclear families accounting for about half of all migrants.

7. Mason Brayman to Parents, Springfield, Illinois, September 14, 1841, Bailhache-Brayman Family Papers, Illinois State Historical Library, Springfield, Illinois; Robert Stuart to John Todd Stuart, April 9, 1834, D. T. Stuart to John Todd Stuart, April 8, 1834, February 19, 1835, Stuart-Hay Papers, Illinois State Historical Library, Springfield, Illinois; E. B. Washburne, ed., *The Edwards Papers; Being a Portion of the Collection of the Letters, Papers, and Manuscripts of Ninian Edwards* (Chicago Historical Society's Collection, Vol. 3), (Chicago: Fergus Printing Company, 1884), 275; John S. Macdonald and Leatrice D. Macdonald, "Chain Migration, Ethnic Neighborhood Formation, and Social Networks," *Milbank Memorial Fund Quarterly*, 42 (January 1964), 82–97; A. Gordon Darroch, "Migrants in the Nineteenth Century: Fugitives or Families in Motion?" *Journal of Family History*, 6 (Fall 1981), 257–77.

8. For an authoritative overview of the role of families within the westward movement, see Kathleen Neils Conzen, "A Saga of Families," in Clyde A. Milner II, Carol A. O'Connor, and Martha A. Sandweiss, eds., *The Oxford History of the American West* (New York: Oxford University Press, 1994), 314–57.

9. Springfield *Sangamo Journal*, February 22, 1834; Eblen, "Nineteenth-Century Frontier Populations"; Howard P. Chudacoff, "A Reconsideration of Geographical Mobility in American Urban History," *Virginia Magazine of History and Biography*, 102 (October 1994), 501–18, esp. 506. According to Howard P. Chudacoff and Tamara K. Hareven, "From the Empty Nest to Family Dissolution: Life Course Transitions into Old Age," *Journal of Family History*, 4 (Spring 1979), 69–83, esp. 81, "most female and male children left their families of orientation by about age 22 or 23."

10. Consult James P. Allen, "Migration Fields of French Canadian Immigrants to Southern Maine," *Geographical Review*, 62 (July 1972), 366–83, for a discussion of the concept of migration fields. D. W. Meinig, *The Shaping of America: A Geographical Perspective on 500 Years of History*, Vol. 2, *Continental America, 1800–1867* (New Haven, CT: Yale University Press, 1986), 229, noted that, in general, "The Midland stream spread westward rather more slowly" than the others, which was true of Springfield in particular.

11. Caroline H. Dall, "Pioneering," *Atlantic Monthly*, 19 (April 1867), 403–16, esp. 407, 414.

12. Jean H. Baker, *Mary Todd Lincoln: A Biography* (New York: Norton, 1987), 4–6, 12–13, 16, 49; J. Duane Squires, "Lincoln's Todd In-Laws," *Lincoln Herald*, 61 (Fall 1967), 121–28.

13. Baker, *Mary Todd Lincoln*, 22, 24, 25, 31, 57, 67; Squires, "Lincoln's Todd In-Laws," 122; Power, *Early Settlers*, 715–17; Justin G. Turner and Linda Levitt Turner, *Mary Todd Lincoln: Her Life and Letters* (New York: Fromm International Publishing, 1972), 7; Joan Cashin, *A Family Venture: Men and Women on the Southern Frontier* (New York: Oxford University Press, 1991), provides a sophisticated and sensitive analysis of the westward movement in the South.

14. Manuscript U.S. Census, Springfield, Illinois, 1850; Power, *Early Settlers*, 696–97, 715–17; Wallace, *Past and Present*, 43, 44–45.

15. Stuart was born in November 1807. Power, *Early Settlers*, 696–97; Wallace, *Past and Present*, 44–45.

16. Baker, *Mary Todd Lincoln*, 40, 48; Squires, "Lincoln's Todd In-Laws," 123; Power, *Early Settlers*, 46, 278–79.

17. Wallace, *Past and Present*, 49; Wilson and Davis, *Herndon's Informants*, 252, 432.

18. Baker, *Mary Todd Lincoln*, 74, 78, 79; Squires, "Lincoln's Todd In-Laws," 123; William Townsend, *Lincoln and His Wife's Home Town* (Indianapolis: Bobbs-Merrill, 1929), 69, 75.

19. *Collected Works*, II, 313; Power, *Early Settlers*, 466; Squires, "Lincoln's Todd In-Laws"; John J. Duff, *Abraham Lincoln, Prairie Lawyer* (New York: Bramwell House, 1960), 78–96.

20. The total real wealth of Lincoln's Todd in-laws—John Todd, John Todd Stuart, Ninian W. Edwards, and William S. Wallace—was $40,500 in 1850, equivalent to more than $ 700,000 in 1991 dollars; John J. McCusker, *How Much Is That in Real Money? A Historical Price Index for Use as a Deflator of Money Values in the Economy of the United States* (Worcester, MA: American Antiquarian Society, 1992), 332. Meanwhile, Lincoln himself reported no real property in the Manuscript U.S. Census, Sangamon County, Illinois, 1850.

21. Manuscript U.S. Census, Springfield, Illinois, 1850, linked with officeholding data for the period 1845–1855 in *History of Sangamon County, Illinois* (Chicago: Inter-State Publishing, 1881), 274–83, 566–67, 679.

22. Springfield *Sangamo Journal*, August 25, 1832, August 31, 1833, January 11, 1834, February 7, 1835, March 26, November 26, 1836, April 15, 1837, July 31, 1840; Springfield *Illinois State Register*, July 9, July 31, 1831; Earl Schenck Miers, ed., *Lincoln Day by Day: A Chronology,*

1809–1865 (Washington, DC: Lincoln Sesquicentennial Commission, 1960), I, 93; Michael Burlingame, ed. *An Oral History of Abraham Lincoln: John G. Nicolay's Interviews and Essays* (Carbondale: Southern Illinois University Press, 1996), 30.

23. Springfield *Morning Courier*, November 4, 1840; Springfield *Sangamo Journal*, February 9, 1832, February 6, 1836; December 6, 1939, September 5, 1849; Paul M. Angle, *"Here I Have Lived": A History of Lincoln's Springfield* (Springfield: Abraham Lincoln Association, 1935), 87–88.

24. Springfield *Sangamo Journal*, December 17, 1836.

25. Springfield *Sangamo Journal*, July 19, 1832, December 17, 1836, April 12, July 12, December 6, 1839, April 15, 1842. Thomas Dublin, "Rural-Urban Migrants in Industrial New England: The Case of Lynn, Massachusetts, in the Mid-Nineteenth City," *Journal of American History*, 73 (December 1986), 623–44, analyzes the role of boarding during the transition from farms to cities.

26. Springfield *Sangamo Journal*, December 15, 1832, July 12, 1839, September 2, 1840.

27. Wilson and Davis, *Herndon's Informants*, 588–91; Speed, *Reminiscences of Abraham Lincoln*, 589–90; William H. Herndon and Jesse W. Weik, *Herndon's Life of Lincoln*, ed. Paul M. Angle (Cleveland: World, 1942), 91; Power, *Early Settlers*, 285; John G. Nicolay and John Hay, *Abraham Lincoln: A History* (New York: Century, 1890), I, 25; Benjamin P. Thomas, *Lincoln's New Salem* (New York: Knopf, 1954), 85; Robert L. Kincaid, "Joshua Fry Speed—1814–1882: Abraham Lincoln's Most Intimate Friend," *Filson Club History Quarterly*, 17 (April 1943), 63–123, esp. 64, 87.

28. Speed, *Reminiscences of Abraham Lincoln*, 3, 4; Wilson and Davis, *Herndon's Informants*, 590; Kincaid, "Joshua Fry Speed," 16, 64, 65.

29. Wilson and Davis, *Herndon's Informants*, 477, 588.

30. Speed, *Reminiscences of Abraham Lincoln*, 21–22, 23, 83.

31. Wilson and Davis, *Herndon's Informants*, 590; James and Sarah McConnell to James and Sarah Smith, Springfield, Illinois, September 8, 1849, James and E. F. McConnell Papers, Illinois State Historical Library, Springfield, Illinois.

32. Burlingame, *Oral History of Abraham Lincoln*, 18–20; Wilson and Davis, *Herndon's Informants*, 205, 267; Power, *Early Settlers*, 165, 613.

33. Rendered thirty years later, Butler's account of Lincoln's early years in Springfield is hopelessly confused, in particular his claim that Lincoln boarded with him for eight years and that Butler paid off all of his debts. But independent sources confirm that Butler "clothed and boarded Lincoln for years—paid his debts"; Burlingame, *Oral History of Abraham Lincoln*, 22–23; Wilson and Davis, *Herndon's Informants*, 267, 447.

34. Burlingame, *Oral History of Abraham Lincoln*, 22–23; Wilson and Davis, *Herndon's Informants*, 267, 447.

35. Miers, *Lincoln Day by Day*, I, 89; David Herbert Donald, *Lincoln* (New York: Simon and Schuster, 1995), 73.

36. *Collected Works*, I, 107; Miers, *Lincoln Day by Day*, I, 93; Duff, *Abraham Lincoln, Prairie Lawyer*, 53–61.

37. *Collected Works*, I, 143, 154, 158–59, 181, 184, 195, 208; Miers, *Lincoln Day by Day*, I, 119; Burlingame, *Oral History of Abraham Lincoln*, 26. Cullom Davis, "Abraham Lincoln, Esq.: The Symbiosis of Law and Politics," Seventh Annual Lincoln Colloquium, 1992, offers the basic analysis of the relationship between law and politics in Lincoln's career.

CHAPTER 15

1. Sangamon County Commissioners Record, Illinois State Archives, Springfield, Illinois, June 4, 1821.

2. Sangamon County Commissioners Record, September 8, 1829. In 1839, the Springfield City Council received a petition with 239 signatures; Springfield City Council, Minutes of the Council Meeting, 1838–1861, Sangamon Valley Collection, Lincoln Library, Springfield, Illinois, May 27, 1839.

3. Sangamon County Commissioners Record, March 7, 1827, December 3, 1833, March 3, 1834.

4. Sangamon County Commissioners Record, March 7, 1827, December 3, 1833, March 3, 1834; Sangamon County Estray Notices, 1821–1830, Illinois State Historical Library, Springfield, Illinois; Paul Simon, *Lincoln's Preparation for Greatness: The Illinois Legislative Years* (Norman: University of Oklahoma Press, 1965), 26.

5. Sangamon County Commissioners Record; Springfield *Sangamo Journal*, February 9, 1832; John Carroll Power, *History of the Early Settlers of Sangamon County, Illinois* (Springfield: Edwin A. Wilson, 1876), 38, 40.

6. Sangamon County Commissioners Record, June 4, 1821, June 4, 1832, March 4, 1834; Sangamon County Indentures of Apprenticeship, Illinois State Historical Library, Springfield, Illinois; Manuscript U.S. Census, Springfield, Illinois, 1850.

7. Sangamon County Indentures of Apprenticeship; Springfield *Sangamo Journal*, July 6, 1833.

8. Springfield *Sangamo Journal*, September 17, October 8, 1846; Springfield *Illinois Journal*, April 9, 1851; Sophonisba P. Breckinridge, *The Illinois Poor Law and Its Administration* (Chicago: University of Chicago Press, 1939), 18, 22; Cullom Davis and Daniel W. Stowell, "A New Look at Lincoln," Abraham Lincoln Institute of the Mid-Atlantic, 2000.

9. Sangamon County Commissioners Record, March 18, 1825.

10. Power, *Early Settlers*, 36; Springfield *Sangamo Journal*, March 23, 1833, July 5, 1834.

11. Springfield *Sangamo Journal*, April 12, 26, 1832.

12. Springfield *Sangamo Journal*, November 24, 1832, August 9, September 6, 1834, December 17, 1836, June 7, 1839; Michael Burlingame, ed. *An Oral History of Abraham Lincoln: John G. Nicolay's Interviews and Essays* (Carbondale: Southern Illinois University Press, 1996), 33; Paul M. Angle, *"Here I Have Lived": A History of Lincoln's Springfield* (Springfield: Abraham Lincoln Association, 1935), 42.

13. Springfield *Morning Courier*, November 4, 1840; Springfield *Sangamo Journal*, February 2, 1831; *Springfield Illinois State Register*, December 30, 1840, April 2, 1845.

14. Springfield *Sangamo Journal*, July 12, 29, 1837; *Compendium of the Enumeration of the Inhabitants and Statistics of the United States . . . from the Returns of the Sixth Census* [U.S. Census of 1840] (Washington, DC: Thomas Allen, 1841), 87. Betty Blackmar, "Rewalking the 'Walking City': Property Relations in New York City, 1780–1840," *Radical History Review*, 21 (Fall 1980), 131–48; and David Montgomery, "The Working Classes of the Pre-Industrial American City, 1780–1830," *Labor History*, 9 (Winter 1968), 3–22, review social conditions in early "walking cities."

15. Springfield *Sangamo Journal*, April 10, December 15, 1832, April 7, 1840; Springfield *Illinois State Register*, May 21, July 31, 1841; Manuscript U.S. Census, Springfield, Illinois, 1850. Richard L. Bushman, "Family Security in the Transition from Farm to City, 1750–1850," *Journal of Family History*, 6 (Fall 1981), 238–56, esp. 247, considers the mingling of rural agriculture and urban refinement within a broader context.

16. Springfield *Sangamo Journal*, May 7, 1840; Springfield *Illinois State Register*, October 15, 1841.

17. Springfield *Sangamo Journal*, March 26, 1836; Springfield *Illinois State Register*, August 6, 1841.

18. Springfield *Sangamo Journal*, April 26, May 10, 17, 1832.

19. Springfield *Sangamo Journal*, June 21, 1834; Springfield City Council, Minutes of the Council Meeting, April 29, 1839, June 4, 1847.

20. Lincoln attended eleven of the twenty-seven meetings during his tenure on the town board. Springfield City Council, Minutes of the Council Meeting, June 24, July 11, August 9, October 1, 1839, March 16, April 7, 20, 1840; "Lincoln—Trustee of the Town of Springfield," *Bulletin of the Abraham Lincoln Association*, (June 1937), 3-7.

21. Springfield City Council, Minutes of the Council Meeting, April 20, 1840; "Lincoln—Trustee of the Town of Springfield."

22. For the "joining" ethic, consult Daniel J. Boorstin, *The Americans: The National Experience* (New York: Random House, 1965), 49–112; and Timothy R. Mahoney, *Provincial Lives: Middle-Class Experience in the Antebellum Middle West* (New York: Cambridge University Press, 1999), 213–56. This list includes all thirty-two voluntary associations founded in Springfield up to 1850, as reported in any of the town's newspapers. There were eleven fraternal, seven temperance, six political, five civic or benevolent, and three religious organizations. Gerald Gamm and Robert D. Putnam, "The Growth of Voluntary Associations in America, 1840–1940," *Journal of Interdisciplinary History*, 29 (Spring 1999), 511–57, esp. 549.

23. Springfield *Sangamo Journal*, November 27, 1834, January 17, 1835.

24. Springfield *Sangamo Journal*, December 13, 1834, September 10, 1836, February 2, 1837; Springfield *Illinois State Register*, April 21, 1841; Joseph Wallace, *Past and Present of the City of Springfield and Sangamon County, Illinois*, (Chicago: S. J. Clarke, 1904), I, 48; Jeff G. Gavin, *Past Sites of Springfield: A Historic Guide to the Downtown Area*, typescript, Sangamon Valley Collection, Lincoln Library, 1980, 11.

25. Springfield *Sangamo Journal*, April 12, 1832, Angle, *Here I Have Lived*, 26.

26. Springfield *Sangamo Journal*, March 19, 1846; Springfield *Illinois Journal*, June 1, 1853;

Springfield *Western Farmer*, November 1, 1839; Springfield *Illinois Journal*, August 27, 1850; Manuscript U.S. Census, Springfield, Illinois, 1850; Mason Brayman to Parents, September 14, 1841, Bailhache-Brayman Family Papers, Illinois State Historical Library, Springfield, Illinois; Mason Brayman to Sister, January 13, 1845, Bailhache-Brayman Family Papers, Illinois State Historical Library, Springfield, Illinois; Willis D. Moreland and Erwin H. Goldenstein, *Pioneers in Adult Education* (Chicago: Nelson-Hall, 1985).

27. Springfield *Sangamo Journal*, December 7, 1833, March 4, 1842, April 22, 1852; Angle, *Here I Have Lived*, 201; Thomas F. Schwartz, "The Springfield Lyceum and Lincoln's 1838 Speech," *Illinois Historical Journal*, 83 (Spring 1990), 45–49; Joseph F. Kett, *Rites of Passage: Adolescence in America, 1790 to the Present* (New York: Basic Books, 1977), 111; Moreland and Goldenstein, *Pioneers in Adult Education*, 38, 44, 45; Carl Bode, *The American Lyceum* (Carbondale: Southern Illinois University Press, 1968). Seven of the ten founding officers can be located in the Manuscript U.S. Census, Springfield, Illinois, 1850, and county histories.

28. Springfield Mechanics Union Book, Illinois State Historical Library, Springfield, Illinois; Springfield *Sangamo Journal*, April 1, July 1, 1837. Of Springfield's 458 gainfully employed residents, 322 practiced manufactures and trades; *U.S. Census of 1840*, 87.

29. Springfield Mechanics Union Book, Illinois State Historical Library, Springfield, Illinois; Miers, *Lincoln Day by Day*, I, 130; Bruce Laurie, *Artisans into Workers: Labor in Nineteenth-Century America* (New York: Noonday Press, 1989).

30. Springfield Mechanics Union Book; Springfield *Illinois State Register*, August 4, 1842, May 17, 1844.

31. Springfield Mechanics Union Book. Fifty of the 101 members appeared in the Manuscript U.S. Census, Springfield, Illinois, 1850.

32. This portrait of Springfield's "joiners" focuses on all 350 Springfield men who appeared in at least two of the U.S. censuses of 1840, 1850, and 1860. Exactly 100 of them were identified in the town's newspapers and county histories as officers of a voluntary association sometime before 1860.

33. Springfield *Sangamo Journal*, April 13, 1842; Henrietta C. Jones, "Illinois Women: Stories of the Pioneer Mothers of Illinois," Women's Exposition Board, 1893, Illinois State Historical Library, Springfield, Illinois, 8. Gamm and Putnam, "Growth of Voluntary Associations," 523, conclude that "The average city directory reported 2.1 associations per 1,000 population in 1840." By that criterion, Springfield's population of 4,533 in 1850 should have supported 9.5 voluntary associations. Thirty-one voluntary associations functioned before 1850, although not all of them were still extant in that year.

34. Springfield *Morning Courier*, November 17, 1840; Robert H. Wiebe, "Lincoln's Fraternal Democracy," in John L. Thomas, ed., *Abraham Lincoln and the American Political Tradition* (Amherst: University of Massachusetts Press, 1986), 11–30.

35. Speed, *Reminiscences of Abraham Lincoln*, 23, 34; Burlingame, *Oral History of Abraham Lincoln*, 36.

36. Burlingame, *Oral History of Abraham Lincoln*, 26.

37. Roy P. Basler, ed., *The Collected Works of Abraham Lincoln* (New Brunswick, NJ: Rutgers University Press, 1953), II, 220–22.

38. *Collected Works*, II, 220–22; Springfield *Illinois State Journal*, March 29, 1854; Manuscript U.S. Census, Springfield, Illinois, 1850, linked with Manuscript Poll Books, Springfield, Illinois, Illinois State Historical Library, Springfield, Illinois, 1848, and leadership rolls of thirty-one voluntary associations published in local newspapers during the period.

CHAPTER 16

1. Roy P. Basler, ed., *The Collected Works of Abraham Lincoln* (New Brunswick, NJ: Rutgers University Press, 1953), III, 512.

2. Daniel Walker Howe, "Why Abraham Lincoln Was a Whig," *Journal of the Abraham Lincoln Association*, 16 (Summer 1995), 27–38, esp. 28; Joel H. Silbey, "'Always a Whig in Politics': The Partisan Life of Abraham Lincoln," *Papers of the Abraham Lincoln Association*, 8 (1986), 21–42; and Michael F. Holt, "The Democratic Party, 1818–1860," in Arthur M. Schlesinger Jr., ed., *History of U.S. Political Parties* (New York: Chelsea House, 1973), I, 497–571, esp. 498, 499, 513; John Ashworth, *"Agrarians and Aristocrats": Party Political Ideology in the United States, 1837–1846* (Cambridge, Eng.: Cambridge University Press, 1987), 64; Daniel Walker Howe, *The Political Culture of the American Whigs* (Chicago: University of Chicago Press, 1979), 13.

3. Harry L. Watson, *Liberty and Power: The Politics of Jacksonian America* (New York: Noonday Press, 1990), 273.

4. Howe, *Political Culture of the American Whigs*, 20, 21, 211.

5. Springfield *Sangamon Journal*, September 29, 1832; Robert V. Remini, *Andrew Jackson and the Bank War* (New York: Norton, 1967), 109–53.

6. Vandalia *Illinois State Register and People's Advocate*, January 5, 1838; Watson, *Liberty and Power*, 244.

7. Springfield *Sangamon Journal*, June 4, 1846; Springfield *Illinois State Register*, July 28, 1848. As one Lincoln scholar put it, "Why central Illinois became Whig is a question that has long troubled historians. The subject invites investigation via modern techniques"; G. S. Boritt, *Lincoln and the Economics of the American Dream* (Memphis: Memphis State University Press, 1978), 314, n. 2.

8. Douglas L. Wilson and Rodney O. Davis, eds., *Herndon's Informants: Letters, Interviews, and Statements About Abraham Lincoln* (Urbana: University of Illinois Press, 1998), 77; Springfield *Sangamon Journal*, February 2, 1831; Theodore Calvin Pease, *Illinois Election Returns, 1818–1848*, Vol. 18 of *Collections of the Illinois State Historical Library* (Springfield: Illinois State Historical Library, 1923), xviii–xxvi; Theodore Calvin Pease, *The Frontier State, 1818–1848*, Vol. 2 of Clarence Walworth Alvord, ed., *The Centennial History of Illinois* (Chicago: A. C. McClurg, 1922), 33–51; Richard P. McCormick, *The Second American Party System: Party Formation in the Jacksonian Era* (Chapel Hill: University of North Carolina Press, 1966), 257–58, 277–78.

9. Springfield *Sangamon Journal*, April 12, 1832, August 30, 1834, January 3, 1835; Paul Simon, *Lincoln's Preparation for Greatness: The Illinois Legislative Years* (Norman: University of Oklahoma Press, 1965), 9.

10. Charles Maltby, *The Life and Public Services of Abraham Lincoln* (Stockton, CA: Daily Independent Steam Power Print, 1884), 44–45.

11. Springfield *Sangamon Journal*, November 26, 1836; Springfield *Illinois State Register*, November 9, 1839; Simon, *Lincoln's Preparation for Greatness*, 32, 35–38, 47, 50–52; G. S. Boritt, *Lincoln and the Economics of the American Dream*, 305; John H. Krenkel, *Illinois Internal Improvements, 1818–1848* (Cedar Rapids: Torch Press, 1958), 65–76; Robert P. Howard, *Illinois: A History of the Prairie State* (Grand Rapids: Eerdmans, 1972), 193–202; Rodney O. Davis, "'I Shall Consider the Whole People of Sangamon my Constituents': Lincoln and the Illinois General Assembly," in George L. Painter and Linda Norbut Suits, eds., *Abraham Lincoln and the Political Process* (Springfield: Lincoln Home National Historic Site, 1992), 13–23.

12. Pease, *Illinois Election Returns*, xxx–xxxiv, xli; Pease, *Frontier State*, 70–91, 147, 252–56; McCormick, *Second American Party System*, 281–82.

13. Springfield *Sangamo Journal*, August 11, September 22, 1832, August 30, 1834, April 18, 1835, April 9, May 14, June 18, 1836; Wilson and Davis, *Herndon's Informants*, 77.

14. Springfield *Sangamo Journal*, June 20, October 24, 1835, June 18, 1836, June 25, July 23, 27, October 8, 1836; Springfield *Illinois State Register*, August 31, 1839; Springfield *Old Hickory*, April 16, 1840; Jonathan M. Atkins, "The Presidential Candidacy of Hugh Lawson White in Tennessee, 1832–1836," *Journal of Southern History*, 58 (February 1992), 27–56; Richard P. McCormick, "Was There a 'Whig Strategy' in 1836?" *Journal of the Early Republic*, 4 (Spring 1984), 47–70; Joel H. Silbey, "Election of 1836," in Arthur M. Schlesinger Jr. and Fred L. Israel, eds., *History of American Presidential Elections, 1789–1968* (New York: Chelsea House, 1971), I, 577–600.

15. Springfield *Sangamo Journal*, April 18, May 9, 1835, December 10, 1836; Wilson and Davis, *Herndon's Informants*, 480. Whig support peaked in Springfield in 1836 at 62 percent and in Illinois in 1840 at 48.9 percent. The table is calculated from Manuscript Poll Books, Sangamon County, Illinois, 1832–1848, Illinois State Historical Library, Springfield, Illinois. Under the state's constitution, voters were not required to vote in the election districts in which they lived, and there was a special procedure for such "absentee voting"; *Illinois Laws* (1823), sec. 3. As a result, an unknown number of nonresidents may have voted in Springfield's presidential elections. The poll books considered here are therefore useless in estimating precise rates of voter turnout in Springfield. The table reveals rates of retention among Whigs and Democrats in pairs of elections without estimating rates of turnout in each election or each pair of elections. During presidential elections, Springfield opened three "polls" for the convenience of voters. All of Springfield's poll books for the presidential elections of 1832 to 1848 survive except for one poll in 1840. As a result, about one-third of all voters cannot be linked from 1836 to 1840 or 1840 to 1844. However, all three polls were held at the same location, the courthouse, and therefore a voter's inclusion in the missing poll book had no geographic basis and was probably random. For another study that links the poll books of 1840 and 1844, see

Paul F. Bourke and Donald A. DeBats, "Individuals and Aggregates: A Note on Historical Data and Assumptions," *Social Science History*, 4 (Spring 1980), 229–50.

16. *Sangamo Journal*, August 5, 1837, July 7, April 28, 1838, April 12, 1839; Vandalia *Illinois State Register and People's Advocate*, April 20, 1838. Anti-Junto Whigs won 6–8 percent of the vote for state representatives in August 1838; Pease, *Illinois Election Returns*, 321. For Whigs' antiparty instincts, see Ronald P. Formisano, "Political Character, Antipartyism and the Second Party System," *American Quarterly*, 21 (Winter 1969), 683–709; Howe, *Political Culture of the American Whigs*, 50–53; and Lynn L. Marshall, "The Strange Stillbirth of the Whig Party," *American Historical Review*, 72 (January 1967), 445–68.

17. Peter Temin, *The Jacksonian Economy* (New York: Norton, 1969), 113-28; Pease, *Frontier State*, 306–7, 311; Boritt, *Lincoln and the Economics of the American Dream*, 41–50; Krenkel, *Illinois Internal Improvements*, 150–176.

18. Springfield *Sangamo Journal*, May 27, 1837, April 12, 1839, April 8, July 29, September 19, 1842.

19. Springfield *Sangamo Journal*, January 20, 1838, October 7, 1842, January 26, February 23, March 30, 1843; Springfield *Illinois State Register*, November 9, 1839; Mason Brayman to Parents, September 14, 1841, Bailhache-Brayman Family Papers, Illinois State Historical Library, Springfield, Illinois. Earl Schenck Miers, ed., *Lincoln Day by Day: A Chronology, 1809–1865* (Washington, DC: Lincoln Sesquicentennial Commission, 1960), I, 129.

20. Springfield *Sangamo Journal*, August 8, 1835, July 22, 1837, October 11, 1839; Springfield *Illinois State Register*, October 12, 1839; Pease, *Illinois Election Returns*, xxxvi–xxxvii, xxxix, xl; McCormick, *Second American Party System*, 282–83, 285–86, 287; Paul M. Angle, *"Here I Have Lived": A History of Lincoln's Springfield* (Chicago: Abraham Lincoln Book Shop, 1935), 60, 62, 109; Simon, *Lincoln's Preparation for Greatness*, 275. Stephen L. Hansen, *The Making of the Third Party System: Voters and Parties in Illinois, 1850–1876* (Ann Arbor, MI: UMI Research Press, 1980), 1–3, challenges McCormick's evaluation of the effectiveness of the convention system before the emergence of the Republican Party.

21. *Collected Works*, I, 201–3; Springfield *Sangamo Journal*, October 11, 1839; Springfield *Illinois State Register*, May 1, August 14, September 9, 1840, August 11, 1843; Springfield *Old Hickory*, September 14, 1840.

22. *Collected Works*, I, 159–79, 184, 203–5, 206; Springfield *Illinois State Register*, May 1, August 14, September 9, 1840; Michael Burlingame, ed., *An Oral History of Abraham Lincoln: John G. Nicolay's Interviews and Essays* (Carbondale: Southern Illinois University Press, 1996), 39; Miers, *Lincoln Day by Day*, I, 143–46; Cullom Davis, "Abraham Lincoln, ESQ.: The Symbiosis of Law and Politics," Seventh Annual Lincoln Colloquium, 1992.

23. Vandalia *Illinois State Register and People's Advocate*, January 5, 1838; Springfield *Illinois State Register*, November 5, 1841, August 11, 1843; Springfield *Sangamo Journal*, January 13, November 6, 13, July 28, September 8, 1838, January 28, 1840; Springfield *Old Hickory*, May 13, 1840.

24. Vandalia *Illinois State Register and People's Advocate*, September 14, 1838; Springfield *Illinois State Register*, April 17, 1840; Springfield *Old Hickory*, August 17, 1840.

25. Springfield City Council, Minutes of the Council Meeting, 1838–1861, Sangamon Valley Collection, Lincoln Library, Springfield, Illinois, April 19, 20, 21, 22, 1841; Springfield *Sangamo Journal*, June 25, 1836, April 30, 1841, March 18, July 22, 1842; Springfield *Illinois State Register*, April 22, August 5, November 11, 1842.

26. Springfield *Sangamo Journal*, October 22, 26, 1841, July 22, 29, 1842.

27. Springfield *Illinois State Register*, March 25, August 11, 1842.

28. Springfield *Illinois State Register*, March 17, March 24, 1843.

29. *Collected Works*, I, 319; Benjamin P. Thomas, "Lincoln: Voter and Candidate," *Bulletin of the Abraham Lincoln Association*, (September 1934), 3–9, esp. 6–7; Joseph Nathan Kane, *The American Counties* (New York: Scarecrow Press, 1962), 129; Dumas Malone, ed., *The Dictionary of American Biography* (New York: Charles Scribner's Sons, 1943), VIII, 245; Baker, *Mary Todd Lincoln* (New York: Norton, 1987), 136.

30. Springfield *Sangamo Journal*, March 30, 1843, June 13, 1844; Springfield *Illinois State Register*, August 18, November 17, 1843.

31. Springfield *Sangamo Journal*, January 4, 1844; Springfield *Illinois State Register*, February 16, 23.

32. Springfield *Illinois State Register*, February 16, 23, March 15, 1844; Miers, *Lincoln Day by Day*, I, 223.

33. In 1850, 29 percent of adult white men in Springfield were immigrants. Irish immigrants represented 9.1 percent and German immigrants 8.4 percent; Manuscript U.S. Census, Springfield, Illinois, 1850; Springfield *Illinois State Register*, May 14, 1841, June 21, 1844. In 1860, Stuart was the gubernatorial nominee of the Union Party, which included the remnant of the American Party in Illinois; Arthur Charles Cole, *The Era of the Civil War, 1848–1870*, Vol. 3 of Clarence Walworth Alvord, ed., *The Centennial History of Illinois* (Chicago: A. C. McClurg, 1922), 196.

34. Springfield *Illinois State Register*, July 17, 1840, June 4, 1841, June 21, 1844; Springfield *Sangamo Journal*, July 24, 1840, September 16, 1847.

35. Springfield *Illinois State Register*, April 12, May 15, June 7, August 16, 1844; Springfield *Sangamo Journal*, July 25, 1844; Charles Sellers, "Election of 1844," in Schlesinger and Israel, *History of American Presidential Elections*, I, 747–861, esp. 789.

36. Springfield *Illinois State Register*, July 19, August 1, 9, 1844; Springfield *Sangamo Journal*, August 8, 22, 29, October 31, 1844.

37. Springfield *Illinois State Register*, August 9, 16, 1844; Springfield *Sangamo Journal*, August 1, 29, 1844; Angle, *Here I Have Lived*, 129–30.

38. Vandalia *Illinois State Register and People's Advocate*, June 15, 1838; Springfield *Sangamo Journal*, February 26, 1846, August 6, 1847.

CHAPTER 17

1. Roy P. Basler, ed., *The Collected Works of Abraham Lincoln* (New Brunswick, NJ: Rutgers University Press, 1953), I, 78, 289.

2. *Collected Works*, I, 108–115; Major L. Wilson, "Lincoln and Van Buren in the Steps of the Fathers: Another Look at the Lyceum Address," *Civil War History*, 29 (September 1983), 197–211; Mark Neely, "Lincoln's Lyceum Speech and the Origins of a Modern Myth," *Lincoln Lore*, 1776 (February 1987), 1–3; Thomas F. Schwartz, "The Springfield Lyceum and Lincoln's 1838 Speech," *Illinois Historical Journal*, 83 (Spring 1990), 45–49; Louis Filler, *The Crusade Against Slavery, 1830–1860* (New York: Harper, 1960), 78–81. Leonard L. Richards, *"Gentlemen of Property and Standing": Anti-Abolition Mobs in Jacksonian America* (New York: Oxford University Press, 1970); Michael Feldberg, *The Turbulent Era: Riot and Disorder in Jacksonian America* (New York: Oxford University Press, 1980), 43–53; and David Grimstead, *American Mobbing, 1828–1861: Toward Civil War* (New York: Oxford University Press, 1998), 33–71, provide overviews of antiabolitionism within the context of antebellum rioting in general.

3. *Collected Works*, I, 108–115.

4. Springfield *Sangamo Journal*, February 15, 1844; Springfield *Illinois Journal*, May 1, June 13, 1849; R. W. D[iller] to Mary Lanphier, March 13, 1848, in Charles H. Lanphier, *Glory to God and the Sucker Democracy: A Manuscript Collection* (Privately Printed, 1973), Vol. 2; Jean H. Baker, *Mary Todd Lincoln: A Biography* (New York: Norton, 1987), 75–9, 202–3, 210.

5. Power, *Early Settlers*, 748.

6. Douglas L. Wilson and Rodney O. Davis, eds., *Herndon's Informants: Letters, Interviews, and Statements About Abraham Lincoln* (Urbana: University of Illinois Press, 1998), 133, 445; Baker, *Mary Todd Lincoln*, 79, 82; J. Duane Squires, "Lincoln's Todd In-Laws," *Lincoln Herald*, 61 (Fall 1967), 121–28; Karen Lystra, *Searching the Heart: Women, Men, and Romantic Love in Nineteenth-Century America* (New York: Oxford University Press, 1989), 160.

7. Wilson and Davis, *Herndon's Informants*, 443; Lystra, *Searching the Heart*, 31; Ellen K. Rothman, *Hands and Hearts: A History of Courtship in America* (New York: Basic Books, 1984), 57, 72; Daniel Scott Smith, "Parental Power and Marriage Patterns: An Analysis of Historical Trends in Hingham, Massachusetts," *Journal of Marriage and the Family*, 35 (August 1973), 419-28; Baker, *Mary Todd Lincoln*, 85–86.

8. Wilson and Davis, *Herndon's Informants*, 443; Rothman, *Hands and Hearts*, 57, 72; Lystra, *Searching the Heart*, 157. Ruth Painter Randall, *Mary Lincoln: Biography of a Marriage* (Boston: Little, Brown, 1953), 36–51; and Douglas L. Wilson, "Abraham Lincoln and 'That Fatal First of January,'" *Civil War History*, 38 (June 1992), 101–30, offer persuasive rebuttals of Herndon's improbable account.

9. *Collected Works*, I, 268, 269; Justin G. Turner and Linda Levitt Turner, *Mary Todd Lincoln: Her Life and Letters* (New York: Fromm International Publishing, 1972), 27; Wilson and Davis, *Herndon's Informants*, 133; Wilson, "That Fatal First," 123.

10. Roy P. Basler, "The Authorship of the 'Rebecca' Letters," *Abraham Lincoln Quarterly*, 2 (March 1942), 80–90; David Herbert Donald, *Lincoln* (New York: Simon and Schuster, 1995), 90–93.

11. W. J. Rorabaugh, "The Political Duel in the Early Republic: Burr v. Hamilton," *Journal of the Early Republic*, 15 (Spring 1995), 1–23; Joanne B. Freeman, "Dueling as Politics: Reinterpreting the Burr-Hamilton Duel," *William and Mary Quarterly*, 53 (April 1996), 289–318.

12. Springfield *Sangamo Journal*, May 23, 1835, July 28, 1838, February 19, 26, March 5, 19, 1841; Earl Schenck Miers, ed., *Lincoln Day by Day: A Chronology, 1809–1865* (Washington, DC: Lincoln Sesquicentennial Commission, 1960), I, 93; Wilson and Davis, *Herndon's Informants*, 451; Nicole Etcheson, "Manliness and the Political Culture of the Old Northwest, 1790–1860," *Journal of the Early Republic*, 15 (Spring 1995), 59–77; Donald, *Lincoln*, 92.

13. John J. Duff, *Abraham Lincoln, Prairie Lawyer* (New York: Bramwell House, 1960), 53–61; Paul M. Angle, *"Here I Have Lived": A History of Lincoln's Springfield* (Springfield: Abraham Lincoln Association, 1935), 115–16.

14. *Collected Works*, I, 302–3; Donald, *Lincoln*, 91-92; Baker, *Mary Todd Lincoln*, 96–97. James E. Myers, *The Astonishing Saber Duel of Abraham Lincoln* (Springfield: Lincoln-Herndon Building Publishers, 1968), provides the fullest narrative of the duel.

15. Baker, *Mary Todd Lincoln*, 94–97; Douglas L. Wilson, *Honor's Voice: The Transformation of Abraham Lincoln* (New York: Knopf, 1998), 165–92.

16. *Collected Works*, I, 305; Wilson and Davis, *Herndon's Informants*, 624, 665; Wilson, "That Fatal First"; Rothman, *Hands and Hearts*, 78–79.

CHAPTER 18

1. Walter B. Stevens, *A Reporter's Lincoln*, ed. Michael Burlingame (Lincoln: University of Nebraska Press, 1998), 94–95.

2. Stevens, *Reporter's Lincoln*, 65.

3. Stevens, *Reporter's Lincoln*, 94–95.

4. Important overviews of the emerging middle class include Stuart M. Blumin, "The Hypothesis of Middle-Class Formation in Nineteenth-Century America: A Critique and Some Proposals," *American Historical Review*, 90 (April 1985), 299–338; Burton J. Bledstein, *The Culture of Professionalism: The Middle Class and the Development of Higher Education in America* (New York: Norton, 1976); Paul E. Johnson, *A Shopkeeper's Millenium: Society and Revivals in Rochester, New York, 1815–1837* (New York: Hill and Wang, 1978); Mary P. Ryan, *Cradle of the Middle Class: The Family in Oneida County, New York, 1790–1865* (New York: Cambridge University Press, 1981); Stuart M. Blumin, *The Emergence of the Middle Class: Social Experience in the American City, 1760–1900* (New York: Cambridge University Press, 1989); Steven Mintz, *Moralists and Modernizers: America's Pre-Civil War Reformers* (Baltimore: Johns Hopkins University Press, 1995). Kathryn Kish Sklar, "Victorian Women and Domestic Life: Mary Todd Lincoln, Elizabeth Cady Stanton, and Harriet Beecher Stowe," in Cullom Davis, Charles B. Strozier, Rebecca Monroe Veach, and Geoffrey C. Ward, eds., *The Public and the Private Lincoln: Contemporary Perspectives* (Carbondale: Southern Illinois University Press, 1979), 20–37; Rodney O. Davis, "Abraham Lincoln: Son and Father," Edgar S. and Ruth W. Burkhardt Lecture Series, Knox College, Galesburg, Illinois, 1997; Kenneth J. Winkle, "The Middle-Class Marriage of Abraham and Mary Lincoln," American Historical Association, Pacific Coast Branch, 1998; and Jean H. Baker, "The Lincoln Marriage: Beyond the Battle of Quotations," Robert Fortenbaugh Memorial Lecture, Gettysburg College, 1999, all examine the impact of various middle-class values on the Lincoln marriage.

5. U.S. Department of Commerce, *Historical Statistics of the United States: Colonial Times to 1970* (Washington, DC: Bureau of the Census, 1975), I, 457. Excellent introductions to the household economy include Christopher Clark, *The Roots of Rural Capitalism: Western Massachusetts, 1780–1860* (Ithaca, NY: Cornell University Press, 1990); Christopher Clark, "Household Economy, Market Exchange and the Rise of Capitalism in the Connecticut Valley, 1800–1860," *Journal of Social History*, 13 (Winter 1979), 169-89; Bruce Laurie, *Artisans into Workers: Labor in Nineteenth-Century America* (New York: Noonday Press, 1989), 15–46; Mary Beth Norton, *Liberty's Daughters: The Revolutionary Experience of American Women, 1750–1800* (Glenview, IL: Scott, Foresman, 1980), 3–39; Jeanne Boydston, *Home and Work: Housework, Wages, and the Ideology of Labor in the Early Republic* (New York: Oxford University Press, 1990); Glenna Matthews, *"Just a Housewife": The Rise and Fall of Domesticity in America* (New York: Oxford University Press, 1987), 3–35; John Mack Faragher, *Women and Men on the Overland Trail* (New Haven, CT: Yale University Press, 1979), 40–65; and John Mack Faragher, *Sugar Creek: Life on the Illinois Prairie* (New Haven, CT: Yale University Press, 1986).

6. Manuscript U.S. Census, Sangamon County, Illinois, 1840; *Compendium of the Enumeration*

of the Inhabitants and Statistics of the United States . . . from the Returns of the Sixth Census [U.S. Census of 1840] (Washington, DC: Thomas Allen, 1841), 87, 302–7.

7. Peter Temin, *The Jacksonian Economy* (New York: Norton, 1969), 17–22, 68–69; and Douglass, C. North, *The Economic Growth of the United States, 1790–1860* (New York: Norton, 1966), 136–37, consider the "Jacksonian boom" of the 1830s. Important studies of middle-class family formation include Nancy F. Cott, *The Bonds of Womanhood: 'Woman's Sphere' in New England, 1780–1835* (New Haven, CT: Yale University Press, 1977); Carl N. Degler, *At Odds: Women and the Family in America from the Revolution to the Present* (New York: Oxford University Press, 1980); Steven Mintz and Susan Kellogg, *Domestic Revolutions: A Social History of American Family Life* (New York: Free Press, 1988), 43–65; Matthews, *Just a Housewife*, 35–65; Boydston, *Home and Work*; Ryan, *Cradle of the Middle Class*; Blumin, *Emergence of the Middle Class*; and William L. Barney, *The Passage of the Republic: An Interdisciplinary History of Nineteenth-Century America* (Lexington, MA: D. C. Heath, 1987), 73–115.

8. Elizabeth McDowell Hill, "Illinois Women: Stories of the Pioneer Mothers of Illinois," Women's Exposition Board, 1893, Illinois State Historical Library, Springfield, Illinois, 24.

9. Springfield *Sangamo Journal*, March 8, 1832, July 6, 1833.

10. Springfield *Sangamo Journal*, December 17, 1836, November 20, 1845; Springfield *Illinois Journal*, May 8, 10, 1850.

11. Springfield *Sangamo Journal*, June 11, December 17, 1836; Douglas L. Wilson and Rodney O. Davis, eds., *Herndon's Informants: Letters, Interviews, and Statements About Abraham Lincoln* (Urbana: University of Illinois Press, 1998), 453; Charles Sellers, *The Market Revolution: Jacksonian America, 1815–1846* (New York: Oxford University Press, 1991).

12. Springfield *Illinois Journal*, May 10, 1850, March 25, April 17, May 31, 1851, February 7, 1852, June 24, 1853, April 21, May 2, 1854; Mrs. Stuart to daughter Elizabeth, May 14, 1855, Stuart-Hay Papers, Illinois State Historical Library.

13. *Sixth Census*, 87; J.D.B. DeBow, *The Seventh Census of the United States, 1850* (Washington, DC: Robert Armstrong, 1853), 727–78; Joseph C. G. Kennedy, *Population of the United States in 1860* [Eighth Census] (Washington, DC: Government Printing Office, 1864), 105–6.

14. Matthews, *Just a Housewife*, 35–65; Richard L. Bushman and Claudia Bushman, "The Early History of Cleanliness in America," *Journal of American History*, 74 (March 1988), 1213–38.

15. Cott, *Bonds of Womanhood*; Mintz and Kellogg, *Domestic Revolutions*, 43–65; Matthews, *Just a Housewife*, 35–65; Ruth Bloch, "American Feminine Ideals in Transition: The Rise of the Moral Mother, 1785–1815," *Feminist Studies*, 4 (June 1978), 100–26; Linda K. Kerber, "The Republican Mother: Women and the Enlightenment—An American Perspective," *American Quarterly*, 28 (Summer 1976), 187–205; Baker, "Lincoln Marriage," 10.

16. Data compiled from Manuscript U.S. Census, Sangamon County, Illinois, 1850. The analysis includes all 921 white adult male household heads living in Springfield in 1850. This study defines middle-class families as all households headed by white adult males who practiced productive but nonmanual occupations—"head work" rather than "hand work"—primarily in commerce, the professions, services, and public office. The remaining families, whose heads engaged in manual occupations, such as manufacturing, building, labor, transportation, and agriculture, or were nonproductive, represent Springfield's working class. In 1840, one-fourth of all Springfield families belonged to the middle class, and this cohort remained stable until 1860. The midpoint of these two decades, 1850, provides a representative look at the middle class in Springfield. White adult male household heads practicing nonmanual but productive occupations in Springfield represented 28.4 percent in 1840, 26.5 percent in 1850, and 27.4 percent in 1860; Manuscript U.S. Census, Sangamon County, Illinois, 1840, 1850, and 1860. It is possible but not particularly helpful to identify a small upper class in Springfield consisting of the top decile of wealthholders as reported in the U.S. Census. Such a quantitative definition, however, reveals only minor differences between the middle and upper classes. Upper-class men were on average three years older than middle-class men, employed two servants rather than one in their homes, and were more heavily native-born—90 percent.

17. Roy P. Basler, ed., *The Collected Works of Abraham Lincoln* (New Brunswick, NJ: Rutgers University Press, 1953), I, 496.

18. Manuscript U.S. Census, Sangamon County, Illinois, 1850, linked with Manuscript Poll Books, Sangamon County, Illinois, 1848, Illinois State Historical Library, Springfield, Illinois, 1848. To determine the outlines of Lincoln's circle of acquaintances in Springfield, I matched the names of all voters who appeared in either the 1850 or 1860 U.S. manuscript census with the indexes in *Collected Works*; and Earl Schenck Miers, ed., *Lincoln Day by Day: A Chronology, 1809–1865* (Washington, DC: Lincoln Sesquicentennial Commission, 1960). This seemed the only feasible method of

matching the nearly 3,000 names with all surviving written records dealing with Lincoln. By including only those acquaintances whose names appeared in written records, this analysis overlooks Lincoln's more casual acquaintances and focuses on those who were important enough to appear in Lincoln's correspondence and personal records.

19. Jean H. Baker, *Mary Todd Lincoln: A Biography* (New York: Norton, 1987), 4, 6, 12, 32–34, 37, 40–45, 55, 62–63; Ruth Painter Randall, *Mary Lincoln: Biography of a Marriage* (Boston: Little, Brown), 1953), 23, 25. Richard C. Wade, *The Urban Frontier: The Rise of Western Cities, 1790–1830* (Cambridge, MA: Harvard University Press, 1959), offers a succinct examination of social and cultural life in Lexington and other early western cities.

20. Baker, *Mary Todd Lincoln*, 99–100; Michael Burlingame, ed., *An Oral History of Abraham Lincoln: John G. Nicolay's Interviews and Essays* (Carbondale: Southern Illinois University Press, 1996), 27. John Modell, Frank F. Furstenberg Jr., and Theodore Hershberg, "Social Change and Transitions to Adulthood in Historical Perspective," *Journal of Family History*, 1 (Autumn 1976), 7–32, esp. 18, note that "Frequently, household formation did not occur until the early 30s for nineteenth-century males, and a delay between marriage and the establishment of a separate household was frequent. During this period, the newlyweds resided in the home of parents or boarded with another family."

21. Springfield *Sangamo Journal*, August 9, 1839, April 10, June 19, 1840; Springfield *Illinois State Register*, October 12, 1839; Jeff G. Gavin, *Past Sites of Springfield: A Historic Guide to the Downtown Area*, typescript, Sangamon Valley Collection, Lincoln Library, 1980, 10.

22. Manuscript U.S. Census, Springfield, Illinois, 1850, linked with *Marriage Records, Sangamon County, Illinois, 1821–1840* (Springfield: Sangamon County Genealogical Society, 1987).

23. David Hackett Fischer, *Growing Old in America* (New York: Oxford University Press, 1977), 98–99; Baker, *Mary Todd Lincoln*, 102–3; Randall, *Mary Lincoln*, 83.

24. Wayne C. Temple, *By Square and Compasses: The Building of Lincoln's Home and Its Saga* (Bloomington, IL: Ashlar Press, 1984), 1–3, 8; Thomas J. Dyba and George L. Painter, *Seventeen Years at Eighth and Jackson*, 2nd ed. (Lisle, IL: IBC Pubications, 1985), 7, 10; Baker, *Mary Todd Lincoln*, 103.

25. Springfield *Illinois State Register*, July 1, 1842.

26. Michael Burlingame, *The Inner World of Abraham Lincoln* (Urbana: University of Illinois Press, 1994), 268-355; and Baker, *Mary Todd Lincoln*, 99–162, present the most recent and comprehensive analyses of the Lincolns' domestic life in Springfield, while reaching starkly different conclusions.

27. Miers, *Lincoln Day by Day*, I, 281. Between 1850 and 1860, 28.7 percent of Springfield's household heads fell from the middle class to the working class; Manuscript U.S. Census, Sangamon County, Illinois, 1850 and 1860.

28. Paul Angle, ed., *Herndon's Life of Lincoln* (Cleveland: World, 1942), 345.

29. Henry B. Rankin, *Intimate Character Sketches of Abraham Lincoln* (Philadelphia: J. B. Lippincott, 1924), 117, 164; Burlingame, *Inner World of Abraham Lincoln*, 273; Davis, "Abraham Lincoln: Son and Father," 13–14; Rosalind Rosenberg, *Divided Lives: American Women in the Twentieth Century* (New York: Hill and Wang, 1992).

30. Rankin, *Intimate Character Sketches*, 53, 58; Robert H. Wiebe, "Lincoln's Fraternal Democracy," in John L. Thomas, ed., *Abraham Lincoln and the American Political Tradition* (Amherst: University of Massachusetts Press, 1986), 11–30.

31. Burlingame, *Inner World of Abraham Lincoln*, 321.

32. *Herndon's Life of Lincoln*, 342–43, 345; Burlingame, *Inner World of Abraham Lincoln*, 274.

33. Davis and Wilson, *Herndon's Informants*, 349; *Herndon's Life of Lincoln*, 343, 349; Stevens, *Reporter's Lincoln*, 119; Burlingame, *Inner World of Abraham Lincoln*, 271–72, 274, 320; Ruth Painter Randall, *Mary Lincoln: Biography of a Marriage* (Boston: Little, Brown, 1953), 79; Davis, "Abraham Lincoln: Son and Father," 14.

34. Burlingame, *Inner World of Abraham Lincoln*, 271–72, 274, 320; Christopher Lasch, *Haven in a Heartless World: The Family Besieged* (New York: Basic Books, 1977).

35. Springfield *Illinois State Journal*, September 18, 1855; Burlingame, *Inner World of Abraham Lincoln*, 277.

36. Burlingame, *Inner World of Abraham Lincoln*, 274–75, 276, 279; Justin G. Turner and Linda Levitt Turner, *Mary Todd Lincoln: Her Life and Letters* (New York: Fromm International, 1987), 50.

37. Springfield *Illinois State Journal*, May 8, 1850, July 12, 1853, April 2, 1855; Springfield *Illinois State Register*, September 5, 1845; Turner and Levitt Turner, *Mary Todd Lincoln*, 59; James and

Sarah McConnell to James and Sarah Smith, September 8, 1849, James and E. F. McConnell Papers, Illinois State Historical Library, Springfield, Illinois;

38. Davis and Wilson, *Herndon's Informants*, 597; Turner and Turner, *Mary Todd Lincoln*, 46, 59, 61.

39. Davis and Wilson, *Herndon's Informants*, 407, 512, 646; Dyba and Painter, *Seventeen Years at Eighth and Jackson*, 10; Burlingame, *Inner World of Abraham Lincoln*, 274–75, 276, 279; Davis, *Abraham Lincoln: Son and Father*, 14–16.

40. Davis and Wilson, *Herndon's Informants*, 407, 443, 453; William L. Barney, *The Passage of the Republic: An Interdisciplinary History of Nineteenth-Century America* (Lexington, MA: D. C. Heath, 1987), 88; Burlingame, *Inner World of Abraham Lincoln*, 268.

41. Davis and Wilson, *Herndon's Informants*, 63, 348–49; 443, 445, 623; Davis, "Abraham Lincoln: Son and Father," 5; Baker, "Lincoln Marriage," 26.

42. Burlingame, *Inner World of Abraham Lincoln*, 268–355.

43. These data include white adult household heads who lived in Springfield in 1850 and divorced between 1850 and 1860; Manuscript U.S. Census, Sangamon County, Illinois, 1850, linked with Divorce Index, Sangamon County, Illinois, 1850–1860, Illinois Regional Archives Depository, University of Illinois–Springfield, Springfield, Illinois. For the circle of Lincoln's acquaintances, consult note 13. Lincoln, as a lawyer, represented many couples in divorce proceedings, which undoubtedly increased the proportion of his acquaintances who divorced during the 1850s. Stacy Pratt McDermott, "Dissolving the Bonds of Matrimony: Women and Divorce in Sangamon County, Illinois, 1837–1860," in Daniel W. Stowell, ed., *In Tender Consideration: Women, Families, and the Law in Abraham Lincoln's Illinois* (Urbana: University of Illinois Press, forthcoming), provides an essential overview of attitudes toward divorce in Sangamon County. John Mack Faragher, *Sugar Creek: Life on the Illinois Prairie* (New Haven, CT: Yale University Press, 1986), 79–86, discusses divorce within a rural community.

CHAPTER 19

1. Douglas L. Wilson and Rodney O. Davis, eds., *Herndon's Informants: Letters, Interviews, and Statements About Abraham Lincoln* (Urbana: University of Illinois Press, 1998), 185. Mario M. Cuomo and Harold Holzer, eds., *Lincoln on Democracy* (New York: Harper, 1990), summarize current interpretations of Lincoln's commitment to democratic values.

2. Richard Hofstadter, "Abraham Lincoln and the Self-Made Myth," in *The American Political Tradition and the Men Who Made It* (New York: Vintage, 1948), 93–136, esp. 95, 97; Joel H. Silbey, "'Always a Whig in Politics': The Partisan Life of Abraham Lincoln," *Papers of the Abraham Lincoln Association*, 8 (1986), 21–42, esp. 37. Merrill D. Peterson, *Lincoln in American Memory* (New York: Oxford University Press, 1994), provides the best overview of changing Lincoln historiography.

3. *Illinois Constitution of 1818*, art. 2, sec. 27; *Illinois Constitution of 1848*, art. 6, sec. 1; *Illinois Laws* (1849), 71. In 1850, 921 of Springfield's 4,533 residents were white adult males; Manuscript U.S. Census, Sangamon County, Illinois, 1850.

4. Kenneth J. Winkle, "The Voters of Lincoln's Springfield: Migration and Politial Participation in an Antebellum City," *Journal of Social History*, 25 (Spring 1992), 595–611, esp. 6, 12.

5. Kenneth J. Winkle, "The Second Party System in Lincoln's Springfield," *Civil War History*, 44 (December 1998), 267–84, esp. 279; Manuscript Poll Books, Sangamon County, Illinois, 1850–60, linked with Manuscript U.S. Census, Sangamon County, Illinois, 1850 and 1860.

6. Standard accounts of Lincoln's election to Congress include Donald W. Riddle, *Lincoln Runs for Congress* (New Brunswick, NJ: Rutgers University Press, 1948); Mark E. Neely Jr., "Lincoln and the Mexican War: An Argument by Analogy," *Civil War History*, 24 (March 1978), 5–24; and David Herbert Donald, *Lincoln* (New York: Simon and Schuster, 1995), 113–15. John Todd Stuart won the Third Congressional District in 1838 and 1841; John J. Hardin, Edward D. Baker, and Abraham Lincoln won the Seventh District in 1843, 1844, and 1846, respectively. Whigs lost the district in 1848. Winkle, "Second Party System," 272–77.

7. Henry C. Whitney, *Life of Lincoln* (New York: Baker and Taylor, 1908), I, 169.

8. Roy P. Basler, ed., *The Collected Works of Abraham Lincoln* (New Brunswick, NJ: Rutgers University Press, 1953), I, 349.

9. *Collected Works*, I, 350.

10. Springfield *Sangamo Journal*, November 20, 1845; *Collected Works*, I, 351–54. Lincoln lost

Putnam, Marshall, and Woodford, with about 40 percent of the vote, but won the remaining eight counties with 58 percent; Theodore Calvin Pease, ed., *Illinois Election Returns, 1818–1848* (Springfield: Illinois State Historical Library, 1923), 159.

11. *Collected Works*, I, 351–52.

12. Winkle, "Voters of Lincoln's Springfield," 606.

13. *Collected Works*, I, 352–54.

14. Springfield *Sangamo Journal*, February 26, 1846.

15. *Collected Works*, I, 356–57.

16. Springfield *Sangamo Journal*, February 5, 26, March 5, 1846; Springfield *Illinois State Register*, May 8, 1846; Earl Schenck Miers, ed., *Lincoln Day by Day: A Chronology, 1809–1865* (Washington, DC: Lincoln Sesquicentennial Commission, 1960), I, 267; Riddle, *Lincoln Runs for Congress*, 155; Donald, *Lincoln*, 114.

17. *Collected Works*, I, 347; Springfield *Sangamo Journal*, June 4, 1846; Springfield *Illinois State Register*, May 8, 1846; Miers, *Lincoln Day by Day*, 266, 273, 274; Neely, "Lincoln and the Mexican War," 13.

18. Springfield *Illinois State Register*, August 11, 1848.

19. *Collected Works*, I, 382–84. Allen C. Guelzo, *Abraham Lincoln: Redeemer President* (Grand Rapids, MI: Eerdmans, 1999), 143–60, provides the most convincing portrait of Lincoln's religious skepticism.

20. *Collected Works*, I, 389–91; Springfield *Sangamo Journal*, June 18, August 13, 1846; Springfield *Illinois State Register*, August 7, 1846.

21. Michael Burlingame, ed., *An Oral History of Abraham Lincoln: John G. Nicolay's Interviews and Essays* (Carbondale: Southern Illinois University Press, 1996), 38; John J. Duff, *Abraham Lincoln, Prairie Lawyer* (New York: Bramwell House, 1960), 97–117.

22. Springfield *Illinois State Journal*, October 28, 1847; Jean H. Baker, *Mary Todd Lincoln: A Biography* (New York: Norton, 1987), 136–38.

23. *Collected Works*, I, 465–66; Baker, *Mary Todd Lincoln*, 141.

24. *Collected Works*, I, 420–22; Springfield *Illinois State Journal*, February 18, 1847; G. S. Borit, "Lincoln's Opposition to the Mexican War," *Journal of the Illinois State Historical Society*, 67 (February 1974), 79–100. Donald W. Riddle, *Congressman Abraham Lincoln* (Urbana: University of Illinois Press, 1957), provides the fullest account of Lincoln's single term in Congress.

25. Springfield *Illinois State Register*, January 7, 14, 1848; Springfield *Illinois State Journal*, January 12, 1848; Neely, "Lincoln and the Mexican War"; Borit, "Lincoln's Opposition to the Mexican War."

26. *Collected Works*, I, 431, 446–47; Springfield *Illinois State Register*, April 11, 1845; Springfield *Illinois State Journal*, April 6, 1848; William H. Herndon and Jesse W. Weik, *Herndon's Life of Lincoln*, ed. Paul M. Angle (Cleveland: World, 1942), 226; Mark Neely, "Did Lincoln Cause Logan's Defeat?" *Lincoln Lore*, 1660 (June 1976), 1–4; Riddle, *Congressman Abraham Lincoln*, 113–27, offers the best single account of the 1846 election in the Seventh District.

27. Springfield *Illinois State Register*, May 19, June 23, July 28, August 11, 1848; Borit, "Lincoln's Opposition to the Mexican War," 93, 95.

28. Springfield *Illinois State Journal*, August 2, 1848; Borit, "Lincoln's Opposition to the Mexican War," 95.

29. Springfield *Illinois State Journal*, August 5, September 6, 1848; Davis and Wilson, *Herndon's Informants*, 348, 468; Burlingame, *Oral History of Abraham Lincoln*, 28; Borit, "Lincoln's Opposition to the Mexican War," 95.

30. Springfield *Illinois State Register*, August 11, 1848.

31. *Collected Works*, I, 518–19.

32. Manuscript Poll Books, Sangamon County, Illinois, Illinois State Historical Library, Springfield, Illinois, 1846 and 1848; Borit, "Lincoln's Opposition to the Mexican War," 95. Harris received 49.8 percent of the vote, Logan 49.1 percent, and Wright 1.1 percent.

33. Springfield *Illinois State Register*, October 8, 1847. Basic introductions to the Free Soil Party include Frederick J. Blue, *The Free Soilers: Third Party Politics, 1848–1854* (Urbana: University of Illinois Press, 1973); David Potter, *The Impending Crisis, 1848–1861* (New York: Harper, 1976), 51–89; Louis Filler, *The Crusade Against Slavery, 1830–1860* (New York: Harper, 1960), 186–91; Richard H. Sewell, *A House Divided: Sectionalism and Civil War, 1848–1865* (Baltimore: Johns Hopkins University Press, 1988), 22–39; Richard H. Sewell, *Ballots for Freedom: Antislavery Politics in the United States, 1837–1860* (New York: Oxford University Press, 1976), 170–201; and Aileen S.

Kraditor, "The Liberty and Free Soil Parties," in Arthur M. Schlesinger, Jr. ed., *History of U.S. Political Parties* (New York: Chelsea House, 1973), I: 741–81.

34. Springfield *Illinois State Journal*, October 25, 1848; Springfield *Illinois State Register*, September 8, 29, 1848.

35. *Collected Works*, I, 347–48, 468, 501–16; Springfield *Illinois State Journal*, August 23, 1848; Harry E. Pratt, *The Personal Finances of Abraham Lincoln* (Springfield, IL: Abraham Lincoln Association, 1943), 101.

36. *Collected Works*, II, 3, 13; Riddle, *Congressman Abraham Lincoln*, 140; Neely, "Did Lincoln Cause Logan's Defeat," 4.

37. Linking the voters of 1848, listed in poll books, with the U.S. Census of 1850 permits a comparison of the personal characteristics of Whigs and Democrats. Record linkage reveals that only about one-fourth (24.2 percent) of the voters of 1848 remained in Springfield long enough to appear in the 1850 census. Of the 1,838 voters, only 444 were still living in Springfield in 1850. As a rule of thumb, death claimed about 2 percent of the American population per year during the nineteenth century, so death probably accounted for only 4 percent of these disappearances. Migration out of Springfield must have claimed the remaining voters. Interestingly, Whigs and Democrats disappeared from Springfield at nearly identical rates. In 1850, 23.8 percent of the Whig voters appeared in the U.S. Census, as did 23.9 percent of the Democrats. Considerably more of the Free Soil voters, 38.5 percent, persisted between 1848 and 1850, but they numbered only 15 voters. Manuscript Poll Books, Sangamon County, Illinois, Illinois State Historical Library, Springfield, Illinois, 1848, linked with Manuscript U.S. Census, Sangamon County, Illinois, 1850.

38. Springfield *Illinois State Register*, October 29, 1841, April 17, 1844; Springfield *Sangamo Journal*, January 5, 1839, March 30, 1843; Springfield *Illinois State Journal*, April 1, 1847.

39. Springfield *Sangamo Journal*, August 11, 1838. Kenneth J. Winkle, "The Second Party System in Lincoln's Springfield," *Civil War History*, 84 (December 1998), 267–84, provides a more detailed analysis of the occupations of Whig and Democratic voters in 1848.

40. Springfield *Illinois State Register*, July 17, 1840, June 4, 1841; Springfield *Sangamo Journal*, July 24, 1840; Springfield *Illinois Journal*, September 16, 1847.

41. Springfield *Illinois Journal*, November 15, 1848; Springfield *Illinois State Register*, September 29, 1848. For a more detailed analysis of the birthplaces of Whig and Democratic voters in 1848, consult Winkle, "Second Party System in Lincoln's Springfield.".

42. *Collected Works*, I, 477; Springfield *Illinois State Journal*, November 29, December 6, 1848; Manuscript Poll Books, Sangamon County, Illinois, Illinois State Historical Library, Springfield, Illinois, 1844 and 1848.

CHAPTER 20

1. Paul Finkelman, "Slavery and the Northwest Ordinance: A Study in Ambiguity," *Journal of the Early Republic*, 6 (Winter 1986), 343–70; Peter Onuf, "From Constitution to Higher Law: The Reinterpretation of the Northwest Ordinance," *Ohio History*, 94 (Winter/Spring 1985), 5–33; James E. Davis, *Frontier Illinois* (Bloomington: Indiana University Press, 1998), 101, 116–17; David Brion Davis, "The Significance of Excluding Slavery from the Old Northwest in 1787," *Indiana Magazine of History*, 84 (March 1988), 75–89; Eugene Berwanger, *The Frontier Against Slavery: Western Anti-Negro Prejudice and the Slavery Extension Controversy* (Urbana: University of Illinois Press, 1967), 7–29; William L. Barney, *The Passage of the Republic: An Interdisciplinary History of Nineteenth-Century America* (Lexington, MA: D. C. Heath,1987), 65.

2. Paul Finkelman, "Slavery, the 'More Perfect Union,' and the Prairie State," *Illinois Historical Journal*, 80 (Winter 1987), 248–69; Robert P. Howard, *Illinois: A History of the Prairie State* (Grand Rapids, MI: Eerdmans, 1972), 130–31; Davis, *Frontier Illinois*, 116–17.

3. Theodore Calvin Pease, *The Frontier State, 1818–1848*, Vol. 2 of Clarence Walworth Alvord, ed., *The Centennial History of Illinois* (Chicago: A. C. McClurg, 1922), 47, 49; Howard, *Illinois*, 131; Davis, *Frontier Illinois*, 166–67; Finkelman, "Slavery and the Northwest Ordinance," 369.

4. Roy P. Basler, ed., *The Collected Works of Abraham Lincoln* (New Brunswick, NJ: Rutgers University Press, 1953), III, 511, IV, 62, VII, 281; Douglas L. Wilson and Rodney O. Davis, eds., *Herndon's Informants: Letters, Interviews, and Statements About Abraham Lincoln* (Urbana: University of Illinois Press, 1998), 457; Paul Simon, *Lincoln's Preparation for Greatness: The Illinois Legislative Years* (Urbana: University of Illinois Press, 1965), 128–29; Benjamin Quarles, *Lincoln and the Negro* (New York: Oxford University Press, 1962), 16–19.

5. Manuscript U.S. Census, Sangamon County, Illinois, 1830; Sangamon County Commissioners Record, Illinois State Archives, Springfield, Illinois, March 7, 1827, March 4, 1834; Sangamon County Indentures of Apprenticeship, Illinois State Historical Library, Springfield, Illinois; Richard E. Hart, "Honest Abe and the African Americans: A Groundbreaking Study of How Blacks in Early Springfield Influenced Lincoln's Views on Race and Society," *Illinois Times*, 23 (February 12, 1998), 6–11, esp. 7; Richard E. Hart, "Springfield's African Americans as a Part of the Lincoln Community," *Journal of the Abraham Lincoln Association*, 20 (Winter 1999), 35–54, esp. 41; Elmer Gertz, "The Black Laws of Illinois," *Journal of the Illinois State Historical Society*, 56 (Autumn 1963), 454–73, esp. 466.

6. Springfield *Sangamo Journal*, December 17, 1836; Manuscript U.S. Census, Springfield, Illinois, 1840; Sangamon County Indentures of Apprenticeship, Illinois State Historical Library, Springfield, Illinois.

7. Thomas William Taylor to Pascal P. Enos, April 26, May 15, 1830, Pascal P. Enos Papers, Illinois State Historical Library, Springfield, Illinois; Sangamon County Commissioners Record, Illinois State Archives, Springfield, Illinois, December 6, 1831; Springfield *Sangamo Journal*, March 2, 1833.

8. Springfield *Sangamo Journal*, September 24, 1836, July 3, 1840, May 9, 1844; Springfield *Illinois Journal*, November 14, 1850.

9. *Collected Works*, I, 48, II, 498; Simon, *Lincoln's Preparation for Greatness*, 130; LaWanda Cox, *Lincoln and Black Freedom: A Study in Presidential Leadership* (Urbana: University of Illinois Press, 1985), 117–31. In his last public address on April 11, 1865, Lincoln announced that he would prefer that suffrage "were now conferred on the very intelligent, and on those who serve our cause as soldiers"; *Collected Works*, VIII, 403.

10. Springfield *Sangamo Journal*, April 28, 1838, February 18, 1842; Springfield *Illinois State Register*, August 15, 1845. Foster claimed to have lived in Springfield for "two or three years" but was not listed in the Manuscript U.S. Census, Sangamon County, Illinois, 1840, compiled less than two years earlier.

11. P. J. Staudenraus, *The African Colonization Movement, 1816–1865* (New York: Columbia University Press, 1961), 27–29; Floyd J. Miller, *The Search for a Black Nationality: Black Emigration and Colonization, 1787–1963* (Urbana: University of Illinois Press, 1975), 54–90; Leonard P. Curry, *The Free Black in Urban America, 1800–1850: The Shadow of the Dream* (Chicago: University of Chicago Press, 1981), 232–37; Louis Filler, *The Crusade Against Slavery, 1830–1860* (New York: Harper, 1960), 20; George M. Fredrickson, *The Black Image in the White Mind: The Debate on Afro-American Character and Destiny, 1817–1914* (New York: Harper and Row, 1971), 6-32; Leon F. Litwack, *North of Slavery: The Negro in the Free States, 1790–1860* (Chicago: University of Chicago Press, 1961), 20–24.

12. Springfield *Sangamo Journal*, November 17, 1832, August 31, 1833.

13. Springfield *Sangamo Journal*, August 23, October 4, 18, November 2, 1839; Springfield *Illinois State Register*, October 5, 1839, July 10, 1840; Sangamon County Indentures of Apprenticeship; Davis, *Frontier Illinois*, 258.

14. Springfield *Sangamo Journal*, August 23, October 4, 18, November 2, 1839, January 23, 1845; Springfield *Illinois State Register*, October 5, 1839, July 10, 1840, January 17, 1845; Springfield *Illinois Journal*, June 1, 1852; Manuscript Poll Books, Sangamon County, Illinois, Illinois State Historical Library, Springfield, Illinois, 1848.

15. Springfield *Illinois State Register*, November 5, 1847, February 18, 1848; Springfield *Illinois Journal*, May 25, 1848; Manuscript U.S. Census, Springfield, Illinois, 1850; Elder S. S. Ball, *Liberia: The Condition and Prospects of That Republic; Made from Actual Observation* (Alton, IL: Printed at the "Telegraph" Office, 1848), 12, 14; Hart, "Honest Abe and the African Americans," 10–11; Hart, "Springfield's African Americans," 52; Miller, *Search for a Black Nationality*, 54, 140–41; Curry, *Free Black in Urban America*, 232–36; Litwack, *North of Slavery*, 24–27.

16. Springfield *Sangamo Journal*, January 25, February 4, 1842; Springfield *Illinois Journal*, June 14, 21, 1850, November 2, 22, 1852; Hart, "Springfield's African Americans," 52–54.

17. Springfield *Sangamo Journal*, June 25, 1836, October 28, 1837; Springfield *Illinois State Register*, June 7, 1844; Filler, *Crusade Against Slavery*, 78–81; Leonard L. Richards, *"Gentlemen of Property and Standing": Anti-Abolition Mobs in Jacksonian America* (New York: Oxford University Press, 1970); Michael Feldberg, *The Turbulent Era: Riot and Disorder in Jacksonian America* (New York: Oxford University Press, 1980), 43–53.

18. *Collected Works*, I, 74–75, IV, 65; Simon, *Lincoln's Preparation for Greatness*, 132–34.

19. *Collected Works*, I, 260, 320, 323; Joshua F. Speed, *Reminiscences of Abraham Lincoln and Notes of a Visit to California* (Louisville: John P. Morton, 1884), 39–40; Robert L. Kincaid, "Joshua

Fry Speed—1814–1882: Abraham Lincoln's Most Intimate Friend," *Filson Club History Quarterly*, 17 (April 1943), 63–123, esp. 67, 69.

20. Donald W. Riddle, *Congressman Abraham Lincoln* (Urbana: University of Illinois Press, 1957), 164, 166, 171–72, 178-79. Allen C. Guelzo, *Abraham Lincoln: Redeemer President* (Grand Rapids, MI: Eerdmans, 1999), 123–38, offers an insightful analysis of the development of Lincoln's views on slavery and race.

21. John J. Duff, *Abraham Lincoln, Prairie Lawyer* (New York: Bramwell House, 1960), 86–87.

22. Duff, *Abraham Lincoln, Prairie Lawyer*, 130–49; David Herbert Donald, *Lincoln* (New York: Simon and Schuster, 1995), 103–4; Filler, *Crusade Against Slavery*, 200.

23. Springfield *Sangamo Journal*, November 7, 1835; *Illinois Constitution* (1848), Art. XIII, Sec. 16; Arthur Charles Cole, ed., *The Constitutional Debates of 1847* (Springfield: Illinois State Historical Library, 1919), xxvi–xxvii, 201–2; Arvarh E. Strickland, "The Illinois Background of Lincoln's Attitude Toward Slavery and the Negro," *Journal of the Illinois State Historical Society*, 56 (Autumn 1963), 474–94, esp. 486; Litwack, *North of Slavery*, 70–71; Berwanger, *Frontier Against Slavery*, 44–45; Finkelman, "Slavery and the Northwest Ordinance," 368.

24. Cole, *Constitutional Debates of 1847*, xxvi–xxvii, 203, 209, 213, 219; Sangamon County Indentures of Apprenticeship; Janet Cornelius, *Constitution Making in Illinois, 1818–1970* (Urbana: University of Illinois Press, 1972), 40–41.

25. Cole, *Constitutional Debates of 1847*, xxvi–xxvii, 203, 209, 213, 219, 873–74.

26. Springfield *Sangamo Journal*, March 16, April 20, 1848; Litwack, *North of Slavery*, 70–71; Strickland, "Illinois Background of Lincoln's Attitude toward Slavery," 486–87.

27. Analysis of support for the restrictive clause in Springfield is based on the 252 voters who participated in the constitutional referendum in March 1848 and remained in the city long enough to appear in the 1850 census; Manuscript Poll Books, Springfield, Illinois, Illinois State Historical Library, Springfield, Illinois, 1848, linked with Manuscript U.S. Census, Springfield, Illinois, 1850.

28. Manuscript Poll Books, Springfield, Illinois, 1848, linked with Manuscript U.S. Census, Springfield, Illinois, 1850; Cole, *Constitutional Debates of 1847*, 861; Gertz, "Black Laws of Illinois," 466; James P. Jones, "The Illinois Negro Law of 1853: Racism in a Free State," *Illinois Quarterly*, 40 (Winter 1977), 5–22.

29. Manuscript U.S. Census, Springfield, Illinois, 1850; Springfield *Illinois Journal*, April 1, 1854.

30. Manuscript U.S. Census, Springfield, Illinois, 1850; Cole, *Constitutional Debates of 1847*, 217; Barney, *Passage of the Republic*, 67. Illinois law defined a "mulatto" as anyone of at least one-fourth African ancestry; Gertz, "Black Laws of Illinois," 466.

31. Springfield *Sangamo Journal*, September 6, 1834; Hart, "Honest Abe and the African Americans," 9.

32. Springfield *Illinois Journal*, January 23, 1850; Manuscript U.S. Census, Springfield, Illinois, 1850; Larry Gara, "The Underground Railroad in Illinois," *Journal of the Illinois State Historical Society*, 56 (Autumn 1963), 508–28; Hart, "Springfield's African Americans," 47. Basic overviews of the Compromise of 1850 and the Fugitive Slave Law include David Potter, *The Impending Crisis, 1848–1861* (New York: Harper, 1976), 90–120; Holman Hamilton, *Prologue to Conflict: The Crisis and Compromise of 1850* (Lexington: University of Kentucky Press, 1964); Stanley W. Campbell, *The Slave Catchers: Enforcement of the Fugitive Slave Law, 1850–1860* (Chapel Hill: University of North Carolina Press, 1968); Filler, *Crusade Against Slavery*, 192–217; and Richard H. Sewell, *A House Divided: Sectionalism and Civil War, 1848–1865* (Baltimore: Johns Hopkins University Press, 1988), 22–39. Jenkins also appears in historical records as Jimison Jenkins.

33. Springfield *Illinois Journal*, January 17, 22, 23, 25, 1850.

34. Springfield *Illinois Journal*, March 28, April 14, 1851.

35. *Collected Works*, II, 130–32; Mark Neely, "American Nationalism in the Image of Henry Clay: Abraham Lincoln's Eulogy on Henry Clay in Context," *Register of the Kentucky Historical Society*, 73 (January 1975), 31–60; Michael Vorenberg, "Abraham Lincoln and the Politics of Black Colonization," *Journal of the Abraham Lincoln Association*, 14 (Summer 1993), 23–45, esp. 26; Staudenraus, *African Colonization Movement*, 242–43; G. S. Boritt, "The Voyage to the Colony of Linconia," *The Historian*, 37 (August 1975), 619–33; Mark E. Neely, Jr., "Abraham Lincoln and Black Colonization: Benjamin Butler's Spurious Testimony," *Civil War History*, 25 (March 1979), 77–83; George M. Fredrickson, "A Man but Not a Brother: Abraham Lincoln and Racial Equality," *Journal of Southern History*, 41 (February 1975), 39–58; Don E. Fehrenbacher, "Only His Stepchildren: Lincoln and the Negro," *Civil War History*, 20 (December 1974), 293–310; Gary R. Planck, "Abraham Lincoln and Black Colonization: Theory and Practice," *Lincoln Herald*, 72 (Summer

1970), 61–77; Jason H. Silverman, "'In Isles Beyond the Main': Abraham Lincoln's Philosophy on Black Colonization," *Lincoln Herald*, 80 (Fall 1978), 115–22. Arthur Zilversmit, "Lincoln and the Problem of Race: A Decade of Interpretations," *Papers of the Abraham Lincoln Association*, 2 (Summer 1980), 22–45, esp. 34–38, provides a succinct historiographical review of Lincoln's attitudes.

36. *Collected Works*, II, 130–32.

37. *Collected Works*, II, 298–99.

38. Manuscript U.S. Census, Springfield, Illinois, 1850 and 1860; J.D.B. DeBow, *The Seventh Census of the United States, 1850* (Washington, DC: Robert Armstrong, 1853), 702; Joseph C. G. Kennedy, *Population of the United States in 1860* [Eighth Census] (Washington, DC: Government Printing Office, 1864), 87.

39. Manuscript U.S. Census, Springfield, Illinois, 1860; Roberta Senechal, *The Sociogenesis of a Race Riot* (Urbana: University of Illinois Press, 1990).

40. Wilson and Davis, *Herndon's Informants*, 597; Lloyd Ostendorf and Walter Oleksy, *Lincoln's Unknown Private Life: An Oral History of His Black Housekeeper, Mariah Vance, 1850–1860* (Mamaroneck, NY: Hastings House, 1995), 23, 34, 36; Hart, "Springfield's African Americans," 46; Quarles, *Lincoln and the Negro*, 194–95; Roy P. Basler, "Lincoln, Blacks, and Women," in Cullom Davis, Charles B. Strozier, Rebecca Monroe Veach, and Geoffrey C. Ward, eds., *The Public and the Private Lincoln: Contemporary Perspectives* (Carbondale: Southern Illinois University Press, 1979), 38–53, esp. 49. Vance reputedly worked part-time for the Lincolns between 1850 and 1858 and then full-time until she moved to Danville, Illinois, in November 1860. The Manuscript U.S. Census, Springfield, Illinois, 1860, however, records her living at home with her husband, Henry, a laborer, and nine children in June 1860. The same census shows two white servants, a boy and a girl, living with the Lincolns. In 1923, Mary Miner Hill reminisced that the Lincolns had a "colored servant" but puts the date at 1861, when the family left for Washington, three months after Vance moved to Danville; Mary Miner Hill Memoirs, 1923, Illinois State Historical Library, Springfield, Illinois.

41. Springfield *Sangamo Journal*, December 17, 1832; John Carroll Power, *History of the Early Settlers of Sangamon County, Illinois* (Springfield, IL: Edwin A. Wilson, 1876), 58, 303, 517; Lloyd Ostendorf, "The Story of William Florville, Mr. Lincoln's Barber," *Lincoln Herald*, 79 (Spring 1977), 29–32.

42. Manuscript U.S. Census, Springfield, Illinois, 1850 and 1860; Ostendorf, "Story of William Florville"; Quarles, *Lincoln and the Negro*, 26–28.

43. Quarles, *Lincoln and the Negro*, 243–44.

CHAPTER 21

1. Springfield *Sangamo Journal*, June 3, 1842; Springfield *Illinois Journal*, January 7, December 1, 1851, April 27, 1853, June 18, 1855; Springfield *Illinois Journal*, November 1, 1856; *Compendium of the Enumeration of the Inhabitants and Statistics of the United States . . . from the Returns of the Sixth Census* [U.S. Census of 1840] (Washington, DC: Thomas Allen, 1841), 85; J.D.B. DeBow, *The Seventh Census of the United States, 1850* (Washington, DC: Robert Armstrong, 1853), 715; Joseph C. G. Kennedy, *Population of the United States in 1860* [Eighth Census] (Washington, DC: Government Printing Office, 1864), 99.

2. Springfield *Sangamo Journal*, July 16, 1846; Springfield *Illinois Journal*, April 6, 21, July 4, 1849, August 9, 1850; Springfield *Illinois State Register*, July 26, 1849; Springfield City Council, Minutes of the Council Meeting, 1838–1861, Sangamon Valley Collection, Lincoln Library, Springfield, Illinois. May 25, 1860, January 16, 1861; Charles E. Rosenberg, *The Cholera Years* (Chicago: University of Chicago Press, 1967), 101–72; Richard L. Bushman and Claudia Bushman, "The Early History of Cleanliness in America," *Journal of American History*, 74 (March 1988), 1213–38.

3. Springfield *Sangamo Journal*, December 2, 1842, August 7, 1845, April 13, 1847; Springfield *Illinois Journal*, April 2, 25, May 17, 1851, October 6, 1853, May 12, 15, June 18, 1855; Springfield *Illinois State Journal*, September 9, 1855; Springfield *Illinois State Register*, April 30, 1847.

4. Springfield *Illinois Journal*, April 26, 1849, September 26, 1850, June 15, September 3, 1853, July 17, 20, 1854; Springfield City Council, Minutes of the Council Meeting, May 2, 1840.

5. Springfield *Illinois Journal*, July 16, 1851; Springfield *Illinois State Journal*, June 12, 1856; Ruth Painter Randall, *Lincoln's Animal Friends* (Boston: Little, Brown, 1958), 106–14; "Man's Best Friend," *For the People: A Newsletter of the Abraham Lincoln Association*, 1 (Autumn 1999), 6.

6. Springfield *Sangamo Journal*, April 26, 1832, May 13, 1847; Springfield *Illinois Journal*, November 11, 1847, July 31, 1850, May 6, 7, 12, September 7, November 23, 1853, April 5, 13, June 28, July 9, 20, 1854; Springfield City Council, Minutes of the Council Meeting, August 7, 1857,

September 9, 1859. Paul J. Gilje, *The Road to Mobocracy: Popular Disorder in New York City, 1763–1834* (Chapel Hill: University of North Carolina Press, 1987), 224–32, reviews a larger city's experience with dogs and hogs.

7. Springfield *Sangamo Journal*, May 30, 1849, May 17, 1851; Manuscript U.S. Census, Springfield, Illinois, 1850 and 1860; Kenneth J. Winkle, "The Voters of Lincoln's Springfield: Migration and Politial Participation in an Antebellum City," *Journal of Social History*, 25 (Spring 1992), 595–611. Mark Wyman, *Immigrants in the Valley: Irish, Germans, and Americans in the Upper Mississippi Country, 1830–1860* (Chicago: Nelson-Hall, 1984), provides an essential overview of immigration to the upper Mississippi Valley before the Civil War. Christopher Elliot Wallace, "The Opportunity to Grow: Springfield, Illinois During the 1850s," Ph.D. dissertation, Purdue University, 1983, 78–131, provides a statistical portrait of German and Irish immigrants in Springfield during the 1850s.

8. Springfield City Council, Minutes of the Council Meeting, December 11, 1846, April 28, 1849, May 23, July 9, August 6, 18, September 3, 1855, October 6, 1856; Springfield *Illinois Journal*, September 26, 1849; Springfield *Illinois State Register*, August 25, 1843.

9. Springfield *Illinois Journal*, May 11, June 22, 1848, September 5, 15, 1849, April 12, June 20, 1851, September 7, 1852; Springfield *Illinois State Journal*, August 17, September 20, December 15, 1855; Springfield *Illinois State Democrat*, December 29, 1858; Eric H. Monkkonen, *The Dangerous Class: Crime and Poverty in Columbus, Ohio, 1860–1885* (Cambridge, MA: Harvard University Press, 1975).

10. Springfield *Illinois Journal*, April 13, 1852, June 7, 15, November 28, 1853; Springfield *Illinois State Democrat*, September 11, December 29, 1858.

11. Springfield *Sangamo Journal*, November 12, 1841; Springfield *Illinois State Journal*, September 18, 1855.

12. Springfield *Illinois Journal*, June 15, 1853; Manuscript U.S. Census, Springfield, Illinois, 1860; Manuscript U.S. Census, Springfield, Illinois, 1850, linked with *Marriage Records, Sangamon County, Illinois, 1841–50* (Springfield: Sangamon County Genealogical Society, 1988), and *Marriage Records, Sangamon County, Illinois, 1851–1860* (Springfield: Sangamon County Genealogical Society, undated).

13. Springfield *Illinois Journal*, July 2, 1853, May 6, 1854; Joseph F. Kett, *Rites of Passage: Adolescence in America, 1790 to the Present* (New York: Basic Books, 1977), 223.

14. Jonathan Bailhache to Wife, January 12, 1843, Bailhache-Brayman Family Papers, Illinois State Historical Library, Springfield, Illinois; Springfield *Illinois Journal*, August 22, 1849, September 18, 1855.

15. Springfield *Sangamo Journal*, May 15, 1832; Springfield *Illinois Journal*, July 15, 1851, January 8, April 22, 1852, January 4, 1854; Springfield City Council, Minutes of the Council Meeting, September 17, 1849; Michael B. Katz, *The Irony of Early School Reform: Educational Innovation in Mid-Nineteenth-Century Massachusetts* (Cambridge, MA: Harvard University Press, 1968).

16. Springfield City Council, Minutes of the Council Meeting, October 5, 1844, March 31, 1845, April 4, 1857, April 30, June 4, 1860; Springfield *Illinois Journal*, April 17, 1851, May 3, June 21, 1852, January 18, May 14, September 29, December 20, 1853, February 25, May 6, September 5, 1854. Roger Lane, *Policing the City: Boston, 1822–1885* (Cambridge, MA: Harvard University Press, 1967), provides a pioneering analysis of the development of an urban police force during the nineteenth century.

17. Manuscript U.S. Census, Springfield, Illinois, 1850 and 1860; Sangamon County Circuit Court, Criminal Docket, 1850 and 1860, Illinois Regional Archives Depository, Sangamon State University, Springfield, Illinois. The overall rate of criminal prosecutions in both 1850 and 1860 was 23 per 1,000. This data includes only prosecutions, and the crime rate was certainly higher. Police may also have practiced selective prosecution of violent crimes as the decade progressed.

18. Springfield *Morning Courier*, January 26, 1841; Richard L. Bushman, *The Refinement of America: Persons, Houses, Cities* (New York: Vintage, 1992), xi–xix; John F. Kasson, *Rudeness and Civility: Manners in Nineteenth-Century Urban America* (New York: Hill and Wang, 1990); Karen Halttunen, *Confidence Men and Painted Women: A Study of Middle-Class Culture in America, 1840–1870* (New Haven, CT: Yale University Press, 1982); Daniel Walker Howe, "American Victorianism as a Culture," *American Quarterly*, 27 (December 1975), 507–32; Richard Sennett, *Families Against the City: Middle Class Homes of Industrial Chicago* (Cambridge, MA: Harvard University Press, 1970).

19. Springfield *Sangamo Journal*, April 13, 1843; Springfield *Illinois Journal*, June 1, 1849, May 15, 1854; Manuscript U.S. Census, Springfield, Illinois, 1860; Henry B. Rankin, *Intimate Character*

Sketches of Abraham Lincoln (Philadelphia: J. B. Lippincott, 1924), 162; Walter B. Stevens, *A Reporter's Lincoln*, ed. Michael Burlingame (Lincoln: University of Nebraska Press, 1998), 193; Bushman, *Refinement of America*, 258, 260; Thomas J. Schlereth, *Victorian America: Transformations in Everyday Life* (New York: Harper, 1991), 133;

20. Springfield *Illinois Journal*, June 6, 1849; Douglas L. Wilson and Rodney O. Davis, eds., *Herndon's Informants: Letters, Interviews, and Statements About Abraham Lincoln* (Urbana: University of Illinois Press, 1998), 452, 513; Steven M. Gelber, "Do-It-Yourself: Constructing, Repairing and Maintaining Domestic Masculinity," *American Quarterly*, 49 (March 1997), 66–112, esp. 71.

21. Halttunen, *Confidence Men and Painted Women*, 59–61, 104–106; Bushman, *Refinement of America*, 120–22, 273–79; Thomas J. Dyba and George L. Painter, *Seventeen Years at Eighth and Jackson*, 2nd ed. (Lisle, IL: IBC Pubications, 1985), 7, 9.

22. Mrs. Stuart to Daughter Betty, January 21, February 25, May 14, December 14, 1855, March 6, 1856, Stuart-Hay Papers, Illinois State Historical Library, Springfield, Illinois; Mason Brayman to Sarah Brayman, February 22, 1852, Bailhache-Brayman Family Papers, Illinois State Historical Library, Springfield, Illinois; Justin G. Turner and Linda Levitt Turner, *Mary Todd Lincoln: Her Life and Letters* (New York: Fromm International Publishing, 1972), 48–49; Harry E. Pratt, *The Personal Finances of Abraham Lincoln* (Springfield: Abraham Lincoln Association, 1943), 91, 94; Jean H. Baker, *Mary Todd Lincoln: A Biography* (New York: Norton, 1987), 113.

23. Howe, "American Victorianism as a Culture"; Schlereth, *Victorian America*; Ruth Bloch, "American Feminine Ideals in Transition: The Rise of the Moral Mother, 1785–1815," *Feminist Studies*, 4 (June 1978), 100–126; Glenna Matthews, *"Just a Housewife": The Rise and Fall of Domesticity in America* (New York: Oxford University Press, 1987), 35–65; Jeanne Boydston, *Home and Work: Housework, Wages, and the Ideology of Labor in the Early Republic* (New York: Oxford University Press, 1990), 75–119; Stuart M. Blumin, *The Emergence of the Middle Class: Social Experience in the American City, 1760–1900* (New York: Cambridge University Press, 1989), 138–91; Mary P. Ryan, *Cradle of the Middle Class: The Family in Oneida County, New York, 1790–1865* (New York: Cambridge University Press, 1981), 145–85.

24. Richard Easterlin, "Population Change and Farm Settlement in the Northern United States," *Journal of Economic History*, 36 (March 1976), 45–75; Robert V. Wells, "Family History and Demographic Transition," *Journal of Social History*, 9 (Fall 1975), 1–21; Robert V. Wells, *Uncle Sam's Family: Issues in and Perspectives on American Demographic History* (Albany: State University of New York Press, 1985), 28–56; Robert V. Wells, *Revolutions in American's Lives: A Demographic Perspective on the History of Americans, Their Families, and Their Society* (Westport, CT: Greenwood Press, 1982), 91–149; Carl N. Degler, *At Odds: Women and the Family in America from the Revolution to the Present* (New York: Oxford University Press, 1980), 210–26; Ryan, *Cradle of the Middle Class*, 155–65.

25. Data on fertility by decade is based on Manuscript U.S. Census, Springfield, Illinois, 1850, linked with *Marriage Records, Sangamon County, Illinois, 1841–50* (Springfield: Sangamon County Genealogical Society, 1988), and *Marriage Records, Sangamon County, Illinois, 1851–1860* (Springfield: Sangamon County Genealogical Society, undated). Data on the period of childbearing is based on a sample of all 130 white adult men who persisted in Springfield in two or more decennial U.S. censuses between 1830 and 1860 and for whom information on place of birth, date of arrival, date of marriage, and number of children appears in John Carroll Power, *History of the Early Settlers of Sangamon County, Illinois* (Springfield: Edwin A. Wilson, 1876), 9; Joseph Wallace, *Past and Present of the City of Springfield and Sangamon County, Illinois* (Chicago: S. J. Clarke, 1904); and Newton Bateman and Paul Selby, eds., *Historical Encyclopedia of Illinois . . . and History of Sangamon County* (Chicago: Munsell Publishing, 1912). Springfield *Illinois Journal*, December 9, 1852, March 18, 1853; Springfield *Illinois State Journal*, September 26, 1855, June 14, 15, 1856, January 20, 1857; Springfield *Illinois State Democrat*, December 8, 1858; Degler, *At Odds*, 210–26.

26. The Lincolns observed the following birth intervals: Robert/Eddie = 2.4 years; Eddie/Willie = 4.8 years; Willie/Thomas = 2.3 years, for an average of 3.2 years. Kathryn Kish Sklar, "Victorian Women and Domestic Life: Mary Todd Lincoln, Elizabeth Cady Stanton, and Harriet Beecher Stowe," in Cullom Davis, Charles B. Strozier, Rebecca Monroe Veach, and Geoffrey C. Ward, eds., *The Public and the Private Lincoln: Contemporary Perspectives* (Carbondale: Southern Illinois University Press, 1979), 20–37, provides a crucial, pathbreaking analysis of the Lincolns' fertility.

27. Sklar, "Victorian Women and Domestic Life," 30–31; Dyba and Painter, *Seventeen Years at Eighth and Jackson*, 26.

28. Wilson and Davis, *Herndon's Informants*, 407, 453, 597; Walter B. Stevens, *A Reporter's Lincoln*, ed. Michael Burlingame (Lincoln: University of Nebraska Press, 1998), 193; Bloch, "Rise of

the Moral Mother"; Baker, *Mary Todd Lincoln*, 120; Rodney Hessinger, "Problems and Promises: Colonial American Child Rearing and Modernization Theory," *Journal of Family History*, 21 (April 1996), 125–43, esp. 131. Stephen M. Frank, *Life with Father: Parenthood and Masculinity in the Nineteenth-Century North* (Baltimore: Johns Hopkins University Press, 1998), 121, 126, notes that "Positive valuations of children's play greatly expanded in the 1830s," and "Within the upper and middle classes, fathers who acted as play partners with young children were quite common."

29. Roy P. Basler, ed., *The Collected Works of Abraham Lincoln* (New Brunswick, NJ: Rutgers University Press, 1953), I, 391; Nancy Schrom Dye and Daniel Blake Smith, "Mother Love and Infant Death, 1750–1920," *Journal of American History*, 73 (September 1986), 329–53; Bloch, "Rise of the Moral Mother"; E. Anthony Rotundo, "American Fatherhood: A Historical Perspective," *American Behavioral Scientist*, 29 (September/October 1985), 7–25, esp. 12; E. Anthony Rotundo, "Body and Soul: Changing Ideals of American Middle-Class Manhood, 1770–1920," *Journal of Social History*, 16 (Summer 1983), 23–38, esp. 31; Rodney O. Davis, "Abraham Lincoln: Son and Father," Edgar S. and Ruth W. Burkhardt Lecture Series, Knox College, Galesburg, Illinois, 1997. Ryan, *Cradle of the Middle Class*, 155–65, analyzes the "routine and intense maternal vigilance" that Victorians instilled in middle-class mothers.

30. Manuscript U.S. Census, Mortality Schedule, Springfield, Illinois, 1850; Wells, "Family History and Demographic Transition"; Ann Douglas, "Heaven Our Home: Consolation Literature in the Northern United States," in David E. Stannard, ed., *Death in America* (Philadelphia: University of Pennsylvania Press, 1975), 49–68; Maris A. Vinovskis, "Angel's Heads and Weeping Willows: Death in Early America," in Michael Gordon, ed., *The American Family in Social-Historical Perspective* (New York: St. Martin's Press, 1978), 546–63; Halttunen, *Confidence Men and Painted Women*, 124–52; Ruth Painter Randall, *Mary Lincoln: Biography of a Marriage* (Boston: Little, Brown, 1953), 139–45.

31. Wilson and Davis, *Herndon's Informants*, 389, 452, 485; Michael Burlingame, *The Inner World of Abraham Lincoln* (Urbana: University of Illinois Press, 1994), 296.

32. Alton *Illinois Temperance Herald*, October 1838; Ronald G. Walters, *American Reformers, 1815–1860* (New York: Hill and Wang, 1978), 123–43, provides the best concise survey of the antebellum temperance movement. See also Steven Mintz, *Moralists and Modernizers: America's Pre-Civil War Reformers* (Baltimore: Johns Hopkins University Press, 1995), 72–76; Joseph R. Gusfield, *Symbolic Crusade: Status Politics and the American Temperance Movement* (Urbana: University of Illinois Press, 1963), 36–60; and Ian R. Tyrrell, *Sobering Up: From Temperance to Prohibition in Antebellum America, 1800–1860* (Westport, CT: Greenwood Press, 1979).

33. Springfield *Sangamo Journal*, December 22, 1831; Springfield *Sangamo Journal*, February 2, March 2, 1833, February 7, March 7, 1835; Alton *Illinois Temperance Herald*, March 1838; Wilson and Davis, *Herndon's Informants*, 452; Paul Simon, *Lincoln's Preparation for Greatness: The Illinois Legislative Years* (Norman: University of Oklahoma Press, 1965), 165–66, 201–2, 279–80; Paul M. Angle, "Lincoln and Liquor, Part One," *Bulletin of the Abraham Lincoln Association*, 27 (June 1932), 3–8, esp. 5–6. Jed Dannenbaum, *Drink and Disorder: Temperance Reform in Cincinnati from the Washingtonian Revival to the WCTU* (Urbana: University of Illinois Press, 1984), 16–179, provides a solid overview of the temperance movement in a major midwestern city. Don Harrison Doyle, *The Social Order of a Frontier Community: Jacksonville, Illinois, 1825–70* Urbana: University of Illinois Press, 1978), 212–26, describes the experience of a nearby Illinois community.

34. Springfield City Council, Minutes of the Council Meeting, 1838–1861, Sangamon Valley Collection, Lincoln Library, Springfield, Illinois, April 5, May 27, December 9, 11, 24, 1839, April 7, 1840; Angle, "Lincoln and Liquor, Part One," 4.

35. This and succeeding profiles of Springfield temperance leaders link identifiable leaders of the Springfield Temperance Society, the Washington Temperance Society, and the Sons of Temperance with Manuscript U.S. Census, Springfield, Illinois, 1850. Walters, *American Reformers*, 129–34. Compare Dannenbaum, *Drink and Disorder*, 32–68.

36. Springfield *Sangamo Journal*, December 17, 1841, February 4, June 3, 1842, February 12, April 30, August 20, 1846; Alton and St. Louis *Missouri and Illinois Temperance Herald and Washingtonian*, January, February 1842; Alton *Illinois Temperance Herald and Washingtonian*, May 1842; Sangamon County Temperance Union Society, Records, 1847–50, Illinois State Historical Library, Springfield, Illinois; Angle, "Lincoln and Liquor, Part One," 7.

37. Wilson and Davis, *Herndon's Informants*, 389, 395, 452, 775; Sangamon County Temperance Union Society, Records.

38. *Collected Works*, 273, 279.

39. *Collected Works*, 273, 279.

40. Angle, "Lincoln and Liquor, Part One," 9. William H. Townsend, *Lincoln and Liquor* (New York: Press of the Pioneers, 1934), 52–62, provides the fullest overview of Lincoln's involvement with the Washingtonian movement. George M. Fredrickson, "The Search for Order and Community," in Cullom Davis, Charles B. Strozier, Rebecca Monroe Veach, and Geoffrey C. Ward, eds., *The Public and the Private Lincoln: Contemporary Perspectives* (Carbondale: Southern Illinois University Press, 1979), 86–98, analyzes Lincoln within a "rational-legalistic" reform tradition.

41. Springfield *Sangamo Journal*, July 13, 1847; Springfield *Illinois Journal*, May 4, June 1, July 13, 1848, October 6, 1851, May 19, 1853; Springfield *Illinois Organ*, March 22, 1853; Wilson and Davis, *Herndon's Informants*, 452; Walters, *American Reformers*, 133–38; Dannenbaum, *Drink and Disorder*, 69–105.

42. Springfield *Illinois Journal*, January 1, 1852, February 23, 1854.

CHAPTER 22

1. Roy P. Basler, ed., *The Collected Works of Abraham Lincoln* (New Brunswick, NJ: Rutgers University Press, 1953), II, 270; Springfield *Illinois Journal*, April 16, 18, 20, 1850, April 14, 1852, February 23, 1854; William H. Townsend, *Lincoln and Liquor* (New York: Press of the Pioneers, 1934), 63; Paul M. Angle, "Lincoln and Liquor, Part Two," *Bulletin of the Abraham Lincoln Association*, 27 (September 1932), 3–9.

2. Springfield *Illinois Journal*, July 11, 1851, February 2, 19, September 13, 1853, May 9, 1854; Townsend, *Lincoln and Liquor*, 3.

3. Springfield *Illinois Journal*, April 26, 30, June 7, October 21, 1852; William E. Gienapp, *The Origins of the Republican Party, 1852–1856* (New York: Oxford University Press, 1987), 13–35; David Potter, *The Impending Crisis, 1848–1861* (New York: Harper, 1976), 141–44; Roy and Jeannette Nichols, "Election of 1852," in Arthur M. Schlesinger Jr. and Fred L. Israel, eds., *History of American Presidential Elections, 1789–1968* (New York: Chelsea House, 1971), II, 921–1003.

4. Springfield *Illinois Journal*, May 23, June 19, August 8, 1854, April 11, 1855; Angle, "Lincoln and Liquor," 5; David Herbert Donald, *Lincoln's Herndon* (New York: Knopf, 1948), 66–69.

5. Tyler Anbinder, *Nativism and Slavery: The Northern Know Nothings and the Politics of the 1850s* (New York: Oxford University Press, 1992), 3–31; Gienapp, *Origins of the Republican Party*, 92–94.

6. Springfield *Illinois Journal*, July 25, September 6, October 2, 1854; Springfield *Weekly Capital Enterprise*, August 19, 1854; John P. Senning, "The Know-Nothing Movement in Illinois," *Journal of the Illinois State Historical Society*, 7 (April 1914), 7–33.

7. *Collected Works*, II, 228, 232, 404; Springfield *Illinois Journal*, January 15, 1854; Potter, *Impending Crisis*, 145–76; Louis Filler, *The Crusade Against Slavery, 1830–1860* (New York: Harper, 1960), 228–32; Richard H. Sewell, *A House Divided: Sectionalism and Civil War, 1848–1865* (Baltimore: Johns Hopkins University Press, 1988), 40–55; Richard H. Sewell, *Ballots for Freedom: Antislavery Politics in the United States, 1837–1860* (New York: Oxford University Press, 1976), 254–65; Larry Gara, "Slavery and the Slave Power: A Crucial Distinction," *Civil War History*, 15 (March 1969), 5–18; William E. Gienapp, "The Republican Party and the Slave Power," in Robert H. Abzug and Stephen E. Maizlish, eds., *New Perspectives on Race and Slavery in America: Essays in Honor of Kenneth M. Stampp* (Lexington: University Press of Kentucky, 1986), 51–78; Michael F. Holt, *The Rise and Fall of the American Whig Party: Jacksonian Politics and the Onset of the Civil War* (New York: Oxford University Press, 1999), 765–803.

8. Gienapp, *Origins of the Republican Party*, 161, 163–64; Sewell, *Ballots for Freedom*, 265–77; Filler, *Crusade Against Slavery*, 230–32; Potter, *Impending Crisis*, 225–65; Michael F. Holt, *The Political Crisis of the 1850s* (New York: Wiley), 139–81.

9. *Collected Works*, III, 512; Arthur Charles Cole, *The Era of the Civil War, 1848–1870*, Vol. 3 of Clarence Walworth Alvord, ed., *The Centennial History of Illinois* (Chicago: A. C. McClurg, 1922), 128–29; Gienapp, *Origins of the Republican Party*, 122–23.

10. *Collected Works*, II, 255, 256, 266.

11. *Collected Works*, II, 284–85; Springfield *Illinois Journal*, November 9, 1854, June 5, 1855; Springfield *Illinois State Journal*, November 7, 1855; Senning, "Know-Nothing Movement," 17; Cole, *Era of the Civil War*, 131, 136, 137; Gienapp, *Origins of the Republican Party*, 125–26, 290; Angle, "Lincoln and Liquor," 5; Townsend, *Lincoln and Liquor*, 69–70. James Gourley recalled that Lincoln "took no part in the great temperance move in 18[55] when an act of the Legislature was passed and Submitted to the People"; Douglas L. Wilson and Rodney O. Davis, eds., *Herndon's*

Informants: Letters, Interviews, and Statements About Abraham Lincoln (Urbana: University of Illinois Press, 1998), 452.

12. *Collected Works*, II, 323; Wilson and Davis, *Herndon's Informants*, 705; Matthew Pinsker, "Senator Abraham Lincoln," *Journal of the Abraham Lincoln Association*, 14 (Summer 1993), 1–21; Gienapp, *Origins of the Republican Party*, 287.

13. *Collected Works*, II, 316–17.

14. Springfield *Illinois State Journal*, July 11, 1855, May 8, 1856; Michael F. Holt, "The Politics of Impatience: The Origins of Know Nothingism," *Journal of American History*, 60 (September 1973), 309–31; Gienapp, *Origins of the Republican Party*, 287; Anbinder, *Nativism and Slavery*, 52–74; Cole, *Era of the Civil War*, 143–44, 340–43.

15. Springfield *Illinois State Journal*, May 10, 1856; Gienapp, *Origins of the Republican Party*, 294; Anbinder, *Nativism and Slavery*, 194–219; Cole, *Era of the Civil War*, 143–46; Don E. Fehrenbacher, *Prelude to Greatness: Lincoln in the 1850s* (Stanford, CA: Stanford University Press, 1962), 19–47; Stephen L. Hansen, *The Making of the Third Party System: Voters and Parties in Illinois, 1850–1876* (Ann Arbor, MI: UMI Research Press, 1980), 47. The profile of the signers of the Sangamon County call is based on Manuscript U.S. Census, Springfield, Illinois, 1850, linked with Manuscript Poll Books, Sangamon County, Illinois, Illinois State Historical Library, Springfield, Illinois, 1848. Among the 129 signers, 41 were listed in the U.S. Census of 1850 of Springfield, and 29 were listed in both the U.S. Census of 1850 and the poll books from 1848.

16. Gienapp, *Origins of the Republican Party*, 316–17, 413–23; Anbinder, *Nativism and Slavery*, 220–45; Hansen, *Making of the Third Party System*, 75–102; Roy F. Nichols and Philip S. Klein, "Election of 1856," in Schlesinger and Israel, *History of American Presidential Elections*, II, 1007–94.

17. *Collected Works*, II, 379; Springfield *Conservative*, August 14, October 9, 16, 1856; Springfield *Illinois State Democrat*, August 1, 1860; Senning, "Know-Nothing Movement," 19.

18. Springfield *Illinois State Journal*, November 5, 1856; Justin G. Turner and Linda Levitt Turner, *Mary Todd Lincoln: Her Life and Letters* (New York: Fromm International Publishing, 1972), 46.

CHAPTER 23

1. Don E. Fehrenbacher, *The Dred Scott Case: Its Significance in American Law and Politics* (New York: Oxford University Press, 1978); David Potter, *The Impending Crisis, 1848–1861* (New York: Harper, 1976), 267–96.

2. Roy P. Basler, ed., *The Collected Works of Abraham Lincoln* (New Brunswick, NJ: Rutgers University Press, 1953), II, 405–6.

3. *Collected Works*, II, 405; Eric Foner, *Free Soil, Free Labor, Free Men: The Ideology of the Republican Party Before the Civil War* (New York: Oxford University Press, 1970).

4. Don E. Fehrenbacher, *Slavery, Law, and Politics: The Dred Scott Case in Historical Perspective* (New York: Oxford University Press, 1981), 244–72; Don E. Fehrenbacher, *Prelude to Greatness: Lincoln in the 1850s* (Stanford, CA: Stanford University Press, 1962), 106–12; Allan Nevins, *The Emergence of Lincoln* (New York: Charles Scribner's Sons, 1950), I, 250–79; Richard H. Sewell, *Ballots for Freedom: Antislavery Politics in the United States, 1837–1860* (New York: Oxford University Press, 1976), 347–48.

5. *Collected Works*, 461–69.

6. Douglas L. Wilson and Rodney O. Davis, eds., *Herndon's Informants: Letters, Interviews, and Statements About Abraham Lincoln* (Urbana: University of Illinois Press, 1998), 163, 267, 438, 442.

7. *Collected Works*, III, 51–52; Fehrenbacher, *Prelude to Greatness*, 121–42; Christopher N. Breiseth, "Lincoln, Douglas, and Springfield in the 1858 Campaign," in Cullom Davis, Charles B. Strozier, Rebecca Monroe Veach, and Geoffrey C. Ward, eds., *The Public and the Private Lincoln: Contemporary Perspectives* (Carbondale: Southern Illinois University Press, 1979), 101–120.

8. *Collected Works*, II, 281, III, 14, 96, 113; George M. Fredrickson, "A Man but Not a Brother: Abraham Lincoln and Racial Equality," *Journal of Southern History*, 41 (February 1975), 39–58; Don E. Fehrenbacher, "Only His Stepchildren: Lincoln and the Negro," *Civil War History*, 20 (December 1974), 293–310.

9. Springfield *Illinois State Democrat*, November 3, 1858, April 10, June 13, 1860; Breiseth, "Lincoln, Douglas, and Springfield," 118; Bruce Collins, "The Lincoln-Douglas Contest of 1858 and

Illinois' Electorate," *Journal of American Studies*, 20 (December 1986), 391–420.

10. William H. Herndon and Jesse W. Weik, *Herndon's Life of Lincoln*, ed. Paul M. Angle (Cleveland: World, 1942), 93–94; Henry B. Rankin, *Intimate Character Sketches of Abraham Lincoln* (Philadelphia: J. B. Lippincott, 1924), 60–61.

11. Kenneth J. Winkle, "'The Great Body of the Republic': Abraham Lincoln and the Idea of a Middle West," in Andrew R. L. Cayton and Susan Gray, eds., *Middle Western Regionalism* (Bloomington: Indiana University Press, forthcoming). This summary includes only speeches that are extant and are included in *Collected Works*, III, 400–554. Between his speeches at Columbus, Ohio, on September 16, 1859, and Dover, New Hampshire, on March 2, 1860, Lincoln delivered seventeen speeches in Kansas, Wisconsin, Illinois, Indiana, Ohio, New York, Connecticut, Rhode Island, and New Hampshire.

12. *Collected Works*, III, 438, 440.

13. *Collected Works*, III, 446.

14. *Collected Works*, III, 438–62; G. S. Boritt, "The Right to Rise," in Davis, Strozier, Veach, and Ward, *Public and Private Lincoln*, 57–70; Geoffrey C. Ward, *Lincoln and the Right to Rise* (Springfield: Sangamon State University, 1978); Richard Hofstadter, "Abraham Lincoln and the Self-Made Myth," in Richard Hofstadter, *The American Political Tradition and the Men Who Made It* (New York: Knopf, 1948), 93–136.

15. *Collected Works*, III, 471–82.

16. Herndon and Weik, *Herndon's Life of Lincoln*, 368; Rankin, *Intimate Character Sketches of Abraham Lincoln*, 368; Waldo W. Braden, *Abraham Lincoln, Public Speaker* (Baton Rouge: Louisiana University Press, 1988), 55.

17. *Collected Works*, III, 535–36, 547, 550; Braden, *Abraham Lincoln, Public Speaker*, 54; David Herbert Donald, *Lincoln* (New York: Simon and Schuster, 1995), 237–40.

18. In addition to the four major candidates, the Radical Abolition Party nominated Gerrit Smith, a congressman from upstate New York, and advocated an immediate end to slavery throughout the nation. The abolitionists were influential only in northern New England and won only 1 percent of the presidential vote. Potter, *Impending Crisis*, 405–47; Elting Morrison, "Election of 1860," in Arthur M. Schlesinger Jr. and Fred L. Israel, eds., *History of American Presidential Elections, 1789–1968* (New York: Chelsea House, 1971), II, 1097–1152; Reinhard H. Luthin, *The First Lincoln Campaign* (Cambridge, MA: Harvard University Press, 1944), 136–67.

19. Fehrenbacher, *Slavery, Law, and Politics*, 289-94; James L. Huston, *The Panic of 1857 and the Coming of the Civil War* (Baton Rouge: Louisiana State University Press, 1982), 238–39; Morrison, "Election of 1860."

20. David C. Mearns, *The Lincoln Papers* (Garden City, NY: Doubleday, 1948), I, 235–37; Luthin, *First Lincoln Campaign*, 139, 157–66.

21. James M. McPherson, *Ordeal by Fire: The Civil War and Reconstruction*, 2nd ed. (New York: McGraw-Hill, 1992), 131–33; Potter, *Impending Crisis*, 405–47.

22. *Collected Works*, IV, 55, 57, 60, 82, 89–90, 91.

23. Potter, *Impending Crisis*, 405–47; Fehrenbacher, *Slavery, Law, and Politics*, 289–94; Morrison, "Election of 1860."

24. Springfield *Illinois State Journal*, October 11, 19, 23, 1860; Herndon and Weik, *Herndon's Life of Lincoln*, 376–77; Paul M. Angle, *"Here I Have Lived": A History of Lincoln's Springfield* (Springfield: Abraham Lincoln Association, 1935), 243; Jeff G. Gavin, *Past Sites of Springfield: A Historic Guide to the Downtown Area*, typescript, Sangamon Valley Collection, Lincoln Library, 1980, 33.

25. Springfield *Illinois State Journal*, November 10, 1860; Wilson and Davis, *Herndon's Informants*, 486; Angle, *Here I Have Lived*, 246–48.

CONCLUSION

1. John Carroll Power, *History of the Early Settlers of Sangamon County, Illinois* (Springfield: Edwin A. Wilson, 1876), 9; Springfield *Illinois State Journal*, June 1, 17, 1859; Caroline M. Beers, "Illinois Women: Stories of the Pioneer Mothers of Illinois," Women's Exposition Board, 1893, Illinois State Historical Library, Springfield, Illinois, 1; John Mack Faragher, *Sugar Creek: Life on the Illinois Prairie* (New Haven, CT: Yale University Press, 1986), 219–25.

2. Springfield *Illinois State Journal*, October 20, 1859; Power, *Early Settlers*, 9. The list of organizers appears in Springfield *Illinois State Journal*, May 27, 1859. Linkage with the Manuscript U.S. Census, Springfield, Illinois, 1860, reveals that 49 of the 61 organizers lived in Springfield. Contem-

porary estimates put travel time in the vicinity of Springfield at four miles per hour; Timothy R. Mahoney, *River Towns in the Great West: The Structure of Provincial Urbanization in the American Midwest, 1820–1870* (New York: Cambridge University Press, 1990), 198.

3. John W. Smith, *History of Macon County, Illinois, from Its Organization to 1876* (Springfield: Rokker's Printing House, 1876), 144; Power, *Early Settlers*, 62–65, 430; T. G. Onstot, *Pioneers of Menard and Mason Counties* (Peoria, IL: J. W. Franks & Sons, 1902), 135. A host of studies point to 1830 as the turning point between settlement by southerners and the arrival of Yankees and immigrants. See, for example, William V. Pooley, *The Settlement of Illinois from 1830 to 1850*, Bulletin of the University of Wisconsin, History Series, Vol. 1, pp. 287–595, (Madison: University of Wisconsin, 1908); Douglas R. McManis, *Initial Evaluation and Utilization of the Illinois Prairies, 1815–1840* (Chicago: University of Chicago Press, 1964), 17–18; Mark Wyman, *Immigrants in the Valley: Irish, Germans, and Americans in the Upper Mississippi Country, 1830–1860* (Chicago: Nelson-Hall, 1984); Ronald E. Nelson, ed., *Illinois: Land and Life in the Prairie State* (Dubuque: Kendall-Hunt, 1978), 7–8; Douglas K. Meyer, "Illinois Culture Regions at Mid-Nineteenth Century," *Bulletin of the Illinois Geographical Society* 18 (December 1976), 3–13; Douglas K. Meyer, "Southern Illinois Migration Fields: The Shawnee Hills in 1850," *The Professional Geographer*, 28 (May 1976), 151–60.

4. Eric Hobsbawm, "Introduction: Inventing Traditions," in Eric Hobsbawm and Terence Ranger, eds., *The Invention of Tradition* (Cambridge, Eng.: Cambridge University Press, 1983), 1–14, esp. 9; R. D. Miller, *Past and Present of Menard County, Illinois* (Chicago: S. J. Clarke, 1905), 24.

5. Springfield *Illinois State Journal*, October 20, 1859; Power, *Early Settlers*, 9–10. The most prominent Old Settler of all—Abraham Lincoln—stayed in Springfield that day and did not join the festivities; Earl Schenck Miers, ed., *Lincoln Day by Day: A Chronology, 1809–1865* (Washington, DC: Lincoln Sesquicentennial Commission, 1960), II, 264. John Brown seized the federal arsenal at Harper's Ferry on October 16, 1859, with a force of nineteen men, including five free blacks. By the time federal troops recaptured the arsenal two days later, Brown's followers had killed four men and suffered ten deaths themselves. See Stephen B. Oates, *To Purge This Land With Blood: A Biography of John Brown* (New York: Harper, 1970). The Old Settlers' Society lapsed in 1860 and was reorganized in 1868.

6. Roy P. Basler, ed., *The Collected Works of Abraham Lincoln* (New Brunswick, NJ: Rutgers University Press, 1953), IV, 63; James E. Davis, *Frontier Illinois* (Bloomington: Indiana University Press, 1998), 424, 453–54 n. 1, 460 n.28.

The best brief introduction to nineteenth-century migration and persistence remains Stephan Thernstrom and Peter R. Knights, "Men in Motion: Some Data and Speculations About Urban Population Mobility in Nineteenth-Century America," *Journal of Interdisciplinary History*, 1 (Autumn 1970), 7–35. Other important studies include Stephan Thernstrom, *Poverty and Progress: Social Mobility in a Nineteenth-Century City* (Cambridge, MA: Harvard University Press, 1964); Peter R. Knights, *The Plain People of Boston, 1830–1860* (New York: Oxford University Press, 1971); and Peter R. Knights, *Yankee Destinies: The Lives of Ordinary Nineteenth-Century Bostonians* (Chapel Hill: University of North Carolina Press, 1991).

7. Power, *Early Settlers*, 10.

8. *Collected Works*, IV, 236.

9. *Collected Works*, IV, 190; Walter B. Stevens, *A Reporter's Lincoln*, ed. Michael Burlingame (Lincoln: University of Nebraska Press, 1998), 143.

Bibliography

PRIMARY SOURCES

Published Sources

Newspapers
Alton *Illinois Temperance Herald*
Alton *Illinois Temperance Herald and Washingtonian*
Alton and St. Louis *Missouri and Illinois Temperance Herald and Washingtonian*
Daily Springfield Republican
Springfield *Conservative*
Springfield *Daily Evening Independent*
Springfield *Illinois Organ*
Springfield *Illinois Republican*
Springfield *Illinois State Democrat*
Springfield *Illinois Journal*
Springfield *Illinois State Journal*
Springfield *Illinois State Register*
Springfield *Morning Courier*
Springfield *Old Hickory*
Springfield *Sangamo Journal*
Springfield *Sangamo Spectator*
Springfield *Sangamon Journal*
Springfield *State Register and People's Advocate*
Springfield *Weekly Capital Enterprise*
Springfield *Weekly Illinois American*
Springfield *Western Farmer*
Springfield *Western Prairie Farmer, Journal of Agriculture and Rural Economy*
Vandalia *State Register and People's Advocate*

Reminiscences, Biographies, and Local Histories
Burlend, Rebecca, and Edward Burlend. *A True Picture of Emigration*, ed. Milo Milton Quaife. New York: Citadel Press, 1968.
Burlingame, Michael, ed. *An Oral History of Abraham Lincoln: John G. Nicolay's Interviews and Essays.* Carbondale: Southern Illinois University Press, 1996.

Bateman, Newton, and Paul Selby, eds. *Historical Encyclopedia of Illinois . . . and History of Sangamon County.* Chicago: Munsell Publishing Company, 1912.
Carpenter, Francis B. *The Inner Life of Abraham Lincoln: Six Months at the White House.* Boston: Houghton, Osgood, 1878.
Dall, Caroline H. "Pioneering." *Atlantic Monthly*, 19 (April 1867), 403–416.
Herndon, William H., and Jesse W. Weik. *Herndon's Life of Lincoln*, ed. Paul M. Angle. Cleveland: World, 1942.
Hertz, Emanuel. *The Hidden Lincoln: From the Letters and Papers of William H. Herndon.* New York: Viking Press, 1938.
The History of Coles County, Illinois. Chicago: William LeBaron, 1879.
History of Macon County, Illinois. Philadelphia: Brink, McDonough and Co., 1880.
The History of Menard and Mason Counties, Illinois. Chicago: O. L. Baskin, 1879.
History of Sangamon County, Illinois. Chicago: Inter-State Publishing Company, 1881.
Iles, Elijah. *Sketches of Early Life and Times in Kentucky, Missouri and Illinois.* Springfield, IL: Springfield Printing Co., 1883.
Johns, Jane Martin. *Personal Recollections of Early Decatur, Abraham Lincoln, Richard J. Oglesby, and the Civil War.* Decatur: Decatur Chapter Daughters of the American Revolution, 1912.
Lamon, Ward Hill. *Life of Abraham Lincoln, 1847–1865.* Boston: James R. Osgood, 1872.
Miller, R. D. *Past and Present of Menard County, Illinois.* Chicago: S. J. Clarke, 1905.
Rankin, Henry B. *Intimate Character Sketches of Abraham Lincoln.* Philadelphia: J. B. Lippincott, 1924.
Ross, Harvey Lee. *The Early Pioneers and Pioneer Events of the State of Illinois.* Chicago: Eastman Brothers, 1899.

Scripps, John Locke. *Life of Abraham Lincoln.* Chicago, 1860; reprinted, Bloomington, IN: Indiana University Press, 1961.

Smith, John W. *History of Macon County, Illinois, from its Organization to 1876.* Springfield: Rokker's Printing House, 1876.

Speed, Joshua F. *Reminiscences of Abraham Lincoln and Notes of a Visit to California.* Louisville: John P. Morton, 1884.

Stevens, Walter B. *A Reporter's Lincoln*, ed. Michael Burlingame. Lincoln: University of Nebraska Press, 1998.

Wallace, Joseph. *Past and Present of the City of Springfield and Sangamon County, Illinois.* Chicago: S. J. Clarke, 1904.

Whitney, Henry C. *Life of Lincoln*, 2 vols. New York: Baker and Taylor, 1908.

Wilson, Charles Edward. *History of Coles County.* Chicago: Munsell, 1906.

Wilson, Douglas L., and Rodney O. Davis, eds. *Herndon's Informants: Letters, Interviews, and Statements About Abraham Lincoln* (Urbana: University of Illinois Press, 1998.

Personal Papers

Basler, Roy P. ed. *The Collected Works of Abraham Lincoln*, 9 vols. New Brunswick, NJ: Rutgers University Press, 1953.

Emerson, Edward Waldo, and Waldo Emerson Forbes, eds. *Journals of Ralph Waldo Emerson*, 10 vols. Boston: Houghton Mifflin, 1909–1914.

Emerson, Ralph Waldo. *Emerson's Complete Works*, 12 vols. Cambridge, MA: Riverside Press, 1883–1893

Lanphier, Charles H. *Glory to God and the Sucker Democracy: A Manuscript Collection*, 5 vols. Privately printed, 1973.

Mearns, David C. *The Lincoln Papers*, 2 vols. Garden City, NY: Doubleday, 1948.

Washburne, E. B., ed. *The Edwards Papers; Being a Portion of the Collection of the Letters, Papers, and Manuscripts of Ninian Edwards.* Chicago Historical Society's Collection. Chicago: Fergus Printing Company, 1884.

Government Records

Compendium of the Enumeration of the Inhabitants and Statistics of the United States . . . from the Returns of the Sixth Census [U.S. Census of 1840]. Washington, DC: Thomas Allen, 1841.

DeBow, J.D.B. *The Seventh Census of the United States, 1850.* Washington, DC: Robert Armstrong, 1853.

Illinois Constitution of 1818.

Illinois Constitution of 1848.

Illinois Laws.

Kennedy, Joseph C. G. *Population of the United States in 1860* [Eighth Census]. Washington, DC: U.S. Government Printing Office, 1864.

Marriage Records, Sangamon County, Illinois, 1821–1840. Springfield: Sangamon County Genealogical Society, 1987.

Marriage Records, Sangamon County, Illinois, 1841–50. Springfield: Sangamon County Genealogical Society, 1988.

Marriage Records, Sangamon County, Illinois, 1851–1860. Springfield: Sangamon County Genealogical Society, undated.

U.S. Bureau of the Census. *County and City Data Book: 1994*, 12th ed. Washington, DC: U.S. Government Printing Office, 1994.

U.S. Department of Commerce. *Historical Statistics of the United States: Colonial Times to 1970*, 2 vols. Washington, DC: Bureau of the Census, 1975.

Miscellaneous

Ball, Elder S. S. *Liberia: The Condition and Prospects of That Republic; Made from Actual Observation.* Alton, IL: Printed at the "Telegraph" Office, 1848.

Frost, John. *Self-Made Men of America.* New York: W. H. Graham, 1848.

Miers, Earl Schenck, ed. *Lincoln Day by Day: A Chronology, 1809-1865*, 3 vols. Washington, DC: Lincoln Sesquicentennial Commission, 1960.

Offutt, Denton. *A New and Complete System of Teaching the Horse on Phrenological Principles.* Cincinnati: Appleton's Queen City Press, 1848.

Smith, Matthew H. *Successful Folks: How They Win.* Hartford, CT: American Publishing Company, 1878.

Unpublished Sources

Bailhache-Brayman Family Papers, Illinois State Historical Library, Springfield, Illinois.

Barnett, John Tipton. "Biography of the Barnett Family Written by John Tipton Barnett." Illinois State Historical Library, Springfield, Illinois.

Divorce Index, Sangamon County, Illinois, October 1825–October 1899, Illinois Regional Archives Depository, University of Illinois–Springfield, Springfield, Illinois.

Enos, Zimri A. "Springfield Residents Before the Deep Snow." Illinois State Historical Library, Springfield, Illinois.

"Illinois Women: Stories of the Pioneer Mothers of Illinois." Women's Exposition Board, 1893, Illinois State Historical Library, Springfield, Illinois.

James and E. F. McConnell Papers, Illinois State Historical Library, Springfield, Illinois.

Manuscript Poll Books, Sangamon County, Illinois, Illinois State Historical Library, Springfield, Illinois, 1834, 1836.

Manuscript U.S. Census, Adams County, Illinois, 1850 and 1860.

Manuscript U.S. Census, Coles County, Illinois, 1850.

Manuscript U.S. Census, Menard County, Illinois, 1850 and 1860.

Manuscript U.S. Census, Sangamon County, Illinois, 1830, 1840, 1850, and 1860.

Manuscript U.S. Census, Mortality Schedule, Springfield, Illinois, 1850.

Mary Miner Hill Memoirs, 1923, Illinois State Historical Library, Springfield, Illinois.

McLaren, William Riley. "Reminiscences of Pioneer Life in Illinois, ca. 1830–1860." Illinois State Historical Library, Springfield, Illinois.

Pascal P. Enos Papers, Illinois State Historical Library, Springfield, Illinois.

Sangamon County Circuit Court, Criminal Docket, 1850 and 1860, Illinois Regional Archives Depository, Sangamon State University, Springfield, Illinois.

Sangamon County Commissioners Record, Illinois State Archives, Springfield, Illinois.

Sangamon County Estray Notices, 1821–1830, Illinois State Historical Library, Springfield, Illinois.

Sangamon County Indentures of Apprenticeship, Illinois State Historical Library, Springfield, Illinois.

Sangamon County Temperance Union Society, Records, 1847–50, Illinois State Historical Library, Springfield, Illinois.

Springfield City Council, Minutes of the Council Meeting, 1838–1861, Sangamon Valley Collection, Lincoln Library, Springfield, Illinois.

Springfield Mechanics Union Book, Illinois State Historical Library, Springfield, Illinois.

Stuart-Hay Papers, Illinois State Historical Library, Springfield, Illinois.

Secondary Sources

Books

Alger, Horatio, Jr. *Abraham Lincoln, the Young Backwoods Boy; or, How a Young Rail Splitter Became President.* New York: American Publishers, 1883.

Alger, Horatio, Jr. *From Canal Boy to President or the Boyhood and Manhood of James A. Garfield.* New York: H. M. Caldwell, 1881.

Allen, Michael. *Western Rivermen, 1763–1861: Ohio and Mississippi Boatmen and the Myth of the Alligator Horse.* Baton Rouge: Louisiana University Press, 1990.

Anbinder, Tyler. *Nativism and Slavery: The Northern Know Nothings and the Politics of the 1850s.* New York: Oxford University Press, 1992.

Anderson, Dwight. *Abraham Lincoln: The Quest for Immortality.* New York: Knopf, 1982.

Angle, Paul M. *"Here I Have Lived": A History of Lincoln's Springfield.* Springfield: Abraham Lincoln Association, 1935.

Dannenbaum, Jed. *Drink and Disorder: Temperance Reform in Cincinnati from the Washingtonian Revival to the WCTU.* Urbana: University of Illinois Press, 1984.

Ashworth, John. *"Agrarians and Aristocrats": Party Political Ideology in the United States, 1837–1846.* Cambridge, Eng.: Cambridge University Press, 1987.

Atherton, Lewis E. *The Frontier Merchant in Mid-America.* Columbia: University of Missouri Press, 1971.

Baber, Adin, A. *Lincoln with Compass and Chain.* Kansas, IL: privately printed, 1968.

Bailyn, Bernard. *The Peopling of British North America: An Introduction.* New York: Vintage, 1986.

Baker, Jean H. *Mary Todd Lincoln: A Biography.* New York: Norton, 1987.

Baker, Jean H. *"Not Much of Me": Abraham Lincoln as a Typical American.* Fort Wayne, IN: Louis A. Warren Lincoln Library and Museum, 1988.

Barney, William L. *The Passage of the Republic: An Interdisciplinary History of Nineteenth-Century America.* Lexington, MA: D. C. Heath, 1987.

Barton, William E. *The Lineage of Lincoln.* Indianapolis: Bobbs-Merrill, 1929.

Berwanger, Eugene. *The Frontier Against Slavery: Western Anti-Negro Prejudice and the Slavery Extension Controversy.* Urbana: University of Illinois Press, 1967.

Beveridge, Albert J. *Abraham Lincoln, 1809–1858,* 2 vols. Boston: Houghton Mifflin, 1928.

Bledstein, Burton J. *The Culture of Professionalism: The Middle Class and the Development of Higher Education in America.* New York: Norton, 1976.

Blue, Frederick J. *The Free Soilers: Third Party Politics, 1848–1854.* Urbana: University of Illinois Press, 1973.

Blumin, Stuart M. *The Emergence of the Middle Class: Social Experience in the American City, 1760–1900.* New York:

Cambridge University Press, 1989.

Bode, Carl. *The American Lyceum.* Carbondale: Southern Illinois University Press, 1968.

Bogue, Allan G. *From Prairie to Corn Belt: Farming on the Illinois and Iowa Prairies in the Nineteenth Century.* Chicago: University of Chicago Press, 1963.

Boorstin, Daniel J. *The Americans: The National Experience.* New York: Random House, 1965.

Boritt, G. S. *Lincoln and the Economics of the American Dream.* Memphis: Memphis State University Press, 1978.

Bourke, Paul, and Donald DeBats. *Washington County: Politics and Community in Antebellum America.* Baltimore: Johns Hopkins University Press, 1995.

Boydston, Jeanne. *Home and Work: Housework, Wages, and the Ideology of Labor in the Early Republic.* New York: Oxford University Press, 1990.

Breckinridge, Sophonisba P. *The Illinois Poor Law and Its Administration.* Chicago: University of Chicago Press, 1939.

Brown, Ralph H. *Historical Geography of the United States.* New York: Harcourt, Brace and World, 1948.

Burke's Presidential Families of the United States of America, 1st ed. London: Burke's Peerage Limited, 1975.

Bushman, Richard L. *The Refinement of America: Persons, Houses, Cities.* New York: Vintage, 1992.

Campbell, Stanley W. *The Slave Catchers: Enforcement of the Fugitive Slave Law, 1850–1860.* Chapel Hill: University of North Carolina Press, 1968.

Carruthers, Olive. *Lincoln's Other Mary.* Chicago: Ziff-Davis, 1946.

Carson, Gerald. *The Old Country Store.* New York: Oxford University Press, 1954.

Cashin, Joan. *A Family Venture: Men and Women on the Southern Frontier.* New York: Oxford University Press, 1991.

Cawelti, John G. *Apostles of the Self-Made Man.* Chicago: University of Chicago Press, 1965.

Cayton, Andrew R. L. *Frontier Indiana.* Bloomington: Indiana University Press, 1996.

Chandler, Josephine Craven. *New Salem: Early Chapter in Lincoln's Life.* Springfield, IL: Journal Printing Company, 1930.

Chudacoff, Howard P. *How Old Are You? Age Consciousness in American Culture.* Princeton, NJ: Princeton University Press, 1989.

Clark, Christopher. *The Roots of Rural Capitalism: Western Massachusetts, 1780–1860.* Ithaca, NY: Cornell University Press, 1990.

Clinton, Catherine. *The Plantation Mistress: Woman's World in the Old South.* New York: Pantheon, 1982.

Cole, Arthur Charles, ed. *The Constitutional Debates of 1847.* Springfield: Illinois State Historical Library, 1919.

Cole, Arthur Charles. *The Era of the Civil War, 1848–1870,* Vol. 3 of *The Centennial History of Illinois,* ed. Clarence Walworth Alvord. Chicago: A. C. McClurg and Company, 1922.

Coleman, Charles H. *Abraham Lincoln and Coles County, Illinois.* New Brunswick, NJ: Scarecrow Press, 1955.

Cornelius, Janet. *Constitution Making in Illinois, 1818–1970.* Urbana: University of Illinois Press, 1972.

Cott, Nancy F. *The Bonds of Womanhood: 'Woman's Sphere' in New England, 1780–1835.* New Haven, CT: Yale University Press, 1977.

Cox, LaWanda. *Lincoln and Black Freedom: A Study in Presidential Leadership.* Urbana: University of Illinois Press, 1985.

Cressy, David. *Coming Over: Migration and Communication Between England and New England in the Seventeenth Century.* New York: Cambridge University Press, 1987.

Cunningham, John T. *New Jersey: America's Main Road.* Garden City, NY: Doubleday, 1976.

Cuomo, Mario M., and Harold Holzer, eds., *Lincoln on Democracy.* New York: Harper, 1990.

Curry, Leonard P. *The Free Black in Urban America, 1800–1850: The Shadow of the Dream.* Chicago: University of Chicago Press, 1981.

Curti, Merle. *The Making of an American Community: A Case Study of Democracy in a Frontier County.* Stanford, CA: Stanford University Press, 1959.

Danhof, Clarence. *Change In Agriculture: The Northern United States, 1820–1870.* Cambridge, MA: Harvard University Press, 1969.

Davis, James E. *Frontier America, 1800–1840: A Comparative Demographic Analysis of the Frontier Process.* Glendale, CA: Clark, 1977.

Davis, James E. *Frontier Illinois.* Bloomington: Indiana University Press, 1998.

Degler, Carl N. *At Odds: Women and the Family in America from the Revolution to the Present.* New York: Oxford University Press, 1980.

Degregorio, William A. *The Complete Book of*

U.S. Presidents, 4th ed. New York: Barricade Books, 1993.

Donald, David Herbert. *Lincoln*. New York: Simon and Schuster, 1995.

Donald, David. *Lincoln's Herndon*. New York: Knopf, 1948.

Dowd, Gregory Evans. *A Spirited Resistance: The North American Indian Struggle for Unity, 1745–1815*. Baltimore: Johns Hopkins University Press, 1992.

Doyle, Don Harrison. *The Social Order of a Frontier Community*. Urbana: University of Illinois Press, 1978.

Duff, John J. *Abraham Lincoln, Prairie Lawyer*. New York: Bramwell House, 1960.

Dyba, Thomas J., and George L. Painter. *Seventeen Years at Eighth and Jackson*, 2nd ed. Lisle, IL: IBC Publications, 1985.

Dyle, Otto R. *Abraham Lincoln in Decatur*. Washington: Vantage Press, 1957.

D'Emilio, John, and Estelle B. Freedman. *Intimate Matters: A History of Sexuality in America*. New York: Harper and Row, 1988.

Eby, Cecil. *"That Disgraceful Affair": The Black Hawk War*. New York: Norton, 1973.

Egnal, Marc. *Divergent Paths: How Culture and Institutions Have Shaped North American Growth*. New York: Oxford University Press, 1996.

Faragher, John Mack. *Daniel Boone: The Life and Legend of an American Pioneer*. New York: Henry Holt, 1992.

Faragher, John Mack. *Sugar Creek: Life on the Illinois Prairie*. New Haven, CT: Yale University Press, 1986.

Faragher, John Mack. *Women and Men on the Overland Trail*. New Haven, CT.: Yale University Press, 1979.

Fehrenbacher, D. E. *The Changing Image of Lincoln in American Historiography*. Oxford, Eng.: Oxford University Press, 1968.

Fehrenbacher, Don E. *Lincoln in Text and Context: Collected Essays*. Stanford, CA: Stanford University Press, 1987.

Fehrenbacher, Don E. *Prelude to Greatness: Lincoln in the 1850s*. Stanford, CA: Stanford University Press, 1962.

Fehrenbacher, Don E. *The Dred Scott Case: Its Significance in American Law and Politics*. New York: Oxford University Press, 1978.

Feldberg, Michael. *The Turbulent Era: Riot and Disorder in Jacksonian America*. New York: Oxford University Press, 1980.

Filler, Louis. *The Crusade Against Slavery, 1830–1860*. New York: Harper, 1960.

Fischer, David Hackett, and James C. Kelly. *Away, I'm Bound Away: Virginia and the Westward Movement*. Richmond: Virginia Historical Society, 1993.

Fischer, David Hackett. *Albion's Seed: Four British Folkways in America*. New York: Oxford University Press, 1989.

Fischer, David Hackett. *Growing Old in America*. New York: Oxford University Press, 1977.

Fogel, Robert W. *Without Consent or Contract: The Rise and Fall of American Slavery*. New York: Norton, 1989.

Foner, Eric. *Free Soil, Free Labor, Free Men: The Ideology of the Republican Party Before the Civil War*. New York: Oxford University Press, 1970.

Forgie, George B. *Patricide in the House Divided: A Psychological Interpretation of Lincoln and His Age*. New York: Norton, 1979.

Frank, Stephen M. *Life with Father: Parenthood and Masculinity in the Nineteenth-Century North*. Baltimore: Johns Hopkins University Press, 1998.

Fredrickson, George M. *The Black Image in the White Mind: The Debate on Afro-American Character and Destiny, 1817–1914*. New York: Harper & Row, 1971.

Fuller, Wayne. *RFD: The Changing Face of Rural America*. Bloomington: Indiana University Press, 1964.

Gienapp, William E. *The Origins of the Republican Party, 1852–1856*. New York: Oxford University Press, 1987.

Gilje, Paul J. *The Road to Mobocracy: Popular Disorder in New York City, 1763–1834*. Chapel Hill: University of North Carolina Press, 1987.

Glickstein, Jonathan A. *Concepts of Free Labor in Antebellum America*. New Haven, CT: Yale University Press, 1991.

Graff, Harvey J. *Conflicting Paths: Growing Up in America*. Cambridge, MA: Harvard University Press, 1995.

Gray, Susan E. *The Yankee West: Community Life on the Michigan Frontier*. Chapel Hill: University of North Carolina Press, 1996.

Gridley, Eleanor. *The Story of Abraham Lincoln or the Journey from the Log Cabin to the White House*. Chicago: M. A. Donohue, 1900.

Grimstead, David. *American Mobbing, 1828–1861: Toward Civil War*. New York: Oxford University Press, 1998.

Guelzo, Allen C. *Abraham Lincoln: Redeemer President*. Grand Rapids, MI: Eerdmans, 1999.

Gusfield, Joseph R. *Symbolic Crusade: Status Politics and the American Temperance Movement*. Urbana: University of Illinois Press, 1963.

Gutman, Herbert G. *The Black Family in*

Slavery and Freedom, 1750–1925. New York: Vintage, 1976.

Hagan, William T. *The Sac and Fox Indians.* Norman: University of Oklahoma Press, 1958.

Hall, Kermit. *The Magic Mirror: Law in American History.* New York: Oxford University Press, 1989.

Halttunen, Karen. *Confidence Men and Painted Women: A Study of Middle-Class Culture in America, 1840–1870.* New Haven, CT: Yale University Press, 1982.

Hamilton, Holman. *Prologue to Conflict: The Crisis and Compromise of 1850.* Lexington: University of Kentucky Press, 1964.

Hansen, Stephen L. *The Making of the Third Party System: Voters and Parties in Illinois, 1850–1876.* Ann Arbor, MI.: UMI Research Press, 1980.

Holt, Michael F. *The Rise and Fall of the American Whig Party: Jacksonian Politics and the Onset of the Civil War.* New York: Oxford University Press, 1999.

Horwitz, Morton J. *The Transformation of American Law, 1780–1860.* Cambridge, MA: Harvard University Press, 1977.

Howard, Robert P. *Illinois: A History of the Prairie State.* Grand Rapids, MI: Eerdmans, 1972.

Howe, Daniel Walker. *The Political Culture of the American Whigs.* Chicago: University of Chicago Press, 1979.

Hulbert, Archer B. *The Paths of Inland Commerce: A Chronicle of Trail, Road, and Waterway.* New Haven, CT: Yale University Press, 1920.

Hurt, R. Douglas. *The Ohio Frontier: Crucible of the Old Northwest, 1720–1830.* Bloomington: Indiana University Press, 1996.

Huston, James L. *The Panic of 1857 and the Coming of the Civil War.* Baton Rouge: Louisiana State University Press, 1982.

Johnson, Hildegard Binder. *Order Upon the Land: The U.S. Rectangular Land Survey and the Upper Mississippi Country.* New York: Oxford University Press, 1976.

Johnson, Paul E. *A Shopkeeper's Millenium: Society and Revivals in Rochester, New York, 1815–1837.* New York: Hill and Wang, 1978.

Jones, Jacqueline. *Labor of Love, Labor of Sorrow: Black Women, Work and the Family, from Slavery to the Present.* New York: Vintage, 1985.

Josephy, Alvin M., Jr. *The Patriot Chiefs: A Chronicle of American Indian Leadership.* New York: Viking, 1961.

Kane, Joseph Nathan. *The American Counties.* New York: Scarecrow Press, 1962.

Kasson, John F. *Rudeness and Civility: Manners in Nineteenth-Century Urban America.* New York: Hill and Wang, 1990.

Katz, Michael B. *The Irony of Early School Reform: Educational Innovation in Mid-Nineteenth-Century Massachusetts.* Cambridge, MA: Harvard University Press, 1968.

Katz, Michael. *The People of Hamilton, Canada West: Family and Class in a Mid-Nineteenth-Century City.* Cambridge, MA: Harvard University Press, 1975.

Kett, Joseph F. *Rites of Passage: Adolescence in America, 1790 to the Present.* New York: Basic Books, 1977.

Knights, Peter R. *The Plain People of Boston, 1830–1860.* New York: Oxford University Press, 1971.

Knights, Peter R. *Yankee Destinies: The Lives of Ordinary Nineteenth-Century Bostonians.* Chapel Hill: University of North Carolina Press, 1991.

Kohl, Lawrence Frederick. *The Politics of Individualism: Parties and the American Character in the Jacksonian Era.* New York: Oxford University Press, 1989.

Krenkel, John H. *Illinois Internal Improvements, 1818–1848.* Cedar Rapids: Torch Press, 1958.

Lane, Roger. *Policing the City: Boston, 1822–1885.* Cambridge, MA: Harvard University Press, 1967.

Laurie, Bruce. *Artisans into Workers: Labor in Nineteenth-Century America.* New York: Noonday Press, 1989.

Lemon, James T. *The Best Poor Man's Country: A Geographical Study of Early Southeastern Pennsylvania.* Baltimore: Johns Hopkins University Press, 1972.

Lincoln, Waldo. *History of the Lincoln Family: An Account of the Descendants of Samuel Lincoln of Hingham, Massachusetts, 1637–1920.* Worcester, MA: Commonwealth Press, 1923.

Litwack, Leon F. *North of Slavery: The Negro in the Free States, 1790–1860.* Chicago: University of Chicago Press, 1961.

Luthin, Reinhard H. *The First Lincoln Campaign.* Cambridge, MA: Harvard University Press, 1944.

Lystra, Karen. *Searching the Heart: Women, Men, and Romantic Love in Nineteenth-Century America.* New York: Oxford University Press, 1989.

Mahon, John K. *History of the Militia and the National Guard.* New York: Macmillan, 1983.

Mahoney, Timothy R. *Provincial Lives: Middle-Class Experience in the Antebellum Middle*

West. New York: Cambridge University Press, 1999.

Mahoney, Timothy R. *River Towns in the Great West: The Structure of Provincial Urbanization in the American Midwest, 1820–1870*. New York: Cambridge University Press, 1990.

Malone, Dumas, ed. *The Dictionary of American Biography*, 20 vols. New York: Charles Scribner's Sons, 1928–1958.

Maltby, Charles. *The Life and Public Services of Abraham Lincoln*. Stockton, CA: Daily Independent Steam Power Plant, 1884.

Matthews, Glenna. *"Just a Housewife": The Rise and Fall of Domesticity in America*. New York: Oxford University Press, 1987.

Mayo, James M. *The American Grocery Store: The Evolution of an Architectural Space*. Westport, CT: Greenwood Press, 1993.

McCormick, Richard P. *New Jersey from Colony to State, 1609–1789*. Princeton, NJ: D. Van Nostrand, 1964.

McCormick, Richard P. *The Second American Party System: Party Formation in the Jacksonian Era*. Chapel Hill: University of North Carolina Press, 1966.

McCusker, John J. *How Much Is That in Real Money? A Historical Price Index for Use as a Deflator of Money Values in the Economy of the United States*. Worcester, MA: American Antiquarian Society, 1992.

McManis, Douglas R. *Initial Evaluation and Utilization of the Illinois Prairies, 1815–1840*. Chicago: University of Chicago Press, 1964.

McPherson, James M. *Ordeal by Fire: The Civil War and Reconstruction*, 2nd ed.. New York: McGraw-Hill, 1992

Meinig, D. W. *The Shaping of America: A Geographical Perspective on 500 Years of History*, Vol. 1, *Atlantic America, 1492–1800*. New Haven, CT: Yale Univerity Press, 1986.

Meinig, D. W. *The Shaping of America: A Geographical Perspective on 500 Years of History*, Vol. 2, *Continental America, 1800–1867*. New Haven, CT.: Yale University Press, 1986.

Miller, Floyd J. *The Search for a Black Nationality: Black Emigration and Colonization, 1787–1963*. Urbana: University of Illinois Press, 1975.

Mintz, Steven, and Susan Kellogg. *Domestic Revolutions: A Social History of American Family Life*. New York: Free Press, 1988.

Mintz, Steven. *Moralists and Modernizers: America's Pre-Civil War Reformers*. Baltimore: Johns Hopkins University Press, 1995.

Mitchell, Robert D. *Commercialism and Frontier: Perspectives on the Early Shenandoah Valley*. Charlottesville: University Press of Virginia, 1977.

Monkkonen, Eric H. *The Dangerous Class: Crime and Poverty in Columbus, Ohio, 1860–1885*. Cambridge, MA: Harvard University Press, 1975.

Moreland, Willis D., and Erwin H. Goldenstein. *Pioneers in Adult Education*. Chicago: Nelson-Hall, 1985.

Myers, James E. *The Astonishing Saber Duel of Abraham Lincoln*. Springfield: Lincoln-Herndon Building Publishers, 1968.

Nackenoff, Carol. *The Fictional Republic: Horatio Alger and American Political Discourse*. New York: Oxford University Press, 1994.

Neely, Mark E., Jr. *The Last Best Hope of Earth: Abraham Lincoln and the Promise of America*. Cambridge, MA.: Harvard University Press, 1993.

Nelson, Ronald E., ed. *Illinois: Land and Life in the Prairie State*. Dubuque: Kendall-Hunt, 1978.

Nevins, Allan. *The Emergence of Lincoln*, 2 vols. New York: Charles Scribner's Sons, 1950.

New Salem: A Memorial to Abraham Lincoln, 3rd ed. Springfield: State of Illinois, 1937.

Newcomb, Rexford. *In the Lincoln Country: Journeys to the Lincoln Shrines of Kentucky, Indiana, Illinois and Other States*. Philadelphia: J. B. Lippincott, 1928.

Nichols, Roger L. *Black Hawk and the Warrior's Path*. Arlington Heights, IL: Harlan Davidson, 1992.

North, Douglass C. *The Economic Growth of the United States, 1790–1860*. New York: Norton, 1966.

Norton, Mary Beth. *Liberty's Daughters: The Revolutionary Experience of American Women, 1750–1800*. Glenview, IL: Scott, Foresman, 1980.

Oates, Stephen B. *To Purge This Land With Blood: A Biography of John Brown*. New York: Harper, 1970.

Oates, Stephen B. *With Malice Toward None: The Life of Abraham Lincoln*. New York: Harper, 1977.

Oberly, James W. *Sixty Million Acres: American Veterans and the Public Lands Before the Civil War*. Kent, OH: Kent State University Press, 1990.

O'Brien, Michael J. *Grassland, Forest, and Historical Settlement: An Analysis of Dynamics in Northeast Missouri*. Lincoln: University of Nebraska Press, 1984.

Onstot, T. G. *Pioneers of Menard and Mason*

Counties. Peoria, IL: J. W. Franks and Sons, 1902.

Ostendorf, Lloyd, and Walter Oleksy. *Lincoln's Unknown Private Life: An Oral History of His Black Housekeeper, Mariah Vance, 1850–1860.* Mamaroneck, NY: Hastings House, 1995.

Pease, Theodore Calvin. *Illinois Election Returns, 1818–1848,* Vol. 18 of *Collections of the Illinois State Historical Library.* Springfield: Illinois State Historical Library, 1923.

Pease, Theodore Calvin. *The Frontier State, 1818–1848,* Vol. 2 of *The Centennial History of Illinois,* ed. Clarence Walworth Alvord. Chicago: A. C. McClurg and Company, 1922.

Pessen, Edward. *The Log Cabin Myth: The Social Backgrounds of the Presidents.* New Haven, CT: Yale University Press, 1984.

Peterson, Merrill D. *Lincoln in American Memory.* New York: Oxford University Press, 1994.

Pooley, William V. *The Settlement of Illinois from 1830 to 1850,* Bulletin of the University of Wisconsin, History Series, Vol. 1. Madison: University of Wisconsin, 1908, 287–595.

Potter, David. *The Impending Crisis, 1848–1861.* New York: Harper, 1976.

Pratt, Harry E. *The Personal Finances of Abraham Lincoln.* Springfield: Abraham Lincoln Association, 1943.

Prucha, Francis Paul. *The Great Father: The United States Government and the American Indians,* 2 vols. Lincoln: University of Nebraska Press, 1984.

Quarles, Benjamin. *Lincoln and the Negro.* New York: Oxford University Press, 1962.

Rader, Benjamin G. *American Sports: From the Age of Folk Games to the Age of Televised Sports,* 2nd ed. Englewood Cliffs, NJ: Prentice Hall, 1990.

Randall, J. G. *Lincoln the President: Springfield to Gettysburg,* 2 vols. New York: Dodd, Mead, 1945.

Randall, Ruth Painter. *Lincoln's Animal Friends.* Boston: Little, Brown, 1958.

Randall, Ruth Painter. *Mary Lincoln: Biography of a Marriage.* Boston: Little, Brown, 1953.

Remini, Robert V. *Andrew Jackson and the Bank War.* New York: Norton, 1967.

Richards, Leonard L. *"Gentlemen of Property and Standing": Anti-Abolition Mobs in Jacksonian America.* New York: Oxford University Press, 1970.

Riddle, Donald W. *Congressman Abraham Lincoln.* Urbana: University of Illinois Press, 1957.

Riddle, Donald W. *Lincoln Runs for Congress.* New Brunswick, NJ: Rutgers University Press, 1948.

Robertson, James Oliver. *American Myth, American Reality.* New York: Hill and Wang, 1980.

Rodgers, Daniel T. *The Work Ethic in Industrial America, 1850–1920.* Chicago: University of Chicago Press, 1978.

Rohrbaugh, Malcolm J. *The Trans-Appalachian Frontier: People, Societies, and Institutions, 1775–1850.* New York: Oxford University Press, 1978.

Rohrbough, Malcolm J. *The Land Office Business: The Settlement and Administration of American Public Lands, 1789–1837.* New York: Oxford University Press, 1968.

Rooney, John F., Jr., Wilbur Zelinsky, and Dean R. Louder, eds. *This Remarkable Continent: An Atlas of United States and Canadian Society and Cultures.* College Station: Texas A&M University Press, 1982.

Rosenberg, Charles E. *The Cholera Years.* Chicago: University of Chicago Press, 1967.

Rosenberg, Rosalind. *Divided Lives: American Women in the Twentieth Century.* New York: Hill and Wang, 1992.

Rothman, Ellen K. *Hands and Hearts: A History of Courtship in America.* New York: Basic Books, 1984.

Rotundo, E. Anthony. *American Manhood: Transformations in Masculinity from the Revolution to the Modern Era.* New York: Basic Books, 1993.

Ryan, Mary P. *Cradle of the Middle Class: The Family in Oneida County, New York, 1790–1865.* New York: Cambridge University Press, 1981.

Schlereth, Thomas J. *Victorian America: Transformations in Everyday Life.* New York: Harper, 1991.

Sellers, Charles. *The Market Revolution: Jacksonian America, 1815–1846.* New York: Oxford University Press, 1991

Senechal, Roberta. *The Sociogenesis of a Race Riot.* Urbana: University of Illinois Press, 1990.

Sennett, Richard. *Families Against the City: Middle Class Homes of Industrial Chicago.* Cambridge, MA: Harvard University Press, 1970.

Sewell, Richard H. *A House Divided: Sectionalism and Civil War, 1848–1865.* Baltimore: Johns Hopkins University Press, 1988.

Sewell, Richard H. *Ballots for Freedom: Antislavery Politics in the United States, 1837–1860.* New York: Oxford University Press, 1976.

Simon, John Y. *House Divided: Lincoln and His Father*. Fort Wayne, IN: Louis A. Warren Lincoln Library and Museum, 1987.

Simon, Paul. *Lincoln's Preparation for Greatness: The Illinois Legislative Years*. Urbana: University of Illinois Press, 1965.

Spears, Zarel C., and Robert S. Barton. *Berry and Lincoln, Frontier Merchants: The Store That "Winked Out."* New York: Stratford House, 1947.

Staudenraus, P. J. *The African Colonization Movement, 1816–1865*. New York: Columbia University Press, 1961.

Tarbell, Ida M. *In the Footsteps of the Lincolns*. New York: Harper and Brothers, 1924.

Tarbell, Ida M. *The Life of Abraham Lincoln*, 2 vols. New York: Macmillan, 1917.

Temin, Peter. *The Jacksonian Economy*. New York: Norton, 1969.

Temple, Wayne C. *By Square and Compasses: The Building of Lincoln's Home and Its Saga*. Bloomington, IL: Ashlar Press, 1984.

The Oxford English Dictionary, 2nd ed., 20 vols. Oxford, Eng.: Clarendon Press, 1989.

Theobald, Paul. *Call School: Rural Education in the Midwest to 1918*. Carbondale: Southern Illinois University Press, 1995.

Thernstrom, Stephan. *Poverty and Progress: Social Mobility in a Nineteenth-Century City*. Cambridge, MA: Harvard University Press, 1964.

Thomas, Benjamin P. *Lincoln's New Salem*. New York: Knopf, 1954.

Thomas, Benjamin. *Abraham Lincoln: A Biography*. New York: Knopf, 1952.

Thompson, C. M. *The Lincoln Way*. Springfield: Illinois State Journal Company, 1913.

Townsend, William. *Lincoln and His Wife's Home Town*. Indianapolis: Bobbs-Merrill, 1929.

Turner, Justin G., and Linda Levitt Turner. *Mary Todd Lincoln: Her Life and Letters*. New York: Fromm International Publishing Company, 1972.

Tyrrell, Ian R. *Sobering Up: From Temperance to Prohibition in Antebellum America, 1800–1860*. Westport, CT: Greenwood Press, 1979.

Vance, James E., Jr. *The Merchant's World: The Geography of Wholesaling*. Englewood Cliffs, NJ: Prentice-Hall, 1970.

Wade, Richard C. *The Urban Frontier: The Rise of Western Cities, 1790–1830*. Cambridge, MA: Harvard University Press, 1959.

Wallach, Glenn. *Obedient Sons: The Discourse of Youth and Generations in American Culture, 1630–1860*. Amherst: University of Massachusetts Press, 1997.

Walsh, John Evangelist. *The Shadows Rise: Abraham Lincoln and the Ann Rutledge Legend*. Urbana: University of Illinois Press, 1993.

Walters, Ronald G. *American Reformers, 1815–1860*. New York: Hill and Wang, 1978.

Ward, Geoffrey C. *Lincoln and the Right to Rise*. Springfield: Sangamon State University, 1978.

Warren, Louis A. *Lincoln's Parentage and Childhood*. New York: Century, 1929.

Warren, Louis A. *Lincoln's Youth: Indiana Years, Seven to Twenty-one, 1816–1830*. Indianapolis: Indiana Historical Society, 1959.

Watson, Harry L. *Liberty and Power: The Politics of Jacksonian America*. New York: Noonday Press, 1990.

Wayland, John W. *A History of Rockingham County, Virginia*. Dayton, VA: Ruebush-Elkins, 1912.

Wayland, John W. *The Lincolns in Virginia*. Staunton, VA: McClure Printing Company, 1946.

Weeks, Phillip. *Farewell, My Nation: The American Indian and the United States, 1820–1890*. Arlington Heights, IL: Harlan Davidson, 1990.

Weiss, Richard. *The American Myth of Success: From Horatio Alger to Norman Vincent Peale*. New York: Basic Books, 1969.

Wells, Robert V. *Revolutions in American's Lives: A Demographic Perspective on the History of Americans, Their Families, and Their Society*. Westport, CT: Greenwood Press, 1982.

Wells, Robert V. *Uncle Sam's Family: Issues and Perspectives on American Demographic History*. Albany: State University of New York Press, 1985.

White, Richard. *The Middle Ground: Indians, Empires, and Republics in the Great Lakes Region, 1650–1815*. New York: Cambridge University Press, 1991.

Wiebe, Robert H. *The Opening of American Society: From the Adoption of the Constitution to the Eve of Disunion*. New York: Knopf, 1984.

Wilson, Douglas L. *Honor's Voice: The Transformation of Abraham Lincoln*. New York: Knopf, 1998.

Wilson, Major L. *Space, Time, and Freedom: The Quest for Nationality and the Irrepressible Conflict, 1815–1861*. Westport, CT: Greenwood Press, 1974.

Wright, Donald R. *African-Americans in the*

Early Republic, 1789–1831. Arlington Heights, IL: Harlan Davidson, 1993.

Wyatt-Brown, Bertram. *Southern Honor: Ethics and Behavior in the Old South*. New York: Oxford University Press, 1982.

Wyllie, Irvin G. *The Self-Made Man in America: The Myth of Rags to Riches*. New York: Free Press, 1954.

Wyman, Mark. *Immigrants in the Valley: Irish, Germans, and Americans in the Upper Mississippi Country, 1830–1860*. Chicago: Nelson-Hall, 1984.

Zelinsky, Wilbur. *The Cultural Geography of the United States*, rev. ed. Englewood Cliffs, NJ: Prentice Hall, 1992.

Zelizer, Viviana A. *The Social Meaning of Money*. New York: Basic Books, 1994.

Articles

Adams, James W., and Alice Bee Kasakoff, "Migration and the Family in Colonial New England: The View from Genealogies." *Journal of Family History*, 9 (Spring 1984), 24–43.

Allen, James P. "Migration Fields of French Canadian Immigrants to Southern Maine." *Geographical Review*, 62 (July 1972), 366–83.

Angle, Paul M. "Lincoln and Liquor, Part One." *Bulletin of the Abraham Lincoln Association*, 27 (June 1932), 3–8.

Angle, Paul M. "Lincoln and Liquor, Part Two." *Bulletin of the Abraham Lincoln Association*, 27 (September 1932), 3–9.

Appleby, Joyce. "New Cultural Heroes in the Early National Period," in *The Culture of the Market: Historical Essays*, ed. Thomas L. Haskell and Richard F. Teichgraeber III. Cambridge, Eng.: Cambridge University Press, 1993), 163–88.

Atkins, Jonathan M. "The Presidential Candidacy of Hugh Lawson White in Tennessee, 1832–1836." *Journal of Southern History*, 58 (February 1992), 27–56.

Baker, Jean H. "The Lincoln Marriage: Beyond the Battle of Quotations." Robert Fortenbaugh Memorial Lecture, Gettysburg College, 1999.

Basler, Roy P. "Lincoln, Blacks, and Women," in *The Public and the Private Lincoln: Contemporary Perspectives*, ed. Cullom Davis, Charles B. Strozier, Rebecca Monroe Veach, and Geoffrey C. Ward. Carbondale: Southern Illinois University Press, 1979.

Basler, Roy P. "The Authorship of the 'Rebecca' Letters." *Abraham Lincoln Quarterly*, 2 (March 1942), 80–90.

Beales, Ross W., Jr. "In Search of the Historical Child: Miniature Adulthood and Youth in Colonial New England." *American Quarterly*, 27 (October 1975), 379–98.

Bieder, Robert E. "Kinship as a Factor in Migration." *Journal of Marriage and the Family*, 35 (August 1973), 429–39.

Blackmar, Betty. "Rewalking the 'Walking City': Property Relations in New York City, 1780–1840." *Radical History Review*, 21 (Fall 1980), 131–48.

Bloch, Ruth. "American Feminine Ideals in Transition: The Rise of the Moral Mother, 1785–1815." *Feminist Studies*, 4 (June 1978), 100–26.

Blumin, Stuart M. "The Hypothesis of Middle-Class Formation in Nineteenth-Century America: A Critique and Some Proposals." *American Historical Review*, 90 (April 1985), 299–338.

Borit, G. S. "Lincoln's Opposition to the Mexican War." *Journal of the Illinois State Historical Society*, 67 (February 1974), 79–100.

Boritt, G. S. "The Right to Rise," in *The Public and the Private Lincoln: Contemporary Perspectives*, ed. Cullom Davis, Charles B. Strozier, Rebecca Monroe Veach, and Geoffrey C. Ward. Carbondale: Southern Illinois University Press, 1979.

Boritt, G. S. "The Voyage to the Colony of Linconia." *The Historian*, 37 (August 1975), 619–33.

Bourke, Paul F., and Donald A. DeBats, "Individuals and Aggregates: A Note on Historical Data and Assumptions." *Social Science History*, 4 (Spring 1980), 229–50.

Breiseth, Christopher N. "Lincoln, Douglas, and Springfield in the 1858 Campaign," in *The Public and the Private Lincoln: Contemporary Perspectives*, ed. Cullom Davis, Charles B. Strozier, Rebecca Monroe Veach, and Geoffrey C. Ward. Carbondale: Southern Illinois University Press, 1979, 101–120.

Bushman, Richard L., and Claudia Bushman, "The Early History of Cleanliness in America." *Journal of American History*, 74 (March 1988), 1213–38.

Bushman, Richard L. "Family Security in the Transition from Farm to City, 1750–1850." *Journal of Family History*, 6 (Fall 1981), 238–56.

Cherlin, Andrew. "Changing Family and Household: Contemporary Lessons from Historical Research." *Annual Review of Sociology*, 9 (1983), 51–66.

Chudacoff, Howard P., and Tamara K. Hareven. "From the Empty Nest to Family

Dissolution: Life Course Transitions into Old Age." *Journal of Family History*, 4 (Spring 1979), 69–83.

Chudacoff, Howard P. "A Reconsideration of Geographical Mobility in American Urban History." *Virginia Magazine of History and Biography*, 102 (October 1994), 501–18.

Clark, Christopher. "Household Economy, Market Exchange and the Rise of Capitalism in the Connecticut Valley, 1800–1860." *Journal of Social History*, 13 (Winter 1979), 169–89.

Collins, Bruce. "The Lincoln-Douglas Contest of 1858 and Illinois' Electorate." *Journal of American Studies*, 20 (December 1986), 391–420.

Conzen, Kathleen Neils. "A Saga of Families," in *The Oxford History of the American West*, ed. Clyde A. Milner II, Carol A. O'Connor, and Martha A. Sandweiss. New York: Oxford University Press, 1994, 315–57.

Coolidge, John. "Hingham Builds a Meetinghouse." *New England Quarterly*, 34 (December 1961), 435–61.

Darroch, A. Gordon. "Migrants in the Nineteenth Century: Fugitives or Families in Motion?" *Journal of Family History*, 6 (Fall 1981), 257–77.

Davis, David Brion. "The Significance of Excluding Slavery from the Old Northwest in 1787." *Indiana Magazine of History*, 84 (March 1988), 75–89.

Davis, Edwin D. "Lincoln and Macon County, Illinois, 1830–1831." *Journal of the Illinois State Historical Society*, 25 (April/July 1932), 63–107.

Davis, Rodney O. "Abraham Lincoln: Son and Father." Edgar S. and Ruth W. Burkhardt Lecture Series, Knox College, Galesburg, Illinois, 1997.

Davis, Rodney O. "'I Shall Consider the Whole People of Sangamon my Constituents': Lincoln and the Illinois General Assembly," in *Abraham Lincoln and the Political Process*, ed. George L. Painter and Linda Norbut Suits. Springfield: Lincoln Home National Historic Site, 1992), 13–23.

Douglas, Ann. "Heaven Our Home: Consolation Literature in the Northern United States," in *Death in America*, ed. David E. Stannard. Philadelphia: University of Pennsylvania Press, 1975, 49–68.

"Dr. Denton Offutt: Horse Tamer." *Abraham Lincoln Quarterly*, 2 (September 1943), 330–33.

Dublin, Thomas. "Rural-Urban Migrants in Industrial New England: The Case of Lynn, Massachusetts, in the Mid-Nineteenth

City." *Journal of American History*, 73 (December 1986), 623–44.

Dye, Nancy Schrom, and Daniel Blake Smith. "Mother Love and Infant Death, 1750–1920." *Journal of American History*, 73 (September 1986), 329–53.

Easterlin, Richard. "Population Change and Farm Settlement in the Northern United States." *Journal of Economic History*, 36 (March 1976), 45–75.

Eblen, Jack E. "An Analysis of Nineteenth-Century Frontier Populations." *Demography*, 2 (1965), 399–413.

Etcheson, Nicole. "Manliness and the Political Culture of the Old Northwest, 1790–1860." *Journal of the Early Republic*, 15 (Spring 1995), 59–77.

Fehrenbacher, Don E. "Only His Stepchildren: Lincoln and the Negro." *Civil War History*, 20 (December 1974), 293–310.

Fehrenbacher, Don E. "Political Uses of the Post Office," in Don E. Fehrenbacher, *Lincoln in Text and Context: Collected Essays*. Stanford, CA: Stanford University Press, 1987, 24–32.

Finkelman, Paul. "Slavery and the Northwest Ordinance: A Study in Ambiguity." *Journal of the Early Republic*, 6 (Winter 1986), 343–70.

Finkelman, Paul. "Slavery, the 'More Perfect Union,' and the Prairie State." *Illinois Historical Journal*, 80 (Winter 1987), 248–69.

Formisano, Ronald P. "Political Character, Antipartyism and the Second Party System." *American Quarterly*, 21 (Winter 1969), 683–709.

Fredrickson, George M. "A Man but Not a Brother: Abraham Lincoln and Racial Equality." *Journal of Southern History*, 41 (February 1975), 39–58.

Fredrickson, George M. "The Search for Order and Community," in *The Public and the Private Lincoln: Contemporary Perspectives*, ed. Cullom Davis, Charles B. Strozier, Rebecca Monroe Veach, and Geoffrey C. Ward. Carbondale: Southern Illinois University Press, 1979), 86–98.

Freeman, Joanne B. "Dueling as Politics: Reinterpreting the Burr-Hamilton Duel." *William and Mary Quarterly*, 53 (April 1996), 289–318.

Gamm, Gerald, and Robert D. Putnam, "The Growth of Voluntary Associations in America, 1840–1940." *Journal of Interdisciplinary History*, 29 (Spring 1999), 511–57.

Gara, Larry. "Slavery and the Slave Power: A Crucial Distinction." *Civil War History*, 15 (March 1969), 5–18.

Gara, Larry. "The Underground Railroad in Illinois." *Journal of the Illinois State Historical Society*, 56 (Autumn 1963), 508–28.

Gelber, Steven M. "Do-It-Yourself: Constructing, Repairing and Maintaining Domestic Masculinity." *American Quarterly*, 49 (March 1997), 66–112.

Gertz, Elmer. "The Black Laws of Illinois." *Journal of the Illinois State Historical Society*, 56 (Autumn 1963), 454–73.

Gienapp, William E. "The Republican Party and the Slave Power," in *New Perspectives on Race and Slavery in America: Essays in Honor of Kenneth M. Stampp*, ed. Robert H. Abzug and Stephen E. Maizlish. Lexington: University Press of Kentucky, 1986, 51–78.

Glick, Paul C. "The Family Cycle." *American Sociological Review*, 12 (April 1947), 164–74.

Gorn, Elliot J. "'Gouge and Bite, Pull Hair and Scratch': The Social Significance of Fighting in the Southern Backcountry." *American Historical Review*, 90 (February 1985), 18–43.

Graebner, Norman A. "The Apostle of Progress," in *The Public and the Private Lincoln: Contemporary Perspectives*, ed. Cullom Davis, Charles B. Strozier, Rebecca Monroe Veach, and Geoffrey C. Ward. Carbondale: Southern Illinois University Press, 1979.

Gray, Susan E. "Local Speculator as Confidence Man: Mumford Eldred, Jr., and the Michigan Land Rush." *Journal of the Early Republic*, 10 (Fall 1990), 383–406.

Hart, John Fraser. "Facets of the Geography of Population in the Midwest." *Journal of Geography*, 85 (September/October 1986), 201–11.

Hart, Richard E. "Honest Abe and the African Americans: A Groundbreaking Study of How Blacks in Early Springfield Influenced Lincoln's Views on Race and Society." *Illinois Times*, February 12, 1998, 6–11.

Hart, Richard E. "Springfield's African Americans as a Part of the Lincoln Community." *Journal of the Abraham Lincoln Association*, 20 (Winter 1999), 35–54.

Hessinger, Rodney. "Problems and Promises: Colonial American Child Rearing and Modernization Theory." *Journal of Family History*, 21 (April 1996), 125–43.

Hobsbawm, Eric. "Introduction: Inventing Traditions," in *The Invention of Tradition*, ed. Eric Hobsbawm and Terence Ranger. Cambridge, Eng.: Cambridge University Press, 1983.

Hofstadter, Richard. "Abraham Lincoln and the Self-Made Myth," in Richard Hofstadter, *The American Political Tradition and the Men Who Made It*. New York: Knopf, 1948.

Holt, Michael F. "The Politics of Impatience: The Origins of Know Nothingism." *Journal of American History*, 60 (September 1973), 309–31.

Holt, Michael F. "The Democratic Party, 1828–1860," in *History of U.S. Political Parties*, ed. Arthur M. Schlesinger Jr. New York: Chelsea House, 1973), I, 497–571.

Howe, Daniel Walker. "American Victorianism as a Culture." *American Quarterly*, 27 (December 1975), 507–32.

Howe, Daniel Walker. "Why Abraham Lincoln Was a Whig." *Journal of the Abraham Lincoln Association*, 16 (Summer 1995), 27–38.

Hudson, John C. "Cultural Geography of the Upper Great Lakes Region." *Journal of Cultural Geography*, 5 (Fall/Winter 1984), 19–32.

Hudson, John C. "North American Origins of Middlewestern Frontier Populations." *Annals of the American Association of Geographers*, 78 (September 1988), 395–413.

Jones, James P. "The Illinois Negro Law of 1853: Racism in a Free State." *Illinois Quarterly*, 40 (Winter 1977), 5–22.

Jordan, Philip D. "The Death of Nancy Hanks Lincoln." *Indiana Magazine of History*, 40 (June 1944), 103–10.

Kerber, Linda K. "The Republican Mother: Women and the Enlightenment—An American Perspective." *American Quarterly*, 28 (Summer 1976), 187–205.

Kett, Joseph F. "Adolescence and Youth in Nineteenth-Century America," in *The Family in History: Interdisciplinary Essays*, ed. Theodore K. Rabb and Robert I. Rotberg. New York: Harper, 1971), 95–110.

Kincaid, Robert L. "Cumberland Gap, Gateway of Empire." *Filson Club Quarterly*, 15 (January 1941), 25–40.

Kincaid, Robert L. "Joshua Fry Speed—1814–1882: Abraham Lincoln's Most Intimate Friend." *Filson Club History Quarterly*, 17 (April 1943), 63–123.

Kobrin, Frances E. "The Fall in Household Size and the Rise of the Primary Individual in the United States." *Demography*, 13 (February 1976), 127–38.

Kraditor, Aileen S. "The Liberty and Free Soil Parties," in *History of U.S. Political Parties*, ed. Arthur M. Schlesinger Jr. New York: Chelsea House, 1973, I, 741–81.

Laslett, Barbara. "The Family as a Public and Private Institution: An Historical

Perspective." *Journal of Marriage and the Family*, 35 (August 1973), 480-92.

Lewis, Jan. "Motherhood in the Construction of the Male Citizen in the United States, 1750–1850," in *Constructions of the Self*, ed. George Levine. New Brunswick, NJ: Rutgers University Press, 1992.

"Lincoln—Trustee of the Town of Springfield." *Bulletin of the Abraham Lincoln Association* (June 1937), 3–7.

"Lincoln's Land Holdings and Investments." *Abraham Lincoln Association Bulletin*, 16 (September 1, 1929), 1–8.

Macdonald , John S., and Leatrice D. Macdonald. "Chain Migration, Ethnic Neighborhood Formation, and Social Networks." *Milbank Memorial Fund Quarterly*, 42 (January 1964), 82–97.

"Man's Best Friend." *For the People: A Newsletter of the Abraham Lincoln Association*, 1 (Autumn 1999), 6.

Marshall, Lynn L. "The Strange Stillbirth of the Whig Party." *American Historical Review*, 72 (January 1967), 445–68.

McCormick, Richard P. "Was There a 'Whig Strategy' in 1836?" *Journal of the Early Republic*, 4 (Spring 1984), 47–70.

McDermott, Stacy Pratt. "Dissolving the Bonds of Matrimony: Women and Divorce in Sangamon County, Illinois, 1837–1860," in *In Tender Consideration: Women, Families, and the Law in Abraham Lincoln's Illinois*, ed. Daniel W. Stowell. Urbana: University of Illinois Press, forthcoming.

McMurtry, Gerald. "The Lincoln Migration from Kentucky to Indiana." *Indiana Magazine of History*, 33 (December 1937), 385–421.

Meyer, Douglas K. "Illinois Culture Regions at Mid-Nineteenth Century." *Bulletin of the Illinois Geographical Society*, 18 (December 1976), 3–13.

Meyer, Douglas K. "Native-Born Immigrant Clusters on the Illinois Frontier." *Proceedings of the Association of American Geographers*, 8 (1976), 41–44.

Meyer, Douglas K. "Southern Illinois Migration Fields: The Shawnee Hills in 1850." *The Professional Geographer*, 28 (May 1976), 151–60.

Mitchell, Robert D. "The Formation of Early American Cultural Regions: An Interpretation," in *European Settlement and Development in North America: Essays in Honour and Memory of Andrew Hill Clark*, ed. James R. Gibson. Toronto: University of Toronto Press, 1978, 66–90.

Mitchell, Robert D. "The Shenandoah Valley Frontier." *Annals of the American Association of Geographers*, 62 (September 1972), 461–86.

Modell, John, and Tamara K. Hareven, "Urbanization and the Malleable Household: An Examination of Boarding and Lodging in American Families." *Journal of Marriage and the Family*, 35 (August 1973), 467–79.

Modell, John, Frank F. Furstenberg Jr., and Theodore Hershberg. "Social Change and Transitions to Adulthood in Historical Perspective." *Journal of Family History*, 1 (Autumn 1976), 7–32.

Montgomery, David. "The Working Classes of the Pre-Industrial American City, 1780-1830." *Labor History*, 9 (Winter 1968), 3–22.

Mutch, Robert E. "Yeoman and Merchant in Pre-Industrial America: Eighteenth-Century Massachusetts as a Case Study." *Societas: A Review of Social History*, 7 (Autumn 1977), 279–302.

Morrison, Elting. "Election of 1860," in *History of American Presidential Elections, 1789-1968*, ed. Arthur M. Schlesinger Jr. and Fred L. Israel. New York: Chelsea House, 1971), II, 1097–1152.

Neely, Mark. "American Nationalism in the Image of Henry Clay: Abraham Lincoln's Eulogy on Henry Clay in Context." *Register of the Kentucky Historical Society*, 73 (January 1975), 31–60.

Neely, Mark. "Did Lincoln Cause Logan's Defeat?" *Lincoln Lore*, 1660 (June 1976), 1–4.

Neely, Mark. "Lincoln's Lyceum Speech and the Origins of a Modern Myth." *Lincoln Lore*, 1776 (February 1987), 1-3.

Neely, Mark. "The Political Life of New Salem, Illinois." *Lincoln Lore*, 1715 (January 1981), 1–3.

Neely, Mark E., Jr. "Abraham Lincoln and Black Colonization: Benjamin Butler's Spurious Testimony." *Civil War History*, 25 (March 1979), 77–83.

Neely, Mark E., Jr. "Lincoln and the Mexican War: An Argument by Analogy." *Civil War History*, 24 (March 1978), 5–24.

Nichols, Roy, and Jeannette Nichols. "Election of 1852," in *History of American Presidential Elections, 1789-1968*, ed. Arthur M. Schlesinger Jr. and Fred L. Israel. New York: Chelsea House, 1971, II, 921–1003.

Nichols, Roy F., and Philip S. Klein "Election of 1856," in *History of American Presidential Elections, 1789-1968*, ed. Arthur M. Schlesinger Jr. and Fred L. Israel. New York: Chelsea House, 1971, II, 921–1003.

Onuf, Peter. "From Constitution to Higher

Law: The Reinterpretation of the Northwest Ordinance." *Ohio History*, 94 (Winter/Spring 1985), 5–33.

Ostendorf, Lloyd. "The Story of William Florville, Mr. Lincoln's Barber." *Lincoln Herald*, 79 (Spring 1977), 29–32.

Peel, Mark. "On the Margins: Lodgers and Boarders in Boston, 1860–1900." *Journal of American History*, 72 (March 1986), 813–34.

Perkins, Elizabeth A. "The Consumer Frontier: Household Consumption in Early Kentucky." *Journal of American History*, 78 (September 1991), 486–510.

Pinsker, Matthew. "Senator Abraham Lincoln." *Journal of the Abraham Lincoln Association*, 14 (Summer 1993), 1–21.

Pitt-Rivers, Julian. "Pseudo-Kinship." *International Encyclopedia of the Social Sciences*. New York: Macmillan, 1968, VIII, 408–13.

Planck, Gary R. "Abraham Lincoln and Black Colonization: Theory and Practice." *Lincoln Herald*, 72 (Summer 1970), 61–77.

Pond, F. N. "The Memoirs of James McGrady Rutledge." *Journal of the Illinois State Historical Society*, 29 (April 1936), 76–88.

Pond, Fern Nance. "New Salem's Miller and Kelso." *Lincoln Herald*, 52 (December 1950), 26–41.

Pratt, Harry E. "Lincoln in the Black Hawk War." *Bulletin of the Abraham Lincoln Association*, 54 (December 1938), 3–13.

Pratt, Harry E. "Lincoln Pilots the Talisman." *Abraham Lincoln Quarterly*, 2 (September 1943), 319–29.

Price, Edward T. "The Central Courthouse Square in the American County Seat." *Geographical Review*, 58 (January 1968), 29–60.

Purvis, Thomas L. "The Making of a Myth: Abraham Lincoln's Family Background in the Perspective of Jacksonian Politics." *Journal of the Illinois State Historical Society*, 75 (Summer 1982), 148–60.

Reinders, Robert. "Militia and Public Order in Nineteenth-Century America." *Journal of American Studies*, 11 (April 1977), 81–101.

Remini, Robert V. "Election of 1832," in *History of American Presidential Elections, 1789–1968*, ed. Arthur M. Schlesinger Jr. and Fred L. Israel. New York: Chelsea House, 1971), I, 495–515.

Rorabaugh, W. J. "The Political Duel in the Early Republic: Burr v. Hamilton." *Journal of the Early Republic*, 15 (Spring 1995), 1–23.

Rose, Gregory S. "Hoosier Origins: The Nativity of Indiana United States-Born Population in 1850." *Indiana Magazine of History*, 81 (September 1985), 201–32.

Rose, Gregory S. "Information Sources for Nineteenth Century Midwestern Migration." *Professional Geographer*, 37 (February 1985), 66–72.

Rose, Gregory S. "Upland Southerners: The County Origins of Southern Migrants to Indiana by 1850." *Indiana Magazine of History*, 82 (September 1986), 242–63.

Rothenberg, Winifred B. "The Emergence of a Capital Market in Rural Massachusetts, 1730–1838." *Journal of Economic History*, 45 (December 1985), 781–808.

Rotundo, E. Anthony. "American Fatherhood: A Historical Perspective." *American Behavioral Scientist*, 29 (September/October 1985), 7–25.

Rotundo, E. Anthony. "Body and Soul: Changing Ideals of American Middle-Class Manhood, 1770-1920." *Journal of Social History*, 16 (Summer 1983), 23–38.

Scheiber, Harry N. "Urban Rivalry and Internal Improvements in the Old Northwest, 1820–1860." *Ohio History*, 71 (October 1962), 227–39.

Schwartz, Thomas F. "The Springfield Lyceum and Lincoln's 1838 Speech." *Illinois Historical Journal*, 83 (Spring 1990), 45–49.

Sellers, Charles. "Election of 1844," in *History of American Presidential Elections, 1789–1968*, ed. Arthur M. Schlesinger Jr. and Fred L. Israel. New York: Chelsea House, 1971, I, 747–861.

Senning, John P. "The Know-Nothing Movement in Illinois." *Journal of the Illinois State Historical Society*, 7 (April 1914), 7–33.

Silbey, Joel H. "Election of 1836," in *History of American Presidential Elections, 1789–1968*, ed. Arthur M. Schlesinger Jr. and Fred L. Israel. New York: Chelsea House, 1971, I, 577–600.

Silbey, Joel. "'Always a Whig in Politics': The Partisan Life of Abraham Lincoln." *Papers of the Abraham Lincoln Association*, 8 (1986), 21–42.

Silverman, Jason H. "'In Isles Beyond the Main': Abraham Lincoln's Philosophy on Black Colonization." *Lincoln Herald*, 80 (Fall 1978), 155–22.

Sklar, Kathryn Kish. "Victorian Women and Domestic Life: Mary Todd Lincoln, Elizabeth Cady Stanton, and Harriet Beecher Stowe," in *The Public and the Private Lincoln: Contemporary Perspectives*, ed. Cullom Davis, Charles B. Strozier, Rebecca Monroe Veach, and Geoffrey C. Ward. Carbondale: Southern Illinois University Press, 1979, 20–37.

Smith, Daniel Scott. "Parental Power and Marriage Patterns: An Analysis of Historical Trends in Hingham, Massachusetts." *Journal of Marriage and the Family*, 35 (August 1973), 419–28.

Squires, J. Duane. "Lincoln's Todd In-Laws." *Lincoln Herald*, 61 (Fall 1967), 121–28.

Steckel, Richard H. "The Economic Foundations of East-West Migration During the 19th Century." *Explorations in Economic History*, 20 (January 1983), 14–36.

Steinson, Barbara J. "Rural Life in Indiana, 1800–1950." *Indiana Magazine of History*, 90 (September 1994), 203–50.

"Stephen T. Logan Talks About Lincoln," *Bulletin of the Lincoln Centennial Association*, 12 (September 1, 1928), 1–5.

Strickland, Arvarh E. "The Illinois Background of Lincoln's Attitude Toward Slavery and the Negro." *Journal of the Illinois State Historical Society*, 56 (Autumn 1963), 474–94.

Swierenga, Robert P. "The Settlement of the Old Northwest: Ethnic Pluralism in a Featureless Plain." *Journal of the Early Republic*, 9 (Spring 1989), 73–105.

Temple, Wayne C. "Lincoln's Arms and Dress in the Black Hawk War," *Lincoln Herald*, 71 (Winter 1969), 145–49.

Temple, Wayne C. "Lincoln's Military Service After the Black Hawk War." *Lincoln Herald*, 72 (Fall 1970), 87–89.

Thernstrom, Stephan, and Peter R. Knights. "Men in Motion: Some Data and Speculations About Urban Population Mobility in Nineteenth-Century America." *Journal of Interdisciplinary History*, 1 (Autumn 1970), 7–35.

Thomas, Benjamin P. "Lincoln the Postmaster." *Bulletin of the Abraham Lincoln Association*, 31 (June 1933), 3–9.

Thomas, Benjamin P. "Lincoln: Voter and Candidate, 1831–1849." *Bulletin of the Abraham Lincoln Association*, 36 (September 1934), 3–9.

Thomas, Benjamin P. "Old New Salem." *Bulletin of the Abraham Lincoln Association*, 29 (December 1932), 3–9.

Tilly, Charles, and C. Harold Brown. "On Uprooting, Kinship and the Auspices of Migration." *International Journal of Comparative Sociology*, 8 (September 1967), 139–64.

Uhlenberg, Peter. "Changing Configurations of the Life Course," in *Transitions: The Family and the Life Course in Historical Perspective*, ed. Tamara K. Hareven. New York: Academic Press, 1978, 65–97.

Uehara, Edwina. "Dual Exchange Theory, Social Networks, and Informal Social Support." *American Journal of Sociology*, 96 (November 1990), 521–57.

Uhlenberg, Peter. "Death and the Family." *Journal of Family History*, 5 (Fall 1980), 313–20.

Uhlenberg, Peter R. "A Study of Cohort Life Cycles: Cohorts of Native Born Massachusetts Women, 1830–1920." *Population Studies*, 23 (November 1969), 407–20.

Van Deusen, Glyndon G. "The Whig Party," in *History of U.S. Political Parties*, ed. Arthur M. Schlesinger Jr. New York: Chelsea House, 1973, I, 333–493.

Vinovskis, Maris A. "Angel's Heads and Weeping Willows: Death in Early America," in *The American Family in Social-Historical Perspective*, ed. Michael Gordon. New York: St. Martin's Press, 1978, 546–63.

Vorenberg, Michael. "Abraham Lincoln and the Politics of Black Colonization." *Journal of the Abraham Lincoln Association*, 14 (Summer 1993), 23–45.

Wallace, Anthony F. C. "Prelude to Disaster: The Course of Indian-White Relations Which Led to the Black Hawk War of 1832," in *The Black Hawk War, 1831–1832*, 2 vols., ed. Ellen M. Whitney. Springfield: Illinois State Historical Library, 1970–1978.

Walters, William D., Jr. "Time and Town Squares." *Bulletin of the Illinois Geographical Society*, 22 (1980), 18–24.

Warren, Louis A. "Abraham Lincoln's Knowledge of His Ancestry." *Lincoln Lore*, 1308 (May 3, 1954), 1.

Warren, Louis A. "The Shiftless Father Myth." *Lincoln Kinsman*, 32 (February 1941), 1–8.

Warren, Louis A. "Thomas Lincoln Goes to New Orleans." *Lincoln Lore*, 1101 (May 15, 1950), 1.

Waters, John J. "Hingham, Massachusetts, 1631–1661: An East Anglian Oligarchy in the New World." *Journal of Social History*, 1 (Summer 1968), 351–70.

Wells, Robert V. "Family History and Demographic Transition." *Journal of Social History*, 9 (Fall 1975), 1–21.

Wells, Robert V. "The Mortality Transition in Schenectady, New York, 1880-1930." *Social Science History*, 19 (Fall 1995), 399–423.

Wiebe, Robert H. "Lincoln's Fraternal Democracy," in *Abraham Lincoln and the American Political Tradition*, ed. John L. Thomas. Amherst: University of Massachusetts Press, 1986, 11–30.

Wilson, Douglas L. "Abraham Lincoln and 'That Fatal First of January,'" *Civil War*

History, 38 (June 1992), 101–30.

Wilson, Douglas L. "Abraham Lincoln, Ann Rutledge, and the Evidence of Herndon's Informants." *Civil War History*, 36 (December 1990), 301–23.

Wilentz, Sean. "Society, Politics, and the Market Revolution, 1815–1848," in *The New American History*, ed. Eric Foner. Philadelphia: Temple University Press, 1990, 51–71.

Wilson, Major L. "Lincoln and Van Buren in the Steps of the Fathers: Another Look at the Lyceum Address." *Civil War History*, 29 (September 1983), 197–211.

Winkle, Kenneth J. "Abraham Lincoln, Self-Made Man," *Journal of the Abraham Lincoln Association*, 21 (Summer 2000), 1–16.

Winkle, Kenneth J. "'The Great Body of the Republic': Abraham Lincoln and the Idea of a Middle West," in *Middle Western Regionalism*, ed. Andrew R. L. Cayton and Susan Gray (Bloomington: Indiana University Press, forthcoming).

Winkle, Kenneth J. "Ohio's Informal Polling Place: Nineteenth-Century Suffrage in Theory and Practice," in *The Pursuit of Public Power: Political Culture in Ohio, 1787–1861*, ed. Andrew R. L. Cayton and Jeffrey Brown. Kent, OH: Kent State University Press, 1994), 169–84.

Winkle, Kenneth J. "The Middle-Class Marriage of Abraham and Mary Lincoln." American Historical Association, Pacific Coast Branch, 1998.

Winkle, Kenneth J. "The Second Party System in Lincoln's Springfield." *Civil War History*, 44 (December 1998), 267–84.

Winkle, Kenneth J. "The Voters of Lincoln's Springfield: Migration and Politial Participation in an Antebellum City." *Journal*

of Social History, 25 (Spring 1992), 595–611.

Zelizer, Viviana A. "The Social Meaning of Money: 'Special Monies.'" *American Journal of Sociology*, 95 (September 1989), 342–77.

Zilversmit, Arthur. "Lincoln and the Problem of Race: A Decade of Interpretations." *Papers of the Abraham Lincoln Association*, 2 (Summer 1980), 22–45.

Unpublished Sources

"Allen Residence," undated typescript, Sangamon Valley Collection, Lincoln Library, Springfield, Illinois.

Davis, Cullom, and Daniel W. Stowell. "A New Look at Lincoln." Abraham Lincoln Institute of the Mid-Atlantic, 2000.

Davis, Cullom. "Abraham Lincoln, Esq.: The Symbiosis of Law and Politics." Seventh Annual Lincoln Colloquium, 1992.

Gavin, Jeff G. *Past Sites of Springfield: A Historic Guide to the Downtown Area.* Typescript, Sangamon Valley Collection, Lincoln Library, 1980.

"Hill Residence," undated typescript, Sangamon Valley Collection, Lincoln Library, Springfield, Illinois.

McKenzie, Molly. "A Demographic Study of Select New Salem Precinct Residents." Undated typescript, Sangamon Valley Collection, Lincoln Library, Springfield, Illinois.

"The Offutt Store," undated typescript, Sangamon Valley Collection, Lincoln Library, Springfield, Illinois.

"The Second Berry-Lincoln Store," undated typescript, Sangamon Valley Collection, Lincoln Library, Springfield, Illinois.

Wallace, Christopher Elliot. "The Opportunity to Grow: Springfield, Illinois during the 1850s," Ph.D. dissertation, Purdue University, 1983.

Index

Numbers in *italics* indicate photos. Numbers followed by the word "table" indicate the entry's inclusion in tables or charts. Numbers followed by the letter "n" and a number indicate the entry's inclusion in Notes.

Fertility control, 280, 281
Fictive kin, 60, 328n. 1
Fillmore, Millard, 297–98
First Great Migration, 11
Florville, William, 266, 267, 268
Ford, Thomas, 189
Foster, James, 254
Fox tribes
    after Black Hawk War, 90
    assault on, 87–88
    land of, 86
    War of 1812 and, 86–87
Francis, Allen, 115
Francis, Josiah, 115
Francis, Simeon, 114
    in 1844 election, 202, 203
    community improvement and, 184, 275
    convention system and, 203–4
    criticized by Democrats, 203
    on currency, 193
    in lyceum, 180–81
    supporting Lincoln, 115
Fraternal societies, 180
Freeman, Abraham, 36–37
Free Soil Club, 245
Free Soilers, 261, 292
Free soil movement, 245–46
Free Soil Party, 244, 245, 246
Fremont, John C., 295
Fugitive Slave Law, 263, 264, 308

Gambling, 178
Garland, Nicholas, 108
Garland, Nicholas A., 109table
Gender imbalance, 165
    marriage and, 62–63, 149
    of stealers in Sangamon County, 62
Gender roles
    exemplified by Lincolns, 229
    labor and, 13–14, 46–48
    within marriage, 214, 217, 223, 224, 226
Gentry, James, 20, 22
Globe Tavern, 221
    arson of, 270
    Lincoln's in, 219–20
    Todd family in, 167, 207
Gorn, Elliot, 64, 65
Gourley, James, 278, 283, 285, 287, 288
Government
    Lincoln on purpose of, 185
    Sangamon County, 172–75
    Whig Party on function of, 187
    See also Political parties
Graff, Harvey, 70, 72–73, 111
Graham, Mentor, 73, 75, 81–82
Gray, Susan, 143
Great Migration, 1
Green, Bowling, 82, 117–18, 173
Green, William, 99

Greene, Bill, 58
Greene, William, 53, 82, 109table
    on Abe Lincoln, 73, 74
    college education, 96
    as merchant, 108–9
    repaying debts, 105
    on Thomas Lincoln, 140
Grigsby, Charles, 21–22
Grigsby, Nathaniel
    on Abe Lincoln, 19, 20, 75
    on Thomas Lincoln, 135, 137
Grigsby family, 19

Hall, Squire
    marriage, 19, 139, 140
    moving to Illinois, 21
Hamilton, Alexander, 210
Hanks, Dennis (cousin), 15, 18, 67, 319n. 5
    on Knob Creek farm, 11
    labor by, 13, 14
    on Lincoln, 74
    on Lincoln extended family, 139–40
    marriage, 19, 139
    moving to Illinois, 21, 43
    on Thomas Lincoln, 67, 135
Hanks, John (cousin), 43
    in Illinois, 21, 26–27
    labor by, 28–29
    on Lincoln, 18, 251
    as raftsman, 42
Hanks, Nancy. See Lincoln, Nancy Hanks
Hardin, John J.
    on convention system, 237
    death, 242
    political involvement, 199, 235
    Shields affair and, 211–12
Hardin County, Kentucky, 10
Hareven, Tamara, 136–37
Harris, Thomas L., 242
Harrison, George, 91, 92–93
Harrison, William Henry
    African Americans and, 249
    election of 1836 and, 116, 117, 118
    election of 1840, 195, 196
    Treaty of 1804 and, 86
Hawley family, 36
Hay, John, 49, 115–16, 215
Hay, Milton, 184
Herdon, John Rowan, 104
Heredith, Andrew, 45
Herndon, Archer, 115, 191
Herndon, James Rowan, 99, 104
Herndon, John Rowan, 59, 74, 99, 101, 104
Herndon, William, 71, 319n. 5
    1846 convention and, 238
    law practice of, 240
    on Lincoln, x, 94, 100, 127, 151, 208, 224,
        225–26, 287–88
    on Lincoln and Berry's store, 97

marketing crops in, 45–46
merchants in, 50–52, 54–55
occupational ladder in, 121, 122table
population characteristics, 57, 61–62, 327n. 3
single men migrating to, 43–44
Whig vs. Democrat votes in, 187–88
See also New Salem, IL; Springfield, IL
Sangamon County Historical Society, 311
Sangamon County Temperance Union, 288
Sangamon River
  1832 elections and, 84
  Lincoln's speech on, 27
  steamboats on, 79–81
Schools. *See* Education
Scott, Winfield, 88, 290
Secessionists, 308
Second Great Awakening, 284
Segregation, 266
"Self–made man" ethic
  characteristics of, 125–27
  coining of term, 124–25
  defined, 124
  individualism and, 125
  Horatio Alger story of, 127–30
  Lincoln and, *ix–x*, 124–25, 126–27, 130–31
Servants
  African American, 251–52
  Lincolns employing, 218
  Mary Todd Lincoln and, 227–29
Settlement
  commemorating Illinois, 311–12, 314–15
  by merchants, 106
  Shenandoah Valley, 5–6
  in Springfield, Illinois, 35–38, 157–60, 344n. 6
  See also Migration
Seventh Congressional District, 233, 236, 247
Seward, William, 306
Sharp Shooters, 180
Shawnee Indians, 6–7
Shelby, Macklin, 251
Shenandoah Valley, 5–6
Shields, James, 210–12
Short, James, 58, 60, 65, 73, 99
Simon, John Y., *x*, 132, 134
Simon, Paul, 116
Sinco, David, 104
Sinco, Henry, 103, 104
single households, 57, 327n. 3
Sioux tribe, 88
Slavery
  debate on, 257
  in Illinois, 249–50
  Lincoln on, 246–47, 257–60, 264–65, 289, 293, 294–95, 301, 302, 306
  Lincoln's early experiences with, 250–51
  as motive for leaving Kentucky, 11
  political party divisions over, 291–92

runaway slaves under, 254, 263–64
southern settlers, 24
southerners and, 24, 31
in Springfield, 252–53
Wilmot Proviso and, 243–44
See also African Americans
"Slave stampede", 264
Society for the Suppression of Horse Thieves, 177
Sons of Temperance, 288
Southern Democrats, 307
Sparrow, Thomas, 13
Sparrow couple, 18–19
Speeches
  1846 campaign, 238–39
  1860 campaign, 308
  in Cincinnati, OH, 304
  on Dred Scott decision, 298–300
  Farewell Address, 315
  first, on Sangamon River, 27
  "House Divided", 301
  "Lost Speech", 296
  Lyceum, 259
  in Milwaukee, Wisconsin, 305
  in New York City, 306
Speed, Joshua, *167*
  club organized by, 180
  friendship with Lincoln, 166, 168–69
  on Lincoln, *ix*, 73, 157, 184
  on Todd–Lincoln relationship, 208, 210
Spencer County, Indiana, 11–12
Springfield, IL, 29
  African Americans and, 251–53, 260, 262–63, 264, 266
  animals in, 270–72
  becoming state capital, 119–20
  colonization societies in, 254–55
  crime in, 177–78, 273–77, 361n. 17
  divorce in, 230
  economy, 38
  equal rights supported in, 257
  establishment of, 31–32
  family size in, 281
  fires in, 270
  free soil movement in, 245
  growth of, 34–35, 156, 176–77
  honoring pioneer past of, 311–15
  housing in, 164–66, 269
  incorporated as a city, 179
  land acquisition in, 32–34, 342n. 26
  land settlement in, 37–38
  Lincoln moving to, 69–70
  Lincoln purchasing land in, 114
  migration to, 35–37, 272–73
  nativism in, 291
  political violence in, 211
  the poor in, 173–74, 273
  population characteristics, 38–40, 324n. 2
  public health in, 175–76, 269–70

Warren, Louis A., 16, 138
Warrior (steamboat), 88
Washington, George, 7, 101, 286
Washingtonians, 285–288
Washington Temperance Convention, 286
Washington Temperance Society, 285–88
Watson, Harry L., 186
Watson, William W., 166
Weaving, 47
Weber, John, 287
Webster, Daniel, 116, 117
Webster's Spelling, 18
Weiss, Richard, 124
Whig Party, 116
    on "progress", 186–87
    in 1844 elections, 198–203
    on African American immigration, 261
    collapse of, 289, 290
    colonization and, 255
    convention system and, 194
    on currency, 192–94
    decline in support for, 242–49, 292–93
    free soil movement and, 245–46
    on immigrants, 201–2
    Lincoln and, 116, 186, 189, 194–95, 200–1
    member profile, 247–48
    merchants supporting, 82
    on Mexican War, 241–42
    as middle class, 218
    nativism and, 291
    principles of, 83
    on purpose of government, 185
    on slavery, 246
    in Springfield mayoral race, 196, 198
    voter support for, 187–88, 190–92, 204,
       233–34, 349n. 15, 357n. 37
Whig pole, 202–3
White, Hugh Lawson, 116–17, 118, 191
Whitney, Henry Clay, 27, 58, 74, 235
Wide Awake Clubs, 309
Widowhood, 15–17
Wiebe, Robert, 73, 184
Wiley, Clothier E. R., 216

Wiley, S. R., 181
Williams, John, 41, 182
Wilmot, David, 243
Wilmot Proviso, 243–44, 245, 258
Wilson, Douglas, 212
Winnebago tribe, 88, 90
Women
    age difference with spouse, 62–63
    childbearing by, 280
    childrearing by, 282–83
    clubs of, 180
    community cooperation by, 49
    domestic labor by, 46–48, 214
    Lincoln and, 63, 149
    as middle–class housewives, 214, 217, 223,
       224, 226
    scarcity of, 62, 63, 149–50
    voting by, 233
Wright, Erastus, 244
Wyllie, Irvin, 125–26

Yates, Richard, 294, 308
YMCA, 275
Young Men's Institute, 275
Youth
    as "self–made", 124–26
    choosing vocation, 76–77, 119
    as economic asset, 136–38
    forming voluntary associations, 179–80
    mischief by, 274–76
    mortality rate, 283
    orphaned, 174
    paths to adulthood from, 70, 72–73
    pioneer entrepreneurship by, 122–24,
       133–34
    as servants, 227–28
    transition to adulthood, 60, 61
    voting by, 233
    See also Men, single

Zimmerman, Robert, 35–36